The Organizational State

The Organizational State

Social Choice
in National Policy Domains

Edward O. Laumann
David Knoke

THE UNIVERSITY OF WISCONSIN PRESS

Published 1987

The University of Wisconsin Press
114 North Murray Street
Madison, Wisconsin 53715

The University of Wisconsin Press, Ltd.
1 Gower Street
London WC1E 6HA, England

First printing

Printed in the United States of America

For LC CIP information see the colophon

ISBN 0-299-11190-3 cloth; 0-299-11194-6 paper

Contents

Tables

Figures

Foreword

by James S. Coleman

The Federal Government in the United States is a government "of the people, by the people, and for the people." Presidents are elected by popular vote in the nation (filtered through the electoral college), Senators are elected by popular vote in their states, and Representatives are elected by popular vote in their Congressional districts. Cabinet members and agency heads are appointed by the elected president, as are members of the Supreme Court.

But this says nothing about politics. Professors Laumann and Knoke have asked, in this book, how policies were made, in the period 1977–80, in the areas of energy and health. That question is a very different one from the question of how the positions of president and Congress are filled. In answering that question, they have stripped off the skin which covers the policymaking process to expose the anatomy underneath. They see there a structure in which persons are scarcely to be found. There is a structure of events which taken together constitute policies in energy or health. And there are actors who shape these events. But the actors are not persons at all. They are corporate actors: firms, trade associations, federal agencies, trade unions and professional associations, and others. These are the actors who shape public policy in energy and health. Unlike the Congress and the president who have formal authority over public policy, these actors do not represent *persons*; they represent *interests*. There is, of course, some relation between persons and interests; but it is a complex relation, so that policy outcomes result from a different configuration of forces than do election outcomes.

When one sees this anatomy of public policy making, and sees this set of self-selected actors-with-interests behind the set of popularly elected representatives-of-people, a much more complex picture of democratic government in the United States emerges. It is not syndicalism. It is not corporatism (though corporatism has emerged recently in some European countries, with actors like trade associations and trade unions entering much more publicly, or even formally into the policy process). It is a fluid system in which the cast of actors varies from one event to another, and one in which a variety of resources enter into play, ranging from information to money.

There is no political theory which adequately characterizes this complex

process of policy formation. The interplay of popularly elected representatives and self-selected corporate actors; the juxtaposition of one structure
with formal authority and a base in people, with another structure lacking formal authority with a base in interests; the way policy initiatives come into
being, and the way policy issues are resolved; these constitute only minimally
explored terrain.

This book extends greatly the charting of this terrain. By focussing on the
less easily observed and more complex structure of corporate actors with interests which lie behind the formal structure of government, it illuminates the
least well known portions of this overall structure of policymaking. It brings
closer the day in which an adequate theory of the political system, able to
comprehend not only the part with formal authority, but also the part without,
will come into being.

Is this book sociology or political science? Such a question is not of interest
to those who will make use of its results in their everyday affairs. Yet it is a
question of some interest for understanding why theory and research on political systems is often limited to that part of the system with formal authority.
The other part, the structure of self-selected corporate actors with interests, is
closer to the traditional domain of sociological methods and theory than to
political science's traditional domain. Yet the problems studied in this book are
clearly part of the domain of political science. The relative lack of work in the
area covered by this book probably derives in part from this boundary between the two disciplines. Those who use the tools most common on the sociology side of the boundary seldom study problems seen to be on the political
science side; and those occupied with problems on the political science side
have forged their tools for studying actors and actions that are clearly on their
side of the boundary.

Yet social reality does not respect disciplinary boundaries; and, occasionally, social scientists are sufficiently attendant to social reality to ignore them
as well. That is what Professors Laumann and Knoke have done. They have
provided the basis for an understanding of—or a theory of—the political system of the United States, encompassing not only the part with formal authority, but also the part which lies behind it, as that system functions to generate policy. In doing so, they have written a book which future theory and
research on the political system of the United States will not be able to ignore.

James S. Coleman
University of Chicago

Acknowledgments

An undertaking as large, complex, and extended as ours can only be conducted with the assistance and cooperation of many people. Our acknowledgment here cannot begin to repay our enormous debts. Foremost gratitude goes to research assistants who participated in various stages of planning, data collection, coding, and analysis: David Prensky, Bernard McMullan, Yong-Hak Kim, Elisabeth Clemens, Nancy Reaven, Larry Raffalovich, Frank Burleigh, Tony Tam, and Chandra Muller. Invaluable secretarial and administrative assistance was provided by Ray Weathers and Lois Kelly. We are especially grateful to George Rumsey for the fine work he did in preparing the figures and tables. Joanne Miller and Paul Burstein, the two Program Officers at the National Science Foundation, were especially helpful and understanding through the long process of translating our theoretical aspirations and empirical hunches into a doable empirical project.

Numerous colleagues read, commented upon, criticized, or suffered through our various efforts to wring a coherent account from the data: James S. Coleman, Paul Burstein, Peter V. Marsden, Ronald S. Burt, Franz U. Pappi, Joseph Galaskiewicz, William J. Wilson, Christine Wright-Isak, Michael Hout, Sheldon Stryker, Michael Useem, J. Craig Jenkins, Douglas Anderton, Mary Fennell, Mindy Schimmel, Gary Fine, Randall Collins, Charles Bidwell, Alan Sica, Gerald Suttles, William Parish, Andrew Shapiro, and several anonymous reviewers.

Elisabeth Clemens and Yong-Hak Kim must be singled out for their important and sustained contributions to the challenging data-analysis and writing-up phases of the project. Clemens assumed principal responsibility for the historical research on the two policy domains for Chapter 2 as well as for writing up the results of this labor, while Kim assumed primary responsibility for the data analysis and writing of Chapters 10, 11, and 13. He also played a key role in the workup of the theoretical materials for the middle section of Chapter 1 on the actor-event interface. To recognize their contributions, we have included them as co-authors for the relevant chapters. Their diligent preparatory and editorial work on all the other chapters in the book is much appreciated as well.

Our two largest obligations are to the National Science Foundation (SES-8015529) for providing the financial wherewithal to conduct the research, and to the hundreds of organizational leaders who gave generously of their time and wisdom to instruct us in the intricacies of their worlds. We hope that we have fairly reflected those worlds in the pages ahead, however imperfect our understanding may remain.

Edward O. Laumann
University of Chicago

David Knoke
University of Minnesota

The Organizational State

1

Introductory Overview

The executive director of a major petroleum-industry trade association was leafing through the *Federal Register,* his daily ritual of scanning the Washington scene. Buried in the fine print was an apparently innocuous announcement by the Federal Aviation Administration of its intent to promulgate new regulations that would require detailed flight plans to be filed by pilots of noncommercial aircraft. Recently, several planes had gone down, and search and rescue efforts had been hampered by lack of information on the pilots' intended routes. The trade association director muttered, "We've got a problem," and spent a frantic morning on the phone alerting his group's membership to apply pressure on the FAA to set aside the regulation. The executive realized that once detailed flight plans were on record with the FAA, the open-disclosure provisions of the Freedom of Information Act would allow anyone to learn where his member companies' planes were flying on their aerial explorations for oil, gas, and minerals. The alert director's quick mobilization of collective response saved the corporations potentially millions of dollars worth of secret data that might have fallen into the laps of their competitors.

This incident dramatically encapsulates several important features of state policy making: the centrality of large formal organizations; the significance of policy interests in narrowly focused events; the great value of timely and trustworthy information; the activation of policy participants through communication networks; and the mobilization of influence resources to bear upon the

3

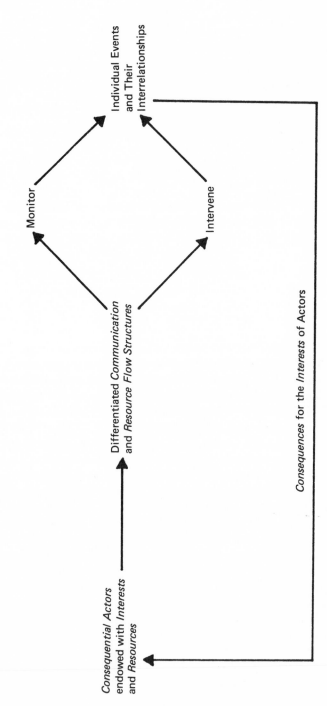

Figure 1.1. The General Model

formal authorities. State policies are the product of complex interactions among government and nongovernment organizations, each seeking to influence the collectively binding decisions that have consequences for their interests. This book reports the results of a five-year study of American energy and health policy making, with particular emphasis on social structure, decision participation, and influence over outcomes. We have developed new analytic perspectives and empirical measures with the view of strengthening our systematic understanding of these complex processes of national decision making.

In this introductory chapter, we will first characterize the variety of approaches that have been proposed to guide the study of state or elite decision making, noting where our approach departs from existing strategies of inquiry to achieve what we believe to be a more theoretically sophisticated and empirically faithful model. After introducing the key definitions and assumptions of our model, we enter an extended discussion of several metamethodological issues raised by our approach. We are primarily concerned with the levels of analysis in terms of which we must proceed and with the innovation of being systematically explicit about the joint analysis of actors and events in a system of action. Finally, we provide a brief overview of the subsequent chapters, stressing their interrelationships within our model of national policy making.

Throughout, two fundamental themes are explored. First, we hope to provide a systematic comparative analysis of two policy domains, energy and health, with reference to the 1970s and to the Carter administration (1977–1980) in particular. Second, this empirical inquiry is conceived within a theoretical framework of sufficient generality to analyze a variety of action systems. We hope to convince the reader of the model's general utility by demonstrating its efficacy in generating empirical insights in two highly distinctive and unrelated political arenas.

Succinctly put, our orienting framework is a *set of consequential corporate actors,* each possessing (1) variable *interests* in a range of *issues* in a national policy domain and (2) relevant mobilizable *resources.* These actors are *embedded* within communication and resource-exchange *networks* (Granovetter, 1985; Marsden and Laumann, 1977). The flows of specialized communications and resources among the actors enable them to monitor, and to communicate their concerns and intentions in, relevant decision-making *events* that, in turn, have consequences for their interests. These events, both in themselves, as unique historical occurrences, and in their interrelationships, have critical import for explaining the behavior of individual actors and their interaction. Figure 1.1 graphically depicts the model.

Other State Policy-making Approaches

Our project departs in important ways from other research approaches to state and elite policy making. In this section we briefly sketch four contexts against which to view our analysis of the social organization of the state.

Recent controversies have swirled around Marxist-inspired analyses of the economic-class basis of the modern state (Block, 1977; Gold et al., 1975; Miliband, 1969; Offe and Ronge, 1975; Poulantzas, 1973; Skocpol, 1980; Therborn, 1976; Wright, 1978). Instrumentalist explanations argue that state policies are determined by the class interests of capitalists and their agents. Structuralist accounts accord the state greater autonomy, depicting policy decisions as reflecting the outcome of struggles between capitalist and working classes or partially determined by social and political forces operating within the state structure itself. Although much of this dispute is conducted at a fairly abstract level, a few empirical efforts have examined the implications of these perspectives. Analyses have addressed both the micro level of state manager-class composition (Dye, 1976) and the macro level, the latter through highly aggregated time series of policy outputs (Griffin et al., 1982; Hicks and Swank, 1984) or detailed historical case studies (Domhoff, 1978; Skocpol, 1979, 1980). None of these analyses track state policy making at the level of organizational populations laying claim to governmental authority on behalf of their interests. Although our project cannot elucidate the class basis of the American state, it cuts directly into that black box to reveal a complex set of interacting private and public institutions. We see policies as resulting from conflicts and contradictions among these organizational players, rather than reflecting the monolithic rationality and clarity of class interests implied by many Marxist images. By studying organizations participating in many policy events across domains, we hope to reveal the underlying social structure and dynamic of state policy making. Perhaps these findings will add substantive fuel to Marxist theoretical debates, despite the differences in conceptual languages.

A second analytic approach conceives of the state in terms of elites whose interests are more organizationally derived than class-oriented (Burton and Higley, 1984; Field and Higley, 1980; Heinz and Laumann, 1982; Knoke, 1981). Mills's (1956) now-classic image of an unaccountable business-government-military power elite dominating the state inspired empirical attempts to identify the players and map their relationships (e.g., Barton, 1975; Domhoff, 1978; Dye, 1976; Hunter, 1959; Moore, 1979; Useem, 1978, 1979, 1984). Much of this research takes the individual as its unit of analysis, tracing career patterns of recruitment to top command posts or delineating discussion networks among core actors (e.g., interlocking corporate directorates). Few studies offer more than anecdotal illustrations of how elite structures affect policy-making activities (but see Galaskiewicz, 1979; Knoke, 1983; Laumann and Pappi, 1976; Laumann et al., 1977; and Perrucci and Pilisuk, 1970, for analyses involving local community elites). Although our project shares the concern of research on elite structures for mapping communication networks, we see organizations rather than natural persons as the core actors at the level of the national state. We further treat network structure as antecedent to policy-event participation and its consequences. Thus, we seek to apply principles of elite social organization more comprehensively.

A third context within which to view our project is the interest group tradition of pluralist political science. Spurred by the explosion of activity in Washington since 1970, recent analyses have concentrated on the origins, prevalence, policy interests, resource endowments, and strategies of those associations and corporate actors as they seek to influence federal policy decisions (Berry, 1984; Schlozman and Tierney, 1983; Walker, 1983). Much of this research is descriptive, and more needs to be learned about how interest groups pursue their policy objectives. Theoretical explanations of the pressure-group system too often emphasize the more formalized aspects of legislation (e.g., "cozy triangles" among executive agencies, congressional subcommittees, and clientele; see Gais et al., 1984) to the relative neglect of less proximate causes (Burstein, 1981; Hayes, 1979; McFarland, 1983; Ripley and Franklin, 1980:4–7). Yet, as Salisbury (1984) so cogently argues, the recent dominance of such institutions as corporations and local governments over mass membership associations in Washington interest representation requires substantial revisions in both descriptive and theoretical accounts of state policy making. Our project was designed, along with a parallel study of Washington representatives (Heinz et al., 1982; Laumann and Heinz, 1985; Nelson et al., 1987), to develop a more sociologically informed approach to interest group behavior. We stress the centrality of network structures among organized interest groups for the exchange of timely policy information and politically useful material resources essential to coalition-formation, influence-mobilization, and bargaining-negotiation processes that ultimately create state policies. In many ways, our emphasis on impacted information and the need to devise governance structures to contain opportunistic behavior runs parallel to that of Williamson's (1975, 1985) transaction cost analysis of economic institutions.

The final approach to which we contrast our project is corporatism. Like pluralism, corporatism gives special attention to organized interests and their relations with the state. Schmitter's definition stressed the "intermediation" function that groups play in a societal corporatist system in which "the constituent units are organized into a limited number of singular, compulsory, noncompetitive, hierarchically ordered and functionally differentiated categories" (Schmitter, 1979:13). Corporatism is most fully developed in European liberal democracies, where peak associations are directly incorporated into governmental deliberations, in return for controlling their fractious mass bases. Most scholars agree that the United States lacks corporatist attributes (Wilson, 1982). Still, the identification of autonomous organizations as key state actors and the insistence that state policies can be understood as a series of negotiations among interest groups are compatible with our own perspective.

In the broad sweep of political sociology and economy, our fundamental theoretical stance may be best characterized as a multiple-elite (Knoke, 1981: 286–88) or managerial-elite perspective (Alford and Friedland, 1985:161–268). Eschewing both pluralistic individualism and Marxist class approaches, we conceive of the modern industrial polity as a complex of formal organizations in conflict with one another over the collective allocation of scarce societal resources. Neither aggregates of persons nor agents of class interests, the large bureaucratic state organizations are effective instruments of domination for those elites who can command their authority. Using power relations within and interorganizational networks among them, state managers and interest group leaders struggle to mobilize political resources that shape public policies beneficial to their organizations' objectives, including the survival of the power structure itself (Alford and Friedland, 1985:25).

From the managerial-elite perspective, the national state is neither a structure for capitalist class rule nor a neutral umpire adjudicating between competing claims of social groups. Rather, the state is an autonomous social formation whose strategies emerge from the basic organizational imperatives of coping with environmental uncertainties, resource scarcities, and socio-legal constraints (Knoke, 1981:288; see Aldrich, 1979, and Scott, 1981, for discussions of organizational autonomy and dependence in strategic-choice conditions). The historical creation of the liberal democratic state—involving greater structural differentiation, increased control over societal resources, and expanded intervention into the economy and society—was accompanied by a parallel transformation of social segments into organized interest groups (e.g., Garson, 1978; Schlozman and Tierney, 1985; Truman, 1951; Walker, 1983). In attempting to maximize their legitimacy and autonomy, state bureaus created stable networks of clienteles, funding sources, and interbureau alliances. The boundaries between the public sector and private interest groups became blurred in the policy-making process (Alford and Friedland, 1985:436).

As state entities took on increasingly significant regulatory functions, dominant interests outside the state sought to secure continuous access to these new centers of power (McConnell, 1966; McNeil, 1978). Interdependent and reciprocal relations between state and private organizations jointly created the modern polity of large-scale bureaucratic hierarchies that centralized increasingly vast amounts of power. Ultimately, only efficient, resource-rich organized interests could gain access to the state managerial elites, as poor and unorganized social groups were relegated to sporadic challenges (Gamson, 1975; Tilly, 1978). Even those interest groups nominally based on mass membership and support—labor unions, political parties, trade associations, voluntary organizations—became dominated by oligarchic elites that controlled the expression of public opinion and participation in their ranks (Michels, 1962; Salisbury, 1984). Thus, the appropriate unit of analysis for studies of policy formation is not the state understood in the institutional sense, but the state as a collection of policy arenas incorporating both governmental and private actors (cf. Parsons, 1969).

A Model for Analysis

Two assumptions underlie the research design. First, we assume that corporate entities—such as trade associations, professional societies, labor unions, public interest groups, government bureaus, and congressional committees— are the key state policy-domain actors. Natural persons are important only insofar as they act on behalf and at the behest of these collectivities.[1] Second, we adopt a social perspective, which assumes that supraindividual structural arrangements among these corporate entities must be taken into account in formulating an adequate explanation of policy domain event participation. These two assumptions jointly guide the following specification of our analytic model.

Policy Domains

In Parsons' (1951:19) succinct definition, a *social system* is a plurality of actors interacting on the basis of a shared symbol system. Membership in any social system under analysis is substantively defined by a criterion of mutual relevance and common fate that stipulates the basis on which members are to take each other into account in their actions. That is, the basis of their mutual relevance to one another or their common orientations to some shared reference point (such as the production of coal for market) serves to mediate their interdependence. Simply put, a *policy domain* is the substantive focus of con-

---

1. Numerous studies of local community politics focus on natural persons as key actors in community decision-making (e.g., Hunter, 1953; Laumann and Pappi, 1976). When we speak of someone playing a decision-making or leadership role as a natural person, we mean to imply that he or she is acting primarily on behalf of his/her unique bundle of personal and social identities and not as a fiduciary agent of a corporate (or organizational) actor. We believe that natural persons themselves are playing less significant roles in national-level politics, even though we do not entirely ignore their importance (cf. Coleman, 1974, 1982).

cern of policy initiatives and debate. More formally a *policy domain* is a subsystem

identified by specifying a substantively defined criterion of mutual relevance or common orientation among a set of consequential actors concerned with formulating, advocating, and selecting courses of action (i.e., policy options) that are intended to resolve the delimited substantive problems in question. (Knoke and Laumann, 1982:256)

A national policy domain is therefore a set of actors with major concerns about a substantive area, whose preferences and actions on policy events must be taken into account by the other domain participants. Numerous policy domains exist in the modern state. Examples include agriculture, housing, education, civil rights, health care, space exploration, law enforcement, national defense—indeed, all arenas into which governmental authority has intruded. Once a substantive criterion is specified, the researcher is in a position to define the core set of actors. Note that this criterion may change over time and even across the set of actors, transforming the definition of what is meant by a particular policy domain with consequent implications for the delimitation of its constituent membership.

To illustrate the point, today we might construe a health matter as referring to any phenomenon affecting the physiological, psychological, or health-related social well-being of an individual or group of individuals. Encompassing mental health issues, such a construction reflects a much more inclusive definition than would have been accepted by most major actors in the policy domain 30 years ago. The identification of this domain is subject to the further restriction that the relevant health policy options include only those currently considered permissible for either the federal government or private organizations with nationally oriented clienteles. Similarly, a national energy policy domain is delineated by the set of all policy options involving the production and allocation of physical power resources that are seriously considered by the federal government and the major private organizations with national markets or supporters.[2]

2. More concretely, we operationally define national health policies to be concerned with: the provision and distribution of medical (including dental) services, pharmaceuticals, and medical devices; prevention and containment of contagion or disease; and screening of food additives, drugs, and medical treatments or procedures for potential hazards. Specifically included within this domain are policies concerned with mental health; the regulation of doctors, dentists, medical technicians, hospital administrators, and other health care providers; the training and certification of such health care providers; the regulation of hospitals, clinics, and other institutions that provide medical services; the regulation of the manufacture and distribution of drugs and medical devices; the financing of providers of health care and the regulation of both public and private health insurance; and the special health problems of identifiable subgroups of the population, including veterans, American Indians, and the elderly. Specifically excluded from the domain are policies concerned with access of handicapped persons to jobs and social services and

The active participants in a policy domain include all consequential organizations that have responsibility for directing, coordinating, or otherwise controlling the creation and distribution of domain values (symbolic or material) pertaining to the subsystem's primary function or to related externalities that are thereby engendered. An organization's consequentiality in a particular domain is established by the extent to which its disclosed intentions and actions are taken into account in the actions of other domain participants. Of particular significance is the set of organizations that occupies the dominant structural position in the subsystem from which influence over collective decision making can be exercised. This set comprises the elite or core organizations of the policy domain.

Delineating Domain Membership

For all practical purposes, the members of a national policy domain are complex formal organizations—such as corporations, confederations, commissions, and committees—rather than natural persons acting in their own right. But such corporate bodies rarely are wholly engaged in policy direction for a given subsystem. Only certain organizational components, particularly those at the executive level, participate in a domain.

We have already noted that the basic analytic criterion determining whether an organization belongs to a subsystem's policy domain is the standard of relevance or fate whereby actors take each other into account in their actions (Knoke and Laumann, 1982). This criterion of mutual relevance effectively excludes any actors whose actions or potential actions are inconsequential in shaping binding collective decisions for the subsystem. Actors with trivial capacities to affect the actions of domain policy-makers thus may be safely ignored by both elite members and analysts. Mere inaction, however, is an insufficient clue to marginality, since some consequential actors can, without any overt action on their part, have their interests taken into account through the reactions of other core members who anticipate their interests in particular policies.

The boundaries between actors in the policy domain and the more periph-

---

occupational safety issues of the kind handled by the Occupational Safety and Health Administration (OSHA).

With respect to energy, we include policies concerned with the production, distribution, consumption, and externalities imposed by the use of fuels for the generation of heat, light, or motive power, whether for ultimate consumption in industrial, commercial, institutional, or residential settings. The fuels include oil, natural gas, manufactured gas (propane), other petroleum byproducts, alcohol, coal, electricity (whether generated by fossil fuel, nuclear fission and fusion, water, or other means), synthetic fuels, biomass, geothermal, wind, water, and solar energy. (See Heinz et al., 1982: I.)

eral members of a subsystem are never rigidly drawn. On the contrary, membership in a policy domain is a continuing collective social construction by the domain actors. Membership is the outcome of continuous negotiations between the consequential actors currently forming the elite, who seek to impose their preferred definitions and requirements for inclusion, and various excluded nonelite actors, who seek the right to participate in collective decision making for the subsystem as a whole.

The specific steps we followed to identify the core actors in the energy and health domains are described in Chapter 3. In brief, they involve counting the frequency with which organizations are mentioned in national news media, their appearances at congressional hearings, and their participation in lobbying and court cases, as well as a final scrutiny of the list by a panel of expert insiders. Through the application of these criteria for domain membership, we identified 217 energy organizations and 156 health organizations as the elite set among which informant interviews were to be conducted.

Structural Relations

The social structure of a policy domain refers to those stable, recurrent patterns of relationships that link consequential actors to each other and to the larger social system. Research on social networks during the past decade indicates that social structure may be usefully conceptualized in terms of the multiple types of ties among system members, the patterning of which, in turn, may be used to identify a subsystem's fundamental social positions and the roles performed by particular organizations.

Contemporary treatments of social networks view the *positions* in a system of social relations as "jointly occupied" by empirical actors (Boorman and White, 1976; Burt, 1977; Sailer, 1978; White et al., 1976). The two prevailing techniques for identifying social positions are structural equivalence and subgroup cohesion. In the approach using the criterion of structural equivalence, two or more actors jointly occupy a structurally equivalent position to the extent that they have similar patterns of ties with other system actors, regardless of their direct ties to each other. The criterion of subgroup cohesion, on the other hand, aggregates only those actors who maintain dense mutual interactions either as "cliques" (maximally connected subsets; see Laumann and Pappi, 1976) or as "social circles" (highly overlapping cliques; see Alba and Moore, 1978). Although important conceptual and methodological differences exist between the two approaches, Burt (1977) has pointed out that the clique approach is a special case of the more general approach of structural equivalence.

Research on interorganizational relations and local community political systems suggests that three generic relationships are especially significant in identifying social structures: information transmission, resource transactions, and boundary penetration.

1. *Information transmission.* Over the course of their research on local communities, Laumann and his colleagues have increasingly emphasized the flow of information about community affairs among elite actors as the primary social network for the resolution of issues (Galaskiewicz, 1979; Laumann and Pappi, 1976; Laumann et al., 1977; Laumann and Marsden, 1982). We can extrapolate this perspective to the national level. The social structure of a national policy domain is primarily determined by the network of access to trustworthy and timely information about policy matters. The greater the variety of information and the more diverse the sources that a consequential actor can tap, the better situated the actor is to anticipate and to respond to policy events that can affect its interests.

2. *Resource transactions.* The resource dependence model of interorganizational relations (Aldrich and Pfeffer, 1976; Benson, 1975; Cook, 1977) begins with the commonplace observation that no organization is capable of generating internally all the resources necessary to sustain itself. Major sources of essential resources, especially information, money, and authority, typically are controlled by other formal organizations. In choosing exchange partners, organizational managers try to minimize the loss of autonomy, which might lead to a takeover by the dominant partner. But supply and demand conditions, resource essentiality (Jacobs, 1974), availability of alternative partners, and other factors can conspire to force some organizations into dependent positions. In this model, an organization's power and influence in a system is a function of its position or location in the overall resource exchange networks generated out of dyadic resource exchanges (see Knoke, 1983).

3. *Boundary penetration.* The third type of actor-to-actor linkage involves relationships serving both instrumental and solidarity-maintenance functions through the shared use of personnel. The more important examples of this mode of coordination include common membership in commissions or confederations or organizations (such as a peak trade association); ad hoc coalitions to pursue limited political objectives; joint operations in research, development, or production (such as a consortium to build a gas pipeline); shared board directorships; or even simple exchanges of personnel. These practices vary along dimensions of superordination-subordination, formalization, duration, and purpose (see Williamson, 1975, 1985).

The Policy Process

What does an elite subsystem oriented to a particular policy domain do when it attempts to influence national policy? Here we shall be primarily concerned with accounting for the policy development process and only secondarily with examining the activities of particular organizations, although the behaviors of the latter are intrinsic to the process.

Broadly following the sequence of events outlined in Smelser's (1962) model of social change, we suggest that the paradigmatic policy process begins with the perception of some disruption or malfunction in the ongoing operations of a subsystem. Actors propose alternative interpretations of the problem and the need for collective action to deal with it. In discussing the problem, policy domain actors communicate their preferred responses to one another, to non-elite audiences, and to governing actors with the authority to make binding decisions for the subsystem. Domain actors or coalitions of actors attempt to persuade the authorities to place the issue on the governmental agenda for resolution. When an issue reaches the agenda, actors mobilize in an effort to influence the outcome of a concrete issue event, which may be part of a larger event scenario. The policy cycle is closed when the authorities select one option to deal with the precipitating policy problem. If implementation of the policy option fails to alleviate the original condition or triggers additional problems, the cycle may commence again, perhaps activating other domain actors' participation (cf. Kingdon, 1984).

We should stress here that we most certainly do not conceive of this process as an approximation of the rational-actor model of decision making so beloved by organizational theorists (compare Allison, 1971). We find much more suggestive the characteristics of the organizational decision-making process proposed by March and Olsen (1976), which stresses the fundamental ambiguities of choice at every stage as actors try to decide what to do. Characteristic ambiguities are inherent in an actor's identification of the problem, definition of the objectives it wants to achieve, and determination of the procedures whereby it proposes to accomplish them. The chief feature of this perspective to which we must pay attention is the *time-dependent nature* of the actors' searches for problems and solutions. Policy processes do not occur in a vacuum, but evolve simultaneously with many others, at various stages of completion, that compete for the scarce attention of domain members. This multiplicity of competing activities places significant constraints on any given policy cycle and must somehow be taken into account in the empirical analysis. The following sections elaborate key features of the approach that inform our empirical analysis.

Problem Recognition

The typical policy process starts when one or more actors label some condition as a problem or issue and draw the attention of other actors to it. The organization itself may be directly experiencing strains in its operations, or it may respond to difficulties encountered by other actors (including nonelites and participants in other subsystems) that are drawn to its attention—for example, by customer complaints or criticism in the mass media. The important point is that a subsystem condition does not become a domain issue until it is recognized as a strain problem by a consequential actor in the policy domain. Nonmembers, including academic observers, cannot meaningfully assert that a subsystem's "objective" conditions are policy issues if they are ignored by such domain actors. Indeed, one criterion of membership in a domain is the willingness of other core actors to accept an organization's assertions about what constitutes an issue.

Problem recognition is clearly a subjective conceptual activity of consequential organizations or, more precisely, of their agents in policy-making roles. Just as we emphasized that membership is a collective social construction of reality, so we argue that the recognition of conditions as policy problems is a continuously constructed social phenomenon, as, indeed, is the entire policy process. Subsequent conditions may stimulate participants' retrospective reinterpretations of earlier activities as having greater or lesser relevance for a problem. Problem recognition thus takes on the flavor of a constantly modified "story," one having a beginning, middle, and end but also, like the old newspapers in Orwell's *1984,* subject to perpetual revision as actors try to make sense of their world and their actions toward it.

Whether an "objective" condition will be labeled and accepted by other domain actors as a legitimate policy issue for subsystem action depends on the result of negotiations among domain members (see Billings et al., 1980; Hermann, 1969; Lyles and Mitroff, 1980). Problem recognition may be highly uncertain when conditions depart markedly from past experience or have traditionally been the province of other subsystems. For example, a major problem for the energy-domain actors during the 1970s was disagreement among themselves as to the root of the "energy crisis"—a real depletion of resources or an artificial imbalance created by governmental interference in the marketplace. Differing beliefs about the nature of the problem clearly affect the types of actors who become involved and the policy alternatives that they champion.

Option Generation

Empirically, the generation of policy options or alternatives may occur simultaneously with issue recognition, but in the proposed analytic model, option generation is a subsequent step. Indeed, in some real cases we may find that the organizations first drawing attention to an issue are not the same actors who subsequently propose various policy options or solutions aimed at eliminating or reducing the strain problem and restoring the subsystem to a new equilibrium.

A *policy option* is the empirical unit act in the policy process. It consists of a statement made by a policy domain actor that advocates that a specific action be taken, either by that actor or by some other authoritative actor, with regard to a socially perceived issue. Most policy options can be cast in the form: "Organization *A* proposes that authority *B* undertake action *X* for reason *Y.*" For example, in 1974 the Association of American Railroads concluded that the Nuclear Regulatory Commission safety standards for casks used to ship nuclear wastes by rail were too low and, therefore, that the Interstate Commerce Commission should change the conditions under which nuclear waste shipments are made.

A domain actor communicates to other core actors, as well as to a larger nonelite "attentive public," its preferred policy option with regard to a specific subsystem problem or issue. Other actors, either differently interpreting the defining problems or perceiving that actor *A*'s proposed alternative might be disadvantageous for themselves or others they care about, offer alternatives to cope with the problem. To illustrate: following the 1979 accident at the Three Mile Island nuclear power plant, some actors proposed a moratorium on new plant construction, others advocated shutting down existing plants as well, and the industry actors wanted to continue operations under tighter safety procedures.

The solutions proffered by domain actors seldom are arrived at by the ideal-typical search procedures of an abstract rational actor who systematically scans all alternatives and selects one that maximizes utility. Rather, organizational option generation more often resembles solutions in search of issues. Organizational routines and standard operating procedures dispose actors toward a stock set of solutions that can be applied across a wide range of problems (see March and Olsen, 1976).

Agenda Placement

Recognition of strain problems and communication of policy options among domain members are necessary for issues to reach the "systematic agenda" (Cobb and Elder, 1972:82; Kingdon, 1984), where the subsystem elites become aware that a condition exists requiring authoritative resolution. If the problem can be dealt with only by some component of the federal government, the next step in the policy process is to place the issue on the governmental agenda. An *agenda* is a formal calendar or docket that specifies the order and time at which matters are to be considered before a final selection is made among the available policy options. The governmental agenda is almost always smaller and more difficult for an issue to reach than is the subsystem agenda. Despite the enormous size and specialization of the federal government, there are more problems seeking the attention of executives, legislators, and regulators than can possibly be seriously entertained in a given period. Advancement onto the governmental agenda typically requires actions by proponents of an issue alternative to increase the salience and political importance of the issue to gatekeeping authorities, particularly by mobilizing politically relevant resources, including coalitions with other actors, to influence authoritative decision-makers. In the process of reaching the stage of formal consideration by authorities, an issue's policy options may have undergone considerable modification and reduction as proponents and opponents negotiate over terms. This process we refer to as *winnowing* the alternatives in preparation for moving the issue onto the agenda.

Events and Scenarios

When an issue reaches a national policy domain's agenda, its subsequent progress can be analyzed in terms of discrete events. An event occurs when a concrete proposal for authoritative action is placed before a decision-making body, such as Congress or a federal regulatory agency. An event typically involves a pro-or-con decision about a single policy option as the solution to an issue. Those actors who favor and those who oppose the particular proposal may be observed marshalling their forces to try to influence the decision outcome. Such variables as the timing of activation, the influence tactics used, and cooperative and competitive interactions among mobilized actors can be investigated. Of particular interest in our research is how the domain social structure determines the time at which core actors become involved in particular types of events.

An event in the energy domain is illustrative. On February 22, 1978, the House Interior Committee reported out a bill to promote the development of coal slurry pipelines. Such pipelines would pump a mixture of crushed coal and water from mines to the users, often over hundreds of miles. Around this event the following actors were mobilized: the coal industry, electric utilities, and construction trade unions, who favored the bill's passage; the railroads, who opposed development because it would cost them lucrative coal-hauling business; and environmental groups and farmers, who opposed the project on the grounds that it would deplete scarce water resources. By asking spokespeople about their organizations' actions before and after the committee reported out the bill, we reconstructed the pattern of activation on this event and related it to the social organization in this sector of the national energy domain.

Discrete events can be concatenated into larger event scenarios that may span considerable time, revealing changing configurations of actors and patterns of action. Events can be chained together because they share some logical similarities, exhibit some temporal proximity and succession, or display some causal connections. To continue the illustration, coal slurry pipeline bills were brought before Congress at least three times during the Carter administration but were never passed. At a higher level of abstraction, these pipeline events can be included in a scenario called "coal industry development" that also includes events pertaining to strip-mining control and reclamation, railroad deregulation, and utility air-pollution standards. The ability to aggregate discrete events into more encompassing equivalence classes gives the researcher greater flexibility in trying to understand how the social organization of a policy domain affects the policy-making process.

Authoritative Decisions

We will have little to say in this book about authoritative decisions, the final stage in the policy process. Political scientists have exhaustively studied the procedures by which laws and regulations are authorized, primarily from an institutional perspective that stresses the motives and interests of proximate decision-makers (such as senators' desires for reelection). In contrast, our research brings a distinct sociological perspective to bear on the selection of outcomes, emphasizing how the social organization of timely and trustworthy information flowing from interested core actors to the proximate authorities defines the nature of the policy debate and its outcome. We do not deny the existence, and the frequently substantial importance, of processes internal to the legislative and executive decision-making organizations, but our primary focus is on the contribution of social structural variation in policy domains to an understanding of ultimate policy decisions.

Metamethodological Issues in the Joint Analysis of Actors and Events in Systems of Action

The foregoing overview of our analytic approach raises a number of critical metamethodological issues that require careful explication.[3] In proposing a framework for analyzing the interface between actors and events, we juxtapose two analytic dimensions, the level of analysis and the phenomenal unit. Our main metatheoretical argument is that since events themselves possess certain absolute and relational properties, the phenomenal facet labeled "event" must be more explicitly incorporated into theory construction. The study of the structure of events has been much neglected in most sociological inquiries, compared with the numerous studies focused on the structure of actors and their institutions. In the following excursus, we show how actors and events can be interfaced at different levels of analysis, with specific examples drawn from the sociological literature. The examples' methodological assumptions and implications are compared and contrasted. The remainder of the book

---

3. This excursus was written in collaboration with Yong-Hak Kim.

demonstrates how the framework can be used to clarify certain theoretical issues and to formulate methodologically appropriate hypotheses.

Theoretical Background

Social theorists have made innumerable attempts to impose some order upon the vast body of sociological research. Efforts to capture the basic analytic tensions in this literature have spawned distinctions between agency and structure (Giddens, 1979:49–95; 1981:162–63), actors and institutions, individual and collective levels of analysis, or, more generally, micro- and macro-sociology.[4] The very number of these somewhat overlapping, but far from consistent, oppositions justifies the conclusion that no single oppositional contrast has proven satisfactory. These synthesizing attempts, moreover, may even have misoriented research and theorizing by confounding two analytically distinct antinomies: the level of analysis (individual vs. collective) at which the theorist is operating and the phenomenal unit (actor vs. event) that the theorist purports to describe or explain.

Our purpose is threefold. First, we propose an overarching framework that compares different theoretical approaches to social phenomena in order to illuminate the fundamental disparities in their theoretical assumptions and methodological implications. Second, in addition to distinguishing between levels of analysis, as the contrasts between micro- and macro-analysis or methodological individualism and methodological holism suggest, we think it useful to draw attention to the signal importance of an additional analytic dimension—the actor-event facet, which includes the interface of the two. Sociologists have focused almost exclusively on actors, relations among actors, and relations among institutions in which actors are embedded, often neglecting the characteristics of the event(s) in which the actors are active. Even in his earliest formulation of action theory, however, Parsons (1937), drew a clear distinction between the unit act, which is an *event* occurring in real time and space, and *actor(s)* who engage(s) in that unit act. Theorists, unfortunately, have often left their focal concerns with the nature of the interface between actors and events implicit and unexplicated. Since events themselves possess certain properties that have consequences for the ways actors behave and are themselves related to one another in distinctively different ways, we

4. Crozier and Friedberg (1980:117) use different terms to describe the actor-structure antinomy, namely, strategic approaches versus system approaches. A somewhat similar antinomy is described as the individualistic versus collectivistic orientation in sociology by Parsons (1961:86), Janowitz (1967:638), and Ekeh (1974:3–19), structural action orientation by Wallace (1975), and structuralism versus individualism by Mayhew (1980, 1981). For a collection of articles that view the micro-macro distinction as a function of particular ways of slicing time and space, see Knorr-Cetina and Cicourel, 1981. See also Collins, 1981:984–89.

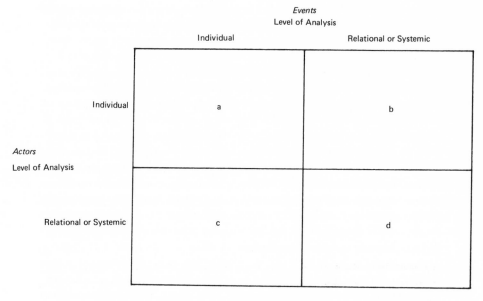

Figure 1.2. A Typology of Frameworks for Sociological Analysis

believe that this phenomenal facet must be incorporated more explicitly into the logic of sociological theory building. Just as network analysis has provided a method for investigating the ties between actors without invoking reified structures, we will argue that this and related structure-detecting techniques, by allowing one to capture the relationship between sets of actors and series of events in an action system, can provide an alternative both to totalizing history and to ahistoricism. Third, after proposing a framework for analyzing the actor-event interface at different levels of analysis, we will demonstrate how this framework can be used to clarify certain theoretical and methodological issues in our research.

Juxtaposing Two Antinomies

Let us first cross-tabulate the two fundamental distinctions involved in analyzing social phenomena in order to construct a fourfold diagram (figure 1.2). We can then identify for each cell a typical class of empirical and theoretical studies that exemplify their authors' distinctive assumptions and emphases regarding actors, events, and level of analysis. Before proceeding, we should make several cautionary remarks. First, the conventional micro-macro distinction often discussed in the literature has little to do with our classification according to the level of analysis because, in our scheme, the units or individual actors are not necessarily natural persons but may include any entity, such as a state, corporate actor, or class, whose actions may be meaningfully described as having a unitary purpose or integrity. (See, for example, Allison, 1971:10–38; Coleman, 1974.) Such entities have often been labeled "macro-variables" in the literature. Similarly, events can be treated as unitary or as a complex ensemble of individual smaller events, depending on the degree to which the analyst stresses the event's relative integrity or autonomy from other events or its interdependencies. Obviously even a "simple" event—for instance, a marriage—could be subdivided indefinitely into subsidiary events that together constitute "the" event.

Second, we use the terms "relational" and "systemic" in a very broad sense that presupposes a hierarchically ordered continuum of increasingly encompassing structural concepts. The term "relation," for example, includes various types of association among elementary units, whether actors or events, whereas "systemic" refers to properties of the whole ensemble arising from the related elements whose properties, in turn, are wholly or in part dependent on those of the whole (Boudon, 1971:2). Finally, this two-by-two diagram does not exhaustively categorize sociological theories, since many are self-reflexive in the sense that they are concerned with actor-actor or event-event relations within a given level of analysis. For example, if one asks how the structure of friendship or the informal communication network is related to the class structure in the society, one is studying actor-actor relations (Laumann, 1966, 1973). If one is concerned with how the business cycle is related to a series of electoral events, one is focusing on the event-event relation (Tufte, 1978).

As we noted, some theorists—for example, those who are especially fascinated with describing the social structure of actors (see, e.g., the citations in Berkowitz, 1982 and Laumann et al., 1978; Laumann and Knoke 1986; Marsden and Laumann, 1984)—emphasize actors and their interrelationships and leave events out of focus, ill-specified, or contingently given. Other theorists, like those who study price movements as market behavior or rational choice in game theoretic settings, focus on attributes of events, but their theoretical emphasis residualizes actors by treating the variability of individual actors' behavior as essentially irrelevant to the modeling effort. Highly restrictive assumptions about an ideal-typical actor, such as a rational profit-optimizer operating in a perfect market, are asserted to be sufficient to deduce adequate empirical predictions of event outcomes (cf. Williamson, 1985).

To make the argument more concrete, suppose we think for a moment of studies that would fall into one or another of the four cells of figure 1.2. We might think of conventional voting studies (e.g., Campbell et al., *The Voter Decides,* 1954) as falling into cell *a.* Actors' voting behavior—the event is a time-specified individual decision to vote for a particular candidate—is explained by reference to the individual actor's "absolute" predispositional properties (Lazarsfeld and Menzel, 1969),[5] such as his or her age, sex, prior political behavior, geographical location, party affiliation, socioeconomic status, and/or personality characteristics. (Some of these attributes—e.g., socioeconomic status—implicitly import a contextual or relational measure into the explanation.) As embodied in much survey research design and public opinion polling, it is assumed that the respondent actor (the individual sampling unit) is free to vary without regard to the behavior of any other respondent in the sample. Each actor is treated as endowed with relatively persistent tendencies to act in certain ways because of certain status or personal characteristics. In short, individuals in this framing perspective are often considered to be independent from their social environment (Blumer, 1948). There is a singular event, having no relationship to any other, and a multitude of actors, but each is treated as analytically independent of all others. Thus, under the strictures of methodological individualism, both actors and events are conceived of as individual-level phenomena.

An example of research belonging in cell *b* can be found in Shepsle's studies of monopoly agenda setting (1979). Criticizing atomistic individualism in *social choice models* for its failure to account for certain equilibrium conditions, Shepsle argues that the institutional structure within which events occur and the relations among these events in the sequential pairwise selection process of options have an "independent impact on the existence of equilibrium and, together with the distribution of preferences, co-determine the characteristics of the equilibrium state(s) of collective choice processes" (1979:28–29). Thus, under certain limiting conditions, an individual actor occupying the role of a monopoly agenda-setter can achieve almost any preferred outcome he wishes, provided that he can appropriately order the sequencing of paired options considered by the voting group operating as a whole under majority rule. The focus of his analysis is on the ordering among events, the chain of decision points in a decision-making process, though Shepsle also attends to the constraints imposed on choice arising out of simultaneous consideration of the constituent actors' utility preferences.

For cell *c,* we suggest that the study by Coleman et al. of the diffusion of innovation among doctors provides a good example. It focuses attention on

5. This terminology is borrowed from Lazarsfeld and Menzel. They use the term "absolute" to indicate that these properties are characteristics of individuals that are obtained without making use of information about the characteristics of the collective or the relationships among these individuals.

the interconnections among actors as they affect a particular event—namely, the adoption of an innovation (Coleman, Katz, and Menzel, 1966). This framing perspective emphasizes the *embeddedness* of actors in larger social entities, such as social networks, in order to explain actors' behavioral and attitudinal characteristics (Galaskiewicz and Marsden, 1978). Granovetter's "The Strength of Weak Ties" (1973) is another example, at a different level of abstraction. The dyadic relation is the unit of the independent variable. Granovetter contends that job information diffuses through weak ties rather than strong ones because "those to whom one is closest are likely to have the greatest overlap in contact with those one already knows, so that the information to which they are privy is likely to be much the same as that which one already has" (1974: 52–53; see also 1973: 1369–73). If Coleman's diffusion theory focuses on the structure of the system of actors, Granovetter examines the kind of relation through which a certain type of information flows. In building a theory of revolution as an event, Skocpol (1979) focuses on the relations between the classes and the state, the relations among the classes themselves, and the relations between the state and other states in the world system. One of her fundamental postulates is that "a revolution is not made [by man], but it comes [when the structural conditions are met]" (Skocpol, 1979: 17). There are no explicit actors making decisions of revolutionary participation in her theory, but only the relations or structures moulding the structural outcome, revolution.

Cell *d* refers to the framework that relates the system of actors to the system of events. An example may be found in White's *Chains of Opportunity: System Models of Mobility in Organizations* (1970), which explores processes through which job seekers and positions are matched. Contrasting cell *d* with cell *a* clarifies the distinctiveness of this framing perspective. Traditionally, research on occupational mobility following the "status attainment model" treated a change of jobs as if it were a purely individual decision, determined by the background characteristics of the individual and those aspects of life history which affect occupational mobility (Coleman, 1985). As often noted, the status attainment model shows us a one-sided view of the world, in which only the supply of job-seekers—not demand or the availability of jobs—is considered. By not taking into account the structure of job opportunities, this model ignores the joint constraints imposed by the relative availability and interest of job-seekers and job-providers. The matching marriage market theory in demography (Becker, 1973, 1974, 1981) is another good example of research belonging to cell *d*. It analyzes the process through which a distribution of available men is matched by that of available women mediated by the interests of both parties. The events in the labor and marriage market examples are the actual points in time at which a job-seeker and -provider are

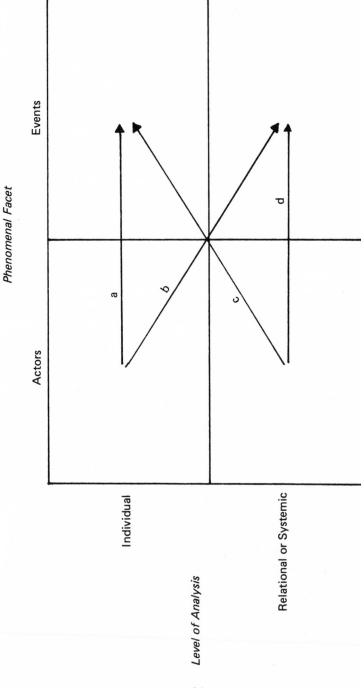

Figure 1.3. An Alternative Depiction of the Typology in Figure 1.2

24

matched or a marriage is contracted. Note that current theories have relatively little to say about the *structuration* of these events beyond rather general references to external factors, such as good or poor states of the economy, that can be assumed to raise or depress the volume of the events at given points in time (Easterlin, 1966, 1970; Evans, 1983; Hogan, 1981).

Smelser's (1962) collective action model, which posits several determinant "value-added" stages between structural conditions and the collective action to reduce structural strain, may be another example belonging to cell *d*. He analyzes the sequence of unfolding value-added events producing the final outcome of collective action. An event or a set of related events initially triggers a disruption of the usual ongoing relationships and thus impairs the usual functioning of the system. A set of actors embedded in a conducive structure attempts to provide onlookers with a context within which the meaning of the strain can be understood to require some form of collective action to change the stressful conditions. This labeling of problems can occur at several levels: values, norms, mobilization of motives for action, and situational facilities (1962:65). Although Smelser clarifies the role of systemic structures in determining the course of the unfolding value-added stages of events, he gives no image of the people who actually execute the sequences (Brown, 1965: 731–33).

Although the current evolutionary theories of organization (Hannan and Freeman, 1977) do not belong to this cell, modifications drawing from neo-evolutionary biology can make them fall into this category. In recent years theories of evolutionary biology, under the name of *biological structuralism*, are undergoing a rapid paradigm change. Instead of treating genetic mutations as random events (genetic atomism), newer theories attempt to build a model of evolution that incorporates certain laws of structural constraints and historical connectedness in explaining them (Collins, 1983). A fruitful future direction for evolutionary theories of organizations would be to consider the historical connectedness of organizational innovations (or structural conduciveness for this connectedness) in explaining the evolution of organizational forms, instead of treating innovations as purely random events.

Another way of depicting the logic of figure 1.2 is presented in figure 1.3. The arrows depict the direction of the move from one phenomenal unit to another while the figure suggests whether one has stayed at the same level of analysis or shifted levels. The letters refer to the cells labeled in figure 1.2. Note that the tendency in social research has been to move from actors as the initial reference point to events, often treated as unproblematic givens. For example, voting studies start out from a predispositional model of actors' inclinations to vote in certain ways. One could conceive of an argument that reverses the logic: that is, it would start from events (e.g., the different at-

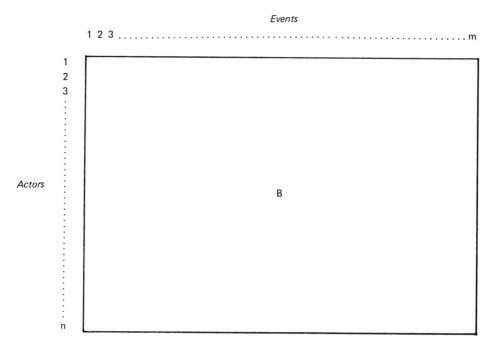

Figure 1.4. The Rectangular Matrix of Actors by Events

tributes of presidential candidates), actively eliciting and orchestrating responses from actors. The relative absence of research emphasizing events and their character as a demand structure for actors' behavior speaks to the relative neglect of explicit theorizing about event structures, particularly when compared with the rich body of work on the social organization of actors. To be sure, certain institutionalist theories represent steps toward a theory of the structuration of events, but many of them, being couched in abstract generalities, are difficult to operationalize empirically.

Structuration of Action Systems

With these preliminaries in hand, we are in position to develop our main argument. To start, we define a rectangular matrix in which the rows are a set of actors (i) and the columns are a set of events (j) in a system of action (see figure 1.4). Entries in the cells of the matrix indicate the nature of the relationship between each actor and event. For example, a *1* might indicate that the actor participated in some way in the event, and a *0*, that it did not. Two critical questions arise immediately: (1) what is the boundary-specifying principle that defines the set of *actors* belonging to the joint space of actors/events? and (2) What is the boundary-specifying principle that defines the set of *events* belonging to the joint space of actors/events? (See Laumann et al., 1983, for an extended discussion of the problem of boundary specification.) As we shall see, the matter is much more complicated than the above questions imply. In fact, there are a multitude of "valid" framing rules for any given system of action, each of which treats the set and subsets of rows and columns in fundamentally different ways. Each alternative has profound implications for selecting the methodology appropriate for empirical analysis.

Before developing this argument about multiple framing principles, we find it useful to form a triangular matrix out of the rectangular matrix depicted in figure 1.4 by taking into account the interrelationships among events and among actors. In figure 1.5, we have added an events-by-events triangular matrix, *A*, that refers to the interrelationships among events (*m*) and an actor-by-actor triangular matrix, *C*, that defines the (dyadic) interrelationships among the actors (*n*). The third-dimensional column indicates the absolute properties of events and actors stacked together, which include variables such as the preferences or the amount of resources of the actor and the public visibility of events. The entries in the matrix itself represent information about the ways actors and events are related to one another in three modalities: within events, within actors, and between actors and events. This is our specification of the individual versus relational level of analysis for a given system of action.

Matrix *C* is familiar to social network analysts who study links among actors. It can readily be interpreted as a symmetrized social choice matrix. Of course, the asymmetric choice matrix, *n* by *n*, would be the customary starting point for a network analysis, but we do not believe that the generality of our argument is lost if we confine attention to the symmetrized submatrix for the sake of simplicity. What may be new for us to think about is the event-by-event matrix, which raises all-too-often-neglected questions about the organization of events and the resulting impact of that organization on the actor-event interface, *B*.

Let us first think about the framing perspective assumed in cell *a* of figure 1.2 as it would apply to the data structure depicted in figure 1.5. In the radically individualist framing of the problem, an event is regarded as a well-defined given (e.g., a presidential election day) and considered merely as a stimulus providing the occasion for the responses arising out of individual actors' predispositions. The event as well as the actors are treated as statistically and sociologically independent units; no information about the relations among the actors in the set (rows) and the events (e.g., the influence of

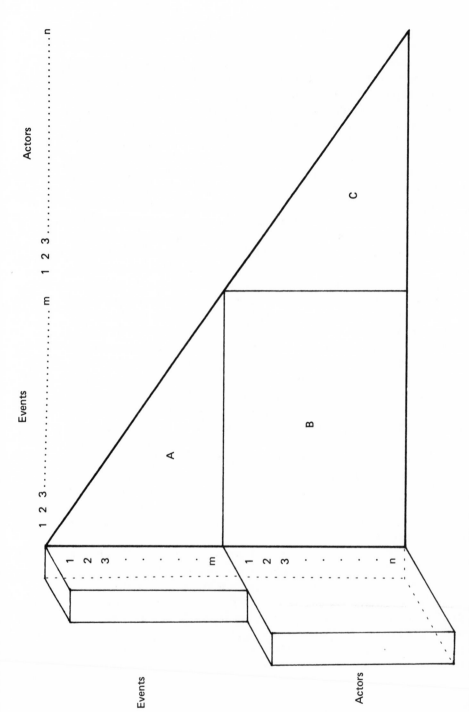

Figure 1.5. A Matrix Representation of the Interface among Events, Actors, and Actors/Events

different events over the course of a campaign on a given actor's maturing decision to vote for a particular candidate) is taken into account. The analysis focuses attention on a single event column vector in figure 1.5 where the rows refer to individual actors endowed with purposive orientations and other individual-level measures of actor characteristics. Even if the investigator should choose to speak of the impact of the social context of a given actor, as indicated, for example, by the preferences of his circle of intimates (see, e.g., Laumann, 1973; Scheuch, 1965), these intimates are, by definition, actors outside the sampling frame constituting the set of actors n, which are sampled as free-standing individuals from the population universe of voters.

Now let us consider the case that introduces selected structural considerations, combining the individual and relational levels of analysis (e.g., cell a plus cell c in figure 1.2). Here we assume that relational information about actor ties contained in triangular matrix C of figure 1.5 can be used, in addition to the individual-level actor information, to explain the behavior of individual actors with respect to a given event (i.e., one of the columns describing an event). Thus, the triangular matrix C in figure 1.5 might describe the dyadic (digraphic or structural equivalent) relations among actors in a communication network. The diagonal elements of the triangle are, using Lazersfeld and Menzel's (1969) term, the relational properties of each actor derived from such a matrix: for example, his centrality in the network.[6] Now, the behavior of individual actors with respect to this given event (e.g., their participation in the event) can be analyzed in terms of the absolute properties of actors (note the third dimension sketched in figure 1.5), the relational properties in the main diagonal, and the pairwise relational properties in the off-diagonal elements of the triangle. The event is still considered to be externally given and independent from all others. A considerable literature has emerged that addresses the methodological issues posed by treating individual- and contextual-level variables of actors in the same analytic framework (e.g., Blalock, 1984; Erbring and Young, 1979).

The literature is less helpful with respect to the structuration of events, since most theorists treat the organization of events as extrinsic to their explanatory problem. Even the most methodologically sophisticated discussions of structural or contextual effects have dealt exclusively with the composition of actors and their surroundings, ignoring the sequencing and structuring aspects of events in which they engage.[7] By contrast, we postulate that events themselves possess properties in the absolute sense of individually character-

---

6. Note that network theorists often call such variables positional variables (e.g., Burt, 1980).

7. For a review of multilevel research, see van den Eeden and Hüttner (1982). See also Erbring and Young (1979).

ized occasions or as *organized contextuality* that have consequences for the ways actors behave. The organized contextuality of an event is based both on its horizontal context (i.e., embeddedness in institutional space) and its longitudinal context (i.e., embeddedness in time). We argue, therefore, that the interconnection of events in these contexts has a fundamental methodological implication for our framing of the data analysis and interpretations of the results.

Empirical Application

Our interest in this conceptualization of the actor-event interface was aroused when we began to design our study of national policy domains, exploring the ways in which actors participated in shaping specific policies over time. Once we successfully resolved the boundary-specification problem of identifying the set of consequential corporate actors in energy and health policy over the past five to 10 years, we were confronted with the task of specifying the set of events around which the actors' activities were organized. We defined an event as a critical, temporally ordered decision point in a collective decision-making sequence that must occur in order for a policy option to be authoritatively selected. Note that this definition involves two analytically separable dimensions—the institutional decision location and historical time—which provide the bases for formulating the principles of linkages among events.

   Thus, two or more events may constitute distinct intermediate points in a chain of related decisions leading to an outcome. Obviously, chains of related decisions will be orchestrated differently, depending on the institutional arena in which the decision-making process takes place. Congressional passage of a bill involves a characteristic series of decision points, such as House and Senate hearings, subcommittee and committee votes, and chamber actions, that follows a predictable, institutionally specified order differing in key respects from the process by which a federal agency comes to promulgate a new regulation. What is permissible for interested parties to do in one institutional arena may not be normatively approved in another because of different institutional rules. Thus, institutionalist theories of government functioning provide at least one significant basis for identifying key events to study and for anticipating the linkages among them.

   The essence of the conceptual framework we propose for the analysis of policy decision making is a structural complex that connects consequential organizational actors with a set of temporally arrayed policy events. To understand how national policy unfolds, one must take into account how organizations perceive and respond to an opportunity structure for affecting policy outcomes that is created by the temporal sequence of policy-relevant events. Because a specific policy event is embedded in the context of other antecedent, concurrent, and impending events, policy analysts must incorporate the entire structure of organizations and events and not focus narrowly upon highly selected instances of either, as do most case studies (e.g., Dahl, 1961).

To be sure, multiple decision-making processes organized around diverse substantive issues claim the attentions of actors participating in a given policy domain. These diverse decision-making activities may be only loosely coupled with one another, if at all, and may proceed with time horizons of days, months, or years. Coupling of events may thus rest on an institutionally prescribed order or on widely shared, cross-cutting concern among the relevant actors about their outcomes.

A simple example of a framing perspective that considers the ways in which the relations among events have impact upon actors would be found in a hypothesis that two events far apart in their institutional settings (one congressional, say, and the other executive) would have a different logic of attracting participants than two events occurring in the same decision-making arena. Another hypothesis might focus attention on the patterns of participation in a scenario of events.[8] For example, the pattern of participation in an institutionally orchestrated scenario would be more orderly than the pattern observed in initiatory events (which by definition lack a fully institutionalized order) or a scenario of events arising from historically significant accidents like the oil embargo of 1973 because the consensually shared institutional norms of the game are inoperative or absent under certain analytically specifiable circumstances.[9]

In addition to the institutional scaffolding that links some events while segregating others, time itself is an ordering principle among events. Events do not occur in isolation, but always are embedded in temporally ordered sequences, which shape the policy responses and initiatives of the core actors and set limits on the outcomes of collective decisions. Two fundamental aspects of time order are worth special mention. First, the mere fact that one event follows another establishes an *incontrovertible* and *irreversible* rela-

8. As a first approximation, we define the scenario of events as a concatenated sequence of events based on content homogeneity. A more elaborate discussion appears in Chapter 9.

9. We have observed that actors participate in scenarios of events in a highly disciplined way. That is, if events in a scenario are statistically independent of each other, as is often assumed in atomistic individualistic models, the expected frequency of participating throughout from the first to the last event is $N \prod_{i=1}^{k} P_i$, where N is the number of actors and k is the number of events in a scenario. The expected frequency of consistent nonparticipation is $N \prod_{i=1}^{k} (1 - P_i)$. We observe, however, that the participation pattern deviates sharply from the random model, indicating the linkage of participation or nonparticipation in a scenario. This suggests the importance of linking events together and taking their relations into consideration in explaining actors' participation in the events. For elaboration see Chapter 11.

tionship between them, seeming to introduce an *ineluctable dependence* of the second on the first that may have to be taken into account in the analysis. Conventional causal thinking is especially congenial to arguments stipulating that a subsequent event is an effect of (i.e., is causally dependent on) a prior event. But what about theories of strategic action that assert that a preferred end-state outcome may "determine" how an actor participates in events leading up to that outcome (see Shepsle, 1979, for example). In this case, the causal order appears to be temporally reversed. Second, an event occurs by definition at a particular point in time that has a distinctive historicity shared with contemporaneous events but serving to distinguish them all from events occurring before and after that historical point. Debates about the desirability of establishing a national health insurance scheme, for example, had very different meanings for the participants in 1948, 1965, and 1980 (Starr, 1982). Similarly, during and immediately after the Arab oil embargo of 1973, events pertaining to energy policy attracted the attention of a far more diverse set of concerned parties and aroused quite different political dynamics than was the case in times of abundant and cheap energy (McFarland, 1984).

Our argument does not claim such profound uniqueness for all events that it logically precludes their systematic analysis or comparison and confines us to narrative accounts of what happened. On the contrary, just as is regularly done for individual actors, we assume that events possess analytic features, such as controversiality, scope of impact, public visibility, and institutional locus, that impose empirical regularities on the political process and permit systematic comparisons. We may use these features in conceptualizing the structuration of events in the submatrix *A* in figure 1.5. Suppose that we input the matrix of these features into a computer algorithm in order to produce the matrix of interpoint distances between all possible pairs of events, as we do in Chapter 10. The proximity of two events indicates that they are similar on the analytically relevant dimensions. One may then hypothesize that the closer the events, the higher the probability that similar actors will be attracted, and vice versa, the similarity of actors being defined by some relations based on the structural equivalence approach. This hypothesis would be a clear example of the kind of analysis that posits an interface between the structure of actors and the structure of events.

Let us look more closely at submatrix *A* in figure 1.5, which represents the interrelationships among events. As a first step, we require that events be arrayed in order of their time of occurrence. Beyond that we are confronted with any number of ways of grouping events (or including them individually) that reflect different frameworks for the structuration of events, none of which enjoys any inherent superiority but each of which leads to quite different images of event structure. For example, one could identify critical events that meaningfully divide the series of events into historical periods. The oil embargo in 1973 in the energy domain or the passage of the Medicare Act in 1965 in the health domain are candidates for critical turning points. Note that the timing of these two cutpoints does not coincide but is justified only in terms of the distinctive historical developments of each domain. If one proposes to *compare* the two domains, then the principle of periodization must be analytically consistent for both even though it leads to different time segments—and therefore different congressional and executive contexts. On the other hand, institutional theories of congressional decision making might argue for the periodicity of the volume of activities over congressional sessions, with peaks in the late spring and fall and troughs in the late summer and late winter. Thus, framing justifies grouping congressional events by month, irrespective of their substantive content, in order to chart the varying volume of participation over time. This way of framing implies that the varying volume of participation affects the scheduling of new events, the deployment of resources by interested parties, and the strategic planning of participation in future events. An actor may participate in a current event in order to ensure his right to play a part in the final event that affects his interest. The decision to participate in the current event would be facilitated if it occurs when there is a low volume of competing activities in the domain. Still another framing tactic might reflect the investigator's interest in grouping events according to their substantive content or relationship to a general policy objective: for example, seeing incidents in the passage of a given bill in terms of a standard cycle of congressional decision making or a common constituency of concerned actors.

Each framing principle generates testable hypotheses concerning the participation of actors and the consequences of different combinations of events. For example, events perceived as sharing substantive content should elicit the attention of similar actors. From an institutionalist perspective, patterns of participation in initiatory events should differ from those in intermediate or late events in that sequence.

Similar remarks, more familiar to network analysts, can be made about the structuration of actor interrelationships. Entries in submatrix C of figure 1.5 can refer to quite distinct types of social relationships—friendship, physical proximity, resource exchanges, authority relations, and so on. Each yields a rather different structural image of the set of actors; it is up to the analyst to provide the theoretical justification for choosing one form of structure over another (see Berkowitz, 1982; Boorman and White, 1976; Laumann and Pappi, 1976: chap. 1; White et al., 1976). Depending on one's notions about the structural differentiation of the social organization, one can identify a rationale for identifying subsets of actors who "belong together" with respect to subsets of events in which they have a particular interest.

Let us illustrate the usefulness of the actor-event interface in explaining organizational participation in the policy domain with more specific examples from cells *a* and *d* of figure 1.2. A naive predispositional framing perspective focuses on actors' individual characteristics (such as general interests and resources) in order to predict their activation by a set of events assumed to be statistically independent. To this model the concept of an actor-event interface adds a consideration of the characteristics of events that attract actors differentially. If one controls for actors' predispositional characteristics, certain events are shown to attract (or demand) particular types of actors. For example, highly visible events may attract different actors than publicly invisible events, even after one controls for organizational monitoring capacity and interests, because highly visible events themselves may entail an inherently different logic of participation (e.g., they may have different implications for strategic participation). Or events occurring at different institutional decision loci attract actors differentially to the extent that they have different implications for the legal mandate, institutional constraints, or institutional norms of the game.

How is the structure of events interfaced with the structure of actors in their policy participation (cell *d*)? In responding to the puzzling question "why are there stable interorganizational relations?" network theorists argue persuasively that the stable relations exist because organizations strive to reduce uncertainty, information costs, and opportunistic behaviors of members by creating relatively stable channels of information inflow and thereby developing certain norms of the game (Leblebici and Salancik, 1982; Williamson, 1975, 1981, 1985). If the institutional norms are strong in a cooperative network, then a set of sequential events constituting distinct points in a chain of related decisions leading to an outcome will attract the actors who are embedded in the same structural locations in the network of actors: for example, members of a subdomain who have high communication density among themselves will be active throughout, from the first to the last events of the scenario. In short, structurally identical events recruit the participation of structurally identical actors, with a possible exception in the strategic participation of some powerful actors who can enjoy the margin of liberty (Crozier and Friedberg, 1980:45–63).[10]

10. The structure of events can be conceived in a number of different ways. That is, there is multiplexity of event structures. In Figure 1.5, for example, the triangle matrix *C* may be a binary matrix, with *1* indicating that the two events belong to the same decision cycle or to the same decision location, and *0* otherwise. The structure of events then can be operationalized with the geometric pairwise distances in *n*-dimensional space calculated from such matrices.

Comparison of several systems of action requires higher-order concepts—Lazarsfeld and Menzel (1969) call them global concepts—that characterize the organizational features of each system of action. For example, we shall be studying the energy and health policy domains as separate entities. One set of results suggests that the structure of communication linkages in the health domain is organized in a well-defined hierarchy, with centrally located actors who mediate communication among the peripherally located actors. In contrast, the energy domain has a more diffuse communication network lacking a coordinating set of actors; actors tend to be located on a wheel that puts them in close proximity with others sharing a narrowly defined concern and farther from every one else. We find interesting differences in the politics of the two domains as a result. Similarly, we study the structuration of the events in each domain. In the health domain, events appear to be sharply clustered on the basis of their specialized content and the institutional loci for their decision making. Events attract narrowly defined constituencies, with little overlap across dissimilar events. In contrast, the energy policy domain processes events lacking much structural differentation in terms of interested parties, content, or institutional loci of decision making. We conclude that the health domain in a given time frame is more institutionalized in its event structure than the energy domain is. Here we assert the testable proposition that the structuration of events in each domain has differing implications for the structuration of the social organization of the actors participating in the domain.

Outline of the Book

Three interrelated themes run through this book. The substantive theme describes, compares, and contrasts the national policy domains in energy and health as they have emerged in the United States in the 1970s as products of distinctive histories of institutional and organizational development. The accent is on understanding the social organization of elite participation in a broadly defined range of policy events, embedded in distinctive institutional arrangements that set the framework for future policy deliberations. The emphasis is on what decisions were made and why, rather than on evaluation of their policy impacts from the perspective of an external observer or concerned citizen. (Policy impacts are, of course, regularly assessed by the interested parties we are studying as part of their ongoing decisions to act.) Drawing on a developing perspective on social choice and the structure of social action, we elaborate a theoretical argument that justifies looking at actors and events in the way we do, in counterdistinction to other modes of inquiry about national decisionmaking. Finally, the methodological theme explores different rationales for adopting given analytic techniques and empirical simplifications that lead us to ask different kinds of questions of our data. The level and unit of analysis are crucial reference points in this discussion. Specific techniques are designed to reveal the underlying structures that coordinate the ways actors and events are orchestrated in the two collective action systems under investigation. That is, the substantive theme is explored from the distinctive vantage points of the theory and methods.

The book is organized into four parts. The first is introductory. This chapter reviews the relevant literature on national elite decision making and introduces our theoretical perspective on the central empirical issues addressed by that literature. While ecumenical with regard to theories of the state, and organizational theory more generally, our theoretical perspective directs attention to the formally constituted corporate actors, both public and private, and their relations with one another as the key figures in national policy making and to the central analytic relevance of events themselves in devising an integrated explanatory account of collective action systems. Introducing our two empirical case studies, Chapter 2 reviews the history of each domain over the past century, with particular attention given to the times at which and interests for which corporate actors were founded and began their efforts to shape policy at the local, state, and national levels of government. Regarding the 1970s, the reader is given a synoptic overview of the main policy controversies and associated decision making events addressed by the most active participants in policy making. The chapter provides a critical reference to the historical and contemporary literature which the reader can use to evaluate the empirical analysis of actors and events presented in subsequent chapters. Chapter 3 describes the study design whereby we identified the core actors in each policy domain and then specified the appropriate individual in each organization to be interviewed for 90 minutes about his or her organization's interests and participation in a wide-ranging set of issues and decision-making events. To give a sense of the diversity of organizational respondents, we present selected descriptive characteristics, including type of organization, age, size, range of participation in various domains, and so on. (Appendix A, in addition, presents detailed characteristics for each respondent organization in the two target populations).[11]

11. Although many of the protagonists are familiar to anyone interested in contemporary national politics, our objective is to provide systematic comparative data about them as they directly relate to the two policy domains in hand. A key notion borrowed from sociological theories of the social system is that given actors play analytically identifiable roles in particular systems of action that permit the analyst to take into account only those attributes having direct relevance to the analysis in hand. Just as one "ignores" (disregards) other features of a man's personality and social characteristics (e.g., his work roles) when focusing on his roles as husband and father in a particular family, it is appropriate to think of a corporate actor's, say a union's, participation in a health controversy as analytically independent from its primary goal of representing its members' interests in negotiating labor contracts.

Parts two and three address corporate actors as individuals pursuing various goals, related to one another through exchange relations, while part four takes up the analysis of events and their outcomes. More specifically, part two considers corporate actors at the individual level of analysis. Two fundamental attributes of individuals are identified and measured: their specific interests in particular policy domains and the resources they control to pursue these interests. In chapter 4 we propose a way of conceptualizing and measuring each actor's scope of interest in a policy domain that, in effect, permits us to define that actor's purposive orientation toward its policy environment. An important byproduct of this technique is the ability to characterize the structure of issue linkages across the population of interested parties, which, in turn, allows us to develop a replicable way of defining the issue publics (i.e., a set of interests and their associated interested parties) that constitute the policy domain in a particular configuration of organized interests. Once suitable analytic techniques are introduced, this latter result nevertheless allows us to move to the collective level of analysis—namely, the characterization of the structure of organized interests in the policy domain. These results permit us to characterize the nature and extent of structural differentiation in each domain: that is, distinctive activities tend to be performed by distinct clusters of actors (Parsons, 1967; Parsons and Smelser, 1956).

Having identified the actors' differentiated interests in the policy domain's concerns, we are in position in Chapters 5 and 6 to consider the nature and extent of actors' resource endowments in pursuing those interests. This is the classic sociological inquiry into the role played by social inequalities in the distribution of scarce resources, directed here toward explaining the results of participation in contests regarding policy objectives. Chapter 5 introduces a lengthy theoretical discussion of the nature of influence in large-scale systems, based on a review of the literature on influence and trust; it concludes with a detailed empirical inquiry concerning the distribution of generalized reputations for influence in the two domains. Comparatively speaking, both domains appear to have sharply unequal influence hierarchies, but each manifests distinctively different patterns of consensus about who counts in their respective domains. The empirical results strongly confirm the theoretical speculation that highly differentiated systems of action require multidimensional rather than unidimensional conceptions of influence structures.

Chapter 6 looks more concretely at the organizational capacity to act by attempting to assess, first, how organizations differ in their ability to monitor and gather relevant information from various actors in the domain relating to their policy interests. Given an adequate monitoring capacity, organizations also differ with respect to the specific resources they control that can be used to reward or punish their supporters and adversaries in the policy-making process. After enumerating these resources and determining their distribution among the relevant actors, we perform a factor analysis and identify three general factors: mobilizable resources (including specialized expertise, personnel, funds, good connections, grassroots mobilization, and opinion mobilization), reputation as an impartial mediator, and authority. These three factors together account for roughly 55 percent of the total variance in the general reputations for influence in each domain.

Part three moves to the collective level of analysis by addressing the structure of relations among actors. Whereas part two stressed the features of individual actors that motivate them to act (i.e., to advance or defend particular interests) and endow them with the resources necessary for effective participation in decision-making events, part three asserts the critical role of timely and pertinent information exchange in orchestrating collective actions. Chapter 7, on dyadic communication, discusses at length the process of information transmission and interpretation and its role in our model of the policy-making process. Recent advances in methods of network analysis permit us to explore detailed hypotheses concerning the patterning of candid-confidential communication links in each policy domain, thereby helping us to understand how interests and resource differentiation among actors organize the communication structure. More important, the techniques we devise to characterize the communication structure in each domain will help us to examine how position in the communication network channels and restricts information flows such that it may shape actor participation and effectiveness in particular decision-making events.

Chapter 8 shifts the analysis of communication structure from the pairwise/dyadic (or micro) level to the global (or macro) level of the domain as a whole. Here we argue that appropriate graphic representations of actors in terms of their relative communication distances will be organized according to two general principles of social organization: centrality/peripherality and interest differentiation. The first principle asserts that centrally located actors in the communication structure act as information aggregators and brokers for the policy domain and have broad-ranging or generalized interests in the issues confronting the domain. In contrast, actors located in the periphery have more specialized and narrowly defined policy concerns. To be sure, a key question is how do actors come to occupy central locations in a communication network? Is it because of their *ex ante* commitment to a broad range of policy concerns, or because their access to diverse information sources induces more generalized concerns? Probably both processes are present in any single instance (Williamson, 1985). The second principle, sectoral differentiation, identifies wedges of the communication structure that are occupied by actors sharing common concerns and exchanging information with respect to those concerns. Actors occupying regions so defined are subjected to selective information exchange, making them highly knowledgeable about certain policy concerns and relatively ignorant about others, although the latter may ultimately have important consequences for their core concerns.

Part four introduces the distinctive element in our analytic framework: a systematic consideration of events as phenomena to be treated jointly with the constituent actors in the system of action. To understand how national policy unfolds, one must take into account how organizations perceive and respond to an opportunity structure created by the temporal sequence of policy-relevant events. Because a specific policy event is embedded in the context of other antecedent, concurrent, and impending events, we must systematically consider the unfolding structure of organizational participation as it is embedded in a structure of events that are tightly or loosely coupled because of institutional, substantive, and historical considerations. Chapter 9 introduces the framework for concatenated event analysis, elaborating our definition of relevant events in several directions. After describing the concept of event scenarios—sets of temporally ordered events having an underlying bias of linkage or interrelationship—we suggest how events may be compared on the basis of analytically abstracted attributes such as relative controversiality, public visibility, scope of impact, institutional locus (i.e., Congress, the courts, or the executive branch), or functional consequence (e.g., regulation, initiation of a program activity, or setting of funding levels). Turning to the empirical analysis, we first take up the problem of specifying a meaningful set of policy events to study in each political domain. A systematic comparison of the ways events differ from one another on various analytic dimensions is presented in order to clarify the biases in the events we chose to study.

A concluding section proposes a novel technique for examining the actor-event interface that accomplishes two analytic purposes. First, we devise more rigorous measures of individual-level event attributes by means of a systematic characterization of the organizational participants they attract or repel. Second, we employ the interrelationships among various analytic features of events we have identified to propose an empirically grounded model of event structuration. Here we answer questions of the following sort: Are controversial events especially likely to enjoy high public visibility and to be broad in scope of impact? Are events dominated by the participation of highly influential private actors more likely to be low in public visibility and controversiality than events dominated by actors of low standing in the influence hierarchy? What might such differences tell us about the strategic behavior of actors with different reputations for influence? Do the two policy domains differ with respect to the degree of linkage between controversy and visibility? If they do, why might that be so?

Chapter 10 continues along the same lines, framing the problem of explaining the participation of individual organizations in policy events from the individualistic point of view. Each organization is characterized in terms of its scope of purposive orientation with respect to the policy domain, relevant resource endowment, including standing in the influence hierarchy, singular locations in the information and resource exchange networks, and scope of participation of individual organizations in the set of policy-making events. A path model used to account for the scope of participation in events is evaluated for each domain. Using a LISREL technique, we achieve reasonably good fits to the observed co-variations among the measures; we observe, however, some provocative differences between the two domains with respect to the role of the exchange networks in explaining the scope of an organization's participation.

Chapter 11 shifts the analysis of events to the relational or collective level as it reviews various means by which events may be linked to one another. Three mechanisms of linkages attract particular attention: institutional, substantive, and temporal. Linking events institutionally refers to the normative legal order that prescribes in advance how decision-making processes in a given institutional arena, like Congress or the Food and Drug Administration, must proceed from initiation to a final authoritative decision by a specified action of an individual or collective decision-maker. Participation of actors is orchestrated by the ground rules prescribed by the institutional arena. Note that the logic of explaining the participation of actors proceeds from features of the events themselves and their linkages instead of from endogenous features of actors, like their interests and internally generated choices based on their interests and resources. Substantive linkage of events rests on their explicitly or implicitly shared commonality of content, irrespective of decision locus or time. Finally, time links events, both vertically and horizontally. Any given event occurs in a particular historical flow of prior and anticipated events that may be specified according to substantive or institutional considerations. Even typically "unrelated" events may be linked by sharing a historical moment—the horizontal feature of time—that defines them as competing for the scarce attention of diverse actors. The chapter concludes with a novel empirical analysis of the pairwise linkages (or dependencies) among events in the energy and health domain as generated by the overlapping or nonoverlapping patterns of co-participation of the consequential actors—an instance of the collective level of analysis of the actor-event interface. The technique permits a rigorous and replicable specification of the organization of significant events in the two domains into socially differentiated subsectors of more or less tightly coupled decision-making processes.

The structure of conflict and consensus is the topic of the next chapter. To this point we have treated actors as having topical interests in various aspects of a policy domain, but no explicit preferences for particular policy outcomes. Such a framing of the problem results in placing mortal enemies in shared arenas of action. By introducing policy preferences, we raise questions about the overarching structure of competition and conflict among actors. The conventional image of policy making assumes that given actors are "ideologically" consistent proponents of particular lines of policy; thus, we should anticipate consistent lineups of actors on each side of a controversy and across the set of controversies confronting a domain. The counterview is that fully mature policy-making domains are highly specialized and pose all sorts of complex side issues and payoffs for various actors. Since the interested parties themselves are complex entities with a multitude of conflicting interests, we should expect highly fluid and easily recombinant alliances that elude unidimensional polarization models in favor of multidimensional structures of conflict. Chapter 12 explores these issues with a technique that takes actors' communication networks *and* preferences into account simultaneously.

Coleman (1973) has proposed a sophisticated model of collective action that is especially congenial to our theoretical and empirical objectives. Using an extensive elaboration of his model, Chapter 13 combines information about actors' interests, resources, and control over events with information about their exchanges of resources to predict, with remarkable success, (1) the actual final outcomes of eight strongly contested event scenarios in each policy domain and (2) the relative overall influence of the actors. Even more provocative theoretically is the opportunity the model affords for examining two rival theories of power—namely, the resource mobilization and the resource deployment approaches to power or influence transactions.

Rather than recapitulate the detailed findings and arguments of the book, the final chapter attempts a retrospective synthesis of the central themes and major conclusions about the social organization of the two national systems of collective action. On this foundation, we then extract a more general formulation of the central assumptions that must undergird an empirically valid model of the organizational state as it has emerged in the late twentieth century in the United States. As a preview of what a more comprehensive conception of the policy structure of the modern state would look like, we analyze some recently available data from a sample of government officials on the interrelationships among the 20 major policy domains with which the national government must deal, using the now familiar techniques introduced in this book. The surprising result of this *Gedankenexperiment* is the suggestion that there is a sharp distinction between those policy arenas most closely associated with the concerns and needs of major public and private organizational actors for financial resources and coordination and those policy domains most pre-occupied with the interests of natural persons in their pursuits as citizens and human beings who work, marry, consume, educate their children—in short, pursue their personal lives. We conclude with some brief remarks regarding the growing disparity between the concerns of positive (or empirically rooted) theories of the state and normative political theory.

2

An Organizational Perspective on Two Policy Domains

with Elisabeth Clemens

The matrix of actors and events at the center of this analysis, the policy domain, is not an ahistorical given but the product of previous political activity. Viewed from this perspective, outcomes are not limited to discrete policy decisions but involve the production and modification of ground rules that determine which issues are acknowledged, how they are linked to others, and which individual and corporate actors are to be recognized as legitimate participants in the policy-making process. The dilemmas and opportunities confronted by participants within a policy domain—indeed, the definition of the domain itself—are products of earlier decisions and nondecisions, what Heclo has called the "policy heritage" (Heclo, 1974). The central task of this chapter is to outline the development of these two policy domains and to account for some of the significant differences that existed between them during the 1970s. At the same time, many of the principal organizational actors in contemporary energy and health policy will be introduced.

As the authors have argued previously, a policy domain or other social system "is substantively defined by a criterion of mutual relevance and common fate that stipulates the basis on which members are to take each other into account in their actions" (Knoke and Laumann, 1982:256). The use of "health" and "energy" as labels for fields of political activity should not be taken to mean that these criteria of relevance are clearly delineated and established for all time. For example, many issues relating to nutrition have been removed from the area of health care to the less prestigious realm of welfare policy and, by way of price-support policies, to the agricultural policy domain. Similarly, energy policy is entangled with questions of regional development, environmental quality, and national security.

Contemporary policy domains are the outcome of a twofold process: the establishment of organizations committed to—and capable of—participation in policy making at various levels of government as well as the framing of "issues" in ways that serve to organize that participation. The significance attributed to organizational, rather than individual, actors does not stem solely from the increased number and size of organizations implicated in contemporary politics. Significant social events have come to be understood as interactions between individuals and corporate actors or among some set of corporate actors (Burt, 1983). In addition, the development of higher education, the mass media, and other institutions has tended to "focus attention on events controlled by ever larger corporate actors" (Coleman, 1973:7). Thus, the scope of citizen concerns has increased enormously in tandem with the growing mediation of political life by a complex network of organizations.

In order to develop this line of argument, it is useful to draw upon two bodies of literature that both, despite their many differences, address the process of policy formation. The first is institutional in character, exploring the growth of state agencies and the ways in which they organize—indeed, elicit—political mobilization and participation (Karl, 1984; Skowronek, 1982). The second emphasizes cognitive and cultural concerns and suggests ways of developing the insight that there is no natural way of framing specific issues or delineating policy domains.

As has been thoroughly documented in works such as Skowronek's *Building a New American State* (1982), political struggles among organized groups have produced not only discrete policy outcomes but transformations of the institutional character of the American state and, hence, the terms in which later debates have been framed. Referring to political reforms of the Progressive era, he argues that "the new American state emerged with a powerful administrative arm, but authoritative controls over this power were locked in constitutional stalemate" (Skowronek, 1982:16). Subsequent debates no longer focused on the federal government's ability to act but on the identity of those directing that activity: Congress, the President, the Civil Service, or various interested private parties.

Much of the political history of the United States during the twentieth century may be understood as a process of more or less incremental state building, a development that this chapter will trace in greater detail for both the energy and the health policy domains. The product has been a highly differentiated political arena in which the stakes necessary for effective participation have become increasingly high. Viewed from this perspective, political history encompasses not only institution building but processes of organizational mobilization and entrenchment as well. Contemporary politics is an activity for corporate actors rather than dedicated individuals or amorphous mass movements (McFarland, 1976; Salisbury, 1984). This organizational activity is effectively patterned by a system of incentives, structured meanings, and embedded resources that may be thought of as the topography of national politics. As Chubb has noted in his recent study of relations between the bureaucracy and interest groups in the formation of energy policy:

> our understanding of these relations is likely to profit if we shift our focus to the role the government plays in structuring them. Interest group activity should *not* be the exogenous variable in explanations of policy-making. The equation should be reversed; the theoretical table should be turned. The influence of private interests should be studied as a dependent variable; the policy needs of the government and the actions of the administration in pursuit of them should become the primary explanatory candidate. (1983:13)

The conception of policy domains as systems of action encompassing both "public" and "private" actors combines political sociology's established concern for the role of interest groups with recent efforts to develop a better understanding of the effects of state activity on the mobilization and direction of political participation (Evans et al., 1985; March and Olsen, 1984). In doing so, however, the approach developed in this book breaks with the traditional interest group literature in a significant way. Perceived group interests are not taken as given—in terms of either functional necessity or ideology—but are understood to be shaped, in large part, by the character of the political domain itself.

A number of recent works in political science and sociology have explored the ways in which the specific character and limited capacity of the political arena affects both the identification of issues and the formulation of "appropriate" solutions (Kingdon, 1984; Polsby, 1984):

> The generation of policy proposals . . . resembles a process of biological natural selection. Many ideas are possible in principle, and float around in a "policy primeval soup" in which specialists try out their ideas in a variety of ways—bill introductions, speeches, testimony, papers, and conversation. . . . Thus the selection system narrows the set of conceivable proposals and selects from that large set a short list of proposals that is actually available for serious consideration. (Kingdon, 1984:21)

To a significant extent, the character of any given winnowing process depends upon the existing set of ground rules, the "definition of the situation." Thus, environmentalists struggled to make the externalities of the fuel industry a relevant issue for the formation of energy policy (Vietor, 1980a) and, to the extent that they succeeded, transformed an ongoing policy debate that had been framed primarily in terms of economic issues and national security. The struggle of organized groups to gain access to and influence within the policy-making process is, at the same time, a contest over the framing of political issues and answers (see Chapter 12 and Gusfield, 1981; Spector and Kitsuse, 1977:75). Demonstrating a similar emphasis on the role of the understanding of a political situation by the actors involved, considerable effort has been devoted to the study of "cognitive maps" as they are used "to derive explanations of the past, make predictions for the future, and choose policies in the present" (Axelrod, 1976:11).

The need to synthesize cognitive or cultural approaches with institutional modes of analysis is not unique to the study of politics; indeed, it has been a major concern in many of the recent developments in organizational theory (Crozier, 1964; March and Olsen, 1984; Meyer and Rowan, 1977). Taken as the starting point for accounts of political history, this theoretical concern suggests the need for a distinctive approach. Rather than focusing on prominent individuals and important events, it is necessary to uncover the paths by which organized groups have been mobilized and the ways in which the terms of political debate have been established and, repeatedly, renegotiated. At any given point in history, policy debates and political struggles may be perceived in terms of a preestablished institutional and cognitive or symbolic context that will, in turn, be transformed over the course of these struggles.

A brief sketch of the character of the energy and health domains in the latter half of the 1970s suggests the variable nature of this cumulative process. In the wake of the "oil shocks" following the Arab-Israeli war of 1973 and the 1979 Iranian revolution, the energy domain was dominated by high-priority issues centering on the need to secure an adequate supply of energy for a wide variety of interested parties. Research and development legislation, administrative reorganization, and wide-ranging regulatory reforms were all on the decision agenda (Chubb, 1983). Many of the active organizations were new to national politics; the number of environmental and citizen interest groups had mushroomed since the late 1960s (McFarland, 1976:2). At the same time, industry groups were confronted with the need to reorganize themselves for a much more public brand of participation than that to which they were accustomed.

A major element in this realignment entailed the shift from the traditional pattern of fuel-specific policy making to debates over "energy policy" as a whole. Subdomains that had developed around the particular interests and problems of oil, coal, nuclear energy, and other fuel types were unsettled by demands that "their" issues now be considered part of broadly aggregated decisions. One element of this more inclusive approach to energy policy was a growing reluctance to continue the system of direct and indirect subsidies— depreciation allowances, quotas, investment credits, and so forth—that had been among the most important factors determining the character of energy industries in the United States since the turn of the century. Attempts to reform government relations with these industries, however, typically resulted in stalemate. At a time when established relations between actors in the domain were disrupted by the suspicious and combative mood that dominated much of U.S. politics in the wake of embargo-related economic crises and the political debacle of Watergate, few were willing to sacrifice present benefits in the hope of devising a fairer and more efficient energy policy in the future.

The international and domestic tensions of the 1970s had a rather different impact on activity within the health policy domain. Already well established, with experienced organizations representing a broad spectrum of interests, the dominant problem faced by this policy domain was the need to adjust in the face of rapidly increasing costs and economic contraction. Relatively few new actors were significant during the period under study; instead, older groups maneuvered to maintain or increase their influence while attempting to protect the interests of their constituencies or staff.

As was the case with energy policy, fundamental reorganization of this sector of government activity was one option; proposals for far-reaching programs of national health insurance received renewed attention during 1977 and 1978. Yet most activity centered on proposals for incremental reforms. Legislation promoting the development of health maintenance organizations (HMOs) promised to change the character of competition in the market for health care services; changes in the administration of federal health care policy—particularly Medicare, Medicaid, and federal subsidization of medical education—challenged the balance of power that had emerged in the wake of the Great Society legislation of the previous decade.

During the 1970s policy-makers in both the energy and the health domains were faced with major political and budgetary problems stemming from the oil embargoes and consistently high levels of inflation. As will be demonstrated in the following chapters, however, the character of organizational activity and debate in the two domains differed in significant ways. Participants in the energy domain faced repeated challenges to the fundamental character of government intervention and private enterprise. Within the health domain, similar challenges were turned aside in favor of a more incremental style of framing problems and making decisions. Many of these differences, we argue, may be traced to the organizational and cultural heritage of the two domains.

Energy Policy in the United States

The Organization of Industries

When speaking of American politics prior to the 1970s, the phrase "energy policy domain" is anachronistic. Until quite recently, the scope of government agencies and legislation rarely extended beyond a single fuel type, nor were energy issues easily disentangled from questions of national security, antitrust regulations, and states' rights. Mirroring these institutional and legislative developments, analyses have tended to trace the course of government policy and intervention with respect to a single industry, such as coal or natural gas. Nevertheless, the ways in which state and federal governments have affected the competitive advantages of various fuels, as well as the concerns motivating these interventions, have exerted a powerful influence on the development of these industries and, consequently, on the character of the political issues that they have inspired. (For an extended treatment of these issues see Chubb, 1983; Goodwin, 1981; and Vietor, 1984).

In order to set the stage for our analysis of contemporary energy politics, we will concentrate on two aspects of the development of this policy domain: the changing dependence of the national economy on various fuel types and the growth of legal and institutional capacities for governing this dependent relationship. The former involves a sequence of discoveries and technical innovations; the latter, the accumulated residue of successive political responses to market-induced or defense-related crises. Taken together, these historical developments help to explain the issues confronted by actors in the energy policy domain in the late 1970s and the range of policy instruments and options available to them.

At the beginning of the twentieth century, coal accounted for 90 percent of the energy consumption of the United States, but this was a recent development (Johnson, 1979:21). Before the large-scale construction of canals and railroads in the first half of the nineteenth century, wood and charcoal had been the nation's primary fuels. In the 1830s new coal-burning technologies prompted entrepreneurs to build canals in order to exploit the great anthracite fields of Pennsylvania. With the availability of an alternative to water power and charcoal, the factory system of manufacturing spread rapidly (Chandler, 1972). Through innovations in transportation and marketing, a later generation of entrepreneurs established coal as the predominant fuel for residential heating through much of the country (Martin, 1976). Thus, the growth of coal production was paralleled by the emergence of powerful industrial and private consumers.

But even as the preeminent position of coal within the national economy was secured, the foundations of an enduring form of interfuel competition were laid. In 1859 the "world's first oil well" was drilled in Pennsylvania, and within a few years John D. Rockefeller, Sr., had founded the Standard Oil Company, which, in all its incarnations, has been a major factor in the domestic and international petroleum industries up to the present day (Davis, 1974:43). Although oil was used initially for kerosene, the development of internal combustion and diesel engines greatly expanded the market for petroleum products, and discoveries in the Midwest transformed an Appalachian enterprise into a nationwide industry (Nash, 1968:2–3). Although coal remained the nation's primary fuel until the 1930s (Johnson, 1979:21), the oil industry soon became vital to the nation's economy and, with greater political consequences, to the military. Although water power and natural gas became important as sources of electricity and residential power, much of the early history of federal intervention in the energy industry relates to problems posed by coal and oil.

In retrospect, however, it is clear that the most consequential actions of the federal government during this period were directed at railroads and manufacturing enterprises rather than at the fuel industries upon which both depended. Although the Bureau of Mines was established as early as 1884, direct links between federal agencies and these industries were fairly sparse. Of greater importance for the politics of energy were legal decisions prompted by the regulation of the railroads, notably the Sherman Anti-Trust Act of 1890, which disallowed "every contract, combination in the form of trust or otherwise, or conspiracy, in restraint of trade or commerce among the several States, or with foreign nations" (Keller, 1981:67). During the same period, the courts affirmed the power of regulatory commissions to determine "reasonable rates" based on the "fair value of property" (Brock, 1984:65).

These legal developments did not lead to political intervention and regulation of the sort observed in the French and German economies during the same period (Keller, 1981:59–64, 69–70). Although increased government regulation of business practices was advocated by factions of the Progressive movement, changes in this direction were blocked by two constitutional considerations: federalism and the Fourteenth Amendment, which guarantees due process, hence protecting the sphere of private contracts. Therefore, in considering the emergence of a national policy domain relating to energy issues, it is necessary to consider the internal organization of the industries and political developments at the state level as well as the expanding activities of national agencies. Although operators in both industries sought to limit production and stabilize prices, the oil industry was aided in this endeavor by its importance for the military and for the economies of a number of states. By contrast, the politics of coal were heavily influenced by the concerns of consumers and organized labor.

The history of the U.S. coal industry has been shaped by the failure of producers to organize themselves. Unlike the relatively concentrated anthracite mining of Pennsylvania, the production of bituminous or soft coal (used primarily by industry) was highly competitive and regionally fragmented. Unable to establish a nationwide trade association, the industry nevertheless had to contend with widespread public hostility toward an alleged "coal trust" and with the government prosecution premised on this image of the industry

(Johnson, 1979:27). Ironically, some of the internal divisions that blocked attempts to organize may be traced to actions by the same federal agencies whose officials repeatedly denied the need for regulation to stabilize the industry. Once secure in its power to set rates for the nation's railroads, the Interstate Commerce Commission consistently established lower rates for the transport of coal to the eastern seaboard from the southern fields, which also had the advantages of better-quality coal, easier mining conditions, and lower labor costs.

The last of these factors—or at least its continued importance —was also a consequence of federal intervention in the coal industry. As early as 1900, national leaders actively promoted arbitration of strikes led by the young United Mine Workers. In 1902 President Theodore Roosevelt forcefully intervened to settle a second strike, and the UMW secured a precedent for recognition by the public and the federal government (Davis, 1974:20). This strengthened the union's position in the producing regions that it controlled and, consequently, heightened the competitive advantages of regions that were more resistant to unionization.

The partial success of organized labor provided a selective incentive for organization on the part of the coal operators. As early as 1898 settlements in the Illinois fields led to the establishment of a price-fixing organization among operators. A decade later Illinois producers led an unsuccessful effort to establish a national trade association. The result was the American Federation of Coal Operators, a regional association representing primarily unionized areas (Graebner, 1973:54–56). Regional divisions remained an obstacle to the organization of the industry and, consequently, a barrier to the establishment of the cooperative—indeed, cooptative—business-government relations achieved by the oil industry during World War I.

When the National Coal Association was finally established in 1917, it represented operators in the Central Competitive Field, a region encompassing Illinois, Indiana, Ohio, and western Pennsylvania (Johnson, 1979:59). As a trade association, however, the NCA was not equal to its task. Coal was produced by hundreds of mines, and before the 1920s, no single firm could claim to control even as much as 3 percent of the market (Johnson, 1979:25). Repeated requests for permission to form combinations to protect price levels were denied. Dependent on selling its product to large industrial buyers as well as residential users, the coal industry was unable to defeat consumer demands for lower prices, particularly once the government began purchasing record amounts for war-related activities. Faced with stiff competition from other producing regions, the NCA led the effort to arrive at some sort of quasi-corporatist arrangement with the federal government during World War I.

In contrast to the experience of the coal industry, the history of business-government relations in the oil industry is strikingly successful. The relative ease of organization within the petroleum industry can be traced in part to characteristics of its production. Initially monopolized by Standard Oil, petroleum became a competitive and unstable industry following the great mid-continental discoveries and the court-ordered breakup of Standard Oil in 1911. Subsequently, Standard Oil's share of the gasoline market (and later the combined production of its former affiliates) declined from 90 percent in 1900 to 40 percent by the late 1920s (Nordhauser, 1979:i). Yet even this diminished level of market control was far beyond that attained by any coal firm, and much of the remaining production was controlled by a handful of large firms, the so-called majors.

The greater level of concentration within the oil industry was complemented by the degree and perception of national dependence on this fuel. Although coal remained the country's primary energy source until the 1930s, the Navy had converted to oil at the turn of the century and, most important, perceived oil, unlike coal, as being in short supply. Not only did the military move to secure its own reserves,[1] but its perception of the oil industry in terms of national security provided the basis for more active and cooperative relationships than those established with coal producers.

Prior to World War I, government intervention addressed two goals: the prosecution of antitrust cases and, more sporadically and at the state level, the regulation of the drilling sprees that followed every major strike, often depressing prices to disastrous levels. The laws governing the extraction of oil (particularly the "rule of capture," which recognized ownership by whomever pumped the oil out first) encouraged rapid exploitation of new discoveries (Nordhauser, 1979:11). Any effort at conservation required poolwide agreements among producers, precisely the sort of combination likely to be condemned as "in restraint of trade" by the courts and producers alike (Nordhauser, 1979:6).

Nevertheless, conservation efforts motivated by military considerations were complemented by the recognized need to prevent waste and stabilize prices in a number of states with economies heavily dependent on oil. As early as 1899 the Texas legislature took steps to regulate drilling, and California followed suit four years later. The most far-reaching program was undertaken in Oklahoma, where new discoveries led to recurrent crises of overproduction. There the nation's first laws prorating the production of oil enabled the Oklahoma Corporation Commission to restrict private oil production (Nash, 1968:15–16). During the same period the Texas Railroad Commission was given the power to regulate oil drilling to prevent physical waste

---

1. In 1911 President Taft set aside federally owned reserves at Elk Hills and Buena Vista Hills in California for the use of the Navy. Woodrow Wilson added the Teapot Dome reservoirs to the Navy's holdings in 1914 (Nash, 1968:17–18).

(Nash, 1968:113), a mandate that eventually was stretched to cover the stabilization of prices. Just as the federal government had developed a regulatory presence on the basis of its constitutional powers over interstate commerce, the states became increasingly involved in cycles of legislation and litigation in their efforts to gain some control over their economies.

Despite high levels of competitiveness and periodic instability prior to World War I, oil producers established the sort of stable, cooperative relationship with the wartime administration that eluded coal operators. In 1915 the Petroleum Division of the Department of the Interior was established to supplement the technical advice provided by the U.S. Geological Survey (Davis, 1974:45–46). Following the onset of the war, the Wilson administration sponsored the Petroleum Advisory Committee (PAC), a group dominated by representatives of the major oil companies and charged with advising the government in its attempts to mobilize the nation's industries. With the U.S. declaration of war, the Council of National Defense, established in August 1916 to oversee industrial mobilization, was transformed into the War Industries Board, and the PAC became the Petroleum War Service Committee (PWSC). Despite the free-market rhetoric that has dominated much of the energy policy debate, the wartime experience established an ideal for business-government cooperation.

In order to meet charges of catering to the interests of private industry in the procurement of fuel for the war effort, Wilson established the U.S. Fuel Administration (USFA); the Oil Division was headed by Mark Requa, an associate of Herbert Hoover (Davis, 1974:47). Under the administration of the USFA, both coal and oil enjoyed unprecedented stability, but the legacies of this close involvement with the federal government differed for the two industries. Wartime legislation, particularly the Lever Act, provided Requa with the authority to fix prices, an effective means of threatening the uncooperative. Instead, he promoted cooperation with the oil companies by establishing an effective committee system responsible for voluntary increases in production and efficiency. Despite repeated clashes with antitrust advocates from the Federal Trade Commission, Requa successfully defended this cooperative movement and gained an increase in the depletion allowances that had been granted to the oil industry in 1913 and 1916. Accepting the argument that these deductions of the cost of discovery were insufficient to cover the expense of replacing exhausted oil properties, Congress included more generous and flexible depletion allowances in the War Revenue Act of 1918 (Nash, 1968:34–36).

In the coal industry, by contrast, rising prices destroyed support for price stabilization schemes. At the same time, the Justice Department successfully prosecuted a number of companies for conspiring to raise prices. Attempts to increase output and regulate prices were also made by the Committee on Coal Production (dominated by representatives of the industry but also including the UMW leader John L. Lewis). In order to defuse demands for price-fixing legislation, the CCP encouraged coal operators to come to a voluntary agreement in 1917 establishing maximum price levels. This strategy backfired. Consumers objected to a price of three dollars a ton, Progressive reformers became agitated at the specter of a "coal trust," and members of the Federal Trade Commission (FTC) were incensed at this attempt to preempt their own investigation into the costs of coal (Johnson, 1979:43).

These reactions aided advocates of government price-fixing; coal was included with foodstuffs and other vital consumer commodities subject to direct regulation under the Lever Act of 1917. As one senator noted, this legislation delegated "greater power over business than was ever before delegated in a free land in the history of the world to the President of the United States" (quoted in Johnson, 1979:51). Industrial self-regulation had faltered in the face of consumer opposition, the Navy's demands for cheap coal, and the political ineptness of the operators themselves. To a far greater extent than in other fuel industries, the interests of industrial and private consumers as well as organized labor influenced the pattern of government intervention in the coal industry.

In contrast to the oil industry, where divisions between the majors and the independent producers were the primary source of intraindustry conflict, the politics of coal reflected the industry's labor-intensive character. Miners were actively recruited for the Fuel Administrator's program to increase coal production following the harsh winter of 1917–18. In return, many of the union's issues were addressed. The Fuel Administration supported UMW demands for grievance procedures, collective bargaining rights, and, in most cases, higher wages, although the UMW did agree to scale back its organizing efforts in the southern fields (Johnson, 1979:78–81).

The end of the war brought a fall in demand as a result of the cancellation of wartime contracts as well as widespread price inflation. Some USFA officials advocated the establishment of peacetime commissions representing business and labor in order to perpetuate the wartime style of (relatively) cooperative problem solving. In a series of meetings during February 1919, business and union leaders agreed to support "a fuel commission of three operators and three miners as advisors to a national fuel administrator who would license all coal industrialists (Johnson, 1979:99). Licensed operators would be able to establish fair trade practices, protected from the threat of antitrust prosecution. This commission was to be one part of a national system of government-supervised industrial self-regulation, a vision akin to Herbert Hoover's idea of the "associative" state (Hawley, 1968:248). But this approach was foreclosed by President Wilson's unwillingness to increase the already unpopular level of government involvement in the economy and, ultimately, by the UMW-led coal strike of 1919.

Echoing the experience of labor organizations throughout the country, the UMW's attempts to exploit economic conditions immediately following the war gave way to defensive activity in the probusiness atmosphere of the 1920s. Despite relatively high incentives for cooperation among organized labor, business, and government, neither the appointment of a federal fuel distributor following the 1927 strikes nor a series of short-lived agreements between the UMW and operators managed to stabilize the unionized sections of the industry (Johnson, 1979:115–22). By 1927 the predominantly southern, nonunionized fields could meet national demand—a troubling situation for northern operators and the union as well as for politicians sensitive to unemployment and labor unrest. In 1928 John L. Lewis of the UMW urged the federal government to stabilize coal production, a policy endorsed by both major parties (Johnson, 1979:128). Thus, at the onset of the Depression, economic conditions had laid the foundations for an uneasy alliance between organized labor and sections of a sharply divided industry.

For the oil industry, wartime cooperation improved its financial situation and helped to overcome its internal divisions. Understandably, there was considerable interest in prolonging this situation. Alfred Bedford, chairman of both Standard Oil of New Jersey and the PWSC, wondered, "If it is so easy for us to work together for our country's sake, I cannot see why, after the war is over, we cannot work together for the good of the industry itself" (quoted in Nordhauser, 1979:5). Apart from expressing a concern for speed, Wilson provided little guidance during reconversion, so business leaders and administrators took the lead in privatizing the newly established system of industrial self-regulation. In March 1919 the PWSC was reconstituted as the American Petroleum Institute (API). Mark Requa was appointed to the board of directors, and another USFA official became the institute's first president. At least in terms of formal organization, the process of postwar reconversion established the foundation for both industrial self-regulation and cooperative relations between government and the oil industry.

Postwar economic conditions, however, did not provide much incentive for self-regulation: "the underlying soundness of the domestic price structure in 1919 to 1920 led many oil men to discount suggestions that anything was seriously wrong as well as arguments that governmental activity could improve conditions. The [*Oil and Gas*] *Journal*'s warning of 1919 that the oil price structure might crumble with the discovery of new oilfields had been hailed with indifference" (Nordhauser, 1979:7). This complacency was shaken by a series of tremendous new strikes occurring in southern California during 1920 and 1921, and, even more disruptive, near Seminole City, Oklahoma. In

July 1927 the Seminole field attained a daily output of half a million barrels. But the oil industry had made few advances toward an effective system of self-regulation and price stabilization; an API study of 1925 had denied the need for any control of production.

Throughout the rest of the 1920s, the oil industry sought to remedy the oil gluts that depressed prices to disastrously low levels. Their efforts concentrated on gaining federal endorsement for voluntary efforts to stabilize prices, but none of the successive Republican administrations were willing to "accept responsibility for revising the antitrust laws and, thus, for raising gasoline prices" (Nordhauser, 1979:33). Following the Teapot Dome scandal of the Harding administration, the federal government distanced itself from close involvement with the industry on market and price-related issues. Yet in 1924, at the urging of conservationists, President Coolidge created the Federal Oil Conservation Board (FOCB), "a cabinet-level committee of inquiry . . . to investigate and report on conditions within the oil industry." For, as Coolidge noted, "the supremacy of nations may be determined by the possession of available petroleum and its products" (quoted in Nordhauser, 1979:18–19).[2]

The FOCB found itself caught between industry representatives desiring limitations on domestic production (which, by raising prices, also increased the value of their foreign reserves), state agencies opposed to any erosion of their authority, and, until 1932, the Hoover administration's reluctance to assert leadership in national economic affairs (Nash, 1968:11). Prior to the ratification of the Interstate Oil Compact in 1935, interstate competition also undermined the efforts of state-level agencies to stabilize oil production. For a brief period in the early 1930s, the FOCB was able to use its economic research agency to establish an informal system of production control based on geographically subdivided estimates of national demand; state agencies adopted these estimates as the basis for mandatory production quotas (Nordhauser, 1979:57). This minimal system collapsed when confronted by a flood of new oil from the east Texas fields. The incoming Roosevelt administration was faced with an industry aware of the need for production regulation (Nash, 1968:129).

The first two years of the Depression made it clear that coal and oil, like

2. Insofar as the oil industry was directly involved in securing the international economic and military position of the United States, antitrust proceedings and other constraints on business activity were often relaxed or dropped altogether (Hogan, 1974). In domestic politics the oil industry secured considerable liberalization of the depletion allowances of 5 percent that were granted to a variety of extractive industries when the national income tax was adopted in 1913. By 1926 the depletion allowance for petroleum had reached 27.5 percent, a tax break premised on the argument that "oil discovered beneath privately owned ground constitutes a capital asset" (Engler, 1961:151). By treating the value of found resources as capital actually invested, the federal government gave the oil industry a major competitive advantage.

many other industries, needed stabilization. The major vehicle for industrial policy in the early New Deal was the National Recovery Administration (NRA) with its industrial codes and advisory committees. However, the experience of various industries with business-government relations during World War I and the 1920s affected their ability to take advantage of this new opportunity for cooperation. Thus, over the 1930s the oil industry developed closer ties with executive agencies and senior members of Congress, whereas coal policy was increasingly influenced by an emerging political alliance between organized labor and the Democratic party.

Even before his inauguration, a delegation of oil executives had conferred with Roosevelt in the hope of rapidly stabilizing the market. At this time debate was organized around two major policy options: greater, and more coordinated, control at the state level or centralized, federal regulation, quite possibly under the guidance of Secretary of the Interior Ickes. Rather than allow itself to be singled out as a problem industry and, potentially, run the danger of being reclassified as a public utility, the oil industry cooperated as the New Dealers implemented their first attempt at national economic policy, the National Industrial Recovery Act (NIRA) of 1933 (Brand, 1983:112).

The API took the lead in drafting an industry code. This was submitted in July 1933, but not without criticism from independent producers, labor, and some major producers. Divisions occurred over the limitation of oil imports, pipeline divestiture, and, above all, price fixing. Faced with the inability of the producers to secure an agreement among themselves, Ickes took over the process of establishing a code for the oil industry that involved production controls rather than price fixing (Nash, 1968:139; Vietor, 1984:24). But despite having been singled out for an industrial recovery policy, by the end of 1933 producers generally voiced a high level of satisfaction with the imposed Oil Code. Thus, when the NIRA was overturned by a series of Supreme Court decisions in 1935, much of the industry supported the rapid implementation of a substitute.

Secretary Ickes, now also administrator of the Oil Code, continued to push for a centralized federal system of regulation, at times advocating policies that suggested the transformation of the industry into a public utility or nationalized enterprise. Roosevelt, however, increasingly supported a moderate approach that combined the promotion of state-level regulation, through instruments such as the 1935 Interstate Compact to Conserve Oil and Gas, and federal supervision of interstate oil transportation under the 1935 Connally Hot Oil Act. Despite the high level of antitrust activity in the late 1930s, the Roosevelt administration actually laid the foundations for a loose system of cooperation between the federal government, state agencies, and oil producers in the interest of stabilizing production and conserving resources (Nash, 1968:153).

Within the oil industry the New Deal served to consolidate the kind of "associative state" (with a considerable element of federal intervention) that had seemed possible in the 1920s. For coal producers the successive Roosevelt administrations brought far greater changes (Davis, 1974:52). By the late 1920s the chronic weakness of the industry had prompted numerous governors to pressure operators to establish fair price codes. A series of union-backed legislative proposals called for the establishment of a national commission to license operators and, therefore, limit production while improving labor conditions (Johnson, 1979:129–32). Throughout the probusiness Hoover administration, the UMW was the most visible and vocal supporter of a national coal policy.

Consequently, the NIRA had more favorable consequences for the coal miners than for the less organized workers in the oil industry. Most significantly, Section 7a protected the rights of labor to organize. Before the implications of this section had been fully worked out, the UMW embarked on a massive membership drive that strengthened its position in previously unionized fields and, more important, succeeded in organizing mines throughout the South. By 1934, with the cooperation of members of the northern Central Competitive Field, the UMW had reduced the north-south price differential, long a potent obstacle to the organization of the industry. That year, thanks in part to the price-fixing provisions of its NIRA code, the coal industry came close to breaking even for the first time since 1927 (Johnson, 1979:201). But this situation was not stable; consumer opposition to the minimum prices combined with price cutting by numerous operators to undermine the Coal Code, which was overturned, along with the rest of the NIRA, by the Supreme Court's 1935 *Schecter* decision.

As in the case of the oil industry, Congress moved rapidly to replace the NIRA codes. But instead of the decentralized system embodied in the Interstate Oil and Gas Compact and the Hot Oil Act (combining state regulation of production and federal supervision of transportation), John L. Lewis of the UMW, along with operators in the Central Competitive Field, advocated direct regulation of the industry. Despite the opposition of southern and western producers, large industrial consumers, the national Chamber of Commerce, and the National Association of Manufacturers, the UMW and its allies secured the passage of the 1935 Bituminous Coal Act (Johnson, 1979:217). Declared unconstitutional because of its labor provisions, the act was replaced by the Bituminous Coal Act of 1937, which created a centralized National Bituminous Coal Commission (NBCC) to regulate competition and enforce minimum prices. But coal prices did not stabilize until after mobilization for World War II, and in 1943 the NBCC was superceded by the Solid Fuels Administration. Dominated by a concern to limit intraindustry competition and uphold the rights of labor, the flurry of legislation during the New Deal failed to establish an effective strategy for managing the coal industry.

During the New Deal itself, government involvement in the generation of

electricity provided the most striking contrast to the decentralized cooperative system developed for the regulation of oil production. The federal government had been in the business of selling electricity since the beginning of
the century; in 1909 Congress required the Army Corps of Engineers to consider possible sites for hydroelectric plants in its river surveys and authorized
the sale of any excess electricity generated from federal irrigation projects
(Davis, 1974:123). In this area, as in so many others, major government involvement had military origins: a dam on the Tennessee River at Muscle
Shoals, Alabama, built to support the manufacture of explosives during World
War I. Following the war, government ownership of this power-generating facility—an obviously commercial property—was something of an anomaly,
and numerous potential buyers were approached. No sale was arranged, however, and on May 18, 1933, Roosevelt signed the Tennessee Valley Authority
Act, which incorporated the Muscle Shoals dam into a plan for the social and
economic development of the entire drainage area. Eventually, the TVA also
became a major supplier of coal-generated electricity and, hence, a sometimes dominating buyer in a region heavily dependent on coal mining. For the
first time in peacetime, the government became a major actor in the production as well as the regulation of energy.

Business-Government Relations and Interfuel Competition: 1940–1974

Prior to the onset of World War II, distinctive patterns of business-government
relations had developed in each of the United States' major energy industries.
For oil producers, relations with the federal government were relatively cooperative, despite the repeated attempts by Secretary of the Interior Ickes to
centralize regulation of the industry. Coal operators, on the other hand, found
themselves subjected to more direct forms of regulation and control; government policy tended to respond to the politically powerful UMW or consumers
rather than to the producers. The TVA was an extreme case of yet another
model of business-government relations, one in which bureaucrats and local
politicians acquired control over electrical utilities, natural gas suppliers, and
other "natural monopolies." The forms of cooperation and control established
during the New Deal had significant consequences for the ability of industries
to turn government intervention in the economy to their own advantage.

These patterns were reinforced by the experience of mobilization for World
War II. For both coal and oil policy, the central problem shifted from the management of economically damaging surpluses to the promotion of maximum
production. Early in the war the possibility of oil shortages prompted the government to use funds from the Reconstruction Finance Corporation to pay for
the construction of two major oil pipelines to the eastern seaboard (Nash
1968:165). In addition to direct funding of construction, the petroleum industry was organized by the establishment of an agency/advisory council system

similar to those created during World War I and advocated by supporters of the "associative state." Along with an industrial advisory body, the Petroleum Industry War Council (PIWC), the Petroleum Administration for War (PAW) regulated the production, transportation, and marketing of oil products. Despite his hostile relations with the industry, Ickes secured immunity from a considerable amount of antitrust policy and enlisted the major oil companies in his attempts to increase the amount of imported oil (Nash, 1968:160, 170).

From the perspective of producers, politicians, and the military alike, the arrangement was successful, and its success raised issues for the future: "By confirming the importance of energy, World War II raised new questions about the manner and means by which industry and government should interact and share authority for the production, pricing, and distribution of fossil fuels" (Vietor, 1984:15). Echoing Mark Requa on the fate of the World War I Fuel Administration, the PAW deputy administrator urged that this arrangement be continued during peacetime. Unlike Requa, he was successful. In 1945 a series of political squabbles led to Ickes's resignation, ending an era of advocacy of direct government intervention in the oil industry (Nash, 1968:182). A year later, as part of Truman's skillfully managed demobilization, the PAW and the PIWC were replaced by the newly created Oil and Gas Division of the Department of the Interior and the National Petroleum Council (NPC), an advisory body supported by member companies.

The official functions of the National Petroleum Council—to provide data and make policy recommendations to the Interior Secretary—were not necessarily its most important. The Council was a forum in which industry leaders could meet and discuss issues of public policy among themselves and with key personnel from the federal bureaucracies involved in petroleum-related matters. In this manner, the Council's quarterly meetings in Washington, and those of its committees, provided opportunities for consensus-building, within the industry and between business and government. (Vietor, 1984:38)

The viability of this form of business-government cooperation was demonstrated as the NPC cooperated with the government during the oil shortages of 1947 and 1948, the Korean War mobilization, and the crisis that followed the nationalization of the Iranian oil industry under Prime Minister Muhammed Mossadeqh in 1951.

The major controversies of this period concerned states' rights rather than private industry. In 1937 Secretary Ickes and the military joined in promoting federal jurisdiction over mineral resources in the tidelands, a three- to 10-mile area immediately offshore. Invoking national security, shortly after the end of the war Truman proclaimed that this area came under federal jurisdiction. Primarily sectional rather than partisan, the tidelands issue was not prominent in the 1948 presidential elections and was obscured by the demands the Korean

War placed on the oil industry and the newly created Petroleum Administration for Defense.

The conflict over jurisdiction resurfaced in the campaign that elected the first Republican president since Hoover. The election of Eisenhower meant an end to Truman's attempts to limit the powers and benefits that had been granted to the oil industry through the advisory council, the depletion allowance, and the minimization of antitrust prosecution with respect to many overseas projects. Instead, Eisenhower sought to decrease the regulatory role of the federal government. In May 1953 he signed the Submerged Lands Act, giving the states title to and ownership of resources within the three- to 10-mile limit. The Outer Continental Shelf Act of the following August secured federal jurisdiction beyond this limit (Nash, 1968:194). A similar withdrawal took place with respect to market regulation; only after years of chronic oversupply did Eisenhower agree to producers' demands for the imposition of quotas on imported oil. Thus, throughout much of the 1950s, the oil industry was left to run itself in cooperation with a sympathetic, but not particularly activist, government.

The situation was quite different with respect to coal. Since the latter part of the New Deal, the primary connection between the coal industry and the federal government was the alliance between the UMW and the Democratic party. Consequently, during the World War II mobilization, the UMW was able to use its political clout to ensure that increased production benefited organized labor rather than the mechanization of mining. At the same time, however, the railroads converted from coal to diesel fuel, while the federal government expended considerable funds on the construction of oil pipelines and, as would become apparent in a most dramatic fashion, the development of nuclear energy. After the war, the flow of natural gas through government-subsidized pipelines, at federally enforced prices, in combination with the influx of cheap foreign oil, undercut coal's position as the primary residential fuel along the eastern seaboard (Vietor, 1980a:3). "Government energy policies were killing the coal industry and draining its profits" (Vietor, 1980b:14).

The major hope for remedying the lack of government support lay in the development of a domestic synthetic-fuel industry; the onset of hostilities gave the U.S. government important patents confiscated from German-owned corporations. Furthermore, in addition to "restructuring energy markets World War II had imbued national security planners with a tremendous respect for the strategic significance of liquid fuel" (Vietor, 1980a:3). Thus, in combination with exploring proposals to establish strategic reserves of petroleum, the Roosevelt and Truman administrations secured passage of the Synthetic Liquid Fuels Act of 1944. Although small amounts of government funding had been allocated to research in this area since the mid 1930s, this legislation approved $30 million for constructing demonstration plants to assess the competitiveness and efficiency of coal-based synthetic fuels. The initial legislation expired during the oil shortage of 1947–48, and the renewal of funding, along with threats of price controls, emerged as part of President Truman's escalating struggle with the oil companies.

Although funding for synthetic fuels continued, advocates of synthetic fuel development were unable to secure further large-scale appropriations. The demonstration projects encountered technical difficulties and, more significantly, the growing opposition of oil companies fearful of competition in a glutted market—a fear that would be heightened by Eisenhower's reluctance to deal with the problem of imported oil. In this struggle the established position of the NPC gave the oil industry a critical advantage. The most fiercely contested issue concerned cost estimates. Public and private estimates did not begin to diverge until 1948, but the differences between various cost projections—particularly those of the Bureau of Mines (BOM) and of the NPC—came to play a critical role in the 1954 decision to terminate the federal synthetic-fuel development project (Vietor, 1980a: 13; see also Wildavsky and Tenenbaum, 1981).

Since the oil industry was nearly unanimous on this point, the synfuels issue was perfectly suited to treatment by the National Petroleum Council. . . . When the council refuted the results of the BOM's demonstration project and recommended against its continuation, it severely undercut the legitimacy of the program. . . . Thus, the negative recommendation from the prestigious National Petroleum Council simply sealed the fate of the federal synfuels program (Vietor, 1980a: 32).

As will be seen, the NPC was not always an effective voice for the oil industry, particularly in cases where the industry had no unified voice. But on issues concerning interfuel competition, NPC representation constituted a powerful advantage.

Faced with their failure to secure the sort of policies that were improving the market position of oil, natural gas, and, on the horizon, nuclear power, coal operators embarked on a project of economic and political consolidation throughout the rest of the 1950s. Early in the decade, mergers between coal companies began to limit the disastrously high level of competition in the industry. By the mid-1950s, operators were able to cooperate in lobbying the government for research and development funding for coal-related projects. Finally, in 1959, the National Coal Policy Conference (NCPC) was established—an umbrella group of coal producers and consumers, including the politically powerful UMW. But coal gained an effective political voice too late to overcome its relative weakness in interfuel competition. At the same time that the NCPC was organized, coal was recognized as an attractive target for diversification, particularly by oil companies; by 1978 "the coal industry had virtually lost its corporate identity" (Vietor, 1980b: 18).

While the coal industry was being politically defeated and institutionally engulfed by oil producers, it was also suffering from the competition of natu-

ral gas in major markets, especially for residential use. By constructing pipelines during World War II, the government created the infrastructure necessary for nationwide distribution; between 1930 and 1960 the production of
natural gas increased tenfold (Nash, 1968:210). Under the Natural Gas Act of
1938, approved prior to the great growth of the industry, the interstate transportation of natural gas came under the jurisdiction of the Federal Power
Commission (FPC). Faced with treatment as a natural monopoly and the possibility of direct, stringent regulation, the gas producers lobbied Congress for
legislative relief.

During the Truman administration, natural gas regulation was caught in a
stalemate between the President and Congress, as well as within the FPC itself, and the situation worsened during Eisenhower's first term. In 1954 the
Supreme Court used the *Phillips* decision to extend the powers of the FPC to
independent gas producers as well as pipeline operators and associated production companies. In October the Natural Gas and Oil Resources Committee
was formed in order to lobby for the Fulbright-Harris bill, which was intended to amend the *Phillips* ruling (Nash, 1968:233). Although it was passed
by Congress, a last-minute charge of industry bribery from Senator Case of
North Dakota caused Eisenhower to veto the bill on ethical grounds. Thus,
despite the existence of a powerful political coalition, natural gas remained a
heavily regulated industry until the period covered by this study.

The entire course of energy politics in the United States serves as a re-
minder that analyses based on market conditions must be supplemented by an
understanding of the role of politically organized economic actors and, ultimately, an understanding of the encompassing symbolic and ideological context. In the case of the deregulation of natural gas, the costs of perceived cor-
ruption outweighed the economic interests of the most powerful economic
actors. The power of political symbolism is obvious when "scandal" is involved, but it is also an important factor in the construction of apparently
objective economic calculations. This is amply illustrated by the history of
civilian nuclear energy development in the United States, particularly when
contrasted with the "economically justified" demise of coal-based synthetic
fuel production.

The development of nuclear energy, unlike that of other energy industries,
has been firmly rooted in the public sector, specifically the military. Early dilemmas stemmed from deregulation rather than regulation—the means by
which this new source of energy would be made available to consumers and
corporations. The product of the secret wartime Manhattan Project, nuclear
energy remained a government monopoly for nearly 10 years, despite the fact
that the Atomic Energy Act of 1946 established a civilian-dominated regulatory system: the congressional Joint Committee on Atomic Energy (JCAE)
and the Atomic Energy Commission (AEC). For the first few years, both were

heavily dependent upon the nuclear physicists. The specialized knowledge necessary for decision making, which insulated the JCAE and the AEC from political pressures for decades, initially served as a barrier to their political efficacy. This situation changed significantly with the onset of the Cold War. Time had allowed a small group of bureaucrats and politicians to acquire some technical knowledge, and, more dramatically, the 1949 explosion of an atomic bomb by the Soviets—three years before the expert advisors of the JCAE had predicted that this would be possible—undermined the influence of expert opinion. The development of nuclear power became entwined with questions of foreign policy and patriotism.

Although the history of nuclear power during the 1950s must be seen within the context of the Cold War, many striking developments were related to civilian use. The AEC sponsored experimental reactors for the generation of electricity, and in 1951 Monsanto and Dow–Detroit Edison applied for permission to develop nuclear plants. Faced with political pressure to develop peaceful applications of this new technology, the AEC approved the construction of a pilot generating plant (Green and Rosenthal, 1963:253) and thereby ended the government monopoly on atomic energy that had been maintained ever since it was first released in a converted squash court at the University of Chicago.

Concern for both civilian development and the consequences of nuclear power for international relations marked the 1950s (Davis, 1974:148). In conjunction with his "Atoms for Peace" plan, Eisenhower supported revisions of the 1946 legislation allowing for "private ownership of reactors under AEC licensing, although nuclear fuels would still be owned by the government and leased to private users." This represented a defeat for Democrats who had urged direct government ownership along the lines of the TVA, but federal policy remained central to the economics of nuclear energy through "pricing policies established by the AEC for nuclear fuel" (Green and Rosenthal, 1963:254).

By the end of the decade, the JCAE and AEC had arrived at an agreement over civilian power development, and "throughout the 1960s, a cooperative and autonomous subgovernment composed of the AEC, the JCAE, and private vendors and power companies promoted the rapid growth of nuclear power" (Chubb, 1983:91). Research funding, subsidies of the cost of producing, transporting and storing fuel, as well as the 1957 Price-Anderson Act, by which the government agreed to underwrite insurance for commercial reactors, "amounted to subsidizing uneconomical plants for their symbolic value" (Davis, 1974:151). Despite opposition to nuclear power development, initially spearheaded by Walter Reuther of the United Auto Workers (UAW), the close relationship between the regulators and regulatees was not seriously threatened until the late 1960s and early 1970s, when local protests against particular plants were incorporated into an emerging national network increasingly opposed to nuclear development in any form (Shapiro, 1984).

Opposition to federal nuclear policy had disruptive consequences for an entire range of fuel-specific policies developed by a host of regulatory agencies and congressional committees. As will be seen in the following section, fuel policies tended to reflect the power of entrenched interest groups as well as broad concerns with international relations and the economy. Neither issue promoted much concern for conservation, a lack of attention reinforced by the political unpopularity of the increased costs that any serious conservation effort would entail. The belief in nuclear power as a cheap and endless source of energy was one factor helping to mask the internal tensions of U.S. energy policy until they became all too apparent in the 1970s.

The Impact of Scarcity: 1968–1980

Popular wisdom traces the transformation of energy policy in the United States to 1973, a year of war between the Arabs and Israelis that prompted the decision of the oil-producing and exporting countries (OPEC) to impose an oil embargo on Israel's allies. But this decision was only the most dramatic of a series of changes that undermined the security and affordability of energy. Indeed, OPEC's ability to disrupt the world economy was itself a reflection of the exhaustion of excess production capacity throughout most of the industrialized world. In the autumn of 1969, the FPC announced that the country faced an impending shortage of natural gas, and curtailments of deliveries to industrial customers began the following spring. During the same period oil producers acknowledged the absence of further additional productive capacity within the United States (Vietor, 1984:199, 275). This surprisingly unanticipated transition from surplus to shortage had enormous consequences for decision making on energy issues.

These decisions were constrained by the presence of firmly entrenched and recently mobilized groups with energy-related interests. Each group promoted its own vision of "energy" problems and policies. Throughout the twentieth century, questions of national security and the continued economic viability of producers had been powerful considerations in the energy policy domain. Represented by the armed forces as well as politically powerful producers' organizations, these positions were consistently recognized. By the late 1960s, however, two additional concerns began to have a significant effect on the development of legislation: consumerism and environmentalism. The appearance of new interested parties served as the entering wedge for a reorganization of business-government relations, changes that were exacerbated by the heightened distrust of established political processes that followed the oil shocks and the Watergate crisis.

The turbulence that has characterized the energy policy domain since the early years of the Nixon administration stands in contrast to the apparent calm of the previous period. Aware that he might be labeled a servant of the oil interests, President Johnson distanced himself from energy issues. In 1963 responsibility for petroleum matters was delegated to the Secretary of the Interior (Cochrane, 1981:384), and the Johnson administration embarked on a course of action in which much was studied but little was changed. In 1967 the Energy Policy Staff was created within the Office of Science and Technology, but despite its mandate to develop a comprehensive and coordinated approach to energy policy (a significant shift from fuel-specific policy making), decision-makers continued to compromise federal policy whenever it "seemed helpful for achieving the Administration's broader goals" (Vietor, 1984:135).

Although the 1960s witnessed considerable integration with industries as well as interfuel mergers (particularly those involving the acquisition of coal companies), changes in the structure of the energy industries were not matched by comparable reforms of federal policy processes. Nor was there much incentive to undertake such reforms. Producers profited from these arrangements, and costs were spread among consumers. Nevertheless, these arrangements were inherently unstable. Perhaps the most fundamental problem was that the relative decline of the productive capacity of oil and gas, particularly domestic, undermined the premise of surplus upon which the entire regulatory system had been constructed.

The first significant changes, however, did not stem from internal strains but from events originating outside the energy policy domain as it was understood at that time. Environmental issues provided one major battleground. New concerns were evident in legislation during the 1960s, and although the Water Quality Act of 1965 and the Air Quality Act of 1967 were not stunning victories for environmentalists, the latter did establish standards based on health criteria as well as cost or technical considerations (Vietor, 1984:230). Far more dramatic reforms followed a major offshore oil leak in the Santa Barbara Channel during January 1969. In the wake of perceived mismanagement by the Department of the Interior, Congress passed the National Environmental Policy Act (NEPA), creating the Council on Environmental Quality as well as providing unprecedented opportunities for citizen intervention by way of the environmental impact statement (Davis, 1974:68). In the absence of major government support for conservation efforts, however, this legislation served to increase the nation's dependence on imported oil. At the same time that air-pollution legislation raised the costs of using coal, particularly from the deep mines of the eastern states, Congress had established a potent tool for delaying efforts to develop alternative energy sources such as nuclear power and the strip mining of low-sulfur coals from the West.

Procedural changes were not limited to environmental issues. In February 1969 Nixon appointed a task force to review the entire oil import quota system. Created as a response to growing congressional disapproval of the program established by Eisenhower, the task force recommended that the quota system be replaced by a tariff, thus abandoning the implicit objective of protecting the "traditional" market shares of independents and majors. This suggestion produced a negative response from both oil companies and members of Congress for whom the ability to secure exemptions was an important political resource. Consequently, Nixon suspended his activities in this area (de Marchi, 1981:400–403). Similar obstacles were encountered by the chairman of the FPC in his efforts to slow the decline of the country's reserves of natural gas. Again, attempts to reform the regulatory process to meet the new conditions of scarcity were hampered by an unwillingness to abandon federally maintained terms of competition among different sectors of the industry. Even the major companies, with the most to gain from increased competition, were opposed to any changes that would diminish regulation of the independent producers for fear that this would undermine political support for total deregulation.

Reacting to the inflationary consequences of financing the Vietnam War and the Great Society, Nixon imposed a nationwide wage-price freeze in August 1971. The first phase of the Economic Stabilization Program involved a freeze on all wages and prices. This was followed by a year in which price increases were allowed to reflect cost increases and then further relaxation of controls until the program expired in 1974—except for oil and, until 1975, health care (Campion, 1984:326). Furthermore, in March 1973 Special Rule No. 1 "reimposed mandatory control over crude oil and product prices—but only for the 24 largest oil companies" (Vietor, 1984:241). These increasingly direct modes of intervention adopted in the early 1970s set the stage for the politics of deregulation that dominated the latter half of the decade.

The Cost of Living Council, charged with administering the Economic Stabilization Program, justified its actions by suggesting that control of prices charged by the largest firms would provide an efficient method of controlling overall prices—an unrealistic assumption given a growing dependence on increasingly expensive, and politicized, foreign oil. Well before the first embargo, exporting nations—led by Col. Moammar Quaddafi of Libya—had successfully demanded price rather than production increases from the major oil companies (Vietor, 1984: 200–201). As early as December 1971, charges of unfair competition began to surface as the FTC began yet another round of investigations of the oil industry. A growing receptivity to reform was apparent in the renewed attempts to promote the development of substitutes for oil, notably oil shale, and in Nixon's proposal of April 1973 to consolidate energy research and regulation in a new cabinet-level agency, the Department of Energy and Natural Resources (de Marchi, 1981:420). This legislation was obstructed by territorial disputes among the JCAE, the House Committee on the Interior, and the Senate Committee on Insular Affairs (de Marchi, 1981:435).

Preexisting dissatisfaction with federal energy policy was heightened by the oil embargo that followed Nixon's decision to resupply the Israeli Air Force in October 1973. This emergency made the unintended consequences of existing policy all too apparent; import policies designed to keep prices low had resulted in increased dependence on foreign oil at the same time that procedural reforms and environmental legislation had created new obstacles to the rapid development of alternative energy sources. Yet the character of the emerging energy policy domain ensured that reform would be a difficult, if not impossible, task.

In the wake of Nixon's failure to establish the Department of Energy and Natural Resources, policy making took place in an institutional arena where influence over issues was highly fragmented among numerous well-developed, entrenched constituencies. The process of change was further hindered by the political atmosphere of the time; post-embargo distrust of business and post-Watergate distrust of the executive branch militated against cooperative action to meet the problems posed by the energy crisis. Well-established working relations between regulatory agencies and industry groups were disrupted, and particularly after the election of Jimmy Carter to the presidency in 1976, new regulations led to greater access, if not necessarily effectiveness, for environmental and public interest groups (Chubb, 1983:99, 134). Organizational reforms in the House of Representatives upset the pattern of working relations between influential members and interest groups. Despite the heightened interest in centralized control, short-term politics rather than long-term planning characterized energy policy throughout the decade.

The 1973 embargo resulted in the Emergency Petroleum Allocation Act. This legislation, involving direct intervention in industry affairs by both administrative agencies and Congress, set the tone for policy over the next years. The Federal Energy Agency was created to administer the extended Phase IV price controls, to allocate supplies, and, following a long tradition of maintaining the status quo, to return market shares within the industry to their 1972 conditions. Reflecting the power of, and the divided opinions within, the petroleum industry, this policy promoted equity within the industry rather than the stimulation of supply. Six months later, the "Buy/Sell List Program" attempted to impose equity by way of mandatory interfirm sales of crude oil (Vietor, 1984:244–45).

The trend toward more interventionist forms of regulation was not restricted to petroleum. Since the early 1960s the Federal Power Commission had been attempting to free itself from the constraints of precedent and to establish the basis for some sort of technically informed, efficient method of regulating natural gas. The landmark 1965 Permian Basin case established area rate making as an alternative to a more traditional firm-specific regulatory approach. As one scholar has commented, however:

the cure was worse than the disease. The Permian case changed the fundamental relationship between the Federal Power Commission and the natural gas industry. In the 1938 Act, Congress had charged the Commission to perform utility rate regulation in a narrow field of interstate commerce. But when the Supreme Court upheld the Permian decision in 1968, it sanctioned federal price control of a major primary industry. (Vietor, 1984:157)

A similar trend toward greater and more active oversight was evident in the growing presence of citizen group intervenors in nuclear development issues and in the successful use of procedures established by NEPA, notably the environmental impact statement, to slow or halt many energy-related projects, particularly those that involved extensive mining of coal in the western states.

Already established as an important point of access for consumer and environmentalist groups, the post-Watergate Congress took the initiative in formulating general policy in the area of energy (Vietor, 1984:249–51). In an effort to retain control over substantive policy issues, Congress passed ever more detailed legislation, addressing issues with a degree of specificity previously reserved for administrative decisions. The mood of political distrust fueled legislative initiatives that threatened to create further obstacles to the development of alternatives to imported oil. In 1974 President Ford vetoed legislation that would have blocked most strip mining. Opposition in both Congress and the courts delayed the construction of the trans-Alaska pipeline, the major hope of U.S. energy policy during this decade.

In addition, the defeat of Ford's final attempt at gradual administrative decontrol, the Energy Independence Act of 1975, expressed political opposition to policies that would expose the U.S. economy to the dynamics of the international oil market. Instead, the Oil and Gas Energy Tax Act, first introduced in 1974 and passed the following year, constituted a direct attack on the structure and privileges of these industries. The 27.5 percent depletion allowance for oil producers, established by the Revenue Act of 1926, was abolished for large firms but retained, at a lower level, for smaller companies. Even Ford's compromise position favoring a gradual decontrol over 30 months was rejected:

In the wake of Watergate, a congressional revolt against Executive power had taken hold. Within weeks of overturning the oil depletion allowance, the House rejected the 30-month plan and voted to extend the Petroleum Allocation Act. The atmosphere was one of reprisal and reprobation. Every compromise was cast as a plum for "Big Oil." To make matters worse, a series of alleged exposes by NBC, Ralph Nader, and a host of newspapers had convinced the public that the energy crisis was a hoax concocted by the oil companies. (Vietor, 1984:251)

In August 1976 the Energy Policy and Conservation Act (EPCA) added direct intervention in the market to the removal of the industry's tax privileges. In order to avoid going into the elections bereft of an energy policy, Ford signed this legislation despite its inclusion of features contrary to his stance on regulation, particularly the provisions for crude oil pricing: "The congressional Democrats who managed the bills had decided to roll back the price of domestic oil and extend controls for at least 40 months" (Vietor, 1984:252). Despite considerable dissatisfaction with this arrangement, EPCA remained in force until 1979, when the combination of the legislation's expiration and the Iranian revolution created an opportunity for major policy initiatives.

By establishing a system analogous to the "vintaging" of natural gas, government presence in the oil industry was further increased. Attacks on industry autonomy were matched by criticisms of industry structure, typified by the Petroleum Industry Competition Act, introduced in 1975. Although this proposal to require major oil producers to divest subsidiary operations including pipelines, refining, and marketing failed to pass, it nevertheless garnered the support of the Independent Gasoline Marketers Council and the National Congress of Petroleum Retailers while receiving only mild opposition from the Independent Petroleum Association of America (Vietor, 1984:221–22). Comparable divisions plagued the natural gas industry as it faced congressional policy initiatives. Yet all this activity accomplished relatively little; in the three years since the first embargo, the contribution of imported oil to domestic consumption increased from 36 to 46 percent (Vietor, 1984:258).

Under the Carter administration, energy policy initiatives continued to pursue the strategies established in the preceding period: attempts to centralize policy making and regulation as well as attacks upon the prerogatives of industry. Although these efforts were more successful than earlier ones, a coherent and effective national energy policy remained out of reach. In discussing energy policy during the Carter period, it is useful to identify three distinct themes: the desire for centralized policy making, the attempts to curb the activities and profits of private industry, and, finally, the need to attend to environmentalist, consumer, and other "liberal" interest groups in Carter's constituency.

Following Gerald Ford's defeat in 1976, Carter's transition team addressed the need for a new energy policy as well as a reorganized administration. James Schlesinger was charged with developing Carter's National Energy Plan, which resulted in the establishment of the Department of Energy (DOE) in October 1977. The organizational reforms envisioned by the new administration were enacted with considerable success; introduced in March 1977, Carter's proposal to establish the DOE, a plan less ambitious than Nixon's proposal for a Department of Energy and Natural Resources, passed both houses with little trouble. These changes were complemented by a major reorganization of the Senate committee system, during which the Committee on Energy and Natural Resources was created as part of an effort to "realign committee jurisdictions to follow more closely the boundaries of perceived policy problems of the 1970s" (Chubb, 1983:72). However, conflict erupted over substantive legislation directly affecting the interests of established actors in the energy policy domain.

During the summer of 1977, Schlesinger, the future "energy czar," directed a comprehensive review of national energy policy. The speed and style of the review process led to the exclusion of many groups—both government agencies and interest groups—as well as a failure to consider important issues. Carter's concern for speed, combined with his belief that "politicization" was a major component of the problem, led to a bypassing of established policy channels: "If a comprehensive plan was to be produced swiftly, the planning team required privacy and thorough control over the process" (Chubb, 1983:232). The plan produced by a small team of economists and lawyers was enormously complex, involving over a hundred legislative proposals and demanding the attention of almost a dozen congressional committees in the 18 months following its introduction (Vietor, 1984:260).

Avoiding consultation also meant foregoing opportunities to build support for the legislation through communication and bargaining. Although a series of conferences had taken place prior to the unveiling of the plan in April 1977, many groups "perceived them as pure salesmanship" (Chubb, 1983:234). In the House, the absence of a developed coalition was overcome by party discipline and Carter's package was passed, with minor changes, within five months. In the Senate, however, southern Democrats actively opposed a central component of the plan, the Crude Oil Equalization Tax. Intended to regulate the price of old oil while gradually decontrolling new sources, thereby providing incentives for exploration while bringing the United States into line with international markets, the legislation was opposed by producers hostile to the threat posed to established market positions and by consumers hostile to decontrol. Much of Carter's legislation was rejected—not only the equalization tax, but the "gas guzzler" tax as well—at the same time that the Senate approved deregulation of natural gas pricing, a move strongly opposed by consumer groups. Thus, with the exception of administrative reorganization, Carter's attempt to implement a coordinated national energy policy was defeated by a combination of entrenched industrial and political interest groups.

The context of energy policy making changed abruptly with the overthrow of the shah of Iran and the consolidation of a revolutionary government under Ayatollah Khomeini in 1979. With the stoppage of Iranian production, world prices rose rapidly, and the Carter administration was again faced with the need to develop a major energy policy initiative. After considerable internal debate, the administration adopted a policy of gradual administrative decontrol combined with legislation imposing a windfall profits tax on producers. Within Congress, the terms of debate concerning the latter were transformed as oil prices skyrocketed, thereby expanding the revenues to be accrued from this tax: "In the ensuing paroxysm of political greed, cooperation within the oil industry broke down (as it did among proponents of the tax that were potential recipients of its revenues). . . . Everyone lobbied for some kind of an exemption. . . . The net effect of this intrafuel brokerage weakened the industry's ability to hold down the aggregate impact of the tax" (Vietor, 1984:269–70). The resulting conference bill created a tiered system that would produce considerable revenues over the period in which domestic prices adjusted to the international market. A similar pattern—a presidential initiative fragmented by congressional politics and, in turn, helping to divide the regulated industry—is evident in the events that led to the passage of the much weakened Natural Gas Policy Act of 1978 (Vietor, 1984:308–11).

Although much of the activity surrounding energy policy during the Carter administration may be seen as an attempt to renegotiate the balance of business-government relations, this established pattern of contention was altered by the increased representation of consumer and environmental interests. The influence of these newly organized groups had been apparent in the first post-Watergate Congress, which was both internally divided and at odds with President Ford over the regulation of strip mining. During the Carter administration, these tensions became increasingly apparent; the need to develop new sources of energy in a period of shortage conflicted with the desire to protect the environment and the consumer. The two concerns complemented one another only on the issue of increased funding for research and development, which, as one scholar has noted, was the most cooperative area of energy policy making during this period (Chubb, 1983:187). With respect to other issues—strip mining, nuclear development, coal slurry pipelines, and synthetic fuel projects—conflicting industrial and environmental interests produced a stalemate that blocked improvement of the nation's energy supply. The struggle was complicated by regional splits as representatives of the consuming states of the Northwest faced politicians from the producing areas of the South and West and the older coal-mining regions of the East attempted to stave off the threat posed by the more accessible, but more environmentally damaging, surface mines of the western states.

Consumers and environmentalists scored their major victories in the area of nuclear development as reforms in the licensing and regulation of nuclear generating plants made investment in this area less certain and more costly. Other legislation established financial incentives for the production of smaller, more fuel-efficient automobiles. But these accomplishments were limited by the failure to implement a coordinated national policy and thereby undermine the position of entrenched groups with respect to fuel-specific policies. Carter was repeatedly defeated in his attempts to halt development of the Clinch River breeder reactor, and although some changes in the regulation of the oil, natural gas, and coal industries were implemented, the final legislation consistently represented a weakened version of the original proposal. The details of these controversies will be discussed in chapters 11 and 12, which explore the linkage of events and the patterns of cleavage within the energy and health domains. As will be apparent, in contrast to the health policy domain during the late 1970s, activity related to energy issues was marked by fragmented participation, enduring conflicts, and a lack of consensus concerning the distribution of influence within the domain. A series of exogenous shocks, the introduction of new groups committed to reframing issues in terms of environmental and consumer considerations, and repeated attempts to consolidate fuel-specific regulations in an integrated energy policy all contributed to the unsettled character of the domain.

As will also become apparent in the history of the health policy domain during this period, even though a perceived crisis appeared to offer an opportunity for major reorganization of these policy domains, established modes of debate and networks of influential organizations limited the extent to which change was feasible.

Health Policy in the United States

Securing the Right to Self-Regulation

Apart from the provision of hospital care for sailors and sporadic attempts to control epidemics, a national politics of health did not exist prior to the 20th century in the United States. Before that time, government involvement in health care occurred primarily at the state or local level. In a broader sense, however, a politics of health was present in the efforts of providers and practitioners to gain advantages both in the market and in their relationships with educational and charitable institutions (Larson, 1977). This period of organizational competition and institution building shaped the situation confronted by national policy-makers during the Progressive era and thereafter.

By the time of the First World War, many of the organizations that continue to be influential had been founded, and the basic framework of the U.S. health care system was established. The preceding century had seen three interrelated developments: the organization of the delivery of care, of medical education, and of the profession itself. Biomedical research did not emerge as a prominent factor in health care until World War II (Campion, 1984: chap. 2). For most of the nation's history, the politics of the profession, as well as debates over the character of hospitals and medical education, were framed by a concern for control over the number and quality of practitioners. In turn, this professional politics had, and continues to have, a powerful influence on the nature of federal intervention and the character of the emerging policy domain.

Of central importance were the relationships established between three types of institutions—hospitals, medical schools, and practitioner organizations. The new prominence of the hospital during the latter half of the 19th century challenged the traditional dominance of solo practitioners in the delivery of care and transformed the terms of professional competition. Prior to this time, medicine had been practiced primarily in private homes or, increasingly, in a physician's office. The first American hospitals were pesthouses or almshouses—charitable institutions, either private or public, serving to house the sick more often than to cure them. But this situation altered with the discovery of antiseptics and anesthetics, the increasing sophistication of diagnostic technology, the training of skilled nurses, and the reform of medical education (Williams and Torrens, 1980:129–30). By 1909 the number of hospitals in the United States was well over 20 times the total in 1873. Their numbers peaked at 7,000 in 1918, although the total number of beds continued to increase (Anderson 1968:27, 30). Technological advances and the demands of an increasingly urban, market-oriented society encouraged the "reconstitution of the hospitals as an institution of medical science rather than of social welfare, its reorganization on the lines of a business rather than a charity" (Starr, 1982:147).

Institutional expansion increased the potential for a division of labor in the delivery of medical care and, with it, the possibility of political conflicts within the medical profession. Usually lacking a permanent house staff, the new hospitals provided opportunities for general practitioners to perform surgery and to take advantage of new therapies and diagnostic technologies. Lack of access to hospital facilities became a major competitive disadvantage and, eventually, an important resource in the profession's attempt to control practitioners. In Britain the guild organization of surgeons, physicians, and apothecaries provided a basic structure for referral and consultation, but there was no precedent for managing relations between general practitioners and specialists in the United States (Stevens, 1971:81). The development of the hospital made possible the division of labor and capital investment central to modern professional medical practice. The regulation of that practice, however, was determined by prolonged—and highly politicized—competition among practitioners and educators.

The transformation of medical education paralleled the development of the modern hospital. During the colonial period, most medical training involved apprenticeship or self-teaching. The first medical school, the College of Philadelphia, was not founded until 1765. By the end of that century, Columbia,

Harvard, and Dartmouth had followed suit (Stevens, 1971:16, 19). But attempts to raise the standards of the would-be profession were frustrated by the rapid expansion of medical schools and the existence of competing forms of medical practice. This proliferation of medical schools undermined attempts both to control the supply of physicians (which, in per capita terms, was exceptionally high) and to establish the authority of European medicine. Over the course of the 19th century, more than four hundred medical schools were founded, although many soon failed. Prior to the Jacksonian period, the majority were affiliated with liberal arts colleges, but proprietary schools accounted for most of the subsequent expansion (Stevens, 1971:24–25). By the time of the Civil War, a medical education might involve anything from a brief course at a commercial school to extended training at a university-based school. Among physicians, a consensus upon which to base the regulation of medical education and practice was effectively absent.

From the 1830s onward the repeal of licensing regulations allowed "medical sects" to establish schools and grant degrees. Graduation from a medical college was the sole legal criterion for practice. The decline of official control meant increased opportunities for practices that physicians trained in European "scientific medicine" had attempted to suppress.[3] Disputes resulting from the increasing institutionalization of alternative types of medicine persisted throughout the century. There was intense feuding among homeopaths, Eclectics, and the "regular" doctors who became known as "allopaths" or practitioners of treatment by opposites. At issue were hospital privileges, access to publicly supported medical schools, and even military service.

These conflicts thwarted efforts to improve the status and income of physicians. Attempts to strengthen the profession's economic position by controlling the supply of physicians were easily, and often correctly, interpreted as attacks upon the vitality of one or another school of medical practice. In addition, limiting the supply of medical personnel was at odds with the interests of most medical schools, particularly proprietary schools, which tended to offer the least instruction to students with the least educational preparation. As will be discussed below, significant educational reform was primarily the prerogative of a handful of elite medical schools, which, regardless of their prestige, lacked the power to enforce their new standards upon other colleges. Hampered by the absence of sufficient political or economic leverage, the task of reforming medical education became entwined with efforts to organize the profession.

3. In addition, the proprietary medical schools—usually requiring less formal education and shorter, even part-time, training than college-based schools—provided opportunities for less affluent (and even female) students to acquire the training required for a career in medicine. Following the great waves of European immigration, members of newly arrived ethnic and religious groups were able to serve their own communities more easily than would have been the case under a formal, university-based system of medical training.

Although the American Medical Association (AMA) was not founded until 1848, professional societies had existed in a number of cities and states since the colonial period. By 1800 there were medical societies in six states, and within 30 years almost every state had some sort of physicians' organization. Members were predominantly allopaths, practitioners of European scientific medicine. Yet the emergence of a health care system dominated by licensed physicians was not an inevitable outcome of the establishment of professional societies. Both hospitals and medical schools were potential institutional alternatives to the system of collegial regulation of private practice that came to dominate the ideology of American medicine (Freidson, 1973). The consolidation of the American health care system involved not only the organization of individual physicians but the gradual cooptation of competing institutions and medical sects.

In time the economic threat posed by the flood of poorly trained "medical doctors" helped to redefine the issues facing the profession; the absence of adequate medical education came to be seen as a greater problem than the wrong sort of medical education. By the 1870s and 1880s, representatives of the more established medical sects joined to urge the establishment of parallel systems of licensing that would recognize each group's autonomy while curbing competition from poorly trained doctors (Starr, 1982:102). Although separate licensing boards were established in a few states, in most cases responsibility was vested in a single board made up of representatives of the different groups. At that time, professional contacts with nonallopathic physicians were grounds for expulsion from most mainstream medical societies. Gradually, however, mutually advantageous political cooperation led to greater interaction both in medical education and in professional societies. Ironically, this did not turn out to be advantageous for the homeopathic and Eclectic doctors: "the more they gained in access to the privileges of regular physicians, the more their numbers declined" (Starr, 1982:107). Although new sects, such as osteopathy and Christian Scientism, emerged, the cooptation of more established groups paved the way for the consolidation of the medical profession.

Attempts were also made to integrate regulatory and educational institutions in order to promote national standards of medical practice. In 1891 state licensing boards were informally linked through a national professional association, the National Confederation of State Medical Examining and Licensing Boards. During the following years, the American Association of Medical Colleges (AAMC) was reorganized, and changes in the bylaws of the AMA strengthened ties with state and county medical societies. By the turn of the century, a network of professional and voluntary associations provided the basis for effective national organizations of educators, physicians, and public officials. The constituency of these organizations, however, limited their ability to push for significant reforms. Although the association of licensing boards was willing to apply pressure to the commercial colleges, it "did comparatively little to assimilate the standards of its own members; like the AAMC, it was not in its interest to antagonize its own membership; nor, indeed, was there unanimity within either organization about the desirability of requiring all schools to maintain the same level" (Stevens, 1971:60).

Although stringent regulation of medical education threatened the financial interests of most schools and the friendly relations among licensing boards, greater control would benefit practicing physicians faced with competition in urban markets. The limitations of state-by-state regulation of medicine were among the first political issues to be faced by the reconstituted AMA, which established a "committee to take up with the U.S. Congress the question of national medical licensing" (Stevens, 1971:61).[4] The subsumption of state licensing under a national system was impeded by local political opposition (often from the state medical societies), and, consequently, attention increasingly focused on national attempts to reform medical education. In 1902 the AMA established its Council on Medical Education. By developing minimum standards for physician training and a system for rating medical schools, the council served as an institutional base for the drive for educational reform.

In its attempts to promote the economic and status concerns of the profession, the AMA emerged as a significant actor in efforts to reform the health care system more generally; consequently, many issues were framed in terms of the profession's concerns. Until World War I the AMA was dominated by prominent medical educators and hospital-based "specialists," who sought to establish a more rigorous and specialized system of medical education. Previously, attempts to improve the quality of medical education had been the concern of educators concentrated at elite medical schools, notably Harvard and Johns Hopkins.[5] Although changes came slowly, reforms were adopted by other university-affiliated schools throughout the remainder of the century. In 1891 the AAMC was reorganized and "set minimum requirements for admission to membership"; by 1896 over one-third of the 155 operating medical schools had joined the organization (Anderson, 1968:31). But, as was the case with hospital-based care at the turn of the century, the role of reformed medical education within the overall health care system remained unclear.

Private foundations provided the resources necessary for thoroughgoing professional reform. For the first time, many nonproprietary schools were able

---

4. Formal interstate agreements were another possible solution. In 1902 four north-central states (Illinois, Indiana, Michigan, and Wisconsin) formed the first system of reciprocal licensing. Although there was a great deal of interest in a national system of reciprocal licensing, this was never achieved, and agreements continue to be made between individual states.

5. Five years prior to the organization of the AAMC in 1876, Harvard instituted written examinations, a graded curriculum, and a three-year program of instruction. Educational prerequisites were made more stringent, and salaries replaced the existing system of student fees to individual professors (Stevens, 1971:41).

to upgrade their facilities and curriculum: "In 1891, the medical schools possessed an estimated $500,000 in endowments. Between 1903 and 1934 nine foundations alone granted medical institutions about $150 million" (Stevens, 1971:56n). Support from the fortunes of the Rockefellers, Carnegies, and others was not limited to the construction of buildings and acquisition of equipment. In 1906 the Carnegie Foundation for the Advancement of Teaching was founded, and four years later—at the suggestion of, but not in cooperation with, the AMA—it sponsored an inspection of all medical schools in the United States and Canada. Abraham Flexner conducted the investigation and, as a representative of one of these new and notoriously wealthy foundations, was able to gain access to most teaching facilities (Starr, 1982:119).

Unlike the previous ratings calculated by the AMA's Council on Medical Education, Flexner's findings were published—including the names of all the schools—along with his recommendation that many should be closed. State licensing boards began to adopt the higher standards set forth by Flexner in his 1910 report and previously advocated by the AMA. Unable to generate the funds necessary to improve their facilities, 36 of the 131 schools in the United States visited by Flexner closed within the next five years (Starr, 1982: 120). With aid of powerful charitable foundations, the AMA gained a measure of control over medical education and, consequently, over the supply of physicians.

In the wake of the Flexner report, medical education in the United States became increasingly standardized. The four-year postgraduate program with laboratory and clinical training, first established at Johns Hopkins in the 1890s, came to be accepted by professionals and expected by regulatory agencies. During the same period, the AMA and other professional societies emerged as the dominant actors in the infant politics of health care. Medical schools and hospitals, although represented by their own organizations, were usually allied with organized physicians, at least until the 1950s, when their interests diverged over the issue of government financing of medical education and health care. Although increasing specialization continued to generate conflicts within the medical profession and the health care industry, the politics of health following World War I was dominated by an issue that had received relatively little attention during the period when the medical profession was striving to organize itself: access.

The Politics of Health on the National Agenda: 1915–1975
Prior to the First World War, the issues that divided, and ultimately organized, the medical profession were the regulation of education, licensing, and access to hospital facilities. For the most part, recourse to politics stemmed from attempts by the profession, led by either educators or practitioners, to acquire legal support for self-regulation. Since the victories of powerful factions

tended to endure to the extent that they became incorporated in law, there was a definite, but limited, incentive for political mobilization on the part of medical practitioners.

The professional politics of the prewar period directly embraced only three of the four central components of a health care system: the development of scientific knowledge, the provision of trained personnel, and the organization of care. Access was not a major concern, although some medical schools established dispensaries to provide clinical experience for their students, and medical sects built clienteles among the rural and lower classes. Attention to the interests of consumers was indirect, a function of attempts to regulate the supply of practitioners allowed to enter the market. During the Progressive period, however, questions of consumer protection and access brought the politics of health onto the national agenda.

In response to the increasing use of pills and manufactured medicines of unknown composition, the AMA initiated a campaign against proprietary medicine in 1900. Journalistic investigations of the pharmaceutical industry and Upton Sinclair's famous expose of Chicago meatpackers produced widespread demand for regulation. This movement drew upon established networks of reformers and activists, including members of settlement houses and other charitable organizations. Characteristically, the AMA preferred private to public regulation and in 1905 established the Council on Pharmacy and Chemistry. The council was provided with its own laboratory to support the AMA's "seal of approval" advertising policy (Starr, 1982:131). In addition, the AMA supported the Pure Food and Drug Act, a relatively weak bill that prohibited the adulteration of drugs and false advertising. Problems of safety and efficacy were not addressed until the rise of consumer activism during the New Deal (Campion, 1984:470).

The fight for drug regulation pitted the pharmaceutical industry against the medical profession and social reformers. The next major health issue to appear on the national agenda provoked a much broader response. In 1913, anticipating the success of workmen's compensation legislation in most of the industrial states, the Association for the Advancement of Labor Legislation, a nationwide organization of reformers and educators, gave top priority to health insurance. The convergence of increasingly advanced, hence expensive, medical technology and the concentration of care in hospitals created a widespread awareness of the need for some sort of prepayment or collective risk bearing (Stevens, 1971: 137). The AALL coordinated efforts that resulted in official investigating commissions in 10 states and the introduction of a standard health insurance bill in 16 (Anderson, 1968:72; Poen, 1979:4).

This proposal found allies within the health care professions. The AMA initially supported this movement, establishing in 1912 the Committee on Social Insurance, chaired by Isaac Rubinow, a socialist and a prominent reformer. In 1916 a joint committee of nursing organizations reported favorably on the principle of health insurance, and a conference of public health officials unanimously endorsed the legislation. Members of the American Hospital Association (AHA) were divided on the merits of government health insurance but "regarded it as an inevitability" and offered to work with state health insurance commissions responsible for studying the matter (Anderson, 1968:82).

Despite this support, health insurance faced considerable opposition. In 1916 the commercial insurance companies organized against public health insurance. They were joined by the American Federation of Labor, led by the ardently voluntaristic Samuel Gompers, numerous employers' associations, and, somewhat unexpectedly, pharmaceutical companies and professional groups fearful of competition from hospital dispensaries (Anderson, 1968:79, 80). Equally important were the internal dynamics of organizations sympathetic to fundamental reforms of health care financing. Particularly within the AMA, growing familiarity with the reform proposals led to a widely shared belief that government health insurance would undermine solo practitioners—the very group that was coming to dominate the organization. Although activity at the national level was suspended during the war, opposition grew within the state societies. In 1919 this resulted in the reorganization of the Committee on Social Insurance and the removal of Rubinow. By 1920 the last bill being considered by a state legislature had failed, and the AMA House of Delegates adopted what would be a long-standing policy:

Resolved, that the American Medical Association declares its opposition to the institution of any plan embodying the system of compulsory insurance which provides for medical service to be rendered contributors or their dependents, provided, controlled, or regulated by any state or the Federal Government. (Quoted in Anderson, 1968:74)

As power within the AMA shifted from prominent educators to general practitioners, the organization abandoned its alliance with the network of policy reformers and social workers. Health insurance was redefined; no longer an "inevitability," it was portrayed as a threat to the fundamental character of medical practice—indeed, to the American way of life. Having so recently secured the collegial regulation of the profession, the AMA and other medical societies emerged as the core of the opposition to further government intervention in the area of health care.

During the 1920s relative political quiet descended upon most of the country. With the defeat of health insurance and growing opposition to most forms of government intervention, changes in the organization of health care once again became matters of professional politics and business strategy. But the political activity of the preceding decades had created significant changes in the conditions of this private politics. Organized physicians were able to take care of most of their internal housekeeping, protected by laws passed during the Progressive years—a time of direct appeal to state power unique in the history of organized medicine.[6] Legislation was used to limit competition rather than to encourage government intervention. In many states organized medicine secured passage of laws against group practice and corporate health plans (Starr, 1982:204; Stevens, 1971:151).

Although the 1920s were a time of significant social and economic change, politicians such as Hoover looked to the development of voluntary methods of regulation—the associational state—in which economic problems would be managed by private trade associations and social welfare would be provided for by enlightened employers, the so-called welfare capitalists.[7] In 1929, the same year that Baylor University founded the first Blue Cross plan for hospital insurance, Congress allowed the Sheppard-Towner Act of 1922 to lapse, thus terminating the first federal program funding health care, in this case for mothers and children. For insofar as medical decision making was to be reserved to health care professionals, private charity was deemed preferrable to government programs.

By the end of the decade, concern for the health of the nation again emerged as a prominent issue. The Committee on the Costs of Medical Care was established with considerable philanthropic support (Poen, 1979:14). Yet apart from the establishment of the National Institute of Health in 1930 to administer the medical research activities of the Public Health Service, responses to health issues were predominantly private. However, the onset of the Depression in late 1929 strained the capabilities of private practitioners and charity to the point of collapse. As the unemployment rate reached 25 percent, local charities found themselves unable to provide medical services for the growing numbers of indigents and aged poor, at the same time that large numbers of physicians faced financial crises as their former patients chose to purchase food rather than health care. Under the Federal Emergency Relief Act of

6. Increasing specialization created tensions within the profession, but the new specialty associations also contributed to the development of private forms of regulation. Most notable was the success of the recently established American College of Surgeons in promoting the standardization of hospital equipment and procedures following the war (Stevens, 1971:91, 119).

7. Although the private solo practitioner has often been portrayed as the embodiment of the tradition of American medicine, challenges to this type of organization of care have always existed. Company-managed employee health programs were well-established in industries like mining and the railroads, while "consumers' clubs" provided prepaid health plans to members of fraternal societies and other predominantly urban organizations. These forms of corporate or contract practice were opposed by professional societies. More enduring alternatives were found in group practices and clinics, particularly in the Midwest, and in the health care plan sponsored by the Kaiser industries of California. Begun to provide care to workers building Grand Coulee Dam, the plan grew with the firm's wartime expansion and eventually served as the basis for Kaiser-Permanente, the largest prepaid medical group in the nation and a model for the development of health maintenance organizations (Hodgson, 1973; Starr, 1982:200–215; Wohl, 1984:161–67).

1933, funds were made available for health care for the aged, and New Deal agencies provided some health care to their constituencies (Litman and Robins, 1984:347; Poen, 1979:18; Starr, 1982:270, 271). Yet despite the apparent need for reform and the support of Federal agencies, Roosevelt refrained from pushing national health insurance, and even passing references to the subject were removed from the Social Security Act. No mass mobilization comparable to the Townsend Clubs' support for old age pensions emerged to challenge the domination of health policy by the interests of the medical profession.

Despite the stalemate on health insurance, the New Deal did introduce important changes in health policy. During the Hoover administration, the Food, Drug and Insecticide Administration was separated from the Bureau of Chemistry, and in 1933 the Food, Drug and Cosmetic Act was introduced in Congress for the first time. Passed five years later in the wake of a drug-related tragedy resulting in a hundred deaths, this legislation extended "federal authority to act against adulterated and misbranded food, drugs, and cosmetic products, banning new drugs until approved by the [newly established] Food and Drug Administration" (Litman and Robins 1984:347). The previous year, the first federally funded agency devoted to the study of a single disease, the National Cancer Institute, had been established. Although organized medicine and conservative factions in Congress blocked progress on health insurance, the federal government greatly increased its presence in the areas of biomedical research and pharmaceutical regulation.

In the late 1930s health insurance reappeared on the national agenda. Faced with growing interest in national health insurance, the AMA moderated its opposition to all insurance plans and began to discuss the forms of voluntary insurance that would be most acceptable. In 1938 it endorsed Blue Cross hospital insurance and four years later approved physician-controlled insurance for physician services such as Blue Shield (Campion, 1984:121). In 1939 Sen. Robert Wagner of New York introduced a bill, based on the recommendation of the National Health Conference of 1938, calling for federally subsidized state medical compensation (Littman and Robins, 1984:347). No action was taken, but during World War II public opinion polls consistently reported high levels of support for the public provision or financing of health care; a 1942 *Fortune* poll reported 74.3 percent in favor of national health insurance (Poen, 1979:30).

The war fundamentally altered the terms upon which health care issues were debated. The wage freeze imposed to control wartime inflation greatly enhanced the importance of fringe benefits—specifically medical benefits—in negotiations between labor and management. Expanded corporate financing of medical care was paralleled by the enormous growth of federally provided health care for servicemen and their dependents. These developments built on, and stimulated, the growth of the hospital- and physician-owned insity had overruled the ideological distaste of the AMA, the AHA, and other professional organizations for *private* health insurance (Starr, 1982:296–97). Initially creatures of the care providers, the largest of these plans, Blue Cross and Blue Shield, emerged as important actors in the making of health policy. Indeed, gradually forced to cut their ties to their original sponsors by political pressures and a series of antitrust cases in the 1970s (Litman and Robins, 1984:227, 354; M. Thompson, 1979:chap. 7), the "Blues" eventually came to advocate limiting the ability of health care providers to set their own prices.

Wartime developments in labor policy deprived the health insurance movement of part of its potential constituency. In addition, the proinsurance coalition organized by Senator Wagner in early 1944 faced an opposition no longer committed to total rejection of public and private health insurance, but willing to formulate conservative alternatives to the reformers' proposals (Poen, 1979:42). The postwar situation also differed in that Harry Truman was now President and, unlike Roosevelt, made the passage of health insurance a major agenda item, particularly during his second term. This level of presidential support was unprecedented. Senator Wagner and his allies put together a coalition that included organized labor, the National Farmers Union, organizations of liberal and black physicians, the National Consumers League, the American Jewish Congress, the NAACP, and the newly established Union for Democratic Action (Poen, 1979:84).[8]

In response to the growing advocacy of national health insurance, the AMA emerged as a potent political actor at the national level, anchoring a loose coalition including the AHA, the American Bar Foundation, the American Dental Association, the Protestant and Catholic hospital associations, the Chamber of Commerce, the National Grange, and other groups opposed to the expansion of government intervention for a variety of economic and ideological reasons. In 1943 the AMA established a Washington office, whereas only six years earlier even a proposal to start a public relations department had been rejected (Campion, 1984:127–28). Following Truman's sponsorship of a health insurance bill in 1949, the need for practical politics brought about the downfall of diehard supporters of private practice within the organization. At the same time, the AMA engaged the services of a public relations firm and,

8. Even the successes of reform groups were often a mixed blessing for the cause of centralized, public health care. Under Truman, most federal health plans were directed by the Federal Security Agency, headed by Oscar Ewing, a strong supporter of national health insurance. The presence of this prominent reformer sparked a controversy when Truman attempted to elevate the FSA to cabinet status, a change later implemented by Eisenhower (Campion, 1984:166). Thus, it is important to recognize that reformers as well as regulatees can capture agencies and, consequently that struggles that appear to be instances of bureaucratic politics (Allison, 1971) may be closely linked to interest group activity.

between 1949 and 1952, spent almost $5 million on a campaign to defeat national health insurance legislation (Campion, 1984:158).

Despite the repeated introduction and strategic reformulation of the Wagner-Murray-Dingell proposals, the only legislative innovations that passed Congress were the AMA-supported Hill-Burton Hospital Construction Act of 1946 and the Hill-Aiken bill of 1949. Drafted in part by representatives of the AHA, the legislation "provided federal assistance to the states to subsidize premium payments on private plans like Blue Cross for persons unable to pay for them" (Poen, 1979:87, 165). Through substitute measures, members of the health care industry and medical professions sought to stave off the direct federal financing of personal medical care that they believed threatened their autonomy.

The repeated failure of national health insurance legislation affected the reform organizations established by its advocates. In 1950 the liberal Committee for the Nation's Health became deeply divided over the proper course of action in a conservative political climate. The faction favoring an emphasis on less controversial reforms such as funding of biomedical research and medical education eventually left the organization. Facing financial crisis, the committee was rescued by the United States Steel Workers and increasingly served the particular needs of organized labor until superseded by a joint AFL-CIO health information office in 1956 (Poen, 1979:177, 207). Thus, a middle-class reform movement, emphasizing research funding, emerged as distinct from popular movements more directly concerned with the expansion of the welfare state.

Although biomedical research and the regulation of pharmaceuticals logically seem to belong to the category of health politics, throughout much of this century they have constituted comparatively calm policy arenas removed from struggles over the organization of care and the training of personnel. Aided by the prodding of the lobby associated with Mary Lasker, federal support of biomedical research increased greatly. The rising level of medical knowledge also resulted in a greater awareness of the risks posed by various substances. The so-called Delaney clause of the 1958 amendments to the Food, Drug and Cosmetics Act of 1938 forbade FDA approval of any food additive "found to induce cancer in man or animal" (Litman and Robins, 1984:350), and further amendments in 1962 strengthened the FDA's control over the pharmaceutical industry.

Shortly after the defeat of the health insurance proposals sponsored by Truman and the congressional trio of Wagner, Murray, and Dingell, reform advocates adopted a politically pragmatic, incremental approach to the problem of health insurance—by way of the aged. As one scholar has noted, this approach created difficulties for the opposition: "it was one thing to write off socialism, but the risks of writing off the aged would give the wise politician some second thoughts" (Marmor, 1970:28). The emergence of the aged as an identifiable constituency for federal funding had been prompted by the growing use of health care as a fringe benefit under union contracts and the vastly increased numbers of private insurance policies taken out by the middle class. Over the course of Truman's two administrations, the number of Blue Cross and Blue Shield policies had grown from 28 to 61 million (Poen, 1979:229). Yet the double burden of being poor and being poor health risks kept these two sources of security beyond the reach of the majority of two population groups: the poor and the elderly. But whereas poor people have rarely been able to organize themselves for persistent legislative lobbying, during the Depression years organizations such as the Townsend Clubs had been the vehicle for the organization of the aged, one of the decisive factors behind the passage of the Social Security Act of 1935.

Insurance legislation specifically for the aged had been drafted as early as 1951, when long-time insurance advocates Wilbur J. Cohen and I. S. Falk persuaded Truman of the usefulness of pursuing a less comprehensive strategy. In 1957, following the passage of disability insurance, representatives of the AFL-CIO persuaded Rep. Aime Forand to introduce a bill providing for "up to 120 days of combined hospital and nursing home care as well as necessary surgery" for aged beneficiaries of Social Security (Campion, 1984:255; Litman and Robins, 1984:349). Congress took no action on the bill, which was endorsed by the AHA and the American Nursing Association. The following year the Forand bill was adopted by a coalition of liberal Democrats and organized labor and became the focus of a nationwide political organizing effort among the elderly (Poen, 1979:27).

At the same time, a council composed of the AMA, the AHA, the American Nursing Home Association, and the American Dental Association studied the issue, concluding that the "health care of the aged does not need improvement." However, their opposition to government health insurance for the aged, supported by the outgoing Eisenhower administration and conservative Republicans, was not doctrinaire. In May 1960 Eisenhower proposed a system of federal assistance to pay for catastrophic illness among the aged, and four months later Congress approved the Kerr-Mills bill, which used federal matching funds to create "a new public assistance category—Medical Assistance for the Aged" (Litman and Robins, 1984:350). The two terms of the Eisenhower administration were also a time of major reorganization of federal involvement in the health care system. In 1953 the Federal Security Agency (FSA) was reorganized and elevated to cabinet status as the Department of Health, Education and Welfare, a change that Congress had repeatedly vetoed under Truman. Thus, the institutional basis for a coordinated federal health policy was greatly strengthened.

In 1960 John F. Kennedy was elected President, a narrow victory attributable in part to the support of organized groups of elderly Americans. Throughout his administration health issues were prominent, particularly the repeatedly defeated King-Anderson bill (a further revision of what one commentator called the "Wagner-Murray-Dingell-Falk-Cohen-Ewing-Ball-Cruikshank-Biemiller-Forand bill"; see Campion, 1984:256), which would have provided health insurance for the elderly through modifications of the social security system. Both supporters and opponents mobilized for a fight of the same proportions as those of the Truman period. Public relations firms were hired, speeches were made, and rallies were held in Madison Square Garden. But the terms of the conflict had shifted significantly. To quote the AMA president in 1961: "Only in the case of the needy or medically needy should government intervene. . . . The King-Anderson program does not provide insurance or prepayment of any type, but compels one segment of our population to underwrite a socialized program of health care for another, regardless of need" (quoted in Campion 1984:256). Just as the New Deal divorced the problem of the aged from those of the indigent by separately institutionalizing Social Security and "welfare," the medical profession sought to protect most of its autonomy by removing the problems of the needy from the much broader issue of the organization and financing of care.

Once the conflict had been framed in terms of the privileged character of the physician-patient relationship and professional responsibility, other aspects of the health care system were left more open to politically mediated change. Legislation such as the Health Professions Education Assistance Act and the Community Mental Health Centers Construction Act of 1963 and the Nurse Training Act of 1964 had increased government presence in the health care system. Federal funding became an important component of medical education and hospital costs. The expansion of government involvement served the interests of educators and hospital administrators and trustees, despite the continued opposition of the AMA and various other professional organizations (Campion, 1984:179).

During the Kennedy administration the King-Anderson bill was blocked by a bipartisan conservative majority on the House Ways and Means Committee. But with the landslide Democratic victory in 1964 following Kennedy's assassination, the passage of some sort of health insurance for the aged was virtually guaranteed. The focus of activity, however, remained the House Ways and Means Committee, where the conservative chairman, Rep. Wilbur Mills, had agreed to cooperate with insurance advocates rather than lose control over the legislation.

Prior to this time Mills's major accomplishment in health policy was the Kerr-Mills legislation of 1960, which created the Medical Assistance for the Aged program, a conservative program administered by the states with federal matching funds. In 1964 he was faced with two alternatives: the King-

Anderson bill, promising 60 days of hospital care to those over 65 regardless of need but virtually no physician services, and two bills proposing the purchase of private health insurance for the elderly needy[9] (Campion, 1984: 271–74). Yet Mills used the power of his position as chairman of Ways and Means to integrate the political options presented by various interest groups and the administration.[10] Unexpectedly, he transformed these mutually exclusive alternatives into components of a much more comprehensive plan. And on April 8, 1965, the House passed H.R. 6675—what Mills described as a "three-layer cake":

Layer one, Medicare Part A, was very close to King-Anderson. It included hospital care for Social Security retirees, financed and administered by Social Security. Layer two, Medicare Part B, came out of the Byrnes bill—a supplemental, voluntary insurance plan covering physician services. It called for financing by uniform premiums from those beneficiaries who elected to participate and a matching contribution from general revenues.

Layer three, Medicaid, grew out of the Eldercare bill, Kerr-Mills, and the AMA's concern for the non-elderly needy. . . . Medicaid liberalized the eligibility requirements of Kerr-Mills and widened it to cover indigent people under sixty-five. It relied on matching federal-state funds and state administration, and permitted the use of private insurance carriers. (Campion, 1984: 275)

The same Congress passed major legislation establishing the Regional Medical Programs, designed to "unite the worlds of scientific research, medical education, and medical care" (quoted in Starr, 1982: 370), as well as a system of neighborhood health centers as part of the War on Poverty.

Once this legislation was passed, the opposition to government intervention that had unified the AMA, the AHA, and numerous other groups foundered on issues of implementation: "Groups in the medical care industry remained active, but their activities were consultative and relatively unpublicized, not those of diehard ideological adversaries" (Marmor, 1970: 88). Thus, as is

9. The AMA's "Eldercare" bill included provisions for federal matching grants to the states whereas the Byrnes (R-Wi) bill mandated a federally administered system. The drafting of the Eldercare bill had involved consultations with "representatives of Blue Cross, Blue Shield, the American Hospital Association, the American Dental Association and the health insurance industry." It was promoted as costing less than the Medicare program while providing more generous benefits to the needy elderly (Campion, 1984: 271–74).

10. Mills's activities as a political broker were evident in the pattern of his consultations with interest groups. A wide variety of public and private interests were consulted on the concerns and technical issues most relevant to their particular situation. The AHA triumphed over the AMA on the issue of reimbursement of hospital-based specialists; payment for the services of radiologists and anesthesiologists was to be included in hospital bills despite the AMA's charge that this would transform specialists into "coerced" employees. The AMA, however, won inclusion of the "usual and customary" fee as the basis for physician reimbursement under Medicare Part B (Marmor, 1970: 66–72).

often the case in U.S. politics, the passage of social reform legislation paved the way for the development of close relations between social service or regulatory agencies and many of the groups initially opposed to the reforms.

For consumers, Medicare and Medicaid had ironic consequences. Intended to aid those who could not afford medical care, the entry of the federal government as a major purchaser of health services resulted in tremendous inflation in the cost of those services. As a compromise with organized medicine, the fee structure of the new programs was based on the notion of "customary" and "reasonable" charges, a concept that allowed the profession to set its prices independently of demand or quality of service. The fee structure also allowed higher compensation for services performed in hospitals, thus providing a disincentive for utilizing more economical methods of care (Starr, 1982:385). The financial impact of the new legislation was severe: even in the year between enactment and implementation, "the rate of increase of physician fees more than doubled" (Marmor, 1970:86), and the government's "share of national health expenditures jumped from 26 to 37 percent between 1965 and 1970" (Starr, 1982:384).

The ramifications of the Medicare and Medicaid legislation were not limited to changes in the access to and price of health care. The massive influx of government funding created large incentives for entrepreneurial behavior in an area of the economy that had been strongly influenced by a self-image of professionalism. In 1968 and 1969 the Hospital Corporation of America, the Humana Corporation, National Medical Enterprises, and a number of other health care businesses were founded. Over the next decade, the health provider industry grew rapidly and became an attractive target for acquisition by major corporations. With striking rapidity, policy-makers confronted the rise of what numerous authors have dubbed the "medical-industrial complex" (Starr, 1982:428–36; Wohl, 1984:1, 19).

The political consequences of these changes in the economics of health care were soon apparent. Addressing a press conference in July 1969, Nixon declared: "Unless action is taken within the next two or three years . . . we will have a breakdown in our medical system" (Starr, 1982:381). Yet the character of the national health policy domain made it unlikely that the necessary actions could actually be taken. Despite their opposition to the initial legislation, the health professions and industry were unwilling to let go of the profits that Medicare and Medicaid spending brought. Although both Nixon and the Kennedy Democrats attempted to revive national health insurance plans, entrenched organizations stood between these proposals and any fundamental reorganization of publicly provided health care. This tension between rising costs and interests in the established organization of care remained the major source of dynamism (and stalemate) in this policy domain for the rest of the decade.

The Fight for Cost Containment

In January 1975 President Ford refused to reintroduce the health insurance plan sponsored by the Nixon administration, warning that he would veto any new spending legislation. Combined with inflationary trends grounded in the increased domestic and military budgets of the Vietnam War era, the oil shocks of 1974–75 highlighted the need for cost containment in all areas of government activity. In the case of national health policy, however, a simple freeze on new spending was insufficient, since many programs had built-in tendencies toward cost escalation. Although significant expansion of federal programs was politically unlikely, there were considerable incentives to reform national health policy in the interests of greater efficiency, economy, or equity.

During the period explored in this study, cost containment was the most prominent theme in health policy debates, but this common concern did not dictate a single solution. Furthermore, not all areas of federal spending were equally affected by the economizing mood of the late 1970s, and even fewer programs have remained untouched by the Reagan administration. Specific issues will be explored in greater detail below, but the following discussion will help to locate the organization of the health policy domain within the politics of the period.

Although few, if any, were satisfied with the state of national health policy, changes were difficult to implement throughout the 1970s. The task of curbing the price of medical care fell to Richard Nixon, who had defeated the Democrats responsible for the passage of Medicare and Medicaid. Responding to the problem of inflation, Nixon secured passage of his Economic Stabilization Program; the wage-price freeze remained in effect for health care until 1975. Action on health issues was also necessary to fend off the movement for national health insurance, an increasingly popular issue being championed by a potential challenger for the presidency, Sen. Edward Kennedy (Starr, 1982: 394–95). In order to provide affordable medical care without greatly increasing federal regulation, the Nixon administration advocated the development of health maintenance organizations (HMOs), prepaid group practices emphasizing preventive medicine and cost efficiency. Encountering conflict over funding, the Health Maintenance Act did not pass until 1973, and an amendment providing for HMO reimbursement under the Medicare program did not secure approval until 1979, despite considerable support from the organized elderly.

Although the AMA forcefully opposed federal aid to new forms of health care delivery, physicians rapidly adapted to the new emphasis on market competition with the development of "preferred provider organizations" and "independent practice associations," designed to capture a clientele while avoiding the need to impose bureaucratic controls over private practice. Similarly, the stability of community and charitable hospitals, often associated with religious groups, has been undermined by the striking growth of proprietary hospitals. As the latter skimmed off the most "profitable" forms of care, pooled-risk forms of financing became increasingly problematic. Yet there was no government initiative proportionate to the enormous innovations in the organization of the health care industry.

Stalemate, rather than quiescence, characterized political activity during the Ford and Carter administrations. In late 1974 Gerald Ford inherited the presidency of the United States along with a demoralized Republican party and a Democrat-dominated Congress. Anticipating renewed political hegemony following the 1976 elections, the Democrats instead found themselves divided between Carter's executive initiatives and an often hostile, sometimes liberal Congress. Action in the area of health was further complicated by the fact that Carter—like Nixon before him—recognized potential competition for the presidency in Sen. Edward Kennedy, one of the leading advocates of national health insurance and related reforms.

This period of legislative stalemate was, nevertheless, a time of significant executive reorganization. Programs were consolidated, and divisions between policy arenas were institutionalized. In 1976 Medicare and Medicaid were moved from the Social Security Administration (Litman and Robins, 1984:354). They were combined, along with eight other programs, in the Health Care Financing Administration (HCFA), a new agency responsible for the bulk of federal expenditures in the health area. The remaining programs were consolidated in the Public Health Service. These changes were implemented by executive order obviating the need for congressional approval. Further reorganization took place in 1980 when the Department of Health, Education and Welfare was divided into the Departments of Education and of Health and Human Services (HHS).

Although these changes in the executive branch suggested the possibility of a more coordinated health policy, Congress continued to favor a host of entitlement programs that served the needs of specific—often well-organized and vocal—constituencies. Early in 1976 Congress opposed Ford's attempt to consolidate Medicaid and 15 categorical programs into a system of block grants to the states, which would no longer be required to provide matching funds (Bowman, 1976:487–91). These programs included state-run comprehensive health services; maternal and child health services; and blood separation centers. In 1975 Ford had vetoed a bill extending funding for these programs, but Congress overrode his decision despite warnings of excessive cost. In 1977 Congress passed the Health Services Extension Act—only a one-year reauthorization, since various congressional committees planned to reevaluate these programs during 1978 (Congressional Quarterly Almanac,

1978:611–16). Further reauthorization of most programs was approved in October 1978.

Despite strong congressional support for continued spending on a variety of health services, there was little agreement on the appropriate extent or character of control over this spending. During the early 1970s new regulatory agencies included professional standards review organizations (PSROs) and a national network of health systems agencies (HSAs) charged with administering the certificate-of-need program (designed to limit capital expenditures on the part of hospitals). By the late 1970s, however, these regulatory agencies were under attack from organized medicine, the hospital industry, and a sizable number of legislators disillusioned with this approach to regulation. The system had been threatened by Ford's previous attempt to replace Medicaid and various categorical programs with block grants, a change that would have given state governments more flexibility but lower funding at the expense of congressional control over the disbursement of funds (Bowman, 1976:487–491). Despite a one-year reprieve under the Health Services Extension Act, the reauthorization bill for the HSAs went down to an unexpected defeat in 1978.

When formulating policy, legislators have some degree of choice between delegating authority for administration to other agencies or promulgating very specific rules and requirements. Throughout the 1970s there was little in the way of mutual trust between Congress and the executive, making the former unwilling to grant much administrative autonomy to the latter. But whereas in the early part of the decade this led to the establishment of numerous agencies intended to promote control of federal programs at the regional or community level, during the Carter administration Congress attempted to exert more direct control over health policy. With regulatory agencies in disarray, and at times defunct, spending became the preferred mechanism for congressional influence.

This tendency is evident in the struggles over funding for the National Institutes for Health. Although the proposed budget continued to expand, by the end of this period Congress attempted to set ceilings on the allocations for individual institutions, traditionally an in-house decision by the NIH. Similarly, controversy over laboratory work involving recombinant DNA led Congress to discuss restructuring the NIH oversight system. In this case, however, there was no agreement on an appropriate method of regulation to replace the reliance on collegial systems. Consequently, genetic engineering continues to be regulated in a piecemeal fashion by the NIH, the Environmental Protection Agency (EPA), the Occupational Safety and Health Administration (OSHA), and various other federal agencies.

The move toward tighter congressional control was also apparent in the struggles over manpower policies. Although the AMA and other professional societies denounced the initial federal contributions to medical education, their fear of oversupply was diminished by the greatly increased demand for health care services following the passage of Medicare and Medicaid in 1965. In 1971 a similar program of federal subsidies for nursing schools was begun. Yet by the late 1970s, continuing shortages of physicians in inner city and rural areas suggested that distribution of manpower, not supply, was the real problem. Faced with predictions of a surplus of physicians, particularly specialists, by the end of the century, congressional liberals attempted to ensure that federally subsidized medical education would provide basic health care for the neediest populations.

Provisions addressing physician distribution were attached to the Health Manpower Authorization bill passed by the House in mid-1975. The Senate took no action that year on the legislation, which required that students repay capitation support given on their behalf unless they practiced in medically underserved areas following their graduation. The next year the Senate considered a bill that would require medical schools to allot more places for students who had accepted scholarships in return for a period of service and that established a national council to allocate residency positions by region and specialty. Following fierce opposition from medical schools and professional societies, a greatly weakened authorization bill was eventually passed. In return for capitation support, medical schools had to allocate 35 percent of first-year residency positions to primary care as well as reserving places for third-year students transferring from foreign medical schools. The latter provision was dropped a year later after numerous elite medical schools elected to forego federal support rather than comply with it.

The use of spending as a direct instrument of congressional policy making was limited, but not entirely prevented, by the opposition of powerful interest groups to increased regulation. Although liberal legislators lacked political support for actively altering the distribution of physicians, something that closely resembled a consensus existed in favor of curbing the overall costs of health care in the United States. With the apparent failure of PSROs and HSAs as mechanisms for limiting expenditures, both Congress and President Carter sought alternative strategies for controlling the growth of all, but particularly government, spending on health care.

To a certain extent this represented a continuation of earlier policies. Attempts were made to improve the competitiveness of the health care system, including relaxation of the requirements for federal assistance to HMOs. Suggestions for general, as well as catastrophic, national health insurance continued to be debated. By 1979 this issue had become one of the major points of confrontation between Carter and presidential contender Edward Kennedy. In a period of economic recession, however, initiation of major new spending programs was not likely, and most of the controversy centered around various proposals for limiting the growing cost of Medicare, Medicaid, and other federal health programs. As was the case with manpower policy during this period, many of the proposals involved fairly direct legislation of standards for

the health care industry rather than the establishment of new regulatory
bodies.

In 1977 President Carter submitted his Hospital Cost Control bill to Congress. This legislation proposed a 9 percent ceiling on the growth of hospital
revenues during 1978 as well as a $2.5 billion nationwide limit on new hospi-
tal construction. The bill met with strong opposition from representatives of
the hospital industry and organized medicine, who argued that capping costs
in this manner would diminish the quality of care. Moved by either a desire for
greater fiscal economy or a willingness to limit the profits earned by hospitals
and physicians, many members of Congress were sympathetic to the intent of
the legislation, but few were enthusiastic about its decidedly cumbersome
character. By the end of 1977, only one of the four congressional committees
with jurisdiction over this bill had reported it out of committee. Carter's bill
was too moderate to gain the support of politicians and groups interested in
major health care reform, yet it generated intense opposition by virtue of the
proposed limitations on the discretion of physicians and hospital trustees in
setting prices and expanding facilities.

In an attempt to defuse the widely shared feeling that something had to be
done about hospital costs, the health provider industry announced a voluntary
cost containment program on January 30, 1978. Two days later Rep. Dan
Rostenkowski (D-Ill.) introduced a bill allowing for a one-year trial of the voluntary system, to be replaced with mandatory controls if the hospital industry
failed to keep costs within prescribed limits. Yet nothing was agreed upon during the 1978 sessions, and in late 1979 plans for federal involvement in hospital cost control were effectively killed when the House rejected the current
administration proposal (a weakened version involving voluntary controls
with mandatory back-up limits), instead creating a commission to study hospital costs.

Following the collapse of Carter's cost containment initiative, Kennedy began to take independent action on his national health insurance plan and, one
might note, on his upcoming campaign for the Democratic presidential nomination. Yet there was relatively little support, outside of organized labor and
traditional liberal groups, for instituting new and costly health care programs
before the escalating costs of Medicare and Medicaid had been brought under
some semblance of control. Eventually, the political stalemate was broken
with the establishment of a payment system organized on an average-cost-per
basis: diagnostic related groups, or DRGs. This regulatory innovation did not
alter the organization of health care in a direct and fundamental manner.
Nevertheless, by tying the issue of cost containment to initial diagnoses—an
area of decision making traditionally shielded from state policy by professional prerogatives—this legislation significantly altered the terms of con-
testation within the health policy domain. Indeed, since 1980 the medical profession has come to see itself as increasingly embattled. Reflecting a variety

of essentially financial concerns, particularly growing government expenditures, the rising cost of insurance, and the expanded role of profit-making corporations, health policy has continued to attract a high level of activity, although a coalition powerful enough to secure fundamental reforms has yet to emerge. But as one recent discussion of the fate of the medical profession concluded:

there is no reason to believe that medicine's basic position of dominance, its key position in the health care system, will change. It will have considerably less control over the economics of health care, however, and will have to struggle to maintain its strong voice in policy-making and in the governance of the organizations in which its members work. (Freidson, 1985:32)

To the extent that this diagnosis is correct, it may be that significant changes will occur first in the process rather than in the products of policy formation. And, as will be argued throughout, it is precisely such changes that an organizational perspective on political life is best suited to detect.

Organizational Mobilization and Symbolic Negotiation

As we stated at the beginning of this chapter, contemporary policy domains are the product of a twofold process of mobilization and symbolic negotiation. Thus, the recognition of an issue entails some form of judgment as to whether it will be understood as an appropriate object of political action—and hence a possible reason for collective mobilization—or whether it will be embedded within the sphere of private decision making. At the same time, the existence of concerned parties, whether individual or corporate, is in many cases a prerequisite for the identification of events or issues and their definition as demanding some form of collective decision. In the chapters that follow, we attempt to capture something of the nature of this constant interplay between systems of actors and systems of events.

With the power of hindsight, however, the consequences of particular patterns of organization and the specific outcomes of repeated bouts of negotiation over the framing of issues are strikingly apparent. Numerous counterfactuals may be posed: had the geopolitical position of the United States been less significant, would oil and nuclear power be privileged industries compared with those dependent on other fuel sources? Would the United States have such a high rate of infant mortality compared with other advanced industrial democracies had welfare policy not been institutionally and rhetorically removed from questions of health? Although answers to such questions are inevitably elusive, the analyses developed throughout this book suggest ways in which the consequences of the system of corporate actors and the establishment of linkages among issues may be captured in a more concrete fashion.

3

Study Design and Data Collection

The introductory discussion of the actor-event interface and the historical sketches in the preceding chapter may well appear to belong in separate books. Yet the theoretical challenge addressed throughout this book requires that an attempt be made to integrate very general arguments concerning relations among systems of actors and events with an appreciation of the historically grounded and temporally ordered nature of the world in which and for which actions are taken. More specifically, this research addresses the character of the two distinctive worlds within which energy and health policy are formed. Despite the recognition of a cost-related "crisis," the health domain has been relatively stable in recent years, and the attention paid to health issues by the general media has declined since the passage of Medicare in the 1960s. By contrast, the energy domain was a highly controversial and visible policy arena during the 1970s as a result of the events following the OPEC cartel's rapid escalation of the price of crude oil. Efforts by three successive administrations to implement new energy policies, often with unintended and conflicting implications, created a level of activity and flux that was unparalleled in the more settled health domain. These contrasting conditions produced diverse patterns of domain structure and thus offer a unique opportunity to draw inferences about general and idiosyncratic processes in national policy domains.

Identifying Core Organizations

The key challenge against which the success or failure of this study will be measured involves the comprehensive identification of the consequential organizational actors, public and private, interested in the energy and health policy domains. In discussing the theoretical and empirical problems of specifying the boundaries of social systems and networks, Laumann et al. (1983) suggest that analysts have focused on one or more of the following components: actors, relations, or activities (events). The choice of a definitional focus fixes certain features of a network or system while allowing the remaining features to vary empirically. Thus, the choice of definitional focus must be made explicit in order to avoid circular procedures whose results depend entirely on the rule of inclusion used to define the population of domain actors. For instance, it is scarcely informative to learn that a social system constructed by a snowball sampling procedure is well connected or "integrated."

The most commonly used definitional tactic employs a selection rule based on some attribute or characteristic of actors. Two particularly well-worn methods for determining social system boundaries are the *positional* approach and the *reputational* approach. In the positional approach, the membership test refers to the presence or absence of some attribute, most commonly the occupancy of a position in a formally constituted group. The reputational approach, on the other hand, utilizes the judgments of knowledgeable informants to delimit the set of participant actors. These two approaches are sometimes combined (see Laumann and Pappi, 1976).

Identifying actors on the basis of individual characteristics leaves the nature of their interconnectedness, as well as the participation patterns of actors in events, empirically free to vary. It is, however, of little more than descriptive interest to learn about the distributions of actors on the positional characteristics used to delimit membership. For the case in hand, there simply is no generally recognized membership list to use in defining the relevant population of domain actors. Although one could imagine consulting a panel of experts who would nominate the actors to be included on the basis of their reputed influence in the policy domain, we dismissed this procedure as being far too dependent on the adequacy of our selection of expert panelists (for whom there is also no generally recognized comprehensive listing).

The second definitional focus selects actors on the basis of participation in a social relationship of a specified type. The relational approach to boundary definition includes the procedure known as snowball sampling (Erickson, 1978). In this procedure, one initially identifies a small set of individual actors; the networks or chains of contact in this set are then traced until some criterion of termination or network closure is satisfied. Although this was a possible strategy for our research, we concluded that there were too many un-

answered questions concerning the identification of the initial set of actors
and meaningful cutoff points to achieve analytic closure (an additional problem was the expense of pursuing farflung chains of contact across the national
scene). Furthermore, the relational approach to boundary definition has been
used infrequently, and there is only limited experience to guide its application. Moreover, use of a relational approach rules out certain questions about
the morphology of the network, since the method fixes or constrains these relational features.

The third strategy, which we adopted, defines a set of events or activities on
the basis of a criterion of substantive relevance. Participation in these events
identifies a relevant set of actors, and the social relationships among them define the system to be examined. The classic formulation of an inclusion rule
based on participation in some activities is Dahl's (1961) decisional method
for determining membership in a community elite. Of course, use of this or a
related approach means that both the composition of the social system (in
terms of the attributes of actors) and the relational patterns within it are empirically at issue. However, although this strategy uses participation in fixed
events as the basis of selection, participation in other related events is not constrained by the inclusion rule.

More specifically, we used multiple methods of tagging the actors' activities in the policy domain in order to identify the core set of actors through a
process of triangulation. First we specified, as concretely as possible (see
"Policy Domains" in Chapter 1), the substantive content associated with the
domain during the 1970s. We then devised systematic procedures for scanning
the participation of organizational actors in events and activities having relevance to that broadly inclusive substantive content. The five tactics described
below were most effective in tagging relatively visible participation in congressional and judicial matters of relevance to energy and health policy making.
Because of the large number of executive agencies and establishments and the
enormous number of executive actions,[1] we did not attempt a systematic
search of this branch of government. Happily, as we shall learn in Chapter 5,
there is a reasonably high correspondence between our counts of organizational participation in congressional and judicial actions and those relating to
executive branch activities. But it is worth remembering that our procedures
probably underestimated the extent of organizational participation in executive branch deliberations. Compensating for this bias, we should point out
that significant policy-making initiatives by the executive branch typically require the consent of the congressional or judicial branch (or both) whose activities we tracked fairly carefully. More routine executive actions are typi-

1. The *Federal Register,* for instance, devotes over 80,000 pages a year to reporting intentions
to act and actions of the executive branch. These activities are difficult to track systematically
without prohibitively expensive monitoring procedures.

cally elaborations of established policies or straightforward applications of policies to particular cases (which are, in any case, almost always subject to judicial, if not congressional, review).

We thus used multiple criteria of participation to identify the population of core organizational actors in each domain. Lists of all nonfederal organizations active during the Carter administration (1977–1980) were compiled from five sources: (1) a computer-generated set of abstracts from eight major newspapers and news magazines covering all regions of the country, selecting all items describing energy or health issues at the federal level;[2] (2) all energy- or health-related hearings before major congressional subcommittees, tallying all organizational appearances to testify or submit written testimony;[3] (3) a computer-generated search of *amicus curiae* participants in energy or health cases before the federal appellate courts;[4] (4) lobbyist registrations explicitly for health or energy legislation, as reported monthly by the *Congressional Quarterly Almanac;*[5] and (5) additional names suggested

2. The news sources were the *New York Times, Chicago Tribune, Washington Post, Los Angeles Times, Houston Chronicle, Atlanta Constitution, Seattle Times,* and *Time* magazine. The computer abstracts were generated by the New York Times's *Information Bank* by requesting the joint occurrences of "federal laws and legislation" and "energy" or "health" as key-word descriptors. Approximately 1,000 energy and 800 health abstracts were produced for the 1977–1980 period.

Each abstract was scanned to identify the key organizational participant(s) and their activities regarding a given policy matter, the subject of the abstracted news story. Disregarding multiple abstracts of a single story appearing in different newspapers, we gave each organization mentioned a score of *1* for its appearance in a news item. These were cumulated to measure the frequency of mentions of each organization in the news media (see Appendix A, column 12).

3. The annual compilations of the *Congressional Information Service* were consulted for the 95th and 96th Congress (in session during 1977–1978 and 1979–1980, respectively). These recorded more than 450 energy-related hearings by 11 subcommittees and more than 152 health-related hearings by six subcommittees. For each hearing summarized by the CIS, the organizational affiliations of all witnesses were tallied on index cards. If an organization sent more than one witness to a given hearing, their collective presences were counted as a single appearance. If a witness affiliated with one organization (e.g., the president of a corporation) was designated as testifying on behalf of another organization (e.g., a trade association), only the latter organization was credited with an appearance at that hearing. Two types of witnesses were ignored in this compilation: (1) federal agencies, which were identified by other means (see below); and (2) numerous local organizations represented at hearings held in the local community.

4. The search was conducted using "energy" and "health" as key words. Of the cases identified in this manner, 167 and 115 were found to be related to substantive or procedural issues in energy and health policy respectively.

5. Lobby registration requirements were tightened somewhat by the 95th Congress (1977–1978) but still remained ambiguous. Although lobbyists are expected to register if their activities are directed at Congress, no executive branch lobby registration is required (see Ornstein and Elder, 1978: 95–115). The *Congressional Quarterly* compilation of congressional registrations is the most complete source available outside Congress itself, but the frequency of registrations is highly unequal, with some organizations appearing almost quarterly and others only once during a two-year Congress. Consequently, we decided to count an organization as registered to lobby

by two panels of domain experts, mainly from journalism and academia.[6]

These five procedures resulted in more than 1,300 organization names in the energy domain and nearly 900 in the health domain, too many to handle effectively in an empirical analysis and undoubtedly including many actors without effective impact on the course of national policy. To reduce the lists to manageable proportions, we imposed the requirement that core actors must appear five or more times across the combination of sources (regarding repeated lobbyist registrations as only one appearance). Finally, we added to the list all major federal agencies, departments, and congressional subcommittees specifically charged with health or energy regulatory, investigative, or legislative authority.

Although the initial lists actually contained 373 organization names (217 in energy, 156 in health), subsequent information indicated that 12 had either been mistakenly included, were wholly owned subsidiaries of other organizations, or did not exist during the period under study. (Seven of the 12 were in the energy domain, and five in the health domain.) Of the 361 legitimate targets, interviews were conducted with 333, for an overall response rate of 92.3 percent (94.3 percent in energy and 89.4 percent in health).[7] Evidence of the comprehensiveness of the initial lists of organizations was provided by the in-

before Congress if it appeared at least once during the four-year interval 1977–1980 and to ignore multiple re-registrations.

6. These experts were identified in part by their prominence in the domain literature and in part by a "snowball" process in which each expert was asked to suggest additional names. In the energy domain, the following persons served as the panel: Russell Boulding, Lynton K. Caldwell, Luther Carter, Joel Darmstadter, Paul Freisma, Martin Greenberger, William Hogan, Milton Holloway, Dorothy Nelkin, and Alvin Weinberg. In the health domain, the panelists were: Odin Anderson, David Drake, Ronald Andersen, Richard Foster, Jeffrey Goldsmith, and Dr. Alvin Tarlov. We are especially grateful for the panelists' willingness to provide this valuable service to the project without remuneration.

In both cases the panelists were mailed preliminary lists containing the names of organizations most frequently appearing in the four sources described above (about 200 energy and 160 health organizations). The panelists were asked to write the names of additional organizations that they felt belonged on the list of "most important" energy or health organizations, with special attention to commissons and task forces not likely to be highly visible to the mass media. (The panelists also vetted a similar initial list of domain issues, described in Chapter 4.) The additional names suggested by the panels were added to the pool accumulated from the other sources.

7. In the energy domain, 12 organizations either refused to be interviewed or deferred their decision until after the field period. The oil industry accounted for the majority of the refusals: Ashland Oil, Exxon, Marathon Oil, Mobil Oil, the Energy Consumers and Producers Association, and the Independent Refiners Association of California. The other six energy refusals came from the New England Electric System, the Potomac Electric Power Company, Burns and Roe Engineering Company, the New Jersey Energy Department, the New York State Public Service Commission, and the Republican Staff of a Senate subcommittee. Another five organizations provided only partial responses: Western Oil and Gas Association, Texas Utilities Company, American Motors, Environmental Defense Fund, and Friends of the Earth.

In the health domain, refusals or deferred decisions were obtained from 16 organizations:

Table 3.1. Distribution of Organization Types by Domain

Organization type	Energy Domain		Health Domain	
	Percent	Number	Percent	Number
Congressional Committees and Subcommittees	10.1	20	5.9	8
Federal Agencies	10.6	21	8.9	12
Associations of State and Local Governments	4.6	9	6.7	9
Research Units	2.0	4	8.2	11
Labor Unions	2.5	5	3.0	4
Trade Associations	24.2	48	8.2	11
Professional Societies	1.0	2	26.0	35
Corporations	33.3	66	4.4	6
Public Interest Groups	11.6	23	28.9	39
TOTAL	99.9	198	100.2	135

formants, who were asked to nominate additional organizations not on the list as "influential and consequential" in the domain. No additional organizations in either domain were mentioned by more than four informants, suggesting that our procedures had satisfactorily identified the core sets. The complete lists of organizations in the energy and the health domains are found in Appendix C, list B. The reader should refer to Appendix A at this time in order to get some idea of the wide range of organizations included in the study and learn something about their salient features: this will be useful in explaining their roles in national policy making. Since the Appendix contains individual-level information, we have been careful to report only information gleaned from publicly available sources or from aggregated information provided by the sample respondents as a whole.

The first column of table 3.1 shows the distribution of the completed en-

American Academy of Orthopedic Surgeons, Cooley's Anemia Foundation, Juvenile Diabetes Foundation, Public Citizen's Health Research Group, ARA Services, Kaiser Foundation Health Plan, Merck, Calorie Control Council, National Eye Institute, National Institute of Environmental Health Sciences, National Institute of Neurological Communicative Disorders and Stroke, the Veterans Administration, and four subcommittee staffs (two Democratic and two Republican). A partial interview was completed with the Veterans of Foreign Wars.

ergy domain interviews across nine broad categories:[8] congressional committees and subcommittees,[9] federal executive branch agencies and independent
establishments (such as EPA), associations of state and local governments,
research units, labor unions, trade associations, professional societies, corporations, and public or consumer interest groups. The third column shows the
distribution of organizations in the health domain.[10]

Interviewing Organizational Informants

A field office was set up in Washington, D.C., during the summer of 1981,
and a staff of interviewers was hired to conduct personal interviews with infor-

8. In both domains, function is an inappropriate basis for categorization, since most organizations engage in numerous activities including research, regulation, advocacy, and referral services. Therefore, we have relied upon a number of analytic distinctions, using each organization's
legal status and type of membership as an aid to our classification. On rather straightforward
constitutional grounds, three types of public organization have been identified: congressional
committees, federal agencies within the executive branch, and associations of state and local officials or agencies. Our fourth category, which includes organizations primarily concerned with
research, spans the public and private sectors—a blurring of formal distinctions that reflects the
reliance of public, for-profit, and private nonprofit organizations on both federal grants and contract work.

In the private sector, organizations have been characterized as primarily producers or consumers. An organization's legal status—notably its incorporation under a particular section of 501(c)
(Internal Revenue Code)—was taken as one factor in determining its classification. Five types of
organization were identified: labor unions involved in production of energy or health care; trade
associations; individual corporations; professional societies and educational associations; and
public or consumer interest groups, including labor unions insofar as they acted as consumers of
health or energy. In the health domain, the final category has been subdivided into organizations
concerned with the provision of research or services and those whose primary activity is political
advocacy.

9. Congressional responsibility for energy matters was spread across some 80 subcommittees
during the decade. However, the bulk of the hearings were conducted by 11 subcommittees of
nine standing committees (five in the House, four in the Senate). We separately interviewed and
recorded the responses of the Democratic and Republican staff informants—hence the 21 actors
in this category (one subcommittee's Republican staff did not function during the period). Full
committees did not take as active a role in the processing of legislation in either domain; hence,
no interviews were conducted with informants from these parent organizations. Thus, the number
of organizations to be interviewed totaled 210, and this figure is used below as the base in calculating the completion rate for the energy domain interviews. However, in some of the analyses
discussed in later chapters, informants were presented with lists of target organizations that
included both the Democratic and Republican staff members of the nine full committees (for
example, when informants were asked to select the most "influential and consequential" organizations in the domain; see Chapter 5). In these cases the total number of targeted organizations
is 228.

10. As in the energy domain, the total number of health organizations for which interviews
were to be obtained was 152, excluding the six congressional full committees. Other lists included 12 full committees (both Democratic and Republican staffs), bringing the total number of
targeted organizations to 164.

mants from each organization on the lists. Although many organizations, particularly corporations, are not headquartered in Washington, most had government liaison offices located in the District.[11] In general, the relevant informant was either an executive director, a vice president for government affairs, or a staff specialist in energy or health matters. For federal organizations, appropriate staff members during the Carter administration were located at their current places of employment and interviewed.

Organization Characteristics

Table 3.2 compares the general types of domain organization on some basic characteristics. In the energy domain, professional societies, corporations, and labor unions are the oldest, with median ages of 60 years or more by 1980. Trade associations averaged about 40 years, and the remaining organizations, including government agencies and subcommittees, were younger (public interest groups averaged less than two decades). The median tenure in office of chief executive officers (CEOs) in 1980, about five years, was lowest for public interest groups and highest for the research units. Comparisons of organization size can be misleading because organizations differ in how they define a participant (employee or member). Voluntary organizations in the energy domain whose members are natural persons, for example, have more than seven times as many dues-paying members as the corporations have paid employees; but, of course, employees work full-time for their company, whereas most members only pay annual dues. The trade associations' memberships are mostly corporate entities; hence, their median value of 2,206 conceals the fact that much larger numbers of individuals are indirectly linked to these groups.

If organization size is equated with staff, the numbers diverge less dramatically across types of organizations. The typical energy corporation allocates 25 staff members to keep track of national policy in all domains. The federal agencies also have large staffs (26 persons), but congressional subcommittees typically employ fewer than five professionals. The trade association staffs are more than twice as large, although many of these persons may be assigned to nonenergy domain tasks. Other organizations have staffs twice as large as the trade associations. However, if total annual budgets are compared, the typical energy corporation ($6.4 billion) and the typical federal agency ($4.3 billion) dwarf the others (labor unions at $55 million, trade associations at $13.2 million, and public interest groups at a bare-bones $2.6 million). Of course, the budgetary lines actually allotted to energy policy activities are likely to be only a tiny fraction of a Fortune 500 corporation's overall operating budget,

11. The 10 percent of target organizations located in other areas were interviewed either at their home office (mostly in the New York–New Jersey area), or by telephone and mail.

Table 3.2. Characteristics of Organizations in the Two Domains

Organization Type	N	Average Date of Founding	Median # Employees or Members	Average Monitoring Capacity[a]	Median CEO Tenure	Average Budget (in 000's)
A. ENERGY DOMAIN[b]						
Congressional Committees and Subcommittees	20	1921	--	4.7	--	--
Federal Agencies	21	1946	--	26.1	--	4,348,000 (N=19)
Associations of State and Local Governments	9	1946	--	9.4	11 (N=6)	2,850 (N=6)
Research Units	4	1934	--	13.5	13 (N=2)	975,800 (N=2)
Labor Unions	5	1921	470,000 (N=4)	8.7	--	55,420 (N=5)
Trade Associations	48	1940	2,206 (N=11)	11.2	7 (N=29)	13,150 (N=48)
Professional Societies	2	1886	33,500	4.4	6	7,400 (N=2)
Corporations	66	1916	56,997 (N=55)	24.6	5 (N=63)	6,385,000 (N=66)
Public Interest Groups	23	1961	463,938 (N=12)	10.2	4 (N=17)	2,640 (N=23)

B. HEALTH DOMAIN[c]

Congressional Committees and Subcommittees	8	1973	--	2.5	--	--
Federal Agencies	12	1967	--	14.0	--	--
Associations of State and Local Governments	9	1970	--	6.7	--	725 (N=8)
Research Units	12	1950	--	5.0	--	45,000 (N=1)
Labor Unions	4	1926	--	7.7	--	16,500 (N=3)
Trade Associations	11	1964	--	9.2	--	2,134 (N=11)
Professional Societies	35	1931	--	4.5	--	2,500 (N=31)
Corporations	6	1913	32,000 (N=5)	17.1	5 (N=5)	31,050 (N=3)
Public Interest Groups	38	1952	--	4.8	--	2,000 (N=34)

[a] Monitoring capacity is a composite measure of an organization's ability to collect various types of information relevant for participation in a policy arena. The measure is the sum of (1) the number of full-time equivalents (FTEs) in Washington monitoring the energy (or health) domain; (2) one-third of the difference between the FTEs monitoring any domain and the number monitoring the energy (or health) domain (differences greater than 30 FTEs were not recognized); (3) the number of FTEs gathering technical data, up to a maximum of 50; (4) one-third the number of in-house counsel up to a maximum of ten persons, i.e., a maximum value of 3.3; (5) the presence or absence of mechanisms for mobilizing grass roots lobbying (1 or 0); (6) the presence or absence of public relations personnel (1 or 0); and (7) the presence or absence of an associated political action committee (1/2 or 0). (See Chapter 6 for an extended discussion of this concept.)

[b] N = 198

[c] N = 135

Table 3.3. Organization Participation in Multiple Policy Domains, by Domain

	Congress. Comms.	Federal Agency	Assoc. of Govts.	Research	Unions	Trade Assocs.	Prof. Assocs.	Corpora- tions	Public Interest Groups	Total
A. ENERGY DOMAIN										
Agriculture	15.0	30.0	44.4	75.0	20.0	16.7	0.0	10.8	23.8	19.1
Civil Rights	0.0	0.0	44.4	0.0	60.0	4.2	0.0	6.2	0.0	6.7
Consumer Rights	15.0	15.0	22.2	0.0	80.0	18.8	0.0	21.5	38.1	22.2
Defense	5.0	5.0	11.1	50.0	20.0	8.3	0.0	20.0	14.3	13.4
Domestic Economic Policy	30.0	35.0	66.7	0.0	80.0	62.5	50.0	67.7	28.6	53.6
Education	5.0	10.0	55.6	25.0	40.0	4.2	100.0	1.5	14.3	9.8
Energy	100.0	90.0	100.0	100.0	100.0	97.9	100.0	100.0	100.0	98.5
Environmental Policy	70.0	70.0	100.0	100.0	80.0	83.3	100.0	83.1	81.0	81.4
Foreign Policy	15.0	30.0	22.2	0.0	20.0	20.0	0.0	27.7	14.3	22.2
Health	25.0	30.0	44.4	50.0	80.0	22.9	0.0	16.9	23.9	24.7
Housing	5.0	15.0	66.7	0.0	60.0	12.5	50.0	4.6	9.5	12.9
International Trade	20.0	50.0	22.2	0.0	60.0	41.7	0.0	40.0	14.3	35.1
Labor Policy	5.0	5.0	55.6	0.0	100.0	20.8	50.0	36.9	4.8	24.7
Law Enforcement	0.0	5.0	66.7	26.0	20.0	10.4	50.0	1.5	19.0	10.3
Social Welfare and Social Security	15.0	10.0	77.8	0.0	100.0	10.4	0.0	13.8	14.3	17.5
Transportation	35.0	50.0	88.9	50.0	40.0	54.2	50.0	60.0	38.1	53.1
Urban Development	10.0	10.0	66.7	25.0	20.0	12.5	50.0	16.9	14.3	17.0
Mean No. of Domains	3.8	4.8	10.1	5.5	10.2	5.2	6.5	5.5	4.7	5.4
Percent Total Effort in Energy	75.5	32.8	37.3	30.3	37.3	54.0	30.0	60.9	50.8	53.3
Number	20	20	9	4	5	48	2	65	21	194

B. HEALTH DOMAIN

Agriculture	12.5	33.3	22.2	8.3	25.0	0.0	8.6	50.0	13.2	14.8
Civil Rights	25.0	25.0	33.3	25.0	100.0	18.2	22.9	0.0	50.0	32.6
Consumer Rights	12.5	75.0	22.2	8.3	50.0	36.4	25.7	16.7	63.2	39.3
Defense	12.5	8.3	11.1	8.3	25.0	0.0	8.6	0.0	5.2	7.4
Domestic Economic Policy	25.0	33.3	33.3	0.0	50.0	45.5	17.1	100.0	34.2	30.4
Education	25.0	25.0	33.3	41.7	75.0	27.3	77.1	16.7	52.6	49.6
Energy	50.0	33.3	44.4	8.3	50.0	9.1	11.4	33.3	26.3	23.7
Environmental Policy	37.5	25.0	66.7	25.0	25.0	27.3	25.7	50.0	23.7	29.6
Foreign Policy	12.5	25.0	0.0	8.3	25.0	0.0	2.9	16.7	7.9	8.1
Health	100.0	91.7	100.0	100.0	100.0	100.0	100.0	100.0	100.0	99.3
Housing	25.0	25.0	44.4	8.3	25.0	9.1	5.7	0.0	42.1	22.2
International Trade	37.5	16.7	11.1	0.0	25.0	36.4	0.0	50.0	7.9	12.6
Labor Policy	25.0	8.3	22.2	8.3	100.0	27.3	17.1	16.7	34.2	24.4
Law Enforcement	12.5	41.7	44.4	0.0	25.0	9.1	5.7	0.0	15.8	14.8
Social Welfare and Social Security	87.5	58.3	66.7	8.3	100.0	72.7	48.6	50.0	63.2	57.0
Transportation	12.5	16.7	44.4	0.0	0.0	9.1	14.3	16.7	28.9	18.5
Urban Development	12.5	25.0	44.4	0.0	25.0	18.2	2.9	16.7	7.9	11.9
Mean No. of Domains	5.3	5.7	6.4	2.6	8.3	4.5	3.9	5.3	5.8	5.0
Percent Total Effort in Health	61.1	58.9	54.2	69.8	34.4	72.6	69.6	71.3	55.9	62.6
Number	8	12	9	12	4	11	6		38	135

but a higher proportion of a lobbying association's funds. Unfortunately, details of the actual expenditures on energy or health policy activities were simply not available.

Domain Activity

Finally, let us compare organizations according to the extent of their involvement in domain activity. Each informant was presented with a list of 17 national policy domains and asked to indicate the ones in which his or her organization "is particularly active" (table 3.3). [12] Not surprisingly, virtually all energy organizations indicated activity in the energy domain, and all health organizations reported activity in health. But few actors are exclusively focused on a single domain. For energy actors, the mean number of domains was 5.4, with environment, domestic economic policy, transportation, and international trade the most frequent additions. The congressional subcommittees were the most restricted, focusing their attention on the energy and environment domains. Among corporations, trade associations, and federal agencies, a majority were active in three additional domains. For organizations active in health policy, the mean number of policy domains was 5.0. Research units displayed the narrowest range of activity, restricting their attention to health and, to a lesser degree, education policy. Unions, by comparison, were active in an average of more than eight additional domains, and the entire group was concerned with civil rights, labor policy, and social welfare issues in addition to health policy.

The informants were asked, "Taking into account (your organization's) efforts to affect national policy in all the areas that you mentioned above, what percentage of this total effort is directed toward national policy on energy/health matters?" [13] As table 3.3 shows, more than half the energy domain organizations' efforts were directed toward national policy activities in that domain, whereas health organizations devoted an average of 62.6 percent of their efforts to issues in that area. Some variation across organization type occurs in the energy domain: congressional subcommittees devoted more than twice the percentage of effort of the federal agencies to energy policy matters, while corporations tend to be more exclusively involved in energy policy than either the trade associations or the other organizations. With the exception of unions, which devoted only one-third of their efforts to health issues, all organization types in the health domain concentrated more than half of their activity in that area. (We shall return to the question of organizational participation in multiple policy domains and its implications for a model of policy making in the organizational state in Chapter 14.)

12. See Appendix B, question A3.
13. See Appendix B, question A4.

In short, these data nicely document the fact that organizations active in each policy domain are, in general, not exclusively engaged in debates about a limited or especially predictable range of policy matters. Many, like corporations and unions, exist to do something else, such as run a business or represent workers in a particular company or industry. Only occasionally do their regular tasks require them to intervene in policy deliberations. Moreover, the principal activities for which they are responsible as corporate actors may involve them in a wide-ranging set of policy concerns, no one of which has much claim on their attention. Even specialized organizations with apparent mandates to participate in national policy formulation are, as we shall learn in Chapter 4, highly selective in their policy efforts. How a corporate actor learns that relevant policy-formulating activities are taking place and the time and circumstances in which it can participate are critical questions to which we will return time and again. Explaining actor participation in specific policy controversies will require us to formulate means for assessing its policy interests, its monitoring capacities, and the resources with which it attempts to affect the policy process in the ways it wants.

Identifying Events

The identification of organizational interests is a prominent element in many works on politics and policy outcomes, but it is only one component of the analysis developed in this study of national policy formation. As was discussed in the introductory chapter, a major concern motivating this research has been the desire to conceptualize events in such a way that they may be subjected to analyses as rigorous as those that social scientists have developed for the study of individual and organizational behavior. Given the long history of the latter endeavor and the relative lack of concern for the former, this effort is, by necessity, exploratory in nature.

In the context of this study, events are defined as temporally located decision points in a collective decision-making process. Every event is understood to involve an authoritative actor who renders a decision at a particular point in time. Thus, events differ significantly from issues, which are more general topics of concern for actors in a domain (see "Identifying Domain Issues" in Chapter 4). Of course, interest in an issue may motivate participation in numerous events, just as participation in the policy process may change the perceptions of an organization's "interests" that inform the actions of its members and representatives. Nevertheless, it is important to maintain the distinction between interest in issues—a characteristic attributed to organizational actors—and the historically specific decision points that constitute events for the purposes of this analysis.

As will be discussed at length in Chapter 9, the existing literature in the social sciences does not provide an established method of identifying and sampling from a population of events defined in this manner. Therefore, in constructing this set of events, we necessarily relied on a purposive strategy of *nonrandom* sampling. Starting from a conception of energy and health policy as sets of decisions concerning the organization of specialized input-through-put-output systems, we selected events from four broad, and roughly parallel, categories in each domain: research, industrial development, regulation, and conservation or consumption in energy; and, in health, biomedical research, the training of personnel, the organization of health care delivery systems, and consumer protection, particularly with respect to the regulation of phar-maceuticals. For the identification of specific events, we drew on the annual reports published in the *Congressional Quarterly* as well as accounts in more specialized news media (see "Identifying Empirical Events" in Chapter 9).

Although it would have been possible to identify events associated with all of the energy and health issues listed in tables 4.1 and 4.2 below, organiza-tional participation was studied only with respect to a subset of these con-cerns. This limitation was necessary so that we could explore the patterns of activity in multiple events related to a single issue or, to use a concept that will organize much of the analysis, over the course of event scenarios. Chapter 9 provides an extended discussion of the formal features that were used to charac-terize individual events and the principles by which events were concatenated into scenarios. A selective overview of the scenarios and their component events is provided in Chapter 11 as well. We shall return to these questions in the final section of the book. The next chapter, however, begins our empirical inquiry with an exploration of the structure of organizational interest in the two domains.

4

The Structure of Issue Linkages and the Scope of Interests

Now that the population of interested actors in each policy domain has been identified, we can turn to the problem of conceptualizing and measuring each actor's scope of interest in its policy domain, which, in an important sense, defines one aspect of that actor's purposive orientation to its environment. What distinguishes our approach from most policy research is that, whereas most investigators have tended to select a particular issue or set of issues for exclusive study, we focus on the embeddedness or relatedness of an issue in the larger constellation of issues confronting a policy domain. Our basic contention will be, first, that issues are linked to one another in the policy domain in systematically different ways with important consequences for the politics of their resolution and, second, that the linkages among issues depend on how those organizations which form an issue's constituency come to link this issue to other issues of interest to them.

At first glance, the fundamental theoretical problem of this chapter appears a simple one: namely, to identify the underlying logic(s) generating the linkages among issues in a broadly defined policy domain. To answer it correctly requires answering other critical questions that have all too often been ignored or, at the very least, not simultaneously addressed in the literature. First, we must ask what features of given issues serve to entail or deny implications for other issues? Then we must learn how such features combine to organize the overall patterning of issue proximities in the policy space. Finally, we must demonstrate what implications, if any, a given organization of issue proximities has for the form and substance of the policy produced in the domain.

At least three general features of issues can be identified that link issues to one another. First, every issue obviously possesses an inherent *substantive* or *conceptual content* that may naturally link it to certain other issues on grounds of a readily acknowledged situational logic. One such linking notion is logical inclusion: for example, the regulation of experimentation on human subjects is logically entailed in the more inclusive issue of the organization of biomedical research, should it arise as an issue at all.[1] Second, every issue eventually comes to occupy an *institutional locus of relevant decision-makers* (with its attendant audience) in which it is typically debated and resolved. Thus, funding issues activate specific congressional appropriation subcommittees whose jurisdictions are defined substantively with respect to particular governmental actors over whose budgets the committees have oversight. Or, the organization of biomedical research is the mandated responsibility of a complex of specific executive agencies—in our illustrative case principally (but not exclusively) NIH. Different issues having a common institutional locus are very likely to be regarded as having implications for one another in the eyes of the decision-makers and other interested parties because of their intertwined propinquity in the decision-making process. And, third, the specific resolution of a particular issue generates a potential or actual flow of harms and/or benefits to an *identifiable set of politically active or inactive individuals and corporate actors,* who are likely to be or become concerned about this flow. To be sure, these actors also possess, in addition, definite, but not necessarily similar, sets of other concerns in which they have coincident or conflicting interests. In this case linkage between two issues arises because the recipients of the harms or benefits perceive that the ways in which both issues are resolved will have similar or contradictory beneficial or disadvantageous effects on them. It is precisely the nature of this socially organized concatenation of diverse other interests around the focal issue of concern among the interested parties that provides the critical driving mechanism linking issues into diversely organized complexes of issues in the policy domain. In other words, issue linkage arises from the ways in which the "natural" constituencies of the several issues are intersected.

The first important point to glean from this discussion is that each of the three features of issues provides an independent, sometimes conflicting basis for linking issues to one another. The second key point is that issues are thus

1. Although two issues may be connected by some conceptual logic, this does not necessarily mean that all actors concerned with one issue will be concerned with the other. We should expect asymmetries in the concerns generated. That is, actors concerned with the conceptually subordinated issue will tend to be interested in the more inclusive one, but the converse is not true.

nearly always embedded in large constellations of issues, the exact nature of which will have significant consequences for the politics of their resolution.

Now it is precisely this emphasis on the embeddedness of single issues in larger issue complexes that distinguishes our approach from most policy research, which has tended to select a particular issue—say, national health insurance or hospital cost containment—for exclusive attention. However detailed the account provided of the unfolding of the policy issue over time, with detailed scenarios of critical decision points and elaborate characterizations of the interested parties, such studies tend to treat the intrusion of "unrelated issues" that have an impact on a given outcome of relevance to the focal issue as little more than fortunate or unfortunate historical accidents. We shall endeavor to demonstrate that more systematic consideration of the organization of the larger policy space in which the focal issue of interest is found should indicate the probable course of its resolution. In sum, then, our argument is that a set of issues possesses differing levels of commonality with respect to each other that are based on conceptual, institutional, and/or sociopolitical similarities and differences. To understand the unfolding issue development of a policy domain, one must be able to characterize the structure of commonality among such a set of issues.

Although sustained attention to the general problem of issue linkage has been rather limited in the literature, the dominant approaches informing policy analysis have all had something to say about the matter, either implicitly or explicitly. Those starting from the premise of an idealized rational actor as policy-maker, for example, would ask how such a rational actor, endowed with complete knowledge of all the objectives to be achieved, the alternative means to these objectives, and the associated costs and benefits of the various means, would construct an optimal policy mix in a given policy domain that maximizes some stipulated standard of the public welfare (cf. Allison, 1971; Moe, 1980). No one, of course, believes that such an actor exists or could exist, because the requirements for information, the stipulated standards of evaluation, and the decision calculus itself are simply too demanding (cf. March and Simon, 1958). The policy produced by such a hypothetical actor, therefore, is intended merely to provide an "idealized" benchmark possessing internal consistency and certain other formal features (e.g., Pareto optimality) against which the empirical situation actually observed can be evaluated. To illustrate this approach with reference to national policy, then, the differential linkages among issues presumably would follow the logic of a rationally designed input-throughput-output system for delivering health care to the nation's population. Functional problems associated with the production of new medical knowledge and its attendant technology, the training of qualified medical and paramedical personnel necessary to staff the organizations of health-care providers, the organization and distribution of health-care providers into appropriate task-performing organizations like hospitals, clinics, HMOs, and solo practices, access to and utilization of these organizations by the population at large, and related matters would all be systematically linked according to the "rational" design of the overall system. In other words, issues would be appropriately linked in greater or lesser proximity strictly as a function of the way the overall system was designed to interrelate these myriad specialized tasks, under stipulated resource and demand constraints. Given its emphasis on normative conceptualization and abstract system rationalization without much concern for concrete institutional realities, this approach is especially congenial with our first basis of issue linkage noted above.

Other, more empirically sensitive analysts adopting the currently fashionable "political economy" approach (see, e.g., Marmor and Christianson, 1982) or its closely related "interest politics" approach (see, e.g., Salisbury, 1970, 1984) would focus attention on the political market for given government policies. In their concern for identifying the set of interested private and public actors who are prepared to demand or supply policy options on the basis of these options' actual or potential impact on actors' own self-defined interests, these analysts direct attention to the coalitional implications of congruent and oppositional interests among the concerned parties. Interestingly enough, they retain the normative rationalists' concern for developing an idealized benchmark against which to evaluate the "distortions in policy making" induced by the superior efficacy that allows the special interests to get their way more often than those who would champion the "public interest" as generally conceived.[2] Rather clearly, their concerns narrowly mirror the institutional and constituency bases of issue linkage noted above.

Identifying Domain Issues

For both domains, initial lists of issues with policy import during the 1970s were compiled from various popular press and academic sources and subsequently consolidated by absorbing minor or narrowly focused topics into broader categories. These preliminary issue lists were sent along with preliminary lists of organizations to the two panels of about a dozen academic and journalistic specialists mentioned in Chapter 3 (n. 6). The panel members were asked to nominate additional issues that had been overlooked. The final sets of 65 energy issues and 56 health issues took their suggestions into account.

The sets of issues were grouped on each questionnaire into four general categories intended to correspond to a rough input-throughput-output se-

2. Marmor and Christianson (1982, esp. pp. 61–216) nicely exemplify such concerns in their discussion of several recent issues in health care policy.

quence (research issues, development issues, regulatory issues, consumption issues). Early in the informant interviews, the interviewer presented a booklet displaying the list of domain issues, along with the instruction to place a checkmark in front of each issue in which the informant's organization had an interest, and then indicate the level of interest on a five-point scale ranging from "minor" to "moderate" to "major interest." (See Appendix B, questions B1–B2.) In coding responses, unchecked issues were coded zero, creating a six-point scale of organizational interest.

Tables 4.1 and 4.2 display the full sets of domain issues presented to informants, clustered according to procedures to be described below. These clusters are presented in the descending order of mean organizational interest (using the 0–5 scale); percentages of organizations expressing moderate to major interest in each issue are also given. The 65 energy issues aggregated into 14 broader but still relatively homogeneous sets, each containing from one to nine issues. The 56 health issues similarly agglomerated into 16 clusters. In the energy domain, the decade-long struggle to decontrol oil and natural gas prices and to define the government's role in energy policy attracted substantially higher concern than any other policy problem. In the health domain, medical funding, health care costs, and disease prevention and control headed the list of issues of greatest organizational concern. Note that no set of issues in either domain attracted more than "moderate" average concern from the entire set of organizations, and the bulk of issues were rated only slightly higher than "minor interest." These aggregate distributions suggest that no issues, even those that were broadly worded, managed to attract widespread attention across the full range of domain participants. Rather, as we shall see below, intense interest tended to be concentrated within small, specialized subsets of organizations.

Measuring Issue Linkage

Now imagine a matrix in which the respondent organizations are listed in the rows and the columns refer to the set of issues confronting the domain. The entries in row i are the 0–5 scores of organization i for each of the issues in which it could express a level of interest. From the vantage point of the linkage among issues, we can determine the extent to which the levels of interest in issue k vary across the set of consequential organizations. The greater the commonality of concern two issues elicit across the set of organizations, whatever its basis in underlying substantive, institutional, or sociopolitical similarities, the higher the correlation to be observed. A negative correlation between two issues, on the other hand, suggests that intense levels of interest in issue j are associated with an absence of interest in issue k, and vice versa.

Table 4.1. Issue Clusters in the Energy Domain

Cluster	Issues	Mean	Percent
1.	OIL AND GAS DEREGULATION ISSUES	3.14	67.5
	Deregulation of domestic oil prices	3.17	68.6
	Deregulation of natural gas prices	3.11	66.5
2.	GOVERNMENTAL ROLE IN ENERGY ISSUES	3.03	67.2
	Creation of the Energy Department	3.14	70.6
	Reorganization of Congressional energy committee structure	2.48	56.2
	Reorganization of federal energy bureaucracies	3.01	68.0
	Role of federal government in formulating comprehensive national energy policies	4.09	87.1
	State and federal control over energy	3.50	76.3
	Public participation in energy policy making	2.91	67.0
	U.S. participation in international cooperative energy arrangements	2.06	45.4
3.	ENERGY INDUSTRY ISSUES	2.53	51.1
	Capital formation in energy industries	2.96	60.3
	Vertical and horizontal divestiture in energy industries	2.09	41.8
4.	COAL ISSUES	2.30	49.0
	Western coal lands leasing	2.05	42.3
	Strip mining of coal	1.95	42.3
	Expansion of U.S. coal production	2.50	54.1
	Coal slurry pipelines	2.09	43.8
	Export of coal and oil from the U.S.	1.90	40.7
	Deregulation of railroad freight rates	1.94	39.7
	Air and water pollution standards	3.29	70.1
	Conversion of power plants from oil and gas to coal	3.13	67.0
	Impact of energy development on local communities ("boom towns")	1.89	41.2
5.	ENERGY CONSUMERS ISSUES	2.25	49.0
	Efficiency standards for buildings, motors, and appliances	2.28	49.5
	Building temperature standards	1.52	32.5
	Conservation of energy consumption	3.61	79.4
	Energy price impact on low-income consumers	2.42	53.6
	Mass transit	1.40	29.9
6.	BIG OIL AND GASOLINE ISSUES	2.24	47.0
	Security of foreign oil supplies	2.43	51.0
	Strategic petroleum reserve	2.12	44.8
	Allocations of petroleum products to states and regions	2.42	51.0
	Allocations to the petroleum industry	2.02	39.7
	Allocation priorities for home heating oil, gasoline, natural gas, and other fuels to consumers	2.46	52.6
	Standby gasoline rationing authority	2.14	45.9
	Gasoline tax and oil import fees	2.11	44.3

Cluster	Issues	Mean	Percent
7.	ELECTRIC UTILITIES ISSUES	2.10	45.2
	Integration of decentralized electricity generation with utility grids	1.95	42.3
	Electric utility rate structure changes	2.46	52.6
	Utility construction work in progress costs	1.88	40.7
8.	ENERGY EXTRACTION AND TRANSPORT ISSUES	2.08	44.5
	Synthetic fuels industry development	3.16	71.6
	Energy Mobilization Board	2.69	59.8
	Alaska lands bill	1.71	33.5
	Transcontinental oil pipeline construction	1.58	32.0
	Alaska-Canada natural gas pipeline construction	1.81	39.2
	Outer Continental Shelf oil and gas exploration	1.96	41.2
	Deepwater tanker ports and LNG facilities	1.64	34.0
9.	RENEWABLE FUELS ISSUES	1.96	42.2
	Research and development of renewable fuels (geothermal, wind power, ocean thermal current, biomass, etc.)	2.57	56.7
	Solar energy commercialization	2.27	51.0
	Municipal garbage-to-fuel	1.55	32.0
	Small-scale hydroelectric generation	1.43	28.9
10.	NUCLEAR POWER ISSUES	1.76	36.9
	Nuclear breeder reactor research and development	1.77	35.6
	Nuclear waste disposal technology	2.24	46.4
	Transportation of nuclear wastes	1.77	38.1
	Nuclear power plant licensing procedures	2.15	46.4
	Nuclear power plant safety	2.03	42.8
	Nuclear power plant insurance	1.46	29.9
	Security of nuclear power plants	1.60	35.1
	Reorganization of the Nuclear Regulatory Agency	1.56	32.0
	Nuclear fusion research and development	1.27	25.8
11.	MANPOWER ISSUE	1.40	31.4
	Energy manpower education and training	1.40	31.4
12.	URANIUM ISSUES	1.37	27.8
	Uranium mill waste disposal	1.45	29.9
	Uranium commercialization	1.28	25.8
13.	AUTOMOBILE ISSUES	1.26	25.0
	Automobile engine design	0.99	19.1
	Automobile fuel efficiency standards	1.46	29.9
	Gasohol industry development	1.81	37.6
	Solar satellite research	0.76	13.4
14.	SMALL OIL AND GASOLINE ISSUES	1.20	21.5
	Independent refinery construction	1.19	19.1
	Service station franchises	0.92	16.5
	Oil company price overcharges to consumers	1.50	28.9

Table 4.2. Issue Clusters in the Health Domain

Cluster	Issues	Mean	Percent
1.	MEDICAL FUNDING ISSUES	3.15	67.2
	Medicare/Medicaid reimbursements for health personnel	2.89	62.4
	Medicare/Medicaid funding	3.29	69.2
	National health insurance	3.28	69.9
2.	HEALTH COSTS ISSUES	2.56	54.9
	Certificates of need	2.14	44.4
	Health maintenance organizations (HMOs)	2.49	55.6
	Health planning	3.12	67.7
	Hospital cost containment	2.79	57.9
	Professional standards review organizations, PSROs	2.26	48.9
3.	PREVENTION AND CONTROL ISSUES	2.54	58.7
	Disease control programs	2.08	47.4
	Preventive care	2.99	69.9
4.	BIOMEDICAL RESEARCH ISSUES	2.21	46.1
	Biomedical research programs, e.g., targeted disease funding	2.85	61.9
	National Institutes of Health funding	2.83	56.4
	DNA research	1.29	27.8
	Human experimentation	1.85	38.3
5.	ELDERLY CARE ISSUES	2.04	44.8
	Home health programs	2.13	46.6
	Nursing homes	1.95	42.9
6.	HEALTH PROFESSIONALS EDUCATION ISSUES	2.00	42.9
	Allied health professional training	2.20	46.6
	Health education	2.65	56.4
	Federal aid to nursing schools	1.41	27.8
	Nurse training	1.52	31.6
	Health professional certification	2.08	45.1
	Federal aid to medical schools	1.85	40.6
	Physician training	2.27	51.9
7.	MENTAL HEALTH AND DRUG ABUSE ISSUES	1.97	43.1
	Community mental health centers	1.79	37.6
	Mental health	2.23	49.6
	Drug/alcohol abuse programs	1.89	42.1
8.	ENVIRONMENTAL AND OCCUPATIONAL HEALTH	1.82	39.9
	Environmental health	1.80	41.4
	Occupational health and safety	1.84	38.3

Cluster	Issues	Mean	Percent
9.	PUBLIC HEALTH ISSUES	1.77	37.5
	Community health centers	1.82	39.1
	Rural health care	2.03	44.4
	Migrant health programs	1.17	22.6
	Public health services	2.25	48.9
	Health professional redistribution programs	1.99	43.6
	National Health Service Corps	1.71	35.3
	Emergency health care programs	1.38	27.8
	Federal aid to hospitals	1.81	38.3
10.	PROFESSIONAL ABUSE ISSUES	1.65	33.5
	Medical malpractice insurance	1.61	34.6
	Medicare/Medicaid fraud	1.68	32.3
11.	DISABILITY ISSUE	1.59	35.3
	Developmental disabilities programs	1.59	35.3
12.	MISCELLANEOUS ISSUES	1.57	33.9
	Indian health care	1.20	25.6
	Medical records privacy	1.93	42.1
	Abortion	1.24	24.8
	Maternal and child health insurance	1.89	42.9
13.	DRUG AND DEVICE REGULATION ISSUES	1.56	33.0
	Drug development regulation	1.83	39.1
	Drug industry regulation	1.68	36.1
	Drug labeling regulation, e.g., expiration date labeling, safety brochure inserts	1.82	39.8
	Generic versus brand-name drugs	1.46	30.8
	Medical advertising	1.05	20.3
	Medical device regulation	1.53	31.6
14.	KIDNEY DIALYSIS ISSUE	1.37	27.1
	Kidney dialysis	1.37	27.1
15.	VETERANS AND UNIONS ISSUES	1.11	21.1
	Hospital housestaff unionization	0.92	17.3
	Veterans health care	1.30	24.8
16.	FOOD ADDITIVES ISSUES	0.84	14.1
	Cyclamates	0.68	10.5
	Saccharin	0.90	15.0
	Food additive regulation	1.13	21.1
	Laetrile	0.63	9.8

In general, we should expect positive correlations among the issues because they are all drawn from the same policy domain. And, as we shall see, this is precisely what happens.

The range of the 1,540 correlations in the health domain (56 issues correlated pairwise across 135 organizations), for example, was between +.829 and −.284, and only 6.2 percent of the correlations were negative in sign. Nearly all of these negatively signed correlations were observed between the four biomedical research issues and the other 52 issues in the domain, indicating the highly distinctive character of the parties concerned with the former. The fact that the vast bulk of the correlations among issues are slightly to strongly positive suggests that the issues confronting the policy domains exhibit a degree of mutual coherence and interrelationship in the concerns of the active participants. Only the distinctive problems of biomedical research appear to attract a group of specialized interests that are disjunctive with those of the other domain participants. A similar analysis of the 2,080 correlations in the energy domain (65 issues correlated pairwise across 198 organizations) ranged between +.874 and −.122, with only 1.1 percent of them negative in sign.

Each matrix of organizations-by-issue-interests based on the informants' reports was first submitted to hierarchical cluster analysis to locate distinct subsets of issues based on similar patterns of organizational interests. Hierarchical clustering produces nested subsets with increasing internal heterogeneity as fewer large clusters are identified (see K. Bailey, 1974, for a useful overview of clustering methods). We used an agglomerative approach that locates pairs of highly similar variables (i.e., similar issues based on the patterns of interests expressed by all organizations), then successively adds other variables or clusters of variables to these core clusters, based on the average similarity to the variables already in the initial clusters. The measure of similarity between pairs of issues was the Pearsonian correlation coefficient mentioned above.

Figures 4.1 and 4.2 are dendrograms, or tree diagrams, that reveal how the basic issue clusters would merge if further hierarchical clustering were carried out. (The numerical values for the branches are the average correlation coefficients within sets of merged clusters.) In the energy domain dendrogram, the 14 basic clusters merge into four distinct larger sets, pairs of which also cumulate before the ultimate merger: (1) clusters 1–3 all deal with aspects of the petroleum and natural gas industry; (2) clusters 4–7 emphasize fundamental problems of energy extraction, transportation, and industry-government regulation, closely related to the previous set of clusters; (3) clusters 8–11 are nuclear and electric utility problems, including the training of skilled workers to operate such facilities; (4) clusters 12–14 involve end-uses: automobiles, renewable energy, and consumer energy problems. Although hierarchical

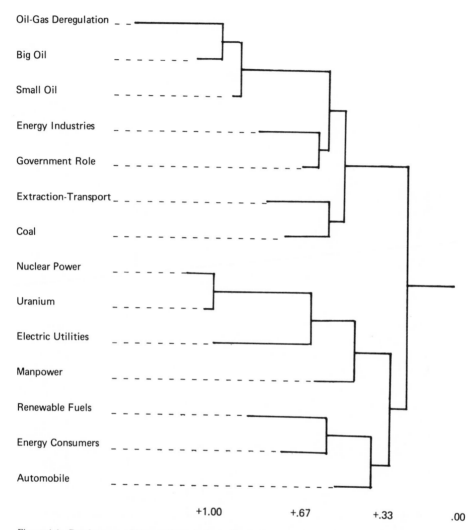

Figure 4.1. Dendrogram of Energy Domain Issue Clusters

clustering suggests which sets of issues are adjacent to one another, in the sense of attracting similar organizational audiences, it fails to convey the overall pattern of proximity and distance among types of issues. A visual demonstration of this situation will be presented shortly.

Turning to the health issue dendrogram in figure 4.2, we observe a similar pattern of higher-level aggregation of issue clusters: (1) clusters 1–4 focus on various aspects of health finances; (2) clusters 5–12 on aspects of the delivery

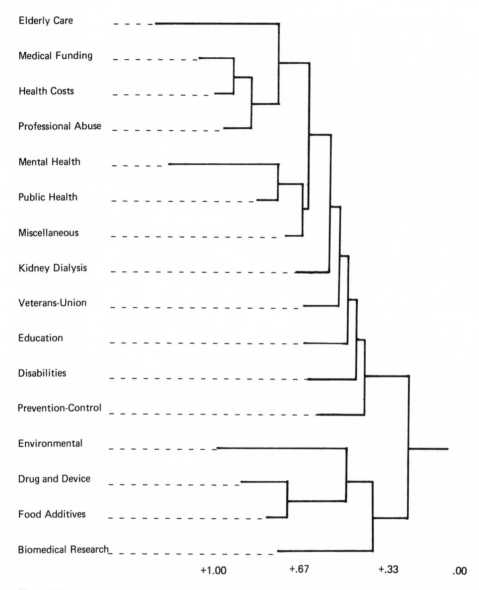

Elderly Care

Medical Funding

Health Costs

Professional Abuse

Mental Health

Public Health

Miscellaneous

Kidney Dialysis

Veterans-Union

Education

Disabilities

Prevention-Control

Environmental

Drug and Device

Food Additives

Biomedical Research

+1.00   +.67   +.33   .00

Figure 4.2. Dendrogram of Health Domain Issue Clusters

of health care; (3) clusters 13–15 on government regulation of medicine; and (4) cluster 16 on biomedical research issues closely linked to government supervision and control.

Although useful for certain analytic purposes (e.g., identifying subsets of issues with relatively high mutual intercorrelations when compared with others), hierarchical clustering does not provide a fully satisfactory means for revealing the overall structure of issue interrelationships, because it yields an essentially unidimensional arrangement among the set of issues according to their relative degree of intercorrelation. We thus turned to another technique, multidimensional scaling (Kruskal and Wish, 1978), which is explicitly designed to produce a multidimensional image or representation of the structure of an intercorrelation matrix. If the original data matrix meets certain conditions, the technique yields a one-, two-, or three-dimensional Euclidean representation of its structure. Sets of issues with high similarity of attracted interest will be located close to each other in a spatial diagram, whereas issues appealing to divergent organizational interests will be plotted far apart. Figures 4.3 and 4.4 display the two-dimensional results for each domain.[3]

The most prominent feature of both domains is the circle or rim pattern in the distribution of issues. That is, no issues occupy the center of the issue spaces of either domain. For the most part the subsets of issues making up each issue cluster are located adjacent to one another, as shown in both figures by the closed lines drawn around them. (In the few cases where overlapping clusters occur, the subsets would be separated when a third dimension is fitted.) Circular configurations are likely to occur when no issue manages to attract the interest of all domain actors in such a fashion that the central issue attains relatively equal covariation with all the other domain issues. The absence of any central issues in either domain indicates that issues attracted the attention of specialized organizational sectors.

In the energy domain, the oil-gas and nuclear-electric issues are located at opposite ends of the first (horizontal) dimension, suggesting a polarization of attention between the two types of fuels. A second (vertical) cleavage appears with the automobile, consumer, and renewable energy issues toward the bottom and coal, extraction, and industry development issues toward the top of the space. The spatial location of the government role issues within the same

3. Multidimensional scalings were performed with the ALSCAL program of Young in the SAS package. The two-dimensional stress value (Kruskal) was 0.26 for the energy domain and 0.25 for health, and the three-dimensional stress was 0.17 for both domains. Although the three-dimensional analyses provided better fits, the two-dimensional patterns are easier to present and do not differ in their gross patterns from the more complex plots.

Clusters of issues are delineated by closed lines in both figures. Membership in a given cluster was determined according to the hierarchical clustering analysis described above. Remember that a cluster contains issues that have relatively higher intercorrelations among themselves than they do with issues located in other clusters.

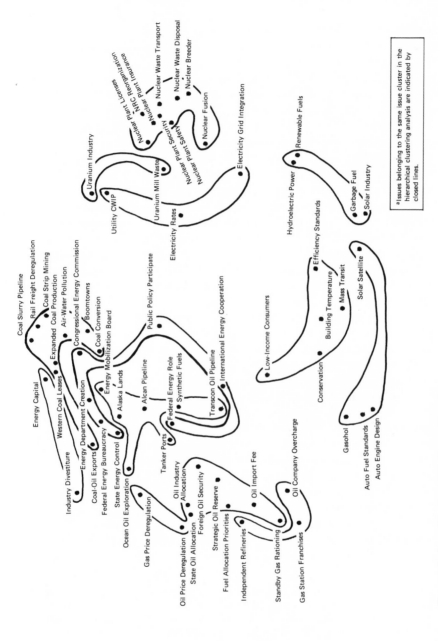

Figure 4.3. Issue Structure of the Energy Domain

Coal Slurry Pipeline
Rail Freight Deregulation
Coal Strip Mining
Expanded Coal Production
Air-Water Pollution
Western Coal Leases
Congressional Energy Commission
Boomtowns
Coal Conversion
Energy Capital
Energy Department Creation
Energy Mobilization Board
Industry Divestiture
Coal-Oil Exports
Federal Energy Bureaucracy
State Energy Control
Alaska Lands
Public Policy Participate
Alcan Pipeline
Ocean Oil Exploration
Tanker Ports
Federal Energy Role
Synthetic Fuels
International Energy Cooperation
Gas Price Deregulation
Oil Industry Allocation
Transcon Oil Pipeline
Oil Price Deregulation
State Oil Allocation
Foreign Oil Security
Strategic Oil Reserve
Oil Import Fee
Independent Refineries
Fuel Allocation Priorities
Oil Company Overcharge
Standby Gas Rationing
Gas Station Franchises

Uranium Industry
Nuclear Plant Licenses
NRC Reorganization
Nuclear Plant Insurance
Nuclear Waste Transport
Nuclear Waste Disposal
Nuclear Breeder
Nuclear Plant Security
Nuclear Plant Safety
Nuclear Fusion
Uranium Mill Waste
Electricity Grid Integration
Utility CWIP
Electricity Rates

Hydroelectric Power
Renewable Fuels
Efficiency Standards
Garbage Fuel
Solar Industry
Low-Income Consumers
Building Temperature
Mass Transit
Conservation
Solar Satellite
Gasohol
Auto Fuel Standards
Auto Engine Design

ᵃIssues belonging to the same issue cluster in the hierarchical clustering analysis are indicated by closed lines.

122

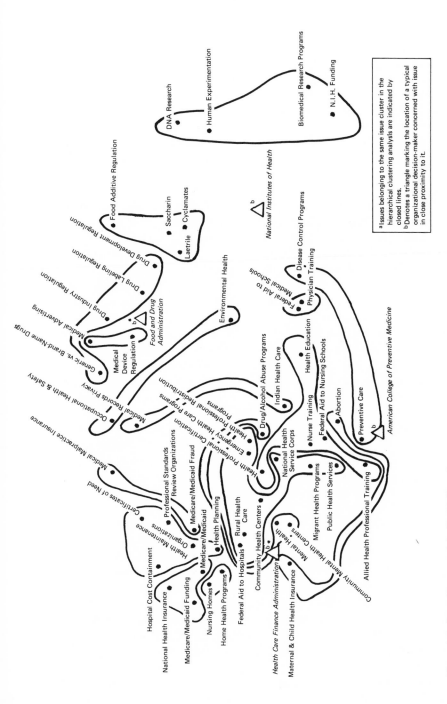

Figure 4.4. Issue Structure of the Health Domain

123

sector as the basic fuel issues (see also figure 4.1) indicates that high concern about what powers the government would acquire over energy policy was concentrated among organizations with the greatest interest in the coal, oil, natural gas, and transportation issues rather than among end-use-oriented actors.

In the health domain, figure 4.4 reveals that the basic issue cleavage lies between such financial issues as Medicare/Medicaid funding and health care costs on the one side and biomedical research issues at the other extreme. The vertical dimension finds issue clusters associated with government regulation (drugs and devices, food additives, and environmental-occupational health) at the opposite end from health care delivery matters (professional education, disease prevention and control, and some public health issues).

In fact, it might be useful to conceive of the elliptical arrangement of the health issues as "hung" on four institutional foci, each located in one of the four quadrants of the space. In the upper righthand quadrant one could locate the issues of particular relevance to the Food and Drug Administration (FDA); in the lower righthand quadrant, roughly halfway between the extreme outliers of biomedical research and physician training, might be located NIH. In the upper lefthand quadrant one can locate the HCFA, while in the lower lefthand quadrant is the American College of Preventive Medicine.

Exact equivalences among the cleavages in the two domains are not easy to identify. For example, the horizontal cleavage in the energy domain polarizes two fuel types (nuclear and petroleum), but the health domain contains nothing analogous (such as contrasting types of diseases). The location of specific issue clusters on opposite sides of an issue space seems to be a function of the particular historical circumstances that bring some issues into greater salience at the time of observation. Perhaps with greater experience in constructing issue spaces, we shall eventually establish underlying uniformities in the placement of issues. But for the present, we can neither generalize the results of two spatial analyses of issues to earlier or later eras nor extrapolate these findings to other national policy domains.

An Actor's Scope of Interest

As discussed in Chapter 1, our argument proceeds on at least two analytic levels: the collective and the individual. The preceding discussion of issue linkage and the one to follow on issue publics adopt a collective or global reference point whereby we try to characterize the global features of the two policy domains and compare how they are similar and different and with what consequences. Here we want to take up the matter of individual-level attributes of actors, which are measured in terms of global-level attributes. We shall use the results of this aside in several subsequent chapters.

An organization's specific profile of expressed interests across the set of domain issues tells us a great deal about its purposive orientation to its policy domain. How particular issue interests are embedded in the large set of issue concerns by the organization itself as well as by other organizations will, according to one of our central hypotheses, be highly consequential in explaining the organization's specific actions and those of the larger collectivity of actors. We shall, in fact, demonstrate that an organization's specific portfolio of issue concerns allows us to anticipate the organization's patterns of exchanges of information, resources, and influence as well as activation in specific policy events (see Chapters 9 and 10).

For present purposes, we want to talk about only one feature of an actor's purposive orientation to its policy domain: namely, its scope of interest. An organization with a narrow scope of interest is one that expresses concern about only a highly circumscribed set of issues when considered in the context of a more broadly inclusive domain of concerns. In contrast, organizations with broad or general scope are those which express wide-ranging concerns across a number of distinctive issue subdomains that may have only the loosest articulation with one another.

We propose to measure an organization's scope of interest by looking at the spread or dispersion of its strongly expressed interests in particular topics in the Euclidean spaces depicted in figures 4.3 and 4.4. As we have already suggested, the interpoint Euclidean distances between the issue nodes in the figures reflect the similarities or dissimilarities among the issues. The adjacent nodes are issues closely linked because of the similar constituencies of interested actors. If an organization is attracted exclusively to issues that are in close proximity, then we can say that its scope of interest is narrow. But if the organization's interest is scattered across the issue space covering a larger area, by definition its scope of interest is wider.

We thus propose to measure the scope of an organization's interest in national energy or health policy as follows. First, calculate the geometric mean of the coordinates of the issue on the X and Y axes in figure 4.3 (or 4.4) for which an organization has expressed a level of interest of *4* or *5*, the two highest levels. Then, sum the squared distances from this mean point to each of the issue locations for which the organization expressed a *4* or greater level of interest.[4] Mathematically,

$$Scope\ of\ interest = \sum_{i=1}^{n}\left[\left(X_i - \sum_{i=1}^{n}\frac{X_i}{n}\right)^2 + \left(Y_i - \sum_{i=1}^{n}\frac{Y_i}{n}\right)^2\right],$$

where n is the number of issues eliciting the organization's strong interest and X_i and Y_i are the coordinates of these issues.

4. One could, of course, simply count the number of issues in which an actor expressed a level of interest of *4* or higher. A simple count measure is heavily reliant on the care with which the issues were selected. One could imagine a situation in which a number of closely related issues

Identifying Issue Publics

Armed with our understanding of issue linkages in the national energy and health policy domains during the 1970s, we shall now turn to a consideration of how consequential actors are organized into *issue publics,* which are defined as subsets of domain organizations that exhibit similar covariations of levels of interest in the entire range of policy issues within the domain. In our conceptualization, organizations that take opposing sides on some or all domain issues may nonetheless be members of the same issue public. This possibility arises because the central relationship is the similarity in the actors' attentiveness to the set of policy issues, and not the extent to which the actors prefer the same positions on these issues. In the energy domain, environmental action associations and electric utility companies may have comparably high levels of interest in nuclear power, pollution, and solar research issues (and similarly low interests in automobile engine design and gasohol production). However, environmentalists and utilities typically adopt opposing policy positions on the particular events that manifest such general policy issues (e.g., the proposed moratorium on nuclear power plant construction following the Three Mile Island accident in 1979).

By considering only the patterning of attentiveness across the full range of domain issues, an issue public classification of organizations can encompass both potential allies and opponents within this single basic unit of social organization. The issue public concept thus delineates the primary subsets of domain organizations within which collaborators and antagonists may crystallize when confronted by specific policy events requiring collective choices. Such oppositional groups embedded within the same issue public are *interest groups* in the usual sense: actors holding a common preference for particular policy event outcomes (e.g., a "pro–nuclear power" interest group that favors fewer regulatory constraints on the construction and operation of power plants, versus an "antinuke" interest grouping that wants more stringent safeguards). An issue public circumscribes those subsets of domain actors that are most susceptible to activation whenever policy events strike at the heart of their interests. Organizations sharing highly similar issue interest profiles are much more likely to mobilize, whether for cooperation or conflict, than are organizations whose interest profiles diverge markedly. Thus, an identification of the issue publics and their organizational composition is the first order of business in a policy domain analysis. Only subsequently can the analysis of emergent interest groups be undertaken.

As persisting subdomains of discourse organized around broadly defined

---

were enumerated in one topical area while another area had only one instance. A specialized actor interested in the first area might have a high count despite its very narrow interest focus.

policy issues, issue publics may constrain or facilitate the development of several important policy processes, including the flow of timely policy information among actors; the progression of items on the policy agenda; the formation of oppositional collective actors (Laumann and Marsden, 1979; see also Chapter 12 below); the planning of resource coordination strategies; the implementation of individual and joint policy influence efforts; and the eventual resolution of specific policy event controversies. We believe that any serious analyses of these policy behaviors must take a domain's issue publics into consideration. Unfortunately, space limitations prevent a thorough examination of issue public relations with all these phenomena. Our more modest aim is to discuss procedures for empirically identifying issue publics in the two national policy domains and to show, in Chapter 8, how they articulate with another fundamental social structural relationship, the communication of policy-relevant information among domain participants.

Related Concepts

Our analysis resides squarely in the context of more general sociological questions about the internal differentiation and integration of complex social systems—the number and nature of social positions and their relations to one another. We cannot review this enormous literature here, but two recent empirical approaches deserve mention for their close parallels to our endeavor. Zeitlín et al. (1976), in a Marxist analysis of the political leadership of Chile's capitalist class, specified a social or class *segment*

as having a relatively distinct location in the social process of production and, consequently, its own specific political economic requirements and concrete interests which may be contradictory to those of other class segments with which, nonetheless, it shares essentially the same relationship to ownership of productive property. (Zeitlin et al., 1976: 1009)

Membership in a class segment was identified empirically by the property interests (land versus corporate capital) to which families or persons were most strongly attached. In this approach, a segment's political interests are to be inferred from the objective relation of actors to the means of economic production. In contrast, our issue public specification requires manifest expressions of concern by the policy actors themselves about a broad range of general domain issues, none of which need be related to the means of production.

Another approach parallel to the issue public concept is Kadushin's notion of a *social circle* (1968; Alba and Kadushin, 1976). Like the issue public, this social formation requires that participants share a concern about a focal set of topics or subjects (e.g., politics, psychotherapy), but the social circle concept further stipulates relatively dense sociometric linkages among actors, such as discussions about the topics among some part of the circle (e.g., Alba and

Moore, 1978). (Unlike the true clique, however, a social circle does not require that all possible direct ties occur.) Rather than define an issue public according to communication relations among its members, we take the question of discussion within and between issue publics as a matter for inquiry. Thus, given subsets of policy domain organizations sharing a focus on broad policy issues, we ask what policy information exchanges occur between these issue publics. Answering this question is the task of the following sections.

Structural Analysis

An analysis of issue publics in national policy domains relies on the structural perspective discussed at length in the first chapter: namely, "an approach to theorizing about, representing, and analyzing social processes which emphasizes their systemic character" (Berkowitz, 1982:vii). In a social system, structure is revealed by the linkages among its key elements, the observed "regularities in the patterns of relations among concrete entities" (White et al., 1976). The particular elements may be actors, objects, events, situations, or various combinations thereof (Breiger, 1974). Social relations have both form and content (Burt, 1982:22). The content of a relation refers to the substantive connections among the elements (e.g., authority, sentiment), whereas its form refers to properties of the ties that exist apart from their particular substance (e.g., intensity, frequency). The present chapter focuses upon one important type of relation—the interest relations that link a core set of policy domain organizations with a set of broadly defined policy issues. The relational content is the attentiveness of actors to the issues and the concern that they express about them; the form is the variation in the intensity of that interest.

The relation between actors and issues identifies a domain's interest groups under criteria of structural equivalence. Two or more actors are structurally equivalent if they exhibit identical patterns of ties to all objects on which relations are assessed (Lorrain and White, 1971). In the present case, when two organizations display the same pattern of interest across the full set of domain issues, they are equivalent and thus jointly occupy the same issue public position within the domain. As a practical matter, empirical organizations seldom have indistinguishable interests, especially where many issues are involved. Thus, the stringent structural equivalence requirements must be relaxed to permit organizations with distinct but very similar interest profiles to be aggregated into the same issue public position.

The initial objectives in an issue public analysis are to determine the apposite number of publics in the domain, the characteristics of the incumbent organizations, and the pattern of the publics' interest in the policy issues that identify these groups. Past research and theory on national policy making is generally silent about the social structure of issue publics. We can, however, state a few *a priori* expectations, drawn from scattered observations in the literature on power structure research and our own speculations.

The guiding hypothesis of this chapter is that national policy domains are internally differentiated into several distinct issue publics, whose constituent organizations exhibit essentially equivalent profiles of interests across the entire range of domain policy issues. This expectation would be refuted if a policy domain is occupied only by a small set of organizations all expressing high interests in every issue—in other words a lack of specialization, yielding an undifferentiated "leading crowd" involved in every facet of domain activity. To be sure, we would expect such results only if domain boundaries are drawn so unrealistically narrowly as to exclude substantial numbers of significant actors. The important questions revolve not around the existence of differentiated issue publics in national policy domains, but around the nature of their composition, their spatial configurations, and their communication patterns.

Composition of Issue Publics. We expect an issue public to consist of heterogeneous types of organizations sharing a common profile of interests across all domain issues. That is, we hypothesize that a public's members will be drawn from the private profit-making, nonprofit, and governmental sectors. Research by political scientists on specialized policy areas indicates the widespread existence of "subgovernments," consisting of small groups of governmental and nongovernmental actors, that dominate routine policy making in these areas (Cater, 1964; McConnell, 1966; Ripley and Franklin, 1980:8–11, 92–94; Walker, 1977). A typical subgovernment involves private sector groups and organizations with the heaviest stakes in the policy outcomes, and congressional committees and subcommittees with principal jurisdictions, and the parallel bureaucracies in the executive branch (this recurrent trinity has earned subgovernments the epithet of "iron triangles" or "cozy triangles"). American policy making blurs the distinction between private and public institutions and finds quite acceptable the continuous access to government officials of those groups most affected by the authorities' actions (Lowi, 1969). The subgovernment phenomenon is alleged to be most prevalent in distributive policies and programs, which confer tangible subsidies upon individuals, groups, and corporations: the cast of characters "is fairly stable over time, and their interactions are marked by low visibility and a high degree of cooperation and mutually rewarding logrolling" (Ripley and Franklin, 1980:21).

Although we anticipate that issue publics will exhibit many of these attributes of subgovernments, we believe that the degree of internal consensus is overstated. Rather, we hypothesize that an issue public will be composed of both potential antagonists and potential coalition partners. For example, in the energy domain, an issue public coalescing around high interest in a particular type of fuel should attract not only major producers and distributors of that fuel, but also end-use organizations such as manufacturers, consumers, and environmental associations, which may have markedly different notions about appropriate pricing and regulatory policies. Although we expect that issue publics will frequently incorporate the subgovernment triumvirates, they will also embrace larger constituencies of interested organizations that are not disposed to the facile accommodation alleged by the political science literature. Thus, issue publics comprise heterogeneous sets of organizations with specialized interests, from whose members potential opposing interest groups may be recruited and mobilized when attempts to influence policy are undertaken.

Spatial Configurations. Social structure is a persisting pattern of relationships among social positions—in the present case the domain's issue publics. The degree to which issue publics overlap one another in their policy interests reveals the degree of centralization within the domain (T. Clark, 1968:580; Freeman, 1968; and Grimes et al., 1976:712, make similar points about community elite participation in issue controversies; see also Laumann and Marsden, 1979). One indispensable procedure for grasping the *Gestalt* of a national policy domain is to array its interest publics in a social space. A two- or three-dimensional display of the proximities among publics will reveal the domain cleavage structure, showing the underlying "fault lines" that differentiate subsets of organizations according to their manifest concerns about the issues. Publics with very similar patterns of high, medium, and low interests in domain issues will be located close to one another in the space, while publics whose issue orientations diverge markedly will be far apart. By inspecting a visual display of the issue publics' locations in the social space, a policy domain analyst can gain much understanding of the issue's characteristic cleavages and their potential for shaping policy actions (e.g., proximate publics are more likely than very distant publics to be drawn into the same issue controversy).

The spatial configurations of domain issue publics may conform to various patterns hypothesized by elitist and pluralist theorists of power structures (Knoke, 1981). We briefly summarize some ideal-typical patterns that might emerge and illustrate them with two-dimensional diagrams in figure 4.5:

• Central administration: The domain's issue publics are all tightly clustered together in the social space, with no peripheral publics located in other regions.
• Linear: The issue space has a single dimension, with various publics arrayed along its entire length according to the degree to which their concerns emphasize a particular defining issue focus.
• Bifurcated: This issue public configuration also involves a single axis of differentiation, but two sets of publics are located at polar ends of this dimen-

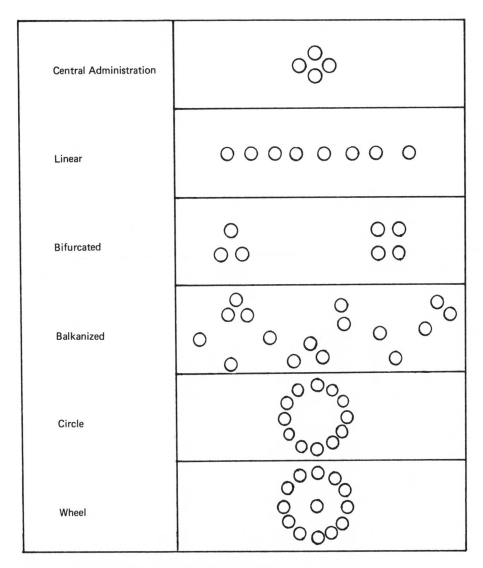

Figure 4.5. Hypothetical Issue Public Spatial Configurations

sion, suggesting either potential antagonists or subdivision into two discrete domains.

• Balkanized: Issue publics are randomly scattered at wide intervals in a multidimensional social space without a discernible ordering principle, implying extremely narrow specialization of interest attention.

- Circle: Issue publics are distributed in two dimensions in the shape of a doughnut with an empty center (or, in three dimensions, along the surface of a hollow sphere). Publics near to one another have more issue concerns in common than publics that are farther apart.
- Wheel: This configuration is similar to the circle, except that the center is occupied by one or more issue publics that share interests with the variety of publics located in the narrowly specialized sectors on the circumference.

The central administration pattern, implied in the classic elite theories of Pareto and Mosca and in Hunter's (1953) study of Atlanta, is most likely in a policy domain with minimal interest differentiation among a small number of positions that preempt all issues. Single-party totalitarian states most clearly exemplify this pattern, as may some national domains where a handful of powerful, consensual actors manage to exclude all other parties from significant involvement. In most American national policy domains, however, we expect that the prevailing norms of relatively open access will make the centrally administered configuration a short-lived phenomenon. Similarly, the linear pattern seems plausible only in those rare instances when a single issue of crisis proportions manages to drive all other domain problems into the distance. Bifurcation into two polarized positions seems likely only when a domain is undergoing differentiation into separate domains, or when the analyst has drawn overly generous boundaries that mistakenly encompass distinct policy arenas. Under routine circumstances, then, only the three multidimensional patterns seem credible as models of domain issue public structures.

The amorphous balkanized pattern was implied by such plural elitist writers as Keller (1963), McConnell (1966), and Rose (1967). They described the American polity as comprising many functionally specialized, largely autonomous hierarchies whose members interact infrequently across institutional boundaries:

These elites do not act cohesively with each other on many issues. They do not "rule" in the sense of commanding the entire nation. Quite the contrary, they tend to pursue a policy of noninvolvement in the larger issues of statesmanship, save where such issues touch their own particular concerns. (McConnell, 1966:339)

If these "strategic elites" attend only to interests touching most directly on their functional performance, the domain will exhibit a fragmented rather than integrated spatial configuration. If, however, an issue public sustains a somewhat broader reconnaissance of its domain, the shading or flowing of its interests into adjacent areas may have the effect of imposing greater structuration upon the space. A circle or rim pattern indicates substantial specialization by each public, but overlapping foci among neighboring positions. For example, nuclear and oil issues tend to create segregated publics. But some electrical utilities operate power plants using both kinds of fuels, and hence they should occupy an intermediate public position. The absence of a central public in the circle implies that no group of organizations exists that maintains diverse interests that are proximate to the full range of domain concerns. Most publics consist of specialists that confine their attention to a delimited span of issues. Thus, every public is drawn away from the center to one side or another of the circle, its specific location depending upon the degree of similarity to or difference from its neighbors.

Theorists working in a radical elitist perspective (Domhoff, 1978; Mills, 1956) argue for the presence of a power elite involved in and controlling all significant policy matters while relegating minor specialists to narrow, peripheral sectors. These power structure researchers have variously identified the core positions as occupied by economic, political, and military elites (Mills, 1956:292), corporation-based foundations and policy organizations rooted in an upper social class (Salzman and Domhoff, 1980), and a large central circle "representative of all major institutions and issue areas" (Moore, 1979:675). Regardless of the particular composition of the core issue publics, the spatial configuration most compatible with these theoretical models appears to be the wheel pattern. The central public or publics are generalist positions that share interests in the full range of domain policy issues, to which the peripheral publics pay only specialized attention.

The preceding identification of domain issue clusters was based on matrices of organizations-by-issue-interests, in which pairwise correlations were calculated for vectors of issues. The issue public concept, however, requires detection of subsets of organizations expressing comparable patterns of interest across all domain issues. Hence, the matrices must be transposed and pairwise correlations must be calculated for vectors of organizations. High positive correlations indicate that a pair of actors share similar patterns of expressed interest across the full range of issues; negative covariation indicates sharply differentiated foci of attention.[5] When hierarchical cluster analyses (S. Johnson, 1967) were performed on the transposed matrices, the results were 13 energy and 14 health issue publics, as shown in figures 4.6 and 4.7. These figures also indicate how the issue publics could be further disaggregated into more narrowly defined subgroups that exhibit higher levels of internal homogeneity with regard to issue interests. However, experience with these more fine-grained specifications suggests that little benefit is to be gained from the greater complexity that such disaggregation produces.

Figures 4.8 and 4.9, on the other hand, indicate how the basic issue publics

5. Note that the correlation coefficient, as a product of standardized scores, takes into account only the similarity between two actors' interest profiles and not the absolute level of their interests. For example, a pair of organizations' interests may be perfectly correlated across the entire set of issues ($r = +1.0$) even though the first actor's interest levels are exactly three points higher than the other's.

MERCHANT SHIPPING

American Institute of Merchant Shipping

MISCELLANEOUS

Institute of Gas Technology
Foster Wheeler Energy
Wheelabrator-Frye
Boeing
New Directions
Mitre Corp
U.S. Labor Party

PIRG—FTC

Public Interest Research Group
Federal Trade Commission

LOCAL GOVERNMENT AND RENEWABLE FUELS

Gas Research Institute	National Consumer Law Center
California Public Utilities Commission	American Bakers Association
American Wind Energy Association	Department of Agriculture
Solar Energy Industries Association	Coalition of Northeast Governors
Hsc on Energy Development and Applications-D	Ssc on Energy Regulation-R
Hsc on Energy Development and Applications-R	American Institute of Architects
Solar Lobby	National League of Cities
Solar Energy Research Institute	U.S. Conference of Mayors
Worldwatch Institute	Gas Appliances Manufacturers Association
Ssc on Energy Conservation and Supply-D	Sheet Metal Workers
Ssc on Energy Conservation and Supply-R	---
Ssc on Energy and Foundations-D	National Audubon Society
Grumann Aerospace	National Association of Counties
---	National Conference of State Legislatures
Consumers Power	Calif Energy Resources Conserv and Dev Comm
Hsc on Oversight and Investigations-D	Hsc on Energy and Power-R
Citizen/Labor Energy Coalition	Hsc on Energy and Power-D

NUCLEAR, ELECTRICAL, ENVIRONMENTAL

Allied General Nuclear Service	General Public Utilities
Hsc on Energy Research and Production-D	Texas Utilities
Babcock and Wilcox	American Public Power Association
General Electric	Natl Assn of Regulatory Utilities Commissioners
American Nuclear Energy Council	Natl Rural Electric Cooperative Association
Atomic Industrial Forum	American Electric Power Service
Ssc on Nuclear Regulation-D	Virginia Electric and Power
Nuclear Regulatory Commission	Tennessee Valley Authority
Ssc on Nuclear Regulation-R	Southern California Edison
Critical Mass Energy Project	National Electric Reliability Council
Environmental Coalition on Nuclear Power	Consolidated Edison
Union of Concerned Scientists	Pacific Gas and Electric
Ssc on Energy Research and Development-D	Public Service Electric and Gas
General Atomic	---
Electric Power Research Institute	KMS Fusions
Rockwell International	Thermo-Electron
Office of Science and Technology	---
Hsc on Energy Research and Production-R	Utility Waste Management Group
National Science Foundation	State Planning Council on Radioactive Waste
---	---
Combustion Engineering	Environmental Action
Houston Lighting and Power	Natural Resources Defense Council
Detroit Edison	Sierra Club
Edison Electric Institute	Council on Environmental Quality
Westinghouse	Hsc on Energy and Environment-D
Northeast Utilities Service	Hsc on Energy and Environment-R
Stone and Webster Engineering	Environmental Policy Center
Commonwealth Edison	National Academy of Sciences

Figure 4.6. Issue Publics in the Energy Domain

AUTO TRANSPORT

Center for Auto Safety
Department of Transportation

MANUFACTURING AND
NATIONAL EXECUTIVE

Chrysler
National Automobile Dealers
 Association
Ford Motor
United Auto Workers
TRW Inc.
United Technologies
America Iron and Steel
 Institute

Dow Chemical
American Paper Institute
Chemical Manufacturers
 Association
National Association of
 Manufacturers
Union Carbide
National Retail Merchants
 Association
National Forest Products
 Association

Resources for the Futures
Office of Management and
 Budget
The White House Office
Council of Economic Advisors
National Governors Association

OIL

Atlantic Richfield
Standard Oil of Ohio
Cities Service
American Petroleum Institute
Sun Oil
Shell Oil
Texaco
Continental Oil
Gulf Oil
Standard Oil of Indiana
Petroleum Industry Research Foundation
Energy Action Education Foundation
Economic Regulatory Administration
Standard Oil of California
American Petroleum Refiners Association
Hampton Roads Energy
Petrochemical Energy Group
Independent Petroleum Association of America

Independent Gas Marketers
Service Station Dealers
American Auto Association
Independent Terminal Operators Association
Society of Independent Gas Marketers
National Council of Farmer Coops
National Oil Jobbers

Union Oil of California
Oil, Chemical and Atomic Workers Union

Tosco
Ssc on Energy and Foundations-R
General Motors
Consumer Energy Council
Consumer Federation of America

New England Fuel Institute

REGULATORY

Chamber of Commerce of U.S.
Department of Commerce
Department of Energy
Ssc on Energy Regulation-D
AFL-CIO
Hsc on Oversight and Investigacions-R

PIPELINES

Foothills Pipelines
Northern Tier Pipeline
National Transportation Safety Board
Rocky Mountain Oil and Gas Association

RAILWAY

Phillips Petroleum
Allied Chemical
Union Pacific
Association of American Railroads

TRANSPORTATION

Interstate Commerce Commission
Ssc on Surface Transportation-D

COAL AND NATURAL GAS

American Natural Resources	Northwest Energy	American Gas Association
Houston Natural Gas	Burlington Northern	Interstate Natural Gas Assn of America
El Paso Natural Gas	U.S. Steel	Columbia Gas System
Montana Power	American Mining Congress	Brooklyn Union Gas
National Economic Research Assn	United Mine Workers	Associated Gas Distributors
AMAX Coal	American Association of Petroleum	Natural Gas Supply Association
Consolidation Coal	Geologists	Republic Geothermal
National Coal Association	National Wildlife Federation	Federal Energy Regulatory Commission
Mining and Reclamation Council	Department of Interior	---
Slurry Transport Association	Environmental Protection Agency	Association of Oil Pipe Lines
Western Governors Policy Office	-------------------------------------	Rio Blanco Oil Shale

135

ISOLATES

American Association of Professional
  Standards Review Organizations
American Insurance Association
Health Industry Manufacturers
  Association
Natl Union of Hospital and Health
  Care Workers
Natl Association of Home Health
  Agencies

FINANCE

American Association
  of Retired Persons/
  National Retired
  Teachers Association
National Council of
  Senior Citizens

Washington Business
  Group on Health
Health Insurance
  Association of
  America
Health Care Financing
  Administration
Ssc on Health-D
Hsc on Health-D
Ssc on Health-R
Hsc on Health-R

Blue Cross and Blue
  Shield Associations
American Hospital
  Association
National Conference
  of State Legislatures
National Governors'
  Association
United Automobile
  Workers

Group Health Associa-
  tion of America
Hospital Corporation
  of America
Federation of Ameri-
  can Hospitals
America Health Care
  Association
National Council of
  Health Care Services

MENTAL HEALTH

American Academy of
  Child Psychiatry
Natl Council of Com-
  munity Mental Health
  Centers
American Psychological
  Association
Assn for the Advance-
  ment of Psychology
Mental Health Asso-
  ciation
Alcohol, Drug Abuse,
  and Mental Health
  Administration
American Psychiatric
  Association
National Women's
  Health Network

Children's Defense
  Fund
National Coalition of
  Hispanic Mental
  Health and Human
  Service Organizations
National Assn of State
  Alcohol and Drug Abuse
  Directors
National Assn of
  Community Health
  Centers

ABORTION

National Abortion Rights Action League
National Urban League

CONSUMERS

American Dietetic Association
American Nurses' Association
National League for Nursing
American Association of Colleges of Nursing

National Association for the Advancement
  of Colored People
National Farmers Union
American Health Planning Association
National Health Law Program
National Association of Counties
Office of the Assistant Secretary for Health
AFL-CIO
American Federation of State, County, and
  Municipal Employees
Service Employees International Union
United States Conference of Mayors
Robert Wood Johnson Foundation
Health Resources Administration

PUBLIC HEALTH

American College of Preventive Medicine
Association of Teachers of Preventive Medicine
American Public Health Association

Assn of State and Territorial Health Officials
Coalition for Health Funding
Ssc on Labor, Health, Education and Welfare-D
Health Services Administration
Hsc on Labor, Health, Education and
  Welfare Appropriations-R
Natl Academy of Sciences Institute of Medicine
Ssc on Health and Science Research-R
Medical Library Association
American Association of Colleges of Pharmacy
United Mine Workers
National Rehabilitation Association

Figure 4.7. Issue Publics in the Health Domain

136

FOOD

Consumer Federation of America
Community Nutrition Institute
Bureau of Foods-Food and Drug Administration

DRUG INDUSTRY

Hoffman-La Roche, Inc.
Merck & Company
Pharmaceutical Manufacturers Association
Food and Drug Administration, Commissioner
  and Staff
Bureau of Drugs-Food and Drug Administration
Pfizer Pharmaceuticals
Upjohn Company

GOVERNMENT

Department of Health and Human Services,   The White House Office
  Secretary's Office   Office of Management and the Budget
Hsc on Health and Environment-D

HEALTH PROFESSIONALS

American Academy of Pediatrics   American Academy of Physician Assistants
American College of Obstetricians and   American Osteopathic Association
  Gynecologists   Chamber of Commerce of the United States
Planned Parenthood Federation of America   American Dental Association
Renal Physicians Association   College of American Pathologists
Association of American Medical Colleges   American Association of Nurse Anesthetists
Council of Teaching Hospitals   American Chiropractic Association
-- American Medical Association
                                            Federal Trade Commission

TARGETED DISEASE 3

American Speech-Language-Hearing Association
National Association for Retarded Citizens
United Cerebral Palsy Associations
Arthritis Foundation
Cystic Fibrosis Foundation
National Hemophilia Foundation
Epilepsy Foundation of America
National Institute of Child Health and
  Human Development-NIH
National Foundation for Iletis and Colitis
Joint Council of Allergy and Immunology
National Society for Autistic Children

TARGETED DISEASE 1

American Association for
  Dental Research
National Institute of
  Dental Research-NIH
American Social Health
  Association
American Cancer Society
Candlelighters Foundation
American Society of Hematology
Endocrine Society
American Diabetes Association
American College of Cardiology
Friends of Eye Research, Re-
  habilitation, and Treatment
American Heart Association

TARGETED DISEASE 2

American Gastroenterological Association
National Kidney Foundation
Citizens for the Treatment of
  High Blood Pressure

HEALTH RESEARCH

American Federation for Clinical Research
National Institute on Aging-NIH
National Institute on Neurological Communicative Disorders and Stroke-NIH
National Institute of Allergy and Infectious Diseases-NIH
National Institute of General Medical Sciences-NIH
National Institute of Arthritis, Metabolism, and Digestive Diseases-NIH
American Society for Microbiology
National Cancer Institute-NIH
Society for Investigative Dermatology
National Institutes of Health, Director and Staff
Environmental Defense Fund
National Institute of Environmental Health Sciences-NIH
American Association of Dental Schools

137

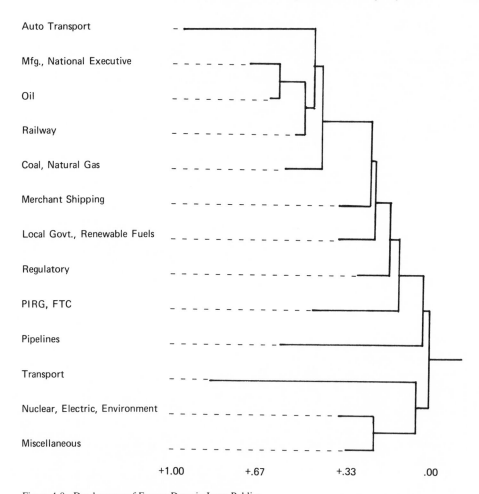

Figure 4.8. Dendrogram of Energy Domain Issue Publics

could be aggregated into yet larger sets of increasingly heterogeneous organizations. For the energy domain, two core clusters are formed, the first involving publics 1–10 and the second publics 11–13. The pattern in which clusters agglomerate may be called "chaining-on" because it resembles the successive addition of links to a chain. In the health domain, a similar pattern of chaining-on occurred.[6] The decision about where to halt the clustering process is

6. The isolate clusters are not shown in figures 4.6 and 4.7 because they do not constitute a common cluster. The five organizations in the isolate clusters of figure 4.7 were actually located in three nonadjacent small clusters that have been grouped together to eliminate these exceptionally small publics, which obscure the relationships among the more significant ones.

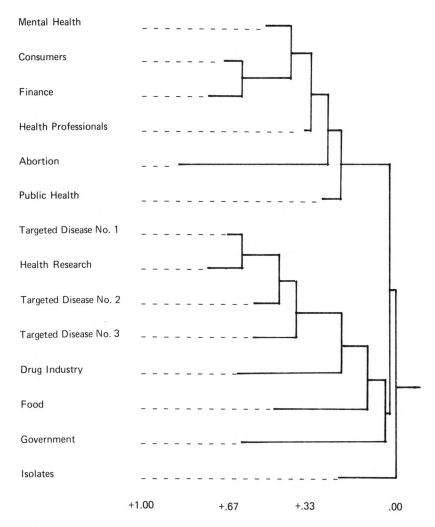

Figure 4.9. Dendrogram of Health Domain Issue Publics

not reducible to a hard and fast rule. Smaller cluster sizes obviously create greater homogeneity at the expense of prolific numbers of issue publics. Our selection of these two sets of 13 and 14 publics reflects our careful consideration of the substantive content of each cluster, as well as the practical need for relatively small numbers of publics that permit manageable analysis and interpretation.

Although the aggregation process was halted in the energy domain after 13 issue publics were formed, six of these are small clusters, having fewer than five members. Four of the seven largest publics appear to be dominated by specific energy sources, as the descriptive labels indicate. This subdivision of the energy domain into distinct fuel types reflects the long tradition of specialization among energy producers (Davis, 1978; Goodwin, 1981; Stobaugh and Yergin, 1979; and see Chapter 2 above). The most significant aspect of the composition of these large publics is the diversity of the organizations they comprise. Indeed, several publics strongly resemble subgovernments in their inclusion of executive bureaus, congressional subcommittees, and client groups. But in contrast to the homogeneous policy preferences described in the political science concept of subgovernments, the issue publics typically contain organizations well known to take opposing views on important policy matters.

The nuclear-electrical-environmental issue public is the clearest example: it comprises the Nuclear Regulatory Commission, Office of Science and Technology, National Science Foundation, National Academy of Sciences, and Council on Environmental Quality, seven House and Senate subcommittees, 25 nuclear or electrical production companies, seven trade associations, and eight planning, antinuclear, or environmental action organizations. Coal and natural gas interests are located in the same issue public despite their obvious differences in physical products. (Note that even with further subdivision of this public, some gas producers and distributors would remain intermeshed with coal industry organizations.) Although no congressional subcommittees appear in the coal-gas public, it contains the Department of Interior, EPA, and the Federal Energy Regulatory Commission of the Department of Energy, as well as the opposing National Wildlife Federation. Similarly, the oil issue public incorporates the major oil companies and trade associations, the small producers, refiners, and distributors, three opposing consumer associations (Energy Action Education, Consumer Energy Council, and Consumer Federation of America), one congressional subcommittee, and the Economic Regulatory Administration unit of the Energy Department. The fourth issue public evidently associated with a specific fuel type is the renewable fuel–local government category. It contains solar, wind, and conservation advocates as well as most of the state and local government associations and nine partisan staffs of eight congressional subcommittees having primary jurisdiction over energy research and development issues.

The three remaining energy issue publics do not seem to represent any specific fuel types. The "miscellaneous" position is an odd assortment of high-tech industries with idiosyncratic interests not matched by the other publics (figure 4.8 indicates that their closest proximity is with the "nuclear, electrical environmental" public). The small regulatory issue public constitutes a critical position of national authority and legitimacy, containing four federal actors, including the Department of Energy, and two peak associations representing the business community (Chamber of Commerce) and labor (AFL-

CIO). As we shall see shortly, this public has policy interests that span virtually the entire domain. Finally, the manufacturing-national executive issue public is composed of several major energy-using corporations and trade associations, particularly those connected with the automobile industry, and four organizations holding important national authority: the White House Office, the Office of Management and the Budget (OMB), Council of Economic Advisors, and National Governors Association.

Turning to the health domain in figure 4.7, we find similar disparities in the sizes of the issue publics. Four publics have three or fewer members, while more than half contain 10 or more. As in the energy domain, several of the larger health publics exhibit considerable internal heterogeneity of organizations, again superficially resembling subgovernments. For example, the public health public contains three congressional subcommittees, a federal agency, eight professional associations or interest groups, a private sector research organization, and a trade union with a strong interest in the health disabilities of its members. Similarly, the health finance public comprises four subcommittees with jurisdiction over insurance policies and a variety of insurance vendors, hospitals, and consumer groups. Clearly, all these parties are unlikely to agree on proposed solutions to the financial exigencies escalating health care costs. Hence, this issue public contains both potential antagonists and coalition confederates likely to be activated whenever health finance issues are brought to the fore.

The four-actor government public appears to be an analogue to a similar cluster within the energy domain. It contains the secretary of HHS, a powerful House subcommittee, the White House Office, and OMB. The policy issues that concern this public, as will be seen below, encompass a substantial portion of the entire domain.[7] The health research public is adjacent to the three targeted disease publics. Most of the NIH units are located in this public, whereas most of the private sector associations concerned with specific disease research and treatment are located in separate publics.

The health professional public contains the powerful AMA as well as several more specialized medical societies and the FTC, whose primary job in health is to regulate professional practices. The mental health issue public constitutes a distinct set of psychological, psychiatric, and mental health care associations along with its primary federal bureaucracy, the Alcohol, Drug Abuse, and Mental Health Administration (ADAMHA). Finally, the heterogeneous consumer public involves several trade unions, state and local government associations, interest groups, and several nursing professional societies.

Hierarchical cluster analyses suggest the presence of a handful of major

---

7. Both the White House Office and OMB failed to complete interviews in the health domain. Given the reported health issue concerns of OMB and President Carter, we felt that they would have been located in the government public.

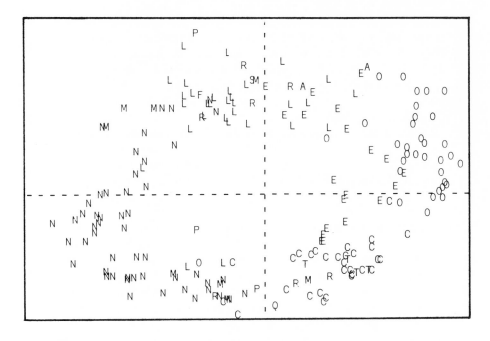

KEY:

O Oil
E Manufacturing, Executive
T Railway
A Automotive Transport
F PIRG, FTC
Q Transport
S Shipping

C Coal, Gas
N Nuclear, Electrical, Environmental
L Local Government, Renewable
R Regulatory
P Pipelines
M Miscellaneous

Figure 4.10. Distribution of Energy Issue Publics

issue publics in each domain composed of specialized organizations, several
of which may take opposing policy stands on the focal issues of concern to the
public. The relationships among a domain's publics are best revealed by spatial
analyses, similar to those performed above on the issues. Figures 4.10 and
4.11 display the two-dimensional solutions for the energy and health domains,
respectively.[8]

8. As before, higher-dimension results provide a better fit to the data but are less easy to display and interpret than the two-dimensional configurations. For the energy domain, Kruskal's

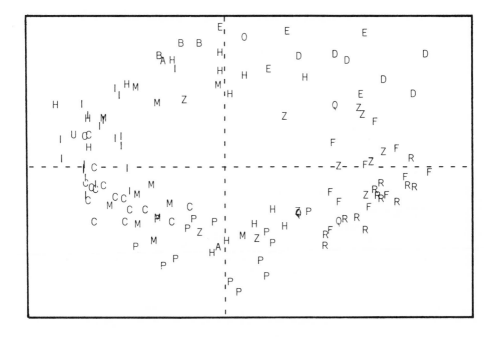

KEY:

P Public Health
R Research
D Pharmaceuticals
E Regulation
U Union
X Home Health
I Insurance
H Health Professionals

C Consumers
M Mental Health
F Fund Raisers No. 1
Q Fund Raisers No. 2
Z Fund Raisers No. 3
B PSRO-Manufacturers
A Abortion-Urban League

Figure 4.11. Distribution of Health Issue Publics

In both domains the issue publics are obviously arrayed in a circle configuration, with an empty center. However, in neither domain do the member organizations of each public cluster tightly around a single point; rather, they spread across large portions of the space in amoebalike fashion and overlap with one another to a considerable degree. These distributions suggest both a specialization of interests within publics and a shading or radiation of atten-

stress was .27 for two dimensions and .19 for three. The health domain's stress values were .28 and .19, respectively.

tion toward the interests of neighboring groups, resulting in fuzzy boundaries between the publics in adjacent sectors of the circle. For the most part, the spatial location of organizations mirrors the positioning of the issues in the earlier multidimensional analyses.

In the energy domain, for example, the oil public is opposite the nuclear-electrical-environmental public, whereas the manufacturing–national executive public is located close to both the oil and the coal-gas publics. The local government–renewable fuels public occupies the space between the oil and nuclear organizations, comparable to the location of renewable fuels and consummers issues in the issue space analysis. Similarly, in the health domain the health research public is nestled among the three targeted disease publics opposite the health insurance, mental health, and consumer publics. The pharmaceuticals and regulatory publics are adjacent to one another but almost directly across from the public health organizations.

As noted above, the absence of any issue public in the center of the circle suggests that no group of organizations maintains a sufficiently broad span of interests to be located equidistant from all the specialist publics occupying the rim. However, in the energy domain, the six organizations making up the regulatory public are in fact positioned on opposite sides of the circle: the AFL-CIO, House investigations subcommittee, Senate energy regulation subcommittee, and Energy Department are embedded in the same sector as the local government–renewable fuels public; the Chamber of Commerce and Department of Commerce are situated within the coal-gas position. (In a three-dimensional solution, these six organizations are placed together at the extreme negative end of the third dimension.) This differentiation, which does not occur for any other energy issue public, implies that the regulatory public may in fact have broad interests spanning the domain, a point to be explored in the next section.

In the health domain, a similar dispersion can be observed for the 15 organizations in the health professional public. These actors are scattered across three of the quadrants of the circle. If the individual organizations were labeled, the AMA and the American Dental Association would appear at the center top of figure 4.11. The FTC and the pathologists' and renal physicians' associations and Planned Parenthood are somewhat to their right. The pediatricians', nurse anesthetists', obstetricians', American medical colleges', and teaching hospitals' associations are located at the bottom center. To the left are the osteopaths, chiropractors, physician assistants, and the Chamber of Commerce. As in the energy domain, the spatial diffusion of an issue public's members may indicate that it encompasses a broad range of interest foci.

The Interests of Issue Publics

The two preceding sections aggregated issues and organizations respectively into clusters of relatively homogeneous equivalence classes and showed how these sets were spatially distributed. This section takes the next logical step: to show the relationship of issue publics to the entire set of domain issues. The basic analysis is a cross-tabulation of the set of issue publics with the set of domain issues, as shown in tables 4.3 and 4.4.

The values in the cells of the tables are standardized scores (Z-scores), calculated as follows: an organization's interest in each issue was coded 0–5 according to its own "no interest–major interest" report. Each organization's Z-score was computed for the set of issues making up an issue cluster (e.g., an organization's average interest in the nine nuclear power issues) by subtracting the mean of all organizations' average interest in the issue cluster and dividing by the standard deviation. Each organization's standard score on that set of issues was thus obtained. Finally, the mean Z-score on the issue cluster was calculated for all organizations in each issue public. Similar procedures were followed for each of the domain issue clusters. Thus, the values reported in tables 4.3 and 4.4 show the relative magnitudes of interest expressed by each issue public in the domain issues. Issue publics with large positive Z-scores have higher than average interest in a set of issues, whereas publics with negative Z-scores focus relatively little attention on that issue cluster.

In the energy domain, the issue interests of most issue publics clearly focus on narrow concerns, with two exceptions. First, the small railway issue public that exhibits exceptionally high levels of interest is not an artifact of a few verbose informants but rather indicates extensive involvement by these organizations in all facets of energy transportation from coal haulage to nuclear waste disposal, as well as intense concern over impending rail freight deregulation. Second, as noted earlier in regard to the spatial configuration of the issue publics, the six-member regulatory public, which includes the Energy Department, also maintains high interests in every domain issue except small oil and the government's energy role (the latter presumably a matter of false modesty, since the regulatory public was itself a major target for actors seeking to modify the federal energy role). These two publics with wide spans of issue attention may help to bridge the more narrowly focused publics that make up the remainder of the energy domain.

The remaining 11 energy publics all display much more circumscribed issue spans. Three publics (shipping, pipelines, transportation) have no major interests at all, suggesting that their organizations are marginal to the energy domain. Four other issue publics have only one or two sets of issues of great concern to them: the auto transport public attends to automobile issues; the local government–renewable fuels public concentrates on consumer and re-

Table 4.3. Issue Public Interests: Energy Domain

	DOMAIN ISSUE CLUSTERS													
Issue Publics	DEREG 1	GOVT 2	IND 3	COAL 4	CONS 5	OIL 6	ELEC 7	EXTR 8	REN 9	NUC 10	MAN 11	URAN 12	AUTO 13	OIL 14
1. Auto Transp	-0.87	-0.48	-1.18	-0.54	0.18	-0.13	-1.21	-0.61	-0.83	-0.82	-0.81	-0.84	1.38	-0.17
2. Mfg, Exec	0.76	0.19	-0.40	0.17	0.49	0.80	0.32	0.03	-0.21	-0.34	-0.29	-0.40	0.56	-0.60
3. Oil	0.74	0.60	0.75	0.02	0.05	1.29	-0.69	0.47	-0.46	-0.72	-0.02	-0.33	0.48	1.70
4. Railway	0.85	1.04	1.37	1.46	0.60	1.35	0.43	0.77	-0.40	0.63	0.35	1.85	-0.10	1.46
5. Coal, Gas	0.38	0.30	0.58	0.63	-0.49	-0.50	-0.08	0.44	-0.53	-0.62	0.29	-0.36	-0.58	-0.89
6. Shipping	-1.66	-1.57	-1.18	-1.10	-1.57	-1.17	-1.21	-1.05	-1.34	-0.98	-0.81	-0.84	-0.99	-1.05
7. Renew	-0.27	-0.49	-0.52	-0.65	0.58	-0.37	0.03	-0.49	0.82	-0.38	-0.16	-0.51	0.12	-0.58
8. Regul	0.50	0.00	0.81	1.07	0.50	0.94	0.46	1.51	0.94	0.99	0.25	0.80	1.01	0.09
9. PIRG-FTC	0.85	-1.20	0.13	-0.58	-0.17	-0.61	-0.44	-0.30	-0.40	-0.38	-0.81	0.24	-0.50	0.62
10. Pipes	-1.53	-1.95	-1.32	-1.39	-1.50	-1.15	-1.21	-0.33	-1.34	-0.96	-0.81	-0.84	-0.79	-0.88
11. Transp	-1.66	-1.98	-1.47	0.06	-1.22	-1.25	-0.44	-1.46	-1.34	-0.70	-0.81	-0.84	-0.99	-1.05
12. Nuclear	-0.58	0.05	-0.18	-0.03	-0.03	-0.51	0.53	-0.25	0.26	1.20	0.18	0.83	-0.25	-0.75
13. Misc	-0.94	-1.04	-1.01	-0.59	-1.31	-0.81	-0.56	-0.83	0.47	-0.17	-0.07	-0.35	-0.15	-1.05
Mean	3.14	3.03	2.53	2.30	2.28	2.24	2.10	2.08	1.96	1.75	1.40	1.36	1.26	1.99
S.D.	1.89	1.39	1.72	1.48	1.43	1.80	1.73	1.43	1.46	1.79	1.72	1.63	1.27	1.53

Table 4.4. Issue Public Interests: Health Domain

Domain Issue Clusters

Issue Publics	FUND 1	COST 2	PREV 3	RES 4	ELD 5	EDUC 6	MENT 7	ENV 8	PUB 9	ABUSE 10	DISAB 11	MISC 12	DRUG 13	DIAL 14	VETS 15	ADDIT 16
1. Mental Health	0.49	-0.14	-0.07	-0.17	-0.29	-0.35	1.13	-0.30	0.18	-0.22	0.42	0.72	-0.08	-0.58	0.13	-0.37
2. Consumers	0.61	0.68	-0.06	-0.72	0.77	0.14	0.45	-0.10	0.81	-0.30	0.09	-0.20	-0.63	-0.42	-0.15	-0.37
3. Finance	0.93	1.15	0.01	-0.82	0.97	0.18	0.53	-0.02	0.29	1.36	0.08	0.44	0.04	0.76	0.46	-0.43
4. Professionals	0.74	0.65	0.25	0.11	-0.32	0.58	-0.27	0.01	0.57	1.06	-0.07	0.58	0.76	0.24	0.95	0.11
5. Abortion	-0.09	-1.10	-0.96	-0.72	-1.08	-0.50	-0.17	-0.50	-0.73	-0.80	-0.89	0.39	-0.73	-0.76	-0.81	-0.68
6. Public Health	-0.20	0.09	0.92	-0.03	0.22	1.05	0.63	0.92	0.69	-0.24	0.31	0.36	-0.11	0.51	0.18	0.26
7. Disease #1	-0.75	-0.89	0.72	1.01	-0.43	0.03	-0.76	-0.41	-0.50	-0.68	-0.48	-0.60	0.05	-0.21	-0.48	0.63
8. Research	-1.55	-1.11	-0.62	1.01	-0.84	-0.28	-0.90	0.13	-0.72	-0.76	-0.41	-0.82	-0.79	-0.46	-0.45	-0.36
9. Disease #2	-1.09	-0.65	0.40	0.03	-0.73	-0.40	-0.42	-0.80	-0.94	-0.65	-0.70	-0.74	-0.71	0.91	-0.20	-0.34
10. Disease #3	-0.00	-1.08	-0.48	0.46	-0.24	-0.87	-0.74	-0.55	-1.01	-0.70	1.04	-0.39	-0.01	-0.76	-0.58	-0.44
11. Drug Industry	-0.49	-0.28	0.07	0.84	-0.55	-0.80	-0.28	0.58	-0.98	-0.45	-0.89	-0.44	1.85	0.27	-0.45	1.26
12. Food	-1.41	-0.53	-1.59	-1.03	-0.37	-1.24	-1.10	-0.60	-0.61	-0.94	-0.89	-0.74	-0.07	-0.76	-0.81	1.96
13. Government	0.67	1.33	1.39	1.68	1.04	2.02	1.69	1.16	2.14	1.77	1.91	2.12	2.19	2.03	1.02	3.38
14. Isolates	-0.69	-0.21	-1.46	-1.27	-0.02	-0.88	-0.76	0.05	-0.86	0.03	-0.66	-0.71	-0.63	0.02	-0.30	-0.64
Mean	3.16	2.56	2.53	2.21	2.04	2.00	1.97	1.82	1.77	1.64	1.59	1.57	1.56	1.37	1.09	0.84
S.D.	1.77	1.69	1.60	1.66	1.89	1.42	1.80	1.66	1.48	1.75	1.79	1.44	1.57	1.79	1.37	1.23

newable fuel issues; the PIRG-FTC duo has high interests in oil and gas deregulation and in the small oil issues; and the miscellaneous subset cares strongly only about renewable fuels. Among the remaining major issue publics, attention is somewhat more widely scattered but still confined mainly to issues that impinge most directly on their functional responsibilities. Thus, the oil public is most concerned about big and small oil, automobile, extraction-transport, deregulation, energy industry, and government role issues. The coal–natural gas public shares some particular interests with the oil public—extraction-transport, deregulation, energy industry, and government roles—but it substitutes coal and manpower training concerns for specific oil issues. The manufacturing–national executive public heavily emphasizes big oil, automobile, electrical, consumer, and oil-gas deregulation issues to the exclusion of other possible concerns. Finally, the large nuclear-electrical-environmental public, which the dendrogram in figure 4.8 reveals to be on the opposite branch from the other main publics, heavily invests itself in electrical, nuclear, and uranium issues, with a smaller concern for renewable fuels and manpower-training problems. Although these matters attract a few publics from the rest of the energy domain, without the involvement of the regulatory and railway publics, the nuclear group would have a unique constellation of interests.

In the health domain the government public, containing the secretary of HHS, spreads its attention across the broader health spectrum just as the energy regulatory group, containing the Energy Department, does in its domain. Another three health publics exhibit high levels of concern for more than half the health domain issues. The health professionals show strong interest in nine issues, concentrating most heavily on abuse, funding, drugs, cost containment, prevention, elderly care, education, public health, and veterans. The public health and the health finance publics both attend to nine issues revolving around medical funding, health costs, professional abuse, mental health, veterans, public health, prevention, and miscellaneous matters. At the other extreme, six of the 14 health publics devote themselves to two or fewer issues reflecting the organizational mandates of their members (e.g., the health research public concentrates solely on biomedical research; the food public gives high attention only to problems related to food additives).

Discussion

Our analysis has been lengthy and intricate, yet we have only sketched the contours of issue publics in national policy domains. Much of the exposition was perforce descriptive, since the concepts, their measures, and the applications to energy and health policy-making organizations had never been attempted before. In the absence of a strong theoretical model to guide the research, we were forced to take a more exploratory approach to identifying the structure of issue publics and their roles in organizing the exchange of policy information. The empirical findings point to several remarkably similar configurations in the two domains:

1. Domain policy issues are spatially distributed in a rim or circle pattern based on the levels of expressed interests by domain organizations.
2. A comparable rim structure obtains in the spatial arrangement of policy organizations based on similarities in their issue interest profiles.
3. Issue publics, defined as subsets of organizations with similar levels of interest in domain policy issues, often resemble subgovernments in embracing both public sector actors and private sector claimants, but they also tend to encompass organizations known to take opposing stances on the resolution of policy controversies.
4. Most issue publics concentrate on a relatively narrow range of policy issues; a few publics, however, maintain somewhat broader spans of high-level attention.

These striking similarities between the energy and health domains are all the more noteworthy in view of our original selection of these two arenas on the presumption that they would exhibit divergent patterns of social organization, given the relatively greater turbulence of policy making in the energy domain during the 1970s. Although differences in detail can be readily identified, the comprehensive structures noted here, and the ones that we will point out in subsequent chapters, suggest that much greater uniformity may prevail across a variety of national policy-making systems than we had initially suspected. The extent to which these convergent empirical findings represent typical features of national policy domain social organization must remain an open question until further experience with a broad set of policy arenas demonstrates their prevalence.

Although our interpretations are grounded in only two empirical instances of national policy domains, the consistency of these findings about issue publics emboldens us to offer here some speculations about basic principles of issue interest structure that may apply beyond the cases at hand. We focus particularly on the two-dimensional spatial arrangements of the issue publics shown in figures 4.10 and 4.11. The emergence of rim structures was anticipated from multiple-elite theories that argue for the preponderance of specialized policy actors that pursue narrowly focused objectives to the exclusion of a wider range of interests that might locate any of them at the center of the issue space. This formal structure appears to be supported by the findings, with the modification that the idiosyncratic interests of individual organizations create a sprawling shape rather than a concise point location for the issue public. The obvious next task is to uncover basic principles that could account for the location of particular issue publics in the overall circular configuration. Ideally, we would like to be able to specify some conditions that would lead to testable propositions, capable of verification or rejection when applied to other national policy domains. Without such a theory, we would be restricted to essentially idiographic explanations for every domain, perhaps grounded mainly in historical circumstances that uniquely determine the number and nature of issue publics and the relationships among them. Although we do not yet have enough depth of experience with policy domain analysis to generate a rigorous theory of the issue public space, we propose below an interpretation based on a generalization from the findings in energy and health.

The arrangement of health publics in figure 4.11 suggests two basic cleavages that tend to cross-cut one another. First, the lower left corner contains publics that tend to favor expansions of liberal welfare-state solutions to the provision of health care (including mental health), in contrast to the other sectors of the circle, which are occupied by actors more oriented toward private health care initiatives and retrenchment of federal involvement in health care funding. Second, the right side of the configuration is dominated by issue publics whose members are most concerned with basic scientific knowledge, whereas those on the left tend to be more involved with applications and delivery of health services. A parallel set of divisions can be detected, in figure 4.10, although they are overlaid by ecological factors inherent in the nature of energy production. The right side of the circle is dominated by publics based on traditional, territorially remote sites for energy production (oil, gas, and coal), while the left side contains the publics focused on diffused-site energy sources (nuclear-electrical and renewable fuels). Interestingly, the various publics concerned with matters of transporting remotely extracted fuels to ultimate consumption sites (e.g., railway, pipelines, and shipping) tend to be located in the middle. This territorial cleavage also represents a science-based differentiation of policy actors, as was noted above for the health domain. A second division, though less distinct than that observed in health, is between consumer groups (located mainly in the upper left sector) and producer groups (scattered elsewhere around the rim, although several manufacturing groups that might be considered energy consumers are nestled snugly between the oil and the coal-gas publics).

To the extent that these results are generalizable at an abstract level, we suggest two implications for cleavage structures that may be expected to emerge in other national policy domains. Most domains will contain some form of input-output cleavage, in which the primary producers of goods or providers of services could be contrasted with the publics consuming their "products." If sufficient care is taken to base the spatial analysis on a large number of domain issues, these differentiated actors are unlikely to be joined together in the same public. Rather, the producing interests and the consuming interests are likely to be arrayed in different, if not polarized, sectors. Conceivably, organizations whose focal concerns lie in the throughput activities of the domain (transportation, fabrication of products from raw materials, interfacing between producers and consumers) will be spatially located at intermediate positions, since they share sets of issues with both sectors.

The second principle of issue public cleavage would appear to fall along a scientific-technical knowledge dimension. Particularly in heterogeneous fields where both researchers and practitioners are pursuing their separate interests, differential attention can focus on funding, regulation, training, ethical standards, and the like. The result may be to contrast those publics most heavily invested in the creation of knowledge with those attending to its applications, as in the health domain, or to contrast publics relying on complex production methods with those using more traditional crafts approaches, as in the energy domain. In contrast to our present concern with what might be called the organization of issue attention among organizational participants according to how it reflects the underlying mode of functional or sectoral specialization in the production process, Chapter 12 will turn to a consideration of the organization of cleavages among participants with respect to the stability and predictability of their preferred policy options across issue topics (e.g., the degree to which actors express generalized support for or opposition to government regulation).

At this time we can offer only general implications from the empirical findings reported in this chapter. The exact nature of cleavages, the composition of issue public sectors, and the way in which the consumer-producer and the science-application dimensions become manifest in a particular policy domain will all be affected by the singular circumstances of given domains. Details will depend upon the unique historical contingencies of the time when observations are made. Despite our suggestions for underlying general principles that structure domain issue publics, no simple or mechanical substitute yet exists to replace painstaking and careful immersion in the particularities of a real domain. Without exposure to these facts, a researcher may overlook crucial nuances that render an interpretation credible and that illuminate situations that might otherwise remain obscure.

5

The Nature of Influence in Policy Domains

The two principal tasks of this chapter are at once theoretical and empirical. First, we review the manifold theoretical and empirical approaches to the study of influence in social systems of various sorts for what they can tell us about the fundamental issues to be taken into account in studying collective decision-making processes in the large systems of actors under discussion. Note is made of the fact that much of the most careful theoretical and empirical work to date has focused on influence processes in two-person (dyadic) interaction. Although theoretical generalization to the multiple-actor setting has been attempted by some, notably Parsons, much of the praxis—that is, the actual exercise of influence in such settings—has been left unspecified and unstudied. The probable complications arising from multiple actors who possess various bases and "amounts" of influence to support conflicting policy preferences (or courses of action) *and* who contend among themselves to be taken into account in the decision-making process have been largely glossed over in the literature. The lessons to be learned from this review of theory and research are many; but the central ones point to the essential nature of influence in large systems as being typically multidimensional in character and as involving questions about the *distribution* of influence among the relevant actors, the structure of *consensus* about this distribution, and the role of *trust* or adversarial power in according influence.

Our second major task is to apply these insights to a comparative study of

152

the two national policy domains. With the multitudes of consequential actors interested in diverse issues and events under study, the reader can readily appreciate the crucial role that the overarching pattern of differentiated influence among the actors can play in facilitating or hindering the tasks of collective decision making. Although we can construct only rough approximations of these two structures of influence with the empirical procedures employed, we hope to demonstrate the considerable power of these tactics in illuminating some of the more obscure corners of national policy making.

Some Theoretical Preliminaries

Banfield's (1961:3) definition of influence as the "ability to get others to act, think, or feel as one intends" provides a useful point of departure for our discussion. Influence, as a concept, has had a long but checkered history in the social sciences, due, perhaps, to the varying attractiveness of its associated intellectual baggage to theorists of different metatheoretical persuasions. Broadly speaking, theorists of power and social control are drawn from two rival but intimately interdependent traditions. Theorists taking their inspiration from the Marxian tradition have viewed with profound suspicion the subjectivist connotations of the term, quite evident in the definition above, with its often latent assumptions of the harmony of interests of the influencer and influencee. Instead, they prefer the more severe concept of power, with its accent on coercion and the subordination of some to the will and caprice of others who possess superior resources to enforce their wishes. Theorists adopting a more functionalist perspective on society that posits a broad harmony of interests undergirding the social order and that questions the capacity of naked coercion to secure compliance and cooperation over the long term have found the concept of influence to be more congenial to their theoretical preconceptions. More recently, both schools of thought have produced adherents of a middle ground that concedes some role to the importance of power *and* influence in explaining collective decision making (e.g., Lenski, 1966). It is to this *rapprochement* of the two perspectives that we hope to contribute.

Parsons' work (1963a; see also Weber, 1947) on the concept of influence as it refers to the process of societal integration is undoubtedly the most ambitious effort to clarify and generalize the analytic underpinnings of the term. Although by no means wholly successful in our view and that of others (see e.g., Baum, 1976; Coleman 1963; Janowitz, 1975; Luhmann, 1979), his work clearly identifies some of the central theoretical issues that must be considered in any serious discussion of influence and power as mechanisms of social control. The 1963 paper on influence was one of a series of papers (1963b, 1968) in which Parsons attempted to clarify, from a macrostructural institutional perspective, the distinctions among four media of societal integrative exchange: money, power, influence, and commitment. Although we do not think it necessary to adopt his entire theoretical apparatus as applied to society (see Parsons, 1961a), in which the paradigm of influence or control is embedded, we do find his discussion of the paradigm highly suggestive for our purposes.

Parsons claims that all the possible ways in which ego (the influencer) can attempt to influence the behavior of another (alter, or influencee) to conform to ego's wishes or intentions may be classified into one of four analytically defined, mutually exclusive modalities. These, in turn, are themselves defined by the intersection of two cross-cutting axes, depicted in figure 5.1. The first axis contrasts the influencer's manipulation of the influencee's own basic orientations to act with the manipulation of the situation in which the influencee finds himself. The second axis refers to whether the sanctions employed are positive or negative from the influencee's point of view. Taking the modes of situational manipulation first, we can speak of ego attempting to manipulate the situation in which alter finds himself in either a contingently positive or a negative way. That is, ego can offer rewards or *inducements* in order to get alter to do his bidding. If alter complies, ego must, of course, deliver the reward or face the prospect of noncompliance in the future because alter will no longer trust him to deliver on his promise. Alternatively, ego can threaten alter with negative sanctions (i.e., punishment) if he should fail to comply with ego's wishes. For Parsons, this contingent negative manipulation of alter's situation to coerce his compliance is the use of *power* in the narrow sense of the term. He notes further that it is an inherently unstable modality of control because if alter complies with ego's request, ego does what he promised to do—nothing. In contrast, positive manipulation imposes an obligation on ego to deliver on his promise each time compliance is elicited. In negative manipulation, alter is constantly tempted to treat ego's threat to punish him as mere bluff. The actual imposition of a negative sanction, then, is ipso facto evidence of the breakdown or failure of a power system to secure compliance.

Let us now turn from the two situational modalities of the exercise of control to the strategies involving ego's direct manipulation of alter—that is, the cases in which ego has influence on alter's actions because of *alter*'s prior orientations or commitments to the situation. In the positive manipulation of alter, alter accepts ego's directions as his own because of his positive belief or trust in ego's superior competence or other attributes that commend ego's suggestions for action as being worthy of being obeyed. For Parsons, the prototypical example of this modality of control is that of voluntary compliance with expert advice: for example, a teacher-student relationship wherein the student believes that the teacher's suggestions and directions are in the student's own best interests. Parsons designated this modality *persuasion* or *influence* as most narrowly construed and emphasized its crucial dependency on

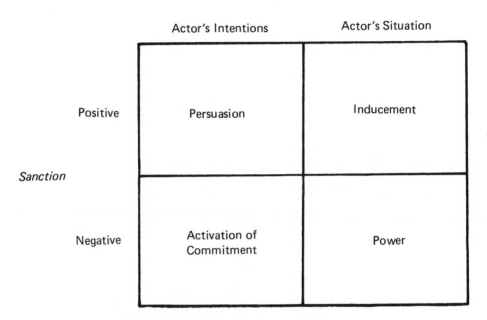

Figure 5.1. Parsons' Paradigm of Influence

the voluntary compliance of the influencee. The negative manipulation of alter by ego involves ego's explicit effort to activate alter's own preexisting commitments to behave in a certain way: for example, ego might point out to a publicly avowed civil libertarian that he should not purchase a house in a neighborhood that is known to discriminate against blacks and Jews attempting to purchase houses there. Note that ego must rely on alter's already being committed to certain orientations for the influence attempt to be successful.

Although the analytical distinctions among the four modalities are readily drawn, Parsons is fully aware that they are usually confounded in the empirical world because actors interested in getting their way are tempted to employ all means at their disposal to secure their ends. In perhaps his most provocative argument, however, he also observes that these modalities possess certain inherent functional incompatibilities that tend to reduce the effectiveness of their joint employment in given situations (see also Etzioni, 1961). For instance, since the use of power tends to engender alienation of the influencee from the influencer, its employment in conjunction with persuasion is likely to be counterproductive.

We have taken the time to review Parsons' argument in some detail because it so nicely exemplifies the complex and often contradictory ways in which the terms "influence" and "power" have been employed in sociological analysis. We are now in a better position to understand the reasons for the highly confused state of the scattered and noncumulative empirical literature devoted to the study of influence and control.

In the 1940s and 1950s, a spate of interesting social-psychological experimental studies, notably the work of Lewin and his associates and of Hovland and his associates (Lewin 1947; Hovland et al., 1953, 1957), explored various conditions affecting the relative efficacy of different techniques of communication and persuasion in modifying the opinions of naive experimental subjects. Considerable attention was devoted to learning, among other things, whether being the first or the last in making a persuasive argument or having an opinion supported by an authoritative, well-respected person or a despised and derogated one conferred relative advantage in modifying opinion over the short or longer term. These and related studies were systematized in an important theoretical synthesis by French and Raven (1959; see also Emerson, 1962). Though they are suggestive, there have, unfortunately, been no empirical studies that have successfully demonstrated the applicability of these carefully controlled and sometimes inconsistent experimental results to naturally occurring influence processes in the social world. Since our research is concerned with organizational actors rather than natural persons, the analytic leap from these studies to ours is even greater than it was for Parsons, who at least had in mind interactions between concrete individual actors. We are thus constrained to view this empirical work on the social psychology of persuasion as offering only a very suggestive analogy that may help us to identify interesting areas for further investigation. In fact, one of the major deficiencies of this tradition for our purposes is that the experimental studies take as given the external validity of the relative ranking of the influencers' influence. That is, reputed prestige differences among would-be opinion-molders are assumed on grounds of face validity before the experiment begins; the experimental studies, with this assumption in hand, only then proceed to examine the consequences of such differences on the influencees. Our problem, in contrast, is precisely to delineate the structure and nature of the influence order in the policy domains of health and energy and only then to examine its consequences for collective decision making.

Another key feature of this tradition in social psychology is its almost exclusive preoccupation with the dyadic process between influencer and influencee. No attention is given to the possible impact of third parties on the outcome of given influence attempts. Since naturally occurring social systems of any interest almost always have a multiplicity of potential sources of influence that may be simultaneously activated with respect to one another, the experimental tradition's almost complete restriction to the two-party case makes the generalizability of its findings especially problematic.

Around the same time that the work in experimental social psychology was going forward, but without much regard to it, sociologists initiated an active research program devoted to studying community leadership and its impact on community decision making. Employing rather ill-defined procedures for identifying and asking "well-placed" informants to identify the reputed community influentials in Atlanta, Georgia, Hunter (1953) in his classic study described the institutional sectors from which they were recruited, their social interrelationships, and the impact of the leaders' preferences on selected community decisions. A flurry of community studies were undertaken in response to Hunter's initiative in efforts to confirm or to challenge his findings (see, e.g., Agger et al., 1964; Dahl, 1961; Gilbert, 1968).

These studies have been subjected to extensive criticism and evaluation (cf. Clark, 1968; Domhoff, 1977; Walton, 1966, 1970), which has resulted in substantial improvements in our understanding of the limitations of the methods employed and of the nature of community decision making more generally. Unfortunately, little progress has been made in our conceptualization and measurement of the structure of influence systems per se (for a notable exception, see Rossi, 1960). Most studies employing the usual reputational techniques to measure influence have adopted a very simplistic model of the underlying influence structure—namely, a simple unidimensional rank-ordering of the influentials on the basis of the number of votes they receive from "well-placed" judges, be they informants or actual members of the set of influentials themselves. Such an approach assumes the structure of influence to be nothing more than an expression of a linear rank-order of the influentials. Although conceiving of an influence hierarchy with many graded positions is a considerable conceptual and empirical advance over confining the analysis to simple asymmetric dyadic exchange, the investigator is still forced to work with an unnecessarily rigid and simplistic notion of the structure of influence.

Consider the case in which a collective decision-making system divides responsibility for issue resolution between two relatively autonomous subsets of actors who are specialized with respect to their membership in one of two policy subdomains (*A* or *B*). The actors empirically arrange themselves into two hierarchies, with a "most influential" actor in each sector and an associated set of actors interested in the policy subdomain who array themselves in a declining order of influence. A unidimensional ordering from the top-ranked to the bottom-ranked, as shown in Figure 5.2, will place the two influential actors in tied or adjacent top ranks, and the others will be intermixed in positions of progressively lower rank.

For an issue confronting policy subdomain *A*, however, the relative influence of an actor in *A* on its resolution should certainly count for more than that of a comparably ranked actor in *B*. Yet it is obvious that in the simple top-to-bottom rank-order of influence, one is constrained to treat two actors tied for a given influence rank as having approximately equivalent impact on the

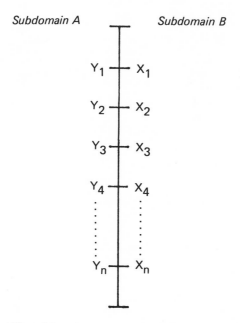

Figure 5.2. A Single Top-to-Bottom Ranked Array of Influentials

policy outcome. Notice how this difficulty can be overcome once one thinks of the structure of influence as multidimensional. In this approach, graphically depicted in Figure 5.3, the two top-ranked actors are located in the center of a dimension that arrays the lesser-ranked actors on their respective sides to reflect their subdomain membership. Issues especially relevant to one or the other subdomain will naturally elicit different rank-orderings of relevant influentials who are activated to resolve them.

Influence, then, is a compound concept when applied to the empirical world in the sense that the grounds (or bases of influence) upon which actors attribute influence to others are manifold in character. An actor may accord influence to another, for example, on the narrow grounds that his special expertise or some other exceptional quality (Weber, 1947, speaks of charisma in this context) allows him to speak authoritatively on matters of common concern, or that he is capable of arguing the merits of a case in a way that articulates or clarifies the influencee's own conception of his stake in a given issue. Or, an actor may take into account the influencer's potential control over valued inducements—such as money, votes, or personnel—that could be advantageously committed, on the one hand, to his or others' purposes, or, on the other hand, to the punishment of those who fail to comply with his wishes. Indeed, as Gamson (1966) observed, even a widely perceived reputation for

Figure 5.3. A Center-Periphery Structure of Influence

influence can itself serve as a basis of influence. Empirical judgments of relative influence among a set of actors inevitably must combine in complex ways all these varied bases of control into summary judgments of the relative consequentiality of given actors for particular issue-resolving deliberations. Such judgments are essential for the various parties to make because they help to orient them to the decision-making process and to organize the sorts of responses believed to be appropriate to support or counter different influence attempts. (See Laumann and Pappi, 1976: chap. 11, and Marsden and Laumann, 1977, for extended discussions of the differential relevance of various influence resources in different community controversies.)[1]

We shall argue further that there are two faces of influence. On the one hand, the structure of influence is fundamentally implicated in the structure of consensus among the relevant actors about who counts or does not count in given policy arenas. The extent and character of this consensus is central to understanding how influence is effective in resolving disagreements over what to do in specific situations. This recognition of the intimate ties between the operation of influence, narrowly or broadly conceived, and the overarching consensus among even contending parties led Parsons (1963a, 1968), Coleman (1963), Luhmann (1979) and others (e.g., Gamson, 1968) to stress the significance of *trust* in influence systems.

Consensus may be either partial or general. If general, then the structure of influence is unambiguously perceived and constitutes a firm framework for organizing influence efforts. Note here, however, that general consensus on who the influential actors are does not prejudge or determine the actual form of the distribution of influence among the relevant actors. That is, general consensus may exist that all the parties are equally influential and thus that their views must be accorded equal weight in deciding what is to be done.

1. Let us emphasize here what has been implicit in our argument: namely, that recognition of an actor's influence in an issue arena by no means implies that all the actors according that recognition necessarily agree with the actor's preferences. The differentiation of influence standing simply identifies those who will be seriously taken into account in collective deliberations about what shall be done. Certain influentials may just as easily serve as negative, rather than positive, reference points for the formation of an influencee's opinions.

Such would be the situation for a collegial deliberative assembly where all actors have an equal vote. Alternatively, there may be general consensus that certain actors enjoy preponderant influence over certain issues, whereas the views of others are of negligible significance. One can imagine many other distributions of influence between these extremes.

Partial consensus implies one of several possibilities. First, it may mean that only subsets of actors agree on who counts in their deliberations and that there are, as a result, discontinuities in the overarching decision-making system that must be bridged by other mechanisms for resolving disputes between subdomains. If the condition of partial consensus does not organize itself even into systemic pockets of consensus, as in the first instance, but reflects a diffuse or generalized lack of agreement among the parties on who matters, then we confront a situation of anarchy and systemic incapacity to resolve any dispute. The Lebanese polity for the past decade exemplifies this situation, as did the U.S. national energy policy domain during the 1970s.

The second face of influence has at least two features of interest: the *constituency* of actors who accord influential standing to given actors and the degree to which the various influentials in an influence system share common constituencies. Consider the case of a small minority of actors who attract the lion's share of positive judgments about their relative influence. On the one hand, one can imagine a situation in which all the participants name the same set of actors as the influentials—here we note that consensus is general and focused on common objects. On the other hand, one can conceive of a situation where a small number of actors attract comparable numbers of deference votes, but each from completely disjoint sets of voters: that is, their respective constituencies do not overlap or intersect. Here consensus is partial but systematically organized. The dynamics of influence processes will surely differ substantially in the two situations. In the first situation, we might expect an elite group to emerge that, once it has decided on a course of action within itself, could anticipate that its wishes would be readily accepted by all the other actors in the system. In the second situation, however, we might expect division into a number of wrangling factions, none of which could expect to speak authoritatively for the system as a whole without the expressed consent of the diversely supported leaders. There is simply no overlapping constituency ready to mediate the various leaders' initiatives.

It is important to note here that consensus and trust are not interchangeable terms, but analytically independent concepts that refer to quite different phenomena. A group may have widespread consensus on "who counts" among themselves but at the same time lack trust in that group of influentials. Conversely, individual actors may come to trust implicitly certain others in whom they repose complete confidence and regard, yet the actors collectively may lack consensus on whom they trust. Figure 5.4 lays out some of the possibilities for the interplay of collective trust and consensus in influence systems.

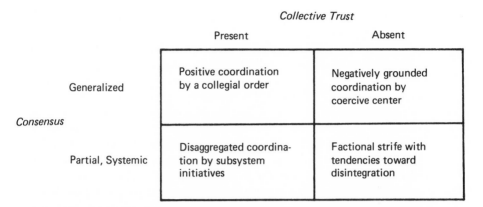

Figure 5.4. Alternative Influence Structures Arising from Different Patterns of Collective Trust and Consensus

In sum, the distribution of influence may be organized in any number of ways. There are the obvious polar contrasts of egalitarian distributions versus those which give a monopoly of influence to one actor whose preferences define the options considered. In addition, there are the cases of complex differentiations of influence among subdomains wherein it is readily recognized that certain actors have special competencies for certain types of issues and that their views should thus count for more than those of people with little or nothing to do with those areas. In such circumstances, one could have multiple leaders who are influential in their respective domains but whose influence is not convertible into domains other than those in which they are regarded as competent.

This discussion, we think, begins to suggest some lines of inquiry and measurement that would profitably expand our analysis of influence by directing attention to two fundamental issues. On the one hand, if it is true that influence depends essentially upon the willingness of other parties to go along with the preferences of an influencer, the issue of consensus becomes critical. That is, to what extent is there a shared perception of who matters or counts in a particular decision situation or more generally? Note here that we are emphasizing the notion of influence as in an important sense *apart from* the realities of institutionally legitimated power, or the right to make binding decisions for others. A decision-making system may assign to certain individuals the right to make binding decisions for others—for example, a congressional committee may be handed responsibility to screen certain proposed health policy initiatives. The members of this committee may not themselves have any special expertise in the matter; their membership arises from extraneous considerations of committee assignment in the House or Senate as a whole. Once on the committee, however, a member enjoys a power base that rests upon his or her right to cast a vote that is binding at critical points in the decision process. It is in this context that influence attempts will be directed toward the member to bring his or her opinion in line with that of the influencer.

But this right to vote—an institutionalized power category in Parsons' approach because it confers the ability to make binding collective decisions—also comes to serve as a basis of influence in the wider system as well. An actor with this power becomes by that fact alone an individual to reckon with, one whose views must be taken into account in other actors' deliberations about what to do to bring about a particular preferred outcome. Powerful actors thus inevitably come to be regarded as influentials in their own right, often coming to possess influential standing on issues quite outside the circumscribed arena in which they hold institutionalized power. Because influence, when effective, operates as the medium of exchange that ties the various disparate elements of a decision-making process together, an inherent feature of influence is its capacity for generalizing from its locus of origin (in specialized expertise, an institutionalized power to decide, or what have you) and achieving ramifying impact on the system as a whole. This generalizing feature typically occurs in ill-defined and poorly understood ways within a given system of influence. It is precisely this essentially unpredictable process of generalization that enables influence to perform its role of systemic integration. That is, it functions to facilitate system integration because no one participating in the system can readily define and agree with others on the precise limits of its applicability and relevance in particular situations. The distribution of power and influence in a given system of collective decision making becomes fully interpenetrated over time.

The Structure of Consensus and Influence in the Energy and Health Policy Domains

With these theoretical preliminaries firmly in mind, we shall illustrate our general argument and propose a methodology for investigating the structure of consensus and influence by analyzing the data we have in hand on the two policy domains. It is useful to recall here that for all practical purposes, we have enumerated and interviewed the entire *population universe* of consequential organizations active in the two policy domains.

After a lengthy discussion in the interview regarding the individual organization's participation in a wide spectrum of energy (or health) issues and its relationships with a variety of organizations active in such matters, we asked the informant the following question (C10a):

As we have indicated, all the organizations on this list are very active and important in the national energy (health) policy area. But we would now like you to check those organizations which stand out as *especially* influential and consequential in formulating national energy [health] policy. (See Appendix B for the complete interview schedule.)

The respondent could "vote" for as many organizations as he or she deemed appropriate. The followup probe (C10b) asked:

Are there any other organizations not on the list that are influential and consequential in formulating national energy [health] policy? Please tell me the names of these organizations.

As mentioned in Chapter 3, no organization that was not on our list received more than four nominations from our respondent organizations.

The first step in analyzing data of this sort is to rank-order the organizations according to the number of votes they received from their colleagues. Since the total number of votes cast by organizations in the energy domain was 9,155 (there were 6,090 in the health domain),[2] any given organization in the energy domain would receive 40.2 votes (37.1 in the health domain) if votes were cast in a random fashion. Such a result is not observed, of course, because of the enormous concentration of votes among relatively few actors. (See Appendix A for a listing of all the organizations, together with the number of votes they received for influential standing (column 3) and the data we employed in selecting organizations to be included.)

The five externally generated pieces of information about organizations listed in Chapter 3 might reasonably be construed as independent evidence for the relative efforts of these organizations to influence national decision making on energy or health policy. They are by no means precisely equivalent or alternative measures of influence standing, because they tap primarily publicly visible efforts at influence and ignore the more informal and subtle modes of exerting influence. Yet one would certainly expect some positive correlation with the number of votes an organization receives. And this is exactly what we find.

Although there is an obvious relationship between the publicity that organizations received in the national press in some one thousand energy articles between 1977 and 1980 and their consequentiality among the active organizations, the linear correlation (Pearson's r) with influence rank is only $-.55$ for energy and $-.50$ for health. The correlation between the influence score (the

2. The average respondent organization in the energy domain cast 50.3 votes (and 46.8 votes in the health domain). This means that roughly 22.1 percent of the target organizations in energy (or 28.5 percent in health) were perceived as falling into the upper tier of a two-tiered influence structure. By analyzing the patterning of the votes, however, we can elicit a far more differentiated view of the structure of influence.

number of votes) and the frequency of appearances before some 450 congressional energy subcommittee hearings (or 153 health subcommittee hearings) during the same period has the same magnitude: $r = -.52$ with influence rank and $+.60$ with "votes" ($r = -.55$ with influence rank and $+.65$ with "votes" in the health domain).[3] The correlation between the influence rank and the number of *amicus curiae* briefs filed is $-.30$ in the energy domain and $-.38$ in the health domain; with "votes," $r = .36$ (energy) and .42 (health).

Table 5.1 displays the results of the regression of influence rank and votes on the number of news articles, hearings, and *amicus curiae* briefs filed by policy domains. Inspection of the standardized regression coefficients for health reveals that "hearings" is a substantially stronger predictor of influence rank and votes than "news articles" or "court cases," achieving more than twice the value of the latter two standardized coefficients.[4] This implies that, in this domain, active participation in the congressional arena of decision making is the most significant factor in achieving influence; newspaper notori-

3. The correlation between the number of votes and number of articles was $+.60$ for energy and $+.50$ for health. Note should be made of the fact that the number of news articles and number of hearings in the energy domain correlate only .31 (and .46 in the health domain). (Correlations here are based on 167 nonfederal organizations in the energy domain and 115 nonfederal organizations in the health domain.)

4. We also examined the impact of two other predictors on influence standing. The first, "mentions," refers to the number of times an organization was mentioned as being in frequent contact with one or another of 23 executive agencies or legislative committees by the highest-level bureaucrat (Senior Executive Service) administering an energy-related agency or the senior legislative aide of an energy-related committee of the House or Senate (there were 20 such agencies or legislative committees for the health domain). This information was secured during a study of Washington representatives undertaken by Laumann and three collaborators (John P. Heinz, Robert Salisbury, and Robert Nelson) that complements the research reported here (Laumann and Heinz, 1985). As part of their larger study, personal interviews were sought in July 1982 with the principal administrators of the most important agencies and congressional committees setting policy in these two domains (and two others, labor and agriculture, unrelated to the present study). During the course of the interview, the respondent was asked to name the nongovernmental organizations with which he or she most frequently had contact on policy-setting matters over the past three or four years.

The second predictor variable examined, "listed," refers to whether or not an organization appears in the *Directory of Washington Representatives* (1982 edition). (Since about 80 percent of the organizations we identified are found in this directory, it is not expected that "listing" will have much predictive value for relative influence standing.) As individual predictors in the energy domain, "mentions" and "listed" are correlated $-.47$ and $-.17$ respectively with influence ranks and .61 and .17 respectively with votes. For the health domain, "mentions" and "listed" are correlated $-.34$ and $-.21$ respectively, with influence ranks, and .37 and .16, respectively with votes. Thus, even though these two variables refer to a time period well into the Reagan presidency and some time after the focal period of the original study, we nevertheless observe a substantial correlation, particularly of "mentions," with the influence rank order. We take this as further evidence of our success in delimiting the relevant sets of active influentials in these policy domains.

Table 5.1. Regression Analysis of Influence Rank and Votes for the Energy and Health Domains by Hearings, News Articles, and Court Filings

Dependent Variable	Independent Variables				
	Constant	Hearings	News Articles	Court	R^2
A. ENERGY DOMAIN					
1. Unstandardized Coefficients					
Influence Rank	179.9**	−3.02**	−6.04**	−4.00	0.45**
Votes	7.74*	1.55**	2.79**	3.07	0.57**
2. Standardized Coefficients					
Influence Rank		−0.39**	−0.43**	−0.04	
Votes		0.45**	0.45**	0.08	
B. HEALTH DOMAIN					
1. Unstandardized Coefficients					
Influence Rank	134.2††	−2.96††	−2.33	−12.04†	0.37††
Votes	1.48	2.05††	2.00†	7.49†	0.52††
2. Standardized Coefficients					
Influence Rank		−0.42††	−0.15	−0.20†	
Votes		0.49††	0.22†	0.21†	

* $p \leq .0002$

** $p \leq .0001$

† $p \leq .005$

†† $p \leq .001$

ety or judicial intervention is of lesser consequence. Substantively, these results make good sense. The dominant policy issue in health for the 1970s has been the levels of public funding for health care.[5] Congress, the final appropriator of such funds, becomes the critical arena for resolving the debate over relative funding levels.

5. For example, the rate of increase over the decade in hospital costs, a major component of overall health costs, has been truly phenomenal. In the United States, hospital expenditures were $27.8 billion (or $133 per capita) in 1970. They rose to $99.6 billion ($430 per capita) in 1980, and, barring major changes in the health care system, are expected to reach $334.6 billion ($1,350 per capita) by 1990 (Freeland et al., 1980; Gibson and Waldo, 1981). The share of national health expenditures devoted to hospital care has also risen from 37.2 percent in 1980 to 40.3 percent in 1980, and it is projected to be 44.1 percent in 1990.

For the energy domain, the relative sizes of the standardized coefficients suggest that "hearings" and "news articles" have substantial and equivalent impact on the number of votes received, whereas the number of *amicus curiae* briefs filed appears to have negligible impact. The dividends in influence standing from active efforts to influence public opinion at large are as rich as those from more targeted efforts to influence Congress, but efforts to influence judicial decision making are of little consequence. This interpretation also makes good sense. The energy domain has been afflicted with a veritable deluge of issues to resolve in the past decade, ranging from fundamental constitutional questions relating to the best ways for the federal government and private enterprise to set national energy policy to myriad conflicting regulatory issues (such as environmental protection versus cost/benefit balances) that have been raised by apparent changes in the availability of reliable sources of energy. The arenas for resolving these disputes are thus widely dispersed throughout government and private spheres of action, and even popular mobilization around proposed solutions becomes a matter of grave concern. Recall, for example, Carter's direct appeals to the nation on the energy crisis in order to mobilize support for his various initiatives, notably the establishment of a Department of Energy.[6]

With slightly less than half of the influence vote variance unexplained by the additive effects of the three initial measures we used to identify the core actors, considerable room remains for other factors to account for influence standing scores. The substantial unexplained residuals also give credence to the notion that other, more informal and less publicly documented processes of influence than those tapped by our public measures of influence attempts play critical roles in formulating and resolving policy disputes.

6. All these interpretations receive additional support from an inspection of the results of the four-variable regression equations that add "mentions," primarily tapping influence attempts directed toward agencies in the executive branch, to predict influence standing. For the cross-domain comparisons, only the unstandardized coefficients are reported here.

	Constant	Hearing	News Articles	Court	Mentions	R^2
Energy votes	9.43**	1.01**	2.49**	3.24	7.32**	0.64**
Health votes	4.00	1.15**	1.78	7.25*	4.44	0.54**

**$p < 0.0001$
*$p < 0.0005$

As we can see, newspaper notoriety contributes more votes in the energy domain than the health domain. Yet "hearings" contributes more votes in the health than in the energy domain. Note also that when the "mentions" variable was added, R^2 for energy increased by 7 percent, and that for health by only 2 percent. Despite the fact that the data for the "mentions" variable were collected two years after the interview, the relative stability of each of the predictors is substantial, suggesting their relative robustness in structuring the influence order.

The Distribution of Influence

Our theoretical introduction pointed to the central significance of the distribution of influence in a social system for its conflict resolution and collective decision making. Surely systems of decision making with a high concentration of influence should function rather differently from those where influence is broadly distributed among the population of relevant actors, who are themselves further differentiated with respect to their preferred policy solutions. The former situation would be congenial to decisive resolution of issues, and even radical changes of course are possible if the central actors are convinced of their wisdom. The latter situation, in contrast, would characterize a pluralized system of collective decision making that might find it difficult to resolve issues in a definitive manner and that would thus tend to prefer compromised and negotiated agreements leading to at best incremental changes over time (cf. Clark, 1968; Lindblom, 1959, 1977; Wildavsky, 1964).

A key empirical question is how to measure the relative amount of influence "possessed" by individual actors with respect to its efficacy or relevance in specific domains of action. We have asserted that influence, almost by definition, possesses a vague and ambiguous quality that varies in its perceived attribution by actors differently circumstanced in the system of action and rests on a multitude of possible foundations (i.e., influence bases). (See Chapter 6 for a more extended discussion of the different resource bases of influence.) In some important sense it is unmeasurable theoretically because its very efficacy in contributing to the coordination of actors' behavior depends on its relative unpredictability of activation and significance of impact on the actions of others. That is, actors may or may not take one another into account in their calculations of whether to do X or Y because they are often uncertain about whether doing so will have positive or negative consequences for what they themselves seek.

Such considerations imply that we cannot expect to develop a strong ratio or interval metric scaling of the influence-ordering of a system of action. Such scaling would be both theoretically and empirically inappropriate—in fact, impossible. We can, however, expect to capitalize on the participants' capacities to discriminate at least roughly between those actors who are especially likely to count in their and others' calculations and those who may be taken less seriously. The degree to which given actors attract positive recognition of their influence and the relative consensus about who matters can give us important clues to the distribution of influence. If we have successfully bounded the relevant set of actors in a policy domain by the procedures we used to identify them, then we can use the distribution of votes across this set of actors as a fair approximation of the extent to which influence is concentrated or dispersed.

Table 5.2 provides a first view of influence dispersion in the two domains by

Table 5.2. The Distribution of Influence Votes across Ranked Quintiles of Organizations

	Number of Votes Cast	Target N	Percent of Votes Cast	Percent Governmental Organizations
A. ENERGY DOMAIN[a]				
Top Quintile	4,294	45	46.9	64.4
Second Quintile	2,392	46	26.1	35.6
Middle Quintile	1,411	48	15.4	22.9
Fourth Quintile	730	44	8.0	4.2
Bottom Quintile	328	45	3.6	0.0
Total	9,155	228	100.0	25.6
B. HEALTH DOMAIN[b]				
Top Quintile	2,999	34	49.0	82.3
Second Quintile	1,721	33	28.1	36.4
Middle Quintile	919	34	15.4	26.5
Fourth Quintile	362	32	5.9	0.0
Bottom Quintile	89	31	1.6	0.0
Total	6,090	164	100.0	29.9

[a] N = 182 respondents
 Average votes cast per respondent = 50.3
 Average votes per target = 40.2

[b] N = 130 respondents
 Average votes cast per respondent = 46.8
 Average votes per target = 37.1

cumulating the number of votes cast for each quintile of organizations (ranked as in Appendix A). In both domains nearly half the votes are cast for organizations in the highest quintiles (a random distribution of votes, of course, would direct only one-fifth of the votes to this category). Although there is a remarkable similarity between the domains on the percentage distribution of votes cast (column 3), there are some hints that the energy domain's influence distribution is somewhat more dispersed (or less concentrated) than the health domain's. Noteworthy also is the substantially higher proportion of government organizations found in the top quintile of the health domain than in the energy domain (82.3 percent versus 64.4 percent; column 4), suggesting again that the health domain's policy making is more formally constituted and managed by governmental actors than is the energy domain.

Figure 5.5 provides a more detailed picture of the unequal distribution of influence votes in the two domains by plotting Lorenz curves of the cumulative proportions of ranked organizations against the cumulative proportions of votes cast. Compare in particular the relative rate of decline of the curves for the top quintiles at the righthand side of the figure (see Schwartz and Winship, 1979), which suggests that the health domain has a somewhat more concentrated distribution at the top than the energy domain does.[7] However, the Gini Indexes for the two curves, measuring the degree of departure from the line of perfect equality, are comparable (.44 and .48, respectively) and reflect relatively concentrated distributions of influence.

The Multidimensional Nature of Influence

Our introductory discussion further suggested that the distribution of influence in a system, contrary to the customary assumption of a unidimensional rank-order, might take a multidimensional form because of systematic differences in the multiple vantage points from which individual actors view the policy domain in action and because of the multiple bases upon which influence may be founded and assessed. To explore the dimensionality of influence in the two policy domains, we turned to a multidimensional scaling analysis of the patterns of influence voting. There are two points of view from which to assess the patterning of voting for influentials: that of the constituency (how similar or different are the sets of actors who vote for particular organizations or targets as being especially influential), and (2) that of consensus (how similar or different the views of the influence order are for each possible pair of voters).

---

7. Schwartz and Winship (1979) observe that when two Lorenz curves do not cross, the Gini Index may be a good measure for comparing the relative degree of inequality between two population distributions. When they do cross, however, the Gini coefficient cannot test whether one distribution has more equality than another. In our case, the two Lorenz curves for health and energy organizations cross each other approximately at the 80th percentile, reflecting the fact that the relative inequality of the two distributions at the bottom is different from that at the top. In such circumstances, Schwartz and Winship suggest that Atkinson's measure of inequality is one of the best measures. Unfortunately, the Atkinson method poses the question of how to select values of e. Since it is beyond the scope of this chapter to analyze our data using a wide range of e values, a procedure recommended by Schwartz and Winship, we adopted the expedient of calculating the standard deviation of the logarithm of votes (SDL) (assigning a value of 0.25 to 0 votes) to supplement the Gini Index as a measure of inequality. This measure is very sensitive to the inequality at the bottom end of the distribution. A comparison of the SDLs, 1.00 for energy and 1.32 for health, reveals that the health distribution at the bottom end is much more unequal than the energy distribution. We are cognizant of the serious defects of the SDL measure enumerated by Schwartz and Winship, but believe it has some utility as a descriptive statistic in this particular situation.

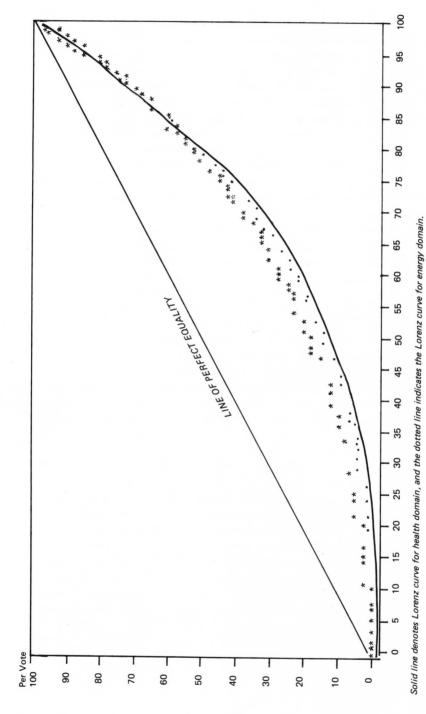

Solid line denotes Lorenz curve for health domain, and the dotted line indicates the Lorenz curve for energy domain.

Figure 5.5. Lorenz Curve for the Distribution of Influence Votes in the National Policy Domains of Energy and Health

Constituency. Consider the data on influence voting as arrayed in an *m* by *n* matrix in which the *m* rows are the choosers (or respondent organizations), the *n* columns are all the targeted organizations for whom the respondent organizations may vote, and the cell entries are either *1* for a vote or *0* for a nonvote. The column total indicates the total number of votes cast for a particular organization (Appendix A, column 3). The specific set of respondent organizations who voted for a given target organization can be called the *constituency* of the target. The first question that naturally arises concerns the varying degrees to which the different target organizations share common constituencies. Among the organizations receiving the most votes—the so-called core influential organizations—it obviously makes considerable difference to the dynamics of the influence process if all receive their votes from essentially the same constituency—that is, all are acknowledged as the central or core influentials to be taken into account by most of the relevant participants—or, in the extreme contrast, if they enjoy recognition of their influential standing by essentially disparate (or relatively nonoverlapping) constituencies. In the latter case, core organizations can be regarded as representing structurally differentiated constituencies or segregated parts of the policy domain. The former situation reflects a potentially more integratively coordinated system of influence in which the participants as a whole, however differentiated their individual interests may be, concede generalized leadership positions to a common core of actors.

But how can we measure constituency overlap and examine its overall organization in the policy domain? We propose, first, simply to count the number of times a given pair of target organizations both received votes or failed to get votes from all the actors casting votes. Operationally, we simply count the number of matched cell entries, either *1*s or *0*s, in every pairing of columns in the matrix described above. Recalling that there is a fixed number of votes (equal to the total number of respondents) in a domain, we can calculate the percentages of overlapping agreement (of both positive votes and nonvotes) between all the constituencies. The average percentage of constituency agreement in the energy domain is 70 percent; in the health domain, 63. These high average levels of constituency agreement in both domains are not really surprising because of the systematic disparities in the numbers of votes cast for the influential organizations. If an organization has by chance factors alone a 20 percent chance of attracting a vote from a given voter (and, of course, an 80 percent chance of failing to get that vote), then for a pair of organizations subject to these chance probabilities, there is a $(.20)(.20) + (.80)(.80)$, or 68 percent, probability of constituency overlap due to chance.

We are, of course, more interested in the amount of constituency overlap among the most influential organizations in the respective domains because it will give us at least a clue about the degree to which the two domains' core influentials attract differentiated constituencies. Looking somewhat arbitrarily at the top 10 organizations in each domain, we observe that the average constituency overlap between the top 10 organizations in the energy domain is 66.0 percent, whereas it is substantially higher in the health domain (75.1 percent). Just as the Lorenz curves depicted in Figure 5.5 (and their associated Gini and SDL indexes) suggested that the health domain has a slightly more concentrated (or unequal) distribution of influence, the higher average percentage of constituency agreement among the most influential organizations in health suggests that there is a less pluralized or constituency-specific set of leaders in the health domain. Coordination of policy formulation and implementation should thus be less controversial and adversarial in the health than in the energy domain. We shall test this inference in subsequent chapters when we examine more systematically actor participation in attempts to influence events in energy or health.

More direct tests of the differentiation of constituencies among these elite organizational actors can be devised. Suppose, for instance, that we assign the voters to one of n mutually exclusive clusters of organizations, membership in which is determined by their shared interests in specified domain issues according to the procedures described in Chapter 4. We can then ask whether these clusters substantially differ among themselves with respect to the number of votes they cast for specific target organizations. That is, a target organization lacking a differentiated constituency, as defined by these differences in expressed interests in domain issues, should attract approximately equal levels of support from all the clusters. To test the significance of the differences among observed proportions, we can then calculate a one-way analysis of variance for each target organization in each domain. Table 5.3 summarizes these results for the 10 most influential organizations in each domain and indicates the clusters which were over- or underrepresented in given constituencies.

For the health domain the AMA and the AHA both selectively recruit their constituencies from the issue-defined clusters of voters, as do the White House Office and the Edison Electric Institute in the energy domain. Can we identify some overarching general principle that might account for such splits in constituency support in the two domains? We think we can: the axis of cleavage in both domains appears to be between producers and consumers. Our analysis of issue publics in Chapter 4 found that the AMA was clustered with organizations representing various health professionals, sometimes called health care providers, whereas the AHA belonged to an issue public predominantly concerned with health insurance issues—in other words, with problems of payment for services rendered. Similarly, we found in the energy domain that the White House Office was clustered with organizations primarily concerned with the end-use costs of energy—notably manufacturing organizations like the automobile and chemical industries and economic enterprise more generally—whereas the Edison Electric Institute was clustered with the utilities: that is, the producers or suppliers. In short, certain key influentials in both domains are differentially attractive to constituencies on the basis of whether they are more concerned with supply-side or demand-side issues with respect to the products (health care services or energy) of their respective production systems.

The alert reader, of course, may well object that the procedure we used cannot definitely establish the *absence* of a differentiated constituency for given targets. One could propose many other substantively meaningful groupings of organizations—for example, public versus private sector organizations—that might, in fact, identify differential voting patterns toward the targets. The results reported in table 5.3 merely help us evaluate the narrow question whether the differentiation in organizations' expressed interests in the policy domain organizes constituency preferences. In defense of this approach, we can only argue that expressed interest differentiation strikes us as an especially important theoretical and substantive basis for structuring constituency differences.

Fortunately, we do not have to leave the issue of constituency differentiation at this unsatisfactory, somewhat ad hoc juncture. By taking a more systematic look at the differences between target organizations' constituencies, we can determine the presence of uni- or multidimensional bases of constituency differentiation. Obviously, at the very minimum, there must be unidimensional differentiation of constituencies because the organizations vary so widely with respect to the number of votes they attract. Whether there is a multidimensional differentiation of the constituencies as well, and what the nature of that differentiation is, are more provocative questions.

To answer such questions, we turn to multidimensional scaling—specifically the Alternating Least Squares Scaling (ALSCAL) algorithm programmed by Forrest Young in the SAS package. As the first step, we calculated all the possible pairwise percentages of constituency agreement among the target organizations for each policy domain. The resulting symmetric matrix of pairwise percentages of constituency agreement can be regarded as estimators of the relative proximities of organizations to one another. These proximities are to be embedded by the computer routine into the smallest number of dimensions in a Euclidean space consistent with an acceptable "goodness of fit" between the original proximity estimates and the computer-derived Euclidean interpoint distances. The resulting graphic representation of the Euclidean space provides a "picture" of the original data matrix such that points (representing given organizations' locations) in close proximity are known to have highly overlapping constituencies (i.e., high percentages of pairwise constituency agreement), and points at greater distances from one another have lower levels of constituency agreement.

Table 5.3. The Differentiation of Constituencies among the 10 Most Influential Organizations in National Energy and Health Policy

Organization	Percent of Total Possible Votes Received	Significance Level	Interest Groups Overvoting for Target	Interest Groups Undervoting for Target
A. TOP TEN MOST INFLUENTIAL ORGANIZATIONS IN THE NATIONAL ENERGY DOMAIN				
1. Department of Energy	.83	N.S.	--	Pipe Lines[a]
2. The White House Office	.81	.03	--	--
3. American Petroleum Institute	.78	N.S.	--	--
4. Office of Management and the Budget (OMB)	.77	N.S.	--	--
5. Senate Committee on Energy and Natural Resources--Democrats	.76	N.S.	--	--
6. Senate Committee on Energy and Natural Resources--Republicans	.73	N.S.	--	--
7. American Gas Association	.68	N.S.	--	--
8. Edison Electric Institute	.66	.03	Nuclear and Electrical[b]	Pipe Lines[a]
9. Subcommittee on Energy and Power--Democrats (House Committee on Interstate and Foreign Commerce)	.64	N.S.	--	--
10. Exxon Corporation	.62	N.S.	--	--
B. TOP TEN MOST INFLUENTIAL ORGANIZATIONS IN THE NATIONAL HEALTH DOMAIN				
1. American Medical Association	.90	.02	--	Health Research[c] Targeted Disease #2[d]
2. Secretary, Department of Health and Human Services	.85	N.S.	--	--
3. Office of Management and the Budget (OMB)	.85	N.S.	--	--
4. The White House Office	.84	N.S.	--	--
5. Subcommittee on Health and Environment--Democrats (IFC Committee)	.78	N.S.	--	--
6. Subcommittee on Health--Democrats (Ways and Means)	.76	N.S.	--	--

7. Subcommittee on Labor, Health, Education, Welfare--Democrats (House Appropriations)	.75	N.S.		--
8. American Hospital Association	.73	.01	Finance[e]	--
9. Senate Subcommittee on Labor--Democrats (Appropriations Committee)	.70	N.S.		--
10. Senate Finance Committee--Democrats	.70	N.S.		--

[a]Includes Foothills Pipelines, Northern Tier Pipeline, National Transportation Safety Board, and Rocky Mountain Oil and Gas Association.

[b]Includes Allied General Nuclear Service, House on Energy Research and Production-D, Babcock and Wilcox, General Electric, American Nuclear Energy Council, Atomic Industrial Forum, Senate Subcommittee on Nuclear Regulation-Democrats, Nuclear Regulatory Commission, Senate Subcommittee on Nuclear Regulation-Republican, Critical Mass Energy Project, Environmental Coalition on Nuclear Power, Union of Concerned Scientists, Senate Subcommittee on Energy Research and Development-Democrats, General Atomic, Electric Power Research Institute, Rockwell International, Office of Science and Technology, House on Energy Research and Production-Republicans, National Science Foundation, Combustion Engineering, Houston Lighting and Power, Detroit Edison, Edison Electric Institute, Westinghouse, Northeast Utilities Service, Stone and Webster Engineering, Commonwealth Edison, General Public Utilities, Texas Utilities, American Public Power Association, National Association of Regulatory Utilities Commissioners, National Rural Electric Cooperative Association, American Electric Power Service, Virginia Electric and Power, Tennessee Valley Authority, Southern California Edison, National Electric Reliability Council, Consolidated Edison, Pacific Gas and Electric, Public Service Electric and Gas, KMS Fusion, Thermo-Electron, Utility Waste Management Group, State Planning Council on Radioactive Waste, Environmental Action, Natural Resources Defense Council, Sierra Club, Council on Environmental Quality, House on Energy and Environment-Democrats, House on Energy and Environment-Republicans, Environmental Policy Center, and National Academy of Sciences.

[c]Includes American Federation for Clinical Research, National Institute on Aging-NIH, National Institute of Neurological Communicative Disorders and Stroke-NIH, National Institute of General Medical Sciences-NIH, National Institute of Arthritis, Metabolism, and Digestive Diseases-NIH, American Society for Microbiology, National Cancer Institute-NIH, Society for Investigative Dermatology, National Institutes of Health, Director and Staff, Environmental Defense Fund, National Institute of Environmental Health Sciences-NIH, and American Association of Dental Schools.

[d]Includes American Gastroenterological Association, National Kidney Foundation, and Citizens for the Treatment of High Blood Pressure.

[e]Includes American Association of Retired Persons/National Retired Teachers Association, National Council of Senior Citizens, Washington Business Group on Health, Health Insurance Association of America, Health Care Financing Administration, Senate Subcommittee on Health-Democrats, House Subcommittee on Health-Republicans, Senate Subcommittee on Health-Democrats, House Subcommittee on Health-Republicans, Blue Cross and Blue Shield Associations, American Hospital Association, National Conference of State Legislatures, National Governors' Association, United Automobile Workers, Group Health Associations of America, Hospital Corporation of America, Federation of American Hospitals, America Health Care Association, and National Council of Health Care Services.

175

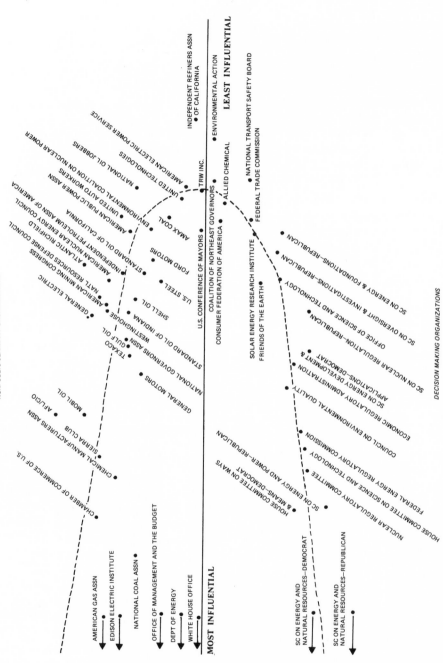

NONPUBLIC CLAIMANT ORGANIZATIONS

DECISION MAKING ORGANIZATIONS

MOST INFLUENTIAL

LEAST INFLUENTIAL

CHAMBER OF COMMERCE OF U.S.

SIERRA CLUB

CHEMICAL MANUFACTURERS ASSN

AFL/CIO

MOBIL OIL

GENERAL MOTORS

NATIONAL GOVERNORS ASSN

GULF OIL

TEXACO

STANDARD OIL OF INDIANA

WESTINGHOUSE

SHELL OIL

AMERICAN MINING CONGRESS

GENERAL ELECTRIC

NATL RESOURCES DEFENSE COUNCIL

ATLANTIC RICHFIELD

AMERICAN NUCLEAR ENERGY COUNCIL

INDEPENDENT PETROLEUM ASSN OF AMERICA

STANDARD OIL OF CALIFORNIA

AMERICAN PUBLIC POWER ASSN

UNITED AUTO WORKERS

ENVIRONMENTAL COALITION ON NUCLEAR POWER

U.S. STEEL

FORD MOTORS

AMAX COAL

UNITED TECHNOLOGIES

NATIONAL OIL JOBBERS

AMERICAN ELECTRIC POWER SERVICE

TRW INC.

U.S. CONFERENCE OF MAYORS

COALITION OF NORTHEAST GOVERNORS

CONSUMER FEDERATION OF AMERICA

ALLIED CHEMICAL

INDEPENDENT REFINERS ASSN OF CALIFORNIA

ENVIRONMENTAL ACTION

NATIONAL TRANSPORT SAFETY BOARD

FEDERAL TRADE COMMISSION

SOLAR ENERGY RESEARCH INSTITUTE

FRIENDS OF THE EARTH

SC ON ENERGY & INVESTIGATIONS—REPUBLICAN

SC ON OVERSIGHT & INVESTIGATIONS—REPUBLICAN

OFFICE OF SCIENCE AND TECHNOLOGY

SC ON NUCLEAR REGULATION—REPUBLICAN

SC ON ENERGY DEVELOPMENT & APPLICATIONS—DEMOCRAT

ECONOMIC REGULATORY ADMINISTRATION

COUNCIL ON ENVIRONMENTAL QUALITY

NUCLEAR REGULATORY COMMISSION

FEDERAL ENERGY REGULATORY COMMISSION

SC ON ENERGY AND TECHNOLOGY

HOUSE COMMITTEE ON SCIENCE AND TECHNOLOGY

HOUSE COMMITTEE ON WAYS & MEANS—DEMOCRAT

SC ON ENERGY AND POWER—REPUBLICAN

SC ON ENERGY AND NATURAL RESOURCES—DEMOCRAT

SC ON ENERGY AND NATURAL RESOURCES—REPUBLICAN

AMERICAN GAS ASSN

EDISON ELECTRIC INSTITUTE

NATIONAL COAL ASSN

OFFICE OF MANAGEMENT AND THE BUDGET

DEPT OF ENERGY

WHITE HOUSE OFFICE

Figure 5.6. Two-Dimensional Smallest-Space Representation of the Influence Structure in the Energy Domain: The Constituency View

Figures 5.6 and 5.7 provide the two-dimensional smallest-space solutions for the constituency structures of the national energy and health domains, respectively.[8] Turning first to the energy domain, we observe that the overall organization of the space can be seen to possess a cometlike structure, with the head of the comet containing a wide variety of low-ranked organizations distributed along a curved, but generally vertically oriented, axis.[9] The two halves of the comet's tail fall on roughly parallel lines along the horizontal axis, and the influential standings of organizations increase as one moves horizontally to the left of the diagram. In short, the horizontal axis roughly arranges the organizations according to their rank-order of influence. The lower half of the tail principally contains various public sector organizations, including House and Senate subcommittees and executive agencies possessing more and more specialized responsibilities in energy policy formulation; the order of influence declines as one moves to the right of the diagram. In contrast, the upper half principally contains private sector organizations, including corporations, trade associations, and public interest groups, who act as claimant organizations in support of or opposition to various policy initiatives, again generally arrayed in declining order of influence as one moves to the right of the space. The vertical axis thus sharply distinguishes between constituencies positively oriented to public sector organizations. The few organizations falling midway on the vertical axis at the lefthand side (including the White House Office and the Department of Energy) are sufficiently popular to attract votes from both sorts of actors; but as we have already noted with respect to the White House Office, they do not necessarily recruit votes in an unbiased fashion from these diverse sectors.

The particularly significant feature of this space is the fact that the tails do not bend back toward each other at the upper end of the influence order, contrary to what one might have expected. This feature of the spatial organization of constituency differentiation tells us that there is a generalized absence of agreement within this policy domain about which organizations really

8. There are 228 organizations mapped in the energy domain and 164 in the health domain, far too many to be labeled individually in the figures without rendering them incomprehensible. We have adopted the expedient of labeling only some of the points with the objective of highlighting the main features of the configurations of organizations.

9. The two-dimensional solution for the energy domain has a slightly high Kruskal stress coefficient of .161. (The coefficient is a measure of the goodness of fit between the proximity estimates and the derived Euclidean distances: 0 indicates a perfect fit.) This figure improves to .116 for the three-dimensional solution. We adopt the two-dimensional solution for discussion here because careful comparison of the two solutions indicates that the three-dimensional solution does not substantially enhance or change our understanding of the underlying organization of the space. These results, however, clearly demand a multidimensional characterization of the constituency structure. A single dimension, presumably reflecting only the rank-order of votes received, would simply provide an unacceptably poor fit to the underlying structure of proximities.

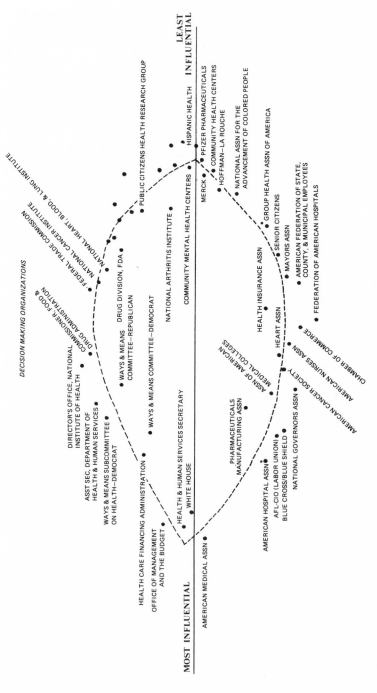

Figure 5.7. Two-Dimensional Smallest-Space Representation of the Influence Structure in the Health Domain: The Constituency View

178

matter in policy deliberations. That is, the constituency structure of the most highly ranked organizations is strongly bifurcated between the public and private spheres. Such a structure of influence implies a polarized adversarial structure in which the "opposing factions" are disinclined to take one another into account in their policy initiatives, with mutual blockage of the collective resolution of their policy differences the most probable outcome. Alternatively, one might find one side's policy solutions imposed on the other. We shall see that bifurcation of constituency differentiation among the highest-ranked actors is absent from the health domain.

Figure 5.7 tells us a broadly similar story about the organization of constituency differentiation in the health domain, but with very important differences as well. The overall shape of the configuration is an ellipse, with a rather pointed end at the pole of the highly influential organizations and a more rounded and heavily populated region at the "low-influence" pole. The horizontal axis arranges the organizations from the highly influential on the left side to the noninfluential on the right. The upper arc primarily contains public sector organizations, whereas the bottom arc consists of private sector claimant organizations.[10] The first noteworthy feature is the tight bunching of the most influential organizations at the point of the ellipse, reflecting the highly overlapping (or undifferentiated) constituencies (see our discussion of table 5.3 above). Second, notice that the arcs do join at the lower-ranked end of the influence hierarchy. Together these features reflect the generalized agreement about who matters in health policy making.

Comparison of these two figures thus suggests that the distribution of influence is considerably more coherent and well orchestrated in the health domain than in the energy domain because it rests on widespread constituency agreement at both the top and bottom of the influence hierarchy. The energy domain manifests far more constituency differentiation with respect to the top influentials.

Consensus. We are now in a position to look at the patterning of influence voting from the vantage point of the second face of influence: consensus among the voters. We inquire here about the nature and extent of the voters' systematic agreement or disagreement with one another on who counts and who does not count in policy formulation. Knowing the nature of the consensus about the influence structure is, for us, logically prior to understanding the adversarial structure with respect to specific policies. To begin answering

10. This flipflop in the vertical orientation of public versus private sector actors in the health domain from that observed in the energy domain has no substantive meaning whatsoever. It arises from minor technical differences in the way the algorithm constructed the Euclidean spatial solutions for the two domains. The fact to remember is that the interpoint distances in a Euclidean space are invariant across rotations of the coordinate axes, which are themselves arbitrary in origin and orientation (cf. McFarland and Brown, 1973).

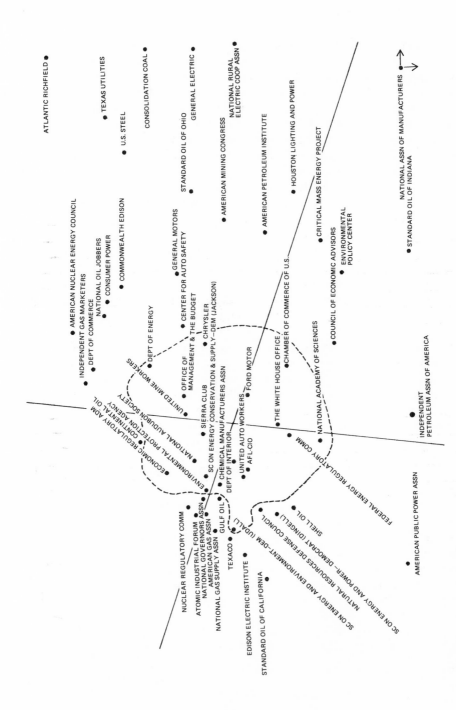

Figure 5.8. Two-Dimensional Smallest-Space Representation of the Consensus Structure in the Energy Domain

180

such questions we first propose to count the number of times a given pair of voters (in the rows of the influence voting matrix described above) agreed in voting for a particular target. Operationally, we simply count the number of matched cell entries, either *1*s or *0*s, in every possible pairing of rows in the matrix. Recalling that there is a fixed number of targets for whom to vote in a domain, we can calculate the percentage of overlap or agreement (both of positive votes and nonvotes) between all pairs of voters. The average percentage of voter consensus in the energy domain is 72.1 percent and in the health domain, 71 percent.[11] Quite clearly, consensus is substantially above chance expectations in both domains. The observed average voter consensus in the health domain, however, is 24.5 percent higher than the average predicted by chance, whereas in the energy domain it is only 20.1 percent higher. Thus, the health domain appears to be slightly more consensual about its influential and noninfluential actors than the energy domain is.

Figures 5.8 and 5.9 provide the two-dimensional smallest-space solutions for the consensus structures of the national energy and health domains, respectively.[12] Turning first to the energy domain, we propose to think of the space as organized in a center-to-periphery pattern of consensus.[13] The inner circle (delineated by dotted lines) includes many, but by no means all, of the most influential public and private-sector organizations, who agree among themselves about the identities of the influentials and the noninfluentials and who also disagree in roughly similar ways with those located in more peripheral locations. These more peripherally located organizations substantially

11. For a standard of comparison, we computed the average expected level of consensus among voters in each domain on the assumption of random voting on the part of all the voters. If voter *A* voted, say, for 25 percent of the target list and voter *B* for 35 percent, then we can compute the random expectation of the two voters' matching votes and nonvotes as $(.25)(.35) + (.75)(.65)$, or 55 percent agreement due to strictly chance matches. The average voter consensus on random match expectations is 52 percent in the energy domain, and 46.5 percent in the health domain.

As one might anticipate, organizations differ considerably among themselves with respect to the degree to which their average observed consensus with the other organizations on who matters exceeds their average expected consensus on chance grounds alone. We found, for the health domain, that the more an organization's profile of expressed interests in 56 issues agreed, on the average, with the profiles of the other organizations' expressed interests, the more that organization exceeded chance expectations in its agreement with the other organizations' perceptions of who matters ($r = .18$, $p < .05$).

12. Again we have far too many organizations (182 in energy and 130 in health) to label them individually without rendering the figures unintelligible. We have selected only some for labeling to highlight the main features of the configurations.

13. Although the two-dimensional solution for the energy domain has a rather high Kruskal stress coefficient (.184), compared with the three-dimensional solution's coefficient of .14, we again found that a careful comparison of the two solutions did not provide evidence that the two-dimensional solution would mislead the observer's understanding of the underlying organization of the space.

agree with those in their immediate vicinity on who matters, but increasingly disagree with those at greater and greater distances from them. The key to understanding the configuration of points is to look for "local regions" where organizations, often sharing some important feature such as being in oil or gas production or being large consumers of energy (like automobile manufacturers or the public utilities), appear to share a common perception of the structure of influence. A careful inspection of the configuration will further reveal the frequent arrangement of apparently similar types of organizations (i.e., similar in policy interests or function) at great distances from one another in rings surrounding the central core region. Such rim arrangements are prima facie evidence that actors with apparently common interests may in fact have very different perceptions of the nature of the influence structure in energy policy.

To illustrate these general precepts of interpretations more concretely, let us first note how the groups interested in environmental defense split into two distinct clusters along the roughly vertical line: the National Audubon Society, Sierra Club, and Natural Resources Defense Council are on the left, falling close to the most influential congressional and executive agencies, whereas the Environment Policy Center and Critical Mass Energy Project fall to the right at considerable distances from the center, perhaps reflecting their more activist and antiestablishment policy postures. Next, notice how the various oil companies and trade associations ring the center at some distance from it. Major oil companies, including Texaco, Gulf, Shell, and Standard Oil of California, are located to the left in a cluster; another cluster of major oil companies (including Arco, Sohio, and Amoco) and the principal trade association, the American Petroleum Institute, are diametrically opposite them to the right of the central core. "Small oil" groups are found in independent niches either at the top of the "oil rim" (National Oil Jobbers and Independent Gasoline Marketers) or at the bottom (Independent Petroleum Association). Such a dispersion reflects the fact that, contrary to the popular perception of a monolithic oil lobby, these organizations are much divided in their policy concerns and preferences and have correspondingly diversified perceptions of the relevant influence structure for realizing their interests. The public utilities also assume a rim organization, with the Edison Electric Institute, the industry's principal trade association, and the National Rural Electric Cooperative Association located at polar extremes on the horizontal axis, and the individual electric utilities scattered throughout the space, reflecting their specialized concerns about energy policy as it affects them in highly circumstantial ways.[14] The nuclear energy organizations also constitute a rim, with the

14. Individual public utilities have, for various historical, locational, and economic reasons, invested in one or another major energy source. Some, like Commonwealth Edison in Illinois, have gone heavily into nuclear energy as a source of energy for their turbines, while others have

Atomic Industrial Forum and Nuclear Regulatory Commission close together on the left, the American Nuclear Energy Council at the top, and General Electric, one of the principal manufacturers of nuclear energy plants, to the extreme right.

There are, of course, indications of the presence of at least some localized regions that appear to include all the relevant major actors in a consensually proximate way. The natural gas groups, for example, are all on the left side of the space (incidentally, we might note, at some considerable distance from the American Petroleum Institute). The coal groups (including U.S. Steel, the American Mining Congress, and Consolidation Coal) are off by themselves to the far right of the space. The three automobile manufacturers (General Motors, Ford, and Chrysler) are close together near the "Naderite" Center for Automobile Safety. And, finally, the three big unions (AFL-CIO, United Auto Workers, and United Mine Workers) are close together near the center, as are the three major congressional subcommittees in energy (labeled according to their respective committee chairmen, Udall, Dingell, and Jackson). As a final observation of some importance to understanding the dynamics of influence in energy policy, note that the U.S. Chamber of Commerce, an umbrella lobbying organization, is located toward the center of the space, reflecting its success in appreciating who the central actors on energy policy are during the Democratic party–dominated Carter period. In stark contrast, the National Association of Manufacturers, another umbrella lobbying organization representing business interests, is isolated at the bottom right of the space. Its extremely peripheral location in the consensus space reflects its highly idiosyncratic conception of the structure of influence in energy. An inference to be tested in Chapter 9 is that such peripheral organizations are unlikely to be actively involved in resolving diverse policy events across the spectrum of policy matters (usually because their interests are so narrowly focused and specialized) or, if active, to be successful in shaping policy toward their preferred outcomes.

Overall, we conclude that the consensus structure for the energy domain is highly differentiated and dissensual with respect to key policy subdomains. Often actors lack a shared perception of who the key influentials are; and, consequently, we can expect volatile coalitions that lack persistence in their support for particular policy initiatives over time (a tendency to be discussed in Chapter 12). In other words, the influence structure lacks a firm shape that stably orients the collectivity of actors to one another in a coherent and gener-

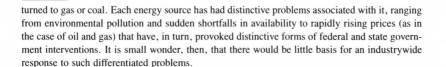
turned to gas or coal. Each energy source has had distinctive problems associated with it, ranging from environmental pollution and sudden shortfalls in availability to rapidly rising prices (as in the case of oil and gas) that have, in turn, provoked distinctive forms of federal and state government interventions. It is small wonder, then, that there would be little basis for an industrywide response to such differentiated problems.

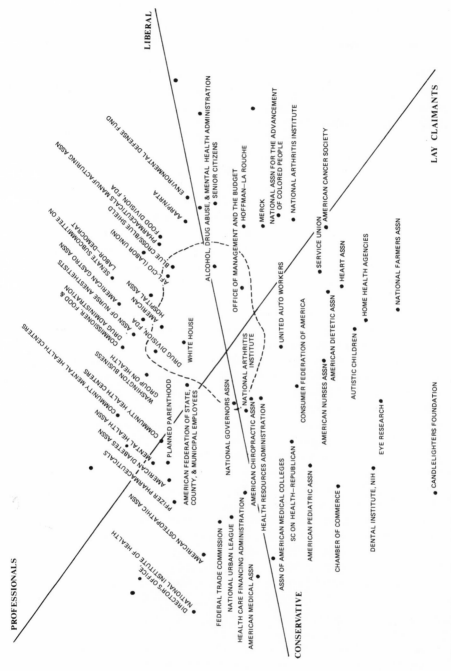

Figure 5.9. Two-Dimensional Smallest-Space Representation of the Consensus Structure in the Health Domain

184

ally shared framework that, in turn, organizes the adversarial structure over specific policies in a predictable or calculable manner from the standpoint of the larger system of collective decision making. Actors with putatively common concerns more often than not lack a shared reference standard that would enable them to anticipate the probable actions of a *delimited* set of significant actors in given policy arenas. That is, they simply could not identify a common line-up of actors to take into account in their own deliberations on policy preferences and tactics.

Worth stressing again is the fact that "consensus" refers here to a common perception of the key players and nonplayers—*not* consensus about particular policy options. The U.S. Chamber of Commerce clearly disagreed with the White House on most of the latter's policy initiatives, yet the Chamber broadly shared the White House's overall view of the domain's significant and not so significant actors. Our working hypothesis, then, is that the Chamber was thus at least in a more favorable position to confront its adversary in specific arenas than were the National Association of Manufacturers or other peripherally located actors, who were likely to identify a wholly different set of actors to take into account in their deliberations on what to do in specific controversies. By sharing the view of the most important actors on who matters, the Chamber enjoys a more favorable competitive position because it can anticipate the sorts of actors its adversaries are likely to take into account and can at least try to devise a strategy that makes use of that information.

Turning to the consensus structure of the national health domain (figure 5.9), we propose once again to interpret its underlying organization in terms of a center-to-periphery structure. As in the energy domain, many of the most influential actors in the health domain cluster together in the center of the space (delineated by dotted lines). In contrast to the energy domain, however, we observe that the more peripheral regions of the health domain are populated by relatively well-defined clusters of "like-minded" actors who broadly share similar organizational characteristics (such as being trade associations, voluntary action groups, or professional associations) or similar postures on national health policy. We have labeled two broad axes of differentiation among the actors that are obliquely oriented to one another, reflecting the tendency for the broadly liberal or conservative policy posture of an organization to be moderately correlated with its general function. What is especially significant here is the fact that the structure of consensus about organizational influence is systematically organized in terms of a broad policy dimension and a "type of organization" dimension. That is, individual actors perceive the influence structure in a systematically biased and, more important, predictable fashion, depending on where they themselves fall on these two dimensions.

What we mean by a "liberal" posture on health policy is a set of policy preferences that would expand the provision of health care to all Americans, regardless of their ability to pay, social characteristics, geographical location, or type of illness (e.g., expansion of the definition of health care to include mental health) through some form of national government subsidy and control. Proponents of such views differ considerably among themselves on the particular means by which these objectives are to be accomplished (e.g., they may support different kinds of national health insurance schemes with varying population coverage) or the sorts of health care that should be covered. At the opposite end, a "conservative" posture supports a set of policy preferences that would limit or curtail government responsibility for the costs of providing health care or for the planning and control of extant or projected health care delivery systems and biomedical research. In general, private sector means for organizing, delivering, and paying for health care are preferred. The second axis essentially distinguishes between organizations representing various professional health care providers, such as the AMA and the Association of Community Mental Health Centers, and those representing various lay groups with general or specialized concerns about the provision of health care, including labor unions, associations for the elderly and retired, and voluntary associations interested in the care, prevention, and cure of specific diseases, such as the American Cancer Society. The only "rim" pattern to be detected in the consensus structure is that of the pharmaceutical companies, which literally encircle the central core of organizations. Even here we can interpret the drug companies' locations in the "lay area" or "professional medical" area as reflecting their relative emphases on prescription or proprietary (over-the-counter) drug sales.

Although these broad principles generally organize the configuration, two interesting clusterings of actors seem to violate them. First, notice that the White House and the AHA are found in close proximity in the center of the space. Surely this violates our precept that professional health care providers like the AHA, especially those with conservative leanings, should be located toward the left side of the space. Yet we find the AHA perceiving the structure of influence in health just as the White House does. The reader will recall from Chapter 2 that one of the major health issues of the Carter administration was its effort in 1977 to impose mandatory cost containment on the rapidly escalating costs of hospital care, which were rising much more rapidly than the overall inflation rate. These apparently uncontrolled costs threatened the very solvency of Medicare/Medicaid. The AHA strongly opposed this initiative and countered with a proposal for voluntary controls and self-regulation. Their strategy, however, was not to mobilize a number of their natural allies among the professional associations of health providers, such as the AMA. Rather, the AHA chose to make its own appeal in a forceful lobbying effort directed toward the principal congressional committees responsible for the legislation. The AHA, in effect, reproduced the White House's view of the principal parties to be taken into account in its effort to forestall the White House initiative. Its perception of the key actors in the health establishment thus deviated from that generally held by the professional associations of health care providers.

The second violation of our general interpretation of this consensus structure concerns the cluster of organizations on the left side of the space around the FTC, including the AMA, the American Osteopathic Association, the National Urban League, and the American Chiropractic Association. Quite surprising is the location of the FTC itself, hardly an actor with an established presence in the health domain, at the vortex of this cluster. Again, an intense controversy during the Carter presidency helps to account for their proximity. Carter appointed Michael Pertschuk, a well-known consumer activist, as FTC chairman in 1977. Under his leadership and with the support of several other recently appointed commissioners, the FTC vigorously expanded its regulatory role in the whole gamut of economic activities of special concern to aroused consumer groups. One sphere that had been more or less ignored by the FTC was the regulation of the practices of professional groups, such as doctors and lawyers. Historically, professional associations, because of their putatively special nature, had been regarded as exempt from the antitrust laws, which were intended to sustain and encourage fair competitive practices in the marketplace. Now the AMA and other professional associations were accused of using their codes of professional ethics, which, among other things, prohibited advertising and laid the basis for suggested minimum fee schedules, to impose unfair restraints on trade. On similar grounds, the AMA's and associated professional associations' efforts to exclude osteopaths and chiropractors from hospital practice were challenged in civil suits in the federal courts. A series of FTC regulations intended to prohibit the AMA and its members from engaging in these practices were bitterly contested by the AMA in the mass media, the judicial system, and Congress. Interested in more information about available medical (and legal) care for the urban poor, the Urban League actively supported the FTC's initiatives. We thus can see how a group of highly interested partisans came to be mutually aware of each other in a delimited subdomain of action, despite their strong disagreements over the policy matters at stake.

We have discussed these two situations at some length because they help enhance our appreciation of the nuances of the underlying consensus order that the smallest-space procedures can help us identify. The following guidelines may direct us in detecting the underlying regularities in different kinds of consensus orders. If policy controversies are sufficiently well defined and enduring to attract a well-delimited set of interested parties, they can cause mutual orientation among the participants and consensus building about who counts in the issue arena. A policy domain characterized by a set of well-orchestrated policy subarenas with few cross-over participants will organize itself into clusters or regions of local consensus, with the participants in multiple subdomains falling somewhere between them. In contrast, a policy domain lacking such well-defined and continuing arenas of disputation is unlikely to possess a consensual order that locates combatants and protagonists in delimited and locally organized regions of mutual awareness. Actors possessing similar functions or interests will be scattered throughout the space in an essentially fortuitous pattern. The consensual order so organized reflects a situation in which actors have difficulty in predicting who the relevant players are and in assessing their relative worth or merit in terms of being taken into account in their own strategic interactions.

Reprise

As we have come to use the term in this chapter, influence has been treated as the emergent crystallization of the summary perceptual judgments of multiple actors engaged in a collective enterprise. That is, we have focused attention on influence in its *morphological* rather than its *processual* aspect. The structure of influence in a particular system is a social fact in precisely the Durkheimean sense that it possesses exteriority and imposes social constraints on individual actors (cf. Durkheim, 1964). Our elaboration of this argument about social facts is that exteriority and social constraint are themselves variably organized in different systems of action. Our central analytic objective is to characterize the organization of a given system's influence structure, for it is this organization that provides the environing and orienting framework within which individual actors organize their own strategic efforts to affect one another's actions. A central tenet of our approach is the necessity of recognizing that actors as individuals and as subsets of a more inclusive system of action may systematically vary in their perception of and consensus about the influence structure, with corresponding consequences for their own actions. To be sure, as the macrostructure of influence itself assumes theoretically different formations, the very nature of collective outcomes will necessarily also be expected to vary.

For the case in hand, we have shown that the influence structure in the health policy domain differs in certain crucial respects from that in the energy policy domain. The health policy domain, for example, appears to be dominated much more by governmental decision-making entities than the energy domain, with its many prominent private sector actors. In addition, consensus about who matters appears to be much more systematically—indeed, almost institutionally—organized in the health domain. We should, however, not lose sight of the fact that the influence structures of the two domains, despite their nearly total disparity in substantive concerns and corporate membership, display remarkably similar formal features as well. Both, for example, are approximately identical with respect to the unequal distribution of influence. Both, in addition, display almost identical correspondences in the way relative influence standings are related to externally grounded criteria of public visibility and participation in decision-making arenas.

Most observers would agree that the 1970s were a decade of relative quiescence in national health policy after the wars over biomedical research support, hospital construction, and national health insurance and Medicare/ Medicaid of the preceding several decades. National energy policy, in contrast, was one of the dominant political and economic preoccupations of the 1970s, a decade of much rancorous strife over the appropriate responses to the energy crisis, the oil embargo of 1973, and the phenomenal escalation of energy prices. The influence structures of these two policy domains rather precisely mirror the differences in their respective historical circumstances. That of energy is ill-defined and balkanized, with many disarticulated arenas for vigorous skirmishes between specialized interests; that is, it is consensually disorganized or unsystematized, in contrast to the well-ordered, predictable patterning of consensus in health. Throughout the 1970s energy policy was in the throes of a rapid move from a highly decentralized and privatized past toward a more centralized structure of decision making.[15] In contrast, national health policy has been successfully institutionalized around long-established governmental actors, including the NIH, the FDA, and various sections of HHS, each having a well-defined clientele of mildly antagonistic supporters and detractors, which often divided over little more than the relative levels of funding among established programs. Both systems do, however, reflect a striking bifurcation in the constituency order between governmental and private sector actors, probably because of the preponderant significance of the preexisting institutionalized decision-making system, which provides a strong reference point for actors to use in distinguishing between the major and minor actors.

---

15. Indeed, one can readily argue that no final settlement was ever achieved with respect to a more centralized national decision-making system in energy policy. From the outset of the Reagan presidency, many initiatives were undertaken to dismantle the regulative machinery proposed by the Carter administration. The most noteworthy was Reagan's expressed intention to dismantle the Department of Energy in favor of the much more decentralized and dispersed set of government actors concerned with various aspects of energy policy that characterized the pre–Carter period.

6

The Organizational Capacity to Act: Monitoring and Resource Endowment

The preceding chapter discussed at length the differentiated structure of influence in energy and health. Organizations were characterized as occupying different positions in a multidimensional influence structure that will be used in subsequent chapters to explain the actor's varying impact on specific decision-making events. This chapter addreseses another question: what attributes of the corporate actors participating in the policy domain explain their relative locations in the influence structure? Broadly speaking, we can draw a distinction between two general categories of resources. The first, monitoring capacity, refers to the resources an organization uses specifically to obtain the information it needs to participate in the policy-making process. The second, which we call "resource endowment," includes the principal types of resources an organizatin can bring to bear in attempting to influence specific policy deliberations. We hope to demonstrate that an organization's monitoring capacity and specific resource endowments go a long way toward accounting for its relative influence standing in the policy domain.

Simply put, an organization's capacity to monitor its environment and its specific resource endowment undergird its capacity to act in the policy domain. Whatever the organization's scope of interests regarding on-going policy deliberations, its resource endowment must permit it to accomplish two key tasks. First, it must be able to monitor the relevant policy environment so that it acquires relevant, timely, and trustworthy information about decision-

190

making events, impending or after the fact, that bear on its interests, as well as information about the larger system, including where necessary resources are to be found, that will help it to advance or defend its interests (cf. Aldrich, 1979:248–55; Aldrich and Pfeffer, 1976). Second, it must have a range of more specific resources, such as money, personnel, reputation for expertise, influence over politically important constituencies, and so on, that together confer that particular reputation for influence (discussed in the last chapter) that other actors will take into account in their own decision-making and related actions.

A crucial assumption motivating the entire analysis of resource endowment, then, is that the flow of information in a policy domain plays the critical role in orchestrating the activities of the participants and in determining the outcome of policy deliberations (cf. Allison, 1971; Deutsch, 1966; Pool, 1983). A striking feature of national policy domains, attested by observational data (Heinz et al., 1982; Laumann and Heinz, 1985), is that the most powerful actors in the domain, typically those who possess the authority to make intermediate or final decisions, are themselves not able to generate their own information but rely heavily on others for the information they need to do their jobs. They thus become the most popular targets of information transmission from all the interested parties—a fact that will be dramatically documented in the next chapter. Judges receive legal briefs designed to present relevant information in the most persuasive light; congressional subcommittee staff depend on claimant groups for the information they give their committee members; and even executive agencies, perhaps to a somewhat lesser extent, must get the information they require from the very actors upon whom they are to confer benefits or harm.

To be of any value, information must be relevant, timely, and trustworthy. Every actor is thus dependent to varying degrees on other interested actors for crucial pieces of information that tell it among other things, when critical events affecting its interests are going to occur or have happened and often with what potential consequences. No actor, however well endowed in organizational resources, has a monopoly on all the information relevant to its concerns. Moreover, even if an organization is the sole source of certain information of relevance to a policy decision, it typically gains nothing from that monopoly until it communicates that information to relevant others, who must be willing to accept its trustworthiness. Herein lies the reason for the remark often made by our informants that reputation as an honest, reliable source of information is an essential asset for any effective—read "influential"—claimant organization. Moreover, reputations for reliable and useful information can be routinely assessed and shared among the relevant actors precisely because representation is a continuing activity. Though there may be complete turnovers in the particular personnel performing the representational activity from one matter to the next, the identities of the concerned organizations change much more slowly. Quite clearly it is in the organizations' long-term interest to make sure that their representatives do nothing to undermine their organizations' claims for veracity.

A peculiar feature of information as a resource, in contradistinction to other sorts of resources like money or personnel, is that it is not consumed or lost in exchange but becomes "possessed" by both the transmitter and the receiver—that is, one cannot "take it back" if circumstances should change. Precisely because of this feature of information exchange, organizations with secrets better kept from general circulation select their representatives carefully to ensure that they exercise "good judgment" in disclosing confidential or damaging information to outsiders. Such organizations are likely to prefer their representatives to be employees, over whom they can exercise greater control and from whom they can expect greater loyalty to their interests, if for no better reason than the agents' dependence for their very livelihoods on the organization's goodwill. If an organization must turn to outsiders because the relevant expertise is not to be found in house, it may prefer to use lawyers, rather than "nonprofessionals," on the premise that lawyers are under a professional obligation to exercise discretion in discussing their clients' business. Organizations lacking such concerns about the circumspect dissemination or acquisition of information may readily turn to outsiders less subject to strictures of professional reticence.

Monitoring Capacity

"Monitoring capacity" refers to the resources an organizaton devotes to scanning its policy task environment for the acquisition of needed information and resources. Organizations regularly hire staff or retain lawyers and other lobbyists and consultants to gather information on the Washington policy scene and to lobby the executive and legislative branches. Even litigation before the federal courts, which imposes unusually demanding information requirements about the relevant facts at issue, is increasingly being used as an instrument to advance the policy objectives of an organization.[1] Monitoring capacity is thus a key instrumentality of an organization's purpose with respect to advancing and defending its policy interests and thus can be expected to vary in its sophistication and scale as a function of the scope and nature of those interests.

---

1. Laumann and Heinz (1985) report that in a sample of 316 nongovernment organizations active in one of four policy domains (health, energy, agriculture, and labor) within the past three or four years, about 64 percent said that they used litigation as a strategy for influencing policy making. This represents a dramatic increase in the willingness to use litigation for such purposes compared with the situation even 20 years ago, when such a tactic was almost unheard of, except for civil rights matters (Zuehl, n.d.).

Organizations, as Laumann and Heinz (1985) demonstrate, vary widely in the degree to which they come to rely on their own staffs as opposed to, or in conjunction with, external representatives (i.e., hired lobbyists, lawyers, public relations consultants, etc.) for monitoring a relevant policy domain.[2] In inventorying 14 specific monitoring and interventionist tasks that monitors perform for nongovernmental organizations, Laumann and Heinz (1985: table 2) found that except for specifically legal tasks like drafting legislation and executive regulations or engaging in litigation, which lawyers on retainer are often hired to do, the majority of the claimant organizations relied exclusively on their own employees to perform these functions. Well under 10 percent of the organizations relied exclusively on external representatives to perform these tasks. Roughly a third used both internal and external representatives in varying combinations to perform the monitoring function, but typically with organizational insiders taking principal responsibility for supervising the monitoring effort.

A troublesome problem arises in attempting to measure an organization's monitoring capacity—at least with respect to its orientation to a specific policy domain—because of the great diversity of organizational forms that are included in the set of consequential domain actors. At one extreme we have business behemoths, like General Motors, Commonwealth Edison, Exxon, and Mobil Oil Corporation, and, on the other, small organizations essentially staffed by volunteers with a few regular employees, like the National Coalition of Hispanic Mental Health and Human Service Organizations. In addition, there are trade and professional associations, public interest groups, labor unions, and federations of corporate actors, each having distinctive organizational structures and ways of doing business. The methodological issue is how to devise a meaningful common metric for comparing such diverse organizations' monitoring capacities. After considerable reflection and pilot work, we hit upon what we think is an effective measure: namely, the enumeration of full-time staff (or their equivalents in volunteer personnel) devoted to different monitoring activities in Washington. While Mobil Oil clearly has much more money to spend in hiring people to perform these tasks than, say, the Sierra Club, Mobil in fact has only a modest staff devoted to monitoring the energy domain, roughly comparable—in numbers at least—to

2. Williamson (1975, 1981, 1985) provides a useful perspective that helps account for an organization's decision to internalize or externalize its monitoring function or to adopt some mixture of task performers. He argues that the principal mechanism driving the organization's decision is the relative transaction cost incurred by performing the task internally under the organization's own hierarchical control as opposed to purchasing the services in a market of autonomous competitors. Although this is an important and fascinating topic, we shall not pursue such an analysis further but shall simply assume that the joint product of internally and externally provided services indexes the organization's relative monitoring capacity.

those of the other active participants in the energy domain. Although a simple head-count obviously ignores possible qualitative differences in competence, the considerable staff turnover in Washington probably results in a fairly equitable distribution with respect to the quality of personnel across the interested parties. Our extensive pilot work certainly did not reveal any organizations enjoying near monopolies on the monitoring talent available in Washington.

Questions D6–D8b, D10–10a, and D13–D15 in Appendix B were designed to elicit detailed information on the staff the organization employed or retained to perform various information-gathering activities regarding the national policy domain of interest. In combination, these questions allowed us to ascertain: (1) the number of full-time equivalent staff members (FTEs) whose regular task involved monitoring the Washington scene about all kinds of national policy issues of interest (general monitors); (2) the number of FTEs devoted to monitoring the Washington scene specifically about issues in national energy or health policy (specialized monitors); and (3) the number of FTEs whose principal responsibility was the gathering of systematic technical data relevant to national energy or health policy (technical staff). The total number of FTEs devoted to these monitoring functions varies between 0 and 102 (with a mean of 7.9 and a median of 4) in the health domain, and between 0 and 266 (with a mean of 16.3 and a median of 9) in the energy domain.

A latent structural variable, monitoring capacity, was calculated according to a LISREL program (Jöreskog and Sörbom, 1981) from these three counts of different types of monitors. As might have been anticipated, we found a positive association between the scope of an organization's interest in the energy (or health) domain (see Chapter 4) and its monitoring capacity. For the energy domain, the zero-order correlation is a modest .44 and, for health, it is .19. These results are consistent with the hypothesis often entertained in the literature (e.g., Aldrich, 1979) that organizations with broad scopes of interest in the policy domain will have a larger monitoring capacity (i.e., more boundary-spanning personnel) in order to scan the more extensive environment that is relevant to their interests.[3] One might well wonder why the correlations are as modest as they are, given the apparent plausibility of the hypothesized linkage. One speculation is that some organizations place more stress than others on the creation of relevant information. Some, because of their general charters, specialize in gathering technical information of rele-

3. We might further expect that organizations with narrower or more specialized scopes of interest will rely more heavily on external monitors for their information and will, in consequence, be located in more peripheral positions in the routine communication network linking actors in the domain. This speculation was examined by Prensky (1985), who found empirical support for it in the health domain (he did not analyze the data for the energy domain). We shall examine monitoring capacity's relation to the volume of communication ties in the policy domain at greater length in the next chapter.

vance to others. For example, Blue Cross/Blue Shield is the principal source of technical information on hospital costs and utilization patterns because of its primary role as the major third-party payer of hospital bills; the American Petroleum Institute, a trade association of the principal oil producers, is a key collator of information on oil reserves and available petroleum-related energy supplies, which it gathers from its membership. Such organizations typically try to avoid becoming overly involved in partisan politics, in part to help reassure others that the information they provide is trustworthy and reliable (but see Wildavsky and Tenenbaum, 1981).

Again one might expect a strong correlation between monitoring capacity and the influence standing of organizations on the plausible grounds that the more influential organizations must have greater monitoring capacity to facilitate the timely exertion of their influence. For the energy domain, the correlation between the number of influence votes received (see Chapter 5) and monitoring capacity is a moderate .54, and for the health domain it is .33. Insight can be gained about this relationship if we examine a little more closely the sorts of organizations that are characteristically found in each of four combinations of influential standing and monitoring capacity (where each of these variables is dichotomized at its median value). As table 6.1 demonstrates, reputation for being influential varies considerably across the different organizational types introduced in Chapter 3. In both the domains government agencies are rated consistently as possessing high levels of influence regardless of their level of monitoring capacity. The exceptions to this generalization are found among associations of state or local governments and research organizations, both of which may have only distant relationships to authorities with formal decision-making powers.

Among the predominantly private organizational types, however, the distribution of monitoring capacity and reputations for being highly influential differs between the two domains. Among organizations involved in the formation of energy policy, trade associations and business corporations together account for more than half of the organizations ranked high on both dimensions. Labor unions tend to be recognized as well-informed participants despite their generally lower monitoring capacity. Professional associations and lay voluntary associations tend to be ranked low with respect to one or both attributes, as do a majority of trade associations despite the high reputation and capacity of a prominent subset of this group.

In the health policy domain, by contrast, the combination of high monitoring capacity and high influence is somewhat more evenly distributed. Among the most striking differences is that lay voluntary associations account for more than 20 percent of this category in health and less than 7 percent in energy. Equally significantly, given the popular image of health policy as dominated by the interests of physicians, only 17 percent of this group ranked high

Table 6.1. Combinations of Organizational Influence Standing and Monitoring Capacity by Type of Organization and Policy Domain

Type of Organization	Energy Domain					Health Domain				
	N	High MC High Infl	High MC Low Infl	Low MC High Infl	Low MC Low Infl	N	High MC High Infl	High MC Low Infl	Low MC High Infl	Low MC Low Infl
Congressional Subcommittees	20	45% / 15%	0% / 0%	55% / 30%	0% / 0%	8	25% / 5%	0% / 0%	75% / 24%	0% / 0%
Federal Agencies	17	53% / 15%	0% / 0%	41% / 19%	6% / 2%	12	67% / 18%	0% / 0%	33% / 16%	0% / 0%
State & Local Governments	10	30% / 5%	30% / 0%	10% / 3%	30% / 5%	9	56% / 11%	11% / 4%	0% / 0%	33% / 7%
Research Organizations	7	14% / 2%	0% / 0%	57% / 11%	29% / 3%	11	45% / 11%	0% / 0%	55% / 24%	0% / 0%
Labor Unions	5	20% / 2%	0% / 0%	60% / 8%	20% / 2%	4	50% / 5%	0% / 0%	05 / 0%	50% / 5%
Trade Associations	46	28% / 22%	11% / 14%	7% / 8%	54% / 42%	11	45% / 11%	18% / 9%	9% / 4%	27% / 7%
Professional Associations	2	0% / 0%	0% / 0%	0% / 0%	100% / 3%	35	17% / 14%	26% / 39%	3% / 4%	54% / 44%
Business Corporations	64	31% / 33%	34% / 61%	9% / 16%	25% / 27%	6	33% / 5%	67% / 17%	0% / 0%	0% / 0%
Lay Voluntary Associations	21	19% / 7%	29% / 17%	9% / 5%	43% / 15%	39	23% / 20%	18% / 30%	18% / 28%	41% / 37%
Total for Each Column	192	60	36	37	59	135	44	23	25	43
Percent of Total	100%	31%	19%	19%	31%	100%	33%	17%	18%	32%

on both dimensions, constituting only 14 percent of the entire set of organizations credited with this combination of attributes. To the extent that these two dimensions capture something of the significance of the various organizations participating in the two domains, health policy would appear to be the product of a much more aggregative process than is energy policy, where business and government are dominant forces.

Resource Endowment

A more vexing problem concerns the conception and measurement of the resource endowment an organization can mobilize in influencing particular policy deliberations in a policy domain. We have already discussed at length in Chapter 5 some of the conceptual and analytic ambiguities in the notion of influence. Here we want to consider the more concrete set of mobilizable resources that organizations control and that presumably undergird their relative influence standings in the national policy domain. Obviously an organization with a large and effectively organized grassroots constituency—the AFL-CIO and the American Association of Retired Persons spring to mind—has a very different basis for its influence in Washington than an organization with a large amount of money to contribute to political campaigns: one of the large drug companies like Pfizer, say, or an oil company like Mobil. Other organizations, such as the American College of Surgeons, may enjoy great influence because of the expertise they can mobilize on a substantive point at issue.

A voluminous literature attempts to develop systematic distinctions among resource bases and to link them to the influence process. Examples include French and Raven's (1959) five bases of power (reward, coercive, referent, legitimate, and expert), with special reference to interpersonal influence processes; Parsons' four media of exchange (money, power, influence, and commitment) at the societal level of analysis and his "influence paradigm" (cf. Galaskiewicz, 1979; Parsons, 1969), and Clark's (1968:57–67) list of 13 resources of power, prestige, and norm formation.[4] Utilizing two generating analytic variables, Laumann and Pappi (1976:185–215) proposed a typology of resources that proved useful in studying community elites. The first variable, the locus of influence base, distinguishes between resources that inhere in the social position of an elite member (e.g., the authority of office) and those that inhere in the personal characteristics of the actor exercising influence (e.g., personal charisma). The second analytic variable is the resource's

4. Clark's 13 resources are money and credit, control over jobs, control of mass media, high social status, knowledge and specialized technical skills, popularity and esteemed personal qualities, legality, subsystem solidarity, the right to vote, social access to community leaders, commitments of followers, manpower and control of organizations, and control over the interpretation of values (see also Gamson, 1968:59–109; Nuttall, Scheuch, and Gordon, 1968:352–56.

effective scope, generality, or convertibility. Here they distinguish between resources that can be used in a wide variety of concrete influence situations as
positive or negative inducements (e.g., money) and those that are restricted
(or particularized) in their efficacy to a limited range of situations. Expertise
on public health policy, for instance, has little direct relevance for resolving
technical questions about reimbursement schemes for hospital costs.

Treating these two axes characterizing influence resources as analytically
independent, dichotomous variables, Laumann and Pappi cross-tabulated
them to form a fourfold typology of resource bases (table 6.2). The eight resources bases were selected so that two of them would fall into each of the
four cells. As they observe (1976:189):

> While not necessarily exhaustive of all the relevant community-level influence re-
> sources, the tabulation does seem to include the salient resources most often discussed
> in the literature. It is especially difficult to construct an exhaustive typology of the
> personal resources. Since power or influence may depend on so many personal charac-
> teristics, even Max Weber (1922:28) characterized power in contrast to authority as a
> concept that is "*soziologisch amorph.*" Robert Michels (1925:65–73) also discussed
> a plethora of "*akzessorische Eigenschaften der Führerschaft*" (accessory characteris-
> tics of leadership).

Unfortunately for us, a major lacuna in the literature on resources appears
to be systematic discussion of the relevant resources that organizations (or
corporate actors) can bring to bear in influencing policy deliberation. To be
sure, one can certainly identify important discussions of organizations' use of
specific resources to advance their ends with respect to their competitors and
others with which they are engaged in antagonistic cooperation (cf. Benson,
1975; Pfeffer and Salancik, 1978), but these discussions are typically ad hoc
and not intended to be systematically comprehensive. As a first approximation
to a systematic identification of the range of resources organizations can use
in advancing their policy claims, we have recast the Laumann-Pappi list of
eight resources in terms that are appropriate for organizations rather than
"natural persons." Each organizational informant was asked the following
question (see Appendix B, question C11 for the extended context):

> Organizations may be regarded as influential and consequential participants in the na-
> tional energy [health] debate because they possess certain characteristics or resources.
> A list of some possibilities appears on Card I. . . .
>
> Would you please select 5 to 10 organizations that you know best and tell me for
> each of them *all* the characteristics or resources on which that organization's influence
> is based? Are there characteristics or resources not on this list that any of these organi-
> zations possess?
>
> 1. Special expert knowledge about the energy [health] field.
> 2. Funds to underwrite efforts to secure support for a proposal.
> 3. Staff or facilities that can be used in an effort to gather support for a proposal.

Table 6.2. Analytical Scheme for Classifying Influence Resources

Effective Scope or Convertibility	Locus of Influence Base	
	Positional (Institutionalized Role)	Personal Characteristics of Incumbent
Generalized	a. Official decision-making authority as elected public official or occupant of a high position in public service	c. General respect as someone who can mobilize the public for good proposals in the interest of the city as a whole
	b. Power of disposal over fluid economic resources, possible giver of credit	d. Honorable broker who can mediate issues in a non-partisan way
Specific	e. Power of disposal over less fluid economic resources, such as land or jobs	g. Good connections with influential persons inside and outside of community
	f. Special expert knowledge of certain limited fields of community interest	h. Influence in certain sub-groups of the population, such as voters of a particular party, members of a voluntary association, and so on

SOURCE: Table 11.1, Laumann and Pappi (1976: 188).

4. Official decision-making authority because of its high position in the government.
5. Good connections to influential organizations.
6. Reputation as an impartial mediator of conflicts about issues.
7. Ability to mobilize its members or employees to support a proposal.
8. Ability to mobilize general public opinion to support a proposal.
9. Other [PLEASE SPECIFY]

The reader can readily translate the listed organizational resources into their equivalents in the original Laumann/Pappi list for community influentials. Although generality versus specificity of scope still makes sense when one is speaking of organizational resoures and their convertibility in various policy-making settings, it is rather more difficult to formulate precisely the organizational equivalent to "personal characteristics of incumbents." To be sure, institutionalized or positional resources, such as the mandated authority to make binding decisions, clearly have a straightforward analogue among corporate actors. The organizational equivalent of idiosyncratic personal characteristics, we suggest, is a situation in which a given organization comes over time to occupy a distinctive niche with respect to a given clientele or constituency and acquire a particular history of participation in politically visible domain events. These together combine to form reputations among domain participants that establish organizations' distinctive trustworthiness and reputability for influence over specific constituencies in given policy deliberations. These more idiosyncratic organizational resources affecting relative efficacy and consequent influence in policy outcomes are clearly analytically separable from those conferred on organizations because of their institutionally prescribed control over authority, funds, employees, and expertise.

To analyze the data gathered by this question poses some challenging issues of conceptualization and technique. First, we lack quantitative indicators for the eight resources that provide meaningful and comparable measures of the amounts of resources under the control of different types of organizations. For instance, although professional and trade associations apparently vary considerably in the sheer amount of money in their annual budgets devoted to national policy affairs, the funds available to even the largest professional or trade associations are quite modest when compared with those potentially available to large business concerns for similar purposes. Or consider the matter of authority, which specifically refers to the formally recognized right to render binding decisions in a specified area of concern. Obviously authoritative entities, such as the offices of the secretary of HHS and the director of the FDA, differ greatly in the scope of their areas of institutionally designated concern. Second, to the extent that the domain is sharply differentiated into relatively autonomous and distinct parts, corporate actors active in one area may have limited information with which to judge the relevant resources of actors active in distant policy subdomains.

Let us think for a moment of organizations as emitting signals of varying intensity and clarity of resolution with respect to the resources they control to the population of interested actors, who are to be regarded as informants. Informant actors in close proximity to a given organization (the target signal source) in terms of shared interests in energy or health policy, institutional arenas of action, information flows, and so on (see Chapters 4, 5, and 7) are in position to attribute specific resources to the signal source as a function of the relative amounts of these resources that it appears to possess on the basis of its past and current participation in the policy subdomain. Organizations possessing considerable amounts of the resource in question are likely to elicit many more judgments from others that they do in fact possess such a resource than those who control only a little of it or lack it entirely. In short, just as we reasoned for the allocation of influence votes in the last chapter, we propose to infer a monotonically increasing amount of the resource from an organization's receiving more votes for possessing the resource in question.

To assess the differential allocation of these resources under the control of various organizations, we first constructed a matrix in which the rows referred to the respective target organizations (or signal sources) and the columns referred to the eight resources that an organization could be said to possess. Cell entries were the total number of votes each signal organization received from all the informant organizations with respect to a given resource. Then, we computed all the pairwise correlations by columns (or resources) across the set of signal organizations (rows). A high positive correlation between two resources, *A* and *B*, means that informants tended to perceive the distribution of resource *A* across the set of organizations as similar to the distribution of resource *B*, whereas a negative correlation between the two resources signifies that the presence of resource *A* is associated with the absence of resource *B* under the control of the same organizations.

Factor analyses (varimax method) of the resulting eight-by-eight correlation matrices for the respective policy domains produce essentially the same three-factor model of differential resource allocation. (See table 6.3 for the factor loadings in each domain.) The factor structure for the health policy domain is more sharply delineated into three distinct factors than the energy domain is.

The first factor, labeled the "mobilizable resource factor," has very high loadings for six resources (which empirically appear to co-vary strongly, though they are readily distinguishable on analytic grounds) and explains the vast bulk (74 percent) of the common variance. The other two factors in the health domain refer to factors defined by only one resource with an exceptionally high loading and no others with even modest loadings, and individually explain approximately equal amounts of variance. Note particularly that in the case of health at least, a reputation for being an impartial mediator or possessing authority is sharply differentiated from the first factor, which refers to the sorts of resources most likely to be mobilized for partisan political purposes by nonpublic claimant organizations. An inspection of the organizations receiving high scores for being impartial mediators in the health domain reveals that they are almost entirely organizations having only modest to low general reputations for influence (see Chapter 5)—two features that comport rather nicely with customary notions about the nature of impartial mediators. (See Appendix A for a listing of the factor scores for the organizations in each domain.) Not surprisingly, the organizations possessing authority are almost always government organizations, either congressional or executive, which lack specific mobilizable resources of the sort associated with the first factor and reputations as impartial mediators. This says that authoritative organizations in the health policy arena tend to be seen as those advocating or implementing particular policy initiatives, rather than as mediators among conflicting policy options.

The factor structure for the energy domain is decidedly more blurred in its differentiation of distinct factors. Although the same six "partisan" resources load very highly on the first factor, we see that a seventh resource, "impartial

Table 6.3. Results from Factor Analyses of Attributed Resource Variables in the Two Policy Domains

	"Mobilizable Resource Factor"		"Impartial Mediator Factor"		"Formal Authority Factor"	
	Energy Domain	Health Domain	Energy Domain	Health Domain	Energy Domain	Health Domain
Special expert knowledge	.95	.92	.07	.27	.24	.11
Funds to support program	.96	.98	.22	.04	.11	.05
Staff or facilities	.96	.98	.22	.14	.14	.10
Good connections	.93	.97	.33	.20	-.13	.10
Ability to mobilize members	.95	.98	.41	.11	-.03	-.07
Ability to mobilize opinion	.83	.93	.28	.12	.23	.18
Official decision-making authority	.10	.10	.23	.05	.97	.99
Reputation as impartial mediator	.47	.19	.81	.98	.43	.18
Variance explained	.78	.74	.04	.12	.15	.11

[a]Factors were rotated using varimax method.

mediator," has a moderate loading (.47) on the first factor as well. The second factor is defined by a similarly high loading on the resource of impartial mediator, but it also draws on "the ability to mobilize members"—a surprising but explicable conjunction, as we shall see. Note that in the case of the energy domain, this second factor of impartial mediation accounts for a very small fraction of the total common variance. Finally, the third factor is defined as "formal authority" (as it was in the health domain), but again we observe, in contrast to health, a moderate loading of the resource of impartial mediator. In short, this resource of impartial mediator loads on all three factors in the energy domain.

A partial explanation for this phenomenon may be found in the prominent role that citizen-based, organized groups advocating environmental protection like the Sierra Club and the National Wildlife Federation played in formulating energy policy during the Carter period. Energy policy was highly controversial and partisan throughout the 1970s, but the environmental advocacy groups enjoyed especially high access to the executive branch under President Carter, who appeared to be especially responsive to their policy inclinations. As a result, these groups had highly ambivalent reputations for influence during this period across the range of interested parties. On the one hand, they claimed to speak for the general public interest in promoting a wise policy for environmental protection against the self-interested rapacity of the special interests, and thus laid a basis for their claim of impartiality. On the other hand, they were increasingly seen to be advocates for antigrowth and antidevelopment policies that adversely affected rational economic planning and full-employment policies. Thus, some informants saw these groups as impartial mediators while others, usually industry groups, saw them as little more than another highly partisan and influential special interest group with no valid claim to impartiality (consistent with this view, they attributed to them the more partisan resource of "ability to mobilize members"). During this period authoritative actors were seeking to construct their mandates for a national energy policy, and thus they were seen, by some at least, as trying to act as mediators among strongly contending factions.

We are now in position to answer a key question: to what extent are the organizations' general reputations for influence (Chapter 5) accounted for by differing levels of these three resource factors? To begin answering it, we computed the following multiple regression equations predicting the number of votes received for being especially influential on the basis of the organizations' three resource factor scores. For the energy domain,

$$A_i = .55 (M_i) + .22 (I_i) + .44 (F_i),$$

and for the health domain,

$$A_i = .53 \, (M_i) + .12 \, (I_i) + .48 \, (F_i),$$

where A_i = attributed influence, M_i = mobilizable resource factor, I_i = impartial mediator factor, and F_i = formal authority factor. All the standardized beta coefficients were significant at the .0001 level, except the one for the impartial mediator factor in the health domain, which met the .05 level of significance. The regression equation accounted for 55 percent of the total variance of attributed influence in the energy domain ($N = 192$) and 54 percent in the health domain ($N = 135$) ($p < .0001$).

From a comparative point of view, the most striking feature of these results is the almost identical patterning of the relative importance of the three resource factors in structuring influence in the two domains, provided, of course, that we are prepared to assume a causal role for the three factors in generating organizational influence. Both formal authority and mobilizable resources, reflecting, respectively, the governmental and private sector sides of the participants in policy deliberations, have about equally strong effects on organizational influence, perhaps with a slight bias in favor of the private sector's resource base in determining influence. Reputation as an impartial mediator has decidedly less impact on enhancing an organization's influence standing. To be sure, one is tempted to point out that the role of mediator appears to play a more salient role in the energy domain than in the health domain. This result may arise from the fact that we observed the two domains at two distinctly different junctures in their institutional development—a period of crisis in the energy domain; one of relative quiescence in the health domain (see Chapter 2). Impartial mediation might be expected to be a scarcer and more valued resource in a highly politicized and polarized domain than in one in which the assignment of institutional roles has been more or less accepted as legitimate and settled by most of the relevant interested parties.[5]

5. We should be wary of overinterpreting these results, which rest, after all, on a number of problematic assumptions about the way our organizational informants went about assigning judgments of the presence or absence of specific resources. Perhaps the most problematic assumption relates to the notion that organizations receiving more attributions of a resource can be assumed to possess more of that resource than those who received fewer such attributions. Certainly organizations differ in their public visibility, and that variability might lead informants, quite independent of the true facts about resource endowment, to attribute more resources to the highly visible and less to the less well known. We believe, however, from evidence reported elsewhere in the book, that most informants, regardless of their own standing in the influence structure and their own visibility, were generally very knowledgeable about domain activities and other domain actors, typically because they themselves were very active in attempting to influence a range of policy outcomes in public and not-so-public forums. We thus have some confidence in our interpretation stressing some important differences between the domains in institutional development because we have collateral information that is consistent with or sustains it.

Concluding Remarks

We have described in this chapter our operationalization of two key organizational attributes—monitoring capacity and resource endowment—that play critical roles in enabling effective organizational participation in policy making. Our summary measure of influence standing (described in Chapter 5) was shown to be closely associated with an organization's specific resource endowments, but it was only very modestly related to monitoring capacity, which performs the dual function of enabling organizations to generate relevant information about the domain (i.e., strict monitoring) and of communicating their intentions to others. We shall turn in the next two chapters to describing the communication structure linking the domain actors in a flow of routine and more candid information exchanges. Armed with a fuller appreciation of the communication network, we will then return to a consideration of how monitoring capacity and resource endowment are implicated in effective participation in domain events.

7

Dyadic Communication

Every night in Washington, as clerks and secretaries head home for the evening's relaxation, the upper-level managers of innumerable agencies, trade associations, and public interest groups begin preparing for some serious partying. At White House state dinners, Georgetown soirees, and Kennedy Center galas, the real business of Washington continues: talk, talk, and more talk. The ceaseless flow of information between policy-makers and claimant organizations knows no distinction between office hours and private time. Such information is the currency with which all types of exchanges are transacted. In the absence of communication, coordinated policy action would become impossible, and the domain would fragment into ineffective, atomized policy actors. Thus, an analysis of the communication networks through which domain information spreads is indispensable to understanding the policy process.

Communication between organizations assists in the construction of collective sociopolitical realities among domain participants. Through continual interactions, actors create and reinforce common frames of reference on which to hang the substantive debates of the domain. Communication serves to develop mutually recognizable terminologies and the rules of the game by which policy disagreements are thrashed out. We do not assert that communication per se induces uniformity of policy preference. Although wishful thinkers believe that conflict erupts only from poor communication, irrecon-

206

cilable interests among domain organizations are likely to persist even in the most crystalline of communication networks. Our point is that the more often domain organizations exchange information, the more sensitized they become to one another's political vocabularies. Thus, the proposed solutions to the growing gas lines created by the oil embargoes of the 1970s tended to stress either the "energy crisis" or the "business as usual" element, depending on whether an actor judged the conditions to call for re-equilibration of the market through unregulated prices or through government price controls. But both paradigms were intelligible to energy domain actors because the dense communication linkages among them had fostered mutual awareness of the alternative points of reference on which solutions to the gasoline shortage could be debated.

Exchanges of policy information are the main way in which organizations cope with a highly uncertain environment in which many actors engage in the competitive and cooperative processes of collective decision making. Information reduces the incalculability of political life by revealing to organizations where they stand in the game. Because no organization has complete control over those events of vital interest to it, its capacity to acquire, digest, and pass along information about the unfolding stream of policy events is indispensable to staying in the game and playing effectively. Many years ago Riesman (1961) noted the ascendancy of the inside dopester in American politics—the information-broker whose ceaseless purveyance of "true facts" greased the wheels of the negotiation, accommodation, and compromise so characteristic of American pluralism. Domain organizations rely heavily upon such agents to keep them apprised of developments that threaten their well-being or offer unexpected opportunities to consolidate gains. Insatiable legions of lawyers, PR men, government affairs specialists, and lobbyists (some 15,000 in Washington, D.C., alone) prowl the corridors of power, ferreting out every smidgen of information bearing on the interests of their employers and clients (Laumann and Heinz, 1985). Some, like Charls Walker, become legends in their own time (Drew, 1978).

If organizations are to have any impact upon the outcomes of collective decisions that affect their interests, they must maintain ready access to potential allies, opponents, and targets of influence efforts. It is no exaggeration to say: no information, no influence. The fundamental social structure of a national policy domain resides in the persistent patterns of communication and exchange of information pertinent to domain affairs among organizations. In the context of community political systems, Laumann et al. (1977:597) asserted, "Communication exchange is an essential precondition to the resolution of local issues" (see also Laumann and Pappi, 1976; Rogers and Kincaid, 1981). Given the unpredictability of many policy events, organizations cannot afford to wait until circumstances thrust these concerns upon their attention. Organizations must establish their communication networks far in advance so that whether the links remain in continual use or lie dormant, such connections can be activated when situations dictate. Some of these information channels are deliberately constructed formal arrangements, such as political action coalitions, data clearing houses, think tanks and research institutes, and inter-agency task forces. Others are more informal paths, involving personal inter-actions between officials activated over luncheons, cocktail parties, and golf outings (Engler, 1961:380). In either case, however, the essential aspect of interorganizational communication is its instrumental, purposive focus on the acquisition of timely and reliable policy-relevant information.

Information Processing

Organizations differ significantly from persons in the ways that they handle information acquired through communication. A widely recognized restric-tion on the rational-actor model of decision making for natural persons is the limited information-processing capacity of individuals (Moe, 1979). Ob-viously, utilities cannot be maximized in a risky environment if the full range of actions and their probable consequences cannot be humanly assessed. A person's attention must inevitably be restricted to a limited set of alter-natives, with an optimal "satisficing" solution the best that can be hoped for (Simon, 1957:xxiv).

Organizations face fewer constraints than persons on their information, al-though, as we shall see below, they also typically seek more data than they can use effectively. As a collectivity of persons, an organization can proliferate numerous boundary-spanning roles, staffed by agents who specialize in inter-acting with other domain organizations' agents. By enlarging the size of its technical and managerial staffs, an organization can more readily cope with an increasingly complex and uncertain information environment. For ex-ample, in 1977 the Edison Electric Institute, the major electrical utility trade association, decided to relocate from New York to Washington, D.C., and to enlarge its advocacy role in response to the increasing politicization of the energy domain. Organizations with larger information-processing staffs—Edison, for example, had 50 staff members devoted to energy-related policy matters in 1980—can more readily maintain extensive communication chan-nels to their domains and thus tap into larger information flows. These organi-zations will come to occupy more central locations in domain communication networks, whereas small organizations will be forced into peripheral positions. This effect is especially true of organizations that invest only a small portion of their total interests in a given domain, such as the KMS Fusion Company (whose main concerns lie in the national defense domain), although some giants, such as the AFL-CIO, can effectively operate in multiple domains.

Organizations can also differ from people in their application of information to the pursuit of their goals. Organizational actions result from complex social interactions taking place within an organization, not from a single intellect's information processing (Wilensky, 1967). When an organization multiplies its communication channels to the external environment and ingests greater volumes of information, it expands the problems of coordination, interpretation, and decision use. With more agents and subunits having partial views and competing claims on the organization's resources, conflicts over priorities erupt. The chance of intelligence failures increases with the number of organizational units involved in the decision process (Wilensky, 1967:57). The information gathered from other domain organizations can be used by an organization's subunits to promote partisan preferences and to impose their particular agenda on the organization as a whole. The more powerful units stand ready to exploit discretion in terms of their own goals. If several primary goals vie for favor—most likely when the organization lacks a strong chief executive officer, a strong unifying ideology, or a dominant board—"the most logical means of reconciling them appears to be a sequential attention to these goals, with each goal attended to periodically" (Mintzberg, 1983:263), presumably at the cost of reduced organizational efficiency and success in influencing domain policies.

Internal heterogeneity and conflicting objectives among an organization's groups, factions, or parties can render much organizational intelligence useless for decision making. Trade associations are especially vulnerable to this problem. The American Petroleum Institute, the AMA, and many others are unable to take stands on some issues because of internal divisions of interest—for example, the oil import quota proposals in the 1970s or abortion on demand. A characteristic response to such deadlocks is the fractioning of an organization into separate entities of greater internal homogeneity.

The bureaucratic politics perspective on organizational behavior (Allison, 1971) points to the way in which interorganizational communication can shape an organization's interests. In contrast to the conventional image of fixed organization goals, an emerging paradigm of decision making by objective argues that "goals are discovered through a social process involving argumentation and debate in a setting where justification and legitimacy play important roles. Not just any sort of goal will be discovered; it will be one that is consistent with shared organizational goals" (Anderson, 1983:214). In effect, organizations, like people, may not know what their attitudes are until they observe their own behavior vis-à-vis other actors. An organization that forges extensive information ties to a domain thereby opens itself to the possibility that its goals will be altered under concerted efforts by other organizations to recruit its participation for joint ventures. For example, an environmental action group with central interests in limiting nuclear power and constraining

land use finds itself actively supporting solar industry development because
its links to renewable fuels organizations raised the salience and compatibility
of alternative fuels strategies with the environmentalists' earlier agenda. In
the extreme case, information generated by some organizations may spawn
entirely new organizations that would not otherwise exist, such as research
outfits and forecasting services. Regulatory decisions sometimes unintentionally create, destroy, or sustain derivative industries—for example, the inefficient small oil refineries nurtured by the crude oil price control entitle-
ments provisions in 1974 (Kalt, 1981:106–7).

   That politics makes strange bedfellows was well understood even before
Charles Dudley Warner coined that aphorism. That communication networks
are essential to putting fellows into the same political bed may be less well
appreciated. A centerpiece of the Carter administration's energy program was
a natural gas price deregulation bill intended to phase out government price
setting. As late as August 1978, more than a year after its introduction, the
bill had attracted only a handful of business supporters, and the conference
report seemed doomed in the Senate. The administration then launched an all-
out sales effort, bringing in hundreds of executives from the paper, textile,
glass, banking, insurance, steel, automobile, construction, and aerospace industries to a series of "summit talks" at the White House. Within two weeks
the Department of Energy handed to wavering senators a list of 55 major industrial and financial corporations and 20 trade associations backing gas deregulation. The Senate impasse broke, and gradual decontrol became the law.
Carter's strategy was to break industry solidarity—for example, splitting off
Chrysler from the other major auto-makers—thus making defections by key
senators acceptable. Some unusual alliances were formed among interest
groups opposing deregulation: Amoco worked closely with Energy Action, a
consumer advocacy group, and the Chamber of Commerce consulted regularly with the AFL-CIO and UAW (Congressional Quarterly, 1979:24–25).
The gas decontrol fight is an excellent illustration of the point that even when
domain organizations typically find themselves on opposing sides of most
issues, they still need to keep open their communication channels for those
occasions when interests coincide. Because most organizations have multiple
interests within a domain and intend to play the game many times, to be effective they must preserve ties to all significant participants.

   Frequently, the recruitment of staff members from other organizations automatically creates strong interorganizational links. The "capture" of regulatory agencies by the very organizations they were established to regulate
has long been remarked (Bernstein, 1955; Huntington, 1950; McConnell,
1966:287–88). One consequence of the intimate iron triangles among agencies, congressional subcommittees, and client organizations is a steady inter-
change of personnel that tends to homogenize viewpoints, reduce the poten-

tial for internal conflict, and enhance the effectiveness of policy-relevant communication. A colorful illustration of how individuals' career lines shape organizational objectives is the curriculum vitae of Craig Hosmer, an 11-term congressman who became the ranking Republican on the old Joint Committee on Atomic Energy. When he left Congress in 1975 to head the American Nuclear Energy Council, the industry was well into its long slide toward stagnation under the triple burden of rising construction costs, slowing consumer demand, and a safety backlash. In a 1977 letter to a Carter senior aide, Hosmer complained that without new reactor orders, "the U.S. nuclear industry will move quickly to extinction." Later that year, sensing that the President was reneging on campaign pledges to promote the streamlining of the nuclear power plant licensing process, and apparently frustrated by Carter's personal vendetta against the Clinch River breeder reactor, Hosmer blasted White House schizophrenia over national nuclear policy in a speech to the Atomic Industrial Forum:

There is the White House symbolized by [energy advisor James] Schlesinger where a courageous effort goes on. . . . And then there is that other White House, populated by no growth counter-culture activists . . . bad guys [trying to] convert the country into a drab, energyless, no-growth sleeping-bag society. That is their goddamned transcendental notion of a great future for the U.S.A. . . . We pray of course . . . the President . . . decisively takes charge of the United States government, grasps its reins, decides where he wants to go, and shuts up or fires any s.o.b. that gets out of line. (Congressional Quarterly, 1979:110)

The licensing reform bill that shortly emerged from the Department of Energy was strongly proindustry and gave Secretary Schlesinger great powers of coordination at the expense of the Nuclear Regulatory Commission and citizen groups.

The preceding examples suggest that organizations participate in national policy domains with objectives that are subject to modification as information from other organizations helps them to define problems, discover goals, and alter tactics. Thus, the decisions an organization reaches on policy matters depend in important ways upon the nature of external communication and how such data are processed by the myriad of internal actors. Fascinating as the effects of information flow are (Mintzberg, 1983:171–217), we unfortunately lack sufficient evidence to analyze these processes. We are forced, therefore, to assume that domain organizations' interests antedate the formation of interorganizational communication networks, while recognizing that the real world is undoubtedly characterized by a continual interplay between internal and external sources of policy preferences.

The Functions of Communication

All communication involves the exchange of information between two or more parties at specific times. Some information is simply broadcast at large through generalized or specialized mass media: no efforts are made to restrict access to particular receivers. Indeed, data may flow well beyond domain boundaries, into the purview of the public at large and even to the attention of academic researchers! Other information is targeted to selected actors with a deliberate intention to prevent its circulation to others. Such communication typically requires restricted-access channels such as memos, telephone conversations, and face-to-face meetings. Although the specific contents of communication are infinitely varied in any domain, the latent functions of communication are to control or reduce uncertainties in an organization's environment (1) by monitoring the on-going stream of domain activity, and (2) by interpreting information for strategic interventions.

Monitoring Function

Organizations gather information about domain events as a form of neutral intelligence about the state of affairs: what interests do other domain participants have in various policy issues, in the substance of forthcoming events; who is likely to participate; when and where will critical decisions be made? Much of this surveillance activity is apparently inductive and exploratory, without overt intention to formulate particular policy choices and actions. Numerous studies find only weak connections between information gathering and decision making:

> In short, mostly organizations and individuals collect more information than they can use or can reasonably expect to use in the making of decisions. At the same time, they appear to be constantly needing or requesting more information, or complaining about inadequacies in information. (Feldman and March, 1981:174)

Organizations create information overloads not because they are stupid, but because information symbolizes their commitment to a rational-choice mode, thus signaling their competence to other domain actors who share this contemporary cultural value (see also DiMaggio and Powell, 1983, and Meyer and Rowan, 1977, for similar observations on symbolic legitimation through rationalized organizational structures). The fact that many data are acquired (or internally digested) too late to have any impact on organizational decision making suggests that information is mostly window dressing that legitimates decisions already made on other grounds (Sabatier, 1978:407).

Monitoring or intelligence requires that organizations cast their nets widely, drawing in an inclusive set of specialists, generalists, allies, antagonists, and neutrals. For example, one of the "Seven Sisters" oil companies reported initiating routine policy discussions with 87 of the 228 energy domain targets, including such potential opponents as the Consumer Energy Council, the Consumer Federation of America, and the Sierra Club. All conceivably informative contacts will be incorporated into a monitoring network in hopes of dredging up every useful shred of information. The pattern of information linkages will be asymmetric, reflecting the broadcast nature of monitoring, which does not require equivalent salience and information reciprocation among exchange partners. That is, given the differing importance that organizations attach to various domains and their differential capacities to process data about their environments, we expect that some organizations will remain unaware of the more marginal actors to whom they are broadcasting. Similarly, some organizations are insensitive to the fact that they are the intended recipients of regular, routine communication. Much of the content flowing through these surveillance channels is relatively innocuous, the sort of information that public relations departments churn out in endless streams: press releases, newsletters, bulletins, annual reports, background briefings, and working papers. Thus, the monitoring function of communication yields information with only limited value for reducing fundamental uncertainties about the domain. The more sensitive material that organizations exchange is restricted to a subset of actors, as described next.

Interpretive Function

Organizations also seek information in order to give meaning to domain events, to interpret the importance of events and their stakes in the outcomes, to evaluate the probable outcomes of decisions and their ramifications for the participants. Specially targeted communication facilitates organizational collaboration, the formation of coalitions, and the forging of collateral ties essential for collective action. In pluralistic polities, the rules of the political game especially encourage interpretive communication, since favorable decisions hinge upon executive and legislative politicking. In the extreme case, the existence of confidential communication channels, through which trustworthy information can be exchanged and jointly interpreted, enables organizations to respond effectively in crisis situations, controlling or reducing the negative impact of disruptive events. For these reasons we should expect the interpretive function of domain communication to explain critical policy behaviors more adequately than the monitoring function.

The monitoring function of communication is constrained by a dearth of meaningful information on costs in relation to performance. The careful cost accounting and allocation measures available to big business corporations have no parallel within the fluid and shifting national policy domains. Here most performance assessments are fragmented judgments based on subjective perceptions (Bower, 1983:37–39). Even "hard" technical or economic data are subject to arbitrary and distorting interpretations. For example, the basic question of how large are America's oil and gas reserves is impossible to answer because of the inherent policy implications in any set of numbers:

> Given the variety of estimates and estimators to choose from, the participants in energy policy pick those that advance their own preferences. Estimates have thus been servants of policy perspectives. We have been able to find no evidence that estimates exert any dominant or independent influence upon policy decisions. The repeated calls for credibility in data as prerequisites to intelligent policy-making mask this fundamental conclusion to which we have been drawn. (Wildavsky and Tenenbaum, 1981:299)

Given the ambiguity of most factual data, then, policy networks emphasize the circulation of impressions about political power—the real poop on which lobbyists have a subcommittee chairman's ear, whose lawyers were seen at a recent state banquet, which coalitions now in formation will have the upper hand in a debate. Gossip is the lifeblood of any collectivity, from politburo to faculty club, in which decisions must be made without benefit of a technocratic system of data management (Bower, 1983:26).

Interpretive communication facilitates organizations' timely intervention into policy events by revealing those times and places in the collective decision cycles where influence efforts can be most cost-effective. To avoid involvement after the outcome is a foregone conclusion, an organization must acquire and internally process policy event data at the right time. The anecdote in Chapter 1 underscores that point: had the trade association director not learned of the FAA regulation until after it went into effect, his efforts to exempt his companies might have been costly or futile. By having a network in place for the exchange of candid, confidential information, an organization can more readily recognize those situations in which concerted action can be consequential for its well-being. Communication apprises other organizations of one's own interests, beliefs, preferences, and intended actions.

Interpretive channels transmit information that alters the probable outcomes of organizations' interventions in policy events. That is, an organization can introduce persuasive information that affects others' behavior. Gamson (1968:73–81, 100–05) has distinguished analytically between inducements, constraints, and persuasions as influence resources (see Parsons, 1969, and Chapter 5 above). Inducements add new advantages to those enjoyed by another actor through the transfer of control over resources: for example, by making a campaign contribution to a candidate through the organization's political action committee (PAC). Similarly, constraints add new disadvantages to a situation, such as damaging information, threats, denunciations, or withdrawal of support (e.g., Environmental Action's "dirty dozen" list of House members with "poor environmental records"). In contrast, persuasion seeks to change an actor's subjective orientation without adding anything positive or negative to a situation. The change may result from a target's conviction about the rightness of the argument or from a prior belief in the expertise of the persuader. In providing new information to a target—as the petroleum trade association members did to the FAA—an organization changes the perceptions of authorities, allies, or opponents. The persuasion may be based on the technical merits of a proposal (e.g., the impact of price deregulation on the supply of natural gas) or on the political consequences of a decision (e.g., how a new health care program will affect the votes of the elderly). The more trustworthy and credible the information source—the higher the persuader's reputation for influence—the greater the capacity of its communications to convince others of a proposal's intrinsic merits (Knoke, 1983). Lobbyists' key tactic is to provide accurate information to indifferent, doubtful, and favorably disposed legislators and executive agency heads. Rarely do lobbyists try to convert their opponents (Fox and Schnitzer, 1981: 168–82; Milbrath, 1963; Ornstein and Elder, 1978:84). Interpretive information on technical performance, economic impacts, industry views and concerns—all enter the persuasion process. This information arms the politicians with reliable data for policy debates.

Choosing between Networks

We have identified two basic functions of communication networks in policy domains. The monitoring function broadcasts information to as many targets as possible and receives information from as many as possible in an effort to dredge up as much factual information as possible. The interpretive function is more selective, targeting those actors that may affect the success of an organization's policy influence efforts with persuasive information. The monitoring function should produce a dense, highly connected network with many asymmetric ties among organizations. The interpretive functions should yield a sparser, more disaggregated, but symmetric matrix of interorganizational connections. The reciprocity of the latter arises from the greater salience of mutual dependence among the subset of actors involved in these information exchanges. For analyzing policy domain activity, the monitoring function is likely to be less useful. It identifies mainly a neutral channel of communication that carries a large "overload" volume of information, having generally lower quality and lower utility for policy interventions. The interpretive function, by contrast, is better at identifying significant policy contents, such as persuasion, strategic interactions, trustworthy support, and solidarity. We prefer to work with this latter network because it is more likely to be strongly related to the sorts of partisan coalitions on policy events that we wish to explain.

The organizational informants were asked to describe two types of communications that they had with the other organizations in the domain. First, they were handed a list of all other domain actors and asked, "Would you please place a check mark *in front of* the name of *all* organizations on this list with whom (your organization) *regularly and routinely* discusses national energy [health] policy matters?" They were then asked to indicate which organization "typically initiates these policy discussions . . . [by checking] under the appropriate heading of WE DO, BOTH, or THEY DO to indicate how the initiation usually occurs" (Appendix B, C1). The results were assembled into an asymmetric matrix of regular-routine communication (RR).

The second communication network was identified by asking informants:

From time to time, organizations face especially sensitive problems in the national energy [health] field, where the judgments of others are valuable in deciding what positions or actions to take. Organizations often develop relationships with other organizations that they trust to exchange sensitive and confidential advice about actions or positions that might be taken.

They were instructed to check off on the list those organizations with which they had such a candid-confidential relationship (CC), noting whether "we give" or "we receive" such advice (Appendix B, C2). In assembling the final form of the CC matrix, we required that both directions of exchange be reported before identifying a channel between a pair of organizations (i.e., both organization A and organization B must state that they both give each other confidential information and receive it from one another). In the few instances where an organization refused to divulge its candid-confidential ties, we imputed such a channel if all four connections existed in the RR matrix.

The communication network thus constructed consists of a square, symmetrized, binary matrix. That is, each row and column of a CC matrix represents one of the domain organizations. A *1* in the row i, column j cell (and its corresponding *1* in the jth row, ith column cell) indicates that a communication tie exists between the pair of organizations. A *0* entry in the pair of cells means that no such candid-confidential tie exists.

Network density is typically measured as the proportion of the actual number of ties among actors to the potential number of ties (Knoke and Kuklinski, 1982:45). Thus, density may range from 0.0 (in a completely unconnected network) to 1.0, where all actors are mutually reachable in one step. Most discussions of total network density ignore difficulties in operationalizing ties. For example, in a hierarchical system, such as an army or another bureaucracy, where only superiors can direct commands to subordinates, the potential number of ties must be calculated in an asymmetric manner. That is, one would want to include those pairs of relations going from a superior to a subordinate, but not the relations in the reverse direction. Under our conceptualization, however, information may flow in both directions between all pairs of policy domain organizations. Thus, to calculate the domain densities for regular-routine and candid-confidential communication, we use the formula:

$$D = \frac{\Sigma \, \Sigma \, z_{ij}}{N^2 - N}$$

where z_{ij} and z_{ji} are the reciprocal ties between actors i and j ($i \neq j$), and N is the number of actors in the network. Density is a measure of the extent to which possible direct ties are realized in a network. It bears little relation to the degree of connectedness (that is, the mutual reachability of pairs of actors through lengthy chains of intermediaries). Indeed, one can find completely connected networks of exceptionally low density. Suppose that each actor is directly connected to only two other actors by bidirectional links. The result is a circular chain with density equal to $2N/(N^2 - N)$, which, for systems of size 25 or greater, yields densities of less than .10. Moore (1979) discovered a huge central circle of 227 members of the American national elite that had a density of only .038. The sparseness was due to a sampling design that selected persons from multiple domains and that permitted heterogeneous discussion contents among the actors.

The RR matrix most closely captures the monitoring function of communication, as it achieves a high density in each domain (.30 in energy and .30 in health) and exhibits considerable asymmetry of inflow and outflow across individual organizations. As expected, the symmetric CC matrix had much lower densities than the RR matrix: only .19 of possible energy and .17 of possible health ties were actually reported in the CC matrix. The national energy and health policy domain densities are similar to those found in two studies of organizations in specialized networks. Knoke and Rogers (1979) examined multiple types of ties among about 10 agriculture agencies in each of 12 Iowa counties and observed average densities of .42 for meetings of the directors, .26 for joint programs, .19 for information and for resource exchanges, .08 for overlapping boards, and .07 for written agreements. Knoke (1983) reported densities among 70 Indianapolis social influence associations and public and private sector organizations of .33 for moral support, .33 for information exchange, and .08 for money exchange. Clearly low-cost relationships such as information exchanges are easier to maintain than high-cost resource exchanges.

Because of the large number of organizations involved (192 in energy and 135 in health), the RR and CC matrices are unwieldy and reveal very little through visual inspection. Some form of data reduction is essential, and two possibilities are available.

Methods for Analyzing Networks

Two general approaches have been developed for analyzing relational data, such as those in the CC communication networks. Both seek to reduce the complexities of matrices involving large numbers of organizations by aggregating or clustering subsets of actors according to differing criteria of similarity. *Structural equivalence* procedures group together two or more actors to the extent that they maintain identical ties with all other actors in the system. Thus, a pair of organizations are structurally equivalent if they communicate with or avoid communicating with the same organizations among the other $N-2$ targets in the domain (Lorrain and White, 1971; White et al., 1976). In a very strong sense, structurally equivalent actors are substitutable for one another and jointly occupy the same structural position within the network. To the extent that a pair of actors maintain different sets of communication partners, they are dissimilar to one another and thus more socially distant within the network (Burt, 1976, 1977). The structural equivalence approach thus argues for data reduction by aggregating those organizations that maintain identical or highly similar direct ties with all other domain organizations. Organizations placed together as structurally equivalent need not, however, be in direct contact with one another under this criterion.

The alternative approach begins with the *graph theoretic* concept that proximity and distance among network actors are a function of their mutual reachability (Harary et al., 1965; Laumann and Pappi, 1976). That is, subsets of organizations are centrally located in a communication network to the extent that they can communicate with others either directly or through relatively few intermediaries. The social distance between actors is measured by "paths," the smallest number of directed communication links necessary to connect a pair. Peripheral organizations are those actors that cannot readily reach many others without lengthy chains of indirect ties. Indeed, at the extreme, isolates completely lack contacts with all other domain participants. The graph theoretic approach argues for a data-reduction strategy that aggregates those organizations which maintain the largest number of short-distance communication links to domain participants. Organizations located close to one another in a social space generated by graph theoretic principles will require shorter average paths to reach others; more distant actors will need lengthier communication paths. Various arguments have been advanced for preferring structural equivalence methods for network analysis (see especially Burt, 1979, who argues that graph theoretic concepts are a special case of structural equivalence). However, we believe that graph theoretic methods are more consistent with our analytic perspective on policy domain communication. Structural equivalence places greater emphasis on the absence of ties between actors in

calculating social distance.[1] That is, mutual avoidance of third parties in communication implies greater similarity in a pair of actors. But in systems involving large numbers of actors, the absence of direct communication linkages may be less a positive, conscious choice than simply a default that arises
from directing scarce organizational resources toward other parties. In contrast, graph theoretic methods emphasize mainly the positive communication
channels created by organizations, both directly and indirectly, through their
partners' ties. Thus, analyses using graph theoretic principles will more real-
istically reflect the choice processes going on within large domain systems.

In addition, structural equivalence implies that organizations grouped into
jointly occupied positions share identical (or highly similar) sources of information. As a result, all organizations in a structurally equivalent location will
be receiving the same information and thus will not be able to supply one
another with uncertainty-reducing data. Clusters generated by graph theoretic
approaches, however, are more likely to bring together organizations with
disparate sources of information—those sources expose their members to a
greater variety of data that could potentially reduce uncertainties about the
policy environment. Typically, we would expect to find that the center of a
graph theoretically defined communication network is occupied by core governmental authorities with dense interconnections among themselves that in
turn proliferate selective ties to the more narrowly specialized sectors of the
domain on the periphery. By serving as a sort of central switching station,
these core positions bring various regions of the space into more or less proximate contact with one another. For these reasons, we find more useful the
graph theoretic procedures for reducing domain communication networks to
manageable size. Before describing the operationalizations, we discuss two
analytic principles for the generation of communication ties between pairs of
organizations in a policy domain.

Structuration Principles

In this chapter, we examine the social organizational processes that generate social distance between pairs of organizations, or dyads, in the candid-
confidential communication networks of the energy and health policy domains. A dyad maintains close proximity through a combination of direct ties

1. We have in mind measures of structural equivalence, such as Euclidean distance (see Burt,
1976), that take into account the covariation across pairs of actors involving both ties present and
ties absent to all third actors in the network. Some alternative measures of structural similarity,
such as the simple matching coefficient or the Jaccard coefficient (see Jardine and Sibson, 1971;
Sokal and Sneath, 1963), specifically ignore the common non-ties. But these operationalizations
are not as frequently used by social network analysts.

and many indirect ties of short path distance. Two general factors may create short distances among organizations. First, *shared interests* in domain policy issues and events form clear bases for mutual interaction. The potential for both cooperation and conflict between organizations having common concerns leads to the formation of communication channels through which interpretive information can flow. Organizations need not agree on solutions to issues and events in order to have much to discuss. Indeed, opponents may have as much reason to exchange candid-confidential information about their intentions as do coalition partners (cf. Laumann and Marsden, 1979). Thus, both allies and antagonists are more likely to find themselves in close proximity than are organizations whose interests are so divergent that they have little to talk about. Second, any social factors that lower the *transaction costs* for communication should result in stronger ties (cf. Williamson, 1985). Information exchanges, especially the more costly candid-confidential ones, require continual effort and commitment of organizational resources to their establishment and maintenance. Therefore, when organizations have similar attributes, their costs for communicating will be lower and the exchange more probable.[2] The principle of homophily—that like attracts like—is well known in the social psychology of friendships and work groups (Kanter, 1977; Laumann, 1966, 1973; Verbrugge, 1979), but has yet to be examined for interorganizational relations.

The principles of shared interests and transaction costs can be expressed as a series of testable hypotheses. The probability that a given pair of policy domain organizations will engage in interpretive communication increases to the extent that:

1. they share common interests in domain issues;
2. they share preferences for the outcomes of policy events;
3. both members have high monitoring capacities;
4. both members have high influence rankings;
5. they are the same "type" of organization (e.g., both are corporations, public interest groups, federal agencies);
6. at least one of the dyad is a public authority organization (congressional subcommittee or federal agency).

2. For example, employees of a professional association are familiar with the organizational structure of such organizations. They can be expected to know where to find their opposite numbers in sister organizations. It is decidedly less obvious to them, however, who occupies positions comparable to their own in huge business concerns, trade associations, or labor unions. Moreover, personnel occupying comparable positions in different types of organizations are likely to be recruited from different social backgrounds, to have had different organizational experiences, and to follow different organizational practices (See Nelson et al., 1987, for documentation on this point). Such differences among personnel will impede easy access and communication across types of organizations, even given shared interests in particular policy issues.

The first two propositions reflect the shared interests principle, and the next three the transaction costs principle. The sixth proposition acknowledges the special role of governmental authorities as targets and instigators of interpretive policy communications. These propositions about dyadic links are intended as *ceteris paribus* relationships: that is, effects upon the social distance between dyads in a communication network after holding constant the impact of all other factors. The next section describes measurement procedures used to test the empirical validity of these expectations.

Measurement

The square, symmetric, binary candid-confidential communication matrix was used to compute path distances between all pairs of domain organizations. Direct ties are paths of distance 1; indirect ties requiring a single intermediary have distance 2; and so forth. (See Chapter 8 for a more detailed explanation of path distance and related concepts.) Table 7.1 shows the distribution of path distances among the dyads in both domains. Both networks are highly connected, with no isolates, and the large majority of the thousands of dyads mutually reachable in two steps or less. The health domain contains notably more distant pairs (10.9 percent requiring two intervening contacts, compared with only 1.2 percent in the energy domain). We can only speculate that the oft-noted turbulence of the energy policy arena placed a higher premium on unfiltered communication.

Each path matrix was submitted to the ALSCAL spatial analysis program, resulting in excellent fits in two dimensions (stress coefficients of .15 for both domains). The results are displayed in figures 8.4–8.7 and discussed in Chapter 8. The coordinate values of the ALSCAL analysis were used to compute the distances between every pair of organizations in each domain, using the standard Pythagorean formula for distance between points in a Euclidean coordinate system. These distance values were the dependent measures used in the linear regression analyses described in the next section.

Values for independent variables in the dyad analyses were obtained from the organizational variables as follows. *Issue correlation* measures the shared interest in domain issues for a pair of organizations by correlating their levels of expressed interest (from "no interest" to "major interest") across 65 energy issues or 56 health issues (see Chapter 4). The higher the correlation, the more similar that pair's pattern of interests across domain issues. *Issue public similarity* is a related measure of common issue orientation, in this case, a 1–0 dichotomy tapping whether the two occupy the same or different issue publics, as discussed above in Chapter 4. The *activity similarity* and *position similarity* measures of shared interests in events were calculated in similar ways. Both are simple matching coefficients that count, respectively, the num-

Table 7.1. Distribution of Path Distances among Domain Dyads in the Candid-Confidential Communication Network

Path Distance	Energy Domain	Health Domain
Disconnected	0%	0%
1	19%	17%
2	80%	72%
3	1%	11%
Total	100%	100%
N	(18,336)	(9,045)

ber of domain events in which a pair of organizations were both actively involved and the number in which they took the same pro/con position. Because the latter value is constrained by the former (i.e., a position cannot be taken unless one is first active), these two measures of shared event interests are highly correlated ($r = .73$ and $.77$ for energy and health respectively).

Turning to measures of transaction costs, *type similarity* is a 1–0 dichotomy that shows whether both members of the dyad belong to the same type of organization, using the nine-category typology presented in Chapter 3. A *government sender* and a *government receiver* pair of dichotomies was used to test whether communication distance varies with the possession of public authority by either dyad partner. For *monitoring capacity* and *influence rank,* rather than create similarity measures on these continuous variables, we directly entered the values of the sending and the receiving organizations. We also explored interaction terms created by multiplying these "main effect" measures, but the resulting coefficients were either insignificant or produced substantively unintelligible values, so we do not report these results in the next section.

Findings on Dyads

The results of the measurements described above appear in the pair of equations reported in table 7.2. The amount of variance in communication distances explained by the entire set of independent variables is noticeably larger in the health domain (31.1 percent) than in the energy domain (25.1 percent).

Table 7.2. Regression of Path Distance Measures on Dyadic Variables

Independent Variables	Standardized Regression Coefficients	
	Energy	Health
Issue Correlation	-.29**	-.17**
Issue Public Similarity	.01	-.02*
Event Activity Similarity	.16**	-.05**
Event Position Similarity	-.14**	-.05**
Organization Type Similarity	-.12**	-.03**
Sender Government Authority	-.16**	-.01
Receiver Government Authority	-.16**	-.01
Sender Influence Rank	.18**	.35**
Receiver Influence Rank	.18**	.35**
Sender Monitoring Capacity	-.02**	-.01
Receiver Monitoring Capacity	-.02**	-.01
Adjusted R-Square	.251**	.311**

* p = <.05
** p = <.0001

This difference is consistent with our previous suggestion that health enjoyed greater structuration during the period under observation. Because of the large number of dyads in each data set, several regression coefficients are statistically significant despite trivial magnitudes. Hence, many of the hypotheses are supported in the formal sense, although a few are substantively unimportant. Note that, with one exception, negative coefficients uphold a hypothesis, since larger values of the dependent variable mean that a dyad is farther apart in the communication space. For example, the negative coefficients for issue correlation ($-.29$ in energy and $-.17$ in health) mean that the more highly the issue interests of a pair of organizations co-vary, the smaller their communication distance. The exception to this relationship concerns the influence rank measure, where small values indicate high rank and large values low rank. Hence, the four positive coefficients reveal that high-ranking organizations tend to be closer together. Two variables that do not receive much support in the equations are the monitoring capacity and issue public similarity measures, none of whose regression coefficients are large or highly significant.

Several contrasts across the two domains are noteworthy. Organizational type is more important in energy than in health (standardized coefficients of $-.12$ and $-.03$, respectively). Being a governmental authority is significant in energy ($-.16$) but not in health ($-.01$). (The identical values for sending and receiving measures of the same variable occur because the CC matrix is symmetric. Multicollinearity is not a problem here because the sender and receiver scores are uncorrelated.) These domain differences imply that energy organizations more often target their policy discussions toward other organizations similar to themselves and toward congressional subcommittees and federal agencies, but that health organizations make more eclectic choices. As shown below, health organizations selected their communication partners on other grounds.

Shared issue and event interests have greater impacts in the energy domain. The magnitudes of energy issue correlation, event activity similarity, and event position similarity coefficients are all much larger than the corresponding health measures. The positive value for similarity in energy event activity is probably due to multicollinearity, as the zero-order correlation is negative. Apparently, shared interests in issues and events are much more important stimulators of communication in the energy domain, where policy-making procedures were less well established and routinized than in the health domain. Energy organizations seem to have sought out for discussion those partners whose concerns most strongly overlapped with their own, but without restricting themselves to those actors sharing outcome preferences on events. In contrast, the driving factor in health domain communication is organizational influence rank. High-ranking senders and receivers are closer together than low-ranking organizations in both domains, but the standardized coefficients are twice as large in health as in energy. Indeed, the energy betas for ranks are much smaller than the beta for issue correlation. Again, these results are consistent with our recurrent finding that the health domain was more highly structured according to centralized, status-oriented principles, whereas the energy domain was more decentralized, amorphous, and fragmented into special interest groupings.

The dyad analyses of the candid-confidential communication network support the basic principles of shared interests and lowered transaction costs in the formation of these basic building-blocks of policy domain interaction. But micro-level communication ties do not paint the complete picture. In the next chapter, we continue to analyze the candid-confidential communication structure from more global perspectives.

8

Global Network Structures

We now shift focus to a higher level of analysis. Previous chapters examined the individual organizations or dyads in each domain. But numerous network analysts argue that a new phenomenon emerges through interactions among discrete participants—the network social structure. Global features may not be consciously visible to the participants, as they involve hundreds or thousands of linkages about which the network actors remain unaware. Nevertheless, "the patterning of linkages can be used to account for some aspects of behavior of those involved" (Mitchell, 1969). Characteristics of the system as a whole can affect the perceptions, orientations, and actions of its organizational components. Relationships between actors, not simply the attributes of these individuals, hold the key to modeling social structures: "The patterning of these relationships . . . may be treated as a complex index of the *mutually determined* actions and *jointly recognized* systematic constraints under which a given system developed" (Berkowitz, 1982:155). By analyzing structural relations at the policy domain level, we can better understand how the overall configuration facilitates or constrains the actions of organizational participants. For example, which organizations have better access to timely information about policy events? What limits the mobilization of resources for use in collective influence efforts? Why are some interest groups more successful than others in affecting the outcome of policy events?

These concerns point to the importance of measuring national policy do-

226

main network structures, the chief task of this chapter. Many distinct structures may link organizations at a given time: economic market relations, governmental authority relations, friendship relations among chief executives, even social-recreational relations! The pattern of relationships in a monetary exchange network will not be identical with that involving common seats on boards of directors. For purposes of explaining domain policy actions, information exchange is the critical relationship. As argued in the preceding chapter, a communication network may be measured by either the asymmetric flow of regular-routine data or the reciprocated exchange of candid-confidential information. Below, we examine the network structures generated by both types of data transactions; later chapters will show how the restricted candid-confidential network helps to explain policy event processes.

Figure 8.1 illustrates some basic features of a hypothetical communication network. Shown is a digraph (directed graph) in which letters represent organizations and arrows show the transmission of information. This digraph was constructed to illustrate a variety of distinct network components. Organization *A* is a network star that receives communication from many others, whereas *K* is obviously an isolate. The subsets (*A, B, C, D*) and (*H, I, K*) are cliques, in which all members directly communicate with one another (i.e., they are mutually reachable without intermediaries). Organizations *E, F, G* are connected to the larger clique by unreciprocated ties to *A*, suggesting that the three are marginally connected to the network. Each of these hangers-on can communicate with clique members *B, C*, and *D* only via an indirect connection through *A*. The path distance between a pair of organizations, as noted in Chapter 7, is the smallest number of linkages required to connect them. For example, *G* can send a message to *B* by a two-step path involving *A* as an intermediary. Organization *F* plays a critical bridging role in allowing communication to flow from the smaller to the larger clique, also in a two-step path. Because the information flows through restricted channels, it is more readily accessible to some members (e.g., *A*) than others (e.g., *G*). Thus, the network structure could account for the greater policy event knowledge and participation of some organizations compared with others.

The existence of many indirect linkages (paths of length two or more) among the network organizations is a common feature of large, sparse networks. Thus, third actors are critical because they permit first and second parties to reach one another (Laumann and Marsden, 1982). By not taking into account the larger domain network structure, we may reach inaccurate conclusions about the ways in which interorganizational relations condition the actions of their participants. (For expositions of the basic principles of network analysis using digraphs, consult any of several treatments: Burt and Minor, 1983; Knoke and Kuklinski, 1982; Laumann and Pappi, 1976:201–5; Marsden and Laumann, 1984.)

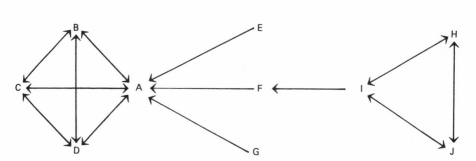

Figure 8.1. Digraph of a Hypothetical Information Exchange Network

The preceding example shows that social network structure, like the cosmos, consists of many intriguing objects. The larger the domain, the more essential it is for an analyst to reduce it to manageable proportions, lest its sheer complexity overwhelm the senses and obscure the underlying structural features. To extend our astronomical metaphor, attention must shift from individual stars to whole clusters or even entire galaxies. A digraph (and its algebraic equivalent, the matrix) can be condensed by grouping together into a single position all those individual organizations that are in some sense identical or equivalent to one another within the particular network under study. For example, if the N oil companies in the energy domain each maintain identical communication ties with the same government agencies, congressional committees, trade associations, interest groups, and other organizations, we might just as well speak of a unitary "oil industry position" within the domain that is jointly occupied by these N individual actors (Burt, 1976). Similarly, other generic types of organizations could be aggregated into single positions, resulting in a much simplified digraph of perhaps a dozen positions rather than nearly 200 original organizations. The condensation would be much easier to depict visually, manipulate algebraically, and interpret substantively.

To perform such data reduction on a network, we have two general approaches, as discussed in the preceding chapter: structural equivalence and graph theoretic. Structural equivalence places in the same position those organizations that maintain identical patterns of direct linkages with all other domain actors. The mutual absence of ties to third parties is as important as their mutual presence in calculating structural equivalence for a given pair of organizations. Graph theoretic methods place organizations in a common position according to their social distances as calculated on the pattern of both direct and indirect paths linking all actors. Here, the pattern of existing ties is the main determinant of proximity or distance among all organizations. Because of their distinct conceptual and methodological bases, the two network reduction methods are likely to yield empirically different network condensations (Burt, 1978). Our preference for the graph theoretic approach, noted in the preceding chapter, stems primarily from its emphasis on the positive choices (both direct and indirect) among communication partners rather than from the avoidance of direct ties that plays a substantial part in the structural equivalence approach.

Applied to an information exchange network, the graph theoretic approach calculates the social distances between pairs of domain organizations as the minimum number of intermediaries through which information must be transmitted from one member of a pair to reach another. The communication structure visually maps organizations with identical patterns of linkages into the same network position, groups those with similar patterns near to one another, and places those with highly discrepant patterns far apart. The precise number of positions in the reduced network depends upon how lenient or stringent the analyst wishes to be in treating proximate organizations. The more generous the criterion, the fewer positions will be identified, and the more organizations will jointly occupy them. Positions close to one another in the communication space contain organizations that are mutually reachable through fewer intermediaries than the members of positions located farther from one another.

Two general principles govern the spatial location of positions in a national policy domain: centrality/peripherality and interest differentiation (see Laumann and Pappi, 1976:138–43, for a related discussion of local community decision-making structures). The centrality/peripherality principle is a formalism that recurs in many types of social networks, such as friendship ties and authority relations. Some actors send and receive many more choices than others, and they tend to target their interactions toward others who enjoy similarly high popularity. The resulting global network structure contains a few central positions occupied by actors that maintain close ties with many others (close in the sense of having low average path distances between them) and a larger number of peripheral positions occupied by actors with lower visibility, fewer ties, and generally tenuous involvement in the system. For national policy domains, we expect the central positions to be dominated (1) by organizations that serve as information brokers, such as peak trade associations and professional societies, and (2) by organizations that possess major governmental authority that makes them the repositories of policy data, such as government bureaus and congressional committees with broad policy mandates. We expect the peripheral positions to be filled by specialist organizations, private sector groups, and those having limited capacities to sustain large volumes of communication (because of scarce resource endowments or low interest in the domain).

The interest-differentiation principle draws upon the relational contents of communication, and specifically the tendency for pairs of organizations that share common interests across a range of domain issues to establish dyadic communication channels. This tendency was documented empirically in the preceding chapter. For the network as a whole, then, organizations with identical or similar interests will use shorter path distances to communicate than will organizations having divergent interests. Not only will the organizations that jointly occupy a position exhibit greater issue interest similarity, but adjacent positions will be more similar in their issue profiles than will the more distant positions. Hence, we would expect to observe a distinct "sectoring" of the communication space, with positions jointly occupied by organizations that hold common interests across the array of domain issues, and a gradually widening disparity as distances increase between positions. The causal mechanism is probably reciprocal: mutual recognition of common interests generates policy discussions among organizational agents, and the formation of durable communication channels promotes the emergence of latent issue concerns among communicating partners. Over time, a stable network results, in which organizations are constrained to interact within delimited patterns that resist changes in either the position or the interests held by the domain members.

Bringing together both the centrality/peripherality and the issue-differentiation principles of communication network structure creates an expected model like that in figure 8.2. The concentric rings represent degrees of centrality; the cross-cutting pie-shaped wedges delimit distinct issue subsectors. Positions are represented by letters, here subsuming two or more individual organizations (although, to the extent that an analyst is willing to tolerate greater internal differentiation among the members of a position, the positions will encompass an area of the communication space rather than a single point).

Thus, position *A* occupies the very center of the space, at a minimum average distance from all the other positions. The organizations occupying *A* presumably invest a portion of their issue interests portfolios in every domain subsector. Moving away from the center, we encounter the more peripheral positions, located in specialized interest sectors. Any position (such as *F*) that lies in close proximity to others (such as *E* and *B*) will share some interests with these neighbors and will communicate with them at a higher rate than it will with more differentiated and more remote positions (such as *I*). We would expect position *F* to engage in more collaborative policy actions and to interact more with other positions in its subsector, to participate less often with positions in adjacent sectors, and to avoid involvement with the positions lying farthest away.

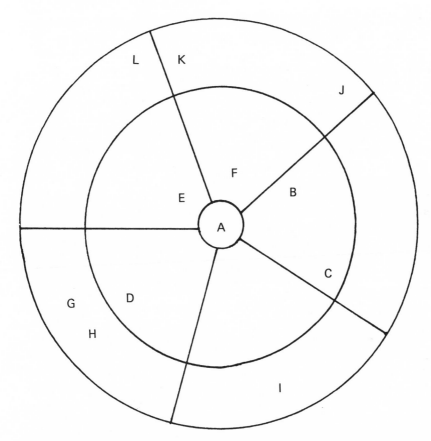

Figure 8.2. Two-Dimensional Schematic of a Communication Network Organized According to Center-Periphery and Issue-Differentiation Principles

Communication among Issue Publics

One way to test the hypothesis that communication patterns covary with domain issue interests is to examine the patterning of communication among groups defined by their issue interests: the issue publics we identified in Chapter 4. These groups were identified by hierarchically clustering organizations according to the correlation coefficient calculated on each pair's profile of interests across the 65 energy or 56 health domain issues. Some 13 energy and 14 health issue publics were identified, consisting of relatively homogeneous sets of organizations.

We permuted the regular-routine communication matrices in both domains into their issue public subsets, then partitioned them into submatrices that reveal intra- and interpublic information exchanges. For these analyses, we believe that the regular-routine communication channels constitute the most publicly visible expression of an organization's policy interests. Hence, the hypothesized linkage between interests and communication is more likely to occur in regular-routine exchanges than in the candid-confidential network, since we had required the later to contain only reciprocated ties.

If our hypothesis is correct, then the partitioned submatrices should exhibit differentially dense ties within and between the issue publics. That is, communications will be structured along issue public lines, with excesses of information exchange among organizations occupying the same public and below-average rates of communication between publics, because interests affect who tells what to whom. If the hypothesis is incorrect, then communication flows will be randomly distributed. Because members of a public have, by definition, highly similar issue interest profiles, we expect to observe higher densities of communication within publics than between publics. Interpublic communication rates will reflect a gradient from higher rates between spatially proximate publics to lower rates among distant publics, where distance is equivalent to dissimilar issue interests. In other words, the fewer interests that two publics have in common, the less often they will exchange policy information. The major exception to this spatial gradient involves those publics containing significant government organizations. Although such governmental publics may not share many of the issue concerns of other domain publics, they are likely to be targeted for excessive communication because of their authority to satisfy claimants' demands for policy decisions. Hence, we expect that the highest rates of interpublic communication will occur between pairs of publics at least one of which contains major governmental actors.

We further expect that the interest-communication links among issue publics will generate differentiated policy roles for these units. Network analysts (Burt, 1976; White et al., 1976) identify generic social roles from patterns of exchange relationships between and within jointly occupied network positions. Indeed, distinctive domain positions can be identified by similarities of exchange relationships among system actors, as we will do later in this chapter with the candid-confidential network. At this point, using the regular-routine matrices overlaid onto positions identified by commonality of interests (i.e., the issue publics), we can classify each public's policy role according to the patterns of communication that its members maintain with themselves and with the other publics. Figure 8.3 displays eight analytic role types, classified according to their inflows, outflows, and internal exchanges of information. We expect most policy domain issue publics to resemble those in the left column, according to our hypothesis that organizations sharing common interests

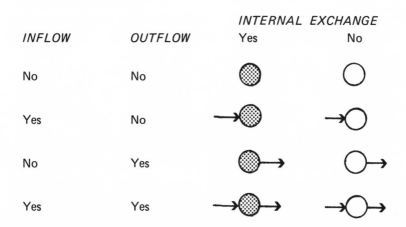

Figure 8.3. Eight Analytic Communication Roles

will tend to discuss policies with one another. These publics will be further differentiated by the presence or absence of regular-routine communication channels to external actors, particularly to publics that contain major governmental authorities. Thus, we hypothesize that issue interest publics act as significant nodes in the exchange of domain policy information, and that they tend to specialize in distinctive policy roles.

Tables 8.1 and 8.2 display descriptive information bearing on some of these relationships. The cell entries in these tables are the communication densities (regular-routine) within or between the domain's issue publics. That is, the proportion of ties present to ties possible is calculated for the various submatrices of the communication network, as partitioned into publics (self-ties of organizations are ignored in estimating densities). Cell densities that equal or exceed the density for the domain as a whole have been circled, to indicate the most heavily used channels in each domain. In the energy domain, six of the seven largest issue publics also have high internal densities (the exception is the miscellaneous grouping), whereas only two of the six smaller issue publics have high intrapublic communication ties. Interpublic communication occurs substantially less often: only 40 percent of all pairs of publics have communication densities above the average for the entire network. Furthermore, energy policy discussion is channeled toward a single public—the six-organization regulatory public that includes the Energy Department. This public maintains substantial sending and receiving ties to every other domain public. The remaining dense communication channels tend to occur, with few exceptions, between publics most similar to one another in their issue interests. For example, issue publics 1 through 5 are highly interconnected (with

Table 8.1. Communication Densities among Energy Domain Publics

Issue Publics Sending Information	Information Publics Receiving Information													
	1	2	3	4	5	6	7	8	9	10	11	12	13	Total
1. Auto Transp	(100)	(42)	25	(50)	30	(50)	30	(58)	(50)	(38)	(75)	25	14	31
2. Mfg, Exec	(39)	(50)	(35)	(39)	29	28	(32)	(62)	22	10	(39)	30	21	33
3. Oil	23	(36)	(56)	(43)	23	(33)	27	(61)	27	19	18	18	12	31
4. Railway	(38)	(39)	(39)	17	(38)	25	23	(75)	13	25	(75)	25	7	32
5. Coal, Gas	(32)	27	28	(40)	(37)	17	25	(55)	10	19	23	26	11	29
6. Shipping	(50)	22	(33)	25	17	--	6	(33)	0	25	0	4	0	15
7. Renew	31	(32)	29	26	25	31	(47)	(46)	20	6	9	(38)	21	33
8. Regul	(58)	(64)	(64)	(79)	(58)	(33)	(51)	(70)	(50)	(46)	(33)	(62)	(38)	59
9. PIRG-FTC	(75)	19	30	13	8	0	20	(42)	0	0	0	12	7	18
10. Pipes	(50)	10	18	25	17	25	5	(33)	0	17	0	7	0	12
11. Transp	(75)	(36)	20	(75)	(32)	0	11	(50)	0	0	(100)	22	21	25
12. Nuclear	25	29	18	27	27	4	(38)	(57)	14	7	17	(60)	27	36
13. Misc	14	17	18	7	10	0	18	24	7	4	14	21	12	15
Total	31	33	31	34	29	16	33	54	18	13	21	36	19	32

234

Table 8.2. Communication Densities among Health Domain Publics

Issue Public Receiving Information

Issue Public Sending Information	1	2	3	4	5	6	7	8	9	10	11	12	13	14	Total
1. Mental Health	(73)	(43)	(39)	16	(46)	(38)	3	13	3	19	10	14	(88)	5	30
2. Consumers	36	(60)	(67)	27	(31)	(50)	11	15	21	13	14	(42)	(89)	29	38
3. Finance	(32)	(60)	(78)	(41)	24	(44)	10	13	28	14	(37)	28	(97)	(40)	41
4. Professionals	17	30	(49)	27	17	(39)	15	19	11	8	(33)	13	(73)	15	28
5. Abortion	(41)	(50)	37	20	(100)	(32)	5	4	0	5	14	(33)	(88)	10	27
6. Public Health	29	(43)	(47)	(33)	18	(48)	22	(42)	21	24	(34)	26	(84)	17	37
7. Disease #1	2	14	14	15	5	(31)	15	22	27	10	18	18	(55)	2	16
8. Research	10	15	11	21	4	(41)	23	(40)	18	23	(32)	18	(54)	3	22
9. Disease #2	3	27	(33)	13	0	(31)	27	18	(33)	12	(33)	0	(58)	7	22
10. Disease #3	17	16	23	9	5	(40)	12	26	12	(39)	17	9	(77)	0	22
11. Drug Industry	10	15	(38)	30	7	(36)	18	(31)	29	14	(100)	(57)	(82)	14	30
12. Food	17	(48)	(37)	22	(33)	(43)	24	23	0	9	(43)	(100)	(92)	7	32
13. Government	(73)	(75)	(96)	(63)	(75)	(73)	(45)	(69)	(50)	(55)	(71)	(75)	(100)	(50)	71
14. Isolates	3	(33)	(45)	12	0	23	0	3	7	0	17	7	(65)	15	18
Total	26	38	45	26	20	42	15	24	19	18	30	26	79	17	31

235

two-thirds of their interposition ties exceeding the overall network density), but none of these five positions communicate at a high level with the remote nuclear-electrical-environmental issue public.

The health domain structures its communication flows among issue publics in a similar fashion. Within-public communication is high: only three of the 14 publics fail to match or exceed the overall density of communication ties (the health professional, first targeted disease, and isolate publics). More than 40 percent of the possible interpublic communication channels exceed the average density, about as often as occurs in the energy domain. Communication between publics is largely channeled toward four publics. The government public, which contains the HHS secretary, maintains high contacts in both directions with all other publics, thus paralleling the pattern of the regulatory position in the energy domain. Clearly, the public that contains the cabinet department most responsible for core domain policies attracts a substantial volume of the policy discussion. Three other health publics—health finance, public health, and consumers—also sustain regular policy discussion contacts at higher than average rates with half or more of the other domain publics. If these four highly involved positions are set aside, the remaining health publics are seen to be tenuously connected to one another. For example, the health research and targeted disease publics do not communicate among themselves at high rates; nor, indeed, do they communicate much with anyone else. Similarly, several other publics in table 8.2 are only sparsely connected to one another if their ties with the four activist positions are ignored. Thus, both energy and health domains exhibit a general pattern of policy communication at the routine-regular level among their issue publics that is strongly skewed to a handful of positions that participate at high rates, while the bulk of publics display only marginal connections.

Policy Roles of Publics

Further insight into the structure of the policy discussion networks can be gained from log-linear analyses of the two density tables. Using procedures and programs developed by Marsden (1980a; 1980b), the observed frequencies of present/absent ties in the square density table were fitted to a quasi-symmetry model, whose estimated effect coefficients are shown in tables 8.3 and 8.4. These models produced excellent statistical fits ($G = 8.25$, $df = 66$; $G = 27.49$, $df = 78$, for energy and health, respectively). A quasi-symmetric model for a square table means that the condition of symmetry (i.e., equal rates of discussion frequency between pairs of issue publics) is approached as closely as possible within the constraints of nonhomogeneity in the marginal distributions (i.e., the number of discussion ties sent and received are not

Table 8.3. Effect Parameters for Quasi-Symmetry Model Fitted to Energy Domain Communication among Issue Publics

	A. Volume Parameter		
Issue Public		$\theta = -1.196$	
	B. Participation Parameters		C. Group Choice Parameters
1. Auto Transp	$\alpha_1 = 1.13$	$\beta_1 = 1.13$	$\gamma_{11} = 2.65$
2. Mfg, Exec	$\alpha_2 = .43$	$\beta_2 = .40$	$\gamma_{22} = .36$
3. Oil	$\alpha_3 = .32$	$\beta_3 = .32$	$\gamma_{33} = .78$
4. Railway	$\alpha_4 = .42$	$\beta_4 = .51$	$\gamma_{44} = -1.32$
5. Coal, Gas	$\alpha_5 = .12$	$\beta_5 = .12$	$\gamma_{55} = .42$
6. Shipping	$\alpha_6 = -.70$	$\beta_6 = -.67$	$\gamma_{66} = 2.57$
7. Renew	$\alpha_7 = -.02$	$\beta_7 = -.03$	$\gamma_{77} = 1.13$
8. Regul	$\alpha_8 = 1.41$	$\beta_8 = 1.23$	$\gamma_{88} = -.60$
9. PIRG-FTC	$\alpha_9 = -1.03$	$\beta_9 = -1.01$	$\gamma_{99} = -.48$
10. Pipes	$\alpha_{10} = -1.10$	$\beta_{10} = -1.00$	$\gamma_{10,10} = 1.70$
11. Transp	$\alpha_{11} = .11$	$\beta_{11} = -.14$	$\gamma_{11,11} = 4.94$
12. Nuclear	$\alpha_{12} = .01$	$\beta_{12} = .00$	$\gamma_{12,12} = 1.60$
13. Misc	$\alpha_{13} = -1.09$	$\beta_{13} = -.87$	$\gamma_{13,13} = 1.17$

equal for a given public; see Knoke and Burke, 1980:48–54, for an explanation of these log-linear hypotheses).

The maximum likelihood parameter estimates in tables 8.3 and 8.4 help to identify the characteristic roles played by each issue public in the policy discussion networks. Theta, the volume parameter, simply reflects the overall number of relations present in the network (the coefficients come from an additive model of the logged expected cell frequencies, hence their positive or negative signs). The alpha and beta parameters reflect differential tendencies of issue publics to engage in policy discussions. A positive alpha indicates a public's "expansiveness," or tendency to initiate many discussions. A positive beta indicates "popularity," or tendency to be sought out by many other pub-

Table 8.4. Effect Parameters for Quasi-Symmetry Model Fitted to Health Domain Communication among Issue Publics

	A. Volume Parameter		
Issue Public	$\Theta = -1.082$		
	B. Participation Parameters		C. Group Choice Parameters
1. Mental Health	$\alpha_1 = -0.19$	$\beta_1 = -0.37$	$\gamma_{11} = 2.66$
2. Consumers	$\alpha_2 = 0.43$	$\beta_2 = 0.48$	$\gamma_{22} = 0.59$
3. Finance	$\alpha_3 = 0.63$	$\beta_3 = 0.89$	$\gamma_{33} = 0.84$
4. Professionals	$\alpha_4 = -0.09$	$\beta_4 = -0.13$	$\gamma_{44} = 0.31$
5. Abortion	$\alpha_5 = -0.06$	$\beta_5 = -0.46$	$\gamma_{55} = 6.91$
6. Public Health	$\alpha_6 = 0.43$	$\beta_6 = 0.69$	$\gamma_{66} = -0.10$
7. Disease #1	$\alpha_7 = -0.83$	$\beta_7 = -0.88$	$\gamma_{77} = 1.03$
8. Research	$\alpha_8 = -0.43$	$\beta_8 = -0.29$	$\gamma_{88} = 1.38$
9. Disease #2	$\alpha_9 = -1.02$	$\beta_9 = -1.13$	$\gamma_{99} = 2.54$
10. Disease #3	$\alpha_{10} = -0.84$	$\beta_{10} = -1.08$	$\gamma_{10,10} = 2.56$
11. Drug Industry	$\alpha_{11} = 0.70$	$\beta_{11} = 0.75$	$\gamma_{11,11} = 7.97$
12. Food	$\alpha_{12} = 0.36$	$\beta_{12} = 0.11$	$\gamma_{12,12} = 7.02$
13. Government	$\alpha_{13} = 2.37$	$\beta_{13} = 2.87$	$\gamma_{13,13} = 2.93$
14. Isolates	$\alpha_{14} = -1.46$	$\beta_{14} = -1.47$	$\gamma_{14,14} = 2.27$

lics for discussion. The gamma parameters are "group choice" effects that indicate the tendency for issue public i to contact public j above or below the rate that would be expected on the basis of volume, inflow, and outflow. A positive gamma on the main diagonal means that an issue public's organizational members tend to choose one another more often than predicted by the theta, alpha, and beta parameters. (The off-diagonal gammas, which are functions of the main diagonal effects, are not shown, to conserve space.)

Using the observed combinations of all three effect parameters, we can classify issue publics in each domain according to their roles in the policy discussion networks. Positions whose alpha and beta parameters are both positive are "carriers" in the sense of having high levels on both the input and output sides. Positions with negative alpha and beta are "isolates" because they underchoose and are underchosen. A negative alpha in conjunction with a positive beta indicates a recipient of communication that does not transmit; the reverse combination depicts a transmitter that does not receive. The third dimension that cuts across these alpha-beta combinations is the sign of the main diagonal gammas, indicating the net tendency for groups to choose or avoid their own occupants as discussion partners. The labels assigned to classifications in tables 8.5 and 8.6 are Marsden's (1980b) terms. Those in *primary positions*, not only have high levels of sending and receiving information from other issue publics, but also interact internally at higher than expected levels. *Brokers* are so designated because when their high input and output rates are held constant, the group's members do not discuss policy matters at higher than expected levels. *Isolated cliques* and *true isolates* both tend to be ignored by other issue publics and to differ from one another only in their degree of internal cohesion.

In the energy domain, the six major issue publics are sharply differentiated in their communication roles. Four of the six occupy primary positions: manufacturing-executive, oil, coal-gas, and nuclear-electrical-environmental. The regulatory issue public performs the major brokerage role for the domain, as might be expected from its extensive ties to and from all other domain publics. If one holds constant its high input and output rates, the regulatory public is seen to have relatively infrequent internal contact. The renewable fuels– local government position is an internally cohesive clique, but it is isolated from the other publics by its low level of communication inflow and outflow. Although the nuclear public is classified as a primary position, its in- and outflow parameters are virtually zero, suggesting that it is largely isolated from other domain participants, a condition implied but not clearly evident in the analyses in Chapter 4 of its organizations' issue interests relative to those of other publics.

In the health domain, the government public occupies a primary role in contrast to the brokerage role played by its regulatory counterpart in the energy domain. Four other publics also occupy primary positions here: the consumer, finance, drug industry, and food publics. More than half the health publics make up isolated cliques. In the health domain, only the public health position plays a brokerage role, and no public is a true isolate.

The final analyses to be reported are three-dimensional plots of the group choice (gamma) parameters from the log-linear quasi-symmetric models. The full set of gamma effect parameters were input to the multidimensional scaling program with a request for a three-dimensional solution (Kruskal's stress was .087 for the energy domain and .387 for health). The six major issue publics in the energy domain are located in four widely separated sectors of the com-

Table 8.5. Classification of Energy Issue Public Policy Discussion Roles, Based on Quasi-Symmetry Model Parameters

OUTDEGREE AND INDEGREE PARAMETERS

	Alpha + Beta +	Alpha − Beta −
Gamma +	Primary Positions 1. Auto Transp 2. Mfg, Exec 3. Oil 5. Coal, Gas 12. Nuclear-Electrical- Environmental	Isolated Cliques 6. Shipping 7. Renew-Local Gov't 10. Pipelines 13. Miscellaneous Low-Status Clique* 11. Transport
GROUP CHOICE PARAMETERS **Gamma −**	Brokers 4. Railway 8. Regulatory	True Isolates 9. PIRG-FTC

* Alpha + Beta −

munication space. The oil and renewable fuels–local government publics are close to one another, as are the coal-gas and manufacturing–national executive pair. The regulatory and the nuclear-electrical-environmental publics are each located in distinct quadrants at considerable distances from the other major publics. As was the case in Chapter 4 with the spatial location of publics according to their interest similarities, the center of the space is essentially vacant, suggesting the absence of any coordinating position that main-

Table 8.6. Classification of Health Issue Public Policy Discussion Roles, Based on Quasi-Symmetry Model Parameters

OUTDEGREE AND INDEGREE PARAMETERS

	Alpha + Beta +	Alpha – Beta –
Gamma +	Primary Positions 2. Consumers 3. Finance 11. Drug Industry 12. Food 13. Government	Isolated Cliques 1. Mental Health 4. Professionals 5. Abortion 7. Disease #1 8. Health Research 9. Disease #2 10. Disease #3 14. Isolates
GROUP CHOICE PARAMETERS		
Gamma –	Brokers 6. Public Health	

tains minimal communication distance to all significant policy actors. Despite its extensive observed communication ties to other publics, the regulatory public lies on the periphery of the domain, once its prolific tendency to emit and attract discussion partners is taken into account.

In contrast, the health domain does not resemble a hollow sphere. The public health position, which was shown to play a broker role, occupies a location at virtually the center of the group choice space. Circling the center are the finance public, the health professionals, a cluster consisting of the drug, re-

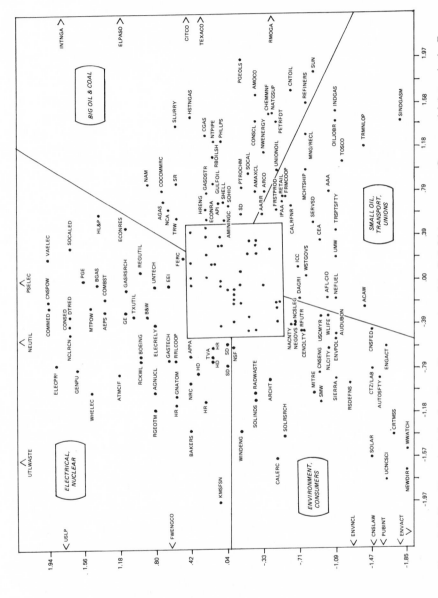

Figure 8.4. Two-Dimensional Smallest-Space Representation of the Path Distances among Consequential Actors in the Energy Domain, Based on the Network of Confidential Information Exchange

242

search, and first targeted disease publics, and another triad comprised of the mental health, consumer, and the government publics. At the farthest peripheries of the sphere are found the second and third targeted disease publics and the food, abortion, and isolate positions. Thus, after adjusting for differential tendencies to choose and be chosen as discussion partners, the health domain offers some evidence that at least one public may serve as a central coordinating position, in contrast to the noticeable absence of such a public in the energy domain.

Candid-Confidential Network Structure

We have uncovered strong evidence that regular-routine information exchanges are structured according to the issue interests of domain organizations. We turn next to analysis of the candid-confidential discussion network, examining the global structures of these selective information exchanges. Here, our primary concern is whether the centrality and sector locations of positions can be explained by the organizational attributes analyzed in preceding chapters. The two matrices of path distances between pairs of domain organizations were submitted to a multidimensional scale analysis (ALSCAL in the SAS package). Because the networks are relatively dense, path distances are short, with all actors being connected by one, two, or at most three steps. Given the numerous ties in the data, the "tie-breaking option" was used to optimize stress. Both the energy and health domain results for two-dimensional solutions yielded stresses of .15.

These two-dimensional plots are shown in figures 8.4 to 8.7. Because of the dense crowding at the center of each diagram, the small insets have been enlarged. The core is clearly dominated by the central political authorities in each domain. For energy, this core set consists of the Energy Department, Interior Department, White House, EPA, and five Senate and House subcommittees (also in the core area are three private sector corporations, but these do not appear to be significant actors, to judge by their influence reputations). Traveling outward from the core toward the periphery, we can readily observe that the energy domain space is subdivided into four distinct sectors: (1) big oil and coal, (2) small oil, transportation, and unions, (3) environmental and consumer groups, and (4) electrical and nuclear ones. (Not shown in the diagram are 17 organizations that are so remote in the communication space as to be plotted beyond the boundaries shown. This set includes such minor players at the U.S. Labor Party, Foothills Pipelines, and the Environmental Coalition on Nuclear Power.)

Within each sector, the positions closer to the core appear to be occupied by aggregative organizations such as the major trade associations or interest groups. For example, the circle adjacent to the core is occupied by the Ameri-

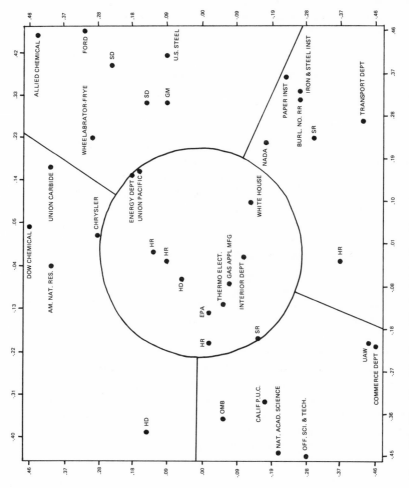

Figure 8.5. Blow-Up of the Central Region of the Two-Dimensional Smallest-Space Solution Depicted in Figure 8.4.

can Petroleum Institute, American Gas Association, Edison Electric Institute, Association of American Railways, National Automobile Dealers Association, American Mining Congress, the AFL-CIO, and various associations of mayors, counties, governors, and state legislators. Also in this first circle are many of the major federal departments, agencies, and congressional subcommittees with sector-specific responsibilities, such as the Interstate Commerce Commission, Department of Transportation, the Federal Energy Regulatory Commission, the Economic Regulatory Administration, the Nuclear Regulatory Commission, the National Science Foundation, and the Department of Agriculture. The more peripheral regions of each sector are occupied by individual claimant organizations, either corporations or narrowly defined trade associations and interest groups. The overall image of the energy domain conforms to the ideal-typical center-periphery and sector principles. Specifically, the core is dominated by those governmental actors with the most broad-reaching policy mandates; the first circle is dominated by the major special interests of particular sectors, and the peripheries are occupied by the minor claimants. In effect, the aggregative interest groups serve as intermediate communication filters that link the peripheries with the core.

That the two-dimensional communication structure differentiates domain organizations along a center-periphery dimension can be easily demonstrated by correlating actors' distances from the center of the space with their influence reputation ranks. The correlation coefficient is $+.46$ (recall that a low rank value indicates a high rank placement). The correlation of distance with actual number of "votes" received is $-.42$. Both correlations indicate that proximity to the center of the communication space is an important factor in peers' judgments of organizational ability to be influential and consequential in domain affairs.

In the health domain a similar core-periphery pattern occurs, as figures 8.6 and 8.7 reveal. The core set consists of HHS, the White House Office, OMB, the Health Resources Administration, the Health Services Administration, HCFA, the FDA commissioner, one Senate subcommittee, and four private sector interest groups (including the Robert Wood Johnson Foundation). Away from the center, the candid-confidential communication space appears to be subdivided into five distinct sectors: (1) health clients, (2) consumer regulatory groups, (3) health care and pharmaceutical companies, (4) specialty health providers, and (5) governmental health mission agencies (mostly NIH units). About a dozen organizations are not shown in the diagram because of their remote locations from the center, such as the medical librarians' association, fundraisers for cystic fibrosis, and allergy immunology research, the Women's Health Network, and the Hispanic health organization.

As in the energy domain, positions closer to the core are occupied by speciality aggregate organizations, such as the AMA, AHA, Blue Cross/Blue

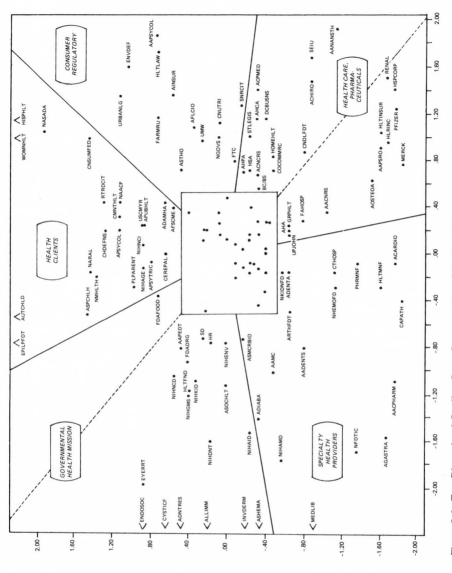

Figure 8.6. Two-Dimensional Smallest-Space Representation of the Path Distances among Consequential Actors in the Health Domain, Based on the Network of Confidential Information Exchange

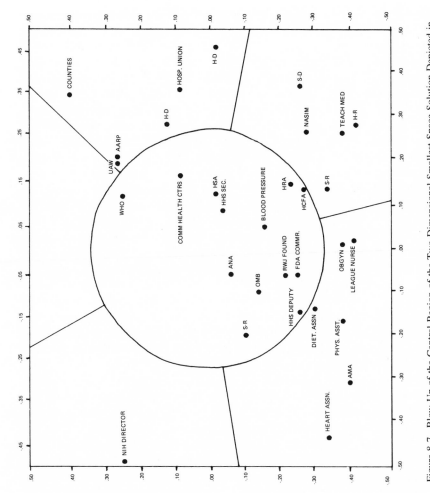

Figure 8.7. Blow-Up of the Central Region of the Two-Dimensional Smallest-Space Solution Depicted in Figure 8.6.

247

Shield, the American Association of Retired Persons (AARP), and associations of counties and state governors. Most of the major federal agencies and congressional subcommittees are located close to the core. As in the energy domain, the overall pattern suggests a core dominated by governmental agencies with broad health policy responsibilities, an array of specialized interest sectors whose inner regions are dominated by the major special interest associations and agencies and whose peripheries are occupied by minor claimants. The core-periphery structure of the health domain communication network is also organized along influence reputation lines. Its correlation with influence rank is .64 and with number of votes is −.60. The lower correlation in energy implies that communicative activities provide a less significant basis for influence reputation in energy than in health. We have already noted in Chapter 5 that there is a weaker consensus about "who matters" among energy domain actors.

In Figure 8.6, a dashed line has been drawn from the upper left to lower right, bisecting the health discussion space into two broad regions. To the left are located groups mainly concerned with the provision of health services; to the right are groups largely concerned about health care delivery and consumption. This producer-consumer cleavage is less obvious in the energy domain, probably because the numbers of actors are not so evenly balanced. In effect, the preponderance of energy producers means that the consumer groups are squeezed into the lower left quadrant of Figure 8.4. But the general pattern is consistent across both domains: organizations involved in the production of a good or service maintain closer communication with one another (about candid and confidential policy matters), as do organizations concerned about the consumption side. Notice, however, that the communication space is organized quite differently from the interest space, described in Chapter 4. Because both producers and consumers may have similar issue interest profiles, they tend to be intermixed within the same issue public (e.g., both nuclear utilities and environmental groups occur in the same cluster in figure 4.8). But similarity of issue concerns is not sufficient to organize candid-confidential information sharing. Rather, groups tend to confine their information exchanges to others sharing their policy outcome preferences. Hence, producers are more likely to speak to other producers, and consumers to other consumers, with the result that the producer-consumer cleavage, which is obscured when one examines only issue interests, emerges clearly in the policy communication analysis. How these patterns of policy discussion affect the pursuit of collective decisions is the subject of the following chapters.

9

Events, Singular and Multiple: A Framework for Concatenated Event Analysis

An Event-Structured Framework

The essence of the framework we are proposing for analyzing policy decision making is a structural complex that connects consequential organizational actors with a set of temporally arrayed political events. To understand how national policy unfolds, one must take into account how organizations perceive and respond to an opportunity structure for affecting policy outcomes that is created by the temporal sequence of policy-relevant events. Because a specific policy event is embedded in the context of other antecedent, concurrent, and impending events, policy analysts must incorporate the entire structure of organizations and events and not focus narrowly upon single instances of either, as do most case studies (e.g., Dahl, 1961).

Central to an analysis of an organizations-events complex is the flow of trustworthy and timely information about events among a set of actors with interests in the outcome of the events. This communication structure among actors oriented toward a common policy area, described in the preceding two chapters, is a critical factor in explaining the dynamic unfolding of the policy process from initiation through completion. The information flowing through the communication structure may be scientific and technical, such as factual data about energy resource reserves (but see Wildavsky and Tenenbaum, 1981, on the problematic nature of such "facts"), or it may be sociopolitical, such as messages from potential allies or adversaries about their probable response to an organization's actions.

All policy actors, but especially organizations charged with proximate decision-making roles in democratic polities, have vast needs for valid, useful, and up-to-date information. Complex formal organizations, whose prosperity and very survival may be at stake in the outcome of policy controversies, develop elaborate organs to monitor the environment continuously for potential opportunities and threats (Wilensky, 1967).

As important as the trustworthiness of information sources is the timeliness of the information that is transmitted. Since the policy process consists of a sequence of events in which organizational intervention is possible at various points, organizations must constantly search for maximum impact points. The ability to frame policy choices by the judicious transmission of targeted information may be greater for some events in the policy process than for others. Organizational contributions to politicians' campaigns, most commonly funneled nowadays through PACs, are best seen not as attempts to "buy" favorable policy outcomes but as insurance for access to proximate decision-makers at appropriate moments, when the presentation of an actor's factual or political information concerning an event may be most persuasive in influencing its outcome.

The framework for concatenated event analysis that we develop below is intended to serve several analytic objectives.[1] First, we want to call attention to the variety of criteria that can be used to concatenate events into scenarios. The four fundamental types of scenarios that we ultimately identify can be used to explain the distinct patterns of policy development in a given domain. We shall argue that each type of scenario is associated with distinct configurations of elements in the policy process. These configurations include the characteristic ways in which policy options are placed on the agenda for authoritative action, the distinct patterns of participation by interested parties over the course of the policy cycle, the larger sociopolitical context within which the scenario events are embedded, the structure of adversary relations among the participants, and the final resolution of the process.

To develop the full implications of an event-structured policy framework, we must first expand on what is meant by an event and its corollary, an event scenario.

Defining Events

As a practical matter, an actor's involvement in an issue is directly observable through its participation in concrete activities, such as advocacy of or lobby-

---

1. The reader might find it useful to review at this point the theoretical discussion in Chapter 1 ("Metamethodological Issues in the Joint Analysis of Actors and Events in Systems of Action"), which develops the concept of the actor-event interface and the manifold ways in which it can be studied methodologically.

ing for a particular policy option. An important analytic problem in any empirical investigation of the issue resolution process thus becomes the rationale for ordering the concrete activities in a collective decision-making system in relation to each other and to more abstract and generalized concepts, such as the underlying issues.

In Chapter 1 we identify events as the basic markers in the policy process. An event is a critical, temporally located decision point in a collective decision-making sequence that must occur in order for a policy option to be finally selected. Every event is understood to require an authoritative actor—be it a House subcommittee, the House as a whole, an executive officer, a judge, or even an influential actor in the private sector—to render a discretionary decision in a delimited time frame. Events may be "linked" to one another as distinct points in a chain of related decisions leading to a specific outcome. Each intermediate decision event in a chain is a necessary but not sufficient gatekeeper through which an option must move (and sometimes in the process be modified or transformed) in order to emerge as the final policy option selected for implementation. The decision-making process may be terminated by a negative decision at any event in the chain.

Obviously, some events in the chain may be of greater significance for shaping the final outcome than others. What happens, for instance, in the initial House subcommittee hearings and the deliberations over the drafting of a bill may be of greater consequence in deciding its content than what happens when a congressionally approved measure reaches the White House for presidential signature. These characteristics of events, then, provide the framework or rationale for the activities undertaken by actors in the policy domain in seeking to influence policy outcomes. Particular events elicit distinctive sorts of actions that are appropriate to them. Efforts to assist a legislative aide on the specific wording of a provision are quite acceptable in the congressional context, but such assistance is strictly illegitimate when directed toward the law clerk of a Supreme Court Justice writing the majority opinion on a case.

Classifying Events

Events do not occur in isolation, but are embedded in temporally ordered sequences. These sequences, or scenarios, provide the basic data for the analysis of policy decisions. For the purposes of this chapter, events are treated as stimuli, characterized by analytic features, that elicit participation from interested actors. The sequence and timing of events shape the responses and initiatives of the core actors and set limits to the outcomes of collective decisions. To understand how events orchestrate the unfolding policy process, we must attend to the characteristics of events that are most likely to affect systematically the involvement of actors in the domain. In a subsequent chapter (Chapter 11), we will discuss some theoretical perspectives that suggest how events come to be organized into orderly configurations with predictable consequences for the participation of interested actors.

Policy events are classified primarily in terms of their consequences for the organization of the policy domain.[2] Under the federal constitutional system, three generic types of events—identified by their functional focus—are likely to occur in every policy domain:

1. Program-initiating or -terminating events: By definition these events are one-time occurrences that signal the start or end of some new activity. They may range from simple executive proclamations adding a minor function to an ongoing agency to major congressional actions creating new cabinet-level departments. The typical event is an enabling decision that calls a new entity into existence and establishes its purposes and authoritative relationships with other actors.
2. Regulative events: These events concern authoritative actions that apply treatment principles to particular cases or promulgate new interpretations of rules carrying the force of law. At the national policy level, most regulative events revolve around specific regulatory agencies charged with the social control of public and private institutions.
3. Funding events: These events concern the national budgetary process in which ongoing programs are given annual allocations to expand, contract, or maintain current levels of activity. Derivative funding events concern grants and contracts from public to private sector organizations for specific goods or services.

These three types of events can occur in precisely this order. For example, the creation of the Department of Energy in 1977 from pieces of other agencies was clearly a program-initiating event, as was the appointment of James Schlesinger as the first secretary. Within the Energy Department, however, the power to set energy prices, to regulate mergers and securities acquisitions, and to set oil pipeline rates was reserved to the independent five-member Federal Energy Regulatory Commission. Thus, decisions made by FERC with respect to dozens of energy companies' requests for economic relief are classified as regulative events. Finally, a \$6.2 billion authorization for Energy Department civilian research and development, vetoed in 1977 by President Carter because it continued the funding of the Clinch River nuclear breeder

---

2. Our central concern is with the consequences of each event at time t for the character of the policy domain at some $t + 1$. Thus, funding decisions are of interest because they prolong or discontinue the activities of specific agencies and affect the status of participating organizations as collaborators, beneficiaries, or cost-bearers. Our categorization of events in terms of their consequences for the framework of the policy domain should be distinguished from other typologies that emphasize the *substantive* consequences of policy decisions. For example, Lowi (1964) has categorized policies as regulatory, distributive, or redistributive.

reactor, is considered one in a series of annual funding events.

Other event characteristics can affect organizational involvement. Among the most important are an event's decision-making locus, public visibility, scope, and controversiality. *Decision-making locus* identifies the event's authoritative actor as a decision-maker in Congress, the executive branch, or the judiciary, although a more precise description may be used when necessary. *Public visibility* refers to the amount of attention devoted to an event by an audience, whether the general public, the mass media, or the more restricted population of interested core actors.[3] The *scope* of an event is indexed by the number and variety of actors interested in the substantive content of the event.[4] Although visibility and scope are generally correlated, they are analytically distinct concepts. For example, capitalization of nuclear power plants is an event with broad scope in its potential impact on consumer utility rates and employment opportunities, yet it has very low visibility outside the electric utility and construction industries.

Controversiality is revealed by the depth of polarization of interested actors into opposing camps.[5] A highly controversial event—which may, but need not, have very high visibility and broad scope—pits bitter antagonists against each other in unyielding opposition; subsequent events in the decision cycle may come to be noncontroversial as a wide consensus builds on the preferred outcome.

The relationships among events' decision-making locus, functional focus, visibility, scope, and controversiality are not theoretically specified from our perspective. Covariation can be determined empirically but is taken here as a given. Instead, these analytic characteristics of events can be used to generate hypotheses about the patterning of organizational participation and the structuration of events themselves. Before turning to these questions, we must first develop a procedure for joining or concatenating discrete events into larger sequences.

3. Operationally, we measured the amount of attention given to an event in the print media by the number of news articles about it published six months before and six months after it occurred in our sample of abstracts from eight newspapers and magazines (described in Chapter 3).

4. We shall defer operationalization of the scope of impact of an event to Chapter 10. We introduce the notion here for the sake of analytic completeness.

5. Operationally, the degree of polarization between interested actors favoring opposing outcomes was measured by the number of organizations taking the minority position on the event. We felt that the mere presence of one or two opposing actors, rather than the proportion of active participants who adopted the minority position, was the appropriate measure of controversiality. First, it avoids the troublesome assumption that all actors are of equivalent weight and influence—a highly problematic one given our results in Chapter 5 and 6. Second, by design, events were selected across different stages in the cycle of policy resolution. We observed that as events approached their final resolution, opposition tended to decline as more and more objectionable features of a policy were eliminated to accommodate the opposition's wishes.

Event Scenarios

We stated above our belief that understanding the national policy process requires us to analyze the complex that connects organizations with events. This perspective requires that we establish equivalences among a set of events extending through time on the basis of their greater or lesser similarity. In other words, we need to adopt some criterion of concatenating discrete events into larger sequences, which we label *event scenarios*. Various criteria for concatenation can be proposed, and the choice of a procedure is mainly a question of the researcher's purposes. We have identified four possible criteria:

1. Causal dependency or institutional ordering: Events are linked according to a formal (legitimate/institutionalized) "logic of decision making" by which a prior event is a necessary and sufficient condition for a subsequent event. Mainstream political science employs this criterion to chain together the events by which a congressional bill becomes law (e.g., introduction, committee referrals, hearings, reports, floor debates, amendments, voting, conferences, revoting, presidential signature; see Oleszek, 1978:15).
2. Content homogeneity: Events are joined together on the basis of identical or similar content, at times latent rather than manifest. Thus, events that incorporate the same scientific or technical problems and solutions could be placed in an equivalence class despite being spread across time (e.g., various efforts to enact national health insurance or to treat nuclear wastes).
3. Audience-participant continuity: This criterion relies upon the reappearance of the same core actors from event to event. The illegitimacy of this approach for certain theoretical purposes is discussed below.
4. Expert evaluation: According to this criterion, the judgment of knowledgeable insiders is used to identify linked series of events. This expert evaluation draws upon persons, including some of the policy-makers themselves, with a thorough familiarity with a given policy domain. Their "cognitive maps" (Axelrod, 1976; Roos and Hall, 1980) and perceptions of the organization and interrelationship of events are assumed to approximate those of another set of knowledgeable insiders, the participating organizations.[6]

Since our analysis seeks to explain how core actors become involved in domain policy making, concatenation of events into scenarios according to any

6. This assumption was tested by analyzing the consistency of organizational participation across scenarios identified by informed observers. After defining the proximity between a pair of events as the logodds ratio based on organizational participation (see Chapter 11 for details), we input the event-by-event matrix of interpoint distances into the hierarchical clustering algorithm. The results showed that a set of events grouped into a scenario by informed observers were placed in the same cluster by the hierarchical clustering algorithm, confirming the reliability of the expert judgment method.

of the first three criteria is undesirable. Causal dependency is useful as far as it goes, but it yields short chains of events with very limited generality. The criterion of content homogeneity tends to impose an external, "social engineering" perspective on events and ignores the subjective understanding of the situation held by the core actors. An audience-participant continuity procedure comes closer to reflecting the perceptions and beliefs of the domain actors but, in using the observed pattern of involvement to concatenate events, a tautology is built in. If the behavior of core actors is used to construct scenarios, these scenarios then cannot be usefully applied to the analysis of core actors' behavior.

Thus, for certain analytic purposes, expert evaluation is the best way to concatenate events into scenarios. The cognitive world views held by consequential organizations (i.e., their managers) form "conceptual lenses" (Allison, 1971:2), the frames of reference and assumptions that actors use to interpret the meaning of events in terms that are amenable to collective action. Any policy process is a continuously constructed and negotiated social phenomenon, not some concrete "objective" situation that can be observed in the same manner as the objects of a natural science (Gusfield, 1981). Therefore, informed experts' knowledge of the linkages among events is the preferred criterion for concatenating empirically observable events into successively larger and longer scenarios to be used in analyzing domain core actors' involvement.

Classifying Event Scenarios

Just as single events can be classified according to various attributes, event scenarios that consist of two or more temporally ordered events can be classified according to some common features. The elementary type of scenario from which all other types are compounded is the self-limiting *standard decision cycle*. We refer to what the civics texts describe as the "customary" or usual sequence of prescribed events followed in passing a bill through Congress to the President, promulgating an executive agency's regulation in the *Federal Register,* or taking a court case through the appellate process to the Supreme Court. On occasion significant departures from such a process may occur, but only when the rules are explicitly suspended. The basic cycle is orchestrated by a set of formal rules specifying each step that must be completed before moving on to the next. We say that such a cycle is self-limiting in the sense that rules also specify when action on a measure must terminate because time has run out—for instance, at the close of a session of Congress. All the prescribed steps must be traversed all over again the next session if the measure is to be enacted into law. Because these steps are a matter of public knowledge, interested parties can organize their efforts accordingly. The many case studies of congressional action on various pieces of legislation nicely document the changing character of the interested parties and their activities over the course of these standard cycles (Bailey, 1950; Kingdon, 1984:195–98). To study the participation of public and private actors over the course of a standard cycle, the investigator must simply select the intermediate decision points of most significance to the cycle's progress and examine the activities of the interested parties that are related to these focal events.

The second type of scenario is called a *consummated recurrent standard cycle* because decision making about essentially identical substantive matters mut be done on a regular or recurrent basis over time. Annual authorization and appropriation bills for executive agencies exemplify such scenarios. To study these scenarios parsimoniously, one can identify the critical intermediate decision event in each of several years to glean some sense of the stability of the decision processes over time with respect to particular substantive issues. Such a cycle is always consummated: that is, authorization bills must be passed every year even if the amounts being appropriated may change dramatically.

In the third type of scenario, an *unconsummated recurrent standard cycle,* we observe the recurrent submission of a piece of legislation proposing the adoption of a new policy initiative that fails to garner sufficient support for passage. Comprehensive national health insurance in the health domain and the coal slurry pipeline bill in the energy domain have been considered repeatedly by Congress but without success. Again we propose to tag "marker" decision events in each unconsummated cycle to investigate the changing fortunes of such measures.

Finally, we can speak of the most complex type of scenario, a *constructed scenario,* which combines decision events from a number of collateral decision cycles into a coherent whole: that is, significant actors regard a set of policy options as joined by some broader policy objective or coalition-building strategy. President Carter's efforts to curtail gasoline consumption involved a variety of measures requiring action by disparate congressional and executive agencies: the imposition of novel taxes (e.g., higher excise taxes on gas-guzzling cars and higher gasoline taxes), the changing of executive regulations on permissible emission standards and automobile fuel standards, the reduction of the speed limit on interstate highways, and the enactment of standby authority to impose gasoline rationing in the event of critical fuel shortages. In this example, the scenario events were both initiatory and regulative, but it is feasible for a constructed scenario to consist entirely of events of one type. Recurrent standard cycles are most likely to consist solely of funding events, since these appear with predictable regularity, but funding events may also be embedded in the more heterogeneous constructed or unconsummated recurrent standard scenarios.

Identifying Empirical Events

Literally hundreds of events during the 1970s were relevant to national policy making in energy and health. It was obvious from the very beginning that we could not study all, or even most, intermediate events in all the standard cycles of interest to us. While one could postulate, in theory, a population universe of policy-relevant events in each policy domain during a stipulated time frame from which to sample a subset for study, the creation of such a comprehensive listing of events was simply not feasible. Much more problematic theoretically, we had no theory for treating a given event as more or less important than, or as important as, any other. Obviously, critical events having massive ramifications for a policy domain occur rarely, whereas the myriad of daily, routine decision-making events can be seen as shaping the major thrusts of policy development only if taken in the aggregate. In other words, although it is quite reasonable to assume "one person, one vote" in sampling the population of voters participating in an election, there is no comparable rationale for a sampling design that treats the population of decision-making events in such a fashion. Thus, a simple sampling design yields too few significant and too many routine events, but there is no theoretically motivated method at hand for stratifying such a population of events into more meaningful categories.

Because we eventually identified a much larger number of discrete events for study (81 in energy and 85 in health) than had been attempted before, we inevitably had to rely on a purposive (nonrandom) sampling of events based upon an extensive reading of documentary sources. We were particularly fortunate in having available the excellent "year in perspective" reports on energy or health policy prepared by the staff of the *Congressional Quarterly*. We also selectively reviewed the more specialized news media, such as the *American Medical News*, the *Federal Register*, federal court opinions, and the set of news abstracts we had collected using the New York Times Abstract Service (see Chapter 3). We particularly wanted to avoid paying exclusive attention to events that attracted great public attention, because many events having broad implications for policy escape public scrutiny, being the province of highly specialized, "insider" deliberations regularly canvassed only by the specialized news media.

To ensure the fullest possible coverage of events, we stipulated that events should relate, in roughly equal measure, to one of four broad categories of topics in each domain. The categories were derived from conceptualizing the systems for producing and distributing energy and health care to ultimate consumers as loosely articulated input-throughput-output systems with specialized corporate actors responsible for different aspects of supply and demand.

Thus, in the energy domain we sought events related to issues in energy research, the development of energy industries, the regulation of energy-producing companies, and the conservation and reorganization of energy consumption by intermediate and ultimate consumers. Similarly, in the health domain we sought events related to issues in biomedical research, the training of health personnel, the organization of health care delivery systems, such as hospitals and HMOs, and consumer protection.[7]

In describing the events selected for study from congressional standard decision cycles, it was necessary to establish a method for determining their temporal location within scenarios—that is, for dating events. Events themselves are formally defined with respect to a discrete act of decision making, such as a vote in Congress that can be dated to the hour and minute of its occurrence. But organizational participation in an event—lobbying, testifying, and so forth—takes place over a loosely bounded period of days or weeks. We therefore adopted the pragmatic rule of dating congressional events by the month the first committee or subcommittee (House or Senate) issued its report recommending passage of a particular measure and the month the conference committee (comprising both House and Senate members) issued its compromise version of the measure. In unconsummated scenarios, we selected the month the first committee in either the House or Senate voted against recommending passage of the measure and continued this process for each of the subsequent years in which the measure was under consideration. For consummated scenarios, we selected the month in which the first committee reported out a bill to its chamber in each new session. These cycles typically concern appropriations measures, which must originate in the House by constitutional provision, and therefore the House committee report was usually selected as the focal event.

When decision-making cycles involve executive agencies or the judiciary as the authoritative actors, it is more difficult to identify appropriate intermediate events. Although just as orderly and prescribed as congressional sequences, these events are often less well publicized and documented in public sources. Therefore, we dated executive agency events by the month in which a regulation was formally promulgated in the *Federal Register* or the month in which the President publicly announced his nomination for an executive position. In the case of judicial decisions, we specified either the time when the

7. Referring to Appendix B, the reader will note that the sets of issues discussed in Chapter 4 are also classified into these four categories. The listing of issues in each category, however, is much more comprehensive than the listing of events in the comparable class of events. Since we were interested in identifying multiple events to constitute scenarios and had only enough time to inquire about a limited number of such events, we decided to use only a subset of issues, for which we could then identify a relevant set of events for further inquiry.

case was first filed for action in a lower federal court or the time when the Supreme Court agreed to hear a case on appeal.

For constructed scenarios, which involve heterogeneous authoritative actors, we selected single events from the early stages of various standard decision cycles. Typically, constructed scenarios were dated by the initial hearings reviews or held by congressional committees, subcommittees, or executive agencies, or by filing dates for court cases. Broadly speaking, the energy policy domain was more extensively institutionalized and routinized in the decade under study than was the energy domain, which had just begun receiving systematic attention from the national elite. Therefore, health policy events were more often concatenated into constructed scenarios. We consistently followed the above procedures in selecting events from the recent past (i.e., the Carter years, 1977–1980). In the more distant past, to avoid the consequences of fallible recall, we selected conclusionary events—for example, the actual passage of the act by Congress as a whole, rather than events preceding final passage. For these early events, an informant merely had to recall that the organization actively participated in some (unspecified) events leading up to the final congressional, executive, or judicial action.

For each event, the informant indicated whether the organization had an interest in the event and, if so, the level of activity, timing of involvement, position taken, involvement in formulating the policy or its alternatives, and collaboration with other organizations on that option (see Appendix B, B3–B13). This information thus permits us to reconstruct both the histories of the individual events and the event activation profiles of every organizational actor in the domain. We were quite successful in identifying events that attracted the attention of our informant organizations. In the energy domain, an average of 22 percent of the organizations participated in each event, with a range between 0 and 94 percent across the 81 events; in the health domain, an average of 19 percent of the organizations participated, with a range between 2 and 41 percent across 85 events. In terms of the aggregate of consequential organizations in each domain, organizations participated in an average of 17.9 out of 81 events in the energy domain and an average of 16.1 out of 85 in the health domain. (For a listing of all the targeted events in each domain, see Appendices C and D, cards B, D, E and F. More detailed descriptions of events may be found in the appendix to Chapter 11.)

The Analytic Differentiation of Sets of Unique Events

But how can we grasp the overall structure of so many unique events that differ according to formal features as well as substantive content and time of occurrence? Again we can turn to multidimensional scaling for radical data

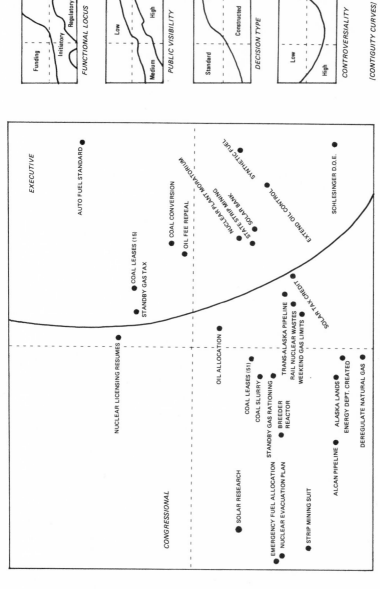

Figure 9.1. Multidimensional Scalogram Analysis of 81 Energy Events on Their Characteristics

*There are fewer than 81 points plotted in the figure because multiple events in many scenarios occupied identical locations in the analytic space, being distinctive only with respect to time of occurrence (which was not included here as a differentiating characteristic).

reduction that clarifies our understanding of the interrelationships among these many events. For each domain, a matrix was constructed with the 81 (85) events in the rows and five formal event attributes in the columns (decision-making locus, public visibility, controversiality, functional focus, and type of decision cycle). The data were subjected to multidimensional profile analysis, using the Guttman-Lingoes MSA-I program (Lingoes, 1973). This program analyzes an n-chotomous regular data matrix and produces a Euclidean space by partitioning subjects (in this case policy events) into n-chotomous categories over all items (attributes) simultaneously (Lingoes, 1973:219).

Figures 9.1 and 9.2 show the two-dimensional representation of these event proximities. The larger diagrams display the decision-making loci: "contiguity curves" mark the cleavages between events with a congressional locus and those with an executive-judicial locus.[8] The small inserts to the right of the figures display the same pattern of points as the larger diagrams, but with different contiguity curves delineating the distribution of formal features within the event space. For example, congressional events in the health domain fall into the upper half of the space and executive and judicial-branch events into the lower half. Highly controversial events tend to fall on the right side and less controversial events on the left side. The orientation of the contiguity curves to one another gives a rough idea of the way in which the five analytic dimensions are correlated with one another.[9] Thus, as the reader can determine from comparing the overlap of the regions of relevant contiguity curves, congressional events tend to be more controversial and publicly visible than executive-judicial events are. Interpretation of the other dispersion patterns is left to the reader.

Another use for these results, to be described in the next chapter, will be the determination of the relative scope of an organization's participation across the set of events differentiated according to these multiple analytic distinctions. To anticipate our argument in the next chapter, we contend that we can assess the scope or range of an organization's participation across the multitude of events more appropriately by examining the spread or dispersion of participation in different types of events than by simply counting the number of events in which the organization was active. It should require substantially

8. There were too few judicial events to warrant distinguishing them from the others. Consequently, we combined them with the events in the executive branch.

9. See table 9.1 below for the intercorrelation matrices of the five formal characteristics of events in each domain, together with other attributes whose measures will be described in a subsequent section. The reader will observe in table 9.1 that the two domains decidedly differ with respect to the way the analytic features of their events co-vary with one another. For instance, whereas public visibility is moderately correlated (.50) with controversiality in the health domain, the two characteristics are negligibly correlated (.13) in the energy domain.

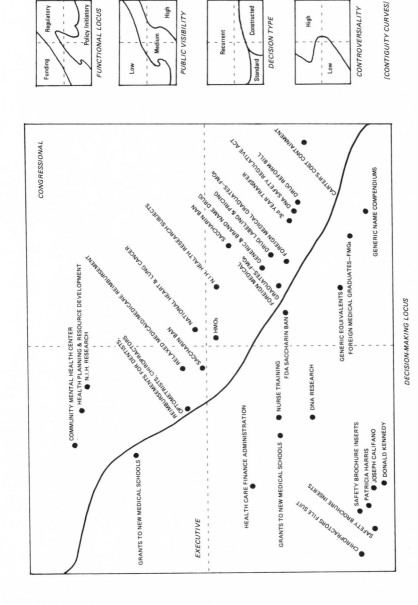

FUNCTIONAL LOCUS
Funding | Regulatory
Policy Initiator

PUBLIC VISIBILITY
Low | Medium | High

DECISION TYPE
Standard | Recurrent
Constructed

CONTROVERSIALITY
Low | High

[CONTIGUITY CURVES]

CONGRESSIONAL

CARTER'S COST CONTAINMENT
DRUG REFORM BILL
DNA SAFETY REGULATIVE ACT
3rd YEAR TRANSFER
FOREIGN MEDICAL GRADUATES—FMGs
GENERIC & BRAND NAME DRUG
DRUG LABELING & PRICING
GENERIC & BRAND NAME DRUG
SACCHARIN BAN
FOREIGN MEDICAL GRADUATES—FMGs
N.I.H. HEALTH RESEARCH SUBJECTS
NATIONAL HEART & LUNG CANCER
RELAXED MEDICAID/MEDICARE REIMBURSEMENT
REIMBURSEMENTS FOR DENTISTS,
OPTOMETRISTS, CHIROPRACTORS
N.I.H. RESEARCH
HEALTH PLANNING & RESOURCE DEVELOPMENT
COMMUNITY MENTAL HEALTH CENTER

GENERIC NAME COMPENDIUMS
FOREIGN MEDICAL GRADUATES—FMGs
GENERIC EQUIVALENTS
FDA SACCHARIN BAN
SACCHARIN BAN
HMOs
DNA RESEARCH
NURSE TRAINING
GRANTS TO NEW MEDICAL SCHOOLS
HEALTH CARE FINANCE ADMINISTRATION

DECISION-MAKING LOCUS

GRANTS TO NEW MEDICAL SCHOOLS

DONALD KENNEDY
JOSEPH CALIFANO
PATRICIA HARRIS
SAFETY BROCHURE INSERTS
SAFETY BROCHURE INSERTS
CHIROPRACTORS FILE SUIT

EXECUTIVE

*There are fewer than 85 points plotted in the figure because multiple events in many scenarios occupied identical locations in the analytic space, being distinctive only with respect to time of occurrence (which was not included here as a differentiating characteristic).

Figure 9.2. Multidimensional Scalogram Analysis of 85 Health Events on Their Characteristics

greater organizational resources and greater generality of interest in a policy domain to motivate participation across analytically distinct sectors. Simple counts of the number of events in which an organization participated can be misleading because they could be concentrated in a narrow range of institutional loci and types of events requiring little in the way of differentiated resource capacities or interests for participation.

To this point we have characterized events as unique occurrences that can be meaningfully compared according to analytic features such as decision-making locus, relative public visibility, or controversiality. In constructing an explanatory tale, we can treat events as possessing attributes—much like actors—in order to transcend their historical and substantive uniqueness. We can ask, for example, whether events having high public visibility are also likely to be highly controversial events, and whether events having these two features are more likely to occur in congressional settings than in courts. There are, of course, many more features of these events that we could examine with the view to developing an empirically grounded model of how distinctive features of events are interrelated and with what consequences. At this stage of the analysis, we treat each event as fully independent of the others. Nothing in our methodology requires interdependence among events, although they may be linked into scenarios according to various analytic schemes. Thus, the relation between a number of events in which an organization participates remains open to empirical investigation and theoretical interpretation. The reader should refer to our metatheoretical discussion of the actor-event interface in Chapter 1 for an elaboration of this argument.

The following section describes a two-stage analysis of the actor-event interface. The first stage permits refined measurement of additional theoretically significant features of the events based on data drawn from our populations of informant organizations. The second allows us to estimate an empirical model of how certain variations among events significantly depend on other features of these events. We shall learn that the interrelationships of event features in the two domains differ in theoretically suggestive ways. Since logit analysis, the procedure we employ, is complex and requires intricate data manipulation, in the interest of theoretical clarity we shall direct primary attention to the results at the expense of displaying all the intermediate structural equations and data manipulations.

Characterizing Events by Participation Patterns: A Two-Stage Logit Analysis

Recall for a moment the data matrix representing the actor-event interface (matrix *B*) in Figure 1.5. In the energy domain, we have a rectangular matrix with 198 rows for the organizational actors and 81 columns for the energy events. Similarly, in the health domain, the matrix has 135 rows and 85 columns. Cell entries are *1* if an organization participated in an event or *0* if it did not.[10] The third dimension of the matrix contains each organization's attributes, replicated for every event. These attributes include their issue interests (Chapter 4), influence standings (Chapter 5), monitoring resources (Chapter 6), and communication position (Chapter 8). A fourth dimension of the matrix involves characteristics of the events themselves, such as their visibility, scope, controversiality, interest level, time, and location. Our task is to explain policy actors' involvement in domain events as a function of both organizational attributes and event characteristics.

Because two distinct levels of analysis are involved, we proceed in two stages. In the first stage, the unit of analysis is the set of domain organizations. For each event, we estimate a separate multivariate logistic regression equation, in which the dependent variable is an organization's dichotomous participation in that specific event, and the independent variables are the four organizational attributes. The estimated coefficients indicate the impact of organizational characteristics upon the likelihood of participation in that specific event. In the second stage, the unit of analysis shifts to the set of domain events. We estimate seven ordinary least-squares (OLS) regression equations, in which each dependent variable is one of the coefficients from the first-stage logistic analysis and the independent variables are the event characteristics. The resulting estimated OLS coefficients reveal the interaction effect of organizational and event characteristics upon policy participation. That is, how does variation in event characteristics affect the impact of organizational attributes on the likelihood of an organization's participating in a policy event?

Stage One: Organizational Participation

A dichotomous dependent variable (participant/nonparticipant) violates important assumptions for ordinary linear regression, particularly the normal distributions of the dependent variable and the error term (Kerlinger and Pedhazur, 1973:47–48). Fortunately, an alternative nonlinear functional form is available—the logistic function, whose properties are well known and suitable for the problem at hand. For each policy event, we specify a general logistic regression equation with the following form:

$$P_i = \frac{(exp(Z_i))}{[1 + exp(Z_i)]}$$

10. Informants were shown the entire list of events and asked which ones their organization "had a particular interest" in. (See Appendix B, question B3.) For those events, the informant indicated whether the organization was actively involved (whether it had a preferred outcome) or was not active on the issue despite its particular interest. For the present analysis we classified all domain organizations on all the events as either active participants or inactive, regardless of the reason. (Organizations that did not exist at the time were treated as missing data on that event.)

where P_i is the probability that the dependent variable takes a particular value (either 1 or 0 in the dichotomous case of participating in an event), and Z_i is an expression of the form:

$$Z_i = b_0 X_0 + b_1 X_1 + b_2 X_2 + \ldots + b_k X_k + \ldots + b_n X_n$$

where each b_k is the estimated effect of an X_k organizational attribute (including a constant, or intercept, term X_0). The logistic regression coefficients are analogous to OLS regression estimates, although the nonlinear relationship of P_i to each X_k makes the interpretation of the impact of a change in X_k on P_i less straightforward (Aldrich and Nelson, 1984:42).

The independent variables in the logistic equations are measures of organizational attributes drawn from the previous chapters. An organization's level of monitoring resources and its communication pattern are measured as simple scalar variables. The monitoring resource scale is the number of FTE staff available to an organization for surveillance of the domain's policy activities (see Chapter 6 and Appendix A, column 8). Communication position simply reflects the total number of organizations that contact it through the regular-routine channels (the "in-degree"). Both variables reflect the organizations' attributes on single dimensions.

The other independent variables in the stage-one analysis are conceptualized in two-dimensional form and thus cannot be measured by simple scalar variables. In Chapter 4 we found that the issue publics in both domains were arrayed in a rim structure (see figures 4.10 and 4.11). We now measure an organization's relative interest in two distinctive clusters of issues by measuring its Euclidean distance from two fixed points on the rim of the circle (as denoted by asterisks in each figure). For the energy domain, the fixed points are the Energy Department's Economic Regulatory Administration (in the oil issue public, point coordinates 1.37 and 0.47), and the National Association of Counties (in the renewable fuels local government public, coordinates -0.34 and 0.90). For the health domain, the fixed points are the HCFA (in the finance public, coordinates -1.7 and .31) and the Bureau of Foods of the FDA (in the food public, coordinates 1.4 and 1.7). The greater the distance from a fixed point to an organization, the less likely is that organization to share the interest concerns of the public closest to the fixed point. For example, the American Petroleum Institute is close to the first fixed point, whereas the Nuclear Regulatory Commission is on the opposite side of the space. Thus, the API has a small Euclidean distance and the NRC has a large distance on the first issue dimension. We would expect that any events in which oil issues were at stake would stimulate the participation of organizations with small distances on this variable, whereas events in which nuclear issues were involved would increase participation among organizations with large distances on this variable. Similar interpretations apply to the effect of distance from the fixed point along the second axis of the two-dimensional issue space.

Comparable procedures operationalize each organization's influence standing. In figures 5.6 and 5.7 in Chapter 5, two asterisks in each diagram denote fixed reference points. The distance of an organization from the fixed point located at the left center measures its relative standing in the overall influence rank-order, while the distance from the fixed point at the righthand side (upper center for energy and lower center for health) measures an organization's proximity to the relatively uninfluential private-claimant sector of the space.

Now consider event 5. We know for every organization whether or not it participated in that event. We also know their distances from the first and second fixed points in both the issue public and influence-standing spaces. We hypothesize that the probability of an organization's participation in this event (or any other domain event) is a joint function of its distance from the four fixed points, its monitoring resources, and its communication position. In the case of the issue-public variables, if event 5 aroused the passions of a distinctive issue public, say the oil public, then organizations in close proximity to the ERA are predicted to be likely participants and everyone else to be unlikely participants. Net of the effects of the other variables in the logistic regression equation for event 5, we expect to find a significant coefficient for close proximity to ERA. That finding would tell us that event 5 possessed a highly localized/specialized interest content that attracted participation only by actors with specialized interests. On the other hand, events that involved many organizations which were widely dispersed around the issue public space will produce an insignificant logistic regression coefficient for the distances from the ERA, because the active organizations are randomly scattered around the point. That finding would indicate that event 5 had generalized interest throughout the policy domain, despite its apparent substantive content relating to oil energy policy. A similar interpretation would apply to coefficients obtained for the second issue public distance variable, as well as the two influence-standing distance measures. In the latter instances, a significant coefficient indicates that an event is dominated by highly influential actors— an "elite event"—or as dominated by a chorus of lower status claimant actors in the private sector.

Space limitations prevent us from displaying the seven b_k coefficients for every one of the 81 energy and 85 health equations. However, we can summarize their overall pattern. In both domains, the first issue public distance variable produced the most statistically significant coefficients (in 58 energy event equations and 38 health event equations). That is, proximity or distance from the first fixed point (ERA in the oil public or HCFA in the finance public) increased or decreased organizational participation in about half the policy events. In other words, organizations tended to become involved in those events in which they had a high level of interest and to avoid participating in events in which they had little interest—not exactly a surprising relationship. The next important variable in both domains was the communication position measure (in-degree). It was significant in 36 energy and 31 health event equations. In almost every equation, the in-degree coefficients had positive signs, indicating that organizations having higher levels of contact with other domain members were more likely to participate in policy events. The third most frequently significant coefficients were the second issue distance dimensions (21 energy and 23 health event equations). The logistic constant parameter was significant in 28 energy and 22 health equations. Its substantive interpretation is that significantly more than zero organizations participated in about a quarter of the domain policy events, after one has controlled for other organizational attributes. Finally, very few of the equations yielded significant coefficients for monitoring resources (4 each in both domains), the first influence rank dimension (14 energy, 1 health), or the second influence rank measure (7 energy, 3 health). Thus, issue interest and communication position seem to be the most important characteristics that dispose organizations toward involvement in domain events.

Stage Two: Organization-Event Interactions

In the second-stage analysis, each of the b_k coefficients for the 81 energy or 85 health event equations is treated as the dependent variable in the OLS regression equation of the form:

$$b_j = a_0W_0 + a_1W_1 + a_2W_2 + \ldots + a_hW_h + \ldots + a_mW_m$$

where the a_h are estimated effects of several W_h event characteristics (including a constant term W_0). An OLS specification is appropriate, since the b_j logistic equation coefficients from the first-stage analysis take on continuous rather than dichotomous values across the set of event equations.

Seven event characteristics are used as independent variables in the seven regression equations estimated for both domains: the event's visibility, scope, controversiality, and interest levels, the date on which it occurred, whether it was a policy-initiating or other type of event, and whether it happened in a full congressional committee or elsewhere (the latter two measures are dichotomous). Table 9.1 shows the intercorrelation matrices for these event characteristics.

The two domains differ in several respects in the way that their event features co-vary with one another. For example, controversial events co-vary with higher public visibility in the health domain, but with wider scope in the energy domain, although with about the same magnitude of interest in both

Table 9.1. Correlations among Event Characteristics

	Visibility	Scope	Controversy	Interest	Date	Initiatory
ENERGY DOMAIN						
Scope	.26					
Controversy	.13	.37				
Interest	.21	.33	.60			
Date	-.50	-.05	.27	.21		
Initiatory	-.02	-.09	.01	.14	.03	
Full Committee	.01	.10	.28	.14	.03	.15
HEALTH DOMAIN						
Scope	.05					
Controversy	.50	-.01				
Interest	.01	.35	.45			
Date	-.34	-.11	.14	.08		
Initiatory	.28	.12	.34	.17	-.27	
Full Committee	-.02	.03	.27	.14	.38	-.14

domains. The moderately strong correlation of date and visibility ($-.50$ in energy and $-.34$ in health) is to some degree an artifact of our selecting those events before 1977 that attracted greater media attention.

Table 9.2 reports the results of the standardized coefficients from the second-stage OLS regressions. The multiple R^2s tend to be small and are nonsignificant in several equations. Scope of event is consistently the most significant effect across equations, whereas controversiality and visibility are seldom important predictors. Marked contrasts appear in comparisons of parallel equations for the two domains.

The logistic constant term equation, showing net participation levels, is increased in the energy domain by both public visibility and event scope. That is, energy organizations tend to participate more in policy events that attract much media attention (the causal order may be reciprocal) and a dispersed set of issue publics. Neither factor is important in the health domain, but fewer organizations are involved in controversial events and full-committee actions.

None of the energy characteristics interact with monitoring resources, but the health equation shows three significant variables. Possession of more resources leads to greater participation by health organizations in events that have wider scope, are policy-initiating, and involve fewer interested groups. Thus, monitoring resources appear to affect participation only in rather dispersed and specialized situations. Communication location does not interact

Table 9.2. Standardized OLS Regressions of First-Stage Logistic Equation Coefficients upon Event Characteristics

Logistic Coefficients	Event Characteristics							
	Visibility	Scope	Controversy	Interest	Date	Initiatory	Committee	R^2
ENERGY DOMAIN								
Constant	.28**	.68***	.17	−.17	.05	−.04	.12	.54***
Resources	.21	.22	.18	.01	.21	−.10	.15	.15**
Indegree	.23	.35**	−.10	−.04	.38**	.08	.12	.17**
Issue D1	−.42***	−.74***	−.03	.28**	−.13	.00	.06	.63***
Issue D2	−.02	−.09	.26	.18	−.02	.13	−.10	.08
Influence D1	−.05	.29**	−.11	−.25	.42***	.22*	−.03	.26***
Influence D2	−.10	−.38***	−.25*	.31*	−.34**	−.07	−.23*	.28***
HEALTH DOMAIN								
Constant	−.27	−.06	−.43**	.06	−.18	.18	−.24*	.36***
Resources	−.20	.47***	.26	−.52***	−.06	.36***	.14	.43***
Indegree	.11	.01	.01	.14	.18	.18	.09	.13
Issue D1	.13	−.61***	.14	.28*	.24*	.01	.01	.42***
Issue D2	.12	.32**	.41*	−.67***	.24*	.01	.01	.35***
Influence D1	.17	−.04	.21	.05	−.02	−.20	.26	.20
Influence D2	−.01	.17	−.04	−.03	−.17	.08	.01	.08

* $p < .05$
** $p < .01$
*** $p < .001$

with events in the health domain and has only a small effect in the energy domain, with broader scope and later events increasing the participation levels of organizations that maintain greater policy contacts in the domain.

In both domains, several event characteristics interact with an organization's distance from the first dimension in issue space. The −.74 scope and −.43 visibility coefficients indicate that events of broad scope and high visibility increase the participation of organizations close to the fixed point (nearer to the ERA). Thus, organizations with strong interest in oil policy events are more likely to participate in broad-scope and highly visible events, whereas groups with stronger interest in nuclear policy events are more prone to involvement in narrow-scope and less visible ones. In the health domain, a similar interpretation applies only to event scope, as the visibility effect is not significant. In both domains the effect of having a large number of organizations with interests in an event is to increase participation among groups more distant from the fixed point. Event date has a slightly positive effect only in the health domain.

In the energy domain, no variables were significant in the equation for the second issue distance dimension coefficients, but in the health domain equation the effects of scope and interest were the reverse of the first dimension. Neither of the health domain influence distance equations yielded significant findings, but the energy domain equations produced several systematic effects. Participation increased among influential organizations when events were broader in scope, more recent, and initiatory. Participation decreased among energy organizations close to the uninfluential claimants whenever events had narrow scope, low controversiality, high interest, an earlier date, and a locus other than a full committee.

In sum, the findings from the two-stage logistic regression analysis indicate that some event characteristics exert systematic effects upon the way some organizational attributes affect policy event participation. These effects are not identical across the two policy domains, further evidence that the structuration of policy making differed markedly during the era under study. In the following chapters we probe more deeply into the interface between organizations and events.

10

Organizational Participation in Decision-Making Events

with Yong-Hak Kim

To this point in our discussion, we have directed analytic and empirical attention to three key elements in our explanatory scheme. First, we identified in Chapter 3 the most consequential actors in a policy domain and noted in the following three chapters those attributes of the organizations that should prove most useful in explaining the actors' differential involvements in policy decision making. More specifically, we measured the purposive orientations of the actors in a policy domain by assessing the general and specific character of their interests in a comprehensive range of policy controversies (Chapter 4) and then identified various sorts of resources under their control, including their differing capacities to monitor the policy environment and to mobilize relevant resources to influence the actions of other actors (Chapters 5 and 6), that enable actors to participate influentially in policy deliberations. Next, we shifted our level of analysis to the dyadic and systemic level in order to examine the organization of information and resource exchanges among the actors

This chapter is a condensed version of our article, "Organizational participation in national energy and health policy: a new perspective," which appeared in the *American Sociological Review* 50 (1985): 1–19. We especially want to acknowledge the helpful comments of Douglas Anderton, Paul Burstein, James S. Coleman, Mary Fennell, Joseph Galaskiewicz, Peter V. Marsden, Franz U. Pappi, Mindy Schimmel, William J. Wilson, and anonymous reviewers for the *American Sociological Review* on an earlier version of the paper presented at the Midwest Sociological Society meetings in Chicago, April 18–21, 1984.

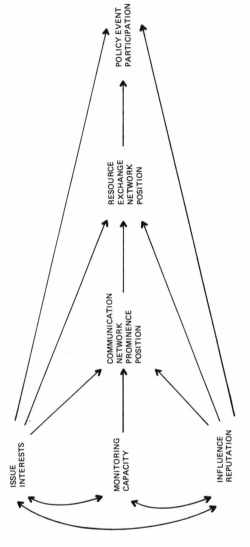

Figure 10.1. Schematic Diagram of Causal Relations in a Model for National Policy Domains

POLICY EVENT
PARTICIPATION

RESOURCE
EXCHANGE
NETWORK
POSITION

COMMUNICATION
NETWORK
PROMINENCE
POSITION

ISSUE
INTERESTS

MONITORING
CAPACITY

INFLUENCE
REPUTATION

that bind or separate them in the pursuit of their diversified interests (Chapters 7 and 8). Finally, in Chapter 9 we described a set of decision-making events over the past seven to 10 years that selectively elicited the actors' attention because of their potential to advance or harm their interests.

We are now in a position to combine these key elements according to the various framing perspectives we discussed in the introductory chapter to see what light they can shed on the nature of collective decision making about national policy in the United States and on our theorizing about such systems more generally. This chapter adopts the framing perspective of the individual level of analysis. The analytic model depicted in figure 10.1 explains the scope of participation of individual organizations in various policy events as a causally postulated function of certain generalized attributes of these organizations. For present purposes we shall ignore how the events in the policy domain might be interrelated in various scenarios as discussed in Chapter 9 and focus instead on the entire set of events in each of our two policy domains regarded (or framed) as discrete and independent opportunities in time for actors to participate in policy formation. Subsequent chapters will pose other framing perspectives from which to explore the interrelationships among actors, relations, and events in collective decision-making systems.

Issue Interests

Let us begin with the element at the top left of Figure 10.1. Each corporate actor is characterized as possessing a profile of *issue interests* across the full range of domain public policy issues. Our objective is to measure its scope of issue interests. Chapter 4 describes at length the rationale for the selection of the issues in each domain and for the structuration of issue linkage within a domain (see especially the discussion of figures 4.3 and 4.4). An actor's interest in a domain issue, the reader will recall, defines the level of concern and attention that it is prepared to exercise regarding the issue's resolution. An organization's issue interests are predetermined within the model; that is, their origins lie outside the model's explanation, presumably in some combination of historical and intraorganizational power dynamics. Remember that interest in an issue does not refer to an organization's policy preferences (pro or con). At this point in the analysis, we are not concerned with which side of an issue the actor favors, but only with the actor's level or intensity of concern about the issue generally. An appropriate level of interest is the precondition for expending scarce resources in efforts to affect the outcome of specific policy domain events involving that issue.

An organization's issue interest scope within a policy domain defines, in an important sense, that actor's orientation toward its environment. What distinguishes our approach from most policy research is that whereas other investigators tend to select a particular issue or small set of issues for exhaustive study, we emphasize the embeddedness or relatedness of every issue within the entire constellation of issues confronting the policy domain. We basically contend, first, that the systematic linkages among issues have important consequences for the politics of their resolution and, second, that such linkages are structurally arranged according to the ways in which organizations form constituencies for the various issues.

As we argued at length in Chapter 4, issues can be linked together by at least three general features. First, every issue possesses an inherent *substantive* or *conceptual content* that may connect it with certain other issues on grounds of logical implications that would be widely recognized and accepted by most participants and observers. For example, biomedical research issues logically entail the related question of regulating human subject experimentation. Second, every issue eventually comes to occupy an *institutional locus* of relevant decision-makers (with its attendant audience), in which it is typically debated and resolved. For instance, funding issues typically are handled by Congress, whereas regulatory issues are the province of executive regulatory agencies. Third, the specific resolution of a particular issue generates a potential or actual flow of harms or benefits to an *identifiable constituency* of politically active or inactive individuals and corporate actors, who are likely to become concerned about this flow. To the extent that another issue activates approximately the same constituency of interest groups, the two matters may become linked by social interpenetration of the interested parties. Thus, the nuclear waste disposal issue stirs the interests of plant manufacturers, utility companies, municipal and state governments, and citizen groups, in addition to relevant federal agencies and congressional subcommittees. Many of these organizations have comparable concerns about utility rate regulations, thereby tying together the nuclear waste and utility rate issues. To summarize, we argue that policy domain issues exhibit varying degrees of commonality with respect to one another based upon their conceptual, institutional, or constituency similarities and differences.

Using the results of the spatial representation of issue linkages described in Chapter 4, we measured the scope of every organization's interests in its national policy domain as the degree of dispersion among the issues in which it expressed high interest (see the appendix to this chapter for details of the calculation). Basically, an organization's *issue interest scope* measures the degree of dispersion across the issue space among those issues in which the organization had a high degree of interest. The higher an organization's score, the more widely separated are the issues in which it had a major interest; the lower its score, the more concentrated is its attention on a small, "localized" region of the issue space.

Monitoring Capacity

The second predetermined variable in figure 10.1 is the organization's endowment of relevant *monitoring resources,* discussed at length in Chapter 6, that can be deployed to tap the flow of policy information among the domain participants. The model is silent about the sources of such resources, but they presumably stem from the organization's position in economic markets, the size and wealth of its membership, and its access to public revenues. Just as we expect an actor's issue interests to shape its participation in domain policy events, so we posit that the magnitude of the staff devoted to monitoring the policy environment imposes varying limits on event participation. For present purposes, we take account only of an organization's internal staff resources. As indicated in the appendix to this chapter, organizational monitoring capacity consists of three variables measuring the number of FTEs employed to monitor the Washington scene about all types of policy matters, the number assigned specifically to energy or health policy concerns, and the number hired to gather technical data relevant to the domain.

Influence Reputation

A closely related predetermined variable is the organization's *influence reputation,* which is defined as the consequentiality in affecting policy decisions that is attributed to it by other domain actors. We argued in Chapter 5 that influence is a social mechanism by which one actor persuades another to modify its behavior by communicating information that changes the perceived connections between a policy decision and its outcome (Parsons, 1969). An organization's imputed influence varies, in part, with the trustworthiness and credibility of the information about its interests and intentions that it communicates to other domain participants. Influence reputations probably reflect both past impact and anticipated future performances in shaping collective domain policy decisions, although the model does not depict these sources. As a causal variable, influence reputation "can be wielded judiciously in an organization's efforts to avoid dependence and promote its interests" (Knoke, 1983).

The challenging problem, of course, is the conceptualization and measurement of the various power resources that an organization may bring to bear upon particular policy domain deliberations. Obviously, an organization with a large and effectively organized mass membership constituency, such as the AFL-CIO, has a very different basis for its influence in Washington than an organization with a large amount of money to contribute to political campaigns, such as Mobil Oil or Pfizer Pharmaceuticals. Yet another organization may enjoy great influence over events because it possesses much expertise on the substantive points at issue—for example, the American College of Surgeons or the Environmental Policy Center. No completely satisfying way of comparing such disparate power resource bases has yet been proposed. We believe, however, that we have made a fairly persuasive case in Chapter 5 that reputed influence standing among the consequential domain organizations, measured simply by the number of times an organization was cited as consequential by the other participants, taps the relative weight that an organization is likely to receive in policy deliberations.

In Chapter 6 we demonstrated that these scores are well predicted by a linear combination of eight specific types of attributed resources. That analysis provided further support for our contention that influence reputation is a reasonable summary measure on which to compare organizations' power bases.

Position in Communication and Resource Exchange Networks

The three antecedent variables in figure 10.1 are hypothesized to affect an organization's locations within two intervening structural variables—the *confidential communication network* and subsequently the material *resource exchange network*. When a policy event arises from an authoritative action, such as a congressional bill or a federal regulatory rule, it becomes a crucial source of uncertainty for policy domain participants. An event's outcome may adversely affect an organization's vested interests, or it may provide new opportunities for gaining material and ideological benefits. In trying to manage these uncertainties, an organization attempts to establish predictable, stable networks of interorganizational information and resource exchanges that enable it better to negotiate its external policy environments. Hence, the model shows that a broader range of issue interests, a higher monitoring capacity, and a more substantial influence reputation all lead to an organization's becoming more centrally located within both the communication and the resource exchange networks. Our depiction of communication network position as causally prior to resource exchange network location reflects our best judgment about the temporal sequence of linkage formation. That is, creating low-cost discussion ties to other domain actors is a precondition for more costly exchanges of valued goods and services such as physical facilities, staff, and technical-scientific data.

A central tenet of the interorganizational network perspective we have been advancing holds that organizations forge links with one another to gather and transmit relevant information and resources bearing upon their specific policy concerns. The approach further asserts the strong proposition that the embeddedness of actors in particular exchange networks facilitates and constrains their actions in ways that cannot be wholly explained by measuring actor-level attributes alone (Marsden and Laumann, 1977). In other words, an organization's *communication network location* specifies an intervening mechanism by which the organization converts its purposive interests, its monitoring resource endowments, and its influence reputation into active participation in policy events.

As described in Chapter 7, we gathered detailed information on the confidential exchange of information among our population of consequential actors. We were thus able to determine the prestige prominence of an organization's location within the communication network, as detailed in the appendix to this chapter (Burt, 1980; Coleman, 1972, 1973; Hubbell, 1965). Prestige prominence takes into account the quality of other organizations with which an actor exchanges information (Knoke and Burt, 1983). We chose this measure of network position over many alternative measures of centrality and prestige prominence for two reasons. First, we have strong theoretical grounds for paying attention to the asymmetric direction of information flows between organizations. Communication inflows, with respect to both volume and source, should play key roles in inducing or constraining an organization's policy participation in the domain. Second, we believe that the prestige prominence measure best combines the volume and source features of an organization's linkages to others in an intuitively obvious manner. A higher prestige prominence score means that an organization is more advantageously located within the domain communication network. This measure taps an actor's structural relationship with the other organizations in the domain and should not be confused with the measure of an organization's influence standing, which rests on a simple count of the number of votes others actors give a focal actor for being especially influential in policy deliberations.

In calculating an organization's prominence within the network of material resource exchanges, we first had to combine the considerable data on various types of interorganizational exchanges. The appendix to this chapter discusses operationalizations for six types of relations. Matrices describing these exchanges were summed to create a single matrix of generalized resources exchange. Then, each organization's prestige prominence score was computed in the same fashion as the communication network position scores described above. A higher score on the *resource exchange network location* variable means that an organization is more advantageously located within that network.

Scope of Event Participation

The ultimate dependent variable to be explained by the causal model is the scope of an organization's active participation in the decision-making events within a policy domain that were described in Chapter 9. This theoretical concept is operationalized by procedures similar to those for the issue interest scope variable above. As noted in that chapter, we carefully selected these events so as to include a comprehensive range of substantive events over an extended period of time—events that tapped both different intermediate stages in the process of policy formation and distinctive decision-making arenas in Congress, the executive branch, and the judiciary.

To avoid confounding the event participation scope variable with the issue interest scope variable described above, and thus artificially inflating their covariation, we did not measure event proximities in terms of their joint organizational constituencies or issue commonalities. Instead, we used five formal features of each event: its decision-making locus, public visibility, controversiality, functional locus, and type of decision cycle. A multidimensional spatial profile analysis arrayed the domain events according to their degree of similarity across these five formal attributes. Figures 9.1 and 9.2 show the two-dimensional representation of these event proximities for the two policy domains.

The same operational procedures used to calculate the issue interest scope variable were used to compute organizational scores on the *event participation scope* variable (see appendix to this chapter). The basic justification for looking at the scope of organizational event participation in this fashion is that discrete domain policy events occur in very disparate decision arenas. These loci vary in the ease by which organizations can monitor them and in the nature of the resources most relevant to their resolution. An organization's ability to participate in many or few events depends upon what the organization brings into the domain in the way of scope of issue interests, monitoring capacity, influence reputation, and embeddedness in the communication and resource exchange networks. We hypothesize that the greater the distance between events in terms of their formal attributes, the heavier the demands imposed upon an organization for effective participation. Thus, only organizations that are well positioned in terms of the independent variables in figure 10.1 will be able to participate in a wide range of domain policy events.

The analytic model in figure 10.1 hypothesizes an ultimate set of linkages from all three predetermined factors and both intervening structural variables to the organization's participation across the set of domain policy events. The presence of direct linkages from all antecedents simply reflects the absence of strong theoretical expectations or prior empirical research on the process that would permit a specification of differential impact. If the assumed importance of the social choice approach to policy making is correct, we would expect to observe that the two network variables substantially mediate the causal impact of the more distal antecedent attributes. However, at the present state of knowledge, estimation of the relative importance of the relationships in the model is entirely an empirical question.

Estimates of the Causal Model

In this section we describe the empirical estimates of our causal model, applying the preceding measures of variables to the theoretical concepts in figure 10.1. The statistical method used is LISREL V, a computer program for maximum likelihood structural and measurement equation estimates, which incorporates multiple indicators for latent variables, such as the monitoring capacity measure (Jöreskog and Sörbom, 1981). Figures 10.2 and 10.3 display the standardized parameter estimates from the LISREL V analyses of the energy and health domains. Both models produced reasonably good fits to the observed covariations among the measures ($\chi^2 = 9.30$, $df = 13$ for energy; $\chi^2 = 18.55$, $df = 13$ for health; the adjusted goodness-of-fit indices are .968 and .908 for energy and health, respectively). The substantive interpretation of these results is discussed in parallel for both models.

The three indicators constituting the latent construct of domain monitoring capacity exhibit essentially equivalent patterns in both domains: the number of domain-specific staff has the largest loading, the number of technical staff has the smallest loading, and the overall Washington monitoring staff has an intermediate value. The three predetermined variables (monitoring capacity, issue interests, and influence reputation) are all positively intercorrelated, although the magnitudes of covariation are notably higher in the energy than in the health domain. This tighter connection among interests and resources implies that energy organizations may require larger resource endowments in order to become broadly concerned about domain policy issues, whereas the more institutionalized nature of the health domain may not require extensive resource holdings in order to sustain broad issue concerns.

In both domains influence reputation has a very substantial impact on communication network position. As expected, the more influential an organization is perceived to be, the more prominent its position within the exchange of confidential policy information. The effect of reputation is somewhat higher in health than in energy, perhaps reflecting the more unsettled conditions in the latter domain. Net of this relationship, issue interests also exert modest positive effects on communication location: the more widespread an organization's policy interests, the more prominent its communication position. This effect is marginally greater in energy than in health. Surprisingly, in neither domain does monitoring capacity have a significant impact on any endogenous variable, once the effects of other measures are taken into account. That is, organizations with both large and small monitoring staffs have essentially identical advantages within the structural exchange networks and equivalent rates of policy event participation. Altogether, the predetermined variables account for 63 and 73 percent of the variation in communication network location in the energy and health domains, respectively.

Turning to organizational locations in the material resource exchange net-

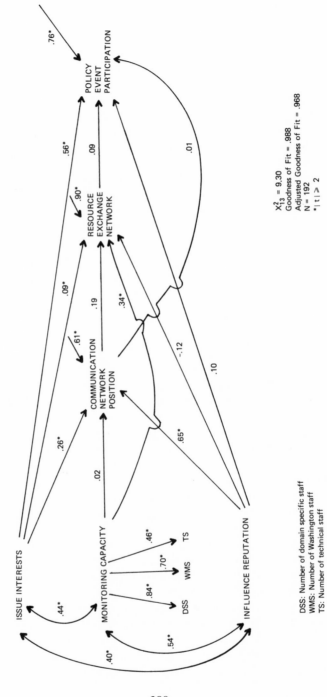

$X_{13}^2 = 9.30$
Goodness of Fit = .988
Adjusted Goodness of Fit = .968
N = 192
*|t| ≥ 2

DSS: Number of domain specific staff
WMS: Number of Washington staff
TS: Number of technical staff

Figure 10.2. A Causal Diagram of Organizational Activation in National Energy Policy Making

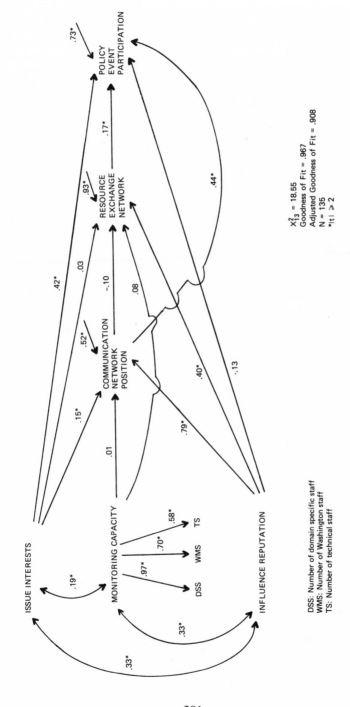

DSS: Number of domain specific staff
WMS: Number of Washington staff
TS: Number of technical staff

$X_{13}^2 = 18.55$
Goodness of Fit = .967
Adjusted Goodness of Fit = .908
N = 135
*|t| > 2

Figure 10.3. A Causal Diagram of Organizational Activation in National Health Policy Making

281

works, we observe contrasting patterns in the two domains. Contrary to expectations, prominent location in the confidential communication network does not significantly increase prominence in the exchange of resources in either domain. The effects of the predetermined variables differ across the domains: in health, a high influence reputation enhances an organization's prominence as a resource exchange partner; in energy, having a broader array of issue interests appears to promote a slightly advantageous exchange location. Since neither equation explains much more than 10 percent of the total variance, clearly other factors not included in this model must be affecting the material resources exchange structure.

Finally, the two domains differ markedly in the effects of the antecedent variables on organizational policy event participation. The scope of issue interests exerts a substantial effect in each domain; the broader the scope of an organization's issue interests, the wider the range of policy events it actively pursues. But for energy organizations, issue interest scope is the only variable achieving a significant relationship. These results support our initial expectations about the unstructured, noninstitutionalized nature of the energy domain in the 1970s. In contrast, the health domain exhibits significant net relationships from both measures of network location. Indeed, the .44 coefficient from the confidential communication network position rivals the issue interests' .42 impact. These relationships indicate that the more prominent a health organization is within either the communication network or the resource exchange network, the more likely it is to participate in a diverse range of policy events, *net of its concerns with policy issues*. Influence reputation does not exert a direct effect on event participation, but its indirect effect through the two structural measures is substantial $((.79 \times .44) + (.40 \times .17) = .42)$. That is, the more reputedly influential a health organization is, the more active it will be in policy events because of its prominent position within the network structures. In the energy domain, influence reputation confers no such differential advantage, either directly or indirectly. Despite these substantively different causal relationships, the two domains are similar in that the explanatory variables account for roughly the same amount of variation in policy event participation (.42 in energy and .47 in health).

The different empirical results from estimating the causal model in the two domains offer strong support for our contention that the health domain was more institutionalized than the energy domain during the period under investigation. The implications of these findings are discussed further in the concluding section.

Discussion

The results of the empirical analyses supported several initial speculations about the differential social organization of the energy and health national policy domains. The contrasting magnitudes of estimated relationships in the causal models can be attributed to differences in the institutionalization of policy participation processes. Our initial model was premised on the crucial impact of timely, trustworthy exchanges of policy-relevant information upon organizations' decisions to participate in policy events. This expectation proved to be correct in the health domain but not in the energy domain during the era under investigation. The absence of a significant effect from communication network position for energy organizations implies that the domain exacted relatively lower transaction costs for the acquisition of information than did the health domain. Some evidence to support this conclusion comes from a related study of Washington representatives, conducted during the first Reagan administration (Laumann and Heinz, 1985). Respondents were asked about the sources of published information on which they relied. Energy representatives were somewhat more likely to rely upon daily newspapers and trade or professional journals than were health representatives; the latter made greater use of computerized data bases, the *Federal Register, Congressional Record,* and reference books. If these results can be projected back to the preceding decade, they suggest that energy policy information was more accessible through widely disseminated sources.

Our research shows that organizational self-interest is a prime factor affecting the scope of policy event participation in both domains. The broader the range of domain issues in which an organization has a substantial concern, the wider the space of policy events in which it becomes involved. However, when the policy domain is more institutionalized, advantageous locations near the center of key social networks make important independent contributions to mobilizing organizational participation. In this context, institutionalization means that a domain has become a routinized, calculable, well-integrated system where the rules of legitimate policy participation are well understood and accepted by all players. Because information about critical events is more impacted (i.e., embedded in less accessible sources) in such domains, network location plays an important structural role in converting an organization's purposive orientations and material resources into activation on decision-making events. To some extent, an advantageous position in the communication network enables an organization to overcome some of the higher costs of obtaining relevant information within a more institutionalized domain.

In turbulent, rapidly changing, and unstable policy domains where the norms of participation have not been clearly demarcated, the social structure may be too fluid to have much value in shaping policy participation. To judge from the history of the energy domain during the 1970s, any organization with a modicum of interest in the policy issues could easily enter into the debates. The territorial bases of energy production (Davis, 1978), unlike the geographically dispersed provision of health services, generated more divisive and contentious controversies within Congress, itself a territorially organized entity. The Nixon-Ford-Carter era can be read (Goodwin, 1981:395–636) as a prolonged struggle over the rules of the game: whether centralized political direction or decentralized market forces would predominate in the allocation of energy resources. Periodic efforts to centralize energy policy, under a federal "czar" (as in James Schlesinger's politically inept "master plan" at the beginning of the Carter administration) or through wage-price and allocation controls (Nixon's response to inflation and the oil embargo), were bitterly fought from many sides, often creating strange coalitions of interest groups on particular events. By the end of the decade, marketplace solutions had triumphed and were further consolidated under Reagan (Kash and Rycroft, 1984:256–79). The highly visible nature of these struggles, further publicized by the mass media, drove the costs of information acquisition in the energy domain considerably below those of the health arena. As a result, privileged locations within the energy communication network conveyed no especial advantage in mobilizing an organization's involvement. In effect, simply having a policy interest was enough to stimulate participation.

A major revelation of this research was the absence of any direct effects of resource possession on event participation. Monitoring capacity (as indexed by staff sizes) and influence reputation did not directly increase event involvement in either domain, contrary to our initial expectations that well-endowed organizations would exhibit broader ranges of participation net of their substantive policy issue interests. Influence reputation among health organizations, however, did translate into more prominent locations within the two structural networks, leading ultimately to the expansion of policy activation. Apparently, at least among elite organizations operating at the core of the national decision-making systems, large resource endowments are not essential for participation efforts. Of course, resource holdings may be critical in enhancing an actor's ability to influence the outcome of collective decisions, but that relationship is the subject for another analysis. At present, we can be fairly confident in concluding that when an organization believes that its interests are at stake, it will attempt to influence the direction of such a decision regardless of the resources available for that effort.

Appendix to Chapter 10

Scope of issue interests. Each organization's scope of issue interests was calculated by: (1) finding all the issues on list A (Appendices C and D) in which
its informant indicated a greater than moderate level of interest (scores of 4 or
5); (2) calculating for those issues the mean of the coordinates generated by
the two-dimensional ALSCAL solution depicted in figure 4.3 or 4.4 (i.e., the
mean location of the average issue in which the organization had high interests); and (3) summing the squared distances of its high-interest issues from
that mean location. The formula for scope of issue interest is:

$$\sum_{i=1}^{n} \left(X_i - \sum_{i=1}^{n} \frac{X_i}{n} \right)^2 + \left(Y_i - \sum_{i=1}^{n} \frac{Y_i}{n} \right)^2$$

where n is the number of issues in which the organization had high interests
and (X_i, Y_i) are the coordinates of the issues.

Monitoring capacity. Three types of employees were classified by informants: (1) general monitors, the number of FTEs on the staff "whose regular
task involves monitoring the Washington scene about all kinds of national
policy issues of interest to it"; (2) specialized monitors, the number of FTEs
devoted to watching the Washington scene about either national energy or
health policy issues; and (3) technical staff, the number of FTEs "whose principal responsibility is the gathering of systematic technical data" that are relevant to either energy or health policy issues. In the analyses reported in this
chapter, the number of specialized monitors was subtracted from the number
of general monitors to avoid an artificially inflated correlation between these
indicators when estimating a latent structural measure of overall organizational monitoring capacity. See Chapter 6 for an extended discussion of this
measure.

Influence reputation. See Chapter 5 for a discussion and analysis of the
method used to measure influence reputation.

Structural location in the confidential communication network. Chapter 7
describes the construction of the matrix representing the communication links
among actors through which confidential information about national policy
was exchanged. This matrix was used to calculate prestige prominence scores
for every domain organization. An actor is prominent within an exchange network to the extent that its relations with other organizations make it especially
visible. Within the generic concept of prominence, two subclasses can be distinguished by the nature of the relationships that render an organization's network position visible: centrality prominence and prestige prominence (Knoke
and Burt, 1983). Centrality measures assume *symmetrical* relations of reciprocated ties between actors and emphasize the sheer volume of the link-

ages. In contrast, prestige measures are based on the assumption of *asymmetric* relations of directed exchanges and emphasize the quality of relations. Prominence in a network derives from being the *target* of many actors or being the target of actors who are themselves the target of many actors. The quality of relations takes into account the structural contexts within which a given volume of an organization's contacts occur. A contact has high quality to the extent that it increases the diversity of the others in a focal organization's primary network. Consider, for example, two organizations, both connected with the same number of others. Suppose that the first organization's contacts themselves have relations with many other organizations, while the second organization's contacts are all otherwise isolates. In this case, the first organization has higher prestige prominence because it has higher-quality connections; the second has low prominence because its relations connect it only with peripheral actors.

The formula for the prestige prominence score of the *i*th organization is:

$$P_i = \sum_{j=1}^{N} C_{ij} P_j$$

where C_{ij} is a square matrix of network relations (normalized to sum to 1.0 over row elements within column j), and P_j is the *j*th organization's prestige prominence score. Prominence scores were computed as a routine eigenvector problem, meaning that each organization's prestige prominence was determined jointly with every other organization's prominence.

Resource exchange network. Informants were asked to indicate the other domain organizations with which their group engaged in a variety of transactions: (1) receiving "technical or scientific information relevant to the issues"; (2) giving "substantial funds as payments for services or goods, or as contributions or membership fees"; (3) receiving such funds; (4) permitting other organizations to use its staff and facilities when those groups do not have such staff and facilities available to them; (5) using staff and facilities of other organizations; and (6) belonging to the same trade association or organizational councils. (See Appendix B, questions C3–C8.)

As might be expected, for each matrix constructed from these responses, some exchanges were not reciprocated. If organization *A* said that it used facilities owned by organization *B*, but *B* did not report that it allowed *A* to use them, then the relationship was measured as unreciprocated. We assigned a score of *1* to unreciprocated reports and *2* to reciprocated reports, on the assumption that reciprocated reports imply a greater salience and value of the exchange tie to both parties. Some of the matrices were transposed to make the row organizations the recipients of resources compatible across types of exchanges. Then all matrix elements were summed pairwise to form a final nonbinary matrix. Prestige prominence scores for every organization in each domain were computed by procedures identical to those described above for the communication network.

Scope of event participation. Every event sampled for each domain was classified on five categoric variables: decision-making locus, public visibility, controversiality, functional focus, and type of decision cycle, described in Chapter 9. In each domain, a matrix was constructed with events in the rows and the five formal event attributes in the columns. The data were subjected to multidimensional profile analysis, the Guttman-Lingoes MSA-I program (Lingoes, 1973). This program is designed to analyze an n-chotomous rectangular data matrix and to produce a Euclidean space by partitioning subjects (in this case, policy events) into n-chotomous categories over all items (attributes) simultaneously (Lingoes, 1973:219). Using the two-dimensional coordinates from the event profile analysis, organizational scores on the scope of event participation were calculated following procedures described above for the calculation of scope of issue interest.

11

The Structure of Event Linkages

with Yong-Hak Kim

This chapter attempts an initial formulation of a theory of participation across pairs of formally independent and temporally distinct events within a policy domain. Thus, its content is analogous to Chapter 7's discussion of communication links (dyadic ties) between pairs of actors in a policy domain. Here we shift the analytic focus from unit events, which are of central concern in Chapters 9 and 10, to pairs of events. Each of the 81 energy events and 85 health events can be treated as a free-standing opportunity to act. Each is characterized by features that selectively elicit or discourage the participation of actors in the domain. In Chapter 9's discussion of event scenarios, however, we noted that some events were drawn from institutionally or substantively integrated sequences of decision-making actions that might serve to orchestrate the nature of an actor's participation over the set of events within a scenario. In other words, as we have argued for actors, there is a crucial systemic aspect to analyzing the impact of events on action.

The key analytic premise of this chapter is that pairs of events may be seen as varying along a continuum of actor participation. At one pole, the events may be treated as entirely independent of one another (i.e., participation of actors in one event is random with respect to their participation in the other). At the other pole, the two events are completely dependent on one another, either in the *causal* sense that the first event is a necessary and sufficient condition for the second or in the *strategic* or purposive sense that an actor's preference for the outcome of the second event constrains its behavior concerning the first. The contribution of this chapter is to use a pairwise analysis of organizational participation in events to identify a variety of attributes associated with the presence of linkages among events.

To proceed with the analysis, we need to devise a measure of the degree to which a pair of events are mutually dependent. Initially, dependence is understood in a formal sense as the extent to which participation in one event predicts involvement in another, although various substantive interpretations of this measure will be introduced in the discussion that follows. Although one might think of a number of ways to measure the linkage of events, we believe that our theoretical purposes are best served if we operationalize the concept of event interdependency as the degree to which actors overlap or avoid participation in any pairing of events. Note that we take no formal notice here of the temporal ordering of the paired events, because it is an open question whether events are linked causally (and therefore must be considered in strict temporal order) or whether they are linked by purposive or strategic considerations whereby the anticipation of later events can exert constraints on prior events. It is incumbent on the analyst to specify the assumptions about temporal ordering underlying his or her theory of action. Having acknowledged the problematic theoretical status of temporal order, we now attempt an exploratory empirical measurement of its importance as a determinant of organizational action.

Measuring Event Linkage

There are four possible ways in which an organization can respond to a pair of events. An organization may (1) participate in the first event and continue to participate in the second event; (2) participate in the first event but not the second event; (3) not participate in the first event but become active in the second event; or (4) remain inactive throughout. To measure the degree of dependency between a pair of events (L_{ij}), we shall use the logodds ratio: $L_{ij} = log\,(a*d/b*c)$, where a, b, c and d refer to the cell frequencies in figure 11.1.[1] The calculation of logodds ratios converts the binary actor-by-event matrix in Figure 1.5 (whose cell entries are *1* if an organization participates in an event or *0* if it does not) to the event-by-event matrix. The latter matrix is our dependent variable, which will be explained by substantive and formal features of

---

1. We have chosen the logodds ratio as a measure of association between a pair of events because it is invariant with respect to the relative number of cases that appear in each column or row; that is, it is insensitive to the number of participants in each event. Controlling the marginal distribution is of concern because of the great variability in the rates of participation across events (see Chapter 9). We added .5 to the cells with 0 frequencies because the odds ratio is undefined whenever zero cells occur.

Event B

	Participate	Not Participate
Participate	a	b
Not Participate	c	d

Event A

Figure 11.1. Event Linkages Defined on the Basis of Participation Pattern

the events analyzed in all possible pairings. For the two domains under study, we calculate logodds ratios for 3,240 (81 × 80/2) and 3,570 (85 × 84/2) event pairings.

In energy, the logodds ratios range from −2.6 to 6.0, with a mean of 0.86. In health, they range from −2.6 to 6.9, with a mean of 1.08.[2] If actors on the average participate randomly, we would observe a mean of 0. The moderate positive deviation of the average from the random expectation in both domains suggests that the systems of actors and events are at least loosely coupled. Because a negative logodds ratio also represents a systematic dependence between two events in the sense that inactivity in one event is nonrandomly associated with activity in the other, we also calculated the average of absolute logodds ratios. In energy, the average of the absolute logodds ratios was 1.0, and in health, 1.16. Both represent only modest increases over

2. To give the reader some sense of how the log transformation normalizes the skewed distribution of odds ratios, the following conversion table is provided. Note, for instance, that the maximum logodds ratio in energy, 6.0, is 403.4 before taking the log. This large odds ratio results, of course, from the division of a small denominator ($b \times c$) into a large nominator ($a \times d$).

Logodds	Odds Ratios
1	2.7
2	7.4
3	20.1
4	54.6
5	148.4
6	403.4

Table 11.1 Participation Pattern of Actors in Events in a Hypothetical Policy Domain

		A	B	C	D	E	F	G	H	I	J	K
						Actors						
Events	1	0	0	0	0	1	1	1	1	1	1	0
	2	0	0	0	0	1	1	1	1	1	1	1
	3	1	1	1	1	0	0	0	0	0	0	1
	4	1	1	1	1	0	0	0	0	0	0	0

the means just reported, reflecting the fact that most pairs of events are positively dependent in the sense that actors tend to be either co-present or co-absent for any given pairing of events. Some degree of patterned participation across sets of events was anticipated, of course, since the events were drawn from two domains of presumably interrelated concerns. A similar analysis of participation in events drawn from wholly unrelated policy concerns (such that there is no coherent or systematic patterning of actor participation from one event to another) would produce an average logodds approximating zero. A negatively signed logodds ratio is likely to occur when the paired events are drawn from disjunctive policy domains such that participation in one event precludes participation in the other.

To arrive at a better understanding of the logodds ratio in this context, consider a hypothetical domain with four events (table 11-1). Participation in an event by an actor is indicated by *1;* failure to participate, by *0.* Analyzing the example in two ways, as a single set and partitioned in two blocks, clarifies the empirical character of event structures and policy domains. A negative logodds ratio is observed for a pair of events drawn from different blocks, yet the within-block logodds ratios are positive (e.g., event 1 is negatively linked with Event 3 and 4, but it is positively linked with event 2). The average logodds ratio for the entire system tends to be close to zero. Thus, attention to the patterned participation elicited by events draws attention to a dimension of social organization that may not be apparent in analyses focused on organizational attributes alone or direct interorganizational ties.

The problems of partitioning raised by this example are closely related to the constructed, if not arbitrary, character of policy domains. As was discussed in Chapter 2, the historical development of policy domains involves a continuing process of legitimation and symbolic framing whereby actors and issues are included or excluded from a domain at a given time. Thus, despite their obvious implications for physical well-being, nutrition is addressed primarily under the rubric of agricultural policy and occupational health is typically viewed as a labor issue. Using logodds ratios, it is possible to assess the accuracy with which various policy domains have been identified. Returning to our study, 17.7 percent of the logodds ratios within the energy domain are negative in sign, whereas in health only 11.1 percent are negative. This means that an energy event, on the average, is negatively linked with 14.1 out of the possible 80 events. An average health event is negatively matched with 9.2 other events out of the total 84.

There is little systematic pattern in the distribution of the negative logodds ratios in the energy domain. For instance, a congressional action calling for a 10-year extension of the federal nuclear accident insurance program (event 304; see no. 14 in the appendix to this chapter) had 39 negative logodds ratios, the largest number in energy. These results indicate that this event attracted a very specialized set of actors. At the other extreme, a bill proposed to encourage the development of synthetic fuel technologies had no event linked with a negative logodds ratio (event 205: no. 9). In health, however, the distribution of negative logodds ratios is more systematic. Biomedical and personnel events are the major sources of negative logodds ratios with other domain events. The two personnel events involving Donald Kennedy and Patricia Harris (events 410 and 116 respectively: no. 6) have the largest numbers of negative pairings (29 and 28, respectively). Biomedical research events also tend to have negative dependence. For example, DNA research (event 107: no. 5) and NIH research (event 117: no. 3) have 26 and 24 negative matches, respectively. Our earlier findings showed similar patternings of negative coefficients of biomedical issues with the other domain issues (see Chapters 4 and 7).

It is obvious that the varying degrees of event linkage or dependence in each domain arise because actors participate in events selectively. For the purposes of this analysis, we propose to reverse the usual causal argument that actors participate in events for reasons stemming exclusively from their own calculations of self-interest. Instead, we postulate here that events, individually and collectively, possess institutional, historical, and other features that elicit or repress actors' participation. In sharp contrast to the preceding two chapters, we propose to infer the logic of actors' selective participation in domain decision making from the vantage point of the event(s). In other words, we analyze the pattern of participation by focusing *exclusively* on event characteristics without considering the properties of the actors, such as their interests, resources, or interrelationships as communication partners. In an important sense, we are adopting a version of the institutionalist or normative theorist's approach that stresses the critical role played by the interpretation of events' symbolic meanings and normative structure in the explanation of social action.

As we noted in the introductory chapter, the literature is not especially forthcoming with respect to the structuration of events or the process of generating event linkage. Indeed, most theorists have treated the relational properties of events as extrinsic to their explanatory problem. As a first step toward developing propositions to explain event linkages, we propose to explicate, metaphorically speaking, the role of homophily/homology among events. In discussing the mechanisms generating communication ties in Chapter 7, we argued that actors with similar (homophilous) characteristics (e.g., similar interest profiles or influence ranks) tend to communicate with one another more than those with dissimilar characteristics. With respect to event linkage, we suggest a proposition of comparable generality: events with similar characteristics tend to attract the same set of actors.[3]

The importance of event homophily for actors' participation can be demonstrated easily. For example, two events with similar substantive content but occurring in different institutional contexts (e.g., one event in the congressional and the other in the executive arena) operate under different institutional rules of access and participation. Congressional passage of a bill involves a series of decision points, including hearings, committee votes, and chamber actions, that follow a predictable, institutionally specified order. This order differs in key respects from the process by which an executive agency initiates a new regulation. Once actors become partisans in a congressional debate, institutional norms encourage them to remain active participants through all the major stages of a bill's passage through Congress. Failure of an actor to appear at an intermediate decision point may cause other actors to infer (i.e., interpret the irregular action as meaning) that the actor is not really committed to the bill in question and therefore discount the actor's earlier actions. Thus, it is often necessary for an organization to participate consistently in a chain of related events if the organization wishes to ensure its right to play a part in the anticipated final stages of the bill's passage. On the other hand, although it is normatively appropriate for an actor to submit written comments or an oral argument on a proposed regulation by a federal agency that requests them in the *Federal Register*, it is normatively impermissible to have *ex parte* communication with the decision-makers once the hearing period is over. Even more stringent restrictions are observed on advocates' communications with judges. Thus, the institutional context in which an event occurs not only influences the actor's perceptions and interpretations of the event but also constrains or specifies their participation in that and other linked events (Wildavsky, 1962).

---

3. An actor-oriented perspective would formulate this proposition by reversing the causal direction: actors tend to participate consistently in a set of events with similar characteristics because they activate similar interest calculations.

Measuring Event Similarity

Our methodological strategy for specifying the role of event homophily is to develop mapping rules for relating similar events on the bases of their shared institutional or temporal characteristics by assessing the extent to which the paired events attract or discourage the participation of the same actors. The rationale underlying this analysis is that events possess certain interevent properties that have consequences for the ways in which actors respond within and across events. In Chapter 9 we showed how certain event characteristics, such as controversiality, scope, and political consequences, have significant effects on the participation of actors despite their differing interests as well as types and amounts of resource endowments. By shifting the level of analysis from the individual to the dyadic level, we shall now try to see if, taken in combination, these event characteristics have significant effects on our measure of event dependence, the logodds ratio. Given the absence of a literature concerning the mechanisms of event linkage generation, we have adopted an exploratory and inductive approach. Predictor variables, including political consequence, decision locus, decision type, controversiality, scope, scenario, and institutional time, have been selected on the basis of plausibility alone.

Except for institutional time, all the predictor variables are defined and operationalized in Chapter 9. *Institutional time* refers to two different institutional time frames: congressional term or presidential (executive) administration. Two dummy variables were used to indicate whether a pair of events occurred in the same Congress (*1* if the paired events occurred within the same two-year congressional term; *0* otherwise) or four-year presidential term (coded likewise). The theoretical justification for including institutional time is based on the frequent observation that a change in presidential administration or congressional membership is often associated with a new balance of understandings about basic policy orientations and preferences. For instance, the first Reagan administration inaugurated a major transformation of Carter's generally proregulatory policy orientations and introduced a more consistently antiregulatory stance. The historical overview of the two policy domains in Chapter 2 showed that the vicissitudes of fundamental policy orientations are often related to changes in presidential administrations. Thus, we expect that a pair of events occurring within the same presidential administration will have a higher degree of mutual dependence than a pair of events occurring across two or more presidential terms. The inference is that the same institutional environment reduces uncertainty and opportunity costs, and thus produces higher incentives for stable and consistent participation (or nonparticipation). We also expect the same argument to hold for a pair of events occurring within the same Congress as opposed to one involving two Congresses. Again the regularized sequencing of events according to the congressional calendar serves to reduce uncertainty for the participants and to homogenize the strategic considerations taken into account by actors when deciding whether to participate or not.

In the cases of controversiality and scope, we dichotomized the distributions of scores into high and low. Other qualitatively defined event characteristics were dichotomized as follows: decision location (congressional versus executive and judicial) and decision type (standard/recurrent versus constructed/consummated). For any pairing of events, this results in four possible combinations: high-high, high-low, low-high, and low-low (or a similar permutation of the qualitative labels for the other variables). If the dependent variable (i.e., the logodds ratio) was not symmetric, one would need three dummy variables to determine the unique cell effects of these four combinations.[4] Since the logodds ratio is symmetric, however, the effect of the high-low combination is identical to that of the low-high match. This produces only three distinguishable combinations. For this reason we created only two dummy variables, high-high and low-low, to avoid linear dependence in the matrix of independent variables. In the case of scenarios (of which there are 21 and 22 categories in energy and health, respectively), we created one dummy variable, *1* indicating that a pair of events were in the same scenario, *0* that they were not. For institutional time, we coded (1) a pair of events as being in the same Congress or not, and (2) a pair of events as being in same presidential administration or not. Similarly, for functional focus we coded one dummy variable, *1* indicating that a pair of events had the same functional focus (i.e., whether they were both initiatory, funding, or regulatory) or *0* that they did not.

In general, we hypothesize a positive effect of event homophily on pairwise event dependence. We expect, for instance, that a pair of events belonging to the same chain of related decisions leading to an outcome (i.e., a scenario) will produce a higher degree of event dependence, primarily because of their homogeneous content and because of institutionally grounded expectations about the participation behavior of interested parties. (We discussed in Chapter 9 the significance of this variable in orchestrating actors' participation.) We also expect that a pair of events embedded in the same institutional context—that is, the same decision-making locus (either the congressional or executive arena)—will generate higher logodds ratios as a result of the actors' tendency to specialize in one institutional arena because of its distinctive information requirements and institutional rules of access. Historical (or institutional) time is another important basis of event dependence, as discussed

---

4. When the independent variables are dichotomous, the estimation of a regression model using three dummy variables is the same as the estimation of the following model: $Y_{ij} = a + b_1 X_i + b_2 X_j + b_3 X_i X_j$. See Lincoln (1984) for more details.

in the introductory chapter. Presumably, the closer in real time two events occur, the more similar the historical circumstances characterizing the two events. Thus, an actor's calculations about whether to participate in two events are likely to be more similar the closer in time they take place, net of all other considerations of similarity and dissimilarity. It is quite difficult, however, to predict the signs of the controversiality and scope variables. One might speculate that a pair of controversial events would induce lower participation linkages because of real or anticipated burn-out effects (Coleman, 1957) arising from continuing hostile actions among parties that usually are constrained to come to some *modus vivendi* over time. The old bromide "one doesn't want to get into too many fights with one's neighbors" applies here.

Empirical Results

Table 11.2 reports the regression coefficients for the energy and health domains. Sixteen percent and 31 percent of the variance in the logodds ratios were explained in energy and health, respectively. The more systematic variation in the measure of event dependency in health may indicate that actors' participation is more structured in the health domain than in the energy domain, a finding consistent with our argument about the relatively greater degree of institutionalization and stability in the health domain. Recall that we also found in Chapter 7, that communication linkages among actors were more systematically determined in health than in energy.

One of the most striking findings concerns the importance of the scenario variable in making events mutually dependent. Net of all other variables, belonging in the same scenario increases the logodds ratio by 2.14 in energy and 2.27 in health. (The appendix to this chapter presents brief historical descriptions of the 28 energy and 23 health scenarios and their outcomes, together with the set of events constituting each scenario.)[5] This finding provides strong evidence for Chapter 9's speculative discussions of the role of scenarios in orchestrating actors' participation. When a set of events are concatenated into a scenario, we observe remarkably high consistency in the domain actors' participation: that is, the set of actors active in the initial event remain active to the final event, and, conversely, those actors inactive in the first event remain so. Relatively few join in the middle of the sequence of events, and fewer still enter, exit, and reenter—a pattern that suggests a strategy of intervention that almost no one follows.[6]

The dummy variable referring to whether or not a pair of events occurred in

---

5. In energy, there are seven scenarios composed of a singleton event; in health, only one scenario is composed of a single event.

6. Inspection of the patterning of participation in all scenarios with three or more events supports this generalization. Less than 10 percent of the actors active in a given scenario exhibit

Table 11.2. Regression of Event Linkage Measures on Relational Event Characteristics

Independent Variables	Regression Coefficients			
	Energy		Health	
Intercept	.77**		.44**	
Both events are controversial	.03	(.01)	−.12*	(−.05)
Both events are not controversial	−.06	(−.03)	.13**	(.06)
Both events have high scope	−.04	(−.01)	.36**	(.11)
Both events have low scope	.02	(.01)	.53**	(.26)
Both are Congressional events	−.08	(−.04)	.24**	(.11)
Both are Executive events	.04	(.01)	.07*	(.01)
Both are standard/recurrent events	.04	(.01)	.08*	(.04)
Both are unconsummated/constructed events	.01	(.00)	.05**	(.02)
Share political consequences	.03	(.02)	.17**	(.08)
Share the institutional calendar of Presidential term	.02	(.01)	.01	(.01)
Share the institutional calendar of Congressional term	.16**	(.07)	.03	(.01)
Belong to the same scenario	2.14**	(.39)	2.27**	(.43)
Adjusted R^2	.16**		.31**	

* $p < .01$

** $p < .001$

Standardized Coefficients are in parentheses

the same Congress increased the logodds ratios significantly in the energy domain. In fact, this variable is the only significant variable in energy other than the scenario variable. This indicates that participation in energy was influenced by the institutionally organized congressional calendar and points as well to the important role played by events, typically described as exogene-

---

irregular patterns of participation. One suspects that even these cases may be errors of reportage rather than indications of strategic behavior. Consistency of action across related events seems to be the name of the game in both domains.

ous shocks, in reframing the energy policy issues confronted by successive Congresses.

In health, decision locus does affect event dependence significantly, supporting the general principle of event homophily. It is interesting to note, however, that a pair of events occurring in Congress has a stronger effect on event linkage (.24) than a pair taking place in the executive branch (.07), which suggests that the health domain actors selectively participated in events with different institutional rules of access, and that the tendency for actors to specialize in one institutional arena is a little stronger for congressional events than executive ones. No such tendency is observed for the energy domain, suggesting that event structuration in energy was not so distinctively driven by the formal institutional sectors of the domain—perhaps another symptom of its general lack of institutionalization.

Health events with the same political consequences, whether they are both initiatory, regulatory, or funding events, have a higher degree of interdependence, when one controls for all other predictor variables, than pairings with mixed political consequences. Different types of politically consequential events appear to attract or repel distinctive subsets of repeat players. That is, initiatory, regulatory, or funding events tend to draw repeat players for those sorts of decision tasks, net of all the other features that make them similar or different.

Interestingly enough, as anticipated, a pairing of controversial events reduces dependence. We interpret this finding as resulting from the effects of the participants' actual or anticipated burn-out in committing resources in contested matters that have, by their very nature, a fairly high likelihood of going wrong for the plurality of actors on the losing side. That is, in institutionalized policy domains, the danger of losing face or damaging one's reputation for being effective or influential makes an actor especially wary of entering contested matters. In other words, since a controversial event usually involves bigger stakes and therefore attracts greater participation at the same time that it also requires more resources to participate, actors tend to avoid participation in multiple controversies.

But no such tendency is observed in energy, and we must ask ourselves why. We speculate that burn-out effects and caution in entering controversial events are more likely in more institutionalized policy arenas, where one's reputational standing is more readily converted into successful influence. Such a resource is not likely to be as easily risked in events with uncertain or potentially adverse outcomes. In a less institutionalized domain, controversy is a generalized condition and, at the same time, actors have considerably less clarity regarding what is being risked by engaging in repeated conflicts. Reputations for influence are unstable and fluid; momentary losses of face caused by a lost battle may be regained in the next controversial encounter. Recall our observation in Chapter 5 that consensus about the influentials was much less extensive in the energy domain than in health and that influence standing played no role in predicting the scope of participation in broadly diversified events (see Chapter 10).

In health, two events with the same scope of impact tend to increase the logodds ratios. The high-high match increased the logodds ratios by .36, and the low-low match by .53, again supporting the principle of event homophily. Alternatively put, a pair of events with a high-low or low-high match tends to depress the number of co-present or co-absent actors. This means that high- and low-scope pairings of events, net of the other features considered, attract disjunctive sets of actors. That is, high-scope events attract (or exclude) the same actors, whereas low-scope events attract a different audience of actors who overlap one another in confronting such events. This pattern of participation is logically similar to that in the hypothetical example presented in table 11.1 in that between-block logodds ratios (in this case a high-low or low-high scope match) are negative while within-block logodds ratios are positive.

Concluding Remarks

This chapter has demonstrated that there is patterned interdependence among events in each policy domain, even if one uses rather minimal pieces of information about the events themselves. This demonstration has important substantive and methodological implications. The main substantive finding is that the participation of the health domain actors is more systematically structured by conjoint or disjunctive features of events than that of the energy actors. Being embedded in the same scenario, however, is the most important predictor explaining dependence among events in both domains. Building on the methodological consequences of this finding, the next chapter adopts the scenario as the unit of analysis in order to study the structure of consensus and cleavage in the two policy domains. Once we take the principal source of observed event dependence more fully into account, we shall see that domain activities as organized into scenarios become very loosely coupled with the viewpoints of the many domain actors—indeed, almost disarticulated from them. How is such specialized differentiation of actor participation integrated into more coherent patterns of consensus and cleavage? This is the crucial question about the governance and integration of the modern state, and it is to this issue that we now turn.

Appendix to Chapter 11

Asterisks indicate the eight major controversies in each domain used in event analyses in subsequent chapters.

Energy Domain

Energy Research

1. *Geothermal energy:* In 1974 Congress approved funding for a multi-agency effort to research, develop, and demonstrate the feasibility of geothermal energy. (Event 101).

2. *Automobile research:* In an effort to reduce the nation's dependency on oil, Congress passed legislation funding the research and development of electric-powered automobiles and advanced automobile engines. Ford vetoed both bills, but Congress overrode his veto on the electric automobile legislation. (Events 102, 103)

3. **Clinch River breeder reactor:* First authorized in 1970, the Clinch River breeder reactor was intended to demonstrate a new nuclear technology. During the Carter administration, however, the President repeatedly vetoed appropriations for the project. In April 1978 the House Science Committee set the stage for another confrontation. Rejecting a Carter administration proposal to amend the Energy Department authorization by removing any commitment to the financing of such demonstration projects, the committee voted to continue funding the Clinch River reactor. The following month the Senate Energy Committee endorsed funding for an alternative breeder technology, but for the fourth year running the Senate failed to enact Energy Department legislation. In 1979 the House Science Committee continued its opposition to Carter by voting increased funding for the reactor. (Events 104, 106, 107, 108, 110)

4. **Nuclear waste disposal:* As on-site storage for nuclear waste filled up, the increasing transport of nuclear waste led a number of railroads to request exemptions from carrying this cargo; the Interstate Commerce Commission rejected these requests. Faced with political opposition to the development of geologically stable, permanent depositories for nuclear waste, in December 1979 the Senate Energy Committee reported a bill requiring the energy secretary to establish long-term interim storage facilities above ground. The following year the House passed significantly different legislation calling for a demonstration project on underground waste disposal. Encountering controversy over the inclusion of military wastes and state veto provisions, only legislation dealing with low-level wastes managed to pass Congress. (Events 105, 109, 111)

Energy Industry Development

5. *Oil pipelines:* In 1968 Atlantic Richfield struck oil on Alaska's North Slope, and five years later, following numerous injunctions secured by environmentalist groups, Congress passed legislation authorizing the construction of the Trans-Alaska pipeline but defeated an amendment that would grant the pipeline immunity from suits brought under the National Environmental Policy Act. In 1977 Congress approved an agreement "in principle" with the Canadian government to build an Alaska-Canada natural gas pipeline. (Events 201, 209)

6. *Solar industry:* In 1974 Congress approved funding for research and development of solar power to heat and cool buildings. A similarly noncontroversial bill was considered in 1977 when the House Public Works Committee reported a bill providing for demonstration of solar technology in federal buildings. As part of Carter's National Energy Plan, tax credits for the installation of solar technologies (as well as insulation and a variety of renewable power sources) were approved in 1978. During the same period, Congress also authorized funding for the development of solar photovoltaic cells and for a "solar bank" to subsidize low-interest loans for the installation of solar technologies. (Events 202, 207, 208, 212, 215)

7. *Coal leasing:* Concern for environmental effects and a fair return on land leased from the federal government led Congress to consider a number of reforms. In 1975, after a prolonged struggle in which additional controls on strip mining were defeated, leasing procedures were revised to ensure greater production and a higher percentage of revenue for the states. Three years later Congress approved a trade of leased lands for less environmentally fragile sites elsewhere in the West. (Events 203, 324)

8. *Uranium enrichment:* Threatening to end a 30-year government monopoly, in May 1976 the Joint Committee on Atomic Energy reported a bill allowing private industry to engage in the enrichment of uranium. Although the House passed the bill, the Senate failed to bring this legislation to the floor. (Event 204)

9. *Energy Mobilization Board; Synthetic fuels:* In 1977 Congress approved loan guarantees for the development of synthetic fuel technologies. Despite his support for this program, Carter vetoed the legislation because it included funds for the Clinch River breeder reactor. Legislation promoting the development of shale oil was defeated in 1978, but the Iranian crisis of the following year prompted Congress to support the synthetic fuels industry with federal loans, subsidies, and guarantees. The creation of an Energy Mobilization Board, proposed in 1979, would have facilitated energy development projects by overriding state laws and environmental regulations, but a coalition of liberal Democrats and states-rights Republicans in the House defeated the conference report. In September 1980 Congress approved the appointment of

John Sawhill to head the new U.S. Synthetic Fuels Corporation. (Events 205, 211, 213, 214, 216)

10. *Oil and gas exploration:* The Outer Continental Shelf Act of 1953 had given the federal government jurisdiction over lands between the offshore state boundaries and the edge of the shelf (up to 200 miles offshore). Faced with proposals to start drilling in the Atlantic and in the Gulf of Alaska, efforts were made to amend the original legislation to include stricter environmental protection. These moves were blocked by the Ford administration, but in 1978 Congress passed legislation increasing federal control over bidding (by authorizing exploratory studies of the areas to be leased) and environmental protection requirements. The same year the House Interior Committee reported a bill removing considerable Alaskan acreage from oil and gas exploration as part of the Alaska Native Claims Settlement Act of 1971. This legislation was passed in November 1980. (Events 206, 210)

Energy Regulation

11. *Natural gas prices and profits:* Natural gas prices were controlled by Nixon's wage-price freeze of 1971. Subsequent legislation attempted to reform the regulatory system, bringing intra- and interstate prices into line with one another. This effort was opposed by consumer groups. In the face of the severe winter of 1976–77, Carter was granted power to order transfers of gas between regions, but his National Energy Plan of 1977 advocated deregulation. Despite intense disagreement, in August 1978 a House-Senate conference committee reported compromise legislation providing for the deregulation of natural gas pricing. The bill was approved by Congress and signed into law that November. In 1979 deregulated natural gas, like oil, was subjected to a windfall profits tax. (Events 301, 311, 312, 317, 319, 323, 328)

12. *Oil prices and profits:* Nixon's wage-price freeze of 1971 imposed price controls on domestic oil and natural gas. With modifications, these remained in force until 1974. The following year, rejecting Ford's policy of "conservation by price," Congress passed the Energy Policy and Conservation Act, which continued federal control over oil prices and extended it to new discoveries. In 1976 price controls were removed from a number of petroleum products as well as from oil recovered from stripper wells. Continuing this move toward market pricing, in 1977 the House considered, but ultimately rejected, a tax to raise domestic oil prices to international market levels. In April 1979 Carter announced the gradual decontrol of oil prices and asked Congress to approve a tax on resulting windfall profits. Two months later, the House Ways and Means Committee reported a bill taxing deregulated oil and gas profits; Congress approved amended legislation in March 1980. (Events 301, 306, 308, 309, 316, 325, 328)

13. *Petroleum allocation:* Faced with the disappearance of excess domestic production capacity, in 1973 Congress required the mandatory allocation of

oil and oil products to maintain the distribution of supplies that had existed in 1972. Following the imposition of the oil embargo in November 1973, Congress gave the President emergency allocation and pricing powers, but Nixon vetoed the bill. The 1979 Iranian crisis provoked similar action, and Congress gave the President power to impose gasoline allocation plans on states that failed to develop their own conservation program. (Events 302, 303, 413)

14. *Nuclear insurance:* The 1957 Price-Anderson Act, which provided limited liability and federal subsidies for the insurance of the nuclear industry, was due to expire in August 1977. In 1974 Congress approved a one-year extension of the act, which was vetoed by President Ford on the basis of cost considerations. In 1975 legislation was passed extending the act for 10 years, at which time the government's role as an insurer would be phased out and the liability limit gradually increased. (Event 304)

15. *Energy administration:* In 1973 Nixon sought to consolidate energy projects in a new Department of Energy and Natural Resources. This effort failed, but the following year Congress abolished the Atomic Energy Commission, dividing its research and regulatory functions between the Energy Research and Development Administration and the Nuclear Regulatory Commission. In 1977 Congress approved the creation of the Department of Energy, a less encompassing organization than that proposed by Nixon. The conflicts stemming from this reorganization were manifested in a series of personnel problems; James Schlesinger resigned in 1979, to be replaced by Charles Duncan. (Events 305, 314, 318, 330)

16. *Petroleum industry divestiture:* In 1975 a Senate amendment requiring horizontal and vertical divestiture of major oil and gas companies was defeated, but by a surprisingly small margin. Two modified versions of the amendment were also rejected. The following year the Senate Judiciary Committee reported a bill calling for vertical divestiture of major oil companies, but this legislation failed to pass Congress. (Events 307, 310)

17. **Strip Mining and Reclamation:* Efforts by environmentalists to enact a surface mining control and regulation act were thwarted four times during the Ford administration by a coalition of industry, utility, and administration interests. In 1977, however, passage of the Surface Mining Control and Reclamation Act imposed fairly strict regulations on the mining industry; enforcement was funded by legislation the following year. In July 1979 the Senate Energy Committee reported a bill allowing states to develop their own strip-mining regulations independent of federal law. The legislation was approved by the Senate but was allowed to die in the House and, in the following year, in conference. That year the Supreme Court agreed to hear cases challenging the 1977 legislation. (Events 313, 321, 329, 334)

18. *Coal slurry pipeline:* Coal operators sought a grant of eminent domain to acquire the rights of way needed for a coal slurry pipeline from the western

fields. The bill was supported by coal companies, the Carter administration, and labor groups, but opposition from the railroads and environmentalist groups delayed the House bill in committee for a year in 1977. Although the bill was reported the next year, the legislation was defeated in the House. (Events 315, 320)

19. *Nuclear plant licensing:* As part of a reorganization of nuclear regulation and reevaluation of the industry's prospects, in June 1978 the House Commerce Committee reported a bill streamlining licensing procedures, including provisions for a pilot program to cover the expenses of citizen intervenors. The legislation was opposed by industry groups, environmentalists, and state governments, and Congress failed to take action. In the wake of the Three Mile Island accident, however, the NRC imposed an 11-month moratorium on licensing nuclear plants, which was lifted in February 1980. (Events 322, 332)

20. **Nuclear plant safety:* In May 1979, prompted by growing criticism of the nuclear regulatory system and the accident at Three Mile Island, a House subcommittee called for a six-month moratorium on nuclear plant construction. This was passed by the Interior Committee, but defeated by the House in November 1979. Also in May the Senate Environment Committee reported a bill to shut down nuclear power plants in states without an approved nuclear emergency evacuation plan. Congress passed this legislation in June 1980. (Events 326, 327)

21. *Railroad deregulation:* In December 1979 the Senate Commerce Committee reported legislation deregulating railroads and allowing them to set rates for shipping coal. Measures to protect captive shippers were included in the bill passed the following September. (Event 331)

22. *NRC Reorganization:* Another consequence of the Three Mile Island accident was a reorganization of the Nuclear Regulatory Commission giving greater authority to the chairman at the expense of the earlier collegial mode of decision making. The plan was introduced in March 1980 and, in the absence of strong congressional opposition, went into effect the following June. (Event 333)

Energy Consumption

23. *Speed limit:* As part of the conservation effort prompted by the oil embargo, Nixon requested and Congress passed legislation withholding federal highway funds from any state failing to adopt a 55-mile-per-hour speed limit for all vehicles. (Event 401)

24. *Taxes and fees:* Pursuing a policy of conservation by price, in 1975 Ford imposed a fee on imported oil and petroleum products. This was overturned by congressional legislation, which Ford then vetoed. Seeking to develop an alternative approach, the House Ways and Means Committee included a gasoline tax (tied to the level of consumption) in the Energy Conser-

vation and Conversion Act of 1975. This provision was killed in the House, which, two years later, also rejected Carter's proposal for a standby gasoline tax to be implemented if consumption rose above target levels. Subsequently, Carter imposed a fee on imported oil, which was later overturned in suits filed by industry and consumer groups. In 1980 Congress voted to repeal the fee and later overrode Carter's veto of this action. (Events 402, 403, 405, 410, 418, 419)

25. *Coal conversion:* Carter's 1977 National Energy Plan proposed taxes as incentives for the conversion of industrial plants to coal. The legislation was weakened as it passed through Congress, first requiring conversion only when it involved low costs and, by the time it was passed in 1978, mandating only that new plants be designed to use coal. In 1979 the EPA adopted stricter air-pollution standards for newly built coal-fired power plants, thereby adding to their cost. In 1980 Congress considered legislation to subsidize the conversion of power plants to coal, but no action was taken that year. (Events 404, 409, 414, 420)

26. *Automobile fuel standards:* Carter's 1977 National Energy Plan included a "gas-guzzler" tax on cars and light trucks not meeting the fleet average for miles per gallon. This passed the House, but without the rebates on fuel-efficient cars that Carter had requested. After much wrangling in the Senate, a more moderate tax was passed in 1978, by which time the Transportation Department had announced stricter automobile fuel efficiency standards. Faced with considerable protest from automobile manufacturers, the federal government began to take a less strict approach; in 1979 the EPA announced a one-year postponement of its new air-pollution standards for vehicles, and the following year Congress passed legislation giving the auto industry greater flexibility in meeting the fuel efficiency standards. (Events 406, 407, 416, 417)

27. **Standby gasoline rationing program:* The 1975 Energy Policy and Conservation Act required the President to submit emergency plans for congressional approval. In 1979 the Senate Energy Committee reported unfavorably on Carter's proposal to include mandatory weekend closings of gas stations in the emergency plan. That April, without making a recommendation, the House Commerce Committee reported legislation proposed by Carter for standby rationing of gasoline. In an amended form, this legislation was approved by the Senate but was killed in the House. Long gas lines in the summer of 1979 prompted Congress to pass revised legislation giving the President emergency powers, including authority to create a standby gasoline rationing program. (Events 411, 412, 415, 421)

28. *Utility rate structure:* The 1977 National Energy Plan proposed that the federal government establish guidelines for state regulation of electric utilities and encourage conservation by banning declining rates for major customers

and related practices. After considerable amendment in Congress, legislation was passed requiring state regulatory agencies to consider the use of energy-saving methods and price structures. (Event 408)

Health Domain

Biomedical Research

1. *Cancer and heart funding:* Throughout the 1970s Congress renewed its commitment to funding medical research. In 1971, funds were authorized for the "war on cancer." In 1977 and 1978 Congress debated reauthorization of funding for the National Cancer Institute and the Heart, Blood and Lung Institute, which eventually passed, along with provisions for increased attention to issues of medical ethics and greater HEW authority with respect to testing for carcinogenic substances. (Events 101, 108, 111)

2. *Targeted disease funding:* Over the 1970s federal funding of medical research became increasingly directed as Congress showed signs of what Sen. Thomas Eagleton dubbed "the disease of the year" syndrome. In 1974 the National Institute of Aging was created, despite charges that it duplicated many existing programs. Two year later Congress authorized funding for research on arthritis, diabetes, and digestive diseases. (Events 102, 103, 106)

3. *Control of NIH funding:* In addition to authorizing funds for specific diseases, some members of Congress also sought to increase their control over the general NIH budget. The fiscal 1980 reauthorization bill for the NIH originally included a controversial proposal allowing Congress to establish appropriation ceilings for individual institutes. Initially approved by the House Subcommittee on Health and the Environment, this provision was defeated both in the Senate and in conference. (Events 114, 117, 118)

4. *Human experimentation:* Some members of Congress, notably Sen. Edward Kennedy, sought greater control over the specific character of NIH-funded research through the establishment of an oversight committee on experimentation. After considerable infighting within Congress and among agencies, the 1973 National Research Act established the temporary National Commission for the Protection of Human Subjects in Biomedical and Behavioral Research. In 1978 legislation reauthorized the commission's funding for four years and extended its oversight to include projects sponsored by the Defense Department and the Central Intelligence Agency. (Events 104, 105, 112)

5. *DNA Regulation:* In March 1978 the House Commerce Committee approved legislation extending the 1976 NIH regulations for recombinant DNA research and establishing a commission to study genetic-engineering technologies. After a period of considerable controversy, concern about the possible dangers of such experiments dissipated, and all proposed legislation was eventually tabled by Congress. (Events 107, 109, 110, 113)

6. *Personnel:* As part of a major reorganization of the Carter administration in July 1979 (stemming in part from ongoing controversies between the

White House staff and the cabinet), the secretary of HEW, Joseph Califano, was fired and replaced by Patricia Harris. Earlier that year Donald Kennedy, the director of the FDA and a major advocate of restrictions on saccharin, nitrates, and other additives, resigned. (Events 115, 116, 410)

Manpower Issues

7. *Nurse training:* The 1971 Comprehensive Nurse Training and Facilities Act extended the federal funding of nursing education, including both construction and capitation grants, that had begun in 1964. Although congressional support for these programs remained strong throughout the 1970s, Presidents Ford and Carter both vetoed funding legislation, claiming that the programs were too expensive and that any shortage of nurses had been corrected. In 1979 Carter finally agreed to the extension of funding for nurse training at a lower level. (Events 201, 211, 212, 214, 215)

8. *Funding of physician education:* Major federal contributions to medical education began with the Health Professions Educational Assistance Act of 1963. By the 1970s continued commitment to such funding was influenced by concern over an anticipated shortage of physicians, particularly in family and general practice specialties. In a highly contested series of reauthorizations, Congress sought to impose requirements such as practice in underserved areas as the basis for continued funding. In 1978 Carter announced that he would cut back construction grants to medical schools that failed to limit class sizes to federal standards. By the end of the decade, the perception of an imminent surplus of physicians led to the reduction of federal grants for capitation support and construction. (Events 202, 204, 213, 218)

9. *Regulation of physician training:* In 1976 medical school funding was reauthorized with a number of controversial provisions requiring medical schools to accept third-year transfers from foreign medical schools and to reserve over one-third of first-year residency positions for primary care training. Restrictions on the status of foreign medical graduates were tightened. A number of prominent medical schools chose to forgo capitation support rather than comply, causing Congress to relax the third-year transfer requirements. In 1980 attempts were made to relax restrictions on the status of foreign medical graduates. That same year, the report of the Graduate Medical National Advisory Committee provided further support for efforts to discourage the overall expansion of many medical specialities while drawing attention to problems in the regional availability of health care. (Events 205, 206, 207, 208, 209, 210, 217, 219)

10. *Collective bargaining for housestaff:* In April 1976 the House Subcommittee on Labor-Management Relations began consideration of legislation amending the National Labor Relations Act to include hospital housestaff. Hearings continued through the following April, when the measure was tabled. (Events 203, 216)

Organization of Care

11. *Professional Standards Review Organizations:* As part of the 1972 Social Security amendments, Congress created a network of PSROs to regulate the quality and cost of care provided by federally funded programs. Although quite controversial, the program was reauthorized under the Carter administration. In 1979 reforms expanded membership in PSROs while curtailing their responsibilities. (Events 301, 322)

12. *Health Maintenance Organizations:* As part of an effort to control the costs of medical care, the Nixon administration proposed federal aid for the development of HMOs. Subsequent legislation relaxed the requirements for federal aid and improved the competitiveness of this alternative organization of care. The program had considerable support but was buffeted by the conflicting demands of those who saw it as a method for returning health care to the free market and those concerned with the needs of underserved populations. In October 1979 the Senate Finance Committee moved to improve HMOs' competitiveness by reporting legislation that would allow them to receive reimbursement from Medicare and Medicaid. (Events 302, 304, 314, 315, 325)

13. *National health planning system:* In 1974 Congress authorized the creation of a network of health systems agencies to limit health care costs. The certificate-of-need program was established to limit capital expenditures and encountered strong opposition from medical professionals interested in acquiring new technologies such as CAT scanners. The program was reauthorized in 1977 and 1979, but attempts to institute stricter regulation the following year were defeated. In 1979 an amendment prevented states from passing certificate-of-need legislation stricter than federal law. (Events 303, 305, 308, 311, 319)

14. *Community health programs:* On the last day of the 1978 session, Congress reauthorized funding for community mental health programs. Major legislative reforms waited until 1979, when Carter introduced the Mental Health Systems Act, which provided greater autonomy for local and state agencies in administering the federally funded program. These reforms were vigorously opposed by representatives of community health centers, and disagreement between House and Senate Committees caused any substantive legislation to be put aside until 1980, when the House Commerce Committee reported Medicare and Medicaid amendments reforming the reimbursement procedures for home health programs and community mental health centers. In May the same committee reported reauthorization legislation for community mental health programs. (Events 306, 312, 318, 328, 329, 331)

15. *Medicare and Medicaid reforms:* In 1977 Carter enacted a major executive reorganization, in part to improve coordination between the Medicare and Medicaid programs through the creation of the Health Care Financ-

ing Administration. Throughout the rest of the decade, most related reforms addressed methods for improving the cost effectiveness of the programs as well as authorizing their extension to additional health care providers such as midwives, dentists, optometrists, and chiropractors. The terms upon which HMOs were able to participate were also liberalized. (Events 307, 323, 324, 326, 327, 330)

16. *Rural health care:* In November 1977 Congress approved legislation designed to address the problems of underserved rural areas (particularly by reimbursing nurse practitioners) without threatening the control of physicians over the majority of Medicare and Medicaid disbursements. Demonstration projects in underserved urban areas were also authorized. (Events 310, 313)

17. **Hospital cost containment:* In response to rising health costs, particularly federal expenditures on Medicare and Medicaid, Carter proposed a mandatory ceiling on hospital costs. This met with fierce opposition from the health industry and a lack of enthusiasm from legislators, who felt that the system would be unworkable. Legislation was kept in committee for most of this period and decisively killed in 1979. Throughout the episode, hospital associations led the opposition, while Democratic support was split both by alternative proposals for a national health care system and by the insistence that labor costs be excluded from the cost ceiling. Later in 1979 the House Commerce Committee reported legislation providing for voluntary limits, with a standby mandatory plan, but the bill failed to pass. Congress continued to consider ways of limiting Medicare and Medicaid disbursements through a prospective payment system. (Events 309, 316, 317, 321)

18. *Chiropractors:* In 1979, charging that there was a conspiracy to force them out of business, representatives of chiropractors filed suit against the AMA and a number of other organizations and individuals. The case was settled out of court. (Event 320)

Drug Regulation

19. *Cyclamates:* In 1969 the FDA banned most sales of products containing cyclamates. Although the relationship between cyclamates and cancer in humans had never been proven definitively, the ban was upheld by administrative courts in 1976 and again in 1980. (Events 401, 415)

20. **FDA ban on saccharin:* In March 1977 the FDA proposed a ban on saccharin based on test results produced by the Canadian government. In November, following massive opposition from producers and consumers, Congress approved an 18-month moratorium on the ban. In 1979 the House voted to extend the moratorium for two years, but the Senate failed to act. Although the FDA could have reimposed the ban at that point, it decided to wait for congressional action. (Events 403, 404, 413, 416)

21. *Drug labeling and generic equivalents:* Until 1978 legislation allowing the substitution of generic equivalents for brand-name drugs had appeared in

several bills, but always in conjunction with proposals concerning the development and marketing of new drugs. In 1978 the issues were separated, and the Substitute Prescriptions Drug Act was introduced. The legislation was opposed by producers, who claimed that it threatened the quality of pharmaceuticals, and by the FTC and FDA, which preferred state rather than federal regulation on this issue. Although hearings were held, no further action was taken. (Events 402, 406, 407, 409, 411)

22. *Drug regulation reform:* In 1977 and 1978 the Senate held subcommittee hearings on legislation that would facilitate new drug licensing by granting approval on the basis of generic equivalents as well as giving the FDA commissioner greater authority to remove hazardous drugs from the market. The proposal stalled in committee in 1978, and the following year a revised version was passed by the Senate but failed to be taken up by the House. (Events 405, 408, 414)

23. *Safety brochure inserts:* In 1979 the FDA announced its intention to require safety brochures to be inserted in 375 prescription drugs. The following year the requirement was reduced to cover only 10 prescription drugs. (Events 412, 417)

12

The Structure of Conflict and Consensus

Readers concerned with analyzing conflict and consensus over the resolution of policy issues in a domain may well ask how our approach deals with such matters. In light of the multitude of parties, both public and private, actively engaged in controversies over diverse policy issues, is it possible to specify principles that organize interested parties in a stable structure of cleavage and cooperation? Shouldn't we expect, on the contrary, a fluid structure of almost random coalitions and oppositions for each contested event across the issue and event structures described in Chapters 4, 9, and 11? Given a system of fluid coalitions, agreement or opposition between any pair of parties interested in a given event would depend solely on calculations of the marginal advantages and disadvantages of each policy option. Such calculations are unlikely to provide very consistent bases for ordering preferences across corporate actors, save, perhaps, for those whose organizational mandate is to be ideologically consistent even with respect to the most arcane "technical" questions.

Typologizing Controversies

Despite a voluminous literature devoted to the description and analysis of political controversies at all levels of government, there appears to be little convincing evidence that ideology, class or status interest, or even sectoral position in the economy provides sufficiently general grounds for differentiating corporate actors into distinctive opposition groups. Of course, there have been various efforts to classify issues with respect to the politics of their resolution. Reacting to the dominance of substantive categories in the design of most case studies in the political science literature, Lowi (1964:689) identified "policies in terms of their impact or expected impact on the society." He proposed a typology corresponding to three major forms of government activity (distribution, regulation, and redistribution) that resembles the system of event classification used in this study (initiatory, regulatory, and funding). Yet two important differences merit discussion. First, reflecting both the understandings of political actors and observed variations in patterns of participation (see table 3.3), this research has employed substantive categories (health, energy, domestic economy, and so forth) as the basis for a first-order disaggregation of policy-making activity in the United States.

Within these substantively defined policy arenas, events have been classified in terms of their functional consequences. Unlike Lowi (1964:711), we have paid relatively little attention to redistributive policies, in which, by definition, "there will never be more than two sides and the sides are clear, stable, and consistent." We encountered little evidence of this type of policy conflict, a finding that may reflect the specific character of the energy and health domains, in which the broad scope and highly differentiated character of government involvement facilitated the framing of conflicts as struggles over marginal adaptations of existing policy. An awareness of the high degree of preexisting politicization of the issues that concern interest groups and private citizens is also evident in the use of an event category that has no equivalent in Lowi's typology: initiatory events.

Laumann and Heinz (1985:471–74) argue that issues have two properties that are of special relevance to how they are formulated, debated, and resolved. First, issues can be distinguished according to their relative positions along a continuum that ranges from those concerning matters that are unprecedented and not likely to arise again to those that concern the continuation of previously established rules, procedures, and case precedents, sometimes generating whole bookshelves of written documentation. The former are situations in which the rules about who can and will participate, the symbolic framing of the issues at stake, and the means to resolve them are unknown beforehand and must be negotiated during the evolving debate. The latter, in contrast, resemble iterative games in which the parties are known repeat players conversant with the rules of participation and possessed of a fairly well worked through payoff matrix of costs and benefits (Riker and Ordeshook, 1973). Second, Laumann and Heinz distinguish between issues concerning governmental actions that are designed to facilitate the interests of particular individuals or groups with no readily apparent detrimental effects

	Episodic	Recurrent
Facilitative	(1) Fluid coalition with no opposition	(2) Iron triangle
Oppositional	(3) Fluid coalitions of strange bedfellows ("sport" expressive issues, e.g., abortion)	(4) Stable coalitions of polarized opponents (e.g., labor policy)

Figure 12.1. A Cross-Tabulation of Types of Issues

for any identifiable organized interests,[1] and other issues concerning governmental actions that would clearly advance the interests of some parties at the expense of others.

To explore the implications of these event characteristics for the consensus/cleavage structure of a domain, these two continua may be dichotomized and cross-tabulated to form the fourfold table depicted in figure 12.1. Although Laumann and Heinz were primarily concerned with the implications of these four types of issues for the sorts of Washington representatives most likely to act in behalf of interested parties, we want to point to their implications for the stability of the consensual/oppositional structures of policy domains. In the case of episodic/facilitative events, we expect a diverse chorus of interested parties with little organized opposition. Being unprecedented and non-recurrent, such events rarely organize participants into predictable and enduring consensual groupings. Facilitative/recurrent issues, however, tend to produce the much-discussed "iron triangles" (Heclo, 1978; Ripley and Franklin, 1980), in which a stable set of interested private parties enjoy close working relationships with the executive agency and possibly the congressional oversight (sub)committee responsible for a particular policy area. In such

1. Obviously, since any governmental action is likely to cost money, there is a sense in which facilitative actions must necessarily be done at the expense of taxpayers and of other possible facilitative actions that might have been undertaken in their stead. We contend, however, that overarching budgetary constraints do not generate explicit adversarial activity at the points of substantive debate. Budgetary oversight is exercised in a different congressional or executive (e.g., OMB) decision-making context where generalized budgetary constraints are in focus (see Padgett, 1981; Wildavsky, 1975). We rarely observe, for example, testimony against increased appropriations for programs devoted to research on a specific disease, although it is obvious that the more spent on one disease, the less is available to be spent on others.

Related to this point, a news story in the *New York Times* (February 25, 1986) observed that it is rare for parties to lobby for changes in the tax code that would remove tax advantages for their competitors. As one of Washington's most experienced lobbyists remarked, "I think there's a sort of comity or protocol among the boys. You work like hell for what you want, but you don't go out and fight against someone else's perk. You think, 'There, but for the grace of God, go I.'"

situations, opponents are few, disarticulated, and aroused only when "things go too far" in benefiting the established coalition. Examples are the association of the targeted disease publics with the relevant NIH institutes and the collaboration between manufacturers, utilities, and other business firms interested in nuclear energy development and the Atomic Energy Commission (converted in 1974 into the Nuclear Regulatory Commission and the Energy Research and Development Administration) until the Three Mile Island disaster and the struggle over the Clinch River reactor disrupted the relationship.

Episodic/oppositional issues, by definition, occur irregularly and, although they may arouse passionate debate at the time, usually leave little residue in continuing working coalitions of opposed factions. In sum, they are what Laumann and Pappi (1976:164–67) call *consummatory* or *expressive* issues.[2] Such issues are concerned with

the maintenance or change in the organization of basic values, commitments, and orientations that guide or control [community affairs]. Such controversies, sometimes termed "status politics" (cf. Lipset, 1963), are usually highly charged with emotional affect and have an "all or none" nature that usually precludes or makes very difficult negotiated settlements among the contending parties. (Laumann and Pappi, 1976:164)

Exemplars of such expressive issues were the antiabortion initiatives in the late 1970s. Aspects of the debates over environmental harm arising from nuclear waste disposal, coal strip mining, and coal slurry transport in the energy policy domain also share some features of a consummatory controversy.

Recurrent/oppositional issues—often related to Lowi's notion of redistributive politics—lay the foundation for stable oppositional coalitions of interested parties that are prepared to do battle time and again to defend their claims against their opponents. The lines drawn between labor and management on domestic labor policy (see Laumann et al., 1986) exemplify stable polarized oppositional structures. Debates over national health insurance schemes and over deregulation of gas prices or environmental impact regulations approximate this type of polarized opposition.

Of course, there is no a priori basis for assigning issues to particular types of controversy (although some issues clearly have more "natural" affinities to

2. In contrast, Laumann and Pappi (1976:164) define *instrumental issues* as those "concerned with controversies over the differing allocation of scarce resources, such as land, jobs, and money. Lipset (1963) and others have spoken somewhat more narrowly of 'class politics' when discussing such issues. For such issues, there usually is a fairly obvious calculus of costs and benefits to various interested parties. As a result, a fairly straight-forward, even quantitative, analysis of objective interest differentiation is facilitated. Conflict over such issues tends to be moderate, often characterized by bargaining and compromise among the contending parties. The specific outcome is the direct result of their relative power or influence. Some political scientists have even thought it possible to devise means for the 'rational' or 'optimal' resolution of such controversies."

certain types than others). In fact, a central objective of the communicative activities within a policy domain is the negotiation of the symbolic terms in which a particular decision-making contest will be debated (Gusfield, 1981). Different symbolic framings of an issue confer competitive advantages and disadvantages on various interested parties. For example, groups interested in increasing funding for existing research programs on specific diseases seek to frame the issue as a routine/facilitative decision with no apparent losers. Actors in favor of adding a new disease program to the responsibilities of the NIH portray the matter as novel but essentially facilitative in impact, again with no apparent losers. Opponents to such initiatives, however, will try to get the matter framed in ways that emphasize the zero-sum character of the decision and will try to identify and rouse other potential losers who might be adversely affected if the decision making proceeds unopposed.

Symbolism in the Structuring of Cleavage

Certain actors may come to be specialized as ideological labelers who "clarify" the meaning of a particular controversy for the various participants by the stands they take, as Lofland's (1969) normal and deviant "smiths"—e.g., teachers and policemen, respectively—do in producing conformists and deviants (see Hirsch, 1986, for a parallel argument). That is, their participation and commentary in an event sequence may establish a specific ideological significance and, in turn, serve to mobilize sympathizers and antagonists on the basis of ideology, irrespective of the event's substantive content. Thus, in the energy domain the participation of the Sierra Club or Friends of the Earth calls for action by other groups sympathetic to "protecting the environment from the rapacity of the special interests" and for appropriate counteraction and claims by their ideological opponents.

The ways in which custody of the symbolic content of the domain is distributed among its participants will impose limits on the range of arguments that are permissible, legitimate, and likely to be accepted as valid frames for the controversy in any given situation. Regular participants in the decision-making process will typically have the advantage in proposing framings of the issue, whereas outsiders or occasional participants will experience difficulty in getting their definitions of the situation accepted as valid. This system provides stability and predictability for the participants (and outside observers) with respect to how particular event episodes are likely to be processed symbolically.

What does this perspective on the symbolic framing of events tell us about the structuration of consensus and opposition among the participating actors? The first implication is that policy domains are likely to differ among themselves with respect to the relative frequency and salience of different types of

issues. Those domains which have a superfluity of events defined as facilitative, whether episodic or recurrent in nature, will experience a relatively
low incidence of structured stable oppositional groupings of interested parties. The accent will be on collaborative or cooperative relations among the
most interested parties, and conflict will be confined to disagreements over
matters of detail and implementation in apportioning costs and benefits. Decision making, in short, will be regarded as technocratic and nonideological.
Bargaining and negotiating among the parties will be featured, with the
widely shared expectation that net benefits will accrue to all over time, though
some costs may be disproportionately borne by some at any given time (cf.
Laumann and Marsden, 1979). The second implication is that to the extent
that issues arousing stable opposition groups come to predominate, we will
observe high predictability of preferred outcomes across the set of participants; that is, we will be able to identify disjoint sets of actors who share preferred outcomes on a set of issues that are specifically opposed to one another.
In the simplest case of bipolar opposition, actors will fall into two mutually
opposed camps. Linkages across scenarios in such a policy domain should be
high, whereas scenario linkage in a facilitatively organized domain should be
low, suggesting that decision making is loosely coupled or disarticulated.

Applying this perspective to our two policy domains, we shall argue that
the health policy domain works on issues, whether episodic or recurrent, that
have usually been conceived as broadly facilitative, with no apparent losers.
No one is against providing high-quality health care to all Americans, regardless of ability to pay. Yet this overarching symbolic consensus among most
participants does not preclude sharp disagreements about how this generally
valued objective is to be implemented. There is substantial ideological conflict
over the role of the federal government as a guarantor of this ideal in the form
of the recurrent debates over national health insurance. But this division between those who prefer, on ideological grounds, private or public insurance
schemes does not readily translate into organizing the division of opinion on
the many other issues being processed in the domain. The only other ideologically structured issue, that between pro-choice and pro-life proponents, is not
widely accepted as a "health issue" by the principal actors in the domain (as
reflected in the very low rate of expressed interest in the issue; see table 4.2).
We thus expect that an actor's preference on one policy issue will tell us little
about its preference on another and that participation across event scenarios
will be very loosely articulated: that is, an actor's participation in one scenario
will tell us little about its likelihood of participation in another. The policy
domain being highly institutionalized (or, in other words, structurally differentiated with respect to decision-making responsibilities), individual actors
are quite knowledgeable about who is responsible for what sorts of policy decisions and can act accordingly, restricting their participation to those events
in which they can readily perceive one of their interests at stake. Uncertainty

about unexpected twists in policy making is low, thus reducing the need to engage in broad participatory activity in order to keep a weather eye on one's interests.

With respect to the energy domain, we observe an overarching symbolic dissensus that is rooted in ideological and self-interested positions that more or less coincide. In an important sense the energy domain was in the process of an attempted transformation during the 1970s. Unprecedented initiatives proposing new governance structures through which the federal government would play a more central coordinating role dominated decision-making discussions. Polarization occurred. On one side were those actors who advocated these changes as necessary in the face of the prolonged energy crisis and its resulting domestic inflation and harm to the nation's defense posture. On the other side were actors who demurred and preferred to retain the decentralized governance structure of the past or preferred an even more systematically sustained deregulation. This cleavage corresponded almost exactly to the government agencies that would gain regulative authority (and their supporters among the public interest groups) and those private corporations that would be regulated. The latter group's explicit self-interests were embedded in an ideological rhetoric of free enterprise that stressed the beneficence of free-market forces in disciplining uneconomic behavior in contrast to the incompetence of government regulation and planning for achieving these ends. We thus expect greater coherence in the postures adopted by the participants regarding various policy initiatives; that is, we anticipate greater predictability of actors' preferences across scenarios. Participation linkage across scenarios should also be relatively higher than in the health domain because the generalized uncertainty about the implications of these initiatives for specific actors made generalized participation more likely as a defensive measure.

Scenario and Cleavage Linkage

Chapter 11 has already introduced the means by which we can assess the linkage of participation across scenarios. Recall that we measured the degree to which participation in two events was positively or negatively linked or independent by the logodds ratio of co-participation and co-absence over the two presence/absence cells (see figure 11.1). By extension, we can use the same procedure to calculate logodds ratios for scenarios by designating an actor as participating in a given scenario if it appears as a participant in any one of the events constituting the scenario, and absent otherwise.[3] In general, both domains manifested low levels of scenario interdependence. In the energy do-

3. Recall that we have already demonstrated in Chapter 11 that the vast majority of actors either participate across all the events in a scenario or remain inactive throughout. Very few selectively participate (i.e., enter and exit and/or reenter).

main, the average of the logodd ratios was 0.85, and in health, 1.06. Both rose slightly when we calculated the averages of the absolute logodds ratios: 1.0 in energy and 1.1 in health. The larger incremental increase in energy than in health reflects the greater disjunction between participation across scenarios, notably between nuclear and oil scenarios (see figures 12.2–12.9 below). (We calculated the average, since a negative logodds ratio indicates the same degree of systemic dependency as a positive logodds ratio of the same magnitude.) Some 11 percent of the logodds ratios were negative in sign in the health domain, and 18 percent were negative in the energy domain. Negatively signed ratios were concentrated in the pairings of biomedical research scenarios with scenarios external to that subdomain; in the energy domain, the negatively signed ratios were not clustered in any patterned way. Such a pattern of negative linkages in the health domain is quite consistent with our observation in Chapter 4 concerning the negative linkage of expressed interest in biomedical issues with expressed interest in all the other health issues. The biomedical subdomain appears to constitute a policy domain with its own distinctive actors and concerns, lacking any systemic coordination with other parts of the health domain. In contrast, the energy domain in the late 1970s lacks any symptoms of systematic subdivision into relatively autonomous regions, despite a long history of fuel-specific policy making.

Although we observe support for the proposition that the energy decision-making scenarios exhibited somewhat more interdependence than those in the health domain, in both domains participation across scenarios was only very loosely coupled. This fact gains in significance when we examine the extent to which actors' preferences for particular outcomes co-vary across the scenarios because it tells us that we can expect only small numbers of common actors in randomly drawn pairs of scenarios. To put it another way, if the average rate of participation in scenarios is about 20 percent of the total population of consequential actors in a policy domain, then we can expect that only 4 percent (.20 × .20) of the actors will jointly appear by chance in any two scenarios having these rates of participation. Given that participation patterns are only slightly tied across scenarios (the average logodds ratios are somewhat larger than chance), we can expect only a few more common actors across pairs of scenarios than would be predicted by chance. (Even though overlapping membership across pairs of scenarios is rare, it may still be the case that common members are disproportionately drawn from the more influential set of actors. Such a pattern might introduce some potential for coordination of outcomes across policy matters.)

We now turn to another question: to what extent do actors' preferences in one scenario co-vary with their preferences in another? Strictly speaking, this refers to behavioral or revealed preferences and not to attitudes or "true" preferences. An actor reveals its preference in a given event only if it participates in its resolution on a particular side (including an explicit fence-straddling position). The actor may harbor strong views about most of the events we asked about, but only those in which it acted will count in the analysis. To calculate the correlation matrix of preferred outcomes across the set of scenarios, we assigned an actor to a preferred outcome on the basis of the first event in the scenario in which it acted with an expressed preference. In only a handful of cases did we observe actors who changed their preferences during the course of the scenario's resolution. Because of the negligible number of switchers, there is no reason to believe that this simplifying decision rule, which ignored changing preferences, systematically biased the results. Of the 210 correlations in the energy domain (21 × 20/2), we found 29 percent that were significant at $p < .05$ level or less. Of the 231 correlations in the health domain (22 × 21/2), we found only 16 percent that were significant at the $p < .05$ level or less. A higher percentage of significant correlations is observed in energy for two reasons. First, substantially larger numbers of domain actors in energy expressed clear preferences vis-à-vis each scenario than in health. The number of organizations with expressed preferences ranges from 26 to 87 in energy, but only from 7 to 56 in health. Thus, the intercorrelations between organizational positions in a pair of scenarios are more likely to be significant solely on statistical grounds because of the larger Ns. Second, the nonrandom sampling of scenarios resulted in an overrepresentation of nuclear scenarios, which were highly intercorrelated among themselves and with a number of other scenarios.

In sum, we observe only modest evidence of linkages among scenarios with respect to participation and preferred outcomes in both domains. To be sure, a small subset of scenarios are closely interconnected and manifest consistent cleavage organization, but persistent cleavages appear very much to be the exception to the rule. In fact, we find that in the overwhelming majority of scenarios, the actors all expressed a preference for the winning outcome. One interpretation of these results would suggest that technocratic and strategic, rather than systematically ideological, considerations drive actors' participation in most policy controversies in these two domains.

In Chapter 4 we discussed how individual actors had distinctive portfolios of issues in which they had vested interests. Thus, each actor's portfolio of expressed interest in issues effectively links these interests to one another in distinctive ways. Actors sharing issue portfolios constitute issue publics that are, in turn, linked in greater or lesser proximity to one another as a result of their variable overlapping interests. Linkage of events is therefore in part a function of the concatenation of individual actors' interests. Moreover, the events themselves are linked to events in the past on various grounds, co-occur in the present with other events that compete for attention or frame political debate, and are linked to future (anticipated) events on various grounds provided by substance or institutional logic. In acting strategically with respect to given events, every actor constructs a unique web of linked events and interests that influences the decision to participate and choice of side.

An alternative explanation of the low level of connectedness of participation and preferences points to the important distinction between intraorganizational and publicly revealed preferences. Throughout the book our argument has been that our data refer primarily to the final stages of long processes in which options proposed by various interested parties are progressively winnowed, leaving only a handful of "viable" alternatives to be placed on the formal governmental decision agenda. Although actors often have well-articulated preferences for particular outcomes, participants in the endgame must engage in a form of strategic action in which selecting a course of action entails an evaluation of the implications (linkages) of each option for the actor's other current or future objectives, subject to the constraint of their past actions. Such considerations oftentimes support the strategic endorsement of the winning option despite strong initial and continuing preferences for some other alternative. The actor settles for the "least bad" outcome when it faces the prospect of losing anyway and especially when it may win even minor concessions by going along. The hope is that one can redress the balance of costs and benefits in future interactions on other issues. Calculations that lead to joining the winners are especially likely in recurrent events under generally nonadversarial conditions (figure 12.1). Only events that are episodic (nonrecurrent) or have clear winners and losers tend to lead the opposing sides to fight to the bitter end.

The Structure of Consensus and Cleavage

To this point our argument would seem to imply that there is very little coherence or pattern in the multifaceted controversies and selective choruses of agreement arising in the two domains. To the contrary, however, we do expect to observe highly patterned structures of consensus and cleavage in both domains. To appreciate this surprising contention in the face of the low connectedness of participation and preferences across scenarios, we must recall our repeated emphasis on the structuration of linkages among actors with respect to their policy interests, information exchanges, and involvement in institutionalized decision-making arenas. In Chapter 8 we contended that the flow of candid and confidential information follows well-worn and enduring channels among mutually trusted actors sharing common interests and broadly similar postures toward issues of importance to them. That is, actors regularly turn to trusted others for interpretive and strategic information concerning "what is going on" and "what is to be done." Timely information gained from these confidential exchanges helps to orchestrate the individual actors' strategic policy interventions. The pattern of confidential exchanges in a given policy domain constitutes the *enduring* structure or scaffolding in which all the actors are embedded and, as a result, granted easy or limited access to relevant information on topics of interest to them. Analogously, we might speak of such a structure as a crystal that is left intact or subjected to breakage along different fault lines, depending on the blows it receives from various policy-relevant events.

Figures 12.2–12.17 indicate the sets of supporters and opponents activated in the most hotly contested scenarios in each domain. (Brief descriptions of the controversies depicted can be found in the appendix to Chapter 11.) The actors' locations coincide with their positions in figures 8.4 and 8.6, which depict the confidential communication networks in energy and health. The contiguity curve drawn in each figure attempts to segregate the proponents (indicated by triangles) from the opponents (indicated by squares). "Errors" occur when one observes opponents on the supporters' side of the curve, or vice versa. What is remarkable is how clearly delineated the supporter and opponent sectors are in each contested matter. (Where the participants are clustered, the former sector is identified by a dotted line, the latter by a dashed line.) Yet the patterns of cleavage shift dramatically from scenario to scenario as the symbolic content changes. Also noteworthy is the fact that the contiguity curve always traverses the center box containing the actors most active in the communication network (who are also among the most influential actors—see Chapter 5). Note that the curve divides actors in the central box into opposing sides, reflecting the active role these peak organizations play in mediating the conflict as they place opposing parties in relatively close communicative proximity to one another. In general, the farther from the center of the space along some axis, the more completely the sector is dominated by either opponents or supporters of a particular outcome.

Before discussing several cases in greater detail, it is worth recalling the argument in Chapter 8 that the structures of confidential communication flows are organized into core and peripheral regions. The periphery, moreover, is clearly divided into sectors occupied by organizations performing principal roles as various sorts of producers and consumers of energy or health care, with various government and peak private organizations occupying the intermediate or central region as brokers (or occasionally initiators) of various policy options. In the case of the energy domain, we see in figure 8.4, moving in a clockwise direction from the righthand corner, sectors concerned with big oil and coal production; small oil, transport, and unions; environmental and consumer groups; and finally the nuclear industry and electrical utilities (the latter falling between the nuclear and coal producers) in the upper lefthand to upper central region. Similarly sorting out various producer and consumer interests in the health domain, we observe in the upper central and righthand sectors of figure 8.6 the principal consumers of health care; then the major third-party payer groups; the hospital and pharmaceutical industries; specialty health (medical) providers; and, finally, in the upper lefthand corner, the biomedical research establishment.

Inspection of the scenarios in which near unanimity of opinion predominated (not shown) discloses that the like-minded choruses of approval or opposition occupy distinct subregions of the space; that is, the active members of the chorus on a given scenario are never widely scattered across the entire policy domain. Thus, consensus and cleavage across various scenarios can be systematically related to distinctive subregions that have broadly shared symbolic meaning for the actors that populate them. In an important sense, then, local regions are circumscribed by the terms of the shared symbolic framing of a particular set of policy concerns.

Returning to the analogy of breaking a crystal, we know that given the structure of the crystal, how it splits depends on the strength and precise incidence of the chisel blow. Similarly, much of the strategic action of event participants, including even the question of who decides to participate and on what side, concerns the negotiation of how the issue will be framed so that it selectively energizes the interests and actions of certain domain members in behalf of particular outcomes and discourages others from entering the deliberations. A consensual chorus results when the generally accepted frame successfully neutralizes the mobilization of potential opponents by stressing the facilitative, nonadversarial character of the policy question.

In the energy domain, figures 12.2–12.4 describe partisan participation in three nuclear energy events (funding for the Clinch River nuclear breeder reactor, nuclear waste storage plans, and the moratorium on nuclear power plant construction). The correlations of participants' positions are quite high across these three events (from $r = .50$ to $r = .92$), reflecting the consistency with which the environmentalist groups in the lower lefthand region challenged the manufacturers of nuclear equipment and the public utilities with heavy nuclear investments, which were concentrated in the upper center and upper right portions of the confidential communication space. The proenvironmental coalition penetrated deeply into the core region on the first two events, receiving aggressive support from key governmental actors in the White House, Energy Department, and OMB. Only on the nuclear plant moratorium question, following the Three Mile Island accident, did the antinuke forces fail to garner support from central governmental actors. The key sponsors of the amendment were lodged within a House subcommittee, but the full House decisively defeated the proposal in a vote that occurred after the Nuclear Regulatory Commission had already decided not to issue new permits until the TMI accident was fully investigated. The three events show that a nuclear energy subdomain had clearly coalesced into a bipolar opposition structure.

The two coalitions—augmented or decremented from event to event by interested actors that entered or left in response to distinctive features of particular events—squared off in a rancorous fight over the future of the American nuclear industry. By the end of the decade, a convergence of safety, cost, and environmental issues had torn apart the cozy triangle among private capital, the Atomic Energy Commission, and congressional oversight committees of the 1950s and 1960s—a triangle that had once promised electricity "too cheap to meter."

Figures 12.5–12.9 display contiguity curves for environmental, natural gas, oil tax, coal strip-mining, and gasoline rationing events in the late 1970s. The proponents of these options fall into broadly regional clusters, generally consisting of environmental and consumer organizations (including labor unions) in the lower and left portions of the communication space, opposed by energy producers and large-scale consumers in the upper right portions. The actual composition of the blocks shifts so dramatically from event to event that only small percentages of actors participate in pairs of events. Their positions show little consistency across events, averaging correlations of only +.19, with the exception of standby rationing and the windfall profits tax (where 38 jointly active organizations lined up almost identically on both events: $r = .86$). Despite this heterogeneity at the organizational level, the overarching cleavage structure of the energy domain is clearly visible on inspection of the event contiguity maps.

Regarding the controversy over deregulation of natural gas (Figure 12.7), one of the largest and bitterest fights of the decade, we observe a diffuse structuring of the opposition groups. Although deregulation proponents are tightly clustered with their own kind, the opponents are scattered throughout the proponents' subregion, including such significant actors as the U.S. Chamber of Commerce, General Motors, and Commonwealth Edison. Noticeably absent from the opponents' coalition are major governmental actors, all of which had lined up behind the compromise deregulation bill (which stretched out final deregulation until 1985) by the time Congress passed it in late 1978. Noteworthy is the split between big oil and the utility interests on the one hand and small oil and a number of industrial consumers on the other. The latter were allied with a variety of labor and consumer groups. The environmentalists were relatively inactive.

The Windfall Profits Tax Act of 1979 (figure 12.8) also illustrates the importance of capturing core support for the eventual success of legislative proposals. The issue emerged in early 1979 as the deadline approached for the demise of federal domestic oil price controls, as required in the 1975 Energy Policy and Conservation Act. President Carter announced on national television in April 1979 that he would begin gradually phasing out oil price controls on June 1. By raising the average price of a barrel of domestic oil from

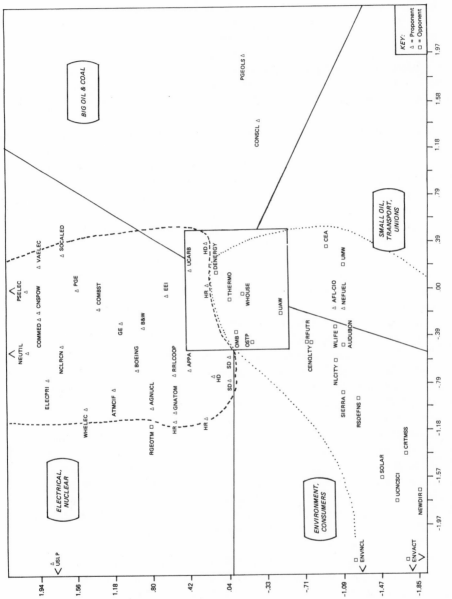

Figure 12.2. Controversial Events in the Energy Domain: Clinch River Breeder Reactor

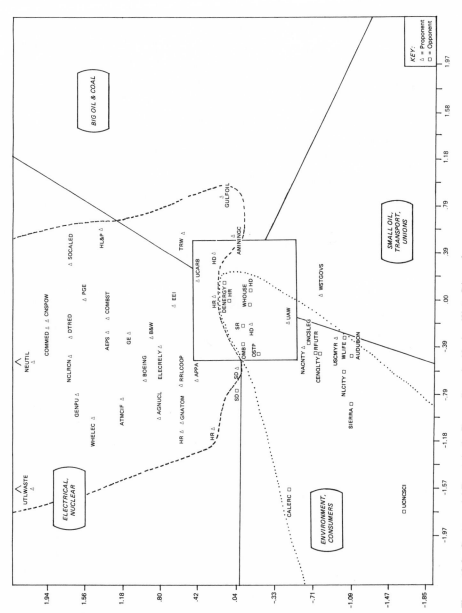

Figure 12.3. Controversial Events in the Energy Domain: Nuclear Waste Disposal

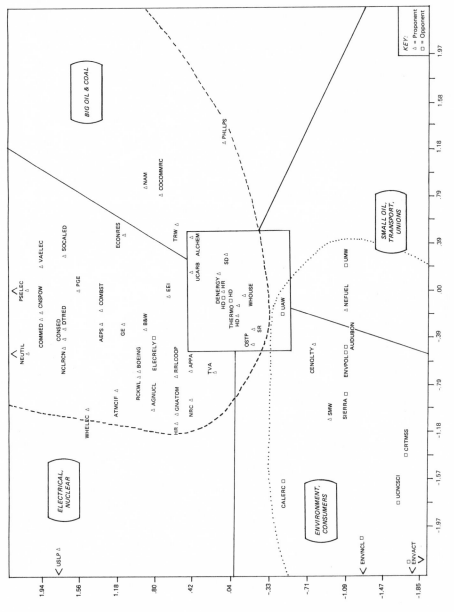

Figure 12.4. Controversial Events in the Energy Domain: Moratorium on Nuclear Plant Construction

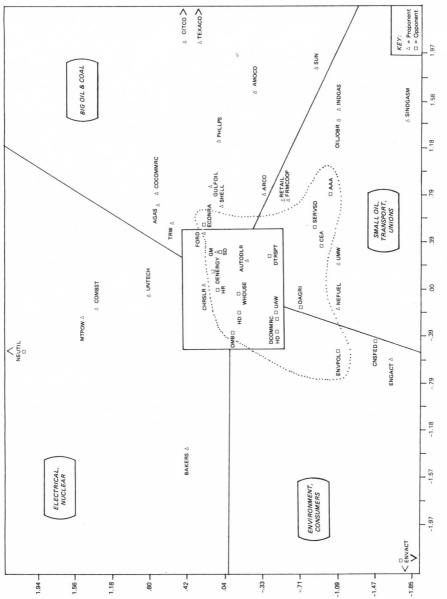

Figure 12.5. Controversial Events in the Energy Domain: Standby Rationing Plan

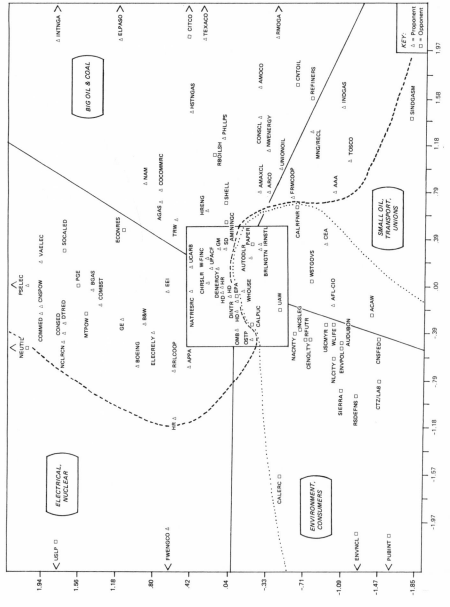

Figure 12.6. Controversial Events in the Energy Domain: Energy Mobilization Board

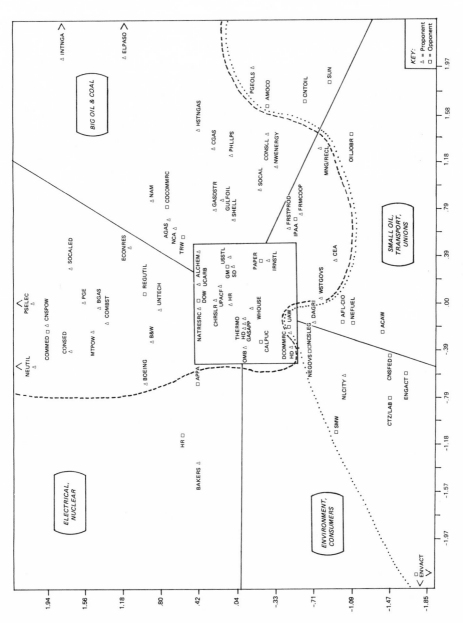

Figure 12.7. Controversial Events in the Energy Domain: Natural Gas Deregulation

329

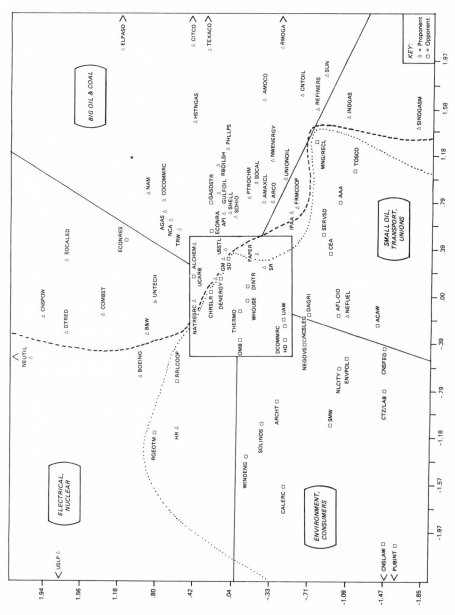

Figure 12.8. Controversial Events in the Energy Domain: Tax on Windfall Profits

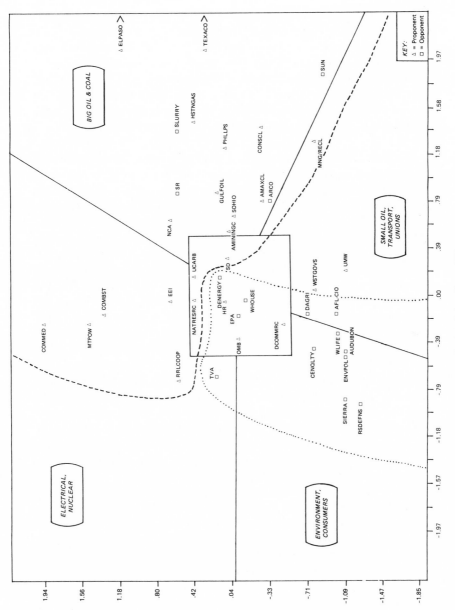

Figure 12.9. Controversial Events in the Energy Domain: Strip-Mining Control Plan

331

$9.50 to the then–world market price of $16.00, Carter hoped to spur additional production and to reduce imports through "price conservation." He also called on Congress to collect some of the "huge and undeserved windfall profits" that U.S. oil companies would realize when domestic prices rose to world levels (soon to skyrocket as the Iranian revolution squeezed world supplies). Carter wanted revenues to be collected through 1982 by an Energy Security Trust Fund and paid out to help low-income families pay their fuel bills, to fund mass transit, and to underwrite the development of the synthetic fuels industry.

As Figure 12.8 shows, the windfall profits tax proposal divided the policy domain almost exactly in half. Producer industry associations and corporations were unanimously opposed to all provisions of the act. In favor were major executive agencies, allied to consumer groups, state and local governments, labor unions, alternative fuels associations, and some environmentalists. In producing the final law, the Carter administration yielded enough concessions to make it palatable to its opponents. Instead of the 70 percent tax rate requested by Carter, Congress settled on 30 percent for newly discovered oil and gave further breaks to independent producers. The total revenue program was drastically scaled back, with the tax to end by 1988 or once $227 billion had been collected, whichever came first. The largest portion of the revenues was earmarked for corporate and personal income tax reductions, with smaller shares to low-income families and mass transit. As a final sop to big oil, no funds were to be spent on synfuel development.

Turning to the health domain, we observe that the first three figures (figures 12.10–12.12) refer to issues related to the funding of biomedical research or to biomedically-linked regulatory matters. Supporters and opponents are *selectively* activated in the broad regions of the space populated with actors whose mandates are especially concerned with such matters. Each scenario elicited a distinctive set of participants, with relatively limited overlap with scenarios that would generally appear to be substantively related. Figure 12.14 (referring to the cost containment issue, one of the premier controversies of the period) arrays the hospital establishment against government and lay actors concerned with paying for rapidly rising hospital charges. The controversy over a national health plan (figure 12.15) produced a similar regional patterning of opposing sides, but the proponents are more homogenously distributed with their own kind, whereas the opponents are scattered among the proponents, but only in a subregion of the proponent cluster. In general, one can draw radii from the center of the space that roughly delineate sectors in which opponents or supporters are concentrated. The key point, of course, is that these radii shift location and orientation as the matter at hand changes.

A superb instance of the process of frame negotiation is found in the great cost containment controversy of 1977[4] (Figure 12.14), in which President Carter through the White House Office and OMB, together with his Democratic allies in the relevant House and Senate subcommittees, proposed mandatory cost caps on hospital charges. The strategy was to single out hospital charges in an effort to control the rising level of government expenditures on health care and, perhaps, in hopes of driving a wedge between traditional allies in the medical establishment. The AHA, with its allies in various sectors of the hospital industry, the drug industry, and even the AMA (which did not have a direct stake in the issue, since doctors' charges would not be subject to this control, but which was ideologically opposed to increased government regulation) counterattacked with a proposal for voluntary price control by the hospitals themselves. Note that none of the specialty professional associations actively opposed the Carter proposal except for the pathologists, an almost exclusively hospital-based group. Given the rapidly increasing cost of employee medical insurance premiums, the financial interests of many members of the U.S. Chamber of Commerce might have been better served by a mandatory cap, but it nevertheless supported the AHA initiative, presumably on the basis of ideological opposition to government-imposed price regulation. Blue Cross/Blue Shield was founded by the AHA and AMA and subsequently enjoyed close ties with them, perpetuated by overlapping boards of directors and frequent exchanges of personnel. It actively supported the AHA's position, but the association of private (for-profit) health insurers remained inactive. The latter were, to say the least, ambivalent on the issue because of conflicting ideological and financial considerations. One suspects that Blue Cross/Blue Shield was subjected to cross-pressures that were resolved in favor of voluntary cost containment because of its special relation to the AHA.

Only some of the unions most closely allied with Carter supported his initiative; the AFL-CIO and UMW were silent, since their party loyalties and general interest in curtailing rising costs were offset by the concern that cost containment legislation might threaten the wages of health care workers. In fact, the coalition supporting mandatory control was drawn from the Democratic side of the congressional subcommittees, executive agencies, such as HCFA and OMB, confronted with escalating hospital charges in the Medicare and Medicaid budgets, the associations of state and local government officials responsible for providing health care to citizens on welfare and public assistance, and various associations of senior citizens especially concerned with maintaining the financial viability, while expanding the coverage, of the Medicare program. As the debate over Carter's hospital cost containment plan ex-

4. See "The Fight For Cost Containment" in Chapter 2 for a synopsis of these events.

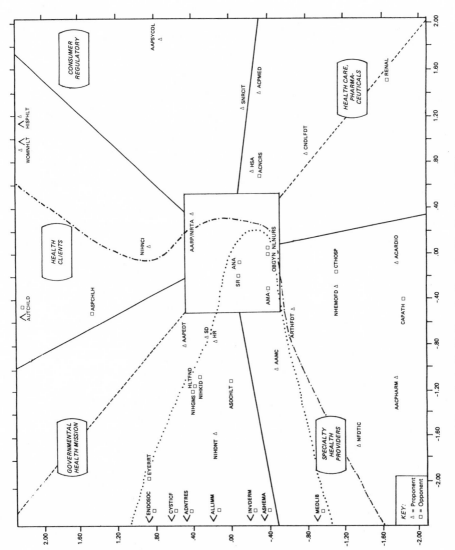

Figure 12.10. Controversial Events in the Health Domain: Control of Funding for the NIH

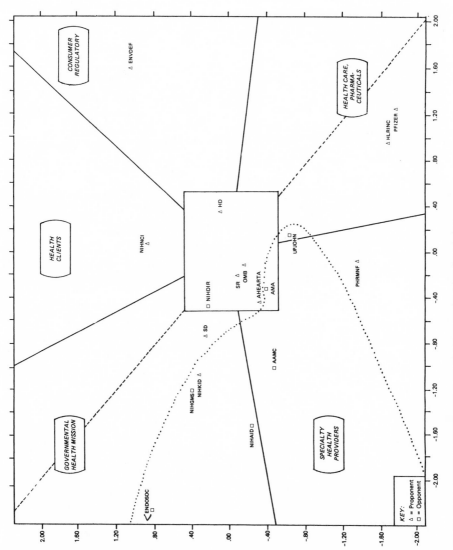

Figure 12.11. Controversial Events in the Health Domain: DNA Regulation

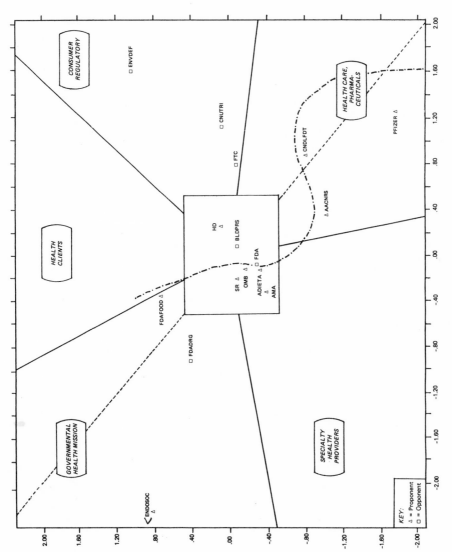

Figure 12.12. Controversial Events in the Health Domain: FDA Ban on Saccharin

336

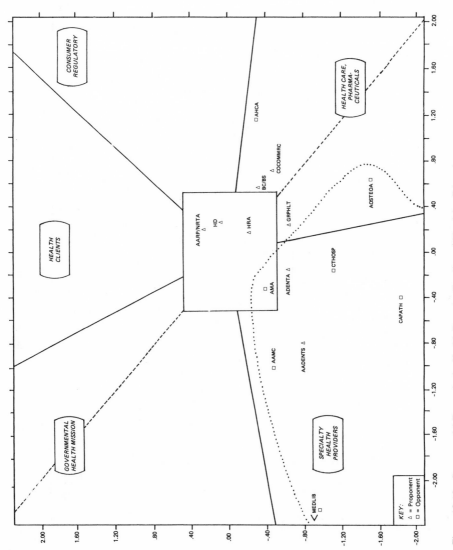

Figure 12.13. Controversial Events in the Health Domain: Funding of Physician Education

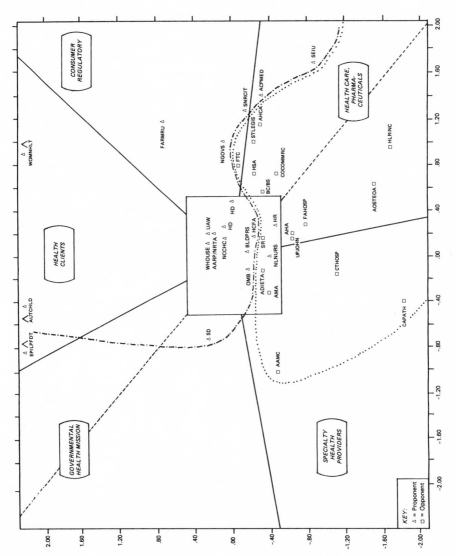

Figure 12.14. Controversial Events in the Health Domain: Hospital Cost Containment

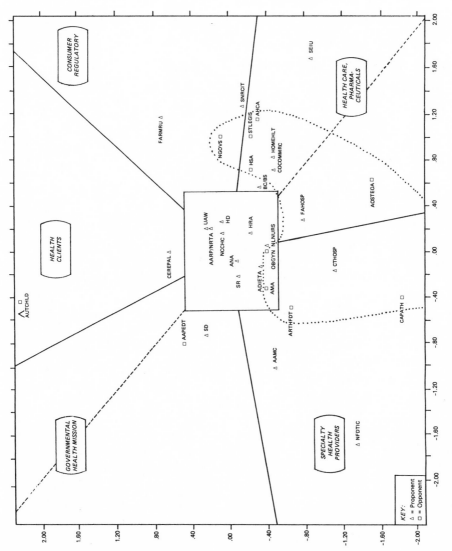

Figure 12.15. Controversial Events in the Health Domain: National Health Planning System

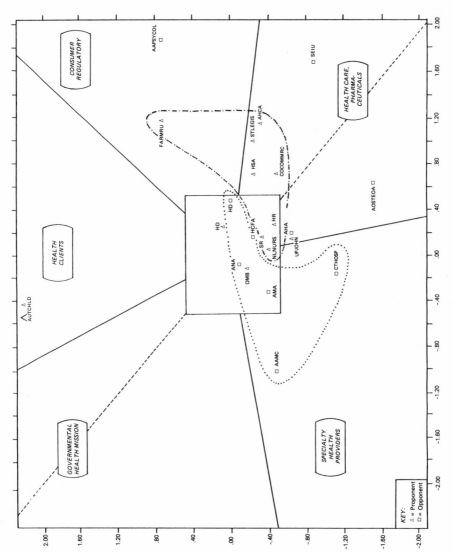

Figure 12.16. Controversial Events in the Health Domain: Medicare and Medicaid Reforms

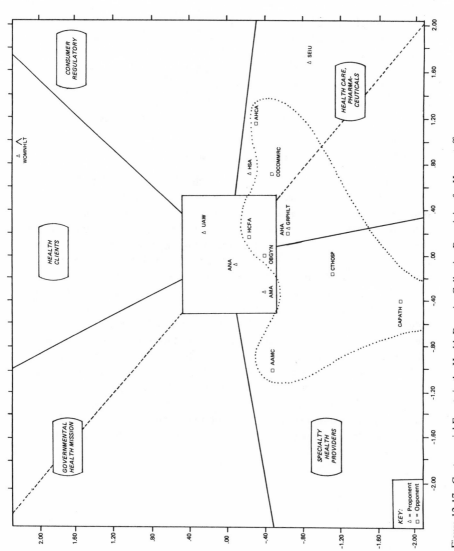

Figure 12.17. Controversial Events in the Health Domain: Collective Bargaining for Housestaff

tended through the next two years, support for the plan was severely eroded. Increasingly aware that it was a partial, and extremely cumbersome, response to the rising cost of health care, a number of congressional Democrats threw their support to the voluntary plan proposed by the hospital industry. Others, led by Sen. Edward Kennedy, became more zealous in insisting on a system of national health insurance as the only equitable and effective method of controlling costs and, consequently, the level of government expenditures.

Concluding Remarks

The principal conclusion of this chapter is the remarkable orderliness in the patterning of consensus and cleavage in the two policy domains. It is not, however, an orderliness easily comprehended by one or two broad analytic distinctions that refer simply to pervasive ideological disagreements among the actors or to master corporate identities with known and unchanging interests. This order is best thought of as a multidimensional structuring of distinctions among interested parties that are selectively activated during the ongoing discourse on what is to be done in a sequence of events. Each actor possesses an array of corporate interests, resources, and linkages with others—that is, strategic considerations—that embeds it in a multidimensional structure of commitments selectively activated by features of the events being processed in an interactive fashion to which each actor contributes and responds. To study such structures more effectively, we must devise more sophisticated methods for analyzing the multidimensionally organized interface of events and actors that preserve its global character. The next chapter takes the final step in our analysis by proposing a strategy for predicting controverted outcomes in policy deliberations on the basis of a model of exchanges of influential communication and resources.

13

Event Outcomes

with Yong-Hak Kim

In this chapter, we explore both the emergence of resource exchange relations among consequential actors and their implications for the outcomes of events. At the system level, this chapter addresses the actor-event interface, building on our key premise that the structure of actors and the structure of critical policy events are mutually interpenetrated complexes. We shall argue that relations among actors arise through their efforts to optimize their interest in event outcomes. The emergent characteristics of the system of events—that is, the outcomes—are determined in part by these emergent relations among actors. And insofar as specific outcomes influence the course of events, this chapter provides further elaboration of our arguments concerning the role of social organization in the continuous process of reframing policy alternatives and, hence, reconstituting policy domains.

In preceding chapters we have emphasized that state policies are the product of complex interactions among government and nongovernment organizations, each seeking to influence collectively binding decisions that have consequences for their respective interests (Laumann, Knoke, and Kim, 1985). In this chapter we attempt to account for the determination of state policies or

We would like to give special thanks to James S. Coleman for his contributions to the development of the mathematical models discussed in this chapter.

event outcomes as the consequence of the network structure by which public and private organizations are *mutually interpenetrated.* To do so, we first develop mathematical models through the extension of Coleman's exchange model (Coleman, 1972, 1973, 1977) in order to explain formally the emergence of resource exchange relations among private sector and government organizations. We then use the structure of private-public interpenetration derived from the model to predict the outcome of events. To do so, however, it is necessary to consider a number of alternative substantive interpretations of the exchange relations among organizations and their implications for the analysis of participation in policy-making processes. In the following discussion, we compare two possible interpretations of resource exchange: resource mobilization and resource deployment.

The penetration of private organizations into governmental policy-making processes has often been studied by resource mobilization theorists. Although a number of studies have stressed the importance of the amount of resources mobilized by interest groups, few have examined the relative effectiveness of resource expenditure in influencing event outcomes (Gamson, 1975, 1980; Goldstone, 1980; Ragin, Coverman, and Hayward, 1982:239). In recent years, the polity model of resource mobilization has challenged the validity of the commonly assumed positive correlation between amounts of resources mobilized and event (movement) outcomes (Gamson, 1975; Oberschall, 1973; Tilly, 1978). This perspective highlights the role of political alliances between interest groups and government organizations as an intervening mechanism through which the relative effectiveness of mobilized resources is determined (Gamson, 1975:15; Ragin, Coverman, and Hayward, 1982:238–52; Tilly, 1978:52–90). Tilly, for instance, argues that without a channel to reach the core of the polity, mobilized resources are likely to evaporate on the street (Tilly, 1978; Zald and McCarthy, 1979:5).

Although there has been increasing attention to the importance of interorganizational relations among interest groups and government organizations (e.g., Zald and McCarthy, 1979), few have explained formally how the fine texture of the interorganizational field arises and the consequences of the resulting network for event outcomes. Although the Tillian perspective correctly recognizes the importance of formal organizations and their relations with the government, empirical studies stimulated by this perspective have serious shortcomings. First, researchers have typically dealt with a single, well-focused event and examined the ways in which the resources mobilized by an interest group or movement organization affect the polity with respect to the outcome of that event (e.g., Ragin, Coverman, and Hayward, 1982). It is insufficient, however, to focus on single events and examine the presence or absence of pairwise relationships between private and public organizations because the polity is an arena in which *multiple* events are simultaneously pursued by numerous public and private organizations.[1]

Second, the Tillian polity model revolves around the one-way penetration of interest groups into the government. Thus, "the policy needs of the government and the actions of the administration in pursuit of them" are totally ignored (Chubb, 1983:13). Interest groups and government organizations mutually coopt, cooperate, and collide with one another in the pursuit of different goals. Consider, for instance, the attempts of antinuclear movement organizations to influence state policy. In May 1979, prompted by the growing criticism of the nuclear regulatory system and by the accident at Three Mile Island, the Subcommittee on Energy and Environment reported a bill calling for a six-month moratorium on nuclear plant construction. Having mobilized a large number of antinuclear activists, funds, and facilities, interest groups such as the Sierra Club and the Friends of the Earth helped to bring this policy option before governmental decision-making bodies. They then engaged in resource transactions with competing organizations active in this policy area, such as the Natural Resources Defense Council, the Union of Concerned Scientists, and the Environmental Center, and with government organizations controlling policy outcomes, such as the Environmental Protection Agency, the Nuclear Regulatory Commission, and the Subcommittee on Energy and Power. Government organizations also mobilized resources and "biases of interest" in order to pursue their own goals. In fact, this legislation activated a large proportion of the energy-domain organizations, with government and environmental groups favoring the moratorium while oil and nuclear companies opposed it. None of these organizations worked alone. They used the interorganizational links of communication and resource exchange to pursue their interests (see figure 12.4).

Thus, to explain event outcomes, we must extend the polity model in order to take into account the entire set of network relations among private interest groups and public organizations in a national policy domain. To do so, we develop two mathematical models of collective action—the resource deployment model and the resource mobilization model—and apply them to the pol-

---

1. Realizing the narrowness of studies focused on a particular movement organization and its mobilization processes, McCarthy and Zald (1977) developed a new concept, "social movement industries." Based on Von Eschen, Kirk, and Pinard's (1971) empirical findings, they argue, for instance, that the civil rights movement in Baltimore was not sponsored by the Congress of Racial Equality alone, but by a set of movement organizations pursuing similar goals. Although the concept of "social movement industries" opens a new way of understanding the process of resource mobilization as well as interactions among organizations, it fails to capture the relations among interest groups constituting different social movement industries and their interorganizational relations with government and other "nongovernment" organizations.

icy domains under study. These models build upon the theoretical elaboration of the resource dependent perspective. Resource dependence theorists have mainly focused on how organizations strive to obtain or *mobilize* resources from the environment for their survival. They have tended to ignore, however, how organizations allocate or *deploy* scarce resources to other organizations to pursue their goals. An earlier work by Selznick (1949) on TVA's cooptive strategy exemplifies the importance of resource deployment to external factors that are *potentially* dangerous for the organization. In studying resource transactions in the policy domains, we argue that organizations not only mobilize resources but also deploy resources to buffer the environmental threat as well as to make dependent relations of other organizations so that they can ask the latter to join a collective action pursuing their goals. In the following section, techniques drawn from network analysis are used to develop formal representations of the mechanisms of resource mobilization and resource deployment. Under the assumption of rational choice, each model attempts to explain the emergence of interorganizational relations of resource exchange among consequential corporate actors. It also attempts to explain the "unintended consequences" of purposive action emerging at the system level—that is, event outcomes.

Resource Exchange Networks in the National Policy Domains

Although the importance of interorganizational relations is well recognized, few have formally explained how and why such a network structure emerges, with the notable exceptions of Coleman (1973, 1977), Marsden and Laumann (1977), and Pappi and Kappelhoff (1984). A brief review of studies of interorganizational relations reveals that they fall into two basic categories: one descriptive and the other explanatory. The former are concerned with mathematical elaborations of *descriptive* measures of network structures, including indices of multiplexity, connectedness, centrality, and prestige. The conceptualization and measurement of centrality, the detection of cliques or structurally equivalent actors, and the depiction of proximities among sets of actors are of focal concern. By contrast, explanatory studies use these descriptive measures to predict behavioral characteristics of the members of the network or to explain systemic characteristics of the network as a whole. What is lacking in the literature is any causal explanation of how the network structure emerges.

We extend earlier works of Coleman (1973, 1977) and Laumann and Marsden (1977) as follows. Whereas previous modeling efforts identified the equilibrium condition of actors' control over events after the exchange of control of events, we specify the equilibrium condition of resource exchanges. Earlier models conceptualized the sociometric relations of dependence as the product of pregiven and fixed matrices of interest and control. According to these models, dependence relations among actors arise because those who control events are different from those who are interested in them. For example, if A controls an event impinging on B's interest, then B depends on A (interest dependence). Since the structure of interest and the structure of control are given and fixed, the product of these two matrices is also fixed. We relax this assumption of fixed dependence and conceptualize resource dependence as a process that moves toward equilibrium. This process reflects not only the structural differentiation of interest and control but also the relative power of interacting actors. Since the notion of power plays an important role in our model, we shall review briefly the systemic concept of power to compare and contrast our structural concept of power with other concepts.[2]

There are three quite different approaches to the conceptualization of power in the network literature. First, there are those who view power in terms of pairwise characteristics.[3] According to Emerson's (1962) view of power, the power A has over B (P_{AB}) is equal to B's dependence on A (D_{BA}). If A also depends on B to some extent, the net power of A over B is given by ($P_{AB} - P_{BA} = D_{BA} - D_{AB}$). Although power is equated with dependence, dependence is, strictly speaking, an opportunity structure for A to exercise power over B, not power itself. Crozier's dyadic notion of power also results from the opportunity structure. He argues that "the power of A over B depends on A's ability to predict B's behavior and on the uncertainty of B about A's behavior" (Crozier, 1964: 158). Note that his concept also moves away from "action" to "state," yet remains on the dyadic level of analysis.

Largely on the basis of Emerson's and Blau's (1964:115–42) specification of power-dependence criteria, Jacobs (1974) elaborates two components of dependence: substitutability and essentiality. He succinctly summarizes propositions of exchange theories: A depends on B to the extent that the resources

---

2. Although we use the concept of power to maintain continuity between our newer mathematical developments and prior models that relied on this concept, we recognize that the term "influence" is more appropriate for understanding the nature of systems such as the national policy domain. See Chapter 5 for our theoretical discussion of influence.

3. Reviewing the literature, Lukes argues that the common core underlying the "concept of power' in all debate about power is the notion that "A exercises power over B when A affects B in a [significant] manner contrary to B's interests" (1974:27). He then distinguishes the "conception of power" from the concept of power as referring to different views concerning "what counts as a significant manner" or "what makes A's affecting B significant" in the analysis of social relationships. Based on this important distinction, he reviews two-dimensional conceptions of power and proposes his own conception. He argues that power is exercised only when a double claim is met: "that A acts (or fails to act) in a certain way and that B does what he would not otherwise do" (1974:41). His notion of *exercised power* is based on the dyadic relations of causal actions, whether the power relations occur between two natural persons, between an institution and natural persons, or between two interacting classes.

that come from A are of great value (essentiality) and are not available from alternative sources (substitutability). He views the degree of dependence as a multiplicative function of these two aspects. A common theme in this type of study is that power is a generalized currency between two interacting parties used to equilibrate imbalances of asymmetric exchanges. This view is limited because it does not consider the whole structure of relations in which the dyadic dependence relation is embedded.

Second, there are those who consider power a consequence of the whole network structure.[4] They equate the centrality score of a node with its power because network centrality is considered a manifestation of power (Boje and Whetten, 1981; Hall et al., 1977; Mariolis and Jones, 1982).

The third approach uses the idea of "network vulnerability," which is defined as the effect of the removal of a particular node or line on the network as a whole. Emerson called this "structural dependence" (the dependence of the whole network on the node), to distinguish it from pairwise dependence. Following the work of Emerson, Yamagishi, Gillmore, and Cook (1986) conceptualize the power of an actor as the ratio of the dependence of the network on the actor to the dependence of the actor on the network.

As will be shown, our network concept of power attempts to capture all three aspects of relational power. That is, a node has more power than others in a network because of the multiplicative function of (1) the sum of asymmetric pairwise exchange relations; (2) the centrality of the node in the system; and (3) the structural dependence of the network on the node (network vulnerability). We start with the most fundamental unit, dyadic interactions.

Two Perspectives on Power

To begin with, let F_{AB} equal the resource flow from A to B. There are two fundamentally different, yet equally valid, perspectives from which to view this dyadic resource transaction. These alternatives are based on different understandings of the causes of resource flows: one emphasizes legitimacy and voluntarism, the other dependence and, perhaps, exploitation. From Parsons' perspective,[5] B has power over A because B has the capacity to mobilize resources from A. According to Parsons:

---

4. L. Freeman (1979) provides an excellent review of various measures of centrality: degree-based, betweenness-based, and closeness-based measures.

5. Parsons does not eliminate the possibility of changing alter's intention, but he categorizes this capacity as "persuasion" or "activation of commitment." He uses power more restrictively: "The power of A over B is, in its legitimized form, the 'right' of A, as a decision-making unit involved in collective process, to make decisions which take precedence over those of B, in the *interest of the effectiveness of the collective operation as a whole*" (1967:318; italics ours).

Power . . . is generalized capacity to secure the performance of binding obligations by units in a system of collective organization where the obligations are legitimized with reference to their bearing on collective goals and where in case of recalcitrance there is a presumption of enforcement by negative situational sanctions—whatever the actual agency of that enforcement. (1967:308)

Power, in short, is the "means of acquiring control of the factors in effectiveness" (1967:303) and "the generalized medium of mobilizing resources for effective collective action" (1967:313–14).

The resource dependence model, however, predicts that A has power over B because B depends on A for valuable resources ($P_{ab} = D_{ba}$). How do we synthesize these contradictory claims? If we introduce the interest of actors, both of these seemingly contradictory perspectives turn out to be valid for any given dyadic resource exchange. First, F_{AB} can be viewed as A's giving of resources to B to pursue A's interest. If B controls events of interest to A, A may deploy resources to B to gain control over them. We call A's strategy a "resource deployment strategy" (hereafter *RDS*). From the RDS perspective, A has power over B because B depends on A for valuable resources.

On the other hand, it is equally valid to regard F_{AB} from the point of view of B's interest. That is, B mobilizes resources from A that are effective in influencing event outcomes of interest to B. We call B's strategy a "resource mobilization strategy" (hereafter *RMS*). Power conceived as mobilizable capacity is exactly the same as Parsons' notion of power, once we replace Parsons' phrase "interest of the collectivity" with "interest of B."[6]

The duality of resource deployment and resource mobilization captures the simultaneous operation of the interests of two partners in a given resource transaction; B gives resources to A to coopt A to achieve the outcome of the event of interest to B, and A mobilizes resources from B to use them for A's purposes. We assume that any given transaction reflects this duality.

From the RDS perspective, the owner of resources deploys his resources among those actors who are most effective in accomplishing the outcomes preferred by resource owners. For example, the Sierra Club deploys resources to a congressional subcommittee and to other functionally related governmental actors if they control the outcome of the nuclear plant construction bill in

6. Since Parsons conceptualizes power with reference to symbols and the legitimacy necessary for achieving a common goal of the collectivity, his notion of power, in the last analysis, does not reside in dyadic relations but in the system as a whole (Giddens, 1968:265; Lukes, 1974). Because the social system is seen as an integrated whole based on common normative ordering, there is no such thing as illegitimate power. As money is a circulating symbolic medium, so is power. When power is exchanged with resources valuable for collective effectiveness, the giver of resources (i.e., the performer of the obligation) is left with "nothing of value," except for the expectation that, in other contexts and on other occasions, "he can invoke certain obligations on the part of other units" (Parsons, 1967:309).

which the Sierra Club is interested. The deployer—in this case the Sierra Club—gives resources to the deployees, with the hope that they (as agents) will apply the resources coming from the deployer for the deployer's goals. To provide an alternative interpretation, the deployer delivers resources to the deployees to create the latter's dependence on the former. This dependence enables the former to ask the latter to do something in the former's interest even against the latter's preferences.

Conversely, one may conceptualize the same transaction in terms of *B*'s RMS; *B* mobilizes resources from *A* to pursue *B*'s goals because *A*'s resources are effective in influencing the event outcomes in *B*'s interest. For instance, governmental actors mobilize resources from environmental groups such as the Sierra Club and the Friends of the Earth if the latters' resources are effective in influencing the outcome of nuclear policy.

Because of the identification problem, we constructed separate models based on RMS and RDS. These models will be used jointly to explain the observed resource exchange network. More specifically, we hypothesize that a given resource exchange F_{AB} is the result of *A*'s RDS and *B*'s RMS and the interaction of the two strategies. We present the deployment model first.

Resource Deployment Model

The resource deployment model contains four analytic components: purposive *actors* who possess *resources* and hold preferred *interests* in the positive and negative outcomes of *events*. Actors bargain among themselves, exchanging their resources to gain greater control over the outcomes of those events in which they have greater interest, relinquishing control over events in which they have less interest. More specifically, the model deals with a system of actors who deploy resources to others (agents) who are effective in controlling the outcome of the events that have impact on the actors' own interests. Diagrammatically:

$$\text{ACTOR } j \xrightarrow[C^{*}_{ji}]{\text{deploy}} \text{ACTOR } i \xrightarrow[A_{ik}]{\text{effective}} \text{EVENT } k \xrightarrow[x_{kj}]{\text{interests}} \text{ACTOR } j$$
$$\text{RESOURCES}$$

The model assumes that at equilibrium the amount of resource flow from *j* to *i* depends on the effectiveness of *i* for an event (A_{ik}) and the interest of the former in the event (X_{kj}), adjusted by their relative power.

This linear system of action requires the following assumptions. First, each interested actor has a differential degree of effectiveness in determining the outcome of a given policy option, and the relative effectiveness of each actor is fixed and known to all actors without any information distortion. Second, each organization exchanges resources so as to best satisfy its interests, given its resources and interest in achieving particular outcomes. The model also assumes that there is no structural barrier hindering exchange processes. In short, it assumes a perfect market and perfect rationality of organizations. It also assumes that there is a closed boundary around the system of actors and events. We fully recognize the limitations of these strict assumptions.[7] But we want to use this idealized model as a benchmark against which to explore the complex real world.

Data. The resource exchange network (C^*) was obtained by asking informants to indicate with which other domain organizations their group engaged in a variety of transactions such as "giving confidential information," "giving substantial funds as payment for services or goods," or "permitting other organizations to use its staff and facilities."

For the application of the mathematical models, we selected the eight controversial events in each domain that were discussed in Chapter 12. We assume that the observed resource exchange network represents the equilibrium condition. We further assume that the observed network contains the history of all previous events that occurred in the policy domain. Thus, to best represent entire issue areas,[8] we first carried out a hierarchical clustering analysis based on a matrix of similarities measured by the logodd ratio of actors' levels of participation (see Chapter 11). If two events attracted the same set of participants, the distance between these two events is zero; they belong to the same event cluster. From the dendrogram produced by the clustering technique, we then selected the eight controversial events distributed evenly in the dendrogram. Brief descriptions of these events and their final outcome are provided in table 13.1. Finally, the interest matrix (X) was created by asking informants to express their relative degree of interest in decision-making events relating to national energy or health policy. Once we excluded organizations that did not express any interest in these eight events or that failed to respond to the questions about the exchange relations, 128 energy and 95 health organizations were finally selected for the analysis.[9]

According to the resource deployment model, power is defined as:

$$P_j = C_{j1}^* P_1 + C_{j2}^* P_2 + \ldots + C_{jm}^* P_m$$

In a matrix notation, $P = C^*P$.

---

7. See appendix to this chapter for details.

8. If events were selected from only one issue area, there would be a low level of interest differentiation, and consequently the model would explain only a small portion of the variance of exchange behaviors.

9. The following six-item scale was used to determine interest levels of organizations in the event: interested, active = 5; interested, publicly inactive, position held = 4; interested, active, no position = 3; interested, inactive = 2; interested, publicly inactive, no position held = 1; and uninterested = 0. See Appendix B, question B3.

Table 13.1. Synopsis of Eight Controversial Events in Each Domain

ENERGY EVENTS

CRNR: First authorized in 1970, the Clinch River Breeder Reactor was a demonstration project for a new nuclear technology. During the Carter administration, however, the president repeatedly vetoed appropriations for the project. In April 1979, the House Science Committee set the stage for another confrontation. Rejecting a Carter administration proposal to amend the Energy Department authorization by removing any commitment to the financing of such demonstration projects, the committee voted to continue funding the Clinch River reactor.

NWS: Faced with considerable political opposition to the development of geologically stable, permanent depositories for nuclear waste, in December 1979 the Senate Energy Committee reported a bill requiring the Energy Secretary to establish long-term interim storage facilities above ground.

EMB: As part of his second national energy plan, Carter proposed the creation of an Energy Mobilization Board to facilitate energy development projects, even at the cost of overriding state laws and environmental regulations. In August 1979, two House committees reported bills creating such an agency and the Senate passed related legislation that autumn. Eventually, a coalition of liberal Democrats and states rights Republicans in the House defeated the conference bill.

NGD: Following a year of intense disagreement, in August 1978 a House-Senate conference committee reported compromise legislation providing for the deregulation of natural gas pricing. The bill was approved by Congress and signed into law that November.

NPC: In May 1979, prompted by growing criticism of the nuclear regulatory system and the accident at Three Mile Island, the Subcommittee on Energy and the Environment passed an amendment calling for a six-month moratorium on nuclear plant construction. This was passed by the full committee, but defeated by the House in November 1979.

TWF: In April 1979, Carter announced the gradual decontrol of oil prices and asked Congress to approve a tax on resulting windfall profits. Two months later, the House Ways and Means Committee reported a bill taxing profits from deregulated oil and gas; Congress approved amended legislation in March 1980.

SMCP: The Surface Mining Control and Reclamation Act of 1977 imposed strict federal regulations on the mining industry. In July 1979, the Senate Energy Committee reported a bill allowing states to develop their own strip mining regulations independent of federal law. The legislation was approved by the Senate but was allowed to die in the House and, in the following year, in conference.

352

SRP: Without making a recommendation, in April 1979 the House Commerce Committee reported legislation proposed by the Carter administration for standby rationing of gasoline. In an amended form, this legislation was approved by the Senate but was killed in the House.

HEALTH EVENTS

DNA: In March 1978, the House Commerce Committee approved legislation extending the 1976 NIH regulations for recombinant DNA research and establishing a commission to study genetic engineering technologies. However, all proposed legislation in this area was tabled by Congress.

NIH: The fiscal 1980 reauthorization bill for the National Institutes of Health originally included a controversial proposal allowing Congress to establish appropriation ceilings for individual institutes. Initially approved by the House Subcommittee on Health and the Environment, this controversial provision was defeated both in the Senate and in conference.

CB: In April 1976, the House Subcommittee on Labor-Management Relations began consideration of legislation amending the National Labor Relations Act to include hospital housestaff. Hearings continued through the following April when the measure was tabled.

CGM: In October 1978, the Carter administration announced that it would cut back construction grants to medical schools that failed to limit class sizes to federal standards.

NHP: The Senate Human Resources Committee recommended passage of national health planning legislation in November 1974. Passed by Congress the following month, this bill established a network of local planning agencies responsible for establishing priorities for development and monitoring the use of federal funds.

CCC: During May 1977, the Subcommittee on Health and the Environment of the House Commerce Committee held hearings on Carter's proposal for hospital cost containment but failed to report the legislation. By the end of the year, only the Senate Human Resources Committee had reported the legislation.

HR: In December 1979, the Senate Finance Committee reported legislation establishing new methods of hospital reimbursement through Medicare and Medicaid intended to promote cost efficiency.

FDAS: In July 1977, following an FDA proposal to ban the use of saccharin, the Senate Human Resources Committee cleared legislation establishing an 18-month moratorium on such a ban. This delay was approved by Congress the following November.

353

We now elaborate the implications of power in the resource deployment model. On the dyadic level, the power index captures both "substitutability" and "essentiality" as follows. Because of the constraint $\Sigma_j\, C^*_{ji} = 1.0$, C^*_{ji} is defined as the fraction (or proportional intensity) of i's dependence on j, which reflects the number of alternative sources of resources for i (substitutability). The constraint on the column sum makes the matrix a negatively connected network.[10] If i has many alternative sources of needed resources, the intensity of i's dependence on each of his partners will be weaker. The more j attracts dependence by i through its monopoly of the supply of resources or other methods, the more powerful j becomes. Or, conversely, the C^*_{ji} element is greater to the extent that the sources of i's needed resources are not substitutable. Unlike most 0 or 1 binary network data, this matrix has a continuous scale, because C^* was constructed by adding various resource exchange relations. Thus, the more "essential" the resources of j for i, the more i will depend on j in these exchange relations—thus, the greater the value of C^*_{ji}. In short, power derived from C^* implies the multiplicative function of essentiality and substitutability—the fundamental axiom of power-dependence (Jacobs, 1974).

It also captures system characteristics of the network as a whole. Unlike most centrality scores previously proposed, which tend to measure the volume of the relations involving a node, power in this model captures not only the volume but also the quality of the relations—an important aspect that has to do with the dependence of the whole network on the node (Knoke and Burt, 1983). Suppose that both A and B attract 10 actors' dependence, but those actors that depend on A are themselves the object of strong dependence by many other actors, whereas the actors that depend on B do not have any actors dependent upon them. In this situation, the network as a whole depends on A more than on B, and, accordingly, A is more powerful than B. Power measured by $P = C^*\,P$ thus reflects the idea of network vulnerability. In sum, the concept of power in the resource deployment model includes the multiplicative functions of three important aspects of power-generating mechanisms: pairwise dependence, volume or centrality, and quality of relations.

Estimation. Since information on organizational effectiveness (A) is not available in our data, it has to be estimated by means of regressions (see the technical appendix to this chapter). The rationale for this estimation can be clarified by a simple illustration. According to the resource deployment model, when the Subcommittee on Energy and Environment reports a bill calling for a moratorium on nuclear power plant construction, interested orga-

---

10. The connection is negative "if exchange in one relation is contingent on nonexchange in the other" (Cook et al., 1983:277). If A has four alternative sources for exchange, for instance, then A's relation to the four possible partners is negative because A can substitute partners.

nizations will deploy resources to this subcommittee and other functionally related executive agencies. Given this proposition of the model, the estimation process works logically backward; the resource flows from interested groups to these government organizations are the *indications* of the latters' effectiveness in controlling the outcome of the moratorium bill. If the model closely approximates reality, the effectiveness of the subcommittee and related executive agencies with respect to this nuclear event must be higher than that of other organizations to which resources were not deployed in this instance.

It is precisely because of this tautological estimation method that we cannot test the model directly. There are, however, four alternative ways of checking the model's validity. Three involve indirect tests and one a direct test. First, the vector of power, P, can be correlated with the actors' reputed influence standings, which were measured independently of resource exchange activities.[11] Second, we can compare the observed exchange network with the exchange network predicted by the model. The variance explained by the regression equation then indicates the model's predictive power. Third, the estimated matrix of effectiveness, A, can be tested against our intuitive knowledge of the policy domains. For instance, we can check whether the subcommittee and executive agencies mentioned in the above example appear to have been especially effective with respect to the nuclear moratorium event. Finally, a direct test is possible by using the model to predict the event outcome. According to the model, the probability of a positive outcome of event k is as follows:

$$\Pi_k = .5 + (\Sigma_i \Sigma_j C_{ji}^* A_{ik} \Phi_{jk}) / 2$$

where $\Phi_{jk} = 1$ if j takes a pro position and $\Phi_{jk} = -1$ if j takes a con position. If Π_k is greater than .5, event k should have a positive outcome. A probability of 0, on the other hand, indicates a negative outcome with absolute certainty.

An External Check on the Deployment Model and Related Findings. The correlation of individual power ratings derived from this model with the independently measured reputed influence standings of organizations (see Chapter 5) is a very respectable .58 in energy and .73 in health. Thus, the ability to deploy resources—that is, the capacity to use valuable resources and the location of the dyadic relations used to create dependencies among other organizations—is highly correlated with the reputed influence of individual actors. This finding is consistent with Emerson's postulate of power as the reverse of dependence ($P_{ab} = D_{ba}$). The somewhat lower correlation in the energy domain may imply a lower degree of agreement there concerning the identity of the

11. The reader will recall that an organization's reputed influence is simply the number of times it was cited as consequential by other organizations. See Chapter 5.

organizations that really matter in policy deliberations—a finding documented at length in Chapters 5 and 8.

The dimensions of the estimated *A* matrices are 128 by 8 for energy and 95 by 8 for health. Because of their very large size, it is impractical to present the full estimated matrices here. Instead, we shall present the estimated effectiveness of 21 selected organizations for each of the eight events in each domain. A *1* in table 13.2 indicates that an organization's estimated effectiveness belongs to the top quintile.[12] In inspecting this table, the reader should first note that an actor's estimated effectiveness varies, often quite dramatically, from event to event. And these variations make a good deal of sense. Second, drawing on what the reader now knows about the particular organization's portfolio of interests and resources (see Appendix A, for example), he or she can assess the very considerable plausibility of the high to low rankings of the various organizations' effectiveness for particular events. Inspection of the complete table would disclose no major anomalies in the estimated effectiveness rankings of the organizational actors in each domain.

For instance, the EPA, the White House, and the Department of Energy are estimated to be the most effective with respect to the nuclear power plant event in the energy domain. For other events, their estimated effectiveness was much lower, reflecting the differentiation of organizational effectiveness across event scenarios. To take an example in the health domain, we observe that the various branches of the FDA had the highest effectiveness in the saccharin event. The congruence of the estimated effectiveness with our intuitive knowledge about who should matter in the policy domains generally or with respect to specific issues indirectly supports the validity of the model's proposition that organizations deploy resources to the targets that are effective in controlling the outcome of the events of greatest interest to the deployers.

Table 13.3 summarizes the control exercised by interested organizations over various events. The results are broken down by type of organization and issue public.[13] To put it simply, the control exercised by an organization over any given event is the amount of resources deployed, multiplied by the deployees' (i.e., the targets') effectiveness on that event.

Compare the relative salience of different types of organizations in the two domains. It should be recalled that the organizations were not randomly selected but are the most consequential and active participants in each domain.

12. Since each of the eight estimated effectiveness scores has a highly skewed distribution, the effectiveness scores ranked at the second or lower quintiles are close to zero. For this reason we reported only the first quintile.

13. Organization j's exercised control over the outcome of event, T_{jk}, is $\Sigma_i E(C_{ji}^*) A_{ik} |\Phi_{jk}|$, where $E(C_{ji}^*)$ is j's resource deployment to i expected by the model, A_{ik} is organization i's effectiveness in controlling the outcome of event k, and $|\Phi_{jk}|$ is the absolute value of j's position on event k.

One striking difference between the two domains, noted in table 13.3, is the relative prevalence of business corporations; in energy they constitute 40 percent of the population of consequential actors, but only 4 percent in health. In sharp contrast, 34 percent of the actors in the health domain are professional associations, whereas only 1 percent of the actors in energy are. In energy, business organizations exercise approximately equal amounts of influence across all eight events, whereas professional associations exercise negligible influence on them. This pattern is precisely reversed when we look at the relative effectiveness of these two types of organizations in the health domain. There have been too many overly facile generalizations about the relative significance and efficacy of different types of actors in affecting policy outcomes. This analysis provides strong evidence that such generalizations must be qualified by taking more systematically into account the characteristics of policy domains and the nature of the controversy in which policy deliberations are taking place.

The circled cells in table 13.3 call attention to the highly selective impact of different issue publics, defined in Chapter 4, on particular controversies. As one might have expected, nuclear-related events are strongly influenced by the nuclear, electrical, and environmental issue public; the standby rationing of gasoline, tax on windfall profits, and gas-deregulation events were largely influenced by the oil public; the surface mining control plan mobilized the coal and natural gas public; and so forth. In the health domain, the finance issue public contributed over 40 percent of the total effort exercised on the finance-related events: unionization, cost containment, and hospital reimbursement.

Table 13.4 examines the determinants of reputed influence. Each organization's potential effectiveness (A_{ik}) and the control exercised by each organization over an event through the network of resource deployment were regressed on the number of influence votes it received.[14] Notice the differences in the variance explained in the two domains. In health, 59 percent of the variance of the reputed influence is explained by potential effectiveness and 47 percent by the control exercised through the network of resource deployment. The corresponding R^2s are much lower in energy—29 and 32 percent respectively. The lower explanatory power of the deployment model in explaining the influence hierarchy in the energy domain is consistent with our argument, resting on a variety of pieced-together empirical facts, that the energy domain lacked a well-established influence hierarchy in the 1970s. Note also that, in health,

---

14. The magnitude of the regression coefficients in the leftmost column may be interpreted directly. Since potential effectiveness with respect to each event sums to one across all organizations ($\Sigma_i A_{ik} = 1.0$), the regression coefficients represent the increment of additional influence votes received as potential effectiveness increases by 1 percent.

Table 13.2. Estimated Organizational Effectiveness on Eight Events for Selected Organizations

Names of Organizations	Energy							
	CRNR	NWS	EMB	NGD	NPC	TWF	SMCP	SRP
Standard Oil of California (Chevron)	1	0	0	0	1	0	0	1
Texaco Inc.	0	0	0	0	0	1	0	0
American Gas Association	1	0	0	1	0	0	1	0
American Petroleum Institute	1	0	1	0	1	0	1	0
U.S. Steel Corporation	0	0	0	0	0	0	0	0
American Mining Congress	1	0	0	0	0	1	1	0
National Coal Association	1	0	0	0	0	1	0	0
Edison Electric Institute	1	1	0	1	0	0	0	1
Chamber of Commerce of the United States	1	0	1	1	0	0	1	0
Sierra Club	0	0	0	0	0	0	0	0
The White House Office	0	0	1	0	1	0	0	0
Council of Economic Advisers	0	1	1	0	1	0	1	0
Council on Environmental Quality	0	1	0	0	0	1	1	0
Office of Management and Budget	0	1	1	0	1	0	0	1
Department of Energy	0	1	0	0	1	1	0	0
Economic Regulatory Administration	0	0	1	0	1	0	0	0
Environmental Protection Agency	0	1	0	0	1	1	0	0
Tennessee Valley Authority	0	1	0	0	1	0	0	0
Subcommittee on Energy Development and Applications	0	1	0	0	1	0	0	1
Subcommittee on Energy and Power: Democratic	0	0	1	0	0	0	0	1
Subcommittee on Energy and Production: Democratic	0	1	0	0	1	0	0	1

Health

	DNA	NIH	CB	CGM	NHP	CCC	HR	FDAS
American Medical Association	1	1	0	1	1	1	1	1
American Nurse Association	0	1	0	1	1	0	1	0
American Cancer Society	1	1	0	0	0	0	0	1
Blue Cross and Blue Shield Associations	0	0	1	1	1	1	1	0
Pfizer Pharmaceuticals	1	0	0	0	0	0	0	1
AFL-CIO	0	0	1	0	0	0	0	0
UAW	0	0	0	0	0	1	0	0
American Hospital Association	0	0	1	1	1	0	1	0
Federation of American Hospitals	0	0	1	1	1	1	0	0
FDA: Commissioner	1	0	0	0	0	1	0	1
FDA: Bureau of Drugs	1	0	0	0	0	0	0	1
FDA: Bureau of Foods	0	0	0	0	0	0	0	1
NIH: National Cancer Institute	1	0	0	0	0	0	0	1
NIH: National Institute of Child Care	1	1	1	0	1	0	0	1
NIH: National Institute of General Medicine	1	0	0	0	0	0	0	0
Health Care Financing Administration	0	0	1	0	1	1	1	0
Office of Management and Budget	1	0	0	1	0	1	0	1
The White House Office	0	0	0	0	0	1	1	0
Subcommittee (LHEW): Republican	1	1	0	0	0	0	0	0
Subcommittee (Health and Environment): Democratic	1	0	1	0	0	1	0	1
Subcommittee (Health and Scientific Research)	1	0	0	0	1	1	0	0

Table 13.3. Exercised Control Over the Outcome of Events in Energy and Health Domains by Organizational Types and Issue Publics

				Energy				
	(N)	CRNR	NWS	EMB	NGD	NPC	TWF	SMCP	SRP
Type of Organization									
1. Congressional Subcommittees	10	9.0%	12.7%	6.9%	7.3%	9.2%	3.1%	3.0%	8.1%
2. Federal Agencies	12	15.9%	13.7%	14.9%	6.6%	11.5%	16.5%	27.0%	24.0%
3. Association of State and Local Government	9	0.0%	3.5%	4.0%	4.3%	1.0%	2.2%	1.4%	0.0%
4. Research Unit	1	1.7%	0.0%	0.0%	0.0%	1.5%	0.2%	1.7%	0.0%
5. Labor Unions	5	3.9%	1.4%	2.5%	3.5%	2.9%	3.3%	2.7%	3.6%
6. Trade Associations	24	17.4%	19.9%	22.7%	22.0%	22.2%	22.5%	18.8%	20.0%
7. Professional Societies	1	1.0%	0.0%	0.0%	0.5%	0.0%	0.6%	0.0%	0.0%
8. Business Corporations	51	43.0%	43.4%	44.0%	53.8%	46.7%	49.7%	39.4%	39.7%
9. Public Interest Groups	15	8.1%	5.4%	4.9%	2.0%	5.1%	2.2%	6.1%	4.7%
Sum	128	100.0%	100.0%	100.0%	100.0%	100.0%	100.0%	100.0%	100.0%
By Issue Public									
1. Manufacturing and National Executive	11	12.6%	10.5%	12.6%	17.4%	11.6%	14.2%	9.0%	19.3%
2. Oil	25	1.4%	1.1%	19.5%	16.1%	1.4%	28.7%	11.9%	31.4%
3. Railroad	3	0.0%	0.0%	2.0%	4.4%	3.7%	3.7%	2.9%	2.8%
4. Coal and Natural Gas	21	4.5%	4.0%	18.5%	19.4%	0.8%	22.2%	37.6%	6.0%
5. Local Government, Renewable Fuel	18	4.3%	10.1%	9.3%	12.1%	7.0%	7.6%	3.3%	13.3%
6. Regulatory	5	6.6%	5.4%	7.9%	5.9%	9.8%	8.8%	9.8%	17.0%
7. PIRG-FTC	1	0.0%	0.0%	0.2%	0.0%	0.0%	0.1%	0.0%	0.0%
8. Nuclear, Electrical, Environmental	41	70.0%	68.3%	28.8%	24.3%	65.1%	14.4%	25.6%	10.3%
9. Isolates	3	0.7%	0.6%	1.2%	0.5%	0.6%	0.4%	0.0%	0.0%
Sum	128	100.0%	100.0%	100.0%	100.0%	100.0%	100.0%	100.0%	100.0%

Health

Type of Organization

	(N)	DNA	NIH	CB	CGM	NHP	CCC	HR	FDAS
1. Congressional Subcommittees	7	19.5%	13.3%	0.0%	7.0%	13.7%	19.4%	23.0%	16.2%
2. Federal Agencies (FDA)	9	4.8%	3.2%	16.1%	11.4%	6.8%	18.0%	14.1%	45.9%
3. State and Local Government	4	0.0%	0.0%	0.0%	0.0%	7.4%	6.3%	2.9%	0.0%
4. Government Sponsored Research Units	6	34.7%	13.2%	0.0%	0.0%	0.9%	0.7%	0.0%	0.0%
5. Labor Unions	2	0.0%	0.0%	1.5%	0.0%	0.9%	0.7%	1.1%	0.0%
6. Trade Associations	7	5.1%	2.2%	24.8%	10.5%	14.1%	12.3%	12.7%	0.0%
7. Professional Societies	30	23.5%	42.5%	47.4%	55.7%	37.6%	25.1%	37.0%	24.7%
8. Business Corporations	4	7.2%	0.0%	0.0%	8.0%	5.6%	7.9%	3.4%	2.5%
9. Lay Voluntary Associations	26	5.3%	25.6%	10.2%	7.3%	14.0%	10.3%	5.9%	10.7%
Sum	95	100.0%	100.0%	100.0%	100.0%	100.0%	100.0%	100.0%	100.0%

By Issue Public

	(N)	DNA	NIH	CB	CGM	NHP	CCC	HR	FDAS
1. Mental Health	4	0.0%	0.7%	0.6%	0.0%	2.0%	2.1%	0.6%	0.0%
2. Consumers	9	0.0%	6.1%	8.3%	11.4%	17.4%	5.3%	11.7%	4.4%
3. Finance	15	0.0%	4.4%	45.0%	21.1%	26.1%	43.5%	42.6%	0.0%
4. Health Professionals	14	19.2%	24.9%	46.2%	49.6%	31.6%	24.4%	30.7%	22.0%
5. Public Health	10	12.9%	24.6%	0.0%	8.9%	8.5%	5.6%	0.0%	8.5%
6. Targeted Disease #1	10	6.8%	16.0%	0.0%	0.0%	0.0%	0.0%	0.0%	5.8%
7. Health Research	8	28.8%	6.6%	0.0%	9.0%	0.0%	0.0%	0.0%	0.8%
8. Targeted Disease #2	3	0.0%	0.0%	0.0%	0.0%	0.0%	1.4%	0.0%	2.6%
9. Targeted Disease #3	10	8.7%	13.5%	0.0%	0.0%	5.5%	1.6%	1.0%	0.0%
10. Drug Industry	6	12.3%	0.0%	0.0%	0.0%	0.0%	3.3%	3.4%	31.6%
11. Food	2	0.0%	0.0%	0.0%	0.0%	0.0%	0.0%	0.0%	11.3%
12. Government	3	11.3%	3.2%	0.0%	0.0%	5.1%	12.8%	10.0%	13.1%
13. Isolates	1	0.0%	0.0%	0.0%	0.0%	3.7%	0.0%	0.0%	0.0%
Sum	95	100.0%	100.0%	100.0%	100.0%	100.0%	100.0%	100.0%	100.0%

[1]Organization j's exercised control over the outcome of events, T_{jk}, is $\Sigma_i \ E(C^*_{ji}) \ A_{ik} \ |\phi_{jk}|$, where $E(C^*_{ji})$ j's resource deployment to i the resource exchange network expected by the model, A_{ik} is organization i's effectiveness in controlling the outcome of event k, and $|\phi_{jk}|$ is the absolute value of j's position on event k.

Table 13.4. Regression of Organizational Potential Effectiveness and Exercised Control over Event Outcome on Number of Reputational Influence Votes Received

Energy Domain

Dependent Variable = Reputed Influence Vote

	Potential Effectiveness (A_{ik})	Exercised Control over Outcome (T_{jk})
Constant	16.8**	25.2**
Clinch River Nuclear Breeder Reactor	3.8	-1.9
Nuclear Waste Storage	2.1	8.8
Energy Mobilization Board	5.0*	12.3
Natural Gas Deregulation	2.8	-5.4
Nuclear Plant Construction	8.6**	-2.3
Tax on Windfall Profit	5.8**	3.9
Strip-Mining Control Plan	2.5	18.9**
Standby Rationing Plan	2.8	18.7*
R^2	.29**	.32**

Health Domain

Dependent Variable = Reputed Influence Vote

	Potential Effectiveness (A_{ik})	Exercised Control over Outcome (T_{jk})
Constant	3.6	19.9**
DNA	1.5	7.0*
NIH	2.3	0.1
Collective Bargaining	3.2	-5.0
Cutback Grant to Medical Schools	1.4	0.9
National Health Plan	5.1*	-2.7
Carter's Cost Containment	13.1**	22.0**
Hospital Reimbursement	2.1	0.2
FDA Saccharin Ban	1.9	2.3
R^2	.59**	.47**

The regression equation for the first column is

Reputed Influence Votes$_i$ = Σ_k b_k (A_{ik} * 100).

The regression equation for the second column is

Reputed Influence Votes$_j$ = Σ_k b'_k (T_{jk} * 100).

*p $\leq$ .05
**p $\leq$ .001

[1]Potential effectiveness refers to A_{ik} estimated by the model.

the *organizational attributes* of potential effectiveness explain a larger amount of the variance of the reputed influence than the actual attempts to control the event outcome through the network of resource deployment. In energy, on the other hand, potential effectiveness explains slightly less than the exercised control, indicating that energy domain actors attribute more influence to those organizations who engage actively in resource deployment than to those who are only estimated to be potentially effective in controlling events.

In the health domain, the potential effectiveness of an actor with respect to the cost containment event is the strongest predictor of reputed influence. This is not entirely surprising, given our extended discussion of this event in Chapter 12, in which we pointed out that it attracted by far the highest level of participation, at the same time that it sharply divided the most influential members of the domain. This event was an element of the major controversy in health policy during the Carter administration. The conflict mobilized the AHA, the Federation of American Hospitals, and the AMA, which opposed federal involvement in cost containment, against the executive branch, including the White House and OMB. Active participants in this fight tended to have a higher-than-average attributed influence standing within the domain.

Finally, the model can be tested directly by comparing the predicted event outcomes with the actual outcomes. Table 13.5 shows the percentage of organizations favoring each side, the actual outcome, and the outcome predicted by the model. All eight events in energy are predicted correctly by the model, as are seven out of the eight in health. The merit of this model is particularly apparent in its ability to predict outcomes that are contrary to the simple principle of majority rule, specifically the events concerning hospital cost control and reimbursements to hospitals for Medicare and Medicaid expenses. Although the majority of active participants (20 versus 17 organizations) favored federal intervention in hospital cost containment, the actual outcome of the event was negative. The mobilization of a number of highly influential organizations, many included within the finance issue public, is central to an adequate interpretation of this episode.

In conclusion, the external checks suggest that the predictiveness of this mathematical model is quite good. The model also provides some insights into state policy formation as the product of complex relations of mutually interpenetrated public and private organizations. Attention to the differentiated patterns of resource deployment, as well as the relative standing and location of the deployers and deployees, suggests something of the fine structure of the political realm—a structure that is excluded by definition from studies focused on interest group behavior or bureaucratic politics.

Table 13.5. Percentage of Organizations Favoring "Positive" or "Negative" Outcome, Actual Outcome, and the Predicted Outcome

	Percent Favoring Positive	Percent Favoring Negative	Actual Outcome	Predicted Outcome	Predicted Probability of Positive Outcome (Π_k)
		Energy Domain (N=128)			
CRNR	26.8	16.3	+	+	.58
NWS	30.2	12.9	+	+	.62
EMB	27.4	47.0	−	−	.34
NGD	37.9	20.2	+	+	.60
NPC	10.9	37.8	−	−	.31
TWF	36.7	24.2	+	+	.59
SMCP	21.1	12.3	+	+	.55
SRP	14.9	19.0	−	−	.48
		Health Domain (N=95)			
DNA	10.5	7.4	−	+	.52
NIH	21.1	25.3	−	−	.45
CB	7.4	8.4	−	−	.49
CGM	8.4	7.4	+	+	.54
NHP	22.1	11.6	+	+	.57
CCC	21.1	17.9	−	−	.49
HR	12.6	10.5	−	−	.48
FDAS	10.5	6.3	+	+	.53

$$\Pi_k = .5 + (\Sigma_i \Sigma_j \ C^{**}{}_{ji} \ A_{ik} \ \phi_{jk}) \ /2$$

where $\phi_{jk} = 1$ if j favors positive outcome or

$\phi_{jk} = -1$ if j favors negative outcome.

Π_k ranges from 0 to 1. If Π_k is greater than .5, there should be a positive outcome for event k.

The Resource Mobilization Model

As we have already pointed out, resources flowing from *A* to *B* can also be viewed from the vantage point of *B*, understood as the resource mobilizer. The mathematical format of resource mobilization is identical to the resource deployment model discussed previously. In substantive terms, the mobilization model deals with a system of actors who mobilize other actors' resources; these resources are assumed to be effective in controlling the outcome of the events that impinge upon the interests of the mobilizers. Diagrammatically,

$$\text{ACTOR } i \xrightarrow[C_{ij}^+]{\text{mobilizes}} \text{ACTOR } j\text{'s} \xrightarrow[R_{jk}]{\text{effect}} \text{EVENT } k \xrightarrow[X_{ki}]{\text{interests of}} \text{ACTOR } i$$
$$\text{RESOURCES}$$

If exchange occurs at equilibrium rates, the control of actor j's resources by actor i is given by the product of i's interest in events and actor j's effectiveness with respect to those events, modified by the ratio of i's power to j's efficacy (power). Thus,

$$C_{ij}^{+} = \frac{\Sigma_k R_{jk} X_{ki} P_i}{P_j}$$

In this model, the observed resource exchange matrix is normalized such that the sum of C_{ij}^{+} over i is equal to 1.0. As in the deployment model, resources flow from j to i, but the subject of interest is i: i mobilizes j's resources to pursue i's own interest.[15]

The difference between the two constraints—namely, $\Sigma_i C_{ij}^{+} = 1.0$ and $\Sigma_j C_{ji}^{*} = 1.0$ is crucial. The constraint of the mobilization model defines C_{ij}^{+} as the fraction of j's resources that were controlled by i at equilibrium. In the mobilization model, is compete with each other to mobilize more of j's resources. Power defined as $C^{+}P$ thus refers to the ability to mobilize resources. In the deployment model, by contrast, C_{ji}^{+} reflects the fraction of i's dependence on various js. From the perspective of RDS, js compete with each other to create more dependence by is, and power refers to the ability to deploy resources.

Because of the quasi-symmetric nature of resource exchange relations, however, the results of both models are quite comparable. For this reason, we report only global summary statistics.

The correlation between the individual power ratings derived from this model with the independently measured influence standing is .23 in energy and .59 in health. Both are significantly lower than the corresponding correlations in the deployment model. This indicates that the domain actors in both domains attribute more influence to those who deploy resources than to those who obtain or mobilize resources from other organizations.[16]

The resource mobilization model also predicted correctly the outcome of all eight energy events. It failed, however, to predict the outcome of three health events—DNA, collective bargaining, and cost containment—suggesting that the event outcome in health is less influenced by the resource mobilizers than the deployers. To put it differently, the incorrect predictions in health indicate that those who mobilized resources to affect the outcome of these events were

15. In contrast, the deployment model treated j as giving resources to i in order to advance j's interest; alternatively stated, j attempts to create dependence by i on j in support of j's interest.

16. In fact, the Coalition of Hispanic Mental Health and Human Service Organizations in health, which received only two influence votes, turned out to be the third most powerful actor according to the resource mobilization model. This is an indication that the definition of power as the ability to mobilize resources is less successful in capturing the influence process among actors in the policy domain.

less successful in reality than in the model, implying that the assumption of this model results in an overestimation of the role of resource mobilizers and their power.

In the following section, we attempt to access the relative importance of the resource deployment strategy (RDS) and the resource mobilization strategy (RMS) for the emergence of interorganizational resource transactions.

Duality of Deployment and Mobilization

We can now use the two models jointly to predict the observed resource exchange relations. We hypothesize a given dyadic transaction between two actors, i and j, that reflects the interest of the deployer (the giver), the interest of the mobilizer (receiver), and the joint interest of the two (the interaction term). That is,

$$C_{ij} = b_1 + b_2 D + b_3 M + b_4 D^*M,$$

where C_{ij} is the observed (unconstrained) resource flow from j to i; $D = E(C^*_{ji})^T$ (i.e., the resource exchange predicted by the deployment model, transposed to match the i,j cell); $M = E(C^+_{ij})$ (i.e., the resource exchange predicted by the mobilization model), and D^*M is the interaction term.[17]

Because of the two constraints, $\Sigma_j C^*_{ji} = 1.0$ and $\Sigma_i C^+_{ij} = 1.0$, the expected values of the two models have nice statistical properties. $E(C^*_{ji})$ refers to the probability that j will deploy resources to i (transposed to match the i,j cell), and $E(C^*_{ij})$ refers to the probability that i will mobilize resources from j. The former may be regarded as the column effect and the latter as the row effect (the last term in the above equation is the interaction of the column and row effect).

The regression coefficients are as follows, with standardized beta's in parentheses:

$$\text{Energy: } C = -.08 + \underset{(.05)}{7.6} D + \underset{(.08)}{13.1} M + \underset{(.41)}{4564} D * M \qquad \text{(Eq. 13.1)}$$

$$\text{Health: } C = -.12 + \underset{(.27)}{18.8} D + \underset{(.25)}{16.4} M + \underset{(.30)}{1031} D * M \qquad \text{(Eq. 13.2)}$$

All coefficients are significant at $p < .001$.

Twenty-six percent of the variance in the resource exchange network is explained by the regression estimation in energy; 43 percent in health. One intriguing finding is that the joint interest of the exchange partners is the main

---

17. There are $n * (n-1)$ cases for this regression equation, one for each i,j cell of C matrix, except for the diagonal cells.

factor in generating dyadic resource flows. That is, when the interest of the deployer, *j*, wanting to deploy resources to an effective agent, *i*, is matched by the interest of the mobilizer, *i*, wanting to mobilize resources from the deployer, *j*, the resource flow from *j* to *i* is very likely to occur. We believe that this finding has significant implications for the micro-foundation of the macro-structure—that is, the interorganizational field.

Notice the different contributions of each model in predicting the dyadic resource flow. In energy, the mobilization model explains slightly more variance than the deployment model, whereas the reverse is true in health.[18] This finding, however, has only limited relevance, because resource transactions among different types of organizations may involve different strategies. For instance, one may hypothesize that the resource flows from the private to the public sector reflect the resource deployment strategy of the private organizations rather than the mobilization strategy of the government organizations. To test this hypothesis, we partitioned the *C* matrix and selected the pattern of resource flows from business to government organizations in energy and from professional associations to government organizations in health. The regression coefficients are as follows for each domain.

$$\text{Energy: } C = -.02 + \underset{(.12)}{12.7} \; D^* - \underset{(-.03)}{4.3} \; M + \underset{(.40)}{4137} \; D*M^*$$

(Eq. 13.3)

$$N = 1,122$$

$$\text{Health: } C = -.19 + \underset{(.38)}{27.1} \; D^* + \underset{(.30)}{19.8} \; M^* + \underset{(.26)}{977} \; D*M^*$$

(Eq. 13.4)

$$N = 480$$

($^*p < .001$.)

In energy, 22 percent of the variance is explained; in health, 57 percent. Given the limited number of variables used in the mathematical models and the complexity of strategic behaviors in the real world transactions studied, we consider these results, especially that in health, a good indication of the validity of these models. The lower R^2 in energy may be more evidence for our argument that the social structure in the energy domain is fluid. As expected, the interaction term (i.e., the matched interest) is the most significant factor accounting for most of the variance of resource flows from business organizations (or professional associations in health) to government organizations in both domains. A major finding of this analysis is that the resource deployment strategy within the private sector is more important than the re-

18. When each model is entered alone in the regression equation, R^2 explained by the mobilization model in energy is 12 percent, and the variance explained by the deployment model is 10 percent. In health, the figures are 20 percent and 24 percent, respectively.

source mobilization strategy within the public sector in explaining the resource flow from the private to the public sector. In energy, once one controlled for both the deployment strategy of business organizations and the joint interests of business and government organizations, the mobilization strategy of the government organizations turned out to be an insignificant variable in explaining resource flow. That is, in energy, resources are transferred from business to government organizations not because of the interest of the latter in mobilizing resources from the former, but because of the interest of the former in deploying resources to the latter. In health, however, resource mobilization by government organizations in pursuit of their own interests was also significant in explaining the dyadic resource flows from the private to the public sector.

Concluding Remarks

In this chapter we extended the Tillian polity model of resource mobilization by conceptualizing the polity as an arena in which the consequential actors act collectively in order to influence the outcomes of multiple events (as opposed to single events) through a complex interorganizational field of resource transactions. After pointing out limitations of the resource dependence perspective, which focuses attention on how organizations acquire needed resources in order to achieve their goals, we elaborated the resource deployment perspective, which suggests that organizations strategically allocate valuable resources to other organizations to facilitate collective action. We then developed mathematical models of resource exchange, initially proposed by Coleman (1973, 1977), and applied them to eight controversial events in each domain. The external checks of the models provide impressive support for their validity. For instance, the models predict the outcomes of the controversial events quite accurately. They also provide valuable insights into the nature of influence processes and the interorganizational resource transactions in national policy domains. Most important in this connection, we discover that dyadic resource flows occur when the interest of the resource deployer and the interest of the resource mobilizer are congruent.

Appendix to Chapter 13

Resource Mobilization Model

Coleman's basic exchange model specifies that actors exchange control over events when actors control some events in which they are not interested (but others are) and lack control over some events in which they are interested. Diagrammatically:

$$\text{ACTOR}_i \xrightarrow[C]{\text{control}} \text{EVENT}_k \xrightarrow[X]{\text{interest}} \text{ACTOR}_j$$

He defines the following matrices:

- C is a matrix of the actors' control over events.
- C^* is a matrix of the actors' control at equilibrium.
- X is a matrix of the events' interests for actors.
- P is a vector of the actors' relative power.
- V is a vector of the events' relative value.

Then $P = CV$ and $V = XP$. Thus, $P = CXP$ and $V = XCV$. Verbally, the power of an actor is his proportion of constitutional control of events, with each event weighted by its equilibrium price or value. The value of an event is the powerful actors' interests in it.

Each actor maximizes the product of his interests in events and his final control over them (i.e., actor i maximizes $\Sigma_k C^*_{ik} X_{ki}$). In the process of exchange, i should buy control over that event for which the ratio of his interests to the event's value (X_{ki}/V_k) is at a maximum.

Coleman assumes that each actor allocates his power over event k in proportion to the ratio X_{ki}/V_k, rather than only for that event for which X_{ki}/V_k is at a maximum. Thus, his final control over event k is

$$C^*_{ik} = \left(\frac{X_{ki}}{V_k}\right)(\Sigma_1 C_{i1} V_1) = \frac{X_{ki} P_i}{V_k} \qquad \text{(Eq. 13.5)}$$

The equilibrium prices or values of events can be derived when the demand for the events equals the supply of the events. The total supply of control over the event S consists of the value of all control that exists in the system for that event:

$$(S_k = \Sigma_i C_{ik} V_k) = V_k \qquad \text{(Eq. 13.6)}$$

The total demand in the system for event k is given by the summation of each individual demand:

$$D_k = \Sigma_i X_{ki} \Sigma_1 C_{i1} V_1 \qquad \text{(Eq. 13.7)}$$

At equilibrium,

$$\frac{dV_k}{dt} = K\,(S_k - D_k) = 0 \qquad\qquad \text{(Eq. 13.8)}$$

Thus,

$$V_k = \Sigma_i\, X_{ki}\, \Sigma_1\, C_{i1}\, V_1 = \Sigma_i\, X_{ki}\, P_i \qquad\qquad \text{(Eq. 13.9)}$$

Coleman assumes that (dependent) relations among actors arise because those who control events are different from those who are interested in those events. Mathematically, $Z = CX$—the product of the two pregiven matrices of control and interest. In our extension of this model, we relax this assumption of fixed dependent relations and conceptualize resource exchange as a process that moves toward an equilibrium. That is, whereas Coleman's basic model identified the equilibrium condition of actors' control over events after the exchange of control over events, we specify the equilibrium condition of resource exchanges.

Our extended model introduces an additional matrix and an additional vector. Since the mobilization model is the more direct extension of Coleman's basic model, we present the mathematics of the mobilization model first:

- $P = CE$—The power of organization j is its control of efficacious resources owned by j.
- $E = RV$—The efficacy of resources owned by j is its effectiveness for controlling valuable events.
- $V = XP$—The value of an event is its interest for powerful actors.

The model specifies a system of actors who are trying to control resources that belong to other actors and that are effective in controlling the outcomes of the events that have an impact on the first set of actors' own interests. Diagrammatically,

$$\text{ACTOR } i \xrightarrow[C_{ij}^+]{\text{control}} \text{ACTOR } j\text{'s} \xrightarrow[R_{jk}]{\text{effective}} \text{EVENT } k \xrightarrow[X_{ki}]{\text{interests}} \text{ACTOR } i$$
$$\text{RESOURCES}$$

This model of a linear system of action requires the following assumptions and variables:

1. X_{ki} and the assumption of fixed "cardinal preferences" on the outcomes of particular policies (k). This assumption implies the following: A's interest in event 1 is, say, 1.7 times his interest in event 2, and this preference is assumed not to change throughout the exchange process.
   Definition: proportion of organization i's interest in event k.
   Constraint: $\Sigma_k\, X_{ki} = 1.0$.

2. R_{jk} and the assumption of perfect information. Each interested actor has its own set of resources that have a differential degree of effectiveness in determining the outcome of a given policy. It is assumed that the effectiveness of each actor's resources is fixed and known to every other actor without any information distortion.

Definition: proportion of effectiveness of organization j's resources in determining the outcome of event k.

Constraint: $\Sigma_j R_{jk} = 1.0$.

3. C_{ij}^+ and a behavioral postulate that each organization will exchange resources so as to best satisfy its interests, given its resources and interests and the assumption of a perfect market of free exchange and perfect rationality of organizations. To achieve the outcomes they prefer, organizations mobilize resources by developing a relation of resource exchanges to mutual benefits. It is also assumed that no structural barrier hinders, and no structural conduciveness facilitates, the exchange process.

Definition: the fraction of j's resources controlled by i.

Constraint: $\Sigma_i C_{ij}^+ = 1.0$.

This set of definitions entails the following set of equations:

$$P = CRXP; \qquad E = RXCE; \qquad V = XCRV$$

The equilibrium equation can be derived from Equation (13.5) by multiplying $\Sigma_k R_{jk}$ in both the nominator and the denominator:

$$C_{ij}^+ = \frac{\Sigma_k R_{jk} X_{ki} P_i}{\Sigma_k R_{jk} V_k} = \frac{\Sigma_k R_{jk} X_{ki} P_i}{E_j} \qquad \text{(Eq. 13.10)}$$

Since actors' efficacy is not known, we assume that efficacy equals power. If exchange occurs at equilibrium rates, the control of actor j's resources by actor i is given by the product of i's interest in events and actor j's effectiveness for the events, modified by the ratio of i's power to j's efficacy (power). To put it differently, the amount of control of one actor's resources by another depends on the effectiveness of the former's resources for an event (R_{jk}) and the interest of the latter in the event (X_{ki}), adjusted by their relative power.

Resource Deployment Model

The mathematical format of the resource deployment model is the same as that of the resource mobilization model. Diagrammatically:

$$\text{ACTOR } j\text{'s} \xrightarrow[C_{ji}^*]{\text{deploy}} \text{ACTOR } i \xrightarrow[A_{ik}]{\text{effective}} \text{EVENT } k \xrightarrow[X_{kj}]{\text{interests}} \text{ACTOR } j$$

RESOURCES

1. X_{kj}: Proportion of organization j's interest in event k.
   Constraints: $\Sigma_j X_{kj} = 1.0$.
2. A_{ik} and the assumption of perfect information. Each interested actor has a differential degree of effectiveness in determining the outcome of a given policy.
   Definition: proportion of effectiveness of organization i determining the outcome of event k.
   Constraint: $\Sigma_i A_{ik} = 1.0$.
3. To achieve the outcome of the policies in which actors are interested, they deploy resources by developing a relation of resource exchanges to mutual benefits.
   Definition: the fraction of resources deployed to i by j's or the proportion of i's dependency on j's.
   Constraint: $\Sigma_j C_{ji}^* = 1.0$.
4. There is a set of additional definitions.
   - $P = CE$—The power of organization j is its ability to deploy resources to effective agent i (i depends on j for valuable resources).
   - $E = AV$—The efficacy of i is its effectiveness in controlling valuable events.
   - $V = XP$—The value of an event is its interest for powerful actors.

If exchange occurs at equilibrium rates, resource deployment by actor j to actor i is given by the product of j's interest in events and actor i's effectiveness for the events, modified by the ratio of j's power to i's efficacy (power).

$$C_{ji}^* = \frac{\Sigma_k A_{ik} X_{kj} P_j}{P_i} \quad \text{or} \quad C^*P = AXP \qquad \text{(Eq. 13.11)}$$

In our data, C^* and X are given, but A and P are unknown, and thus must be estimated. Since $C^*P = AXP$ at equilibrium, and $P = CAXP$ or $C^{-1}P = AXP$ (assuming C is invertible), thus $C^{-1}P = AXP = C^*P$. If we assume furthermore that $C = I$—initially, actors retain resources for their own control—then $P = C^*P$. The format of this equation is the same as that of what network theorists call a prestige score (Burt, 1980; Coleman, 1972, 1973; Hubbell, 1965).

Once we solve $P = C^*P$ for P, A can be estimated running m regression equations, where m is the number of actors in the system.

$$C_{ji}^* = \frac{\Sigma_k A_{ik} X_{kj} P_j}{P_i} + \varepsilon_{ji} \qquad \text{(Eq. 13.12)}$$

For example, organization i's effectiveness on event k (A_{jk}) is a regression coefficient for the independent variables, N_{kji}, in the following equation, and there are m such regression equations:

$$
\begin{bmatrix} C_{1i}^* \\ C_{2i}^* \\ C_{3i}^* \\ \cdot \\ \cdot \\ \cdot \\ \cdot \\ C_{mi}^* \end{bmatrix} = A_{i1} \begin{bmatrix} n_{11i} \\ N_{12i} \\ N_{13i} \\ N_{14i} \\ \cdot \\ \cdot \\ \cdot \\ N_{1mi} \end{bmatrix} + A_{i2} \begin{bmatrix} N_{21i} \\ N_{22i} \\ N_{23i} \\ N_{24i} \\ \cdot \\ \cdot \\ \cdot \\ N_{2mi} \end{bmatrix} + \ldots A_{ik} \begin{bmatrix} N_{k1i} \\ N_{k2i} \\ N_{k3i} \\ N_{k4i} \\ \cdot \\ \cdot \\ \cdot \\ N_{kmi} \end{bmatrix} + \begin{bmatrix} e \\ e \\ e \\ e \\ \cdot \\ \cdot \\ \cdot \\ e \end{bmatrix}
$$

where

$$
N_{kji} = \frac{X_{kj}P_j}{P_i},
$$

which is the adjusted interest of j in event k by relative power.

Needless to say, this estimation is necessary because we do not have information about the relative effectiveness of agent organizations (matrix A). If we had all the necessary information—A, X, and C—we could derive a vector of power as well as a vector of efficacy for the actors. The vector of E would provide useful information that previous models could not capture. In the deployment model, power is the ability to deploy resources, and E is the objective quality of being an effective agent. In this case, one can compare P and E and examine the correlations across different types of organizations. In the deployment model, for example, government organizations would have higher E and lower P, whereas business organizations have low E and high P, because the latter organizations deploy resources mostly to government organizations. A two-by-two table of high-P/high-E, low P/high E, and so on would convey interesting information about the nature of the policy domain.

14

The Organizational State

A Retrospective Synthesis

Rather than recapitulate the detailed findings of the previous chapters, here we will summarize the central themes and major conclusions concerning the social organization of the two national systems of collective action. These findings then provide a basis on which to construct, albeit in an exploratory fashion, a more explicit argument with respect to the assumptions that underlie the analysis of political processes from the perspective of organizational activity. Applying the techniques and analytic framework developed throughout the preceding chapters to another, more extensive, set of data will enable us to generate an image that approximates the organization of the entire realm of political activity in the contemporary United States, not simply of a few isolated policy arenas. The results of this exercise suggest the great potential of this type of approach to the empirical study of politics, yet ultimately raise troubling questions about the nature of representation in an organizational state.

Throughout our analyses we were impressed by the degree of convergence across the energy and health domains. We began with a presumption that health would be more institutionalized and energy more fluid. And, in fact, our analyses consistently explained more variance—with respect to both organizational behavior and event outcomes—in the data that were gathered for the health domain. But although the differences that emerged lay in the expected direction, the similarities in structures and processes are too striking to ignore. Hence, in this summary we emphasize common relationships across the domains.

The core populations of national policy domains consist of large numbers of private as well as public organizations. About three-quarters of the hundreds of key actors are nongovernmental collectivities. Their presence in large numbers reveals the limitations of policy-making studies that focus exclusively upon the micro-processes of influence within governmental institutions such as Congress and the executive agencies. Despite their lack of formal decision-making authority, many private participants possess sufficient political clout to ensure that their expressed interests will be taken into account by other actors. This mutual recognition creates and sustains the legitimacy of core actors' involvement in domain issues and events. We did not gather data on the thousands of claimant groups that exist outside the inner core, but we believe that the core private and public sector organizations rarely acknowledge these bit-players as meaningful actors within the policy-making process. Their salience is too low and their costs of entry are too high to secure more than episodic and grudging acknowledgment of their existence by the core actors. In explaining most decisions, the peripheral organizations may be ignored, although their omission may carry negative connotations for normative democratic theory.

Within the group of core participants, however, there exists a relatively dense system of interorganizational interaction. Our analyses of patterns of communication among a highly diverse set of organizations revealed a considerable level of connectedness. For routine communication, the ratio of actual ties to potential ties was .30 in both domains; for confidential communication, the ratio decreased to .19 in the energy domain and .17 in health. None of the actors are isolated, and all are mutually reachable within three steps. As was discussed in Chapter 7, these results are comparable to those reported by studies of communication density within far more homogeneous or functionally interdependent sets of organizations than the group interviewed for this project. And, as was explored in Chapters 10 and 12, these networks of communication serve to orchestrate participation with respect to domain events in ways that remain undetected in analyses restricted to the relationships between the attributes of individual organizations and their political activity.[1]

To specify a large and tightly interconnected set of domain core actors is not

---

1. It should be emphasized that there is not necessarily a "fundamental" structure to which all instances of differentiation and stratification within a policy domain may be reduced. A variety of resources and organizational attributes—money, membership, attitudes, ideology, reputation and so forth—may serve as "distance-generating mechanisms." Indeed, "given a plurality of relationship-specific structures predicated on different principles of organization, structural contradictions are possible features of any complex social system" (Laumann and Pappi, 1976:6–9).

to assert that each possesses identical power and influence within the domain. Indeed, there are large variations in size and wealth between organizational types as well as within each of these categories (see table 3.2). Yet we did not discover strong relationships between resources and overall reputation. Although influence rank is predicted to some degree by "hard" resource holdings (such as money, employees, and public authority) and "soft" resources (such as impartial mediation and public mobilization), the vast majority of core actors within these domains possess sufficient resources to render purely quantitative assessments irrelevant for understanding policy behavior. In fact, one of the resources commonly associated with participation in the making of policy in the theoretical literature—the size of staffs available to monitor ongoing domain activities—proved unrelated to participation in policy events.

Despite the relative absence of a direct relationship between participation and individual organizational attributes, within each domain we uncovered a number of highly differentiated social structures that order the core organizations into central and peripheral positions. One of the most unequal hierarchies is influence reputation ranking. The highest-ranking organizations tend to be governmental actors, generalist trade associations and professional societies, and major corporations. At the bottom are found specialist associations, public interest groups, and similar claimant organizations having either narrow or incidental interests in the domain. An organization's reputation is an amalgam of its past successful influence, present strategic location, and future (anticipated) exploits, with a little misperception thrown in. Within the health domain, however, there was a high degree of consensus on these points. In the energy domain, by contrast, there was a marked bifurcation in the perceptions of organizations' relative standing within the policy arena. Consumer and environmental groups tended to see executive agencies as the most authoritative, whereas business organizations attributed greater influence to trade associations as well as to Congress. We found little evidence that the character of political activity varied systematically among different sorts of organizations, thereby producing the patterns of executive and congressional specialization that have been noted in some studies.

In addition to stratification in terms of attributed influence, both energy and health domains are also highly differentiated along lines of policy interest. No organizations, even generalist government actors mandated to scrutinize and coordinate domain affairs, distributed their attention so as to occupy a central location in the issue space. Instead, issue publics are arrayed like beads on a bracelet. Typically, an organization's substantive goals determine the cluster of issues on which it concentrates its time and effort. Thus, coal companies ignore nuclear power, solar energy, and oil import fees. The norm of fighting for one's own interests but not against another's serves to reinforce a narrow vision of proper partisan conduct for most organizations. Even the environmental interest groups—which perceive dangers in many types of fuel usage—are highly selective in their attention to issues, in large measure because of the need to husband their resources. The result is a substantially balkanized domain structure, with a dozen or more subdomains in which most of the core organizations invest their resources. In the absence of a central subset of actors with diversified issue portfolios, the domain structure is better characterized as elite interest group pluralism rather than centralized coordination. [crucial]

When we turn to the structure of confidential communication within policy domains, however, a core/periphery structure is clearly visible. This system of organization simultaneously reflects levels of participation and influence as well as differentiated concerns and policy preferences. Information exchanges in national policy domains are instrumentally structured at both micro (dyadic) and global (whole system) levels. Organizations generate and sustain ties to one another because of substantive similarities in their issue and event interests. Communication partners are instrumental collective actors, either as potential supporters and opponents or as targets of influence efforts.

The major governmental actors—the White House, OMB, cabinet departments, key House and Senate subcommittees—occupy the center of the communication network. As formal authorities, they are targets of numerous information and influence communications. Arrayed around this core subset are the generalist trade associations, professional societies, and major corporations. They seem to mediate communication between the central authorities and the peripheral specialist actors that occupy the remoter subregions of the communication space. These specialists may be recruited by the generalists to form temporary coalitions or action sets (see Knoke and Burleigh, 1988) in pursuit of specific, limited objectives. In the fight over cost containment, hospital trade associations mobilized selected groups of medical professionals, notably the hospital-based pathologists, while the major physicians' societies, though sympathetic, remained on the sidelines. Similarly, in the incident that opened the first chapter, a decision by the FAA unintentionally generated a working alliance among firms that, typically separated by fuel-specific concerns, shared a set of specialized concerns associated with exploration for new reserves. Thus, the highly differentiated communication networks, in conjunction with the issue interests of the actors, define the constraints within which subsequent policy fights are conducted.

Organizational activation on a specific event is a joint function of the event's characteristics (especially visibility, scope, and controversiality) and the organization's own attributes (particularly its interest in the underlying issues and its location in the communication network). At the same time, neither organizations nor events "possess" attributes in some absolute sense, but take on meanings by becoming embedded in a system of organizational action and interaction through the recognition of events and the construction of scenarios. Thus, collective efforts to influence the outcome of public policy events involve both micro-level (actor-based) and global (system-level) social forces. Because of the interpenetrating nature of these processes, we cannot assign causal priority to either dynamic, nor indeed is this necessarily an appropriate goal for all theory construction (see Chapter 1). One way to visualize this dialectic is to imagine a carpet into which a figure is woven in a contrasting color. When attention focuses on the figure, the background threads recede in salience. Yet one need only flip the carpet over to appreciate that the figure is defined by, and inseparable from, the context upon which it is arranged. Likewise, every event-organization configuration is created by the simultaneous intersection of historical opportunity with actor dispositions: trying to explicate one without the other is folly.

When participation in individual events is aggregated for an organization, the level of its activity within the domain is clearly a function of its scope of interest, interorganizational resource exchanges, and influence reputation, but not its location in the communication network or its monitoring capacity (see Chapter 10). Obviously, activation depends upon certain stable structural properties of the organizations embedded in the policy domain, as well as upon idiosyncratic attributes not investigated in our project. However, in collapsing an organization's activity level across all possible events, to some extent we create an analytic artifact. That is, events actually occur in a temporally distributed succession rather than simultaneously. Characterizing each organization only according to the number of events in which it was publicly active violates this historically contingent process of mobilization. Thus, although we now understand some of the individual- and system-level forces related to domain organizations' participation in policy events, much more work remains to be done on how the timing and sequence of events interacts with actors' attributes to mobilize domain activity. A good place to begin might be modeling organizational event histories in a fashion parallel to the sociology of employment.

Explaining the outcome of policy events is the ultimate focus of our research. From our perspective on the emerging organizational state, one must never neglect the fact that many—indeed, most—decision-making events, even one of considerable consequence, are worked on by only a limited number of actors, and by the endstage of the decision-making process, there is little if any controversy about the policy option that will be implemented. Decisions typically pass into the structure of constraints unremarked, but not, therefore, without considerable consequences for future policy. Indeed, as was discussed in Chapter 12, one very important type of event is defined as recurrent and noncontroversial. Participants in these decision processes are usually recruited from a narrow region of the policy domains, and the mode of decision making is expert and technocratic. In fact, only a very limited number of matters are selected for dispute and public controversy, the result of poorly understood processes whereby key actors come to contest the symbolic framing in which "routine" decisions had heretofore been made.

By limiting the number and range of actors recognized as knowledgeable and legitimate participants, these "routine" understandings of the nature of policy events help to stabilize the organization of policy domains. In addition, however, we selected for detailed analysis eight highly controversial events, spanning diverse issue areas, in each domain. Each event attracted unique constellations of openly partisan organizations. The typical cleavage patterns bifurcate the communication structure: one group of actors favoring the outcome of the policy proposal and a second subset of opponents. Most significantly, these opposition groups form idiosyncratic coalitions across substantively different events. Yet, somewhat paradoxically, it is possible to acknowledge widely varying patterns of organizational participation without abandoning the assumption that some sort of relatively stable social structure nevertheless orders much activity. Social order is not limited to the regular association of specific traits with particular behaviors. For the purposes of this research, it is far more appropriate to conceive of order in relational terms; the proper model is a color wheel rather than a categorical system. Without beginning to overcome all the theoretical and technical obstacles that are entailed, Chapters 12 and 13 sketch the agenda suggested by this perspective.

Finally, we developed exchange models, first proposed by Coleman, and applied them to selected controversial issues in each domain. Despite the level of attention directed toward the collective structure of these two policy domains, the fact that organizations are, at least potentially, autonomous and strategic actors should not be forgotten. Two models of organizational interaction were developed to identify what types of strategic action are of greatest consequence. The operative factors in the resource deployment and resource mobilization models are the domain organization's interests in each event and their relative control over the outcomes of these events through resource exchanges. Assuming the achievement of equilibrium after exchanging resources, tests of the models' effectiveness proved highly accurate in predicting both the organization's power over events and the domain's collective outcomes for every event. Business organizations in energy and professional societies in health proved most influential for collective decisions. The resource deployment and mobilization models jointly identified resource exchanges between pairs of organizations. Interestingly, the interaction term accounted for the greatest part of the variance of resource transactions. Beyond this, however, we discovered that the resource deployment strategy within the private sector was more important than the resource mobilization strategy of government organizations in explaining the resource flow from the private to the public sector.

In conclusion, our research on the social organization of the U.S. national energy and health domains indicates the existence of large, exclusive, highly differentiated communities of policy-making organizations. According to narrowly specified issue agendas, they pursue events through the communication of intent, the mobilization of support, and the targeting of influence efforts. Resource exchanges lie at the heart of the influence system and account for the process of collective decision. Overall, policies are the product of decentralized contention among a plurality of organizations seeking to satisfy their interests by influencing public authorities.

Central Assumptions of an Empirical Model of the Organizational State

Our investigation both reinforces and challenges conventional images of the policy-making process. We find some truth in each of the major approaches to analyzing state behavior: pluralist, managerial, and class (Alford and Friedland, 1985). But none of these perspectives provides a distinctly superior account of the collective decisions with respect to dozens of discrete events involving hundreds of organizational actors. In this section, we discuss the assumptions underlying our conceptualization of the organizational state.

1. *The state is increasingly an organizational state.* In recent years investigations of the state have become a cottage industry within historical-comparative and political sociology. Frequently, analysts begin with a definition of the state as possessing an administrative monopoly over the legitimate means of violence within some defined territory (Weber, 1979:54), but part company over its form, origins, and development. We conceive of the state in advanced industrial capitalist democracies as a long-term product of the steady expansion of sovereignty through increasingly broader jurisdictions and more autonomous complex organizations.

The conditions favoring state formation and nation building are complex and warrant continuing research: population growth and urbanization, technological innovation, legal-cultural institutionalization, military competition in the world system (Chirot, 1985; Hechter and Brustein, 1980; Thomas and Meyer, 1984; Tilly, 1975). In Parsons' (1966) evolutionary paradigm, the increasingly elaborated societal division of labor naturally led to the emergence of a specialized polity charged with performing goal-attainment and coordination functions for the entire society. The spread of rationality norms through both economy and polity abetted the penetration of the bureaucratic arms of the state into arenas previously considered private (Meyer and Rowan, 1977; Scott, 1981; Thompson, 1967; Weber, 1979; J. Wilson, 1975; 1977). Successive revolutions in citizenship increased individual rights in the political, social, and economic domains at the same time that they subjected citizens to expanded state regulation (Bendix, 1964; Wilensky, 1975).

Since the late 19th century, individual persons have been eclipsed as significant social actors by the rise of a social invention, the corporation (Burt,
1975; Coleman, 1974, 1982; Mizruchi, 1982, 1984). These "new persons"
permitted quantities of human and material resources to be assembled and
coordinated on a scale heretofore unimaginable. Changes in the legal codes
and customs legitimated vast centralization and concentrations of wealth and
power. As has been argued throughout this book, the economic and political
behavior of the modern rational-bureaucratic state is better explained by an
organizational perspective that takes account of the constraints confronting
these giant enterprises than by an approach that focuses on individual agents
and their social psychologies.

As giant manufacturing and finance companies came to dominate the economy, they sought to tame unpredictable market contingencies through state
interventions (McNeil, 1978). In a *pas de deux* of countervailing powers,
business and state bureaucracies fed one another's hunger for domination,
while steadily squeezing out any effective form of democratic control that was
not channeled through formal organizations. Whether viewed as class domination and control or as a managerial imperative, these structural transformations left large-scale organizations as the only effective participants in the
fundamental political decisions of mature capitalist societies. Unorganized
groups were reduced to impotent raging at the barred gates to the polity (Gamson, 1975; Tilly, 1978).

2. *The boundaries between public and private sectors are blurred, and irrelevant, even in noncorporatist societies.* Contrary to Weber and other "real-
ists," we do not believe that the state is subject to "relatively clear-cut empirical identification and delineation" (Nordlinger, 1981). The state is not a
unitary actor, but a complex entity spanning multiple policy domains, comprising both government organizations and those core private sector participants whose interests must be taken into account. Both neo-Marxist and liberal theorists converge on this point. Miliband (1969:49–53) specified a set
of institutions that are largely governmental (e.g., executive, civil bureaucracy, military and police), but Wright (1978:210, n. 5) wrote more broadly
of "a complex network of institutions, organizations, and social relationships." Kingdon characterized participants without formal governmental
positions as "outside of government, but not just looking in," arguing that
"the line between inside and outside of government is exceedingly difficult to
draw" (1984:48; see also McConnell, 1966:125, for similar comparisons of
state and private association governance). Intimate consulting and lobbying
relationships, frequent employment interchanges, and open communication
channels between government and interest groups create the inseparably intertwined institutions that constitute the modern state (Berry, 1984; Laumann
and Heinz, 1985; Salisbury, 1984; Schlozman and Tierney, 1985). The so-
called cozy or iron triangles of federal agencies, congressional committees,

and clientele groups so prevalent in pork-barrel politics are another manifestation of the vague boundary between public and private sectors (Heclo, 1978; McConnell, 1966: 217; Ripley and Franklin, 1980).

Governmental actors are distinguishable from private groups by their possession of formal legal authority to make binding decisions for the society as a whole in explicitly circumscribed fields of activity. Outside this limited area, they are as likely to depend on resource deployment strategies, as many private actors. But the fact that most of these decisions reflect substantial influences by interest groups diminishes the significance of this formal distinction among state participants. Although the United States allegedly lags far behind many European nations in delegating public authority to nongovernmental groups (Schmitter, 1979; Wilson, 1982), efforts by Presidents Carter and Reagan to deregulate industries and professions testify to a long-standing fusion of government and private concerns. The historical oscillation between market forces and government centralization, noted by critics such as McConnell (1966:366–52) and Lowi (1969:125–46), makes sense only when we view the state as a complex system of government and nongovernmental organizations that struggle for power and legitimacy in the making of public policies affecting domain participants.

3. *For many events, government organizations are not neutral umpires, but seek to promote their own agendas.* Pluralists such as Dahl (1963) portray the executive and legislature as even-handed judges among disputing interest group claimants. Even Lowi, himself no pluralist, wrote that "the role of government is one of ensuring access, particularly to the most effectively organized, and of ratifying the agreements and adjustments worked out among the competing leaders and their claims" (1969:71). This neutrality fantasy is difficult to maintain in the face of numerous instances in which government agencies intervene actively on behalf of one side or another (Allison, 1971; Kingdon, 1984:23–47; Ornstein and Elder, 1978:117–220). Just as interest groups lobby the authorities in favor of their preferred positions, so governmental agents lobby the interest groups on behalf of policy stances sponsored by the government organizations.

Government organizations may even be divided among themselves over intentions and strategies, particularly in a federated system whose division of powers more readily allows the differing legislative, executive, and bureaucratic branches to be captured by representatives of opposing political and ideological tendencies (Bernstein, 1955). In recent American history, presidential administrations frequently differed from the partisan composition of Congress, while the permanent federal bureaucracy seemingly pursued its own agendas of jurisdictional expansion and consolidation, oblivious to the short-term electoral winds blowing in and out of Washington (Sundquist, 1968).

4. *Policy preferences of organizations reflect mainly nonideological orga-nizational imperatives.* Our analysis is concerned with explaining neither in-ternal organization structures nor organizations' decision-making processes (see Knoke, 1987, on acquisition and allocation of resources in associations). However, in examining collective actions within systems of organizations operating in a policy domain, we make certain assumptions about the micro-level social forces that orient participating organizations toward policy events. In our view the strategic choice model (Astley and Van de Ven, 1983; Child, 1972) offers the best account of the behavior of the large organizations that dominate national policy domains. In this perspective, organization managers are autonomous, proactive agents who continuously construct, enact, and change their organizations' strategies according to their subjective meanings and interpretations imputed to other policy domain participants. As strategic actors, managers adhere to norms of administrative rationality: "As long as we assume that organizations have goals and that those goals have some clas-sical properties of stability, precision, and consistency, we can treat an organi-zation as some kind of rational actor" (March, 1981:215). Rational choice consists of a clearly defined set of alternatives from which one selection can be made that maximizes (or "satisfices"; see Simon, 1976) an organization's benefits net of its costs.

Faced with an often overwhelming diversity of policy events (frequently spanning many domains), organization managers and especially government affairs specialists must decide whether and how to intervene on narrow and pragmatic grounds. Corporate or union security, survival, growth, and adap-tation take precedence over rigid ideological concerns, whether expressed as "free enterprise" or "worker solidarity." Where economic objectives are par-ticularly salient, as in the case of profit-making corporations and trade as-sociations, managers are more likely to focus upon short-term gains and im-mediate firm or industry priorities than upon the general advantage of a "capitalist class."

Even the existence of a potentially class-conscious coordinating action set (Domhoff, 1978; Useem, 1983) does not guarantee that classwide concerns will dominate concrete policy events. When large economic stakes are present, rational managers are more likely to pursue policy outcomes that offer maxi-mum potential payoffs for firm-level goals—such as market share growth, im-port protection, government deregulation, and labor control—than to assert principled stands that, theoretically, would strengthen the capitalist system. Likewise, managers of non-profit-oriented organizations may deviate from ostensibly transorganization ideologies—religious, environmentalist, status group—when confronted by policy events whose ideological implications are unclear or inconsistent with imperatives for organizational survival and pros-perity. A classic example of this dilemma occurred in the Clean Air Act amendment fights of the 1970s (Ornstein and Elder, 1978:155–85). The automotive workers' union allied with its traditional class foes, the auto companies, in efforts to weaken or delay imposition of tougher emission standards. At the same time, a large number of retail merchants supported the bill out of concern that they might be forced to pay the clean-up costs and curb local urban development.

Few events have an unambiguous connection to broad questions of ownership and authority in the relations of production. By lengthy and tenuous chains of reasoning, an omniscient directorate of class theoreticians might be able to detect some fundamental class interest at stake in funding for biomedical research or solar energy tax credits for homeowners. But most domain organizations, even those where class consciousness is exceptionally developed, will be unable to articulate consistent, principled class-based positions across every domain event. Instead, participants largely perceive only the narrow market relations that affect their immediate interests at the economic level (Wright, 1978:90). Even issues in which class conflict is presumably greatest—such as market regulation, plant investment policy, and labor power control—are typically debated by narrow subsets of domain participants rather than by classwide coalitions that pull most of the domain population into the struggle.

When one economic sector's viability is threatened by political events (e.g., proposals to discontinue subsidies for nuclear power plant insurance or demands that strip mines be restored), other capitalist enterprises usually see no connection to their own situation and therefore do not express solidarity with their brother corporations. Indeed, one industry's or enterprises' profits are often another's costs. Hence, events can generate oppositional cleavages among organizations that, theoretically, share fundamental interests. Funding for the development of synthetic fuels pitted the coal and oil industries against one another (at least until the latter engulfed the former through mergers). Policy efforts intended to control the inflation of health care costs have caused the incrementally defined, pragmatic interests of Blue Cross and Blue Shield to diverge from the expressed preferences of the professional and hospital associations responsible for their creation. In addition, many events attract only specialized audiences whose immediate market stakes are jeopardized (e.g., uranium ore enrichment; nuclear fusion research), and consequently remain invisible to most of the domain. As a consequence, we expect to observe little or no manifest expression of class struggle in most domain policy events. Even if most organizations were highly class-conscious actors, they would be unable to determine their positions on events according to fundamental class interests. In other words, fundamental class principles have limited usefulness for explaining observed variations in organizational participation across a variety of events.

5. *Major structural changes in both substantive and procedural matters*

(rules of the game) are generally off the agenda. The dominant belief systems in capitalist democracies tend to deflect challenges to a set of core values, including private ownership of capital, privatization of the surplus, and managerial prerogatives in the workplace. Threats of expropriation rarely affect the course of policy making. But if such fundamental issues are successfully injected into public debate, they have a tremendous potential to transform the polity and society.

During the period covered by this study, U.S. politics did experience one fairly close brush with a radical challenge to these basic premises. As gasoline and fuel oil prices began to escalate after the Arab oil embargo, consumers grew increasingly angry and distrustful of the major oil companies. Public opinion polls uncovered substantial disbelief that the fuel shortages were genuine, and a sizable minority favored a government takeover of oil and other natural resources. In 1975 a handful of liberal senators, led by Phillip Hart (D-Mich.) and James Abourezk (D-S.D.), sponsored a bill that would divest the vertical holdings of the 22 largest oil firms. These corporations controlled the full range of petroleum industry components—from production, transportation, and refining through wholesale and retail marketing—to such an extent that reliable data on production costs, pricing policies, and reserve supplies were simply unavailable to public policy-makers (Wildavsky and Tenenbaum, 1981). Although stopping short of outright nationalization, the liberal senators wanted to radically restructure domestic competition within the petroleum industry. In the smug belief in their own strength, the corporations did little to oppose the divestiture effort. On October 8, 1975, the divestiture amendment was defeated in the Senate by 54 to 45, and another attempt was beaten back two weeks later by 49 to 40. To the oil industry, "the near miss was totally unexpected, like a lightning bolt from the blue" (Sherrill, 1983:273).

The next year a staff report for the Petroleum Industry Competition Act of 1976 concluded in populist tones:

> If it is true that we must have these gigantic corporations to raise capital for new energy, to plan our economic future, that "regulatory" arrangements between unaccountable corporation oligarchs and bureaucrats are preferable to free markets, that our own corporations must wield monopoly power to compete with monopolies sponsored by other nations, then we should give free enterprise a respectful burial and not disgrace an honorable—if much abused—concept by using it to camouflage a system of corporation socialism. . . . Granted, divestiture provides no complete solution to the problem. It offers only a reasonable chance for somewhat lower prices, but it's a measure we owe the world to take. (Sherrill, 1983)

The Democratic party added a plank to its platform supporting vertical divestiture, while its presidential nominee, Jimmy Carter, gave verbal support to horizontal divestiture (preventing companies from owning competing fuel sources). Panicked, the major oil producers launched an all-out counterattack, coordinated by an American Petroleum Institute task force, that featured employee and stockholder mobilization, newspaper and television ad campaigns, and even a three-act musical comedy (sponsored by the Exxon Oil Company) on the virtues of the free enterprise system. Although the prodivestiture forces pushed their bill out of the Senate Judiciary Committee in June 1976, it was later removed from the calendar and never reappeared, the apparent victim of election-year jitters (Sherrill, 1983:317–18). A shaken oil industry accepted a compromise continuation of domestic price controls, albeit with generous ceilings. In this instance, an international crisis provoked an attack on the basic organization of private industry, but not a successful attack. As was evident in the energy policy domain throughout the 1970s, even the best-laid plans for reorganization could founder when confronted with the inertia of the policy network.

6. *Event cleavages reflect the idiosyncratic nature of organizations' interests.* In the absence of an overarching class cleavage—or any other systematic structuring principle—shaping political participation, organizations are free to pursue whatever policy positions they believe will promote their well-being. Organizations with identical goals may draw different conclusions about the stakes in events; organizations holding divergent objectives may find grounds for cooperation. Activity with respect to one event need not constrain organizations' choices in subsequent ones. The result is a low level of consistency between events, in both participation and position taking. Knowing an organization's activity in one event will not predict its participation or position in others, especially as the temporal and substantive content becomes attenuated. Organizations may drop into and out of involvement or switch positions when long- or short-term disadvantages become apparent. At the system level, the bifurcation into opposing collective actors in the case of one event maps poorly onto other events unless they are very closely related (see Chapter 12). The continual movement of organizations into and out of debates, with accompanying shifts in position, creates a fragmented, loosely knit structure rather than two strongly polarized camps.

Events shade and blend into one another, unfolding in indeterminate sequences that allow domain participants to react idiosyncratically to each event. Although organizations learn from their own and others' experiences, and apply these insights to subsequent fights, the lessons that each one draws are likely to differ. An iterative gaming strategy develops, in which organizations continually shuffle from coalition to coalition in opportunistic pursuit of advantage. The scramble to protect and enhance each increment of corporate well-being results in a fluid domain structure that defies an analyst's ability to detect a single underlying structuration principle.

7. *Most collective decisions involve shifting interorganizational coalitions*

and influence interactions. Typical policy domain events attract the active participation of only small numbers of organizations. For the bulk of domain actors, the stakes in any given event are either too small or too ambiguous to warrant participation. Organizational resources are finite, even for the largest corporations, and the system's persistence over indefinite time means that the political game will never be finished. Every organization must limit its involvement, husband its resources, and play for limited gains.

Cooperation among organizations that share a common preference for an event outcome raises the probability that their efforts will produce a favorable decision. Coalitions of organizations pool resources and coordinate their common efforts to overcome their opponents and persuade the public authorities of the merits of their case. Such processes of contention among opposing interest group coalitions, including partisan government organizations, are the key dynamic for any understanding of collective decision making in national policy domains.

The Structure of National Policy Domains

To this point, we have summarized the main assumptions underlying our analysis of the rapidly emerging organizational state in the United States. These propositions stress the critical role played by private and public organizational actors in formulating, selecting, and implementing policies across the various policy domains that make up the modern state. The book has focused on two such policy domains as illustrative vehicles for its argument, but these two are of broad consequence; together, they account for roughly 20 percent of the country's gross national product. Our general conception of the organizational state, however, requires that we say something about how these focal domains are embedded in the more inclusive set of policy domains. Moreover, we should say something more generally about how the domains within this encompassing set are themselves interrelated. Thus, we would like (1) to propose systematic first approximations of the relative proximities of all the major national policy domains to each of the two focal domains, energy and health, and to one another more generally as functions of the varying degrees of overlap of their respective decision-making apparatuses, and (2) to draw out some implications of these structures for a theory of state functioning. We admit that this is a speculative exercise that awaits empirical refinement and testing as more appropriate and persuasive data are brought to bear.

First, let us imagine that two policy domains, health and domestic economy, intersect one another, as depicted in figure 14.1. Each domain consists of a population of consequential actors, as defined by the procedures described in Chapter 3, pursuing a set of variably linked issue topics (and related decision-

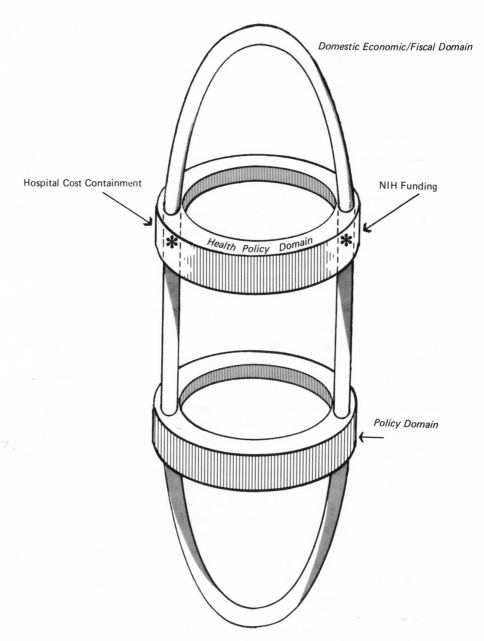

Figure 14.1. A Hypothetical Representation of the Intersection of the Health Policy Domain with the Domestic Economy/Fiscal Domain

388

making events) that organize the substantive content of domain participation, as described in Chapter 4's discussion of issue publics. Let us suppose further that the two domains intersect at those points where the costs to be incurred for health programs impinge on the federal budget, with attendant implications for the domestic economy more generally. In the 1977 debate over mandatory cost caps for hospital charges, for example, participants were recruited from both domains. Those active in the domestic economy domain were inclined to frame the issue of hospital cost containment in terms of its implications for budget deficits and the allocation of scarce funds among competing alternative uses. Actors from the health domain saw the issue from the vantage point of its impact on delivering quality health care and maintaining the economic viability of key capital resources in the health care delivery system. For these actors, alternative uses of scarce funds for nonhealth purposes were largely irrelevant. In short, arguments in the health domain were framed in substantive terms relevant to maintaining or improving national health objectives and the autonomy of key private actors in that domain, whereas arguments in the domestic economic domain were framed in the language of alternative uses for scarce resources and management of the entire economy and the federal budget. The debate over the framing of the problem was intense and consequential because the outcome would effectively determine whether mandatory or voluntary strategies for controlling costs would be seen as more attractive and practical by relevant decision-makers (e.g., those members of Congress most active in the health domain who had to assent to a particular policy option). Thus, the extent of common participation across any given set of domains should suggest the frequency with which various ways of framing issues and identifying alternatives come into conflict with one another. The symbolic framing that ultimately prevails has important consequences for shaping the terms in which debate finally takes place in Congress.

As first approximations of the relative proximities of a wider range of policy domains, we are fortunate to have in hand a study of Washington representation (Laumann and Heinz, 1985; Laumann et al., 1986; Nelson et al., 1987). Data were collected in 1983 according to procedures similar to those we used in 1981. Following a sequential sampling design, this study identified client organizations (our nongovernmental corporate actors), the representatives they employed or retained to represent these organizational interests before the three branches of the federal government, and government officials involved in policy deliberations in four domains (agriculture, energy, health, and labor). The representatives were asked to identify up to five government officials with whom they had most frequent contacts in pursuing their representational activities in a particular policy domain. Approximately 75 governmental officials were interviewed in each domain. These officials ($N = 301$)

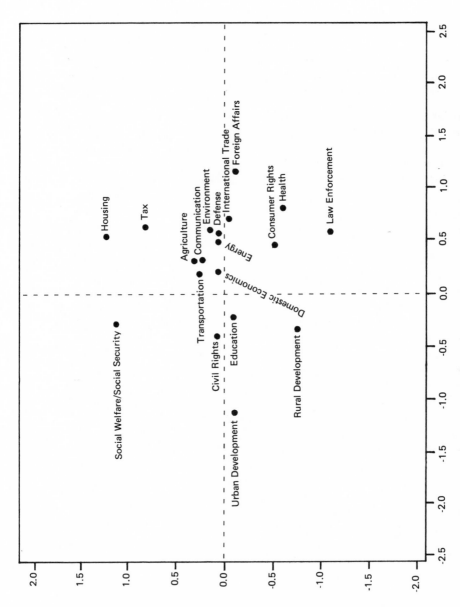

Figure 14.2. Two-Dimensional Smallest-Space Representation of the Relative Proximities of Other National Policy Domains to the Energy Policy Domain

included senators, House members, senior congressional committee staffers, officials in the Government Accounting Office (the congressional oversight agency), and a multitude of senior executive service personnel and political appointments from nearly 60 governmental units in the executive branch, ranging from OMB and the Council of Economic Advisors to the Centers for Disease Control and the Veterans Administration (Nelson et al., 1987). This sample of government officials provides the data we use in analyzing policy domain proximities.

Each official was presented with a list of 20 policy domains and asked to indicate roughly the percentage of time he or she devoted to each over the past year. Although we obtained more refined estimates, we shall dichotomize the responses between those who spent none or less than 5 percent of their time in a policy domain and those who spent more than 5 percent of their time in it.[2] Given the limitations of the data for the purpose in hand, we decided to use a simple overlap measure of proximity between two domains—that is, the raw count of the respondents who devoted at least 5 percent of their time to policy making in *both* domains. Using the multidimensional scaling techniques we discussed before (ALSCAL; see Schiffman et al., 1981), we constructed graphic representations of the energy and health domain proximities to the other policy domains (see figures 14.2 and 14.3), based on the subsamples of government officials nominated by the representatives active in each domain.

In the case of energy, figure 14.2 presents an intuitively appealing portrayal of the tight interrelationships of energy policy with domestic economy, defense, international trade, environment, and transportation.[3] Our discussions in Chapter 2 and elsewhere described the profound concerns engendered by the 1973 oil embargo for our entire military position, the growing environmental concerns aroused by increased dependence on domestic coal and nuclear fuel, and the controversies over cross-country transport of fuels, particularly coal slurry and nuclear wastes. Labor, civil rights, or welfare policies more generally are seen to be distant and essentially unrelated to the critical issues agitating the energy domain—at least in the sense that officials selected for these activities in the energy domain were relatively inactive in those other domains.

In contrast, figure 14.3 depicts the preoccupations of decision-makers in the health domain as rather more loosely coupled with most other policy do-

2. Respondents could add to the list of policy domains if they found none that adequately described their policy activities. Although a handful of topics were mentioned, all could be readily accommodated in our list. We thus have good reason to believe that the list is fairly comprehensive and complete.

3. The two-dimensional solution has a Kruskal stress of .09 and an R^2 of .985, both indications of an excellent fit to the original data matrix.

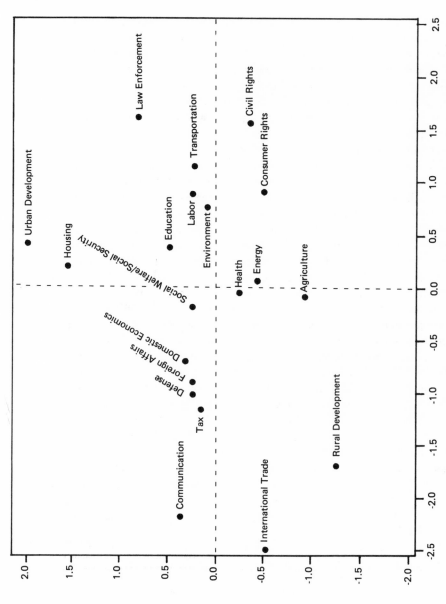

Figure 14.3. Two-Dimensional Smallest-Space Representation of the Relative Proximities of Other National Policy Domains to the Health Policy Domain

mains—that is, at least insofar as such linkages to other policy domains are reflected by government decision-makers' being called to do work in those other domains as well.[4] One can divide the space into roughly two parts: the upper righthand side includes policy domains broadly concerned with social welfare, education, and private citizenship; the lower lefthand side includes policy domains concerned with the functioning of the economy, both domestic and international. As the consumer of some 10 percent of the gross national product, the health domain clearly has very substantial implications for domestic economic policy, tax policy, and even defense (since it is the main rival for scarce government and private economic resources). Note, however, that these implications operate at a distance in that health policy-makers tend to be more specialized in (or restricted to) health policy matters and are thus relatively inactive as general players across policy domains.[5] Thus, participants who are active in both defense and health policy establishments are quite rare. Each of these domains tends to be dominated by its own specialists. Their rival claims on the budget are integrated by actors involved in cross-cutting policy domains such as domestic economy and taxation.

Much more speculative and problematic is our portrayal in figure 14.4 of the proximities of the policy domains, based on the combined sample of government officials from the four domains.[6] A more defensible picture could be derived using officials independently drawn from all 20 policy domains, although even then we would have no way of assessing the relative weight to assign various domains, which obviously differ greatly in their significance, popular attention, and volume of activity. For example, there would seem to be little justification for treating the defense policy domain, which lays claim to a quarter of the federal budget, as being equivalent to housing with its 2 percent of the budget. Yet even budget share is not a sure indicator of relative importance, since comparatively inexpensive policies may still be of critical significance to the citizens' overall sense of justice and satisfaction and to the quality of life that the government is held responsible for providing.

4. Somewhat surprisingly, the two-dimensional solution for health vis-à-vis the other domains is somewhat poorer than that obtained for energy (Kruskal stress $= .16$ and $R^2 = .889$). Both measures of fit indicate an acceptable solution. The relatively poorer fit may be due to the fact that government officials concerned with health policy spend considerably more time on it than they do in other policy domains and, consequently, their links with other domains are more fluid and idiosyncratic.

5. In fact, Nelson et al. (1987: table 6) report that representatives in the health domain tend to devote a substantially larger proportion of their time to working on health policy than those in the other three domains devote to their primary domain.

6. The two-dimensional solution yields rather poor measures of goodness of fit (Kruskal stress $= .27$, $R^2 = .698$), suggesting that a higher-dimensional solution is required. Such a result is hardly surprising given the highly disparate character of the policy domains. Inspection of higher-order solutions does not suggest that the two-dimensional solution misrepresents the fundamental discontinuities in the clustering of the policy domains into relatively disjoint regions.

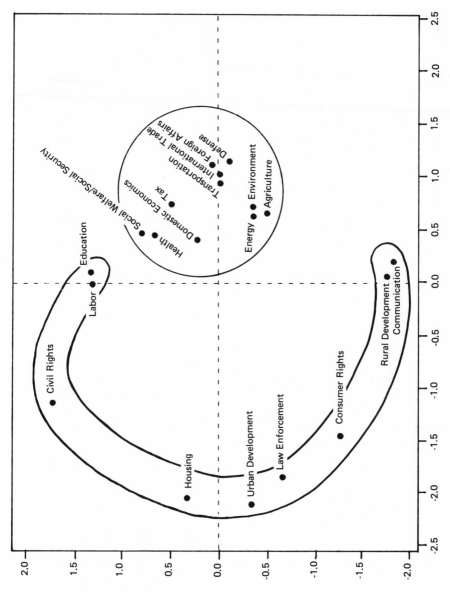

Figure 14.4. Two-Dimensional Smallest-Space Representation of the Relative Proximities of the 20 National Policy Domains of the United States

Despite these caveats and limitations, we find this figure an unusually provocative way of thinking about the differentiation of the polity as a whole.
The organization of the policy domains divides itself into two distinct parts:
(1) a tightly clustered set of policy domains associated with major *organizational actors'* interrelated concerns with the economy and national defense,
both prominent consumers of tax dollars and government effort, and (2) an arc
of policy domains dispersed along a continuum from *personal* or individual
rights of citizenship, work, and learning through various person- or family-
centered rights of economic well-being and civic and domestic security. In
other words, the latter set of domains—dispersed and unintegrated in the
sense that they lack significant numbers of overlapping policy-formulating
actors—are principally concerned with the well-being of natural persons. In
short, there appears to be a fundamental disarticulation in policy formation
and implementation between the polity of organizational actors and their concerns and the polity of persons as citizens and human beings.

Normative Political Theory and the Organizational State

The recognition of the modern state as an organizational phenomenon has informed both the design and the conclusions of this research. Representatives
of corporate actors were identified and interviewed; patterns of relations
among organizations were traced and then related to a wide range of policy
outcomes. At the level of description and explanation, the approach is entirely
appropriate. Yet viewed from the perspective of normative theories of the
state, the assumptions underlying this research are problematic. Throughout
much of the philosophical heritage that informs the concept of representative
democracy, there runs the belief, or fiction, that the state is grounded in a
covenant among individuals and retains its legitimacy by responding to the
wishes of individual citizens as expressed through a variety of electoral
mechanisms. At least initially, the question raised by the characterization of
the state as constituted and enacted by organizational actors may be explored
with respect to problems of political representation: in what sense does this
form of representation secure accountability to the citizens of the nation? Indeed, this question poses in acute form the problem of the level of analysis
with which we began our inquiry. Corporate actors are not simply aggrega-
tions of individual persons that can be dissolved into their component parts at
will. Yet many theorists concerned with the organizational problems of collective action, including rational-choice theorists such as Hardin (1982), Moe
(1980), and Olson (1965), make just such assumptions.

The issues raised by this question may be clarified by contrasting the problem of representation within a political system dominated by corporate actors
with similar analyses developed within the context of theories of social class.

In many cases these arguments start from the assumption that individuals and, more important, sets of individuals, have distinct interests that are (or are not) then represented within the institutions of government. Whether an individual's interests are defined primarily by his or her position within the system of production or are formed by a wider variety of factors such as race, gender, and religiosity (Parkin, 1979), his or her relation to the political sphere is typically mediated by group membership defined in similar terms. This remains true even with the recognition of incompatibility of interests, whether on the part of an entire set of individuals located in "contradictory class positions" (Wright, 1978) or on the part of different "fractions" of a single class (Bourdieu, 1984). Thus, despite possessing considerable analytic power, the varieties of class analysis fail to shed light on the phenomenon of individual interest as simultaneously mediated by multiple organizations and group affiliations. Depending on one's theoretical perspective, this situation seems prone to produce either fragmented selves or disembodied interests. In either case, the relation of natural persons to political outcomes is far from clear.

Just as individuals may be analytically dissolved into multiple self-interests or identities, corporate actors are subject to a variety of divergent and often contradictory interests rather than possessing one master identity that rationalizes and coordinates all their various concerns. Unions must choose to act in behalf of their members as employees of threatened industries, individual consumers of health care, or advocates of larger class or status concerns, just as business corporations must pick and choose among their concerns for cheaper health care for their employees, limited liability for their products, enhancement of market position through protectionist strategies, and the access to potential trading partners made possible by free trade. Simplistic assumptions about unambiguous, typically singular, organizational interests produce misleading models of the polity of organizational interest groups.

Generalizing from these insights, it becomes clear that theories of the modern state must take into account the multifaceted character of the self, or, stated in the terms of Simmel's formal sociology, the web of group affiliations. Similarly, the question of the relation between state and society must be restated. Rather than seeking to identify the essential social location of individuals and the "true" interests associated with each such location, it becomes necessary to pay greater attention to the overall pattern of group formation and political mobilization than has been characteristic of much contemporary political sociology.

The recognition of the individual as, at least in part, the intersection of multiple membership sets is of particular importance for understanding the consequences of the expansion of the modern welfare state. For, with this expansion, a growing number of the spheres of an individual's activity become explicitly politicized. In addition to regional factors and class and religious identities, a growing range of individual attributes have become the basis for the identification of political interests: place of residence, consumption patterns, family size, educational status, and a wide range of beliefs concerning the desirable quality of life.

Viewed optimistically, this development might be taken as the basis for an intensification of a pluralist style of political life. But the evocation of a growing number of "selves," and hence self-interests, by the expanding welfare state raises troublesome issues when contrasted with normative theories of representation in democratic governments. For with the figurative dissolution of the individual into a cluster of self-interests represented by different organizations, the basis for political accountability is thrown open to question. To the extent that political opinion is increasingly mediated by organizational activity within a variety of disjunctive policy domains, the concerns of easily organized interest groups will systematically be represented more effectively in policy-making processes (Olson, 1965). Thus, rather than simply condemning the government as a creature of "the interests," it becomes possible to specify which types of interests are likely to become the foundation of effective organizational participation in a policy arena.

This view of politics as systematically biased pluralist representation must, however, be further modified. For, as has been made clear by the results of this research, the basis for effective political participation by organizations is not purely a product of the size of their constituencies but also a result of their standing within those networks of organizations that have been labeled "policy domains." To the extent that this sort of dynamic prevails in national political life, policy making is increasingly divorced or insulated from the expressed ideals of representative democracy.

Taken together, these characteristics of the "organizational state" suggest a distinctive perspective on the question of the autonomy of the modern state. If one ceases to focus on the capacity of state agencies or the autonomy of government agents with respect to policy making and implementation, the suspected increase in state autonomy may be seen as the flipside of a decline in political accountability due, in large part, to the expanding scope and increasingly organizational character of contemporary political life.

Appendices
References
Index

Appendix A

Characteristics and Network Positions of
Organizations in the U.S. Energy and
Health Policy Domains

APPENDIX A – Characteristics and Network Positions of Organizations in the United States Energy and Health Policy Domains

ID No.	Name of Organization	Abbreviation	(1)	(2)	(3)	(4)	(5)	(6)	(7)	(8)	(9)	(10)	(11)	(12)	(13)	(14)	(15)
ENERGY DOMAIN:																	
Congressional Committees: House																	
1925	Subcommittee (Energy & Environment): Democrats	HDIENG	NEE	4	88	1	5	1	1	2	1	-	-	-	-	-	11
1926	Subcommittee (Energy & Environment): Republicans	HRIENG	NEE	3	73	1	5	1	1	3	1	-	-	-	-	-	31
1937	Subcommittee (Energy & Power): Democrats	HDCENG	LGRF	1	116	1	1	5	5	4	1	-	-	-	-	-	39
1938	Subcommittee (Energy & Power): Republicans	HRCENG	LGRF	1	98	1	2	5	5	5	1	-	-	-	-	-	31
1941	Subcommittee (Oversight & Investigation): Democrats	HDCOVR	LGRF	1	41	2	5	1	1	3	3	-	-	-	-	-	57
1942	Subcommittee (Oversight & Investigation): Republicans	HRCOVR	REG	1	35	2	4	3	3	5	1	-	-	-	-	-	14
1953	Subcommittee (Energy Development & Applications): Democrats	HDSEDV	LGRF	3	65	1	4	3	3	4	1	-	-	-	0	-	8
1954	Subcommittee (Energy Development & Applications): Republicans	HRSEDV	LGRF	1	52	2	4	3	3	5	2	-	-	-	-	-	18
1955	Subcommittee (Energy Research & Production): Democrats	HDSERS	NEE	4	55	2	4	3	3	3	2	-	-	-	2	-	22
1956	Subcommittee (Energy Research & Production): Republicans	HRSERS	NEE	2	49	2	4	3	3	2	1	-	-	-	-	-	30
Congressional Committees: Senate																	
1971	Subcommittee (Surface Transportation): Democrats	SDCTRSP	TRAN	5	31	3	3	1	4	5	4	-	-	-	-	-	5
1975	Subcommittee (Energy Conservation & Supply): Democrats	SDECNS	LGRF	5	75	1	3	1	5	5	4	-	-	-	-	-	4
1976	Subcommittee (Energy Conservation & Supply): Republicans	SRECNS	LGRF	5	67	1	3	1	5	5	2	-	-	-	-	-	1
1977	Subcommittee (Energy Regulation): Democrats	SDEREG	REG	3	83	1	4	3	3	3	1	-	-	-	-	-	76
1978	Subcommittee (Energy Regulation): Republicans	SREREG	LGRF	3	75	1	4	3	5	5	1	-	-	-	-	-	4
1979	Subcommittee (Energy Research & Development): Democrats	SDER&D	NEE	3	64	1	4	3	3	3	1	-	-	-	-	-	13
1987	Subcommittee (Nuclear Regulation): Democrats	SDPNCL	NEE	5	57	2	4	3	3	5	3	-	-	-	-	-	5
1988	Subcommittee (Nuclear Regulation): Republicans	SRPNCL	NEE	5	57	2	4	3	3	5	4	-	-	-	-	-	4
1995	Subcommittee (Energy & Foundations): Democrats	SDFENG	LGRF	5	30	3	4	3	3	5	3	-	-	-	-	-	0
1996	Subcommittee (Energy & Foundations): Republicans	SRFENG	OIL	1	31	3	4	3	3	5	4	-	-	-	-	-	18
Federal Agencies																	
1901	The White House Office	WHOUSE	MNE	1	148	1	1	1	1	4	1	-	-	-	-	-	50
1902	Council of Economic Advisors	CEA	MNE	2	79	1	4	2	4	5	4	-	-	-	-	-	27
1903	Council on Environmental Quality	CENQLTY	NEE	2	72	1	5	1	1	2	2	-	-	-	-	-	23
1904	Office of Management and the Budget	OMB	MNE	1	140	1	5	1	1	2	1	-	-	-	0	-	48
1905	Office of Science and Technology	OSTP	NEE	1	50	2	5	1	1	4	3	-	-	-	-	-	26
1906	Department of Agriculture	DAGRI	LGRF	4	28	3	3	2	5	3	3	-	-	-	-	-	35
1907	Department of Commerce	DCOMMRC	REG	3	33	3	4	1	4	1	1	-	-	-	-	-	16
1908	Department of Energy	DENERGY	REG	1	155	1	1	2	5	5	1	-	-	-	-	-	28
1909	Economic Regulatory Administration	ECONRA	OIL	3	68	1	1	1	5	5	1	-	-	-	-	-	25
1910	Federal Energy Regulatory Commission	FERC	CNG	3	81	1	2	1	1	3	1	-	-	-	-	-	8
1911	Department of Interior	DINTR	CNG	3	98	1	5	1	2	4	2	-	-	-	-	-	27
1912	Department of Transportation	DTRSPT	AUTO	3	52	2	3	1	4	3	1	-	-	-	-	-	14
1913	Environmental Protection Agency	EPA	CNG	5	112	1	2	1	1	1	1	-	-	-	-	-	9
1914	Federal Trade Commission	FTC	ISOL	5	29	3	4	3	3	4	4	-	-	-	0	-	3
1915	Interstate Commerce Commission	ICC	TRAN	5	33	3	4	3	3	4	4	-	-	-	-	-	4
1916	National Science Foundation	NSF	NEE	5	34	3	4	3	3	1	4	-	-	-	-	-	16

ID	Organization																
1917	National Transportation Safety Board	TRSPTSFTY	PIPE	5	17	4	4	3	3	4	5	5	–	–	–	–	1
1918	Nuclear Regulatory Commission	NRC	NEE	5	88	3	3	1	1	3	5	5	–	–	–	–	10
1919	Solar Energy Research Institute	SOLRSRCH	LGRF	4	33	3	4	5	1	3	4	4	–	–	–	–	4
1920	State Planning Council on Radioactive Wastes	RADWASTE	NEE	5	20	4	3	4	2	2	4	3	–	–	–	–	1
1922	Tennessee Valley Authority	TVA	NEE	2	50	2	5	5	5	5	5	3	–	–	–	–	10

Associations of State and Local Governments

ID	Organization																
1801	California Energy Resources Conservation & Development Commission	CALERC	LGRF	2	18	4	3	1	1	5	4	4	0	12	1	1	17
1802	California Public Utilities Commission	CALPUC	LGRF	2	25	3	3	1	2	5	5	5	0	9	2	1	10
1803	Coalition of Northeast Governors	NEGOVS	LGRF	2	18	4	2	1	4	3	3	2	0	4	2	0	25
1804	National Association of Counties	NACNTY	LGRF	2	23	4	4	2	5	3	3	3	0	8	0	0	7
1805	National Conference of State Legislatures	NCSLEG	LGRF	1	23	4	3	5	1	1	4	2	0	6	4	0	17
1806	National Governors Association	NGOVS	MNE	–	68	1	1	1	–	3	3	4	0	33	7	1	25
1807	National League of Cities	NLCITY	LGRF	3	33	3	2	5	5	2	2	3	0	5	2	0	20
1810	United States Conference of Mayors	USCMYR	LGRF	3	37	2	5	3	5	5	2	2	0	6	3	1	11
1811	Western Governors Policy Office	WSTGOVS	CNG	3	32	5	3	5	5	5	1	3	0	0	0	0	29

Research Units

1559	Mitre Corporation	MITRE	ISOL	4	13	5	4	1	1	5	5	5	0	5	0	0	0
1563	National Economic Research Associates	ECONRES	CNG	3	17	2	4	5	1	5	3	5	0	5	1	1	1
1713	National Academy of Sciences	NASCIENCE	NEE	2	43	5	2	1	5	1	4	3	0	5	12	0	9
1721	Resources for the Future	RFUTR	MNE	4	27	3	3	2	1	2	3	4	0	7	2	1	0

Labor Unions

1601	AFL–CIO	AFL-CIO	REG	1	89	1	1	5	5	5	4	4	0	19	9	0	50
1602	Oil, Chemical & Atomic Workers International Union	ACAW	OIL	2	36	1	1	1	1	3	2	3	0	6	0	0	22
1603	Sheet Metal Workers of America	SMW	LGRF	2	10	5	3	4	4	4	2	4	0	5	8	0	26
1604	United Automobile Workers of America	UAW	MNE	2	47	2	1	2	5	5	4	4	0	8	8	0	18
1605	United Mine Workers	UMW	CNG	2	40	4	2	4	4	5	3	3	0	2	6	1	19

Trade Associations

ID	Organization																
1051	American Gas Association	AGASA	CNG	1	124	1	1	5	5	5	1	1	4	29	92	1	18
1052	American Petroleum Institute	API	OIL	3	142	1	1	5	5	5	1	1	6	32	23	1	21
1053	American Petroleum Refiners Association	REFINERS	OIL	5	24	3	2	2	2	2	2	4	0	4	4	0	15
1054	Associated Gas Distributors	GASDSTR	CNG	5	9	5	5	5	5	5	4	5	0	2	4	1	7
1055	Association of Oil Pipe Lines	OILPIPE	CNG	5	7	3	5	5	1	1	5	5	0	4	0	0	4
1057	Gas Research Institute	GASRSRCH	LGRF	5	24	3	4	5	3	3	5	5	1	6	1	0	1
1058	Independent Gas Marketers Council Inc.	INDGAS	OIL	5	16	4	2	4	4	3	3	2	0	12	3	0	21
1059	Independent Petroleum Association of America	IPAA	OIL	4	56	2	1	2	1	1	5	5	1	13	3	1	17
1061	Independent Terminal Operators Association	TRMNLOP	OIL	5	12	5	5	5	2	2	5	5	0	6	0	0	13
1062	Institute of Gas Technology	GASTECH	ISOL	5	5	5	1	5	1	3	1	1	1	9	0	1	0
1063	Interstate Natural Gas Association of America	INTNGA	CNG	3	24	3	2	4	4	4	2	2	0	9	0	0	19
1064	National Oil Jobbers Council	OILJOBR	OIL	4	42	2	1	5	5	4	1	4	3	16	1	1	30
1065	Natural Gas Supply Association	NATGSUP	CNG	5	41	1	2	2	1	1	5	5	1	3	3	0	10
1066	New England Fuel Institute	NEFUEL	OIL	2	12	2	5	5	4	2	2	4	2	11	3	0	26
1067	Petroleum Industry Research Foundation	PETRFDT	OIL	1	19	5	1	1	5	5	5	5	0	4	6	0	0
1068	Rocky Mountain Oil and Gas Association	RMOGA	PIPE	2	23	4	2	5	3	3	2	5	0	7	7	1	29
1069	Service State Dealers of America	SERVSD	OIL	3	17	3	4	2	4	4	3	2	0	5	5	0	20

ID No.	Name of Organization	Abbreviation	(1)	(2)	(3)	(4)	(5)	(6)	(7)	(8)	(9)	(10)	(11)	(12)	(13)	(14)	(15)
	Trade Associations (continued)																
1070	Society of Independent Gasoline Marketers of America	SINDGASM	OIL	4	18	4	2	2	5	5	4	0	7	0	0	1	22
1071	Western Oil and Gas Association	WESTOGA	-	-	17	1	-	-	1	2	2	0	5	0	0	1	12
1150	American Mining Congress	AMININGC	CNG	5	66	1	3	5	1	1	4	2	29	1	1	1	18
1151	Mining and Reclamation Council	MNG/RECL	CNG	5	12	1	1	1	1	1	3	0	4	1	0	1	17
1152	National Coal Association	NCA	CNG	4	104	5	4	4	5	4	1	3	19	39	1	1	19
1153	Slurry Transport Association	SLURRY	CNG	5	9	5	1	1	5	2	1	0	5	2	0	1	2
1250	American Nuclear Energy Council	NCLRCN	NEE	2	59	2	4	3	4	4	5	5	19	0	0	1	15
1251	Atomic Industrial Forum	ATMCIF	NEE	3	69	1	1	5	2	5	4	4	19	0	0	1	14
1350	American Public Power Association	APPA	NEE	1	48	2	1	5	1	4	2	0	21	0	0	1	43
1351	Edison Electric Institute	EEI	NEE	1	121	1	1	1	5	1	1	8	51	10	3	1	17
1352	Electric Power Research Institute	ELECPRI	NEE	1	48	2	1	1	1	1	2	2	20	5	-	-	17
1353	National Association of Regulatory Utilities Commissioners	REGUTIL	NEE	1	29	3	3	1	5	1	2	0	16	1	-	1	13
1354	National Electric Reliability Council	ELECRELY	NEE	3	15	4	2	4	2	3	5	0	7	2	0	0	6
1355	National Rural Electric Cooperative Association	RRLCOOP	NEE	5	42	2	1	1	4	1	1	0	17	4	3	1	35
1356	Utility Waste Management Group	UTLWASTE	NEE	5	5	5	3	1	4	1	3	1	6	0	0	0	2
1450	American Wind Energy Association	WINDENG	LGRF	4	8	4	4	2	2	5	3	0	6	1	0	1	2
1451	Solar Energy Industries Association	SOLINDS	LGRF	5	18	4	2	5	5	2	3	0	12	0	0	1	10
1550	American Bakers Association	BAKERS	LGRF	5	7	5	2	4	2	2	5	0	4	0	0	1	11
1552	American Institute of Merchant Shipping	MCHTSHIP	ISOL	4	7	5	2	2	4	5	5	1	5	0	0	1	0
1553	American Iron and Steel Institute	IRNSTL	MNE	4	26	3	2	2	2	4	5	0	11	0	0	1	33
1554	American Paper Institute Inc.	PAPER	MNE	1	23	4	2	5	4	3	2	1	6	1	2	1	20
1555	Association of American Railroads	AARR	RR	1	104	1	1	2	1	1	4	2	9	1	-	1	19
1556	Chamber of Commerce of the U.S.	COCOMMRC	REG	1	52	2	1	5	1	4	1	2	10	24	-	1	10
1557	Chemical Manufacturers Association	CHEMMNF	MNE	5	92	2	4	5	3	2	3	0	5	1	1	1	3
1558	Gas Appliance Manufacturers Association	GASAPP	LGRF	5	16	5	1	2	1	4	5	0	4	0	1	1	18
1560	National Association of Manufacturers	NAM	MNE	4	19	4	1	2	1	2	2	3	10	32	0	1	8
1561	National Automobile Dealers Association	AUTODLR	MNE	5	13	4	1	5	1	3	5	2	5	0	0	1	22
1562	National Council of Farmer Coops	FRMCOOP	OIL	3	4	2	5	5	4	1	5	0	6	0	0	1	4
1564	National Forest Products Association	FRSTPROD	MNE	3	25	5	2	2	2	4	5	0	5	0	0	1	8
1565	National Retail Merchants Association	RETAIL	MNE	3	13	3	2	2	4	4	5	2	6	0	0	1	9
1566	Petrochemical Energy Group	PTROCHM	OIL	4	25	3	1	4	5	5	4	2	5	0	0	0	9
	Professional Societies																
1050	American Association of Petroleum Geologists	PGEOLS	CNG	3	5	5	3	2	4	5	5	0	7	0	0	0	13
1551	American Institute of Architects	ARCHT	LGRF	2	9	5	4	2	3	2	3	3	3	2	0	1	7
	Business Corporations																
1001	American Natural Resources Company	NATRESRC	CNG	4	20	4	2	2	5	4	3	0	7	1	0	1	23
1003	Atlantic Richfield Company	ARCO	OIL	3	63	1	1	1	2	1	2	1	13	13	3	1	42
1005	Cities Service Company	CITCO	OIL	3	17	4	4	3	3	3	3	0	4	2	0	1	22
1006	Continental Oil Company	CNTOIL	OIL	3	39	2	2	2	2	5	2	0	2	9	0	0	25
1007	El Paso Natural Gas Company	ELPASO	CNG	3	25	3	2	4	4	4	5	2	2	3	0	1	26

Code	Company	Abbrev	Type													
1009	Foothills Pipelines Ltd.	FHPIPE	PIPE	5	5	6	5	3	3	4	5	0	5	0	1	1
1011	Gulf Oil Company	GULFOIL	OIL	4	1	70	5	3	1	3	1	4	8	0	2	7
1012	Houston Natural Gas Corporation	HSTNGAS	CNG	2	4	22	4	5	2	3	3	5	5	0	0	7
1015	Northern Tier Pipeline Company	NTPIPE	PIPE	1	5	12	5	2	3	3	2	2	3	1	0	4
1016	Northwest Energy Company	NWENERGY	CNG	1	3	15	4	1	2	4	1	2	5	0	0	4
1017	Phillips Petroleum Company	PHLLPS	RR	2	4	36	3	3	4	3	2	1	7	0	1	7
1018	Shell Oil Company	SHELL	OIL	1	3	60	4	3	3	4	1	1	6	1	1	4
1019	Standard Oil of California	SOCAL	OIL	2	2	53	5	2	1	1	2	2	6	0	0	13
1020	Standard Oil of Indiana	AMOCO	OIL	1	2	64	5	1	1	1	5	1	8	0	0	10
1021	Standard Oil of Ohio	SOHIO	OIL	1	4	54	5	3	2	1	5	2	8	0	0	8
1022	Sun Oil Company	SUN	OIL	3	4	71	4	4	3	3	4	0	3	0	1	4
1023	Texaco Inc.	TEXACO	OIL	3	4	15	5	5	4	3	3	0	3	1	1	1
1024	Tosco Corporation	TOSCO	OIL	3	4	37	4	4	4	5	3	0	4	1	1	2
1025	Union Oil Company of California	UNIONOIL	OIL	3	2	36	2	4	4	3	1	0	11	0	0	2
1101	AMAX Coal Company	AMAXCL	CNG	3	1	41	2	1	1	5	1	0	5	0	1	2
1102	Consolidated Coal Company	CONSCL	CNG	3	2	50	5	1	1	5	–	0	4	1	0	4
1103	U.S. Steel Corporation	USSTL	CNG	5	3	9	3	5	3	2	4	0	2	0	1	3
1201	Allied General Nuclear Service	AGNUCL	NEE	3	4	20	5	3	3	5	2	0	5	0	0	6
1202	Babcock and Wilcox	B&W	NEE	2	3	12	2	3	1	1	5	0	6	0	1	2
1203	Combustion Engineering Inc.	COMBST	NEE	4	5	14	5	4	4	4	1	2	2	1	1	0
1204	General Atomic Company	GNATOM	NEE	4	1	69	1	1	1	3	3	0	19	2	0	3
1205	General Electric Company	GE	NEE	1	1	64	1	3	1	1	4	3	18	0	1	6
1206	Westinghouse Electric Corporation	WHELEC	NEE	1	1	27	3	5	5	1	5	0	3	0	3	2
1301	American Electric Power Service Corporation	AEPSC	NEE	2	3	6	2	1	3	3	4	0	5	0	0	2
1302	Brooklyn Union Gas	BGAS	CNG	2	4	14	5	1	3	2	4	2	5	0	0	3
1303	Columbia Gas System, Inc.	CGAS	CNG	4	2	39	3	4	1	5	3	2	7	0	2	5
1304	Commonwealth Edison Company	COMMED	NEE	2	2	38	1	4	5	5	5	0	2	1	2	20
1305	Consolidated Edison Company	CONSED	NEE	1	2	9	5	4	2	2	3	0	3	0	0	1
1306	Consumers Power Company	CNSPOW	LGRF	1	4	19	5	3	2	3	2	1	4	1	1	3
1307	Detroit Edison Company	DTRED	NEE	2	3	11	4	5	3	4	3	1	3	1	1	3
1308	General Public Utilities	GENPU	NEE	2	3	3	5	4	2	4	2	0	4	0	1	8
1309	Hampton Roads Energy Corporation	HRENG	OIL	2	5	17	4	2	2	3	3	0	8	0	1	3
1310	Houston Lighting and Power Company	HL&P	NEE	2	4	14	4	2	2	3	5	0	5	0	1	3
1311	Montana Power Company	MTPOW	NEE	4	4	17	4	2	2	3	2	1	1	1	1	4
1313	Northeast Utilities Service Company	NEUTIL	NEE	2	4	32	3	2	4	4	3	1	3	0	1	6
1314	Pacific Gas and Electric Company	PGE	NEE	1	2	10	3	2	2	2	3	1	3	0	0	3
1316	Public Service Electric and Gas Company	PSELEC	NEE	1	3	25	4	4	2	4	5	0	3	0	1	3
1317	Southern California Edison Company	SOCALED	NEE	1	3	18	3	3	2	3	3	0	1	1	0	1
1318	Texas Utilities Company	TXUTIL	NEE	1	4	16	4	4	4	4	3	0	3	0	1	3
1319	Virginia Electric and Power Company	VAELEC	NEE	5	3	16	5	2	3	3	3	1	4	1	1	3
1401	KMS Fusion Inc.	KMSFSN	NEE	4	2	2	4	2	2	5	5	0	5	0	1	0
1402	Republic Geothermal Inc.	RGEOTM	CNG	4	4	2	2	2	4	4	2	0	7	2	1	0
1403	Rio Blanco Oil Shale Company	RBOILSH	CNG	1	2	28	5	4	2	5	3	0	8	0	0	1
1501	Allied Chemical Corporation	ALCHEM	RR	1	4	11	3	2	4	3	4	0	8	0	0	14
1502	American Motors Company	AMMOTORS	–	2	–	25	3	1	–	4	–	0	6	0	1	7
1503	Boeing Company	BOEING	ISOL	4	2	17	3	2	2	4	3	0	6	0	1	19
1504	Burlington Northern Inc.	BRLNGTN	CNG	4	2	25	5	4	4	4	3	0	6	0	1	5
1506	Chrysler Corporation	CHRSLR	MNE	4	2	40	5	2	2	3	5	0	9	2	1	2
1507	Dow Chemical, U.S.A.	DOW	MNE	4	2	46	4	2	2	3	5	0	8	0	1	10
1508	Ford Motor Company	FORD	MNE	5	2	8	5	2	2	3	3	1	14	1	1	1
1509	Foster Wheeler Energy Company	FWENGCO	ISOL	1	4	72	1	4	2	4	2	0	6	0	0	7
1510	General Motors Corporation	GM	OIL	2	5	9	4	5	4	5	4	0	10	0	1	29
1511	Grumman Aerospace Corporation	GRUMMAN	LGRF	5	3	16	4	5	2	3	5	0	6	0	1	0
1512	Rockwell International Corporation	RCKWL	NEE	4	4	16	4	4	4	4	3	0	5	0	1	0

ID No.	Name of Organization	Abbreviation	(1)	(2)	(3)	(4)	(5)	(6)	(7)	(8)	(9)	(10)	(11)	(12)	(13)	(14)	(15)
	Business Corporations (continued)																
1513	Stone and Webster Engineering Corporation	S&WENGIN	NEE	—	4	12	5	—	—	—	3	3	2	9	0	0	1	13
1514	Thermo-Electron Inc.	THERMO	NEE	4	3	3	5	—	3	3	4	3	0	3	3	0	0	34
1515	TRW Inc.	TRW	MNE	2	2	25	3	3	1	4	1	1	1	4	1	0	1	24
1516	Union Carbide	UCARB	MNE	3	3	31	4	2	2	2	1	1	0	3	4	0	1	27
1517	Union Pacific Corporation	UPACF	RR	2	2	13	4	4	5	5	1	2	1	1	3	0	1	30
1518	United Technologies Corporation	UNTECH	MNE	2	2	28	3	4	2	3	2	1	0	5	0	0	1	22
1520	Wheelabrator-Frye Inc.	W-FINC	ISOL	4	4	18	4	3	1	5	1	2	0	8	0	0	1	6
	Public Interest Groups																
1701	American Automobile Association	AAA	OIL	3	3	17	4	5	5	1	3	3	0	5	0	0	1	26
1702	Center for Auto Safety	AUTOSFTY	AUTO	4	4	4	5	4	4	4	5	4	0	5	1	0	1	6
1703	Citizen/Labor Energy Coalition	CTZ/LAB	LGRF	4	4	18	4	1	2	2	2	4	1	3	1	0	1	9
1704	Consumer Energy Council of America	CNSENG	OIL	4	1	17	4	2	4	1	2	3	0	2	2	0	1	0
1705	Consumer Federation of America	CNSFED	OIL	3	3	32	3	2	4	2	3	3	0	13	2	—	1	40
1706	Critical Mass Energy Project	CRTMSS	NEE	4	4	8	5	2	2	2	4	4	0	1	4	0	1	17
1707	Energy Action Education Foundation	ENGACT	OIL	4	4	16	4	2	1	4	5	4	0	14	6	0	1	27
1708	Environmental Action Inc.	ENVACT	NEE	4	4	13	4	2	2	2	2	4	0	1	5	0	1	26
1709	Environmental Coalition on Nuclear Power	ENVNCL	NEE	2	2	4	5	4	2	4	4	5	0	3	0	0	0	25
1710	Environmental Defense Fund	ENVDEF	—	1	1	52	2	—	—	—	4	4	0	13	5	1	1	55
1711	Environmental Policy Center	ENVPOL	NEE	1	1	40	2	1	1	5	4	1	0	51	7	1	1	42
1712	Friends of the Earth	FOEARTH	—	3	3	55	3	—	—	—	2	4	0	21	—	0	1	27
1714	National Audubon Society	AUDUBON	LGRF	5	5	25	5	5	5	1	3	5	0	6	0	1	1	4
1715	National Consumer Law Center	CNSLAW	LGRF	1	1	6	5	4	2	4	4	5	0	6	7	0	2	17
1716	National Wildlife Federation	WLIFE	CNG	5	5	28	1	2	5	5	1	2	0	6	7	2	1	27
1717	Natural Resources Defense Council Inc.	RSDEFNS	NEE	1	1	63	1	4	4	2	1	2	4	41	12	0	1	27
1718	New Directions	NEWDIR	ISOL	5	5	1	5	4	2	4	4	4	0	5	1	0	1	3
1720	Public Interest Research Group	PUBINT	ISOL	5	5	11	5	2	4	2	3	5	0	7	1	0	0	5
1722	Sierra Club	SIERRA	NEE	2	2	91	1	1	5	4	2	2	3	16	6	2	1	24
1723	Solar Lobby	SOLAR	LGRF	4	4	17	4	1	1	5	2	1	0	12	0	2	1	2
1724	Union of Concerned Scientists	UCNCSCI	NEE	4	4	37	2	4	4	2	2	3	3	11	14	1	1	14
1725	U.S. Labor Party	USLP	ISOL	4	4	0	5	4	2	4	2	5	0	5	0	1	0	18
1727	Worldwatch Institute	WWATCH	LGRF	5	5	9	5	5	1	1	3	5	0	3	5	0	1	2

HEALTH DOMAIN:

Congressional Committees: House

ID No.	Name of Organization	Abbreviation	(1)	(2)	(3)	(4)	(5)	(6)	(7)	(8)	(9)	(10)	(11)	(12)	(13)	(14)	(15)
2954	Subcommittee (LHEW): Republicans	HRAHLT	PH	1	1	80	1	3	4	1	5	2	2	—	—	—	—	2
2957	Subcommittee (Health & Environment): Democrats	HDCHLT	GOV	1	1	101	1	3	1	1	3	1	1	—	—	—	—	64
2961	Subcommittee (Health): Democrats	HDWHLT	FIN	5	5	99	1	2	5	1	4	1	1	—	—	—	—	14
2962	Subcommittee (Health): Republicans	HRWHLT	FIN	4	4	83	1	3	4	1	4	2	2	—	—	—	—	13

Congressional Committees: Senate

Code		Abbr	Type								Total
2965	Subcommittee (LHEW): Democrats	SDAHLT	PH	1	91	1	4	1	1 5 2	— — — —	52
2969	Subcommittee (Health): Democrats	SDFHLT	FIN	3	91	1	2	1	1 5 1	— — — —	10
2970	Subcommittee (Health): Republicans	SRFHLT	FIN	5	85	1	5	1	1 5 1	— — — —	16
2974	Subcommittee (Health and Scientific Research): Republicans	SRHHLT	PH	1	78	1	5	3	3 3 1	— — — —	43

Federal Agencies

Code		Abbr	Type			Total
2901	Federal Trade Commission	FTC	HP	1 51	2 3 5 1 2 2	9
2902	Department of Health and Human Services: Office of the Secretary	HHSSEC	GOV	1 111	...	60
2903	HHS: Office of the Assistant Secretary for Health	HHSHLT	CON	2 80	...	21
2904	HHS: Alcohol, Drug Abuse and Mental Health Administration	ADAMHA	MH	4 40	...	10
2905	Food and Drug Administration: Commissioner & Staff	FDA	DRUG	3 69	...	18
2906	FDA: Bureau of Drugs	FDADRG	DRUG	5 36	...	17
2907	FDA: Bureau of Foods	FDAFOOD	FOOD	5 30	...	6
2908	Health Resources Administration	HRA	CON	4 48	...	26
2909	Health Services Administration	HSA	PH	2 39	...	32
2922	Health Care Financing Administration	HCFA	FIN	2 90	...	17
2923	Office of Management and Budget	OMB	GOV	— 110	...	39
2925	The White House Office	WHOUSE	GOV	— 109	...	18

State and Local Governments

Code		Abbr	Type			Total
2703	American Health Planning Association	AHPA	CON	5 28	...	7
2713	National Council of Community Mental Health Centers	CMNTHLT	MH	5 14	...	3
2715	National Council of Community Health Centers	NCCHC	MH	2 15	...	28
2801	Association of State and Territorial Health Officials	ASTHO	PH	5 18	...	1
2803	National Association of Counties	NACNTY	CON	3 38	...	18
2802	National Association of State Alcohol and Drug Abuse Directors	NASADA	MH	4 3	...	0
2804	National Conference of State Legislatures	NCSLEG	FIN	3 35	...	19
2805	National Governors' Association	NGOVS	FIN	4 74	...	14
2806	United States Conference of Mayors	USCMYR	CON	4 45	...	3

Research Units

Code		Abbr	Type			Total
2407	National Academy of Sciences Institute of Medicine	NASIOM	PH	1 60	...	17
2910	National Institutes of Health: Director and associated staff	NIHDIR	RES	4 73	...	10
2911	NIH: National Cancer Institute	NIHNCI	RES	4 51	...	15
2914	NIH: National Institute on Aging	NIHAGE	RES	4 34	...	2
2915	NIH: National Institute of Allergy and Infectious Diseases	NIHAID	RES	5 30	...	0
2916	NIH: National Institute of Arthritis, Metabolism, & Digestive Diseases	NIHAMD	RES	5 36	...	1
2917	NIH: National Institute of Child Health and Human Development	NIHKID	DIS3	2 29	...	16
2918	NIH: National Institute of Dental Research	NIHDNT	DIS1	5 27	...	2
2919	NIH: National Institute of Environmental Health Sciences	NIHENV	RES	4 26	...	1
2920	NIH: National Institute of General Medical Sciences	NIHGMS	RES	5 29	...	7
2921	NIH: National Institute of Neurological and Communicative Disorders and Stroke	NIHNCD	RES	4 28	...	2

407

ID No.	Name of Organization	Abbreviation	(1)	(2)	(3)	(4)	(5)	(6)	(7)	(8)	(9)	(10)	(11)	(12)	(13)	(14)	(15)
Labor Unions																	
2501	AFL-CIO	AFLCIO	CON	4	89	1	1	5	5	2	3	0	22	3	0	1	4
2502	American Federation of State, County and Municipal Employees	AFSCME	CON	4	48	2	1	5	5	1	2	0	5	0	0	1	19
2503	National Union of Hospital and Health Care Employees	NUHHCE	ISO	3	11	4	3	4	2	1	1	0	6	0	0	0	9
2504	Service Employees International Union, AFL-CIO	SEIU	CON	4	10	4	5	3	3	4	5	0	7	0	0	1	12
Professional Societies																	
2701	American Association of PSRO's	AAPSRO	ISO	5	10	4	5	3	3	4	4	0	6	0	0	1	2
2702	American Health Care Association	AHCA	FIN	3	16	4	2	4	4	1	3	0	4	1	4	1	30
2704	American Hospital Association	AHA	FIN	1	95	1	1	5	5	3	2	0	31	8	4	1	39
2705	American Insurance Association	AINSUR	ISO	5	20	1	5	3	3	1	4	0	6	2	0	1	0
2707	Federation of American Hospitals	FAHOSP	FIN	3	59	2	2	5	5	2	2	2	13	2	4	1	27
2708	Group Health Association of America	GRPHLT	FIN	3	43	1	2	5	2	2	4	2	7	0	0	1	4
2709	Health Industry Manufacturers Association	HLTMNF	ISO	4	25	3	3	4	4	3	4	1	5	3	1	1	6
2710	Health Insurance Association of America	HLTINSUR	FIN	2	49	2	1	5	2	1	3	3	19	0	0	1	15
2711	National Association of Home Health Agencies	HOMEHLT	ISO	5	9	2	2	5	5	1	1	0	3	0	0	1	13
2714	National Council of Health Care Services	NCHCARE	FIN	1	5	5	5	3	3	3	3	0	4	0	0	0	45
2716	Pharmaceutical Manufacturers Association	PHRMNF	DRUG	3	72	1	1	5	5	3	4	3	8	0	0	1	16
2101	American Academy of Child Psychiatry	AACPSY	MH	3	3	1	4	5	3	1	5	0	7	0	0	1	5
2104	American Academy of Pediatrics	AAPEDT	HP	2	29	1	5	5	5	2	2	0	12	0	0	1	18
2105	American Academy of Physician Assistants	APASST	HP	2	2	5	4	2	3	4	3	0	2	0	0	1	11
2106	American Association for Dental Research	ADNTRES	DIS1	3	3	3	3	2	2	5	5	0	5	0	0	1	2
2107	American Association of Nurse Anesthetists	AANANSTH	HP	4	3	5	5	3	4	5	5	0	4	0	0	1	10
2108	American Chiropractic Association	ACHIRO	HP	3	7	2	3	3	3	3	2	0	3	0	0	1	9
2109	American College of Cardiology	ACARDIO	DIS1	1	2	4	3	4	4	2	5	0	10	0	0	1	15
2110	American College of Obstetricians and Gynecologists	OBGYN	HP	3	9	4	2	5	4	5	3	1	4	2	0	1	16
2111	American College of Preventive Medicine	ACPMED	PH	3	12	4	3	5	1	3	2	0	7	0	0	1	8
2112	American Dental Association	ADENTA	HP	1	10	4	3	5	5	4	4	0	19	2	0	1	26
2113	American Dietetic Association	ADIETA	CON	3	45	4	5	4	4	1	2	0	13	0	0	1	23
2114	American Federation for Clinical Research	ACLNRSCH	RES	3	6	4	3	2	4	2	2	0	5	2	0	1	8
2115	American Gastroenterological Association	AGASTRA	DIS2	4	4	5	2	2	2	5	5	0	9	0	0	1	6
2116	American Medical Association	AMA	HP	1	117	5	1	4	2	4	5	3	30	24	1	1	68
2117	American Nurses Association	ANA	CON	1	59	2	1	5	5	1	2	1	17	0	0	1	50
2118	American Osteopathic Association	AOSTEOA	HP	1	8	4	4	4	3	3	4	1	3	0	0	1	26
2119	American Psychiatric Association	APSYTRIC	MH	1	44	2	5	4	5	2	2	2	19	0	0	1	4
2120	American Psychological Association	APSYCOL	MH	1	18	1	2	1	4	2	3	4	12	0	0	1	44
2121	American Public Health Association	APUBHLT	PH	3	60	3	1	1	5	2	3	3	11	2	0	1	19
2122	American Society of Hematology	ASHEMA	DIS1	2	2	2	2	3	4	3	4	0	6	0	0	0	14
2123	American Society for Microbiology	ASMCRBIO	DIS2	3	4	5	5	3	4	2	4	0	7	0	0	1	14
2124	American Speech-Language-Hearing Association	ASPCHLH	DIS3	3	1	5	5	3	3	2	2	0	9	0	0	0	9
2125	Association for the Advancement of Psychology	AAPSYCOL	MH	1	1	5	5	3	3	2	4	0	12	0	0	1	21
2126	Association of Teachers of Preventive Medicine	ATCHPM	PH	1	0	5	5	3	3	5	1	0	4	0	0	0	11
2127	College of American Pathologists	CAPATH	HP	4	5	5	3	1	1	1	4	1	5	0	0	1	11

Table of organizations with attribute codes (columns unlabeled in source; numeric values given in image left-to-right order).

ID	Organization	Abbrev	Code														
2128	Endocrine Society	ENDOSOC	DIS1	11	1	0	8	0	5	4	4	4	3	5	2	2	2
2129	Medical Library Association	MEDLIB	PH	5	0	0	6	0	5	4	3	3	5	5	4	4	3
2131	National League for Nursing	NLNURS	CON	42	0	1	6	0	1	2	4	4	2	3	3	18	3
2133	Renal Physicians Association	RENAL	HP	5	0	0	6	0	5	3	3	3	5	5	3	3	3
2134	Society for Investigative Dermatology	INVDERM	RES	2	0	0	6	0	5	5	3	4	5	4	2	1	2
2601	American Association of Colleges of Pharmacy	AACPHARM	PH	13	0	0	4	0	3	4	4	3	3	3	3	9	3
2602	American Association of Colleges of Nursing	AACNRS	CON	15	1	0	4	0	3	4	3	3	5	3	0	16	3
2603	American Association of Dental Schools	AADENTS	RES	5	1	1	6	0	3	5	3	3	5	4	4	14	0
2604	Association of American Medical Colleges	AAMC	HP	34	1	1	24	0	3	2	1	1	1	1	4	76	4
2605	Council of Teaching Hospitals	CTHOSP	HP	30	1	0	0	0	3	4	2	2	5	4	4	16	4

Business Corporations

ID	Organization	Abbrev	Code														
2402	Blue Cross and Blue Shield Associations	BC/BS	FIN	21	1	2	27	1	2	1	1	1	1	1	1	88	2
2403	Hoffman-La Roche, Inc.	HLRINC	DRUG	15	1	1	7	0	1	1	5	5	2	3	4	19	3
2404	Hospital Corporation of America	HSPCORP	FIN	5	1	0	3	0	5	1	4	4	2	2	5	28	0
2406	Merck & Company	MERCK	DRUG	8	1	3	4	0	5	1	3	3	5	5	5	17	0
2408	Pfizer Pharmaceuticals	PFIZER	DRUG	18	1	4	3	0	5	1	3	3	5	4	5	13	4
2410	Upjohn Company	UPJOHN	DRUG	34	1	1	2	0	2	2	3	3	5	3	2	20	3

Lay Voluntary Associations

ID	Organization	Abbrev	Code														
2201	AARP/NRTA	AARP/NRTA	FIN	37	0	0	21	1	1	1	5	5	1	1	4	70	4
2202	Chamber of Commerce of the United States	COCOMMRC	HP	28	0	0	3	0	1	2	1	5	1	1	3	61	0
2203	Children's Defense Fund	CHDEFNS	MH	0	1	2	8	0	2	2	1	5	1	2	0	30	1
2205	Consumer Federation of America	CNSUMFED	FOOD	14	1	2	4	0	2	4	1	4	2	3	1	19	1
2206	Environmental Defense Fund	ENVDEF	RES	6	1	0	10	0	5	2	4	2	3	3	0	25	0
2207	National Abortion Rights Action League	NARAL	ABOR	1	1	0	7	0	4	3	5	5	2	2	0	26	0
2208	National Association for the Advancement of Colored People	NAACP	CON	19	1	1	12	1	3	3	2	3	3	3	3	23	3
2209	National Council of Senior Citizens	SNRCIT	FIN	38	1	2	12	1	3	4	1	5	2	2	3	40	3
2210	National Farmers Union	FARMRU	CON	39	1	0	4	0	4	3	4	3	2	4	2	13	2
2211	National Urban League	URBANLG	ABOR	10	1	0	9	0	4	2	4	4	1	3	2	23	2
2212	Planned Parenthood Federation of America	PLPARENT	HP	0	1	3	15	1	1	1	5	4	1	2	3	40	3
2302	American Cancer Society	ACNCRS	DIS1	6	0	3	3	0	5	5	1	5	2	3	4	71	4
2303	American Diabetes Association	ADIABA	DIS1	10	1	2	12	1	4	1	1	5	2	1	5	45	5
2304	American Heart Association	AHEARTA	DIS1	17	1	0	5	0	1	1	1	5	5	1	2	66	2
2305	American Social Health Association	ASOCHLT	DIS2	4	0	0	7	0	1	5	3	3	3	3	1	2	1
2306	Arthritis Foundation	ARTHFDT	DIS3	26	1	0	10	1	3	3	4	5	3	3	3	23	3
2307	Candlelighters Foundation	CNDLFDT	DIS1	11	0	0	9	0	4	4	5	3	4	4	3	4	3
2308	Citizens for the Treatment of High Blood Pressure	BLDPRS	DIS2	8	1	0	9	0	3	4	3	5	2	3	3	8	3
2309	Coalition for Health Funding	HLTFND	PH	7	0	0	4	0	3	2	1	5	3	3	2	35	2
2310	Community Nutrition Institute	CNUTRI	FOOD	9	1	0	5	0	4	1	4	5	2	4	2	5	2
2312	Cystic Fibrosis Foundation	CYSTICF	DIS3	6	1	0	12	0	3	5	5	4	1	3	2	10	2
2313	Epilepsy Foundation of America	EPILPFDT	DIS3	21	0	0	6	0	5	4	1	5	1	3	3	11	3
2314	Friends of Eye Research, Rehabilitation, and Treatment	EYERRT	DIS1	2	0	0	4	0	3	3	1	5	2	3	2	5	2
2315	Joint Council of Allergy and Immunology	ALLIMM	DIS3	6	0	0	13	0	5	5	1	3	1	5	3	5	3
2317	National Mental Health Association	NMHLTH	MH	11	0	0	0	0	4	3	1	5	2	1	1	39	1
2318	National Association for Retarded Citizens	RTRDCIT	DIS3	5	0	0	8	0	3	4	5	4	1	3	3	22	3
2319	National Foundation for Ileitis and Colitis	NFDTIC	DIS3	19	0	0	6	0	5	1	1	5	5	4	3	1	3
2320	National Health Law Program	HLTLAW	CON	22	0	2	6	1	5	1	3	5	1	5	0	9	0
2321	National Hemophilia Foundation	NHEMOFD	DIS3	5	0	0	10	0	3	3	5	3	5	3	3	6	3
2322	National Kidney Foundation	NKIDNFD	DIS2	15	0	0	9	0	2	4	2	3	5	3	2	24	2

ID No.	Name of Organization	Abbre-viation	(1)	(2)	(3)	(4)	(5)	(6)	(7)	(8)	(9)	(10)	(11)	(12)	(13)	(14)	(15)
	Lay Voluntary Associations (continued)																
2323	National Rehabilitation Association	NREHAB	PH	0	0	8	5	3	2	4	4	5	0	5	0	0	1	0
2324	National Society for Autistic Children	AUTCHLD	DIS3	1	1	4	5	5	3	3	4	5	0	8	0	0	0	34
2325	National Women's Health Network	WOMNHLT	MH	4	4	4	5	5	3	3	5	5	0	5	0	0	1	31
2328	United Cerebral Palsy Associations	CEREPAL	DIS3	1	2	9	4	2	4	3	3	7	0	7	0	0	0	18
2329	Washington Business Group on Health	DCBUSNS	FIN	1	2	32	3	2	4	5	4	2	0	2	0	0	1	17
2409	Robert Wood Johnson Foundation	RWJFDT	CON	2	2	44	2	2	1	5	4	4	0	2	0	0	0	37
2505	United Automobile Workers (UAW)	UAW	FIN	2	4	61	1	1	2	1	1	1	0	10	4	1	0	28
2506	United Mine Workers (UMW)	UMW	PH	4	0	35	2	5	3	5	3	3	0	4	0	1	1	3
2712	Hispanic Mental Health and Human Service Organizations	HISPHLT	MH	0	0	2	5	5	3	3	3	5	0	7	0	0	1	11

(1) Issue Publics are subsets of organizations within a domain that exhibit similar levels of interest across the entire range of policy issues within that domain (see Chapter 4). Codes: ABOR: Abortion. FOOD: Food. CONS: Consumers. GOV: Government. DIS1: Disease #1. DIS2: Disease #2. DIS3: Disease #3. HP: Health Professionals. ISO: Isolates. MH: Mental Health. DRUG: Drug Industry. PH: Public Health. RES: Health Research.

(2) Scope of Interest reflects the dispersion of an organization's interests as measured across a Euclidean space in which the distance between points representing single issues increases with the dissimilarity of the sets of organizations expressing interest in those issues (see Chapter 4).

(3) Number of Influence Votes are equal to the number of organizations in a domain that identified a given organization as "especially influential and consequential in formulating energy (health) policy" (see Chapter 5).

(4) Influence Rank categorizes the Influence Votes into quintiles.

(5, 6, 7) Mobilizable Resources, Impartial Mediation, and Authority are factor scores, presented here by quintiles, resulting from a varimax factor analysis of informants' attributions of eight types of resources to a set of five to ten other organizations in the same domain. These analyses produced very similar three-factor models for both the energy and health domains, although the factor structure is more distinct in the latter case. The first factor, Mobilizable Resources, reflects the attribution of the type of resources likely to be mobilized by nonpublic claimant organizations for partisan purposes. The second factor, Impartial Mediation, measures the extent to which a reputation as an impartial mediator was attributed to the organization, while the third factor indicates the attribution of formal decision making authority (see Chapter 6).

(8) Monitoring Capacity is a composite measure of an organization's ability to collect various types of information relevant for participation in a policy arena (see Chapter 6).

(11) Congressional Hearings records the number of times that each organization appeared at Congressional subcommittee hearings related to energy or health policy (see Chapters 3 and 5).

(12) Newspaper Mentions is the number of times that an organization was named in stories related to energy or health policy that were printed in the following publications: The New York Times, The Chicago Tribune, The Los Angeles Times, The Houston Chronicle, The Atlanta Constitution, The Seattle Times, and Time Magazine (see Chapters 3 and 5).

(13) Amicus Briefs is the number of times an organization participated in filing friend of the court briefs before federal appelate courts. The sample included 167 cases related to energy policy and 115 concerning health issues (see Chapter 3).

(14) Registered Lobbyist indicated by a "1" if the organization was registered as a Congressional lobbyist at least once from 1977 to 1980. This information was obtained from annual listings in Congressional Quarterly (see Chapter 3).

(15) Scope of Activity, ranked by quintiles, reflects the dispersion of an organization's activity as measured across a Euclidean space in which the distance between points representing single events increases as those events are less similar in terms of five formal features: decision-making locus, public visibility, controversiality, functional locus, and type of decision cycle (see Chapters 9 and 10).

Appendix B

Interview Schedule

All cards and lists mentioned in the interview schedule are reprinted in Appendices C and D. Since the interview for the health domain is identical to that for energy except for the issues, events, and organizations discussed, we have not reproduced the interview schedule for the health respondents. We have, however, included the cards and lists used in the health study in Appendix D. To conserve space, we have deleted wherever possible repetitive forms used to facilitate the recording of the respondent's answers.

SOCIAL ORGANIZATION OF NATIONAL POLICY DOMAINS

Energy

Interviewer Number: _____   Organization ID: _____

Organization Type: _____

    Site of Interview: Headquarters Office / Washington Office   [CIRCLE ONE]
                                                      (non-headquarters)

    Policy Domain: Energy / Health   [CIRCLE ONE]

        Organization Informant: _____

        Informant's Title: _____

        Informant's Telephone: _____

        Second Informant (IF ANY): _____

        Informant's Title: _____

        Informant's Telephone: _____

Interviewer: _____

Date: _____

Time: _____

Place: _____

       _____

414

NATIONAL ENERGY POLICY STUDY

As we mentioned in our letter and our discussion over the telephone, our project is interested in studying the process by which national energy policy is made. We have identified (ORGNAME) as a significant actor in this policy-making process. We would like to talk with you today about national energy policy and the role that (ORGNAME) has taken in its development. Since interviews are being carried out with many organizations about national energy policy, we will follow an interview guide to make sure we cover all the questions in the shortest time possible.

☆ ☆ ☆ ☆ ☆ ☆ ☆

PART I: GOALS, PURPOSES AND INTERESTS

A1. First, we would like to ask you a few questions about (ORGNAME) in general. How would you describe the main activities and functions of your organization?

_____

_____

_____

_____

Profit-seeking firm

    (1) development of resources (e.g., research, coal mining, oil exploration, training and professional schools)

    (2) mediation and coordination activities (e.g., wholesalers, interstate pipelines)

    (3) delivery of goods and services to the ultimate consumer (e.g., electric company, private clinics)

Voluntary organization [ASK IF QUALIFIES UNDER SECTION OF 501(c)]

    (4) professional association

    (5) trade association

    (6) public interest group

Government organization

    (7) Congressional committee

    (8) executive department

    (9) independent establishment or corporation

    (10) educational institution

    (11) other

415

GOALS, PURPOSES AND INTERESTS–Continued

A2. In general, would you characterize (ORGNAME's) participation in national policy making as:

_____ (1) a predominant concern

_____ (2) one of several concerns

_____ (3) incidental to its regular business

A3. Organizations can be active in many different areas of national policy making.

[HAND CARD A TO R.]

Could you tell me those policy areas on this list in which (ORGNAME) is particularly active?

[CIRCLE NUMBERS GIVEN BY R.]

1. Agriculture	10. Health
2. Civil Rights	11. Housing
3. Consumer Rights	12. International Trade
4. Defense	13. Labor Policy
5. Domestic Economic Policy	14. Law Enforcement
6. Education	15. Social Welfare/Social Security
7. Energy	16. Transportation
8. Environmental Policy	17. Urban Development
9. Foreign Policy	

A3a. Are there any other national policy areas in which (ORGNAME) is active?

_____

_____

_____

_____

[IF ORGANIZATION IS INACTIVE IN ALL POLICY DOMAINS GO TO B1]

A4. Taking into account (ORGNAME's) efforts to affect national policy in all the areas that you mentioned above, what percentage of this total effort is directed toward national policy on energy matters?

_____% **[RECORD PERCENTAGE]**

416

PART II. NATIONAL ISSUES

Next we want to talk about the important national energy policy issues facing (ORGNAME).

B1.   In which of these national energy issues has (ORGNAME) had an interest in the past 4 to 5 years?

[HAND LIST A TO R.]

Please place a check in front of each issue in which (ORGNAME) has had an interest and then in the columns to the right under the phrase that best reflects the **level** of interest in that issue. If (ORGNAME) has had no interest in a particular issue, just go on to the issue on the next line.

B2a.   Are there any other national energy policy issues in which (ORGNAME) had an interest?

[PROBE TO CHECK IF ISSUE IS REALLY CONTAINED ON LIST A;
IF NOT, RECORD ISSUE NAME IN FULL BELOW AND ASK:]

B2b.   Can you give me the date (year) of this issue?

ISSUE NAME   DATE

_____   _____
_____   _____
_____   _____
_____   _____

B2c.   Please tell me the number that represents the level of interest that (ORGNAME) had in this issue.

_____   1   2   3   4   5
_____   1   2   3   4   5
_____   1   2   3   4   5
_____   1   2   3   4   5

B3.   Now we would like to ask you some questions about energy issues of particular interest to us.

To facilitate our discussion we have identified several events that were important in the area of energy research during the past few years.

[HAND CARD B TO R.]

Please look through this list of events and identify those events in which (ORGNAME) had a particular interest. **[I. SHOULD ENCOURAGE R. TO READ THROUGH LIST EVEN IF R. CLAIMS HIS/HER ORGANIZATION HAD NO INTEREST IN THIS AREA.]** Please tell me the numbers of the events.

[CHECK EVENTS THAT R. INDICATES AND THEN RECORD TOTAL NUMBER OF EVENTS BELOW]

You have identified _____ events. With regard to event number _____, could you please select the phrase in box A that best describes your organization's activity?

[HAND CARD C TO R.]

417

1. Active involvement in the issue; your organization had a particular position on the issue. **[GO to B4]**

2. Active involvement in the issue though your organization did not have a position on the issue; for example, a study with regard to the issue, holding a conference to discuss the issue, etc. **[GO TO B4]**

3. Publicly inactive; because your organization could not come to agreement on a common position. **[GO TO NEXT EVENT]**

4. Publicly inactive; your organization had a position but did not actively pursue it. **[GO TO B5]**

5. Inactive; not a high priority for your organization. **[GO TO NEXT EVENT]**

8. Don't know **[ASK: IS THERE SOMEONE WITH WHOM I COULD SPEAK WHO WOULD BE ABLE TO PROVIDE THIS INFORMATION? RECORD NAME AND GO TO B8]**_____

0. INAP-PRECODED: ORGANIZATION DID NOT EXIST AT THAT TIME.

B4. Did your organization become active before this event or only after the event occurred?

    1. Before **[GO TO B4a]**   2. After **[GO TO B5]**

B4a. Did your organization remain active after the event occurred?

    1. Yes

    5. No

B5. What was your organization's position on this event, was it for or against it?

    1. For **[GO TO B6]**

    2. Against **[GO TO B8]**

    3. Both for and against **[RECORD DETAILS, THEN GO TO B8]**

B6. Was your organization involved in the development of the policy option represented by this event?

    1. Yes **[GO TO B7]**

    5. No **[GO TO NEXT EVENT]**

B7. Did **your** organization formulate this policy option, was it developed in collaboration with others, or did it adopt another organization's policy position?

    1. Formulated alternative policy position . . . .

    2. Collaborated with others . . . .   **[GO TO NEXT EVENT]**

    3. Adopted another organization's policy position . . . .

B8. Did (ORGNAME) advocate an alternative policy?

    1. Yes **[GO TO B9]**

    5. No **[GO TO NEXT EVENT]**

B9. Did your organization formulate this alternative policy position, was it developed in collaboration with others, or did it adopt another organization's policy position?

   1. Formulated alternative policy position

   2. Collaborated with others

   3. Adopted another organization's policy position

[REPEAT QUESTIONS B3–B9 FOR EACH EVENT CHECKED]

[AFTER ASKING QUESTIONS B3–B9 FOR EACH EVENT THAT R. CHECKED, SEE IF STARRED EVENT HAS BEEN CHECKED.

IF R. HAS CHECKED STARRED EVENT, ASK QUESTIONS B10–B13.

IF R. DID NOT CHECK STARRED EVENT, GO TO **ENERGY INDUSTRY DEVELOPMENT**]

	Activity (B3)	When Active (B4) (B4a)	Position (B5)	(B6) Involved Alternative Policy (B8)	Formulated Policy (B7) (B9)
1. Geothermal energy	1. active position 2. active, no position 3. publicly inactive no position [STOP] 4. publicly inactive position held [GO TO B5] 5. Inactive [STOP] 8. Don't know [PROBE] 0. INAP	1. Before 2. After [IF BEFORE] 1. Yes 5. No	1. For [GO TO B6] 2. Against [GO TO B8] 3. Both for and against [RECORD DETAILS; GO TO B8]	1. Yes 5. No [STOP] 1. Yes 5. No [STOP]	1. Formulated 2. Collaborated 3. Adopted 1. Formulated 1. Collaborated 3. Adopted
2. Electric-powered automobiles	Activity (B3) ___	When Active (B4) (B4a) ___ ___	Position (B5) ___	(B6) Involved Alternative Policy (B8) ___ ___	Formulated Policy (B7) (B9) ___ ___
3. Advanced automobile engines	Activity (B3) ___	When Active (B4) (B4a) ___ ___	Position (B5) ___	(B6) Involved Alternative Policy (B8) ___ ___	Formulated Policy (B7) (B9) ___ ___
4. Breeder reactor plant funding	Activity (B3) ___	When Active (B4) (B4a) ___ ___	Position (B5) ___	(B6) Involved Alternative Policy (B8) ___ ___	Formulated Policy (B7) (B9) ___ ___
5. ICC nuclear wastes transport regulation	Activity (B3) ___	When Active (B4) (B4a) ___ ___	Position (B5) ___	(B6) Involved Alternative Policy (B8) ___ ___	Formulated Policy (B7) (B9) ___ ___
6. Continue breeder reactor development	Activity (B3) ___	When Active (B4) (B4a) ___ ___	Position (B5) ___	(B6) Involved Alternative Policy (B8) ___ ___	Formulated Policy (B7) (B9) ___ ___

419

		Activity (B3)	When Active (B4) (B4a)	Position (B5)	(B6) Involved Alternative Policy (B8)	Formulated Policy (B7) (B9)
____	7. Construction halt of breeder reactor	1. active position 2. active, no position 3. publicly inactive no position [STOP] 4. publicly inactive position held [GO TO B5] 5. Inactive [STOP] 8. Don't know [PROBE] 0. INAP	1. Before 2. After [IF BEFORE] 1. Yes 5. No	1. For [GO TO B6] 2. Against [GO TO B8] 3. Both for and against [RECORD DETAILS; GO TO B8]	1. Yes 5. No [STOP] 1. Yes 5. No [STOP]	1. Formulated 2. Collaborated 3. Adopted 1. Formulated 1. Collaborated 3. Adopted

		Activity (B3)	When Active (B4) (B4a)	Position (B5)	(B6) Involved Alternative Policy (B8)	Formulated Policy (B7) (B9)
____ **	8. Breeder reactor termination proposal	____	____ ____	____	____	____ ____ ____

[ASK B10–B13]

		Activity (B3)	When Active (B4) (B4a)	Position (B5)	(B6) Involved Alternative Policy (B8)	Formulated Policy (B7) (B9)
____	9. Nuclear wastes storage	____	____ ____	____	____	____ ____

		Activity (B3)	When Active (B4) (B4a)	Position (B5)	(B6) Involved Alternative Policy (B8)	Formulated Policy (B7) (B9)
____	10. Breeder reactor funding	____	____ ____	____	____	____ ____

		Activity (B3)	When Active (B4) (B4a)	Position (B5)	(B6) Involved Alternative Policy (B8)	Formulated Policy (B7) (B9)
____	11. Underground nuclear wastes	____	____ ____	____	____	____ ____

B10. Now we would like to ask a few additional questions about event number 8, the breeder reactor termination proposal.

In particular, what organizations, if any, did (ORGNAME) join with in trying to influence this event?
[RECORD FULL NAME]

[PROBE: IF GROUP CATEGORY GIVEN, ASK: Can you give me the names of specific organizations?]

	(ORGNAME) Initiated	Other Initiated
_____	____	____
_____	____	____
_____	____	____
_____	____	____
_____	____	____
_____	____	____
_____	____	____
_____	____	____
_____	____	____
_____	____	____
_____	____	____
_____	____	____
_____	____	____
_____	____	____

B10a. **[FOR EACH ORGANIZATION MENTIONED IN B10]** Can you tell me whether (ORGNAME) initiated the joint effort or if the other organization did so?

B11. How would you characterize the activities that (ORGNAME) engaged in during this period? Please indicate all that apply.

[HAND CARD G TO R.]

[CIRCLE ALL THAT APPLY]

(1) Conducted research on a topic

(2) Acted as a clearinghouse of information

(3) Formulated policy alternatives

(4) Provided technical advice

(5) Advocated a policy position

(6) Collaborated with other organizations with long-term interest in this topic

(7) Recruited organizations not usually involved in this topic

(8) Mobilized public opinion using mass media (press releases, advertisements)

(9) Mobilized opinion at the grassroots (letter writing, etc.)

(10) Coordinated the various efforts to influence the outcome

B12. What are the names of the major organizations, including government agencies, which were opposed to (ORGNAME's) position?

_____	1 2 3 4 5 6 7 8 9 10	
_____	1 2 3 4 5 6 7 8 9 10	
_____	1 2 3 4 5 6 7 8 9 10	
_____	1 2 3 4 5 6 7 8 9 10	
_____	1 2 3 4 5 6 7 8 9 10	
_____	1 2 3 4 5 6 7 8 9 10	
_____	1 2 3 4 5 6 7 8 9 10	
_____	1 2 3 4 5 6 7 8 9 10	
_____	1 2 3 4 5 6 7 8 9 10	
_____	1 2 3 4 5 6 7 8 9 10	
_____	1 2 3 4 5 6 7 8 9 10	
_____	1 2 3 4 5 6 7 8 9 10	

421

B13a. Now I would like you to look at this card and tell me what reasons each of these organizations had for their opposition.

[HAND CARD H TO R.]

[CIRCLE APPROPRIATE NUMBERS ABOVE FOR EACH ORGANIZATION]

1. Motivated by private economic gain

2. Tried to enhance its public image

3. Acted in public interest, but misguided

4. Sought to protect or extend its sphere of influence

5. Involved because of its ties to other organizations

6. Represented the interests of its members or clientele

7. Participated as part of an exchange with a different organization on another issue

    (log rolling)

8. Strategic manuever for possible long-range gain

9. Attempted to punish our organization for past actions

10. Automatically took a position opposed to our position

B13b. Are there any reasons not on this list that any organization may have had to be in opposition?
[RECORD NEXT TO APPROPRIATE ORGANIZATION]

B3. Next we have identified several events that were important in the area of **Industry development** during the past few years.

[HAND CARD D TO R.]

Please look through this list of events and identify those events in which (ORGNAME) had a particular interest. **[I. SHOULD ENCOURAGE R. TO READ THROUGH LIST EVEN IF R. CLAIMS HIS/HER ORGANIZATION HAD NO INTEREST IN THIS AREA.]** Please tell me the numbers of the events.

[CHECK EVENTS THAT R. INDICATES AND THEN RECORD NUMBER OF EVENTS BELOW]

You have identified _____ events. With regard to event number _____, could you please select the phrase in box A that best describes your organization's activity?

[HAND CARD C TO R.]

1. Active involvement in the issue; your organization had a particular position on the issue. **[GO to B4]**

2. Active involvement in the issue though your organization did not have a position on the issue; for example, a study with regard to the issue, holding a conference to discuss the issue, etc. **[GO TO B4]**

3. Publicly inactive; because your organization could not come to agreement on a common position. **[GO TO NEXT EVENT]**

4. Publicly inactive; your organization had a position but did not actively pursue it. **[GO TO B5]**

5. Inactive; not a high priority for your organization. **[GO TO NEXT EVENT]**

8. Don't know **[ASK: IS THERE SOMEONE WITH WHOM I COULD SPEAK WHO WOULD BE ABLE TO PROVIDE THIS INFORMATION? RECORD NAME AND GO TO B8]_____**

0. INAP-PRECODED: ORGANIZATION DID NOT EXIST AT THAT TIME.

B4. Did your organization become active before this event or only after the event occurred?

1. Before **[GO TO B4a]**   2. After **[GO TO B5]**

B4a. Did your organization remain active after the event occurred?

1. Yes

5. No

B5. What was your organization's position on this event, was it for or against it?

1. For **[GO TO B6]**

2. Against **[GO TO B8]**

3. Both for and against **[RECORD DETAILS, THEN GO TO B8]**

B6. Was your organization involved in the development of the policy option represented by this event?

1. Yes

5. No **[GO TO NEXT EVENT]**

423

B7. Did **your** organization formulate this policy option, was it developed in collaboration with others, or did it adopt another organization's policy position?

    1. Formulated alternative policy position . . . .

    2. Collaborated with others . . . .   **[GO TO NEXT EVENT]**

    3. Adopted another organization's policy position . . . .

B8. Did (ORGNAME) advocate an alternative policy?

    1. Yes

    2. No **[GO TO NEXT EVENT]**

B9. Did your organization formulate this alternative policy position, was it developed in collaboration with others, or did it adopt another organization's policy position?

    1. Formulated alternative policy position

    2. Collaborated with others

    3. Adopted another organization's policy position

[REPEAT QUESTIONS B3–B9 FOR EACH EVENT CHECKED]

[AFTER ASKING QUESTIONS B3–B9 FOR EACH EVENT THAT R. CHECKED, SEE IF STARRED EVENT HAS BEEN CHECKED.

IF R. HAS CHECKED STARRED EVENT, ASK QUESTIONS B10–B13.

IF R. DID NOT CHECK STARRED EVENT, GO TO *ENERGY REGULATORY ISSUES]*

		Activity (B3)	When Active (B4) (B4a)	Position (B5)	(B6) Involved Alternative Policy (B8)	Formulated Policy (B7) (B9)
____	1. Trans-Alaska oil pipeline	1. active position 2. active, no position 3. publicly inactive no position [STOP] 4. publicly inactive position held [GO TO B5] 5. Inactive [STOP] 8. Don't know [PROBE] 0. INAP	1. Before 2. After [IF BEFORE] 1.Yes 5. No	1. For [GO TO B6] 2. Against [GO TO B8] 3. Both for and against [RECORD DETAILS; GO TO B8]	1. Yes 5. No [STOP] 1.Yes 5. No [STOP]	1. Formulated 2. Collaborated 3. Adopted 1. Formulated 1. Collaborated 3. Adopted
		Activity (B3)	When Active (B4) (B4a)	Position (B5)	(B6) Involved Alternative Policy (B8)	Formulated Policy (B7) (B9)
____	2. Solar heating & cooling	____	____ ____	____	____	____ ____
		Activity (B3)	When Active (B4) (B4a)	Position (B5)	(B6) Involved Alternative Policy (B8)	Formulated Policy (B7) (B9)
____	3. Coal lands leasing procedures	____	____ ____	____	____	____ ____
		Activity (B3)	When Active (B4) (B4a)	Position (B5)	(B6) Involved Alternative Policy (B8)	Formulated Policy (B7) (B9)
____	4. Uranium enrichment	____	____ ____	____	____	____ ____

	Activity (B3)	When Active (B4) (B4a)	Position (B5)	(B6) Involved Alternative Policy (B8)	Formulated Policy (B7) (B9)
_____ 5. Synthetic fuels technologies	1. active position 2. active, no position 3. publicly inactive no position [STOP] 4. publicly inactive position held [GO TO B5] 5. Inactive [STOP] 8. Don't know [PROBE] 0. INAP	1. Before 2. After [IF BEFORE] 1.Yes 5. No	1. For [GO TO B6] 2. Against [GO TO B8] 3. Both for and against [RECORD DETAILS; GO TO B8]	1. Yes 5. No [STOP] 1.Yes 5. No [STOP]	1. Formulated 2. Collaborated 3. Adopted 1. Formulated 1. Collaborated 3. Adopted

	Activity (B3)	When Active (B4) (B4a)	Position (B5)	(B6) Involved Alternative Policy (B8)	Formulated Policy (B7) (B9)
_____ 6. Outer Continental Shelf	_____	_____ _____	_____	_____ _____	_____ _____ _____ _____

	Activity (B3)	When Active (B4) (B4a)	Position (B5)	(B6) Involved Alternative Policy (B8)	Formulated Policy (B7) (B9)
_____ 7. Solar equipment	_____	_____ _____	_____	_____ _____	_____ _____ _____ _____

	Activity (B3)	When Active (B4) (B4a)	Position (B5)	(B6) Involved Alternative Policy (B8)	Formulated Policy (B7) (B9)
_____ 8. Solar tax credits	_____	_____ _____	_____	_____ _____	_____ _____ _____ _____

	Activity (B3)	When Active (B4) (B4a)	Position (B5)	(B6) Involved Alternative Policy (B8)	Formulated Policy (B7) (B9)
_____ 9. Alaska–Canada natural gas pipeline	_____	_____ _____	_____	_____ _____	_____ _____ _____ _____

	Activity (B3)	When Active (B4) (B4a)	Position (B5)	(B6) Involved Alternative Policy (B8)	Formulated Policy (B7) (B9)
_____ 10. Alaska lands bill	_____	_____ _____	_____	_____ _____	_____ _____ _____ _____

	Activity (B3)	When Active (B4) (B4a)	Position (B5)	(B6) Involved Alternative Policy (B8)	Formulated Policy (B7) (B9)
_____ 11 Oil from shale rock	_____	_____ _____	_____	_____ _____	_____ _____ _____ _____

	Activity (B3)	When Active (B4) (B4a)	Position (B5)	(B6) Involved Alternative Policy (B8)	Formulated Policy (B7) (B9)
_____ 12. Solar photovoltaic cells	_____	_____ _____	_____	_____ _____	_____ _____ _____ _____

	Activity (B3)	When Active (B4) (B4a)	Position (B5)	(B6) Involved Alternative Policy (B8)	Formulated Policy (B7) (B9)
_____ **13. Synthetic fuels industry	_____	_____ _____	_____	_____ _____	_____ _____ _____ _____

[ASK B10–B13]

	Activity (B3)	When Active (B4) (B4a)	Position (B5)	(B6) Involved Alternative Policy (B8)	Formulated Policy (B7) (B9)
_____ 14. Energy Mobilization Board	_____	_____ _____	_____	_____ _____	_____ _____ _____ _____

	Activity (B3)	When Active (B4) (B4a)	Position (B5)	(B6) Involved Alternative Policy (B8)	Formulated Policy (B7) (B9)
____ 15. Solar bank	1. active position 2. active, no position 3. publicly inactive no position [STOP] 4. publicly inactive position held [GO TO B5] 5. inactive [STOP] 8. Don't know [PROBE] 0. INAP	1. Before 2. After [IF BEFORE] 1.Yes 5. No	1. For [GO TO B6] 2. Against [GO TO B8] 3. Both for and against [RECORD DETAILS; GO TO B8]	1. Yes 5. No [STOP] 1.Yes 5. No [STOP]	1. Formulated 2. Collaborated 3. Adopted 1. Formulated 1. Collaborated 3. Adopted

	Activity (B3)	When Active (B4) (B4a)	Position (B5)	(B6) Involved Alternative Policy (B8)	Formulated Policy (B7) (B9)
____ 16. U.S. Synthetic Fuels Corporation	____	____ ____	____	____	____ ____ ____

B10. Now we would like to ask a few additional questions about event number 13, the synthetic fuel industry.

In particular, what organizations, if any, did (ORGNAME) join with in trying to influence this event? [RECORD FULL NAME]

[PROBE: IF GROUP CATEGORY GIVEN, ASK: Can you give me the names of specific organizations?]

	(ORGNAME) Initiated	Other Initiated
_____	_____	_____
_____	_____	_____
_____	_____	_____
_____	_____	_____
_____	_____	_____
_____	_____	_____
_____	_____	_____
_____	_____	_____
_____	_____	_____
_____	_____	_____
_____	_____	_____
_____	_____	_____
_____	_____	_____
_____	_____	_____

B10a. [FOR EACH ORGANIZATION MENTIONED IN B10] Can you tell me whether (ORGNAME) initiated the joint effort or if the other organization did so?

426

B11. How would you characterize the activities that (ORGNAME) engaged in during this period? Please indicate all that apply.

[HAND CARD G TO R.]

[CIRCLE ALL THAT APPLY]

　(1) Conducted research on a topic

　(2) Acted as a clearinghouse of information

　(3) Formulated policy alternatives

　(4) Provided technical advice

　(5) Advocated a policy position

　(6) Collaborated with other organizations with long-term interest in this topic

　(7) Recruited organizations not usually involved in this topic

　(8) Mobilized public opinion using mass media (press releases, advertisements)

　(9) Mobilized opinion at the grassroots (letter writing, etc.)

　(10) Coordinated the various efforts to influence the outcome

B12. What are the names of the major organizations, including government agencies, which were opposed to (ORGNAME's) position?

1	2	3	4	5	6	7	8	9	10
1	2	3	4	5	6	7	8	9	10
1	2	3	4	5	6	7	8	9	10
1	2	3	4	5	6	7	8	9	10
1	2	3	4	5	6	7	8	9	10
1	2	3	4	5	6	7	8	9	10
1	2	3	4	5	6	7	8	9	10
1	2	3	4	5	6	7	8	9	10
1	2	3	4	5	6	7	8	9	10
1	2	3	4	5	6	7	8	9	10
1	2	3	4	5	6	7	8	9	10
1	2	3	4	5	6	7	8	9	10

B13a. Now I would like you to look at this card and tell me what reasons each of these organizations had for their opposition.

[HAND CARD H TO R.]

[CIRCLE APPROPRIATE NUMBERS ABOVE FOR EACH ORGANIZATION]

　1. Motivated by private economic gain

　2. Tried to enhance its public image

　3. Acted in public interest, but misguided

　4. Sought to protect or extend its sphere of influence

　5. Involved because of its ties to other organizations

　6. Represented the interests of its members or clientele

　7. Participated as part of an exchange with a different organization on another issue (log rolling)

　8. Strategic manuever for possible long-range gain

　9. Attempted to punish our organization for past actions

　10. Automatically took a position opposed to our position

B13b. Are there any reasons not on this list that any organization may have had to be in opposition? **[RECORD NEXT TO APPROPRIATE ORGANIZATION]**

427

B3. Next we have identified several events that were important in the area of **energy regulation** during the past few years.

[HAND CARD E TO R.]

Please look through this list of events and identify those events in which (ORGNAME) had a particular interest. [I. SHOULD ENCOURAGE R. TO READ THROUGH LIST EVEN IF R. CLAIMS HIS/HER ORGANIZATION HAD NO INTEREST IN THIS AREA.] Please tell me the numbers of the events.

[CHECK EVENTS THAT R. INDICATES AND THEN RECORD NUMBER OF EVENTS BELOW]

You have identified _____ events. With regard to event number _____, could you please select the phrase in box A that best describes your organization's activity?

[HAND CARD C TO R.]

1. **Active involvement in the issue; your organization had a particular position on the issue. [GO to B4]**

2. Active involvement in the issue though your organization did not have a position on the issue; for example, a study with regard to the issue, holding a conference to discuss the issue, etc. **[GO TO B4]**

3. Publicly inactive; because your organization could not come to agreement on a common position. **[GO TO NEXT EVENT]**

4. Publicly inactive; your organization had a position but did not actively pursue it. **[GO TO B5]**

5. Inactive; not a high priority for your organization. **[GO TO NEXT EVENT]**

8. Don't know **[ASK: IS THERE SOMEONE WITH WHOM I COULD SPEAK WHO WOULD BE ABLE TO PROVIDE THIS INFORMATION? RECORD NAME AND GO TO B8]**_____

0. INAP-PRECODED: ORGANIZATION DID NOT EXIST AT THAT TIME.

B4. Did your organization become active before this event or only after the event occurred?

1. Before **[GO TO B4a]**   2. After **[GO TO B5]**

B4a. Did your organization remain active after the event occurred?

1. Yes

5. No

B5. What was your organization's position on this event, was it for or against it?

1. For **[GO TO B6]**

2. Against **[GO TO B8]**

3. Both for and against **[RECORD DETAILS, THEN GO TO B8]**

B6. Was your organization involved in the development of the policy option represented by this event?

1. Yes

5. No **[GO TO NEXT EVENT]**

428

B7. Did **your** organization formulate this policy option, was it developed in collaboration with others, or did it adopt another organization's policy position?

    1. Formulated alternative policy position . . . .

    2. Collaborated with others. . . . .   **[GO TO NEXT EVENT]**

    3. Adopted another organization's policy position . . . .

B8. Did (ORGNAME) advocate an alternative policy?

    1. Yes

    2. No **[GO TO NEXT EVENT]**

B9. Did your organization formulate this alternative policy position, was it developed in collaboration with others, or did it adopt another organization's policy position?

    1. Formulated alternative policy position

    2. Collaborated with others

    3. Adopted another organization's policy position

[REPEAT QUESTIONS B3–B9 FOR EACH EVENT CHECKED]

[AFTER ASKING QUESTIONS B3–B9 FOR EACH EVENT THAT R. CHECKED, SEE IF STARRED EVENT HAS BEEN CHECKED.

IF R. HAS CHECKED STARRED EVENT, ASK QUESTIONS B10–B13.

IF R. DID NOT CHECK STARRED EVENT, GO TO *ENERGY CONSUMPTION]*

	Activity (B3)	When Active (B4) (B4a)	Position (B5)	(B6) Involved Alternative Policy (B8)	Formulated Policy (B7) (B9)
___ 1. Price control on domestic oil and natural gas	1. active position 2. active, no position 3. publicly inactive no position [STOP] 4. publicly inactive position held [GO TO B5] 5. Inactive [STOP] 8. Don't know [PROBE] 0. INAP	1. Before 2. After [IF BEFORE] 1.Yes 5. No	1. For [GO TO B6] 2. Against [GO TO B8] 3. Both for and against [RECORD DETAILS; GO TO B8]	1. Yes 5. No [STOP] 1.Yes 5. No [STOP]	1. Formulated 2. Collaborated 3. Adopted 1. Formulated 1. Collaborated 3. Adopted
	Activity (B3)	When Active (B4) (B4a)	Position (B5)	(B6) Involved Alternative Policy (B8)	Formulated Policy (B7) (B9)
___ 2. Mandatory controls for oil	___	___ ___	___	___ ___	___ ___
	Activity (B3)	When Active (B4) (B4a)	Position (B5)	(B6) Involved Alternative Policy (B8)	Formulated Policy (B7) (B9)
___ 3. Energy emergency allocation powers	___	___ ___	___	___ ___	___ ___
	Activity (B3)	When Active (B4) (B4a)	Position (B5)	(B6) Involved Alternative Policy (B8)	Formulated Policy (B7) (B9)
___ 4. Nuclear accident insurance	___	___ ___	___	___ ___	___ ___

429

	Activity (B3)	When Active (B4) (B4a)	Position (B5)	(B6) Involved Alternative Policy (B8)	Formulated Policy (B7) (B9)
____ 5. NRC created	1. active position 2. active, no position 3. publicly inactive no position [STOP] 4. publicly inactive position held [GO TO B5] 5. Inactive [STOP] 8. Don't know [PROBE] 0. INAP	1. Before 2. After [IF BEFORE] 1.Yes 5. No	1. For [GO TO B6] 2. Against [GO TO B8] 3. Both for and against [RECORD DETAILS; GO TO B8]	1. Yes 5. No [STOP] 1.Yes 5. No [STOP]	1. Formulated 2. Collaborated 3. Adopted 1. Formulated 1. Collaborated 3. Adopted

	Activity (B3)	When Active (B4) (B4a)	Position (B5)	(B6) Involved Alternative Policy (B8)	Formulated Policy (B7) (B9)
____ 6. Price controls on domestic oil	____	____ ____	____	____ ____	____ ____

	Activity (B3)	When Active (B4) (B4a)	Position (B5)	(B6) Involved Alternative Policy (B8)	Formulated Policy (B7) (B9)
____ 7. Horizontal and vertical divestiture	____	____ ____	____	____ ____	____ ____

	Activity (B3)	When Active (B4) (B4a)	Position (B5)	(B6) Involved Alternative Policy (B8)	Formulated Policy (B7) (B9)
____ 8. Price controls on petroleum products	____	____ ____	____	____ ____	____ ____

	Activity (B3)	When Active (B4) (B4a)	Position (B5)	(B6) Involved Alternative Policy (B8)	Formulated Policy (B7) (B9)
____ 9. Price control exemptions on strip-per wells	____	____ ____	____	____ ____	____ ____

	Activity (B3)	When Active (B4) (B4a)	Position (B5)	(B6) Involved Alternative Policy (B8)	Formulated Policy (B7) (B9)
____ 10. Vertical divestiture	____	____ ____	____	____ ____	____ ____

	Activity (B3)	When Active (B4) (B4a)	Position (B5)	(B6) Involved Alternative Policy (B8)	Formulated Policy (B7) (B9)
____ 11. Natural gas price ceiling	____	____ ____	____	____ ____	____ ____

	Activity (B3)	When Active (B4) (B4a)	Position (B5)	(B6) Involved Alternative Policy (B8)	Formulated Policy (B7) (B9)
____ 12. Emergency Natural Gas Act	____	____ ____	____	____ ____	____ ____

	Activity (B3)	When Active (B4) (B4a)	Position (B5)	(B6) Involved Alternative Policy (B8)	Formulated Policy (B7) (B9)
____ 13. Coal strip mining control	____	____ ____	____	____ ____	____ ____

	Activity (B3)	When Active (B4) (B4a)	Position (B5)	(B6) Involved Alternative Policy (B8)	Formulated Policy (B7) (B9)
____ 14. DOE creation bill	____	____ ____	____	____ ____	____ ____

	Activity (B3)	When Active (B4) (B4a)	Position (B5)	(B6) Involved Alternative Policy (B8)	Formulated Policy (B7) (B9)

___ 15. Coal slurry pipeline	1. active position
	2. active, no position
	3. publicly inactive
	   no position [STOP]
	4. publicly inactive
	   position held [GO TO B5]
	5. Inactive [STOP]
	8. Don't know [PROBE]
	0. INAP
		1. Before
		2. After
		
		[IF BEFORE]
		1.Yes
		5. No
			1. For
			   [GO TO B6]
			2. Against
			   [GO TO B8]
			3. Both for and
			   against
			[RECORD
			DETAILS; GO
			TO B8]
				1. Yes
				5. No [STOP]
				
				1.Yes
				5. No [STOP]
					1. Formulated
					2. Collaborated
					3. Adopted
					
					1. Formulated
					1. Collaborated
					3. Adopted

	Activity (B3)	When Active (B4) (B4a)	Position (B5)	(B6) Involved Alternative Policy (B8)	Formulated Policy (B7) (B9)
___ 16. Crude oil equalization tax	___	___ ___	___	___ ___	___ ___
	Activity (B3)	When Active (B4) (B4a)	Position (B5)	(B6) Involved Alternative Policy (B8)	Formulated Policy . (B7) (B9)
___ 17. Natural gas deregulation (House)	___	___ ___	___	___ ___	___ ___
	Activity (B3)	When Active (B4) (B4a)	Position (B5)	(B6) Involved Alternative Policy (B8)	Formulated Policy (B7) (B9)
___ 18. Energy Secretary	___	___ ___	___	___ ___	___ ___
	Activity (B3)	When Active (B4) (B4a)	Position (B5)	(B6) Involved Alternative Policy (B8)	Formulated Policy (B7) (B9)
___ 19. Natural gas deregulation (Senate)	___	___ ___	___	___ ___	___ ___
	Activity (B3)	When Active (B4) (B4a)	Position (B5)	(B6) Involved Alternative Policy (B8)	Formulated Policy (B7) (B9)
___ 20. Coal slurry pipeline	___	___ ___	___	___ ___	___ ___
	Activity (B3)	When Active (B4) (B4a)	Position (B5)	(B6) Involved Alternative Policy (B8)	Formulated Policy (B7) (B9)
___ 21. Strip mining control	___	___ ___	___	___ ___	___ ___
	Activity (B3)	When Active (B4) (B4a)	Position (B5)	(B6) Involved Alternative Policy (B8)	Formulated Policy (B7) (B9)
___ 22. Nuclear regulatory hearing	___	___ ___	___	___ ___	___ ___
	Activity (B3)	When Active (B4) (B4a)	Position (B5)	(B6) Involved Alternative Policy (B8)	. Formulated Policy (B7) (B9)
___ 23. Natural gas deregulation (con-ference)	___	___ ___	___	___ ___	___ ___
	Activity (B3)	When Active (B4) (B4a)	Position (B5)	(B6) Involved Alternative Policy (B8)	Formulated Policy (B7) (B9)
___ 24. Leasing of Federal coal lands	___	___ ___	___	___ ___	___ ___

431

		Activity (B3)	When Active (B4) (B4a)	Position (B5)	(B6) Involved Alternative Policy (B8)	Formulated Policy (B7) (B9)
____ 25. Domestic oil price controls	1. active position 2. active, no position 3. publicly inactive no position [STOP] 4. publicly inactive position held [GO TO B5] 5. Inactive [STOP] 8. Don't know [PROBE] 0. INAP		1. Before 2. After [IF BEFORE] 1.Yes 5. No	1. For [GO TO B6] 2. Against [GO TO B8] 3. Both for and against [RECORD DETAILS; GO TO B8]	1. Yes 5. No [STOP] 1.Yes 5. No [STOP]	1. Formulated 2. Collaborated 3. Adopted 1. Formulated 1. Collaborated 3. Adopted

	Activity (B3)	When Active (B4) (B4a)	Position (B5)	(B6) Involved Alternative Policy (B8)	Formulated Policy (B7) (B9)
____**26. Power plant construction moratorium	____	____ ____	____	____	____ ____

[ASK B10–B13]

	Activity (B3)	When Active (B4) (B4a)	Position (B5)	(B6) Involved Alternative Policy (B8)	Formulated Policy (B7) (B9)
____ 27. Nuclear emergency evacuation plan	____	____ ____	____	____	____ ____

	Activity (B3)	When Active (B4) (B4a)	Position (B5)	(B6) Involved Alternative Policy (B8)	Formulated Policy (B7) (B9)
____ 28. Tax windfall profits	____	____ ____	____	____	____ ____

	Activity (B3)	When Active (B4) (B4a)	Position (B5)	(B6) Involved Alternative Policy (B8)	Formulated Policy (B7) (B9)
____ 29. Coal strip mining control	____	____ ____	____	____	____ ____

	Activity (B3)	When Active (B4) (B4a)	Position (B5)	(B6) Involved Alternative Policy (B8)	Formulated Policy (B7) (B9)
____ 30. Energy Secretary	____	____ ____	____	____	____ ____

	Activity (B3)	When Active (B4) (B4a)	Position (B5)	(B6) Involved Alternative Policy (B8)	Formulated Policy (B7) (B9)
____ 31. Deregulation of railroads, coal freight rates	____	____ ____	____	____	____ ____

	Activity (B3)	When Active (B4) (B4a)	Position (B5)	(B6) Involved Alternative Policy (B8)	Formulated Policy (B7) (B9)
____ 32. Nuclear power plant licensing	____	____ ____	____	____	____ ____

	Activity (B3)	When Active (B4) (B4a)	Position (B5)	(B6) Involved Alternative Policy (B8)	Formulated Policy (B7) (B9)
____ 33. NRC reorganization	____	____ ____	____	____	____ ____

	Activity (B3)	When Active (B4) (B4a)	Position (B5)	(B6) Involved Alternative Policy (B8)	Formulated Policy (B7) (B9)
____ 34. Strip mining control	____	____ ____	____	____	____ ____

432

B10. Now we would like to ask a few additional questions about event number 26, the power plant construction moratorium.

In particular, what organizations, if any, did (ORGNAME) join with in trying to influence this event? **[RECORD FULL NAME]**

[PROBE: IF GROUP CATEGORY GIVEN, ASK: Can you give me the names of specific organizations?]

	(ORGNAME) Initiated	Other Initiated
_____	_____	_____
_____	_____	_____
_____	_____	_____
_____	_____	_____
_____	_____	_____
_____	_____	_____
_____	_____	_____
_____	_____	_____
_____	_____	_____
_____	_____	_____
_____	_____	_____
_____	_____	_____
_____	_____	_____
_____	_____	_____
_____	_____	_____

B10a. **[FOR EACH ORGANIZATION MENTIONED IN B10]** Can you tell me whether (ORGNAME) initiated the joint effort or if the other organization did so?

B11. How would you characterize the activities that (ORGNAME) engaged in during this period? Please indicate all that apply.

[HAND CARD G TO R.]

[CIRCLE ALL THAT APPLY]

(1) Conducted research on a topic

(2) Acted as a clearinghouse of information

(3) Formulated policy alternatives

(4) Provided technical advice

(5) Advocated a policy position

(6) Collaborated with other organizations with long-term interest in this topic

(7) Recruited organizations not usually involved in this topic

(8) Mobilized public opinion using mass media (press releases, advertisements)

(9) Mobilized opinion at the grassroots (letter writing, etc.)

(10) Coordinated the various efforts to influence the outcome

433

B12. What are the names of the major organizations, including government agencies, which were opposed to (ORGNAME's) position?

_____	1	2	3	4	5	6	7	8	9	10
_____	1	2	3	4	5	6	7	8	9	10
_____	1	2	3	4	5	6	7	8	9	10
_____	1	2	3	4	5	6	7	8	9	10
_____	1	2	3	4	5	6	7	8	9	10
_____	1	2	3	4	5	6	7	8	9	10
_____	1	2	3	4	5	6	7	8	9	10
_____	1	2	3	4	5	6	7	8	9	10
_____	1	2	3	4	5	6	7	8	9	10
_____	1	2	3	4	5	6	7	8	9	10
_____	1	2	3	4	5	6	7	8	9	10
_____	1	2	3	4	5	6	7	8	9	10

B13a. Now I would like you to look at this card and tell me what reasons each of these organizations had for their opposition.

[HAND CARD H TO R.]

[CIRCLE APPROPRIATE NUMBERS ABOVE FOR EACH ORGANIZATION]

1. Motivated by private economic gain
2. Tried to enhance its public image
3. Acted in public interest, but misguided
4. Sought to protect or extend its sphere of influence
5. Involved because of its ties to other organizations
6. Represented the interests of its members or clientele
7. Participated as part of an exchange with a different organization on another issue (log rolling)
8. Strategic manuever for possible long-range gain
9. Attempted to punish our organization for past actions
10. Automatically took a position opposed to our position

B13b. Are there any reasons not on this list that any organization may have had to be in opposition?
[RECORD NEXT TO APPROPRIATE ORGANIZATION]

434

B3. Next we have identified several events that were important in the area of **energy consumption** during the past few years.

[HAND CARD F TO R.]

Please look through this list of events and identify those events in which (ORGNAME) had a particular interest. [I. SHOULD ENCOURAGE R. TO READ THROUGH LIST EVEN IF R. CLAIMS HIS/HER ORGANIZATION HAD NO INTEREST IN THIS AREA.] Please tell me the numbers of the events.

[CHECK EVENTS THAT R. INDICATES AND THEN RECORD NUMBER OF EVENTS BELOW]

You have identified _____ events. With regard to event number _____, could you please select the phrase in box A that best describes your organization's activity?

[HAND CARD C TO R.]

1. Active involvement in the issue; your organization had a particular position on the issue. [GO to B4]

2. Active involvement in the issue though your organization did not have a position on the issue; for example, a study with regard to the issue, holding a conference to discuss the issue, etc. [GO TO B4]

3. Publicly inactive; because your organization could not come to agreement on a common position. [GO TO NEXT EVENT]

4. Publicly inactive; your organization had a position but did not actively pursue it. [GO TO B5]

5. Inactive; not a high priority for your organization. [GO TO NEXT EVENT]

8. Don't know [ASK: IS THERE SOMEONE WITH WHOM I COULD SPEAK WHO WOULD BE ABLE TO PROVIDE THIS INFORMATION? RECORD NAME AND GO TO B8]_____

0. INAP-PRECODED: ORGANIZATION DID NOT EXIST AT THAT TIME.

B4. Did your organization become active before this event or only after the event occurred?

1. Before [GO TO B4a]   2. After [GO TO B5]

B4a. Did your organization remain active after the event occurred?

1. Yes

5. No

B5. What was your organization's position on this event, was it for or against it?

1. For [GO TO B6]

2. Against [GO TO B8]

3. Both for and against [RECORD DETAILS, THEN GO TO B8]

B6. Was your organization involved in the development of the policy option represented by this event?

1. Yes

5. No [GO TO NEXT EVENT]

435

B7. Did **your** organization formulate this policy option, was it developed in collaboration with others, or did it adopt another organization's policy position?

    1. Formulated alternative policy position . . . .

    2. Collaborated with others . . . . **[GO TO NEXT EVENT]**

    3. Adopted another organization's policy position . . . .

B8. Did (ORGNAME) advocate an alternative policy?

    1. Yes

    2. No **[GO TO NEXT EVENT]**

B9. Did your organization formulate this alternative policy position, was it developed in collaboration with others, or did it adopt another organization's policy position?

    1. Formulated alternative policy position

    2. Collaborated with others

    3. Adopted another organization's policy position

[REPEAT QUESTIONS B3–B9 FOR EACH EVENT CHECKED]

[AFTER ASKING QUESTIONS B3–B9 FOR EACH EVENT THAT R. CHECKED, SEE IF STARRED EVENT HAS BEEN CHECKED.

IF R. HAS CHECKED STARRED EVENT, ASK QUESTIONS B10–B13.

IF R. DID NOT CHECK STARRED EVENT, GO TO *PART III: COMMUNICATION*]

	Activity (B3)	When Active (B4) (B4a)	Position (B5)	(B6) Involved Alternative Policy (B8)	Formulated Policy (B7) (B9)
____ 1. 55-mph speed limit	1. active position 2. active, no position 3. publicly inactive no position [STOP] 4. publicly inactive position held [GO TO B5] 5. Inactive [STOP] 8. Don't know [PROBE] 0. INAP	1. Before 2. After [IF BEFORE] 1.Yes 5. No	1. For [GO TO B6] 2. Against [GO TO B8] 3. Both for and against [RECORD DETAILS; GO TO B8]	1. Yes 5. No [STOP] 1.Yes 5. No [STOP]	1. Formulated 2. Collaborated 3. Adopted 1. Formulated 1. Collaborated 3. Adopted
____ 2. Imported oil fee	Activity (B3) ____	When Active (B4) (B4a) ____ ____	Position (B5) ____	(B6) Involved Alternative Policy (B8) ____	Formulated Policy (B7) (B9) ____ ____
____ 3. Gasoline tax	Activity (B3) ____	When Active (B4) (B4a) ____ ____	Position (B5) ____	(B6) Involved Alternative Policy (B8) ____	Formulated Policy (B7) (B9) ____ ____
____ 4. Conversion to coal	Activity (B3) ____	When Active (B4) (B4a) ____ ____	Position (B5) ____	(B6) Involved Alternative Policy (B8) ____	Formulated Policy (B7) (B9) ____ ____
____ 5. Standby gasoline tax	Activity (B3) ____	When Active (B4) (B4a) ____ ____	Position (B5) ____	(B6) Involved Alternative Policy (B8) ____	Formulated Policy (B7) (B9) ____ ____

436

	Activity (B3)	When Active (B4) (B4a)	Position (B5)	(B6) Involved Alternative Policy (B8)	Formulated Policy (B7) (B9)
___ 6. "Gas-guzzler" tax	1. active position 2. active, no position 3. publicly inactive no position [STOP] 4. publicly inactive position held [GO TO B5] 5. Inactive [STOP] 8. Don't know [PROBE] 0. INAP	1. Before 2. After [IF BEFORE] 1. Yes 5. No	1. For [GO TO B6] 2. Against [GO TO B8] 3. Both for and against [RECORD DETAILS; GO TO B8]	1. Yes 5. No [STOP] 1. Yes 5. No [STOP]	1. Formulated 2. Collaborated 3. Adopted 1. Formulated 1. Collaborated 3. Adopted

	Activity (B3)	When Active (B4) (B4a)	Position (B5)	(B6) Involved Alternative Policy (B8)	Formulated Policy (B7) (B9)
___ 7. Automobile fuel efficiency standards	___	___ ___	___	___ ___	___ ___

	Activity (B3)	When Active (B4) (B4a)	Position (B5)	(B6) Involved Alternative Policy (B8)	Formulated Policy (B7) (B9)
___ 8. Electric utility rate structure	___	___ ___	___	___ ___	___ ___

	Activity (B3)	When Active (B4) (B4a)	Position (B5)	(B6) Involved Alternative Policy (B8)	Formulated Policy (B7) (B9)
___ 9. Conversion to coal by electric utilities	___	___ ___	___	___ ___	___ ___

	Activity (B3)	When Active (B4) (B4a)	Position (B5)	(B6) Involved Alternative Policy (B8)	Formulated Policy (B7) (B9)
___ 10. Gasoline tax	___	___ ___	___	___ ___	___ ___

	Activity (B3)	When Active (B4) (B4a)	Position (B5)	(B6) Involved Alternative Policy (B8)	Formulated Policy (B7) (B9)
___ 11. Weekend gasoline sales restrictions	___	___ ___	___	___ ___	___ ___

	Activity (B3)	When Active (B4) (B4a)	Position (B5)	(B6) Involved Alternative Policy (B8)	Formulated Policy (B7) (B9)
___ 12. Standby gasoline rationing	___	___ ___	___	___ ___	___ ___

	Activity (B3)	When Active (B4) (B4a)	Position (B5)	(B6) Involved Alternative Policy (B8)	Formulated Policy (B7) (B9)
___**13. Gasoline allocation plan	___	___ ___	___	___ ___	___ ___

[ASK B10–B13]

	Activity (B3)	When Active (B4) (B4a)	Position (B5)	(B6) Involved Alternative Policy (B8)	Formulated Policy (B7) (B9)
___ 14. EPA air pollution standards	___	___ ___	___	___ ___	___ ___

	Activity (B3)	When Active (B4) (B4a)	Position (B5)	(B6) Involved Alternative Policy (B8)	Formulated Policy (B7) (B9)
___ 15. Standby rationing plan	___	___ ___	___	___ ___	___ ___

		Activity (B3)	When Active (B4) (B4a)	Position (B5)	(B6) Involved Alternative Policy (B8)	Formulated Policy (B7) (B9)
____	16. Air pollution standards	1. active position 2. active, no position 3. publicly inactive no position [STOP] 4. publicly inactive position held [GO TO B5] 5. Inactive [STOP] 8. Don't know [PROBE] 0. INAP	1. Before 2. After [IF BEFORE] 1.Yes 5. No	1. For [GO TO B6] 2. Against [GO TO B8] 3. Both for and against [RECORD DETAILS; GO TO B8]	1. Yes 5. No [STOP] 1.Yes 5. No [STOP]	1. Formulated 2. Collaborated 3. Adopted 1. Formulated 1. Collaborated 3. Adopted

		Activity (B3)	When Active (B4) (B4a)	Position (B5)	(B6) Involved Alternative Policy (B8)	Formulated Policy (B7) (B9)
____	17. Automobile efficiency standards	____	____ ____	____	____ ____	____ ____ ____

		Activity (B3)	When Active (B4) (B4a)	Position (B5)	(B6) Involved Alternative Policy (B8)	Formulated Policy (B7) (B9)
____	18. Imported oil fee (court)	____	____ ____	____	____ ____	____ ____ ____

		Activity (B3)	When Active (B4) (B4a)	Position (B5)	(B6) Involved Alternative Policy (B8)	Formulated Policy (B7) (B9)
____	19. Imported oil fee (Senate)	____	____ ____	____	____ ____	____ ____ ____

		Activity (B3)	When Active (B4) (B4a)	Position (B5)	(B6) Involved Alternative Policy (B8)	Formulated Policy (B7) (B9)
____	20. Conversion to coal	____	____ ____	____	____ ____	____ ____ ____

		Activity (B3)	When Active (B4) (B4a)	Position (B5)	(B6) Involved Alternative Policy (B8)	Formulated Policy (B7) (B9)
____	21. Standby gas rationing plan	____	____ ____	____	____ ____	____ ____ ____

438

B10. Now we would like to ask a few additional questions about event number 13, gasoline allocation.

In particular, what organizations, if any, did (ORGNAME) join with in trying to influence this event? **[RECORD FULL NAME]**

[PROBE: IF GROUP CATEGORY GIVEN, ASK: Can you give me the names of specific organizations?]

	(ORGNAME) Initiated	Other Initiated

B10a. **[FOR EACH ORGANIZATION MENTIONED IN B10]** Can you tell me whether (ORGNAME) initiated the joint effort or if the other organization did so?

B11. How would you characterize the activities that (ORGNAME) engaged in during this period? Please indicate all that apply.

[HAND CARD G TO R.]

[CIRCLE ALL THAT APPLY]

(1) Conducted research on a topic

(2) Acted as a clearinghouse of information

(3) Formulated policy alternatives

(4) Provided technical advice

(5) Advocated a policy position

(6) Collaborated with other organizations with long-term interest in this topic

(7) Recruited organizations not usually involved in this topic

(8) Mobilized public opinion using mass media (press releases, advertisements)

(9) Mobilized opinion at the grassroots (letter writing, etc.)

(10) Coordinated the various efforts to influence the outcome

439

B12. What are the names of the major organizations, including government agencies, which were opposed to (ORGNAME's) position?

1	2	3	4	5	6	7	8	9	10
1	2	3	4	5	6	7	8	9	10
1	2	3	4	5	6	7	8	9	10
1	2	3	4	5	6	7	8	9	10
1	2	3	4	5	6	7	8	9	10
1	2	3	4	5	6	7	8	9	10
1	2	3	4	5	6	7	8	9	10
1	2	3	4	5	6	7	8	9	10
1	2	3	4	5	6	7	8	9	10
1	2	3	4	5	6	7	8	9	10
1	2	3	4	5	6	7	8	9	10
1	2	3	4	5	6	7	8	9	10

B13a. Now I would like you to look at this card and tell me what reasons each of these organizations had
for their opposition.

[HAND CARD H TO R.]

[CIRCLE APPROPRIATE NUMBERS ABOVE FOR EACH ORGANIZATION]

1. Motivated by private economic gain
2. Tried to enhance its public image
3. Acted in public interest, but misguided
4. Sought to protect or extend its sphere of influence
5. Involved because of its ties to other organizations
6. Represented the interests of its members or clientele
7. Participated as part of an exchange with a different organization on another issue
   (log rolling)
8. Strategic manuever for possible long-range gain
9. Attempted to punish our organization for past actions
10. Automatically took a position opposed to our position

B13b. Are there any reasons not on this list that any organization may have had to be in opposition?
[RECORD NEXT TO APPROPRIATE ORGANIZATION]

440

PART III: COMMUNICATION

C1a. Here is a list of organizations involved in national energy matters which we have compiled from various sources.

[HAND LIST B TO R.]

Would you please place a check mark **in front of** the name of **all** organizations on this list with whom (ORGNAME) **regularly and routinely** discusses national energy policy matters?

[I. SHOULD MAKE SURE R. MAKES CHECKS IN FRONT OF NAME AND READS ALL COLUMNS]

C1b. Are there any organizations not on this list with whom (ORGNAME) regularly and routinely discusses important energy matters?

[WRITE ORG NAMES MENTIONED BY R.]

NAME	WE DO	BOTH	THEY DO
_____	_____	_____	_____
_____	_____	_____	_____
_____	_____	_____	_____
_____	_____	_____	_____
_____	_____	_____	_____
_____	_____	_____	_____
_____	_____	_____	_____
_____	_____	_____	_____

C1c. Considering the organizations whose names you have checked, would you now indicate if (ORGNAME) typically initiates these policy discussions, if the other organization usually initiates the discussions, or if the discussions are initiated as often by one as by the other. You may just make a check under the appropriate heading of WE DO, BOTH, or THEY DO to indicate how the initiation usually occurs.

With regard to the organizations you additionally mentioned, who initiates the contact about policy matters?

[READ EACH NAME, IF ANY, WRITTEN IN C1b AND RECORD RESPONSE]

C2. From time to time, organizations face especially sensitive problems in the national energy field, where the judgments of others are valuable in deciding what positions or actions to take. Organizations often develop relationships with other organizations that they trust to exchange sensitive and confidential advice about actions or positions that might be taken.

[HAND LIST C TO R.]

Using this list, we would like you to check those organizations with whom (ORGNAME) has such special relationships that involve the trusted exchange of sensitive and confidential advice. First, under the column headed "WE RECEIVE CONFIDENTIAL ADVICE" please check **all** those organizations from whom (ORGNAME) receives such confidential advice. Second, under the column headed "WE GIVE CONFIDENTIAL ADVICE" please check **all** those organizations who come to (ORGNAME) for such confidential advice.

441

C3a. The process of formulating positions on national energy matters often involves the use of technical or scientific information relevant to the issues. Which organizations on the list does (ORGNAME) regularly rely upon as sources of this type of technical and scientific information?

_____	_____	_____	_____	_____
_____	_____	_____	_____	_____
_____	_____	_____	_____	_____
_____	_____	_____	_____	_____
_____	_____	_____	_____	_____
_____	_____	_____	_____	_____
_____	_____	_____	_____	_____
_____	_____	_____	_____	_____
_____	_____	_____	_____	_____
_____	_____	_____	_____	_____
_____	_____	_____	_____	_____
_____	_____	_____	_____	_____
_____	_____	_____	_____	_____

C3b. From what other organizations not on this list does (ORGNAME) receive this type of technical and scientific information?

_____
_____
_____
_____
_____
_____
_____
_____
_____
_____

C4a. Please tell me the numbers of the organizations on this list **to** which (ORGNAME) gives substantial funds as payments for services or goods, or as contributions or membership fees. Indicate which of these transfers of funds are payments for services or goods.

[PLACE 'P' NEXT TO ORGANIZATION NUMBERS WHICH ARE INDICATED AS RECEIVING PAYMENTS]

_____	_____	_____	_____
_____	_____	_____	_____
_____	_____	_____	_____
_____	_____	_____	_____
_____	_____	_____	_____
_____	_____	_____	_____
_____	_____	_____	_____
_____	_____	_____	_____
_____	_____	_____	_____
_____	_____	_____	_____
_____	_____	_____	_____

442

C4b. Now, tell me the organizations on this list **from** which (ORGNAME) receives substantial funds as payments for services or goods, or as contributions or membership fees. Indicate which of these transfers of funds are payments for services or goods.

[PLACE 'P' NEXT TO ORGANIZATION NUMBERS WHICH ARE INDICATED AS GIVING PAYMENTS]

_____	_____	_____	_____
_____	_____	_____	_____
_____	_____	_____	_____
_____	_____	_____	_____
_____	_____	_____	_____
_____	_____	_____	_____
_____	_____	_____	_____
_____	_____	_____	_____
_____	_____	_____	_____
_____	_____	_____	_____

C5a. On occasion, an organizations finds that it needs staff or facilities that it doesn't have readily available but that another organization does have available. Again referring to this list, please tell me the numbers of the organizations that (ORGNAME) **allows to use its** staff and facilities in such situations.

_____	_____	_____	_____
_____	_____	_____	_____
_____	_____	_____	_____
_____	_____	_____	_____
_____	_____	_____	_____
_____	_____	_____	_____
_____	_____	_____	_____
_____	_____	_____	_____
_____	_____	_____	_____
_____	_____	_____	_____

C5b. Now, tell me the organizations on this list that **allow (ORGNAME) to use** their staff and facilities in such situations.

_____	_____	_____	_____
_____	_____	_____	_____
_____	_____	_____	_____
_____	_____	_____	_____
_____	_____	_____	_____
_____	_____	_____	_____
_____	_____	_____	_____
_____	_____	_____	_____
_____	_____	_____	_____
_____	_____	_____	_____

C6a. Still referring to the list, tell me all the organizations whose representatives held a seat on (ORGNAME's) board of directors during the past 4 or 5 years.

———— ———— ———— ————
———— ———— ———— ————
———— ———— ———— ————
———— ———— ———— ————
———— ———— ———— ————

C6b. Does any person in (ORGNAME) hold a seat on the board of directors of any of the organizations on the list?

———— ———— ———— ————
———— ———— ———— ————
———— ———— ———— ————
———— ———— ———— ————
———— ———— ———— ————

C7. To which trade associations or organizational councils on the list does (ORGNAME) belong?

———— ———— ———— ————
———— ———— ———— ————
———— ———— ———— ————
———— ———— ———— ————
———— ———— ———— ————

C8. Does (ORGNAME) belong to any other associations, such as special commissions or panels, at which national energy policy matters are likely to be discussed? Please tell me the names of these associations.

_____
_____
_____
_____
_____
_____
_____
_____
_____
_____
_____

COMMUNICATION–Continued

C9. With which organizations on this list does (ORGNAME) often find itself on opposite sides of the fence on energy isssues?

_____	_____	_____	_____
_____	_____	_____	_____
_____	_____	_____	_____
_____	_____	_____	_____
_____	_____	_____	_____

C10a. As we have indicated, all the organizations on this list are very active and important in the national energy policy area. But we would now like you to check those organizations which stand out as **especially** influential and consequential in formulating national energy policy.

[HAND LIST D TO R.]

C10b. Are there any other organizations not on the list that are influential and consequential in formulating national energy policy? Please tell me the names of these organizations.

_____
_____
_____
_____
_____
_____
_____
_____
_____
_____
_____
_____
_____

445

C11. Organizations may be regarded as influential and consequential participants in the national energy debate because they possess certain characteristics or resources. A list of some possibilities appears on Card I.

[HAND CARD I TO R.]

Would you please select 5 to 10 organizations that you know best and tell me for each of them **all** the characteristics or resources on which that organization's influence is based? Are there characteristics or resources not on this list that any of these organizations possess?

ORG Number			RESOURCE POSSESSED							OTHERS
_____	1	2	3	4	5	6	7	8	9	_____
_____	1	2	3	4	5	6	7	8	9	_____
_____	1	2	3	4	5	6	7	8	9	_____
_____	1	2	3	4	5	6	7	8	9	_____
_____	1	2	3	4	5	6	7	8	9	_____
_____	1	2	3	4	5	6	7	8	9	_____
_____	1	2	3	4	5	6	7	8	9	_____
_____	1	2	3	4	5	6	7	8	9	_____
_____	1	2	3	4	5	6	7	8	9	_____
_____	1	2	3	4	5	6	7	8	9	_____

1. Special expert knowledge about the energy field.
2. Funds to underwrite efforts to secure support for a proposal.
3. Staff or facilities that can be used in an effort to gather support for a proposal.
4. Official decision-making authority because of its high position in the government.
5. Good connections to influential organizations.
6. Reputation as an impartial mediator of conflicts about issues.
7. Ability to mobilize its members or employees to support a proposal.
8. Ability to mobilize general public opinion to support a proposal.
9. Other **[PLEASE SPECIFY]** _____

C12. And now would you indicate the most important characteristics of resources held by (ORGNAME)?

   1   2   3   4   5   6   7   8   9

Other: _____

Other: _____

[C13 FOR ALL GOVERNMENT ORGANIZATIONS ONLY]

C13. As a congressional committee/government agency (ORGNAME) receives many communications from numerous organizations containing information, proposals, and opinions about national energy policy. Most people recognize that (ORGNAME) must be able to select those which are considered reliable and useful sources of such information. Please tell me which organizations on this list (ORGNAME) has found to be the most reliable and useful. You may just tell me the numbers.

_____	_____	_____	_____
_____	_____	_____	_____
_____	_____	_____	_____
_____	_____	_____	_____
_____	_____	_____	_____
_____	_____	_____	_____
_____	_____	_____	_____
_____	_____	_____	_____

446

PART IV: ORGANIZATIONS

Now, we'd like to ask you some questions about your organization.

D1. When was (ORGNAME) founded? _____

D2. Thinking about the past decade, could you tell me about the important events, such as mergers, splits, or major reorganizations in (ORGNAME)? When did each of these events occur?

_____

_____

_____

[IF PROFIT SEEKING FIRM, GO TO D3

IF VOLUNTARY ORGANIZATION, GO TO D22

IF GOVERNMENT ORGANIZATION, GO TO D56]

PROFIT-SEEKING FIRM

[THIS SECTION FOR PROFIT-SEEKING FIRMS]

D3. How many persons does (ORGNAME) employ?

_____ employees

D4. Do you have a list of the members of (ORGNAME's) board of directors that you could give us?
   [GET WRITTEN LIST OF BOARD OF DIRECTORS]

D5. Who is your chief executive officer and when did he become the CEO?

Name _____   Year became CEO _____

[IF D5 IS **1977 OR LATER**, GO TO D5a

IF D5 IS **1977 OR EARLIER**, GO TO D6]

D5a. What did he do before he became CEO?

_____

_____

_____

D5b. Did his predecessor leave the job because he took another job, because he retired, or because of a difference of opinion between him and the board? **[PROBE FOR DETAILS]**

1. Took another job	2. Retirement
[GO TO D5c]	3. Differences of opinion
	4. Other **[GO TO D5d]**

D5c. With whom did he take another job?

D5d. Has he taken another position since he left?

1. Yes **[PROBE FOR WHAT POSITION AND WITH WHOM]**

5. No

8. Don't know

447

D6. Most organizations have someone who is responsible for its dealings with national government and with other organizations about national policy matters that affect (ORGNAME). Who is the principal person responsible for this activity at (ORGNAME) and what is his title.

_____

_____

D7. Does (ORGNAME) have any staff members whose regular task involves monitoring the Washington scene about all kinds of national policy issues of interest to it?

   1. Yes **[GO TO D7a]**   5. No **[GO TO D8]**

D7a. How many full-time equivalent staff members do this?

   _____ full-time equivalents

D7b. More specifically, how many full-time equivalent staff members monitor the Washington scene about national energy policy issues?

   _____ full-time equivalents

D7c. Are any of these staff members headquartered in Washington?

   1. Yes

   5. No

D7d. Have any of these staff members served on the staff of a Congressional committee or been employed by an executive department or independent government agency?

   1. Yes **[RECORD THE GOVERNMENT ORGANIZATION]**

   5. No

D8. Does (ORGNAME) have any staff members whose principal responsibility is the gathering of systematic technical data, such as estimates of utilization of energy services, that is relevant to national energy policy issues?

   1. Yes **[GO TO D8a]**   5. No **[GO TO D9]**

D8a. For which of the following purposes is this technical data gathered? **[INDICATE ALL THAT APPLY]**

   1. Use in internal decision making

   2. Distribution to political decision makers

   3. Dissemination to other organizations in the health field

   4. Dissemination to the general public

   5. Other **[LIST OTHER PURPOSES]**_____

   _____

D8b. How many full-time equivalent personnel gather such technical data?

   _____ full-time equivalents

D9. Firms must make many decisions on how to spend their scarce resources of time, money, and personnel on matters of concern to them. We would like you to estimate the relative amounts of influence that different individuals and groups in your firm have in determining (ORGNAME's) policies on national energy issues. In general, how much influence or say do you think the following individuals or groups have in determining (ORGNAME's) policies concerning national energy issues? [DO NOT ASK ITEM IF INDIVIDUAL OR GROUP DOES NOT EXIST]

	A very great deal of influence (1)	A great deal of influence (2)	Quite a bit of influence (3)	Some influence (4)	Little or no influence (5)	No such individual or group (0)
a. Chief executive officer						
b. Executive in charge of government affairs						
c. Board of directors						
d. Other staff						

D10. Does (ORGNAME) have in-house counsel?

    1. Yes [GO TO D10a]   5. No [GO TO D11]

D10a. How many lawyers are employed in this group?

    _____ lawyers

D11. Litigation is becoming an increasingly prominent method of trying to influence national energy policy. To what extent does (ORGNAME) use litigation as a method for trying to influence national energy policy? Would you say:

    1. Never

    2. Rarely

    3. Sometimes

    4. On a regular or frequent basis

D12. Does (ORGNAME) have any kind of program which is designed to activate persons, such as employees, customers, or franchise owners, in local areas to lobby their own Congressmen and Senators on energy policy issues of interest to your firm?

    1. Yes

    5. No

D13. Excluding commercial advertising, does (ORGNAME) have a designated individual or group that is responsible for public relations?

    1. Yes

    5. No

D14. Does (ORGNAME) have an associated political action committee?

    1. Yes

    5. No

449

D15. We note that your organization has testified at Congressional hearings. Do you ever make use of the following individuals to testify on behalf of (ORGNAME) at Congressional hearings? **[INDICATE ALL THAT ARE USED]**

    1. CEO

    2. Executive in charge of governmental affairs

    3. General counsel

    4. Other staff

    5. Lobbyist or lawyer retained by (ORGNAME) to testify

    6. Expert witness (technical)

    7. Representative from other organizations that you allow to use

       (ORGNAME's) name

    8. Other **[RECORD]**

_____

_____

_____

_____

_____

_____

_____

_____

450

ORGANIZATIONS—Continued

Does (ORGNAME) regularly retain or use any individuals or organizations, such as law firms, government affairs specialists, or trade associations, to do the following things: **[GO DOWN COLUMNS, ASKING ITEMS a, b, c, d, and e, FOR EACH QUESTION]**

	D16 To monitor the Washington scene on developments in energy policy	D17 To help prepare Congressional testimony	D18 To testify before Congressional committees	D19 To testify before executive agencies	D20 To maintain informal contacts with Congressional committees	D21 To maintain informal contacts with executive agencies
a. Does (ORGNAME) regularly retain or use any individual or organization, such as law firms, government affairs specialists, or trade associations . **[IF 5 OR 0, THEN GO TO NEXT COLUMN]**	1. Yes 5. No 6. For special circumstance 0. Don't engage in such an activity	1. Yes 5. No 6. For special circumstance 0. Don't engage in such an activity	1. Yes 5. No 6. For special circumstance 0. Don't engage in such an activity	1. Yes 5. No 6. For special circumstance 0. Don't engage in such an activity	1. Yes 5. No 6. For special circumstance 0. Don't engage in such an activity	1. Yes 5. No 6. For special circumstance 0. Don't engage in such an activity
b. What is the name and location of the individual or organization that you retain or use most extensively?	Name Location	Name Location	Name Location	Name Location	Name Location	Name Location
c. Is that individual or organization a lawyer or law firm, trade association, or what?	1. Lawyer or law firm 3. Trade association 5. Other **[RECORD]**	1. Lawyer or law firm 3. Trade association 5. Other **[RECORD]**	1. Lawyer or law firm 3. Trade association 5. Other **[RECORD]**	1. Lawyer or law firm 3. Trade association 5. Other **[RECORD]**	1. Lawyer or law firm 3. Trade association 5. Other **[RECORD]**	1. Lawyer or law firm 3. Trade association 5. Other **[RECORD]**
d. What is the name and location of any other individual or organization that you retain or use?	Name Location	Name Location	Name Location	Name Location	Name Location	Name Location
e. Is that individual or organization a lawyer or law firm, trade association, or what?	1. Lawyer or law firm 3. Trade association 5. Other **[RECORD]**	1. Lawyer or law firm 3. Trade association 5. Other **[RECORD]**	1. Lawyer or law firm 3. Trade association 5. Other **[RECORD]**	1. Lawyer or law firm 3. Trade association 5. Other **[RECORD]**	1. Lawyer or law firm 3. Trade association 5. Other **[RECORD]**	1. Lawyer or law firm 3. Trade association 5. Other **[RECORD]**

451

VOLUNTARY ORGANIZATIONS
[THIS SECTION FOR VOLUNTARY ORGANIZATIONS]

D22. Are individuals eligible for membership in (ORGNAME)?

    1. Yes [GO TO D22a]   5. No [GO TO D23]

D22a. How many individuals are members?

    _____ individual members

D22b. How many individuals were members in 1977?

    _____ individual members in 1977

D23. Are organizations eligible for membership in (ORGNAME)?

    1. Yes [GO TO D23a]   5. No [GO TO D24]

D23a. How many organizations are members?

    _____ organizational members

D23b. How many organizations were members in 1977?

    _____ organizational members in 1977

D24. Are there eligibility requirements for voting membership?

    1. Yes [GO TO D24a]   5. No [GO TO D25]

D24a. What are these eligibility requirements?

    _____

    _____

    _____

D25. Are there non-voting members also?

    1. Yes

    5. No

D26. Could you tell me what percentage of all the eligible individuals and/or organizations are actually members?

    _____ % of individuals

    _____ % of organizations

D27. What is the current schedule of dues for membership in (ORGNAME)?

[GET WRITTEN SCHEDULE OF DUES]

D28.   What was the annual renewal rate for the membership in (ORGNAME) last year?

_____ %

D28a. Thinking about the last four or five years, has the annual renewal rate for the membership de-creased, been stable, or increased?

1. Decreased

2. Been stable

3. Increased

D29.   Does (ORGNAME) have any volunteer staff?

1. Yes **[GO TO D29a]**   5. No **[GO TO D30]**

D29a. How large is the volunteer staff?

_____ volunteers

D29b. How many full-time equivalents would you say that these volunteers represent?

_____ full-time equivalent volunteers

D30.   How many full-time equivalent paid staff members does (ORGNAME) have?

_____ full-time equivalent paid staff

D31.   Does (ORGNAME) have an elected board of directors or similar group?

1. Yes **[GO TO D31a]**   5. No **[GO TO D32]**

D31a. How many members are there on this board?

_____ members

D31b. Do you have a list of the members of this board that you could give to us?

[GET WRITTEN LIST OF BOARD OF DIRECTORS]

D31c. When does the board meet?

D31d. Are there any standing committees that meet more frequently than the entire board does?

1. Yes **[GO TO D31e]**   5. No **[GO TO D32]**

D31e. What do these committees do?

_____

_____

_____

_____

453

D32. Does (ORGNAME) have an elected body of representatives other than a board of directors that meets periodically?

    1. Yes **[GO TO D32a]**   5. No **[GO TO D33]**

D32a. When does this body meet? _____

D33. Does (ORGNAME) have an elected president or chairman?

    1. Yes   5. No

D34. Who is the chief administrative or staff officer in (ORGNAME)?

    _____

D35. Does this position have a specified term of office?

    1. Yes **[GO TO D36]**   5. No **[GO TO D35a]**

D35a. When did the current chief staff officer take this position?

    Year became chief staff officer _____

[IF D35a IS 1977 OR LATER, ASK D35b THROUGH D35e

IF D35a IS 1976 OR EARLIER, GO TO D36]

D35b. What did the current administrative officer do before he took this position?

    _____

    _____

    _____

    _____

D35c. Did his predecessor leave the job because he took another job, because he retired, or because of a difference of opinion between him and the board? **[PROBE FOR DETAILS]**

    1. Took another job   2. Retirement

    [GO TO D35d]   3. Differences of opinion

                                4. Other **[GO TO D35e]**

    D35d. With whom did he take another   D35e. Has he taken another position
           job?   since he left?
                                          1. Yes **[PROBE FOR WHAT POSITION AND WITH WHOM?]**

                                          5. No

                                        8. Don't know

454

D36. Most organizations have someone who is responsible for its dealings with national government and with other organizations about national policy matters that affect (ORGNAME). Who is the principal person responsible for this activity at (ORGNAME) and what is his title.

_____

_____

D37. Does (ORGNAME) have any staff members whose regular task involves monitoring the Washington scene about all kinds of national policy issues of interest to it?

    1. Yes **[GO TO D37a]**   5. No **[GO TO D38]**

D37a. How many full-time equivalent staff members do this?

    _____ full-time equivalents

D37b. More specifically, how many full-time equivalent staff members monitor the Washington scene about national energy policy issues?

    _____ full-time equivalents

D37c. Are any of these staff members headquartered in Washington?

    1. Yes

    5. No

D37d. Have any of these staff members served on the staff of a Congressional committee or been employed by an executive department or independent government agency?

    1. Yes **[RECORD THE GOVERNMENT ORGANIZATION]**

    5. No

D38. Does (ORGNAME) have any staff members whose principal responsibility is the gathering of systematic technical data, such as estimates of utilization of energy services, that is relevant to national energy policy issues?

    1. Yes **[GO TO D38a]**   5. No **[GO TO D39]**

D38a. For which of the following purposes is this technical data gathered? **[INDICATE ALL THAT APPLY]**

    1. Use in internal decision making

    2. Distribution to political decision makers

    3. Dissemination to other organizations in the health field

    4. Dissemination to the general public

    5. Other **[LIST OTHER PURPOSES]**_____

    _____

D38b. How many full-time equivalent personnel gather such technical data?

_____ full-time equivalents

D39. Firms must make many decisions on how to spend their scarce resources of time, money, and personnel on matters of concern to them. We would like you to estimate the relative amounts of influence that different individuals and groups in your organization have in determing (ORGNAME's) policies on national energy issues. In general, how much influence or say do you think the following individuals or groups have in determining (ORGNAME's) policies concerning national energy issues? **[DO NOT ASK ITEM IF INDIVIDUAL OR GROUP DOES NOT EXIST]**

	A very great deal of influence (1)	A great deal of influence (2)	Quite a bit of influence (3)	Some influence (4)	Little or no influence (5)	No such individual or group (0)
a. Chief staff officer						
b. Executive in charge of government affairs						
c. Board of directors						
d. Elected representatives						
e. Elected president or chairman						
f. Other staff						
g. General membership						

D40. Does (ORGNAME) have in-house counsel?

1. Yes **[GO TO D40a]**   5. No **[GO TO D41]**

D40a. How many lawyers are employed in this group?

_____ lawyers

D41. Litigation is becoming an increasingly prominent method of trying to influence national energy policy. To what extent does (ORGNAME) use litigation as a method for trying to influence national energy policy? Would you say:

1. Never

2. Rarely

3. Sometimes

4. On a regular or frequent basis

D42. Does (ORGNAME) have any kind of program which is designed to activate members in local area to lobby their own Congressmen and Senators on energy policy issues of interest to your organization?

1. Yes

5. No

456

D43. Does (ORGNAME) have a designated individual or group that is responsible for public relations?

    1. Yes

    5. No

D44. Does (ORGNAME) have an associated political action committee?

    1. Yes

    5. No

D45. We note that your organization has testifies at Congressional hearings. Do you ever make use of the following individuals to testify on behalf of (ORGNAME) at Congressional hearings? **[INDICATE ALL THAT ARE USED]**

    1. Chief staff officer

    2. Individual in charge of governmental affairs

    3. General counsel

    4. Other staff

    5. Individual from the general membership

    6. Lobbyist or lawyer retained by (ORGNAME) to testify

    7. Expert witness (technical)

    8. Representative from other organizations that you allow to use

       (ORGNAME's) name

    9. Other **[RECORD]**

457

Does (ORGNAME) regularly retain or use any individuals or organizations, such as law firms, government affairs specialists, or trade associations, to do the following things: [GO DOWN COLUMNS, ASKING ITEMS a, b, c, d, and e, FOR EACH QUESTION]

	D46 To monitor the Washington scene on developments in energy policy	D47 To help prepare Congressional testimony	D48 To testify before Congressional committees	D49 To testify before executive agencies	D50 To maintain informal contacts with Congressional committees	D51 To maintain informal contacts with executive agencies
a. Does (ORGNAME) regularly retain or use any individual or organization, such as law firms, government affairs specialists, or trade associations . [IF 5 OR 0, THEN GO TO NEXT COLUMN]	1. Yes 5. No 6. For special circumstance 0. Don't engage in such an activity	1. Yes 5. No 6. For special circumstance 0. Don't engage in such an activity	1. Yes 5. No 6. For special circumstance 0. Don't engage in such an activity	1. Yes 5. No 6. For special circumstance 0. Don't engage in such an activity	1. Yes 5. No 6. For special circumstance 0. Don't engage in such an activity	1. Yes 5. No 6.For special circumstance 0. Don't engage in such an activity
b. What is the name and location of the individual or organization that you retain or use most extensively?	Name Location	Name Location	Name Location	Name Location	Name Location	Name Location
c. Is that individual or organization a lawyer or law firm, trade association, or what?	1. Lawyer or law firm 3. Trade association 5. Other [RECORD]	1. Lawyer or law firm 3. Trade association 5. Other [RECORD]	1. Lawyer or law firm 3. Trade association 5. Other [RECORD]	1. Lawyer or law firm 3. Trade association 5. Other [RECORD]	1. Lawyer or law firm 3. Trade association 5. Other [RECORD]	1. Lawyer or law firm 3. Trade association 5. Other [RECORD]
d. What is the name and location of any other individual or organization that you retain or use?	Name Location	Name Location	Name Location	Name Location	Name Location	Name Location
e. Is that individual or organization a lawyer or law firm, trade association, or what?	1. Lawyer or law firm 3. Trade association 5. Other [RECORD]	1. Lawyer or law firm 3. Trade association 5. Other [RECORD]	1. Lawyer or law firm 3. Trade association 5. Other [RECORD]	1. Lawyer or law firm 3. Trade association 5. Other [RECORD]	1. Lawyer or law firm 3. Trade association 5. Other [RECORD]	1. Lawyer or law firm 3. Trade association 5. Other [RECORD]

We'd like to end by asking a few questions about (ORGNAME's) budget.

D52. What was your budget last year?

$ _____

D53. We are interested in (ORGNAME's) major sources of revenue. How much did (ORGNAME) earn from each of the following last year?

1. Membership dues $ _____

2. Fees-for-service, such as subscriptions and advertising revenue from (ORGNAME's) publications $ _____

3. Grants from funding agencies $ _____
   [PROBE FOR SOURCES]

4. Major private donors $_____

5. Donations from the general public $_____

6. Other [RECORD SOURCES AND AMOUNTS]

_____

_____

_____

D54. Please give us an estimate of the percentage of (ORGNAME's) budget that was spent on matters related to influencing national policy in all areas of concern to your organization. By this we mean both information gathering about the alternative policies under consideration and the actual efforts to affect the policies that were decided on.

_____ %

D55. Now, please give us an estimate of the percentage of (ORGNAME's) budget that was spent on matters relating specifically to national energy policy.

_____ %

GOVERNMENT ORGANIZATION

[THIS SECTION FOR GOVERNMENT ORGANIZATIONS]

D56. How many persons does (ORGNAME) employ?

_____ employees

D57. How many of these employees are at the professional staff level?

_____ employees at professional staff level

459

Appendix C

Interview Cards and Lists: Energy

SOCIAL ORGANIZATION OF NATIONAL POLICY DOMAINS

Energy

CARDS

CARD A

1. Agriculture
2. Civil Rights
3. Consumer Rights
4. Defense
5. Domestic Economic Policy
6. Education
7. Energy
8. Environmental Policy
9. Foreign Policy
10. Health
11. Housing
12. International Trade
13. Labor Policy
14. Law Enforcement
15. Social Welfare/Social Security
16. Transportation
17. Urban Development

ENERGY RESEARCH ISSUES

1974

May   1. Senate Interior Committee reports a bill for research and development of **geothermal energy** (Congress passes in August).

1975

May   2. Senate Commerce Committee reports a bill to research and develop **electric-powered automobiles** (Congress passes act in August 1976 and overrides Ford's veto).

1976

May   3. House Science Committee reports a bill to research and develop **advanced automobile engines** (Congress passes bill in September, but fails to override Ford veto).

1977

April   *Carter renounces plutonium as nuclear fuel, seeks to redirect* **breeder reactor** *research and cancel the Clinch River demonstration plant.*

June   4. House Science Committee reports an energy research bill containing funds to continue Clinch River **breeder reactor** plant (passed by Congress in September, but Carter vetoes it in November).

October   *Carter proposes that federal government take over responsibility for interim storage of* **high-level nuclear wastes** *until permanent geologic site found by 1985.*

1978

March   5. Interstate Commerce Commission rejects railroads' requests for exemptions on transport of **nuclear wastes.**

April   6. House Science Committee votes to continue development of Clinch River **breeder reactor** (passed by House in July).

August   *Carter agrees to delay decision on Clinch River* **breeder reactor** *and to develop alternative breeder technology, in compromise to get Sen. McClure's signature on natural gas pricing conference report.*

1979

March   *Federal Interagency Review Group recommends further study of* **nuclear wastes** *disposal methods.*

April   7. House Science Committee again refuses to halt construction of Clinch River **breeder reactor** (House passes bill in July).

May   8. Senate Energy Committee endorses Carter proposal to terminate Clinch River **breeder reactor** and to seek alternative design (bill does not reach floor for vote in 1979).

October   *Nevada and Washington State governors close* **low-level nuclear wastes** *dumps in their states.*

December 9. Senate Energy Committee reports a bill to store **nuclear wastes** in above-ground vaults for up to 100 years (Senate passes bill in July 1980)

1980

February *Carter proposes legislation to bury* **nuclear wastes** *underground by mid-1990s; he also creates State Planning Council on Radioactive Waste Management.*

March   10. House Science Committee votes to increase funding for Clinch River **breeder reactor.**

July   11. House Science Committee reports a bill calling for underground **nuclear wastes** disposal demonstration (House approves a bill in December, but no legislation passes before Congress ends).

CARD C

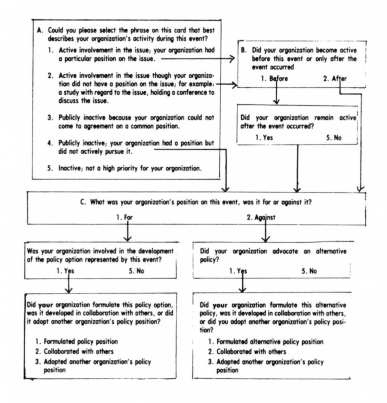

A. Could you please select the phrase on this card that best describes your organization's activity during this event?

1. Active involvement in the issue; your organization had a particular position on the issue.

2. Active involvement in the issue though your organization did not have a position on the issue; for example: a study with regard to the issue, holding a conference to discuss the issue.

3. Publicly inactive because your organization could not come to agreement on a common position.

4. Publicly inactive; your organization had a position but did not actively pursue it.

5. Inactive; not a high priority for your organization.

B. Did your organization become active before this event or only after the event occurred

1. Before   2. After

Did your organization remain active after the event occurred?

1. Yes   5. No

C. What was your organization's position on this event, was it for or against it?

1. For   2. Against

Was your organization involved in the development of the policy option represented by this event?

1. Yes   5. No

Did your organization advocate an alternative policy?

1. Yes   5. No

Did your organization formulate this policy option, was it developed in collaboration with others, or did it adopt another organization's policy position?

1. Formulated policy position
2. Collaborated with others
3. Adopted another organization's policy position

Did your organization formulate this alternative policy, was it developed in collaboration with others, or did you adopt another organization's policy position?

1. Formulated alternative policy position
2. Collaborated with others
3. Adopted another organization's policy position

464

CARD D

ENERGY INDUSTRY DEVELOPMENT ISSUES

1973

June   1. Senate Interior Committee reports a bill to construct the **Trans-Alaska oil pipeline** (Congress passes act in November)

October   **Arab oil boycott;** *Nixon declares Project Independence*

1974

January   2. House Science Committee reports a bill for **research and development** of **solar heating and cooling** of homes and buildings (Congress passes act in August)

1975

November   3. House Interior Committee reports a bill to revise federal **coal lands leasing procedures,** without strip mining control provisions (Congress passes act in June 1976 and overrides a Ford veto)

1976

May   4. Joint Atomic Energy Committee reports a bill to allow private industries to enter the **uranium enrichment** business (House passes bill, but it dies in Senate)

1977

March   5. Senate Energy Committee reports a bill that includes loan guarantees to develop **synthetic fuel** technologies (Congress passes act in October, but Carter vetoes it because the bill contains Clinch River funding)

June   6. Senate Energy Committee reports a bill to tighten rules for oil and gas exploration on **Outer Continental Shelf** (Congress passes act in August 1978)

July   7. House Public Works Committee reports a bill to provide **solar equipment** on federal buildings (Congress passes act in July)

July   8. House Ad Hoc Energy Committee reports a bill that includes **solar tax credits** for equipment (Congress passes act in October 1978)

September   9. Carter announces agreement in principle with Canada to build **Alaska-Canada natural gas pipeline** (Congress approves agreement in November)

1978

March   10. House Interior Committee reports **Alaska lands bill** to remove large acreage from oil and gas exploration (Congress passes act in November 1980)

April   11. Senate Energy Committee reports a bill to require federal government to test three methods to squeeze **oil from shale rock** (Congress kills bill in June)

June   12. House Science Committee reports a bill to develop **solar photovoltaic cells** as a commercially competitive technology (Congress passes act in October)

1979

June   13. House Banking Committee reports a bill to develop a **synthetic fuels industry** with federal loans, subsidies, and guarantees (Congress passes act in March 1980)

August   14. Two House committees report bills to create an **Energy Mobilization Board** to expedite energy development projects (Congress kills bill in conference in June 1980)

November   15. House Banking Committee reports a bill to create a **solar bank** to finance equipment purchases (Congress passes act as part of synthetic fuels program in March 1980)

1980

September   16. Carter nominates John Sawhill to head new **U.S. Synthetic Fuels Corporation** (Congress gives "recess appointments" to board members in October)

465

CARD E
ENERGY REGULATORY ISSUES

1971

August   1. Nixon imposes **price controls on domestic oil** and **natural gas** under authority of Economic Stabilization Act

1973

May   2. Senate Interior Committee reports a bill to require **mandatory controls** to allocate oil and oil products among regions and sectors of petroleum industry (Congress passes act in November)

November   3. Senate Interior Committee reports a bill to give the President **energy emergency allocation powers** (Congress passes bill in March 1974, and Nixon vetoes it)

1974

June   4. Joint Atomic Energy Committee reports a bill for 10-year extension of federal **nuclear accident insurance** program (Price-Anderson) (Congress passes act in September, Ford vetoes it, and a new version passes in 1975)

August   5. Senate revises a bill to create the **Energy Research and Development Authority (ERDA)**, abolishing the old Atomic Energy Commission and creating a **Nuclear Regulatory Commission** to assume its safety and regulatory functions (Congress passes act in October)

1975

March   6. Senate Interior Committee reports an Energy Policy and Conservation Act requiring continuation of federal **price controls on domestic oil**, extending them to "new oil" (Congress passes act in December)

October   7. Senate rejects amendments to require **horizontal and vertical divestiture** of operations of major oil and gas companies

1976

April–June   8. Federal Energy Administration (FEA), in a series of "energy actions" removes **price controls on various** petroleum products, such as residual fuel oil, home heating oil, and diesel fuel

May   9. House Commerce Committee reports an Energy Conservation and Production Act that includes **price control exemptions on stripper wells** (Congress passes act in August)

June   10. Senate Judiciary Committee reports a bill to force **vertical divestiture** on 18 major oil companies (Congress kills bill)

July   11. Federal Power Commission increases **natural gas price ceiling** on new interstate gas, nearly tripling prices

1977

January   *Carter asks for* **emergency natural gas allocation powers** *to deal with natural gas shortages caused by severe winter weather*

January   12. Congress passes **emergency natural gas** act within week of Carter's request, giving him temporary power to order transfers of interstate gas to regions where needed

April   *Carter sends Congress his comprehensive* **National Energy Plan** *involving 113 provisions, with emphasis on cutting oil and natural gas consumption*

April   13. House Interior Committee reports a bill to **control coal strip mining** (Congress passes act in July)

May   14. Senate Governmental Affairs Committee reports a bill to **create a Department of Energy** (Congress passes Act in August)

June   15. House Interior Committee votes to delay for 1 year any consideration of a **coal slurry pipeline** bill

June   16. House Ways and Means Committee reports a bill to impose a **crude oil equalization tax** to raise domestic oil prices to current world prices (Congress kills bill in October)

July   17. House Ad Hoc Energy Committee reports a bill to **deregulate natural gas**, raising prices and bringing all natural gas under federal regulation

August   18. Carter nominates James Schlesinger as first **Energy Secretary** (Senate confirms him)

September   19. Senate Energy Committee sends **natural gas deregulation** bill to floor without a recommendation

ENERGY REGULATORY ISSUES—continued

1978

March   *Carter sends legislation to Congress to streamline* **nuclear power plant licensing** *procedures, cutting time from 10–12 years to 6 years*

March   20. House Interior Committee reports a **coal slurry pipeline** bill (House kills bill in July)

May   21. Senate Energy Committee reports a bill authorizing funds to carry out provisions of the 1977 **strip mining control** act (Congress passes act in July)

June   22. House Commerce Commission reports a bill that includes funds to pay expenses of **citizen intervenors in nuclear regulatory hearings** (provisions withdrawn from bill in October)

August   23. House–Senate conferees sign a report on a compromise **natural gas deregulation** bill calling for phase-out of controls by 1985 (Congress passes act in October)

September   24. House Interior Committee reports a bill to authorize the Interior Secretary to exchange some **leased federal coal lands** in Western states for lands where mining may be less damaging to the environment (Congress passes act in October)

1979

January   **Iranian revolution** *causes worldwide oil shortage*

March   **Three Mile Island** *nuclear power plant accident*

April   *Carter unveils his new energy proposals, including gradual* **decontrol of domestic oil prices** *by October 1981, and asks Congress for* **windfall profits tax**

May   25. House Commerce Committee defeats efforts to extend **domestic oil price controls** for one year, allowing Carter's phased decontrol to take effect

May   26. House Interior Subcommittee votes for a 6-month **nuclear power plant construction moratorium** (Congress kills amendment in November)

May   27. Senate Environment Committee reports a bill to shut down nuclear power plants in states without an approved **nuclear emergency evacuation plan** (Congress passes act in June 1980)

June   28. House Ways and Means Committee reports a bill to **tax windfall profits** on deregulated oil and gas (Congress passes act in March 1980)

July   *Carter vows to* **limit imported oil** *to 1977 levels, about 8.5 millions barrels a day*

July   29. Senate Energy Committee reports a bill to allow states to design their own **coal strip mining control** plans without adhering to the 1977 federal act (Senate passes bill in August 1980, but House committee bottles it up)

July   30. Carter nominates Charles Duncan as **Energy Secretary** to replace Schlesinger (Senate confirms him)

October   *President's Commission on* **Three Mile Island Accident** *issues report calling for changes in way nation's nuclear power plants are built, licensed and operated, but does not call for a moratorium on new plants*

December   *Carter demotes Nuclear Regulatory Commission chair Joseph Hendrie, names John Ahearne acting chair, and asks Congress to* **reorganize the NRC,** *strengthening the chairman's role*

December   31. Senate Commerce Committee reports a bill to **deregulate railroads,** allowing them to set **coal freight rates** (Congress passes act in September 1980)

1980

February   32. Nuclear Regulatory Commission **resumes nuclear power plant licensing** after an 11-month halt following Three Mile Island accident

March   33. Carter submits his **NRC reorganization plan** to Congress, giving chairman more authority in day-to-day operations (plan takes effect in June as Congress does not reject it)

June   *At Vienna summit conference of Western allies, Carter pledges greatly expanded U.S.* **coal production**

October   34. Supreme Court agrees to hear cases challenging 1977 federal **strip mining control** act (no decision yet announced)

ENERGY CONSUMPTION ISSUES

1973

December   1. Congress passes **55-mph speed limit** act

1975

January   2. Ford imposes an **imported oil fee** (Congress suspends his action, Ford vetoes it, a federal court rules it illegal, but Supreme Court upholds Ford in 1976; Ford finally lifts the fee in December 1975 in a compromise over an omnibus energy bill)

May   3. House Ways and Means reports a bill containing a 23 cents a gallon **gasoline tax** (provision killed in June House vote)

1977

January   *Day before leaving office, Ford orders end to gasoline price controls (Carter rescinds order)*

June   4. House Ways and Means Committee reports a bill to tax electric utilities and industries burning oil and natural gas, forcing **conversion to coal** (Congress passes a weaker version with taxing powers in October 1978)

June   5. House Ways and Means Committee rejects Carter proposal for a **standby gasoline tax**

June   6. House Ways and Means Committee reports a "**gas-guzzler tax**" on inefficient automobiles, but without rebates to purchasers of fuel-efficient autos as requested by Carter (Congress passes act in October 1978)

June   7. Transportation Department announces new **automobile fuel efficiency standards,** raising fleet averages at earlier dates than previously scheduled

July   8. House Ad Hoc Energy Committee reports a bill that includes minimal national standards for **electric utility rate structure** (Congress passes a weaker version in October 1978)

November   9. House-Senate conferees report a bill to require **conversion to coal by electric utilities** only when change can be made at low cost and without environmental damage (Congress passes act in November)

1978

August   10. Congress rejects Carter proposal to add 5 cents per gallon to federal **gasoline tax** every year that gasoline consumption target levels are exceeded

1979

March   11. Senate Energy Subcommittee rejects Carter proposal for **weekend gasoline sales restrictions**

April   *Carter orders decontrol of domestic oil prices*

April   12. House Commerce Committee reports Carter's first proposed **standby gasoline rationing** plan (killed by Congress in May)

May   13. Senate Energy Committee reports a bill to give President emergency authority to force conservation on states without a **gasoline allocation plan** of their own (Congress passes act in October)

May   14. Environmental Protection Agency adopts **tougher air pollution standards** for newly built **coal-fired power plants**

July   15. House Commerce Committee reports Carter's second proposed **standby rationing plan,** to take effect whenever a shortfall of 20% lasts at least 30 days (Congress passes act in October)

September 16. Environmental Protection Agency postpones for 1 year its new **air pollution standards** for vehicles

December   *Carter sends Congress the details of his proposed standby gasoline rationing plan*

1980

March   *Carter sends Congress legislation to require electric utility coal conversion for 80 power plants*

March   17. Senate Commerce Committee reports a bill to give auto industry greater flexibility to meet **automobile fuel efficiency standards** (Congress passes act in September)

March   *Carter imposes a $4.62 per barrel imported oil fee*

April   18. Various parties file suit in federal court to block Carter's **imported oil fee** (federal judge overturns fee in May)

May   19. Senate Finance Committee votes to repeal Carter's **imported oil fee** (Congress repeals fee in June, then overrides Carter's veto)

June   20 Senate Energy Committee reports a bill to subsidize the **conversion to coal** of 80 utility power plants (House and Senate pass different versions of bill, no law is enacted by end of 1980 session)

July   21. House Commerce Subcommittee defeats an attempt to block the **standby gasoline rationing** plan (plan goes into effect, to be used when emergency arises)

468

CARD G

1. Conducted research on a topic.

2. Acted as a clearinghouse of information.

3. Formulated policy alternatives.

4. Provided technical advice.

5. Advocated a policy position.

6. Collaborated with other organizations with long-term interest in this topic.

7. Recruited organizations not usually involved in this topic.

8. Mobilized public opinion using mass media (press releases, advertisements).

9. Mobilized opinion at the grassroots (letter writing, etc.).

10. Coordinated the various efforts to influence the outcome.

CARD H

1. Motivated by private economic gain.

2. Tried to enhance its public image.

3. Acted in public interest, but misguided.

4. Sought to protect or extend its sphere of influence.

5. Involved because of its ties to other organizations.

6. Represented the interests of its members or clientele.

7. Participated as part of an exchange with a different organization on another issue (log rolling).

8. Strategic manuever for possible long-range gain.

9. Attempted to punish our organization for past actions.

10. Automatically took a position opposed to our position.

CARD I

1. Special expert knowledge about the energy field.

2. Funds to underwrite efforts to secure support for a proposal.

3. Staff or facilities that can be used in an effort to gather support for a proposal.

4. Official decision-making authority because of its high position in the government.

5. Good connections to influential organizations.

6. Reputation as an impartial mediator of conflicts about issues.

7. Ability to mobilize its members or employees to support a proposal.

8. Ability to mobilize general public opinion to support a proposal.

9. Other.

LIST A

Please place a check in front of each issue in which (ORGNAME) has had an interest and then in the columns to the right under the phrase that best reflects the **level** of interest in that issue. If (ORGNAME) has had no interest in a particular issue, just go on to the next issue.

	Minor Interest 1	2	Moderate Interest 3	4	Major Interest 5
I. ENERGY RESEARCH ISSUES					
_____ 1. Nuclear breeder reactor research and development	_____	_____	_____	_____	_____
_____ 2. Nuclear waste disposal technology	_____	_____	_____	_____	_____
_____ 3. Uranium mill waste disposal	_____	_____	_____	_____	_____
_____ 4. Transportation of nuclear wastes	_____	_____	_____	_____	_____
_____ 5. Automotive engine design	_____	_____	_____	_____	_____
_____ 6. Solar satellite research..............................	_____	_____	_____	_____	_____
_____ 7. Research and development of renewable fuels (geothermal, wind power, ocean thermal current, biomass, etc.)	_____	_____	_____	_____	_____
_____ 8. Nuclear fusion research and development	_____	_____	_____	_____	_____
II. ENERGY INDUSTRY DEVELOPMENT ISSUES					
_____ 9. Synthetic fuels industry development	_____	_____	_____	_____	_____
_____ 10. Solar energy commercialization	_____	_____	_____	_____	_____
_____ 11. Energy Mobilization Board...........................	_____	_____	_____	_____	_____
_____ 12. Capital formation in energy industries	_____	_____	_____	_____	_____
_____ 13. Gasohol industry development	_____	_____	_____	_____	_____
_____ 14. Muncipal garbage-to-fuel	_____	_____	_____	_____	_____
_____ 15. Transcontinental oil pipeline construction	_____	_____	_____	_____	_____
_____ 16. Alaska lands bill	_____	_____	_____	_____	_____
_____ 17. Alaska-Canada natural gas pipeline construction	_____	_____	_____	_____	_____
_____ 18. Outer Continental Shelf oil and gas exploration	_____	_____	_____	_____	_____
_____ 19. Western coal lands leasing	_____	_____	_____	_____	_____
_____ 20. Security of foreign oil supplies	_____	_____	_____	_____	_____
_____ 21. Strategic petroleum reserve	_____	_____	_____	_____	_____
_____ 22. Vertical and horizontal divestiture in energy industries	_____	_____	_____	_____	_____
_____ 23. Energy manpower education and training	_____	_____	_____	_____	_____
_____ 24. Expansion of U.S. coal production	_____	_____	_____	_____	_____
_____ 25. Small-scale hydroelectric generation	_____	_____	_____	_____	_____
_____ 26. Uranium commercialization	_____	_____	_____	_____	_____
_____ 27. Independent refinery construction	_____	_____	_____	_____	_____
_____ 28. Deepwater tanker ports and LNG facilities	_____	_____	_____	_____	_____
III. ENERGY REGULATORY ISSUES					
_____ 29. Deregulation of domestic oil prices	_____	_____	_____	_____	_____
_____ 30. Deregulation of natural gas prices......................	_____	_____	_____	_____	_____
_____ 31. Nuclear power plant licensing procedures..................	_____	_____	_____	_____	_____
_____ 32. Nuclear power plant insurance	_____	_____	_____	_____	_____
_____ 33. Nuclear power plant safety	_____	_____	_____	_____	_____

471

LIST A—continued

	Minor Interest 1	2	Moderate Interest 3	4	Major Interest 5
III. ENERGY REGULATORY ISSUES—continued					
___ 34. Security of nuclear power plants	___	___	___	___	___
___ 35. Reorganization of the Nuclear Regulatory Agency	___	___	___	___	___
___ 36. Strip mining of coal	___	___	___	___	___
___ 37. Coal slurry pipelines	___	___	___	___	___
___ 38. Deregulation of railroad freight rates	___	___	___	___	___
___ 39. Creation of the Energy Department	___	___	___	___	___
___ 40. Air and water pollution standards	___	___	___	___	___
___ 41. Allocations of petroleum products to states and regions	___	___	___	___	___
___ 42. Allocations to the petroleum industry	___	___	___	___	___
___ 43. Role of federal government in formulating comprehensive national energy policies	___	___	___	___	___
___ 44. State and federal control over energy	___	___	___	___	___
___ 45. Reorganization of Congressional energy committee structure . .	___	___	___	___	___
___ 46. Reorganization of federal energy bureaucracies	___	___	___	___	___
___ 47. U.S. participation in international cooperative energy arrangements	___	___	___	___	___
___ 48. Export of coal and oil from the U.S.	___	___	___	___	___
___ 49. Efficiency standards for buildings, motors, and appliances	___	___	___	___	___
___ 50. Integration of decentralized electricity generation with utility grids	___	___	___	___	___
___ 51. Service station franchises	___	___	___	___	___
IV. ENERGY CONSUMPTION ISSUES					
___ 52. Electric utility rate structure changes	___	___	___	___	___
___ 53. Conversion of power plants from oil and gas to coal	___	___	___	___	___
___ 54. Utility construction-work-in-progress costs	___	___	___	___	___
___ 55. Standby gasoline rationing authority	___	___	___	___	___
___ 56. Gasoline tax and oil import fees	___	___	___	___	___
___ 57. Automobile fuel efficiency standards	___	___	___	___	___
___ 58. Allocation priorities for home heating oil, gasoline, natural gas, and other fuels to consumers	___	___	___	___	___
___ 59. Oil company price overcharges to consumers	___	___	___	___	___
___ 60. Conservation of energy consumption	___	___	___	___	___
___ 61. Public participation in energy policy making	___	___	___	___	___
___ 62. Energy price impact on low-income consumers	___	___	___	___	___
___ 63. Building temperature settings	___	___	___	___	___
___ 64. Mass transit	___	___	___	___	___
___ 65. Impact of energy development on local communities ("boom towns")	___	___	___	___	___

472

LIST B

Would you please place a check mark **in front of** the name of **all** organizations on this list with whom your organization **regularly** and **routinely** discusses national energy policy matters?

	WE DO	BOTH	THEY DO
OIL AND GAS INDUSTRY			
Production Companies			
____001. American Natural Resources Company	____	____	____
____002. Ashland Oil Inc.	____	____	____
____003. Atlantic Richfield Company	____	____	____
____004. Champlin Petroleum Company	____	____	____
____005. Cities Service Company	____	____	____
____006. Continental Oil Company	____	____	____
____007. El Paso Natural Gas Company	____	____	____
____008. Exxon Corporation	____	____	____
____009. Foothills Pipelines Ltd.	____	____	____
____010. Gulf Mineral Resources Company	____	____	____
____011. Gulf Oil Company	____	____	____
____012. Houston Natural Gas Corporation	____	____	____
____013. Marathon Oil Company	____	____	____
____014. Mobil Oil Corporation	____	____	____
____015. Northern Tier Pipeline Company	____	____	____
____016. Northwest Energy Company	____	____	____
____017. Phillips Petroleum Company	____	____	____
____018. Shell Oil Company	____	____	____
____019. Standard Oil of California (Chevron)	____	____	____
____020. Standard Oil of Indiana (AMOCO)	____	____	____
____021. Standard Oil of Ohio (SOHIO)	____	____	____
____022. Sun Oil Company	____	____	____
____023. Texaco Inc.	____	____	____
____024. Tosco Corporation	____	____	____
____025. Union Oil Company of California	____	____	____
Trade Associations and Research Firms			
____050. American Association of Petroleum Geologists	____	____	____
____051. American Gas Association	____	____	____
____052. American Petroleum Institute	____	____	____
____053. American Petroleum Refiners Association	____	____	____
____054. Associated Gas Distributors	____	____	____
____055. Association of Oil Pipe Lines	____	____	____
____056. Energy Consumers and Producers Association	____	____	____
____057. Gas Research Institute	____	____	____
____058. Independent Gasoline Marketers Council, Inc.	____	____	____
____059. Independent Petroleum Association of America	____	____	____
____060. Independent Refiners Association of California	____	____	____
____061. Independent Terminal Operators Association	____	____	____
____062. Institute of Gas Technology	____	____	____

LIST B—continued

	WE DO	BOTH	THEY DO

OIL AND GAS INDUSTRY—continued

Trade Associations and Research Firms—continued

	WE DO	BOTH	THEY DO
___063. Interstate Natural Gas Association of America	___	___	___
___064. National Oil Jobbers Council	___	___	___
___065. Natural Gas Supply Association	___	___	___
___066. New England Fuel Institute	___	___	___
___067. Petroleum Industry Research Foundation	___	___	___
___068. Rocky Mountain Oil and Gas Association	___	___	___
___069. Service Station Dealers of America	___	___	___
___070. Society of Independent Gasoline Marketers of America	___	___	___
___071. Western Oil and Gas Association	___	___	___

COAL INDUSTRY

Production Companies

	WE DO	BOTH	THEY DO
___101. AMAX Coal Company	___	___	___
___102. Consolidated Coal Company	___	___	___
___103. U.S. Steel Corporation	___	___	___

Trade Associations and Research Firms

	WE DO	BOTH	THEY DO
___150. American Mining Congress	___	___	___
___151. Mining and Reclamation Council	___	___	___
___152. National Coal Association	___	___	___
___153. Slurry Transport Association	___	___	___

NUCLEAR INDUSTRY

Production Companies

	WE DO	BOTH	THEY DO
___201. Allied General Nuclear Service	___	___	___
___202. Babcock and Wilcox	___	___	___
___203. Combustion Engineering Inc.	___	___	___
___204. General Atomic Company	___	___	___
___205. General Electric Company	___	___	___
___206. Westinghouse Electric Corporation	___	___	___

Trade Associations and Research Firms

	WE DO	BOTH	THEY DO
___250. American Nuclear Energy Council	___	___	___
___251. Atomic Industrial Forum	___	___	___

ELECTRIC AND GAS UTILITIES

Production Companies

	WE DO	BOTH	THEY DO
___301. American Electric Power Service Corporation	___	___	___
___302. Brooklyn Union Gas	___	___	___
___303. Columbia Gas System, Inc.	___	___	___
___304. Commonwealth Edison Company	___	___	___
___305. Consolidated Edison Company	___	___	___
___306. Consumer Power Company	___	___	___

	WE DO	BOTH	THEY DO

ELECTRIC AND GAS UTILITIES—continued

Production Companies

____307. Detroit Edison Company .... ____ ____ ____

____308. General Public Utilities .... ____ ____ ____

____309. Hampton Roads Energy Company .... ____ ____ ____

____310. Houston Lighting and Power Company .... ____ ____ ____

____311. Montana Power Company .... ____ ____ ____

____312. New England Electric System .... ____ ____ ____

____313. Northeast Utilities Service Company .... ____ ____ ____

____314. Pacific Gas and Electric Company .... ____ ____ ____

____315. Potomac Electric Power Company .... ____ ____ ____

____316. Public Service Electric and Gas Company .... ____ ____ ____

____317. Southern California Edison Company .... ____ ____ ____

____318. Texas Utilities Company .... ____ ____ ____

____319. Virginia Electric and Power Company .... ____ ____ ____

Trade Associations and Research Firms

____350. American Public Power Association .... ____ ____ ____

____351. Edison Electric Institute .... ____ ____ ____

____352. Electric Power Research Institute .... ____ ____ ____

____353. National Association of Regulatory Utilities Commissioners .... ____ ____ ____

____354. National Electric Reliability Council .... ____ ____ ____

____355. National Rural Electric Cooperative Association .... ____ ____ ____

____356. Utility Waste Management Group .... ____ ____ ____

SOLAR AND ALTERNATIVE FUELS

Production Companies

____401. KMS Fusion Inc .... ____ ____ ____

____402. Republic Geothermal Inc .... ____ ____ ____

____403. Rio Blanco Oil Shale Company .... ____ ____ ____

Trade Associations and Research Firms

____450. American Wind Energy Association .... ____ ____ ____

____451. Solar Energy Industries Association .... ____ ____ ____

OTHER INDUSTRIES

Production Companies

____501. Allied Chemical Corporation .... ____ ____ ____

____502. American Motors Company .... ____ ____ ____

____503. Boeing Company .... ____ ____ ____

____504. Burlington Northern Inc .... ____ ____ ____

____505. Burns and Roe Inc .... ____ ____ ____

____506. Chrysler Corporation .... ____ ____ ____

____507. Dow Chemical, U.S.A. .... ____ ____ ____

____508. Ford Motor Company .... ____ ____ ____

____509. Foster Wheeler Energy Company .... ____ ____ ____

LIST B—continued

	WE DO	BOTH	THEY DO

OTHER INDUSTRIES—continued

Production Companies

	WE DO	BOTH	THEY DO
____510. General Motors Corporation	____	____	____
____511. Grumman Aerospace Corporation	____	____	____
____512. Rockwell International Corporation	____	____	____
____513. Stone and Webster Engineering Corporation	____	____	____
____514. Thermo-Electron Inc	____	____	____
____515. TRW Inc	____	____	____
____516. Union Carbide	____	____	____
____517. Union Pacific Corporation	____	____	____
____518. United Technologies Corporation	____	____	____
____519. Western Energy Company	____	____	____
____520. Wheelabrator-Frye Inc	____	____	____

Trade Associations and Research Firms

	WE DO	BOTH	THEY DO
____550. American Bakers Association	____	____	____
____551. American Institute of Architects	____	____	____
____552. American Institute of Merchant Shipping	____	____	____
____553. American Iron and Steel Institute	____	____	____
____554. American Paper Institute Inc	____	____	____
____555. Association of American Railroads	____	____	____
____556. Chamber of Commerce of the U.S.	____	____	____
____557. Chemical Manufacturers Association	____	____	____
____558. Gas Appliance Manufacturers Association	____	____	____
____559. Mitre Corporation	____	____	____
____560. National Association of Manufacturers	____	____	____
____561. National Automobile Dealers Association	____	____	____
____562. National Council of Farmer Coops	____	____	____
____563. National Economic Research Associates	____	____	____
____564. National Forest Products Association	____	____	____
____565. National Retail Merchants Association	____	____	____
____566. Petrochemical Energy Group	____	____	____

UNIONS

	WE DO	BOTH	THEY DO
____601. AFL-CIO	____	____	____
____602. Oil, Chemical and Atomic Workers International Union	____	____	____
____603. Sheet Metal Workers of America	____	____	____
____604. United Automobile Workers of America	____	____	____
____605. United Mine Workers	____	____	____

PUBLIC INTEREST AND RESEARCH

	WE DO	BOTH	THEY DO
____701. American Automobile Association	____	____	____
____702. Center for Auto Safety	____	____	____
____703. Citizen/Labor Energy Coalition	____	____	____

LIST B—continued

	WE DO	BOTH	THEY DO
____704. Consumer Energy Council of America	____	____	____
____705. Consumer Federation of America	____	____	____
____706. Critical Mass Energy Project	____	____	____
____707. Energy Action Education Foundation	____	____	____
____708. Environmental Action Inc	____	____	____
____709. Environmental Coalition on Nuclear Power	____	____	____
____710. Environmental Defense Fund	____	____	____
____711. Environmental Policy Center	____	____	____
____712. Friends of the Earth	____	____	____
____713. National Academy of Sciences	____	____	____
____714. National Audubon Society	____	____	____
____715. National Consumer Law Center	____	____	____
____716. National Wildlife Federation	____	____	____
____717. Natural Resources Defense Council Inc	____	____	____
____718. New Directions	____	____	____
____719. Public Citizen	____	____	____
____720. Public Interest Research Group	____	____	____
____721. Resources for the Future	____	____	____
____722. Sierra Club	____	____	____
____723. Solar Lobby	____	____	____
____724. Union of Concerned Scientists	____	____	____
____725. U.S. Labor Party	____	____	____
____726. Wilderness Society	____	____	____
____727. Worldwatch Institute	____	____	____

STATE AND LOCAL GOVERNMENT

	WE DO	BOTH	THEY DO
____801. California Energy Resources Conservation & Development Commission	____	____	____
____802. California Public Utilities Commission	____	____	____
____803. Coalition of Northeast Governors	____	____	____
____804. National Association of Counties	____	____	____
____805. National Conference of State Legislatures	____	____	____
____806. National Governors Association	____	____	____
____807. National League of Cities	____	____	____
____808. New Jersey Energy Department	____	____	____
____809. New York State Public Service Commission	____	____	____
____810. United States Conference of Mayors	____	____	____
____811. Western Governors Policy Office	____	____	____

FEDERAL GOVERNMENT

Executive Office of the President

	WE DO	BOTH	THEY DO
____901. The White House Office	____	____	____
____902. Council of Economic Advisers	____	____	____

LIST B—continued

	WE DO	BOTH	THEY DO

FEDERAL GOVERNMENT—continued

Executive Office of the President—continued

	WE DO	BOTH	THEY DO
____903. Council on Environmental Quality	____	____	____
____904. Office of Management and the Budget	____	____	____
____905. Office of Science and Technology Policy	____	____	____

Executive Departments

____906. Department of Agriculture	____	____	____
____907. Department of Commerce	____	____	____
____908. Department of Energy	____	____	____
____909. Economic Regulatory Administration	____	____	____
____910. Federal Energy Regulatory Commission	____	____	____
____911. Department of the Interior	____	____	____
____912. Department of Transportation	____	____	____

Independent Establishments and Government Corporations

____913. Environmental Protection Agency	____	____	____
____914. Federal Trade Commission	____	____	____
____915. Interstate Commerce Commission	____	____	____
____916. National Science Foundation	____	____	____
____917. National Transportation Safety Board	____	____	____
____918. Nuclear Regulatory Commission	____	____	____
____919. Solar Energy Research Institute	____	____	____
____920. State Planning Council on Radioactive Waste Management	____	____	____
____921. Synthetic Fuels Corporation	____	____	____
____922. Tennessee Valley Authority	____	____	____

HOUSE OF REPRESENTATIVES

Committee on Interior and Insular Affairs

____923. Democratic Party members and staff	____	____	____
____924. Republican Party members and staff	____	____	____

Subcommittee on Energy and the Environment

____925. Democratic Party members and staff	____	____	____
____926. Republican Party members and staff	____	____	____

Subcommittee on Mines and Mining

____927. Democratic Party members and staff	____	____	____
____928. Republican Party members and staff	____	____	____

Subcommittee on Oversight and Special Investigation

____929. Democratic Party members and staff	____	____	____
____930. Republican Party members and staff	____	____	____

Subcommittee on Public Lands

____931. Democratic Party members and staff	____	____	____
____932. Republican Party members and staff	____	____	____

	WE DO	BOTH	THEY DO

FEDERAL GOVERNMENT—continued

HOUSE OF REPRESENTATIVES—continued

Committee on Interior and Insular Affairs—continued

Subcommittee on Water and Power Resources

____933. Democratic Party members and staff . . . . ____ ____ ____

____934. Republican Party members and staff . . . . ____ ____ ____

Committee on Interstate and Foreign Commerce

____935. Democratic Party members and staff . . . . ____ ____ ____

____936. Republican Party members and staff . . . . ____ ____ ____

Subcommittee on Energy and Power

____937. Democratic Party members and staff . . . . ____ ____ ____

____938. Republican Party members and staff . . . . ____ ____ ____

Subcommittee on Health and the Environment

____939. Democratic Party members and staff . . . . ____ ____ ____

____940. Republican Party members and staff . . . . ____ ____ ____

Subcommittee on Oversight and Investigations

____941. Democratic Party members and staff . . . . ____ ____ ____

____942. Republican Party members and staff . . . . ____ ____ ____

Subcommittee on Transportation and Commerce

____943. Democratic Party members and staff . . . . ____ ____ ____

____944. Republican Party members and staff . . . . ____ ____ ____

Committee on Public Works and Transportation

____945. Democratic Party members and staff . . . . ____ ____ ____

____946. Republican Party members and staff . . . . ____ ____ ____

Subcommittee on Oversight and Review

____947. Democratic Party members and staff . . . . ____ ____ ____

____948. Republican Party members and staff . . . . ____ ____ ____

Subcommittee on Surface Transportation

____949. Democratic Party members and staff . . . . ____ ____ ____

____950. Republican Party members and staff . . . . ____ ____ ____

Committee on Science and Technology

____951. Democratic Party members and staff . . . . ____ ____ ____

____952. Republican Party members and staff . . . . ____ ____ ____

Subcommittee on Energy Development and Applications

____953. Democratic Party members and staff . . . . ____ ____ ____

____954. Republican Party members and staff . . . . ____ ____ ____

Subcommittee on Energy Research and Production

____955. Democratic Party members and staff . . . . ____ ____ ____

____956. Republican Party members and staff . . . . ____ ____ ____

LIST B—continued

	WE DO	BOTH	THEY DO

FEDERAL GOVERNMENT—continued

HOUSE OF REPRESENTATIVES—continued

Committee on Science and Technology—continued

Subcommittee on Investigations and Oversight

| ____957. Democratic Party members and staff .... | ____ | ____ | ____ |
| ____958. Republican Party members and staff .... | ____ | ____ | ____ |

Subcommittee on Natural Resources and Environment

| ____959. Democratic Party members and staff .... | ____ | ____ | ____ |
| ____960. Republican Party members and staff .... | ____ | ____ | ____ |

Subcommittee on Science, Research and Technology

| ____961. Democratic Party members and staff .... | ____ | ____ | ____ |
| ____962. Republican Party members and staff .... | ____ | ____ | ____ |

Subcommittee on Transportation, Aviation and Communication

| ____963. Democratic Party members and staff .... | ____ | ____ | ____ |
| ____964. Republican Party members and staff .... | ____ | ____ | ____ |

Committee on Ways and Means

| ____965. Democratic Party members and staff .... | ____ | ____ | ____ |
| ____966. Republican Party members and staff .... | ____ | ____ | ____ |

SENATE

Committee on Commerce, Science and Transportation

| ____967. Democratic Party members and staff .... | ____ | ____ | ____ |
| ____968. Republican Party members and staff .... | ____ | ____ | ____ |

Subcommittee on Science, Technology and Space

| ____969. Democratic Party members and staff .... | ____ | ____ | ____ |
| ____970. Republican Party members and staff .... | ____ | ____ | ____ |

Subcommittee on Surface Transportation

| ____971. Democratic Party members and staff .... | ____ | ____ | ____ |
| ____972. Republican Party members and staff .... | ____ | ____ | ____ |

Committee on Energy and Natural Resources

| ____973. Democratic Party members and staff .... | ____ | ____ | ____ |
| ____974. Republican Party members and staff .... | ____ | ____ | ____ |

Subcommittee on Energy Conservation and Supply

| ____975. Democratic Party members and staff .... | ____ | ____ | ____ |
| ____976. Republican Party members and staff .... | ____ | ____ | ____ |

Subcommittee on Energy Regulation

| ____977. Democratic Party members and staff .... | ____ | ____ | ____ |
| ____978. Republican Party members and staff .... | ____ | ____ | ____ |

LIST B—continued

	WE DO	BOTH	THEY DO

FEDERAL GOVERNMENT—continued

SENATE—continued

Committee on Energy and Natural Resources—continued

Subcommittee on Energy Research and Development

____979. Democratic Party members and staff	____	____	____
____980. Republican Party members and staff	____	____	____

Subcommittee on Energy Resources and Materials Production

| ____981. Democratic Party members and staff | ____ | ____ | ____ |
| ____982. Republican Party members and staff | ____ | ____ | ____ |

Committee on Environment and Public Works

| ____983. Democratic Party members and staff | ____ | ____ | ____ |
| ____984. Republican Party members and staff | ____ | ____ | ____ |

Subcommittee on Environmental Pollution

| ____985. Democratic Party members and staff | ____ | ____ | ____ |
| ____986. Republican Party members and staff | ____ | ____ | ____ |

Subcommittee on Nuclear Regulation

| ____987. Democratic Party members and staff | ____ | ____ | ____ |
| ____988. Republican Party members and staff | ____ | ____ | ____ |

Subcommittee on Resource Protection

| ____989. Democratic Party members and staff | ____ | ____ | ____ |
| ____990. Republican Party members and staff | ____ | ____ | ____ |

Subcommittee on Transportation

| ____991. Democratic Party members and staff | ____ | ____ | ____ |
| ____992. Republican Party members and staff | ____ | ____ | ____ |

Committee on Finance

| ____993. Democratic Party members and staff | ____ | ____ | ____ |
| ____994. Republican Party members and staff | ____ | ____ | ____ |

Subcommittee on Energy and Foundations

| ____995. Democratic Party members and staff | ____ | ____ | ____ |
| ____996. Republican Party members and staff | ____ | ____ | ____ |

JOINT

Office of Technology Assessment

| ____997. Democratic Party members and staff | ____ | ____ | ____ |
| ____998. Republican Party members and staff | ____ | ____ | ____ |

LIST C

Under the column headed "WE RECEIVE CONFIENTIAL ADVICE," please check **all** those organizations from whom your organization receives such advice. Under the column headed "WE GIVE CONFIDENTIAL ADVICE," please check **all** those organizations who come to your organization for advice.

Same as List B

LIST D

Please check those organizations which stand out as **especially** influential and consequential in formulating national energy policy.

Same as List B

Appendix D

Interview Cards and Lists: Health

Health

CARDS

CARD A

1. Agriculture
2. Civil Rights
3. Consumer Rights
4. Defense
5. Domestic Economic Policy
6. Education
7. Energy
8. Environmental Policy
9. Foreign Policy
10. Health
11. Housing
12. International Trade
13. Labor Policy
14. Law Enforcement
15. Social Welfare/Social Security
16. Transportation
17. Urban Development

CARD B

BIOMEDICAL RESEARCH ISSUES—NIH FUNDING, DNA research, Human Experimentation, Targeted-Disease Funding

1971

December   1. **National Cancer Act** established. Bill mandates a "war" on cancer.

1974

March   2. Bill providing for a **National Institute of Aging** within NIH is cleared by Staggers's House Committee.

June   House and Senate hold conference on **National Research Act.** Bill provides for the establishment of national biomedical research training and fellowship programs. The bill would:

    3. authorize 1975 funding for **NIH research** programs.

    4. establish a temporary advisory **National Commission for the Protection of Human Subjects in Biomedical and Behavior Research.** This commission would become permanent in 1976.

    5. prohibit HEW-supported research on **live human fetuses.**

1976

September   6. Legislation providing for **Arthritis, Diabetes and Digestive Diseases** programs is cleared by Rogers Subcommittee on Health and the Environment.

November   *President Carter is elected*

1977

February   7. NIH-mandated ban on **DNA research** rescinded.

March   8. Staggers Committee recommends passage of legislation extending authorities for **National Cancer, and National Heart, Blood and Lung Institutes** through 1981.

July   9. Williams's Senate Committee recommends passage of **Recombinant DNA Safety Regulation Act.** Bill would establish a presidentially appointed commission within HEW to regulate DNA research activities.

1978

March   10. Legislation extending 1976 NIH research guidelines for **DNA Research** is cleared by Staggers Committee. Bill also establishes a commission to study **genetic engineering technologies.**

May   11. Staggers's House Committee clears Biomedical Research bill. Legislation would extend the **National Cancer and National Heart, Blood and Lung Institutes** through 1981.

May   12. Legislation creating a **President's Commission for the Protection of Human Subjects of Biomedical Research** is recommended for passage by Williams's Senate Committee.

December   13. Califano announces new regulations relaxing NIH-mandated safety guidelines for federally funded **DNA Research** projects.

1979

April   14. Kennedy Subcommittee on Health and Scientific Research considers bill to extend authority for the **National Heart, Blood and Lung Institute** and the **National Cancer Institute** through 1983.

July   15. **Joseph Califano** is fired.

July   16. **Patricia Harris** is named **Secretary of HEW.**

July   *Carter demands cabinet members' resignation.*

1980

February   17. House Subcommittee on Health and the Environment recommends passage of **NIH Health Research** legislation. Bill includes provisions requiring **appropriations ceilings** for the individual Institutes as well as **peer review** of research contracts.

May   18. Williams's Senate Committee clears an **NIH Research**-authorization bill **excluding** House provisions for **appropriation ceilings** for the Institutes.

November   *President Reagan is elected*

485

CARD C

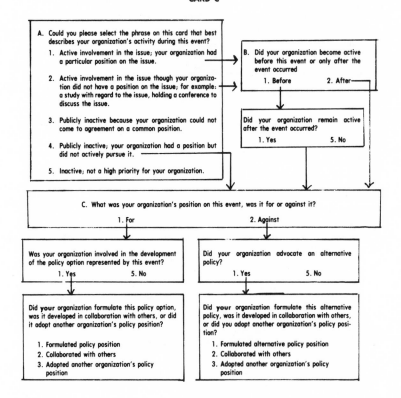

A. Could you please select the phrase on this card that best describes your organization's activity during this event?

1. Active involvement in the issue; your organization had a particular position on the issue.

2. Active involvement in the issue though your organization did not have a position on the issue; for example: a study with regard to the issue, holding a conference to discuss the issue.

3. Publicly inactive because your organization could not come to agreement on a common position.

4. Publicly inactive; your organization had a position but did not actively pursue it.

5. Inactive; not a high priority for your organization.

B. Did your organization become active before this event or only after the event occurred
1. Before   2. After

Did your organization remain active after the event occurred?
1. Yes   5. No

C. What was your organization's position on this event, was it for or against it?
1. For   2. Against

Was your organization involved in the development of the policy option represented by this event?
1. Yes   5. No

Did your organization formulate this policy option, was it developed in collaboration with others, or did it adopt another organization's policy position?

1. Formulated policy position
2. Collaborated with others
3. Adopted another organization's policy position

Did your organization advocate an alternative policy?
1. Yes   5. No

Did your organization formulate this alternative policy, was it developed in collaboration with others, or did you adopt another organization's policy position?

1. Formulated alternative policy position
2. Collaborated with others
3. Adopted another organization's policy position

486

MANPOWER ISSUES—Nurse Training, Physician Training, Foreign Medical Graduates, 3rd Year Medical School Transfers

1971

June   1. Congress clears **Comprehensive Nurse Training and Facilities** legislation. Bill provides for **capitation grants** to nursing schools.

October   2. Congress clears **Comprehensive Manpower Training Act.** Legislation extends grants to research and training facilities, as well as instituting **capitation grants** for medical schools.

1976

April   3. House Subcommittee on Labor-Management Relations considers legislation to amend the National Labor Relations Act to allow **collective bargaining coverage** for hospital interns, residents, and fellows.

May   4. Williams's Senate Committee clears **Health Manpower** legislation. Bill extends federal funding for Manpower programs through 1978.

September   House-Senate Conference Committee votes to recommend passage of **Health Manpower** legislation. Bill extends facility and **capitation grants** to medical schools. Legislation adds provisions requiring:

            5. medical schools to reserve a specified number of positions in incoming classes for **3rd year transfers** from foreign schools.

            6. stricter controls on the immigration and work status of **Foreign Medical Graduates (FMGs).**

            7. medical schools to reserve 35% of first year **residency programs for doctors** entering **primary care fields** of medicine.

November   *President Carter is elected*

1977

January   8. Assistant Secretary of HEW Cooper announces a 4-year phase-in period for **Foreign Medical Graduate (FMG)** provisions mandated in 1976 Health Manpower Act.

October   9. Staggers Committee votes to recommend legislation revising the **3rd year transfer student** provision in the 1976 Health Manpower Act.

December   10. House-Senate Conference Committee reports bill revising provision in 1976 Health Manpower Act regarding **3rd year transfer students.**

1978

May   11. Staggers Committee recommends passage of **Nurse Training Act.** Legislation would extend funding authorities through 1980 for programs included under the Nurse Training Act of 1975.

October   12. House-Senate Conference Committee reports **Nurse Training** legislation.

October   13. HEW begins cutbacks on grants to **new medical schools.**

1979

April   14. Williams's Senate Committee clears **Nurse Training Act.** Legislation extends funding for nurse training programs through 1980.

July   *Carter demands resignation from cabinet members.*

September   15. House-Senate Conference Committee reports **Nurse Training** legislation.

October   16. Education and Labor Committee reports legislation to amend the National Labor Relations Act to provide specific **collective bargaining protection** for medical housestaff.

1980

May   17. Staggers Committee reports bill relaxing immigration restrictions on **Foreign Medical Graduates (FMGs).**

May   18. Health Manpower legislation extending **Health Professional and Nurse Training** program authorities through 1983 is reported by Staggers Committee. Bill also repeals **capitation grants** to medical and nursing schools.

September   19. Results of the **Graduate Medical Education National Advisory Committee (GMENAC)** are presented to Congress.

November   *President Reagan is elected*

CARD E

ORGANIZATION OF CARE—Cost Containment, HMOs, Health Planning, Community Health Services, Rural Health Care, PSROs

1972

November   1. Congress clears legislation mandating establishment of a network of **Professional Standards Review Organizations (PSROs)** to contain hospital costs and guarantee quality of in-hospital treatment.

1973

December   2. House and Senate hold conference on **Health Maintenance Organizations (HMOs).** Bill mandates HEW responsibility for a 5-year plan to assist and develop HMOs.

1974

November   3. Williams's Senate Committee recommends passage of **National Health Planning, Development and Health Facilities** legislation. Bill establishes Health Planning Agencies under HEW, institutes Certificate of Need provisions, and extends state responsibility for regulation of the health care industry.

1976

May   4. Williams Committee reports legislation relaxing restrictions on services offered by **Health Maintenance Organizations (HMOs)** seeking federal aid under the 1973 HMO Act.

November   *President Carter is elected*

1977

February   5. National Academy of Sciences Institute of Medicine urges curbs on the acquisition, use, and cost of **CAT-scanners** through the **Certificate of Need** program under HEW.

March   6. Staggers's House Committee reports **Health Services Extension Act.** Legislation extends funding authority for a variety of health programs including **Community Mental Health Centers** and **Home Health Programs.**

March   7. HEW reorganizes. Changes include placing Medicare and Medicaid programs under the **Health Care Financing Administration**.

March   8. Legislation extending funding for **State Health Planning Agencies** as well as construction grants and loans for health facilities is reported by Staggers Committee.

May   9. Rogers Subcommittee on Health and the Environment hears testimony on **Carter's Hospital Cost Containment** legislation. Bill would set mandatory ceilings on hospital revenues and capital expenditures.

November   10. House-Senate Conference reports **Rural Health Care** bill. Legislation authorizes Medicare and Medicaid reimbursements for **Nurse Practitioners and Physician Assistants.**

1978

May   11. Williams Committee reports **Health Planning** legislation extending **Health Planning Agencies** and **Certificate of Need** provisions. Bill also includes provisions to encourage voluntary cutbacks on unneeded hospital services.

May   Staggers Committee reports legislation authorizing funding for Health Programs through 1981. Bill covers:

   12. **Community Health Centers**

   13. **Rural Health Programs**

   14. **Health Maintenance Organizations (HMOs)**

May   15. Williams Committee reports bill extending assistance to **Health Maintenance Organizations (HMOs)** through 1983. Legislation also includes provisions revising restrictions on HMO membership rates and operation.

October   16. Staggers Committee recommends passage of **Voluntary Hospital Cost Containment** legislation. Bill establishes National Commission on Hospital Costs and provides incentives for cutting back unneeded hospital services.

1979

March   17. Talmadge Subcommittee on Health hears testimony on **Hospital Cost Containment Act.** Bill would provide for voluntary cost controls with a mandatory control backup for hospitals exceeding their voluntary limits.

May   18. Williams Committee reports the **Mental Health Systems Act.** Bill would authorize funds through 1983 for a flexible state-run system of mental health services to replace programs under the Community Mental Health Centers Act.

CARD E—Continued

ORGANIZATION OF CARE—Cost Containment, HMOs, Health Planning, Community Health Services, Rural Health Care, PSROs

1979—*continued*

May   19. Staggers Committee reports bill extending authorities for **Health Planning and Resource Development** programs through 1982. Bill includes provisions for Certificate of Need programs, Voluntary Cost Containment measures, and Health Planning Agencies.

July   20. **Chiropractors** charge the AMA, 12 other organizations, and 1 individual with conspiring to force chiropractors out of business. Suit was filed in U.S. District Court in New York.

July   *Carter demands resignation of cabinet members*

October   21. Staggers Committee reports Carter's revised **Hospital Cost Containment** legislation. Bill provides for voluntary limits on hospital cost increases with a provision for standby mandatory controls.

October   Staggers Committee clears Medicare/Medicaid legislation providing for:

     22. revisions of **Professional Standards Review Organizations (PSROs).**

     23. regulations requiring **second opinions for elective surgery.**

     24. Medicare/Medicaid **reimbursements for nurse-midwives.**

     25. **Medicare/Medicaid reimbursements for Health Maintenance Organizations (HMOs).**

December   Senate Finance Committee reports legislation to establish

     26. New methods of **hospital reimbursements** under Medicare/Medicaid to provide incentives for cost efficiency.

     27. **relaxed Medicare/Medicaid reimbursements** for Home Health programs and Allied Health Professionals.

1980

March   Staggers Committee reports Medicare amendment legislation. Bill includes provisions relating to:

     28. **Home Health programs**

     29. **Community Mental Health Centers**

     30. **Reimbursements for Dentists, Optometrists, and Chiropractors**

May   31. Staggers Committee reports legislation authorizing 1981 appropriations for **Community Mental Health Centers.**

November   *President Reagan is elected*

489

CARD F

DRUG REGULATION—Saccharin, New Drug Development, Generic Equivalents of Brand-Name Drugs, Safety Brochure Inserts, Cyclamates

1969

October — 1. HEW **bans cyclamates.**

1976

April — 2. House subcommittees on Health and the Environment and Consumer Protection and Finance hear testimony on **Prescription Drug Labelling and Price Advertising Act.** Bill would define conditions for the substitution of generic equivalents for brand-name drugs.

November — *President Carter is elected*

1977

March — 3. FDA **bans saccharin.**

July — 4. Williams's Senate Committee clears bill delaying **saccharin ban** for 18 months.

July — Kennedy Subcommittee on Health and Scientific Research hears testimony on proposed amendments to the Food, Drug, and Cosmetic Act to revise regulations of **prescription drug development and use.** Bill would:

5. revise requirements for the **investigation, approval and distribution of new drugs.**

6. provide for regulation of the quality and interchangeability of **generic and brand-name drugs.**

1978

June — 7. Congressional subcommittees on Consumer Protection and Finance and Monopoly and Anti-Competitive Activities hold hearings on legislation allowing pharmacists to fill prescriptions with **generic equivalents.**

June — 8. Kennedy Subcommittee on Health hears testimony on Carter's **Drug Regulation Reform bill.** Legislation would revise procedures for new drug development, investigation, and distribution.

September — 9. FDA announces intention of releasing list of **generic equivalents** of prescription drugs.

1979

April — 10. **Donald Kennedy,** director of FDA, **resigns.**

March — 11. FDA releases compendium **listing generic names** of 2,400 prescription drugs.

June — 12. FDA announces intention to require **safety brochure inserts** for 375 prescription drugs.

July — 13. Staggers's House Committee recommends an extension of the **saccharin ban** moratorium through 1981.

July — *Carter fires cabinet*

September — 14. A revised version of the **Drug Regulation Reform Bill** is reported by Williams's Senate Committee.

1980

February — 15. FDA upholds 1969 **cyclamate ban.**

May — 16. Williams Committee recommends passage of **saccharin ban moratorium** extension.

May — 17. FDA reduces the **safety brochure insert** requirement to cover only 10 prescription drugs rather than 375.

November — *President Reagan is elected*

490

CARD G

1. Conducted research on a topic.

2. Acted as a clearinghouse of information.

3. Formulated policy alternatives.

4. Provided technical advice.

5. Advocated a policy position.

6. Collaborated with other organizations with long-term interest in this topic.

7. Recruited organizations not usually involved in this topic.

8. Mobilized public opinion using mass media (press releases, advertisements).

9. Mobilized opinion at the grassroots (letter writing, etc.).

10. Coordinated the various efforts to influence the outcome.

CARD H

1. Motivated by private economic gain.

2. Tried to enhance its public image.

3. Acted in public interest, but misguided.

4. Sought to protect or extend its sphere of influence.

5. Involved because of its ties to other organizations.

6. Represented the interests of its members or clientele.

7. Participated as part of an exchange with a different organization on another issue (log rolling).

8. Strategic manuever for possible long-range gain.

9. Attempted to punish our organization for past actions.

10. Automatically took a position opposed to our position.

CARD I

1. Special expert knowledge about the health field.

2. Funds to underwrite efforts to secure support for a proposal.

3. Staff or facilities that can be used in an effort to gather support for a proposal.

4. Official decision-making authority because of its high position in the government.

5. Good connections to influential organizations.

6. Reputation as an impartial mediator of conflicts about issues.

7. Ability to mobilize its members or employees to support a proposal.

8. Ability to mobilize general public opinion to support a proposal.

9. Other.

LIST A

Please place a check in front of each issue in which (ORGNAME) has had an interest and then in the columns to the right under the phrase that best reflects the **level** of interest in that issue. If (ORGNAME) has had no interest in a particular issue, just go on to the next issue.

	Minor Interest 1	2	Moderate Interest 3	4	Major Interest 5

BIOMEDICAL ISSUES

____ 1. Biomedical research programs, e.g., targeted-disease funding . . . .

____ 2. DNA research . . . .

____ 3. Human experimentation . . . .

____ 4. National Institutes of Health funding . . . .

MANPOWER ISSUES

____ 5. Allied health professional training . . . . . .

____ 6. Federal aid to medical schools . . . .

____ 7. Federal aid to nursing schools . . . .

____ 8. Health professional certification . . . .

____ 9. Hospital housestaff unionization . . . .

____ 10. Medicare/Medicaid reimbursements for health personnel . . . .

____ 11. Nurse training . . . .

____ 12. Physician training . . . .

ORGANIZATION OF CARE

____ 13. Certificates of need . . . .

____ 14. Community health centers . . . .

____ 15. Community mental health centers . . . . . .

____ 16. Developmental disabilities programs . . . .

____ 17. Disease control programs . . . .

____ 18. Drug/Alcohol abuse programs . . . .

____ 19. Emergency health care programs . . . .

____ 20. Environmental health . . . .

____ 21. Federal aid to hospitals . . . .

____ 22. Health education . . . .

____ 23. Health maintenance organizations (HMOs) . . . .

____ 24. Health planning . . . .

____ 25. Health professional redistribution programs . . . .

____ 26. Home health programs . . . .

____ 27. Hospital cost containment . . . .

493

LIST A—continued

	Minor Interest 1	2	Moderate Interest 3	4	Major Interest 5

ORGANIZATION OF CARE—continued

____ 28. Indian health care ....

____ 29. Kidney dialysis ....

____ 30. Mental health......................

____ 31. Migrant health programs ....

____ 32. National Health Service Corps ....

____ 33. Nursing homes ....

____ 34. Occupational health & safety ....

____ 35. Preventive care ....

____ 36. Professional standards review
organizations, PSROs ....

____ 37. Public health services ....

____ 38. Rural health care ....

____ 39. Veterans health care ....

DELIVERY OF CARE

____ 40. Abortion ....

____ 41. Cyclamates ....

____ 42. Drug development regulation..........

____ 43. Drug industry regulation ....

____ 44. Drug labeling regulation, e.g., expiration
date labeling, safety brochure inserts ...

____ 45. Food additive regulation ....

____ 46. Generic versus brand-name drugs ......

____ 47. Laetrile..........................

____ 48. Maternal & child health insurance ......

____ 49. Medical advertising ....

____ 50. Medical device regulation ....

____ 51. Medical malpractice insurance ....

____ 52. Medical records privacy ....

____ 53. Medicare/Medicaid fraud ....

____ 54. Medicare/Medicaid funding...........

____ 55. National health insurance ....

____ 56. Saccharin ....

494

LIST B

Would you please place a check mark **in front of** the name of **all** organizations on this list with whom your organization **regularly** and **routinely** discusses national health policy matters?

	WE DO	BOTH	THEY DO
PROFESSIONAL ASSOCIATIONS			
___101. American Academy of Child Psychiatry			
___102. American Academy of Dermatology			
___103. American Academy of Orthopaedic Surgeons			
___104. American Academy of Pediatrics			
___105. American Academy of Physician Assistants			
___106. American Association for Dental Research			
___107. American Association of Nurse Anesthetists			
___108. American Chiropractic Association			
___109. American College of Cardiology			
___110. American College of Obstetricians and Gynecologists			
___111. American College of Preventive Medicine			
___112. American Dental Association			
___113. American Dietetic Association			
___114. American Federation for Clinical Research			
___115. American Gastroenterological Association			
___116. American Medical Association			
___117. American Nurses' Association			
___118. American Osteopathic Association			
___119. American Psychiatric Association			
___120. American Psychological Association			
___121. American Public Health Association			
___122. American Society of Hematology			
___123. American Society for Microbiology			
___124. American Speech-Language-Hearing Association			
___125. Association for the Advancement of Psychology			
___126. Association of Teachers of Preventive Medicine			
___127. College of American Pathologists			
___128. Endocrine Society			
___129. Medical Library Association			
___130. Myopia International Research Foundation			
___131. National League for Nursing			
___132. Physicians National Housestaff Association			
___133. Renal Physicians Association			
___134. Society for Investigative Dermatology			
GENERAL INTEREST GROUPS			
___201. American Association of Retired Persons/National Retired Teachers Association (AARP/NRTA)			
___202. Chamber of Commerce of the United States			
___203. Children's Defense Fund			
___204. Common Cause			
___205. Consumer Federation of America			

LIST B—continued

	WE DO	BOTH	THEY DO

GENERAL INTEREST GROUPS—continued

____206. Environmental Defense Fund . . . . ____ ____ ____

____207. National Abortion Rights Action League . . . . ____ ____ ____

____208. National Association for the Advancement of Colored People . . . . . ____ ____ ____

____209. National Council of Senior Citizens . . . . ____ ____ ____

____210. National Farmers Union . . . . ____ ____ ____

____211. National Urban League . . . . ____ ____ ____

____212. Planned Parenthood Federation of America . . . . ____ ____ ____

____213. Veterans of Foreign Wars of the United States . . . . ____ ____ ____

____214. Women's Lobby . . . . ____ ____ ____

HEALTH INTEREST GROUPS

____301. American Brittle Bone Society . . . . ____ ____ ____

____302. American Cancer Society . . . . ____ ____ ____

____303. American Diabetes Association . . . . ____ ____ ____

____304. American Heart Association . . . . ____ ____ ____

____305. American Social Health Association . . . . ____ ____ ____

____306. Arthritis Foundation . . . . ____ ____ ____

____307. Candlelighters Foundation . . . . ____ ____ ____

____308. Citizens for the Treatment of High Blood Pressure . . . . ____ ____ ____

____309. Coalition for Health Funding . . . . ____ ____ ____

____310. Community Nutrition Institute . . . . ____ ____ ____

____311. Cooley's Anemia Foundation . . . . ____ ____ ____

____312. Cystic Fibrosis Foundation . . . . ____ ____ ____

____313. Epilepsy Foundation of America . . . . ____ ____ ____

____314. Friends of Eye Research, Rehabilitation, and Treatment . . . . ____ ____ ____

____315. Joint Council of Allergy and Immunology . . . . ____ ____ ____

____316. Juvenile Diabetes Foundation . . . . ____ ____ ____

____317. Mental Health Association . . . . ____ ____ ____

____318. National Association for Retarded Citizens . . . . ____ ____ ____

____319. National Foundation for Ileitis and Colitis . . . . ____ ____ ____

____320. National Health Law Program . . . . ____ ____ ____

____321. National Hemophilia Foundation . . . . ____ ____ ____

____322. National Kidney Foundation . . . . ____ ____ ____

____323. National Rehabilitation Association . . . . ____ ____ ____

____324. National Society for Autistic Children . . . . ____ ____ ____

____325. National Women's Health Network . . . . ____ ____ ____

____326. Pennsylvania Diabetes Institute . . . . ____ ____ ____

____327. Public Citizen's Health Research Group . . . . ____ ____ ____

____328. United Cerebral Palsy Associations . . . . ____ ____ ____

____329. Washington Business Group on Health . . . . ____ ____ ____

PRIVATE FIRMS, FOUNDATIONS, RESEARCH INSTITUTIONS, & INSURANCE PLANS

____401. ARA Services, Inc. . . . . ____ ____ ____

____402. Blue Cross and Blue Shield Associations . . . . ____ ____ ____

____403. Hoffman-La Roche, Inc . . . . ____ ____ ____

496

LIST B—continued

	WE DO	BOTH	THEY DO
PRIVATE FIRMS, FOUNDATIONS, RESEARCH INSTITUTIONS, & INSURANCE PLANS—continued			
____404. Hospital Corporation of America	____	____	____
____405. Kaiser Foundation Health Plan	____	____	____
____406. Merck & Company	____	____	____
____407. National Academy of Sciences Institute of Medicine	____	____	____
____408. Pfizer Pharmaceuticals	____	____	____
____409. Robert Wood Johnson Foundation	____	____	____
____410. Upjohn Company	____	____	____
LABOR UNIONS			
____501. American Federation of Labor–Congress of Industrial Organi-zations (AFL–CIO)	____	____	____
____502. American Federation of State, County, and Municipal Employees (AFSCME)	____	____	____
____503. National Union of Hospital and Health Care Employees, RWDSU, AFL–CIO	____	____	____
____504. Service Employees International Union, AFL–CIO	____	____	____
____505. United Automobile Workers (UAW)	____	____	____
____506. United Mine Workers (UMW)	____	____	____
EDUCATIONAL ASSOCIATIONS			
____601. American Association of Colleges of Pharmacy	____	____	____
____602. American Association of Colleges of Nursing	____	____	____
____603. American Association of Dental Schools	____	____	____
____604. Association of American Medical Colleges	____	____	____
____605. Council of Teaching Hospitals	____	____	____
TRADE ASSOCIATIONS			
____701. American Association of Professional Standards Review Organizations	____	____	____
____702. American Health Care Association	____	____	____
____703. American Health Planning Association	____	____	____
____704. American Hospital Association	____	____	____
____705. American Insurance Association	____	____	____
____706. Calorie Control Council	____	____	____
____707. Federation of American Hospitals	____	____	____
____708. Group Health Association of America	____	____	____
____709. Health Industry Manufacturers Association	____	____	____
____710. Health Insurance Association of America	____	____	____
____711. National Association of Home Health Agencies	____	____	____
____712. National Coalition of Hispanic Mental Health and Human Service Organizations	____	____	____
____713. National Council of Community Mental Health Centers	____	____	____
____714. National Council of Health Care Services	____	____	____
____715. National Association of Community Health Centers	____	____	____
____716. Pharmaceutical Manufacturers Association	____	____	____

LIST B—continued

	WE DO	BOTH	THEY DO

ASSOCIATIONS OF GOVERNMENT OFFICIALS & ORGANIZATIONS

____801. Association of State and Territorial Health Officials . . . .

____802. National Association of Counties . . . .

____803. National Association of State Alcohol and Drug Abuse Directors . .

____804. National Conference of State Legislatures . . . .

____805. National Governors' Association . . . .

____806. United States Conference of Mayors . . . .

GOVERNMENT ORGANIZATIONS

Executive Branch and Independent Establishments

____901. Federal Trade Commission . . . .

Department of Health and Human Services

____902. Office of the Secretary . . . .

____903. Office of the Assistant Secretary for Health . . . .

____904. Alcohol, Drug Abuse, and Mental Health Administration . . . . . .

Food and Drug Administration

____905. Commissioner and associated staff . . . .

____906. Bureau of Drugs . . . .

____907. Bureau of Foods . . . .

____908. Health Resources Administration . . . .

____909. Health Services Administration . . . .

National Institutes of Health

____910. Director and associated staff . . . .

____911. National Cancer Institute . . . .

____912. National Heart, Blood and Lung Institute . . . .

____913. National Eye Institute . . . .

____914. National Institute on Aging . . . .

____915. National Institute of Allergy and Infectious Diseases . . . . . .

____916. National Institute of Arthritis, Metabolism, and Digestive Diseases . . . .

____917. National Institute of Child Health and Human Development

____918. National Institute of Dental Research . . . .

____919. National Institute of Environmental Health Sciences . . . .

____920. National Institute of General Medical Sciences . . . .

____921. National Institute of Neurological Communicative Disorders and Stroke . . . .

____922. Health Care Financing Administration . . . .

____923. Office of Management and the Budget . . . .

____924. Veterans Administration . . . .

____925. The White House Office . . . .

498

	WE DO	BOTH	THEY DO

GOVERNMENT ORGANIZATIONS—continued
Legislative Branch
HOUSE OF REPRESENTATIVES

Appropriations Committee

	WE DO	BOTH	THEY DO
____951. Democratic Party members & staff	____	____	____
____952. Republican Party members & staff	____	____	____

Subcommittee on Labor and Health, Education and Welfare Appropriations

____953. Democratic Party members & staff	____	____	____
____954. Republican Party members & staff	____	____	____

Interstate and Foreign Commerce Committee

____955. Democratic Party members & staff	____	____	____
____956. Republican Party members & staff	____	____	____

Subcommittee on Health and the Environment

____957. Democratic Party members & staff	____	____	____
____958. Republican Party members & staff	____	____	____

Ways and Means Committee

____959. Democratic Party members & staff	____	____	____
____960. Republican Party members & staff	____	____	____

Subcommittee on Health

____961. Democratic Party members & staff	____	____	____
____962. Republican Party members & staff	____	____	____

SENATE

Appropriations Committee

____963. Democratic Party members & staff	____	____	____
____964. Republican Party members & staff	____	____	____

Subcommittee on Labor and Health, Education, and Welfare Appropriations

____965. Democratic Party members & staff	____	____	____
____966. Republican Party members & staff	____	____	____

Finance Committee

____967. Democratic Party members & staff	____	____	____
____968. Republican Party members & staff	____	____	____

Subcommittee on Health

____969. Democratic Party members & staff	____	____	____
____970. Republican Party members & staff	____	____	____

Human Resources Committee

____971. Democratic Party members & staff	____	____	____
____972. Republican Party members & staff	____	____	____

Subcommittee on Health and Scientific Research

____973. Democratic Party members & staff	____	____	____
____974. Republican Party members & staff	____	____	____

LIST C

Under the column headed WE RECEIVE CONFIDENTIAL ADVICE, please check **all** those organizations from whom your organization receives such advice. Under the column headed WE GIVE CONFIDENTIAL ADVICE, please check **all** those organizations who come to your organization for such advice.

Same as List B

LIST D

Please check those organizations which stand out as **especially** influential and consequential in formulating national health policy.

Same as List B

References

Agger, Robert E., Daniel Goldrich, and Bert E. Swanson
1964 *The Rulers and the Ruled: Political Power and Importance in American Communities*. New York: John Wiley.
Alba, Richard D., and Charles Kadushin
1976 "The intersection of social circles: a new measure of social proximity in networks." *Sociological Methods and Research* 5:77–102.
Alba, Richard D., and Gwen Moore
1978 "Elite social circles." *Sociological Methods and Research* 7:167–88.
Aldrich, Howard E.
1979 *Organizations and Environments*. Englewood Cliffs, N.J.: Prentice-Hall.
Aldrich, Howard E., and Jeffrey Pfeffer
1976 "Environments of organizations." *Annual Review of Sociology* 2:79–105.
Aldrich, John H., and Forrest D. Nelson
1984 *Linear Probability, Logit, and Probit Models*. Beverly Hills, Calif.: Sage.
Alford, Robert P., and Roger Friedland
1985 *Powers of Theory: Capitalism, the State, and Democracy*. Cambridge: Cambridge University Press.
Allison, Graham T.
1971 *Essence of Decision: Explaining the Cuban Missile Crisis*. Boston: Little, Brown.
Anderson, Odin W.
1968 *The Uneasy Equilibrium: Private and Public Financing of Health Services in the United States, 1875–1965*. New Haven: College and University Press.
Anderson, Paul A.
1983 "Decision-making by objection and the Cuban missile crisis." *Administrative Science Quarterly* 28:201–22.
Astley, W. Graham, and Andrew Van de Ven
1983 "Central perspectives and debates in organization theory." *Administrative Science Quarterly* 28:245–73.
Axelrod, Robert (ed.)
1976 *Structure of Decision: The Cognitive Maps of Political Elites*. Princeton: Princeton University Press.
Bailey, Kenneth D.
1974 "Cluster analysis." In David R. Heise (ed.), *Sociological Methodology 1975*, pp. 59–128. San Francisco: Jossey-Bass.

Bailey, Stephen K.
  1950 *Congress Makes a Law.* New York: Columbia University Press.
Banfield, E. C.
  1961 *Political Influence.* New York: Free Press.
Barton, Allen H.
  1975 "Consensus and conflict among American leaders." *Public Opinion Quarterly* 38:507–30.
Baum, Rainer C.
  1976 "Introduction to Part IV: Generalized Media in Action." In Jan J. Loubser, Rainer C. Baum, Andrew Effrat, and Victor Meyer Lidz, *Explorations in General Theory in Social Science: Essays in Honor of Talcott Parsons,* vol. 2. New York: Free Press.
Becker, Gary S.
  1973 "A Theory of Marriage: Part I." *Journal of Political Economy* 81:813–46.
  1974 "A Theory of Marriage: Part II." *Journal of Political Economy* 82 (2, pt. 2): S11–S26.
  1981 *A Treatise on the Family.* Cambridge: Harvard University Press.
Bendix, Reinhard
  1964 *Nation-Building and Citizenship: Studies of Our Changing Social Order.* New York: Wiley & Sons.
Benson, J. Kenneth
  1975 "The interorganizational network as political economy." *Administrative Science Quarterly* 20:229–49.
Berkowitz, Steven
  1982 *An Introduction to Structural Analysis: The Network Approach to Social Research.* Toronto: Butterworths.
Bernstein, Marver
  1955 *Regulating Business by Independent Commission.* Princeton: Princeton University Press.
Berry, Jeffrey M.
  1984 *The Interest Group Society.* Boston: Little, Brown.
Billings, Robert S., Thomas W. Milburn, and Mary Lou Schaalman
  1980 "A model of crisis perception: a theoretical and empirical analysis." *Administrative Science Quarterly* 25:300–316.
Blalock, Herbert
  1984 "Contextual-effects models: theoretical and methodological issues." *Annual Review of Sociology* 10:353–72.
Blau, Peter M.
  1964 *Exchange and Power in Social Life.* New York: Wiley & Sons.
Block, Fred
  1977 "The ruling class does not rule: notes on the Marxist theory of the State." *Socialist Revolution* 7:6–28.
Blumer, Herbert
  1948 "Public opinion and public opinion polling." *American Sociological Review* 13:542–54.

Boje, David M., and David A. Whetten
1981 "Effects of organizational strategies and contextual constraints on centrality and attributions of influence in interorganizational networks." *Administrative Science Quarterly* 26:378–95.

Boorman, Scott A., and Harrison C. White
1976 "Social structure from multiple networks, II: Role structure," *American Journal of Sociology* 81:1384–446.

Boudon, Raymond
1971 *The Uses of Structuralism*. Trans. Michalina Vaughan. London: Heinemann Educational Books.

Bourdieu, Pierre
1984 *Distinction: A Social Critique of the Judgment of Taste*. Cambridge: Harvard University Press.

Bower, Joseph L.
1983 *The Faces of Management: An American Approach to Leadership in Business and Politics*. Boston: Houghton-Mifflin.

Bowman, Elizabeth
1976 "Congress cool to health block grant plan." *Congressional Quarterly Weekly Report* 34, February 28, 1976, pp. 487–91 ff.

Brand, Donald R.
1983 "Corporatism, the NRA, and the Oil Industry." *Political Science Quarterly* 98:99–118.

Breiger, Ronald L.
1974 "The duality of persons and groups." *Social Forces* 53:181–90.

Brock, William Ranulf
1984 *Investigation of Responsibility: Public Responsibility in the United States, 1865–1900*. New York: Cambridge University Press.

Brown, Roger
1965 *Social Psychology*. New York: Free Press.

Burstein, Paul
1981 "The sociology of democratic politics and government." *Annual Review of Sociology* 7:291–319.

Burt, Ronald S.
1975 "Corporate society: a time series analysis of network structure." *Social Science Research* 4:271–328.
1976 "Positions in networks." *Social Forces* 55:93–122.
1977 "Power as a social typology." *Social Science Research* 6:1–83.
1978 'Cohesion versus structural equivalence as a basis for network subgroups." *Sociological Methods and Research* 7:189–212.
1980 "Models of network structure." *Annual Review of Sociology* 6:79–141.
1982 *Toward a Structural Theory of Action: Network Models of Social Structure, Perceptions and Action*. New York: Academic Press.
1983 "Network data from archival records." in Ronald S. Burt and Michael J. Minor (eds.), *Applied Network Analysis: A Methodological Introduction*, pp. 158–74. Beverly Hills, Calif.: Sage Publications.

Burt, Ronald S., and Michael Minor (eds.)

1983 *Applied Network Analysis: A Methodological Introduction.* Beverly Hills, Calif.: Sage Publications.

Burton, Michael G., and John Higley

1984 "Elite theory: the basic contentions." Paper presented at the annual meetings of the American Sociological Association, San Antonio, Tex.

Campbell, Angus, Gerald Gurin, and Warren E. Miller

1954 *The Voter Decides.* Evanston, Ill.: Row, Peterson.

Campion, Frank D.

1984 *The AMA and U.S. Health Policy Since 1940.* Chicago: Chicago Review Press.

Cater, Douglas

1964 *Power in Washington.* New York: Random House.

Chandler, Alfred D., Jr.

1972 "Anthracite coal and the beginnings of the Industrial Revolution in the United States." *Business History Review* 46:141–81.

Child, John

1972 "Organization structure, environment and performance: the role of strategic choice." *Sociology* 6:1–22.

Chirot, Daniel

1985 "The rise of the West." *American Sociological Review* 50:181–95.

Chubb, John E.

1983 *Interest Groups and the Bureaucracy: The Politics of Energy.* Palo Alto, Calif.: Stanford University Press.

Clark, Terry N.

1968a *Community Structure and Decision-Making: Comparative Analyses.* San Francisco: Chandler.

1968b "Community structure, decision-making, budget expenditures, and urban renewal in 51 American communities." *American Sociological Review* 60:66–72.

Cobb, Roger W., and Charles D. Elder

1972 *Participation in American Politics: The Dynamics of Agenda-Building.* Baltimore: Johns Hopkins University Press.

Cochrane, James J.

1981 "Energy policy in the Johnson administration: logical order versus economic pluralism." In Craufurd D. Goodwin (ed.), *Energy Policy in Perspective: Today's Problems, Yesterday's Solutions,* pp. 337–93. Washington, D.C.: Brookings Institution.

Coleman, James S.

1957 *Community Conflict.* Glencoe, Ill.: Free Press.

1963 "Comment on 'The Concept of Influence.'" *Public Opinion Quarterly* 27:63–82.

1972 "Systems of social exchange." *Journal of Mathematical Sociology* 2:145–63.

1973 *The Mathematics of Collective Action.* Chicago: Aldine.

1974 *Power and the Structure of Society.* New York: W. W. Norton.

1977 "Social action systems." In K. Szaniawsk (ed.), *Problems of Formalization in the Social Sciences,* pp. 11–50. Wroclaw Poland: Ossolineum.

1982 *The Asymmetric Society.* Syracuse, N.Y.: Syracuse University Press.

1985 "Micro foundations and macrosocial theory." In Siegwart Lindenberg, James S. Coleman, and Stefan Nowak, (eds.), *Approaches to Social Theory,* pp. 345–63, New York: Russell Sage Foundation.

Coleman, James S., Elihu Katz, and Herbert Menzel

1966 *Medical Innovation: A Diffusion Study.* Indianapolis: Bobbs-Merrill.

Collins, Randall

1981 "On the microfoundations of macrosociology." *American Journal of Sociology* 86:984–1014.

1983 "Upheavals in biological theory undermine sociobiology." In Randall Collins (ed.), *Sociological Theory 1983,* pp. 306–18. San Francisco: Jossey-Bass.

Congressional Quarterly Almanac

1978 "Health Services Centers." *Congressional Quarterly* 34:611–16.

Congressional Quarterly

1979 *Energy Policy.* Washington, D.C.: Congressional Quarterly.

Cook, Karen S.

1977 "Exchange and power in networks in interorganizational relations." *Sociological Quarterly* 18:62–82.

Cook, Karen S., Richard M. Emerson, Mary R. Gillmore, and Toshio Yamagishi

1983 "The distribution of power in exchange networks: theory and experimental results." *American Journal of Sociology* 89:275–305.

Crozier, Michel

1964 *The Bureaucratic Phenomenon.* Chicago: University of Chicago Press.

Crozier, Michel, and Erhard Friedberg

1980. *Actors and Systems: The Politics of Collective Action.* Trans. Arthur Goldhammer. Chicago: University of Chicago Press.

Dahl, Robert A.

1961 *Who Governs? Democracy and Power in an American City.* New Haven: Yale University Press.

1963 *Modern Political Analysis.* Englewood Cliffs, N.J.: Prentice-Hall.

Davis, David H.

1974 *Energy Politics.* New York: St. Martin's Press.

1978 *Energy Politics.* 2d ed. New York: St. Martin's Press.

deMarchi, Neil

1981 "Energy policy under Nixon: mainly putting out fires." In Craufurd D. Goodwin (ed.), *Energy Policy in Perspective: Today's Problems, Yesterday's Solutions,* pp. 395–473. Washington, D.C.: Brookings Institution.

Deutsch, Karl W.

1966 *The Nerves of Government.* New York: Free Press.

DiMaggio, Paul J., and Walter W. Powell

1983 "The iron cage revisited: institutional isomorphism and collective rationality in organizational fields." *American Sociological Review* 48:147–60.

Domhoff, G. William

1977 *Who Really Rules? New Haven and Community Power Reexamined.* Rutgers, N.J.: Transaction Books.

1978 *The Powers That Be: Process of Ruling-Class Domination of America.* New York: Vintage Books.

Drew, Elizabeth

1978 "Charlie." *New Yorker,* January 9, 1978, pp. 32–58.

Durkheim, Emile

1964 *The Rules of Sociological Method.* Trans. Sarah A. Solovay and John H. Mueller; ed. George E. G. Catlin. 8th ed. New York: Free Press of Glencoe.

Dye, Thomas R.

1976 *Who's Running America?* Englewood Cliffs, N.J.: Prentice-Hall.

Easterlin, Richard A.

1966 "On the relation of economic factors to recent and projected fertility changes." *Demography* 3 : 131–55.

1970 "Towards a socioeconomic theory of fertility: survey of recent research on economic factors in American fertility." In Samuel J. Behrman, Leslie Corsa, Jr., and Ronald Freedman (eds.), *Fertility and Family Planning: A World View,* pp. 127–56. Ann Arbor: University of Michigan Press.

Ekeh, Peter P.

1974 *Social Exchange Theory: The Two Traditions.* Cambridge: Harvard University Press.

Emerson, Richard

1962 "Power-dependence relations." *American Sociological Review* 27 : 31–41.

Engler, Robert

1961 *The Politics of Oil: A Study of Private Power and Democratic Directions.* New York: Macmillan.

Erbring, Lutz, and Alice Young

1979 "Individual and social structure: contextual effects as endogenous feedback." *Sociological Methods and Research* 7 : 396–430.

Erickson, Bonnie H.

1978 "Some problems of inference from chain data." In Karl Schuessler (ed.), *Sociological Methodology 1979.* San Francisco: Jossey-Bass.

Etzioni, Amitai

1961 *A Comparative Analysis of Complex Organizations.* New York: Free Press.

Evans, Mariah D.

1983 "Modernization, economic conditions and family formation: evidence from recent white and nonwhite cohorts." Ph.D. dissertation, University of Chicago.

Evans, Peter B., Dietrich Rueschemeyer, and Theda Skocpol

1985 "On the road toward a more adequate understanding of the state." In Peter B. Evans, Dietrich Rueschemeyer, and Theda Skocpol, eds., *Bringing the State Back In,* pp. 347–66. Cambridge: Cambridge University Press.

Feldman, Martha S., and James G. March

1981 "Information in organizations as signal and symbol." *Administrative Science Quarterly* 26 : 171–86.

Field, G. Lowell, and John Higley

1980 *Elitism.* London: Routledge & Kegan Paul.

Fox, Harrison W., and Martin Schnitzer

1981 *Doing Business in Washington: How to Win Friends and Influence Government.* New York: Free Press.

Freeland, Mark, George Calat, and Carol E. Schendler
    1980 "Projections of national health expenditures, 1980, 1985, and 1990." *Health Care Financing Review 1*: 1–27.
Freeman, Jo
    1979 "Resource mobilization and strategy: a model for analyzing social movement organization actions." In Mayer N. Zald and John D. McCarthy (eds.), *The Dynamics of Social Movements*, pp. 167–89. Cambridge, Mass.: Winthrop Publishers.
Freeman, Linton C.
    1968 *Patterns of Local Community Leadership*. Indianapolis: Bobbs-Merrill.
    1979 "Centrality in Social Networks. I. Conceptual Clarification." *Social Networks* 1: 215–39.
Freidson, Eliot
    1970 *Professional Dominance; The Social Structure of Medical Care*. New York: Atherton Press.
    1985 "The reorganization of the medical profession." *Medical Care Review* 42: 11–35.
French, J. R. P., and B. Raven
    1959 "The bases of social power." In D. Cartwright (ed.), *Studies in Social Power*, pp. 150–67. Ann Arbor: University of Michigan Institute for Social Research.
Gais, Thomas L., Mark A. Peterson, and Jack L. Walker
    1984 "Interest groups, iron triangles, and representative institutions in American national government." *British Journal of Political Science* 14: 161–81.
Galaskiewicz, Joseph
    1979 *Exchange Networks and Community Politics*. Beverly Hills, Calif.: Sage Publications.
Galaskiewicz, Joseph, and Peter V. Marsden
    1978 "Interorganizational resource networks: formal patterns of overlap." *Social Sciences Research* 7: 89–107.
Gamson, William A.
    1966 "Reputation and resources in community politics." *American Journal of Sociology* 72: 121–31.
    1968 *Power and Discontent*. Homewood, Ill.: Dorsey Press.
    1975 *The Strategy of Social Protest*. Homewood, Ill.: Dorsey.
    1980 "Understanding the careers of challenging groups: a commentary on Goldstone." *American Journal of Sociology* 85: 1043–60.
Garson, G. David
    1978 *Group Theories of Politics*. Beverly Hills: Sage.
Gibson, Robert M., and Daniel R. Waldo
    1981 "National health expenditures, 1980." *Health Care Financing Review* 3: 1–54.
Giddens, Anthony
    1968 " 'Power' in the recent writings of Talcott Parsons." *Sociology* 2: 257–72.
    1979 *Central Problems in Social Theory: Action, Structure and Contradiction in Social Analysis*. Berkeley: University of California Press.
    1981 "Agency, institution, and time-space analysis." In Karin Knorr-Cetina and Aaron V. Cicourel (eds.), *Advances in Social Theory and Methodology: Toward an*

508   *References*

Integration of Micro- and Macro-Sociologies, pp. 161–74. London: Routledge & Kegan Paul.

Gilbert, Claire W.
1968 "Community power and decision-making: a quantitative examination of previous research." In Terry N. Clark (ed.), *Community Structure and Decision-Making: Comparative Analysis*, pp. 136–56. San Francisco: Chandler.

Gold, David; Clarence Lo; and Erik Olin Wright
1975 "Recent developments in Marxist theories of the capitalist state." *Monthly Review* 27:29–41.

Goldstone, Jack
1980 "The weakness of organization: a new look at Gamson's *The Strategy of Social Protest.*" *American Journal of Sociology* 85:1017–42.

Goodwin, Craufurd D. (ed.)
1981 *Energy Policy in Perspective: Today's Problems, Yesterday's Solutions.* Washington, D.C.: Brookings Institution.

Granovetter, Mark S.
1973 "The strength of weak ties." *American Journal of Sociology* 73:1350–80.
1974 *Getting a Job: A Study of Contacts and Careers.* Cambridge: Harvard University Press.
1985 "Economic action, social structure, and embeddedness." *American Journal of Sociology* 91:481–510.

Green, Harold P., and Alan Rosenthal
1963 *Government of the Atom: The Integration of Powers.* New York: Atherton Press.

Griffin, Larry J., Joel A. Devine, and Michael Wallace
1982 "Monopoly capital, organized labor, and military expenditures in the United States, 1949–1976." *American Journal of Sociology* (Suppl.) 88:113–53.

Grimes, Michael D., Charles M. Bonjean, J. L. Lyon, and Robert L. Lineberry
1976 "Community structure and leadership arrangements: a multidimensonal analysis." *American Sociological Review* 41:706–25.

Gusfield, Joseph R.
1981 *The Culture of Public Problems: Drinking-Driving and the Symbolic Order.* Chicago: University of Chicago Press.

Hannan, Michael T., and John Freeman
1977 "The population ecology of organizations." *American Journal of Sociology* 82:929–64.

Harary, Frank, Robert Z. Norman, and Dorwin Cartwright
1965 *Structural Models: An Introduction to the Theory of Directed Graphs.* New York: John Wiley and Sons.

Hardin, Russell
1982 *Collective Action.* Baltimore: Johns Hopkins University Press.

Hawley, Ellis W.
1968 "Secretary Hoover and the bituminous coal problem, 1921–1928." *Business History Review* 42:247–70.

Hayes, Michael T.
1979 "Interest groups and Congress: toward a transactional theory." In Leroy N.

Rieselbach (ed.), *The Congressional System*, 2d ed., pp. 252–73. North Scituate, Mass.: Duxbury.

Hechter, Michael, and William Brustein
1980 "Regional modes of production and patterns of state formation in Western Europe." *American Journal of Sociology* 85:1061–94.

Heclo, Hugh
1974 *Modern Social Politics in Britain and Sweden.* New Haven: Yale University Press.
1978 "Issue networks and the executive establishment." In Anthony King (ed.), *The New American Political System,* pp. 87–124. Washington, D.C.: American Enterprise Institute.

Heinz, John P., and Edward O. Laumann
1982 *Chicago Lawyers: The Social Structure of the Bar.* New York: Russell Sage Foundation, American Bar Foundation.

Heinz, John P., Edward O. Laumann, Robert Nelson, and Robert Salisbury
1982 "Washington representatives and national policy making." A proposal to the Trustees of the American Bar Foundation. New York: American Bar Foundation.

Hermann, Charles F.
1969 *Crisis in Foreign Policy: A Simulation Analysis.* Indianapolis, Ind.: Bobbs-Merrill.

Hicks, Alexander, and Duane Swank
1984 "On the political economy of welfare expansion: a comparative analysis of 18 advanced capitalist democracies, 1960–1971." *Comparative Political Studies* 17:81–119.

Hirsch, Paul M.
1986 "From ambushes to golden parachutes: corporate takeovers as an instance of cultural framing and institutional integration." *American Journal of Sociology* 91:800–837.

Hodgson, Godfrey
1973 "The politics of American health care." *Atlantic* 232, March, pp. 45–61.

Hogan, Dennis P.
1981 *Transition and Social Change: The Early Lives of American Men.* New York: Academic Press.

Hogan, Michael J.
1974 "Informal entente: public policy and private management in Anglo-American petroleum affairs, 1918–1924." *Business History Review* 48:187–205.

Hovland, Carl I., Irving L. Janis, and H. H. Kelley
1953 *Communication and Persuasion.* New Haven: Yale University Press.
1957 *The Order of Presentation in Persuasion.* New Haven: Yale University Press.

Hubbell, C. H.
1965 "An input-output approach to clique identification." *Sociometry* 28:277–99.

Hunter, Floyd
1953 *Community Power Structure.* Durham: University of North Carolina Press.

Huntington, Samuel T.
1950 "Clientilism: a study in administrative politics." Ph.D. dissertation, Harvard University.

Jacobs, David
1974 "Dependency and vulnerability: an exchange approach to the control of organizations." *Administrative Science Quarterly* 19:45–59.
Janowitz, Morris
1967 "Review of the sociological tradition." *American Sociological Review* 32: 638–40.
1975 "Sociological theory and social control." *American Journal of Sociology* 81:82–108.
Jardine, Nicholas, and Robin Sibson
1971 *Mathematical Taxonomy.* London: Wiley.
Johnson, James P.
1979 *The Politics of Soft Coal: The Bituminous Industry from World War I Through the New Deal.* Urbana, Ill.: University of Illinois Press.
Johnson, S. C.
1967 "Hierarchical clustering schemes." *Psychometrika* 32:241–54.
Jöreskog, Karl G., and Dag Sörbom
1981 *LISREL V: Analysis of Linear Structural Relationships by Maximum Likelihood and Least Squares Methods.* Uppsala: University of Uppsala.
Kadushin, Charles
1968 "Power, influence, and social circles: a new methodology for studying opinion makers." *American Sociological Review* 3:685–99.
Kalt, Joseph P.
1981 *The Economics and Politics of Oil Price Regulation.* Cambridge: MIT Press.
Kanter, Rosabeth Moss
1977 *Men and Women of the Corporation.* New York: Basic Books.
Karl, Barry D.
1984 *The Uneasy State: The United States from 1915 to 1945.* Chicago: University of Chicago Press.
Kash, Don E., and Robert W. Rycroft
1984 *U.S. Energy Policy: Crisis and Complacency.* Norman: University of Oklahoma Press.
Keller, Morton
1981 "The pluralist state: American economic regulation in comparative perspective, 1900–1930." In Thomas K. McCraw (ed.), *Regulation in Perspective,* pp. 56–94. Cambridge: Harvard University Press.
Keller, Suzanne
1963 *Beyond the Ruling Class: Strategic Elites in Modern Society.* New York: Random House.
Kerlinger, Fred N., and Elazar J. Pedhazur
1973 *Multiple Regression in Behavioral Research.* New York: Holt, Rinehart & Winston.
Kingdon, John W.
1984 *Agendas, Alternatives, and Public Policies.* Boston: Little, Brown.
Knoke, David
1981 "Power structures." In Samuel L. Long (ed.), *The Handbook of Political Behavior,* 3:275–332. New York: Plenum.

1983 "Organization sponsorship of social influence associations." *Social Forces* 61:1065–87.

1987 "Resource acquisition and allocation in U.S. national associations." In Bert Klandermans (ed.), *Organizing for Change: Social Movement Organizations Across Cultures.* Greenwich, Conn.: JAI Press.

Knoke, David, and Peter J. Burke

1980 *Log-linear Models.* Beverly Hills, Calif.: Sage.

Knoke, David, and Frank Burleigh

1988 "Collective action in national policy domains: constraints, cleavages, and policy outcomes." *Research in Political Sociology* (forthcoming).

Knoke, David, and Ronald Burt

1983 "Prominence." In Ronald Burt and Michael Minor (eds.), *Applied Network Analysis: A Methodological Introduction,* pp. 195–222. Beverly Hills, Calif.: Sage Publications.

Knoke, David, and James H. Kuklinski

1982 *Network Analysis.* Beverly Hills, Calif.: Sage Publications.

Knoke, David, and Edward O. Laumann

1982 "The social organization of national policy domains: an exploration of some structural hypotheses." In Peter V. Marsden and Nan Lin (eds.), *Social Structure and Network Analysis,* pp. 255–70. Beverly Hills, Calif.: Sage Publications.

1983 "Issue publics in national policy domains." Paper presented at the annual meetings of the American Sociological Association. Detroit, Mich.

Knoke, David, and David L. Rogers

1979 "A blockmodel analysis of interorganizational relations." *Sociology and Social Research* 64:28–52.

Knorr-Cetina, Karin, and Aaron V. Cicourel (eds.)

1981 *Advances in Social Theory and Methodology: Toward an Integration of Micro- and Macro-Sociologies.* London: Routledge & Kegan Paul.

Kruskal, Joseph B., and Myron Wish

1978 *Multidimensional Scaling.* Beverly Hills, Calif.: Sage.

Larson, Magali S.

1977 *The Rise of Professionalism: A Sociological Analysis.* Berkeley: University of California Press.

Laumann, Edward O.

1966 *Prestige and Association in an Urban Community.* New York: Bobbs-Merrill.

1973 *Bonds of Pluralism: The Form and Substance of Urban Social Networks.* New York: Wiley Interscience.

Laumann, Edward O., Joseph Galaskiewicz, and Peter V. Marsden

1978 "Community structure as interorganizational linkages." *Annual Review of Sociology* 4:455–84.

Laumann, Edward O., and John P. Heinz

1985 "Washington lawyers—and others: the structure of Washington representation." *Stanford Law Review* 37: 465–502.

Laumann, Edward O., John P. Heinz, Robert Nelson, and Robert Salisbury

1986 "Organizations and political action: representing interests in national policymaking": Paper presented at the annual meetings of the American Sociological Association, New York.

Laumann, Edward O., and David Knoke
  1986 "Social network theory." In Siegwart Lindenberg, James S. Coleman, and Stefan Nowak (eds.), *Approaches to Social Theory*, pp. 83–104. New York: Russell Sage Foundation.
Laumann, Edward O., David Knoke, and Yong-Hak Kim
  1985 "An organizational approach to state policy formation: a comparative study of energy and health domains." *American Sociological Review* 50:1–19.
Laumann, Edward O., and Peter V. Marsden
  1979 "The analysis of oppositional structures in political elites: identifying collective actors." *American Sociological Review* 44:713–32.
  1982 "Microstructural analysis in interorganizational systems." *Social Networks* 4:329–48.
Laumann, Edward O., Peter V. Marsden, and Joseph Galaskiewicz
  1977 "Community-elite influence structures: extension of a network approach." *American Journal of Sociology* 83:594–631.
Laumann, Edward O., Peter V. Marsden, and David Prensky
  1983 "The boundary-specification problem in network analysis." In Ronald Burt and Michael Minor (eds.), *Applied Network Analysis: A Methodological Introduction*, pp. 18–34. Beverly Hills, Calif.: Sage Publications.
Laumann, Edward O., and Franz U. Pappi
  1976 *Networks of Collective Action: A Perspective on Community Influence Systems*. New York: Academic.
Lazarsfeld, Paul F., and Herbert Menzel
  1969 "On the relation between individual and collective properties." In Amitai Etzioni (ed.), *A Sociological Reader on Complex Organizations*, 2d ed., pp. 499–516. New York: Holt, Rinehart and Winston.
Leblebici, Huseyin, and Gerald Salancik
  1982 "Stability in interorganizational exchange: rulemaking processes of the Chicago Board of Trade." *Administrative Science Quarterly* 27:227–42.
Lenski, Gerhard
  1966 *Power and Privilege: A Theory of Social Stratification*. New York: McGraw-Hill.
Lincoln, James R.
  1984 "Analyzing relations in dyads: problems, models, and an application to interorganizational research." *Sociological Methods and Research* 13:45–76.
Lindblom, Charles E.
  1959 "The 'science' of muddling through." *Public Administration Review* 19:79–88.
  1977 *Politics and Markets: The World's Political-Economic Systems*. New York: Basic Books.
Lingoes, James
  1973 *The Guttman-Lingoes Nonmetric Program Series*. Ann Arbor, Mich.: Mathesis Press.
Lipset, Seymour M.
  1963 "The sources of the 'Radical Right'" & "Three decades of the Radical Right: Coughlinites, McCarthyites, and Birchers." In Daniel Bell, (ed.), *The Radical Right*, pp. 259–337. Garden City, N.Y.: Doubleday.

Litman, Theodor J. and Leonard S. Robins, eds.

1984 *Health Politics and Policy.* New York: John Wiley & Sons.

Lofland, John

1969 *Deviance and Identity.* Englewood Clifs, N.J.: Prentice-Hall.

Lorrain, François, and Harrison C. White

1971 "Structural equivalence of individuals in social networks." *Journal of Mathematical Sociology* 1:49–80.

Lowi, Theodore J.

1964 "American business, public policy, case-studies, and political theory." *World Politics* 16:667–715.

1969 *The End of Liberalism: Ideology, Policy, and the Crisis of Public Authority.* New York: Norton.

1979 *The End of Liberalism: The Second Republic of the United States,* 2d ed. New York: Norton.

Luhmann, Niklas

1979 *Trust and Power.* Trans. Howard Davis, John Raffan, and Kathryn Rooney. Chichester, England: John Wiley & Sons.

Lukes, Steven

1974 *Power: A Radical View.* Essex: Anchor Press.

Lyles, Marjorie A., and Ian I. Mitroff

1980 "Organizational problem formulation: an empirical study." *Administrative Science Quarterly* 25:102–19.

March, James G.

1981 "Decision in organizations and theories of choice." In A. Van de Ven and W. F. Joyce (eds.), *Perspectives on Organization Design and Behavior,* pp. 205–44. New York: Wiley Interscience.

March, James G., and Johan P. Olsen

1976 *Ambiguity and Choice in Organizations.* Bergen: Universitetsforlaget.

1984 "The new institutionalism: organizational factors in political life." *American Political Science Review* 78:734–49.

March, James G., and Herbert A. Simon

1958 *Organizations.* New York: Wiley.

Mariolis, Peter, and Maria H. Jones

1982 "Centrality in corporate interlock networks: reliability and stability." *Administrative Science Quarterly* 27:571–84.

Marmor, Theodore R.

1970 *The Politics of Medicare.* Chicago: Aldine.

Marmor, Theodore R., and Jon B. Christianson

1982 *Health Care Policy: A Political Economy Approach.* Beverly Hills, Calif.: Sage Publications.

Marsden, Peter V.

1980a "Models and methods for characterizing the structural parameters of groups." Mimeographed. Chapel Hill: University of North Carolina.

1980b "Methods for the characterization of role structures in network analysis." Paper presented at conference on Methods in Social Network Analysis, Laguna Beach, Calif.

Marsden, Peter V., and Edward O. Laumann
  1977 "Collective action in a community elite: exchange, influence resources, and issue resolution." In R. J. Liebert and A. W. Imersheim (eds.), *Power, Paradigms, and Community Research,* pp. 199–250. London: Sage.
  1984 "Mathematical ideas in social structural analysis." *Journal of Mathematical Sociology* 10:271–94.
Martin, Albro
  1976 "James J. Hill and the first energy revolution: a study in entrepreneurship, 1865–1878." *Business History Review* 50:179–97.
Mayhew, Bruce
  1980 "Structuralism versus individualism: part I, shadowboxing in the dark." *Social Forces* 59:335–75.
  1981 "Structuralism versus individualism: part II, ideological and other obfuscations." *Social Forces* 59:627–648.
McCarthy, John D., and Mayer N. Zald
  1977 "Resource mobilization and social movements: a partial theory." *American Journal of Sociology* 82:1212–41.
McConnell, Grant
  1966 *Private Power and American Democracy.* New York: Knopf.
McFarland, Andrew S.
  1976 *Public-Interest Lobbies: Decision-Making on Energy.* Washington, D.C.: American Enterprise Institute.
  1983 "Public interest lobbies versus minority faction." In Allan J. Cigler and Burdett A. Loomis (eds.), *Interest Group Politics,* pp. 324–53. Washington, D.C.: CQ Press.
  1984 "Energy lobbies." *Annual Review of Energy* 9:501–27.
McFarland, David D., and Daniel J. Brown
  1973 "Social distance as a metric: a systematic introduction to smallest space analysis." In Edward O. Laumann, *Bonds of Pluralism: The Form and Substance of Urban Social Networks,* pp. 213–53. New York: John Wiley & Sons.
McNeil, Kenneth
  1978 "Understanding organizational power: building on the Weberian legacy." *Administrative Science Quarterly* 23:65–90.
Meyer, John W., and Brian Rowan
  1977 "Institutionalized organizations: formal structure as myth and ceremony." *American Journal of Sociology* 83:341–63.
Michels, Robert
  1925 *Zur Soziologie des Parteiwessens in der modernen Demokratie.* Stuttgart: Alfred Kroner Verlag.
  1962 *Political Parties.* New York: Free Press.
Milbrath, Lester W.
  1963 *The Washington Lobbyists.* Chicago: Rand McNally.
Miliband, Ralph
  1969 *The State in Capitalist Society.* London: Merlin Press.
Mills, C. Wright
  1956 *The Power Elite.* New York: Oxford University Press.

Mintzberg, Henry
1983 *Power in and Around Organizations*. Englewood Cliffs, N.J.: Prentice-Hall.
Mitchell, J. Clyde
1969 "The concept and use of social networks." In J. Clyde Mitchell (ed.), *Social Networks in Urban Situations*, pp. 1–50. Manchester, England: Manchester University Press.
Mizruchi, Mark S.
1982 *The American Corporate Network, 1904–1974*. Beverly Hills, Calif.: Sage.
1984 "An organizational theory of class cohesion: incorporating resource dependence concepts into a social class model of intercorporate relations." *Power and Elites* 1:23–36.
Moe, Terry M.
1979 "On the scientific status of rational models." *American Journal of Political Science* 23:215–43.
1980 *The Organization of Interests: Incentives and the Internal Dynamics of Political Interest Groups*. Chicago: University of Chicago Press.
Moore, Gwen
1979 "The structure of a national elite network." *American Sociological Review* 44:673–91.
Nash, Gerald D.
1968 *United States Oil Policy, 1890–1964*. Pittsburgh: University of Pittsburgh Press.
Nelson, Robert, John P. Heinz, Edward O. Laumann, and Robert Salisbury
1987 "Interest representation in Washington: lawyers, lobbyists, and more." *American Bar Foundation Research Journal* (in press).
Nordhauser, Norman E.
1979 *The Quest for Stability: Domestic Oil Regulation 1917–1935*. New York: Garland Publishing.
Nordlinger, Eric
1981 *On the Autonomy of the Democratic State*. Cambridge: Harvard University Press.
Nuttall, Ronald L., Erwin Scheuch, and Chad Gordon
1968 "The structure of influence." In Terry N. Clark (ed.), *Community Structure and Decision-Making*, pp. 349–80. San Francisco: Chandler.
Oberschall, Anthony
1973 *Social Conflict and Social Movements*. Englewood Cliffs, N.J.: Prentice-Hall.
Offe, Claus, and Volker Ronge
1975 "Theses on the theory of the state." *New German Critique* 6:137–47.
Oleszek, Walter J.
1978 *Congressional Procedures and the Policy Process*. Washington, D.C.: Congressional Quarterly Press.
Olson, Mancur
1965 *The Logic of Collective Action: Public Goods and the Theory of Groups*. Cambridge: Harvard University Press.
1982 *The Rise and Decline of Nations: Economic Growth, and Social Rigidities*. New Haven: Yale University Press.

Ornstein, Norman J., and Shirley Elder
    1978 *Interest Groups, Lobbying and Policymaking.* Washington, D.C.: Congressional Quarterly Press.
Padgett, John
    1981 "Hierarchy and ecological control in federal budgetary decision making." *American Journal of Sociology* 87:75–129.
Pappi, Franz U., and Peter Kappelhoff
    1984 "Abhängigkeit, Tausch und kollektive Entscheidung in eine Gemeindeelite." *Zeitschrift für Soziologie* 13:87–117.
Parkin, Frank
    1979 *Marxism and Class Theory: A Bourgeois Critique.* London: Tavistock.
Parsons, Talcott
    1937 *The Structure of Social Action.* New York: Free Press of Glencoe.
    1951 *The Social System.* Glencoe, Ill.: Free Press.
    1961a "An outline of the social system." In Talcott Parsons, Edward Shils, Kaspar D. Naegele, and Jesse R. Pitts (eds.), *Theories of Society: Foundation of Modern Sociological Theory,* pp. 30–79. New York: Free Press.
    1961b 'The general interpretation of action." In Talcott Parsons, Edward Shils, Kaspar D. Naegele, and Jesse R. Pitts (eds.), *Theories of Society: Foundation of Modern Sociological Theory,* pp. 85–97. New York: Free Press.
    1963a "On the concept of influence (with rejoinder to comments)." *Public Opinion Quarterly* (Spring). (Reprinted in *Sociological Theory and Modern Society* [New York: Free Press, 1967].)
    1963b "On the concept of political power." *Proceedings of the American Philosophical Society* 107:232–62. (Reprinted in *Sociological Theory and Modern Society* [New York: Free Press, 1967].)
    1966 *Societies: Evolutionary and Comparative Perspectives.* Englewood Cliffs, N.J.: Prentice-Hall.
    1967 *Sociological Theory and Modern Society.* New York: Free Press.
    1968 "On the concept of value-commitments." *Sociological Inquiry* 38 (no. 2). (Reprinted in *Politics and Social Structure* [New York: Free Press, 1969].
    1969 *Politics and Social Structure.* New York: Free Press.
Parons, Talcott, and Neil J. Smelser
    1956 *Economy and Society.* New York: Free Press.
Perrucci, Robert, and Mark Pilisuk
    1980 "Leadership and ruling elites: the interorganizational bases of community power." *American Sociological Review* 35:1040–57.
Pfeffer, Jeffrey, and Gerald R. Salancik
    1978 *The External Control of Organizations: A Resource Dependence Perspective.* New York: Harper & Row.
Poen, Monte M.
    1979 *Harry S. Truman Versus the Medical Lobby: The Genesis of Medicare.* Columbia, Mo.: University of Missouri Press.
Polsby, Nelson W.
    1984 *Political Innovation in America: The Politics of Policy Innovation.* New Haven: Yale University Press.

Pool, Ithiel de Sola
1983 "Tracking the flow of information." *Science* 221:609–13.
Poultanzas, Nicos
1973 *Political Power and Social Classes.* London: New Left Books.
Prensky, David
1985 "Interorganizational Structure and Organizational Participation in a National Policy Domain." Ph.D. dissertation, University of Chicago.
Ragin, Charles, Shelley Coverman, and Mark Hayward
1982 "Major labor disputes in Britain, 1902–1938: the relationship between resource expenditure and outcome." *American Sociological Review* 47:238–52.
Riker, William H., and Peter C. Ordeshook
1973 *An Introduction to Positive Political Theory.* Englewood Cliffs, N.J.: Prentice-Hall.
Ripley, Randall B., and Grace A. Franklin
1980 *Congress, the Bureaucracy, and Public Policy.* Revised ed. Homewood, Ill.: Dorsey Press.
Rogers, Everett M., and D. Lawrence Kincaid
1981 *Communication Networks: Toward a New Paradigm for Research.* New York: Macmillan.
Roos, Leslie L., Jr., and Roger I. Hall
1980 "Influence diagrams and organizational power." *Administrative Science Quarterly* 25:57–71.
Rose, Arnold M.
1967 *The Power Structure: Political Process in American Society.* London: Oxford University Press.
Rossi, Peter H.
1960 "Power and community structure." *Midwest Journal of Political Science* 4:390–401.
Sabatier, Paul
1978 "The acquisition and utilization of technical information by administrative agencies." *Administrative Science Quarterly* 23:396–417.
Sailer, Lee D.
1978 "Structural equivalence: meaning and definition, computation and application," *Social Networks* 1:73–90.
Salisbury, Robert H.
1970 *Interest Group Politics in America.* New York: Harper & Row.
1984 "Interest representation: the dominance of institutions." *American Political Science Review* 78:64–76.
Salzman, Harold, and G. William Domhoff
1980 "The corporate community and government: do they interlock?" In G. William Domhoff (ed.), *Power Structure Research,* pp. 227–54. Beverly Hills, Calif.: Sage Publications.
Scheuch, Erwin K.
1965 "Die Sichtbarkeit politischer Einstellungen in altäglichen Verhalten." *Kölner Zeitschrift für Soziologie und Sozialpsychologie* 17:169–24.

Schiffman, Susan., M. Lance Reynolds, and Forrest Young

1981 *Introduction to Multidimensional Scaling: Theory, Methods and Applications.* New York: Academic Press.

Schlozman, Kay L., and John T. Tierney

1983 "More of the same: Washington pressure group activity in a decade of change." *Journal of Politics* 34: 351–77.

1985 *Organized Interests and American Democracy.* New York: Harper & Row.

Schmitter, Phillippe C.

1979 "Still the century of corporatism?" In Phillippe C. Schmitter and Gerhard Lehmbruch (eds.), *Trends Toward Corporatist Intermediation,* pp. 7–52. Beverly Hills, Calif.: Sage Publications.

Schwartz, Joseph, and Christopher Winship

1979 "Welfare approach to measuring inequality." In Karl F. Schuessler (ed.), *Sociology Methodology 1980,* pp. 1–36. San Francisco: Jossey-Bass.

Scott, Richard W.

1981 *Organizations: Rational, Natural and Open Systems.* Englewood Cliffs, N.J.: Prentice-Hall.

Selznick, Phillip

1949 *TVA and the Grass Roots.* Berkeley: University of California Press.

Shapiro, Andrew

1984 "Ideology, capacity and mobilization: the American antinuclear movement." Center for the Study of Industrial Societies, Occasional Paper Series, University of Chicago.

Shepsle, Kenneth A.

1979 "Institutional arrangements and equilibrium in multidimensional voting models." *American Journal of Political Science* 23: 27–59.

Sherrill, Robert

1983 *The Oil Follies of 1970–80.* New York: Anchor Press.

Simon, Herbert A.

1957 *Administrative Behavior: A Study of Decision-Making Processes in Administrative Organization.* 2d ed. New York: Macmillan.

1976 *Administrative Behavior.* 3d ed. New York: Free Press.

Skocpol, Theda

1979 *States and Social Revolutions.* New York: Cambridge University Press.

1980 "Political response to capitalist crisis: neo-Marxist theories of the state and the case of the New Deal." *Politics and Society* 10: 155–201.

Skowronek, Stephen

1982 *Building a New American State: The Expansion of National Administrative Capacities, 1877–1920.* New York: Cambridge University Press.

Smelser, Neil

1962 *Theory of Collective Behavior.* New York: Free Press.

Sokal, Robert R., and Peter H. A. Sneath

1963 *Principles of Numerical Taxonomy.* San Francisco: Freeman.

Spector, Malcolm, and John I. Kitsuse

1977 *Constructing Social Problems.* Menlo Park, Calif.: Cummings.

Starr, Paul
1982 *The Social Transformation of American Medicine: The Rise of a Sovereign Profession and the Making of a Vast Industry.* New York: Basic Books.
Stevens, Rosemary
1971 *American Medicine and the Public Interest.* New Haven: Yale University Press.
Stobaugh, Robert, and Daniel Yergin
1979 *Energy Future.* New York: Random House.
Sundquist, James L.
1968 *Politics and Policy.* Washington, D.C.: Brookings Institution.
Therborn, Goran
1976 "What does the ruling class do when it rules?" *Insurgent Sociologist* 6:3–16.
Thomas, George M., and John W. Meyer
1984 "The expansion of the state." *Annual Review of Sociology* 10:461–82.
Thompson, James D.
1967 *Organizations in Action.* New York: McGraw-Hill.
Thompson, Martin J.
1979 *Antitrust and the Health Care Provider.* Germantown, M.D.: Aspen Systems Corp.
Tilly, Charles
1975 *The Formation of National States in Western Europe.* Princeton: Princeton University Press.
1978 *From Mobilization to Revolution.* Reading, Mass.: Addison-Wesley.
Truman, David B.
1951 *The Governmental Process.* New York: Knopf.
Tufte, Edward R.
1978 *Political Control of the Economy.* Princeton: Princeton University Press.
Useem, Michael
1978 "The inner group of the American capitalist class." *Social Problems* 25:225–40.
1979 "The social organization of the American business elite and participation of corporate directors in the governance of American institutions." *American Sociological Review* 44:553–72.
1983 *The Inner Circle: Large Corporations and the Rise of Business Political Activity in the U.S. and U.K.* New York: Oxford University Press.
1984 *The Inner Circle.* New York: Oxford University Press.
van den Eeden, Pieter, and Harry J. M. Hüttner
1982 "Trend report: multi-level research." *Current Sociology* 30:1–181.
Verbrugge, Lois M.
1979 "Multiplexity in adult friendships." *Social Forces* 57:1286–309.
Vietor, Richard H. K.
1980a *Environmental Politics and the Coal Coalition.* College Station: Texas A & M University Press.
1980b "The synthetic liquid fuels program: energy politics in the Truman era." *Business History Review* 56:1–34.

1984 *Energy Policy in America Since 1945: A Study of Business-Government Relations.* New York: Cambridge University Press.

Von Eschen, Donald, Jerome Kirk, and Maurice Pinard
1971 "The organizational sub-structure of disorderly politics." *Social Forces* 49: 529–43.

Walker, Jack L.
1977 "Setting the agenda in the U.S. Senate: a theory of problem selection." *British Journal of Political Science* 7:423–46.
1983 "The origins and maintenance of interest groups in America." *American Political Science Review* 77:390–406.

Wallace, Walter
1975 "Stru.:ture and action in the theories of Coleman and Parsons." In Peter Blau (ed.), *Approaches to the Study of Social Structure*, pp. 121–34. New York: Free Press.

Walton, John
1966 "Substance and artifact: the current status of research on community power structure." *American Journal of Sociology* 71:430–38.
1970 "A systematic survey of community power research." In Michael Aiken and Paul Mott (eds.), *The Structure of Community Power*, pp. 443–64. New York: Random House.

Weber, Max
1922 *Grundrisse der Sozialökonomie III: Abteilung, Wirtschaft und Gesellschaft.* Tübingen: Verlag von J. C. B. Mohn (Paul Siebeck).
1947 *The Theory of Social and Economic Organizations.* Trans. A. M. Henderson and Talcott Parsons; ed. Talcott Parsons. New York: Free Press of Glencoe.
1979 *Economy and Society: An Outline of Interpretive Sociology.* Ed. Guenther Roth and Claus Wittich. Berkeley: University of California Press.

White, Harrison C.
1970 *Chains of Opportunity: System Models of Mobility in Organizations.* Cambridge: Harvard University Press.

White, Harrison C., Scott A. Boorman, and Ronald L. Breiger
1976 "Social structure from multiple networks, I: Blockmodels of roles and positions." *American Journal of Sociology* 81:730–80.

Wildavsky, Aaron
1962 "The analysis of issue–contexts in the study of decision-making." *Journal of Politics* 24:717–32.
1964 *The Politics of Budgetary Process.* Boston: Little Brown.
1975 *The Politics of Budgetary Process.* 2d ed., Boston: Little, Brown.

Wildavsky, Aaron, and Ellen Tenenbaum
1981 *The Politics of Mistrust: Estimating American Oil and Gas Resources.* Beverly Hills, Calif.: Sage Publications.

Wilensky, Harold
1967 *Organizational Intelligence.* New York: Basic Books.
1975 *The Welfare State and Equality: Structural and Ideological Roots of Public Expenditures.* Berkeley: University of California Press.

Williams, Stephen J., and Paul R. Torrens (eds.)

1980 *Introduction to Health Services.* New York: Wiley.

Williamson, Oliver E.

1975 *Markets and Hierarchies: Analysis and Antitrust Implications.* New York: Free Press.

1981 "The economics of organizations: the transaction cost approach." *American Journal of Sociology* 87:548–77.

1985 *The Economic Institutions of Capitalism: Firms, Markets, Relational Contracting.* New York: Free Press.

Wilson, Graham

1982 "Why is there no corporatism in the United States?" In Gerhard Lehmbruch and Phillipe C. Schmitter (eds.), *Patterns of Corporatist Policymaking,* pp. 219–36. Beverly Hills, Calif.: Sage Publications.

Wilson, James Q.

1975 "The rise of the bureaucratic state." *Public Interest* 41:77–103.

Wohl, Stanley

1984 *The Medical Industrial Complex.* New York: Harmony Books.

Wright, Erik Olin

1978 *Class, Crisis and the State.* London: New Left Books.

Yamagishi, Toshio, Mary Gillmore, and Karen Cook

1986 "Network connections and the distribution of power in exchange networks." Paper presented at a meeting of the Public Choice Society, Baltimore, Md., March 21–23.

Zald, Mayer N., and John D. McCarthy

1979 *The Dynamics of Social Movements.* Cambridge, Mass.: Winthrop Publishers.

Zeitlin, Maurice, W. Lawrence Neuman, and Richard Earl Ratcliff

1976 "Class segments: agrarian property and political leadership in the capitalist class of Chile." *American Sociological Review* 41:1006–29.

Zucker, Lynne G.

1977 "The role of institutionalization in cultural persistence." *Annual Review of Sociology* 42:726–43.

Zuehl, James J.

n.d. *"Amici Curiae and the United States Supreme Court."* Manuscript. University of Chicago, Department of Sociology.

Index

Abortion, 314, 316; issue public, 243
Abourezk, James, 385
Actors: core set in policy domain, 10–11; embedded in social networks, 23, 342; relational properties of, 29–30; in systems of action, 36n. *See also* Organizational actors
Actors and events, joint analysis, 18–35, 94, 249, 342, 343, 377
Actors-by-actors matrix, 27, 34
Actors-by-events matrix, 27, 263–64, 289
Actor-event interface, 33–35, 263. *See also* Actors and events
Adversarial structure, 311, 315–16, 320–42, 377–79; in energy domain, 322–32; influenced by budgetary constraints, 313n; relation to communication network, 210, 248; relation to consensus, 187–88; relation to event charcteristics, 313–14
Aged. *See* Elderly
Agenda, of government actors, 14, 16–17, 382
Agenda-setting, monopoly, 22
AFL, on national health insurance, 79
AFL-CIO, 140–41, 144, 183; on energy policy, 210, 245; on health policy, 333; influence, 197, 275; monitoring capacity, 208; on national health insurance, 83
Agricultural policy domain, 292, 389
Air Quality Act of 1967, 65
Alaska Native Claims Settlement Act of 1971, 302
Alcohol, Drug Abuse, and Mental Health Administration (ADAMHA), 141
Allergy immunology research, 245
ALSCAL, 173, 221, 243, 391; and scope of issue interests, 285. *See also* Multidimensional scaling
American Academy of Orthopedic Surgeons, 99n
American Association for Labor Legislation (AALL), 78
American Association of Medical Colleges, 75, 144; 19th century membership, 76

American Association of Retired Persons (AARP), 197, 248
American Bar Foundation, 82
American Cancer Society, 187
American Chiropractic Association, 187. *See also* Chiropractors
American College of Preventive Medicine, as focus of issue space, 124
American College of Surgeons, 80n, 197, 275
American Dental Association, 32, 144; on health insurance, 84, 86n
American Federation of Coal Operators, 50
American Gas Association, 245
American Hospital Association (AHA), 172, 245, 333; effectiveness, 363; on health insurance, 78, 82, 84; on hospital cost containment, 86, 86n, 186, 363; on Medicare and Medicaid, 86,86n
American Jewish Congress, 82
American Medical Association (AMA), 75–77, 141, 144, 172, 186, 187, 209, 245, 333; attacks on proprietary medicine, 78; Committee on Social Insurance, 78–79; Council on Medical Education, 76, 77; Council on Pharmacy and Chemistry, 78; efffectiveness, 363; "Eldercare" proposal, 86n; on health insurance, 78–79, 81–82, 84; on hospital cost containment, 86, 186, 363; internal politics, 76, 79; on Medicare and Medicaid, 86, 86n; on manpower policies, 90–91; opposition to federal funding of medical education, 85; opposition to reorganization of health care delivery, 88; political activity, 82–83; sued by chiropractors, 309
American Mining Congress, 183, 245
American Motors, 98n
American Nuclear Energy Council, 183, 211
American Nursing Association, on national health insurance, 84
American Nursing Home Association, on national health insurance, 84

523

Event interdependency, 289; measurement, 289–90

Event linkage, 294, 298–99; measured by organizational participation, 289–93; participation across, 288–89; relation to participation, 292–93; types of, 288–89. *See also* Event scenario; Events: concatenated

Event outcomes, system of, 343

Event participation. *See* Organizational participation in events

Event participation scope. *See* Scope of event participation

Events: analytic features, 32–33, 34, 263, 278; as framing principle, 30–31, 32–34; calculation of demand for, 369–70; categories, 108, 111–12, 257–58; clusters, 351; concatenated, 17–18, 250; control over, 295, 346–47, 349, 350, 351, 356, 356*n*, 369–70; critical, 33; decision-making locus, 253, 261, 298; definition, 17–18, 30, 107, 250–51; definition of value, 369–70; differentiated by characteristics, 259–60; embeddedness, 249, 377–78; functional focus, 252, 253; identification, 107–8; identification of sample, 108, 257–59; initiatory, 312; institutional location, 34, 293; structuration, 30; subdivisions, 21; symbolic framing, 316; temporal ordering, 289; theoretical significance, 18, 19, 26; types, 252*n*, 257–58. *See also* Controversiality; Organizational participation in events; Scope of events; Visibility of events

Events-by-events matrix, 26–27, 29, 32–33, 34*n*, 289–90

Event scenario, 108, 254–56, 295–96, 299; constructed, 256; criteria for, 254–55; definition, 17–18; participation in, 31*n*, 296, 296*n*, 317–18; relation to event characteristics, 256; in relation to policy process, 250; singletons, 296*n*; types of, 255–56. *See also* Events: concatenated

Event scenario linkage, 315–19; relation to issue publics, 319–20

Event similarity, measurement, 295

Event structure, 291, 293

Exchange model. *See* Coleman, James S.: Exchange model; Resource exchange

Exchange relations: as resource deployment, 344; as resource mobilization, 344

Expert identification: as basis for concatenating events, 255; as criterion of domain membership, 95, 97–98, 98*n*

Exxon Oil Company, 98*n*, 193; and petroleum industry divestiture, 385–86

Facilitative events, consequences for policy domain, 316

Facilitative/recurrent issues, 313

Factor analysis, of resource allocation, 201–2

Falk, I. S., 84

Farmers, and coal slurry pipeline, 17–18

Federal agencies, 100, 100*n*, 101, 102, 229; in energy domain, 177, 345, 350, 354–55; formal authority, 382; inclusion in sample, 98; influence, 168–69, 195, 376; in policy domain, 140–41, 229, 382; scope of activity, 106; as targets of communication, 224, 232. *See also* Public sector

Federal Aviation Administration, 3, 215, 377

Federal Emergency Relief Act of 1933, and health care for the elderly, 80–81

Federal Energy Agency, 67

Federal Energy Regulatory Commission (FERC), 140, 245, 252

Federal Oil Conservation Board, 55

Federal Power Commission (FPC), 62, 64, 66, 67–68

Federal Security Agency, 82*n*, 84

Federal Trade Commission (FTC), 66, 141, 144, 187, 310; anti-trust activities, 52–53

Federation of American Hospitals, effectiveness, 363

Flexner, Abraham, 76–77

Food and Drug Administration (FDA), 81, 83, 189, 200, 245, 307; Bureau of Foods, 265; and cyclamates ban, 309; and drug regulation reform, 310; effectiveness, 356; as focus of issue space, 124; foundation of, 81; and generic drug legislation, 310; and saccharine ban, 309; and safety brochure inserts, 310

Food issue public, 243

Foothills Pipeline, 243

Forand, Aime, 84

Ford, Gerald: in energy policy domain, 68, 69, 71, 300, 302, 303, 304; in health policy domain, 88, 89, 90, 307

Ford Motor Company, 183

COMPOSED BY G & S TYPESETTERS, INC., AUSTIN, TEXAS
MANUFACTURED BY McNAUGHTON & GUNN, INC., ANN ARBOR, MICHIGAN
TEXT AND DISPLAY LINES ARE SET IN TIMES ROMAN

Library of Congress Cataloging-in-Publication Data
Laumann, Edward O.
The organizational state.
Bibliography: p. 501–521.
Includes index.
1. Lobbying—United States. 2. Pressure groups—
United States. 3. Energy policy—United States—
Decision making. 4. Medical policy—United States—
Decision making. 5. United States—Social policy—
Decision making. 6. United States—Politics and
government—1977–1981—Decision making.
I. Knoke, David. II. Title.
JK1118.L38   1987   324′.4′0973   87-40142
ISBN 0-299-11190-3
ISBN 0-299-11194-6 (pbk.)